A Companion to Twentieth-Century American Drama

Blackwell Companions to Literature and Culture

This series offers comprehensive, newly written surveys of key periods and movements and certain major authors, in English literary culture and history. Extensive volumes provide new perspectives and positions on contexts and on canonical and post-canonical texts, orientating the beginning student in new fields of study and providing the experienced undergraduate and new graduate with current and new directions, as pioneered and developed by leading scholars in the field.

Published

A Companion to Shakespeare's Works

A COMPANION TO

TWENTIETH-CENTURY AMERICAN DRAMA

EDITED BY **DAVID KRASNER**

Blackwell
Publishing

BLACKWELL PUBLISHING
350 Main Street, Malden, MA 02148-5020, USA
108 Cowley Road, Oxford OX4 1JF, UK
550 Swanston Street, Carlton, Victoria 3053, Australia

First published 2005 by Blackwell Publishing Ltd

Library of Congress Cataloging-in-Publication Data

A companion to twentieth-century American drama / edited by David Krasner.
p. cm.—(Blackwell companions to literature and culture)
Includes bibliographical references and index.
ISBN 1-4051-1088-0 (hardcover: alk. paper)
1. American drama—20th century—History and criticism—Handbooks, manuals, etc.
I. Krasner, David, 1952– II. Series.

PS350.C655 2005
812′.509–dc22
2004007690

A catalogue record for this title is available from the British Library.

Set in 11/13pt Garamond 3
by Kolam Information Services Pvt. Ltd., Pondicherry, India
Printed and bound in the United Kingdom
by TJ International Ltd, Padstow, Cornwall

The publisher's policy is to use permanent paper from mills that operate a sustainable forestry
policy, and which has been manufactured from pulp processed using acid-free and elementary
chlorine-free practices. Furthermore, the publisher ensures that the text paper and cover board
used have met acceptable environmental accreditation standards.

For further information on
Blackwell Publishing, visit our website:
www.blackwellpublishing.com

For
Don B. Wilmeth
and
Thomas Postlewait
Pioneers in the Field

Contents

Illustrations

Notes on Contributors

Thomas P. Adler is Professor of English at Purdue University, where he has taught dramatic literature for over 30 years. His publications include *A Streetcar Names Desire: The Moth and the Lantern* and *American Drama 1940–1960: A Critical History*.

Sarah Bay-Cheng is Assistant Professor of English and Theatre at Colgate University. She is the author of *Mama Dada: Gertrude Stein's Avant-Garde Theater* and co-editor of the forthcoming *The False and the Fallen Staff: A Collection of Falstaff Plays from Four Centuries*.

Annemarie Bean is Assistant Professor of Theatre at Williams College. She is currently writing a book on the performances of miscegenation through the development of female impersonation in American blackface minstrelsy.

Deanna M. Toten Beard is Assistant Professor of Theatre Arts at Baylor University. Her research specialty is American theatre history and dramatic literature in the period 1900 to 1930. She has published previously on the topic of experimental performance.

Murray Biggs teaches English and Theatre Studies at Yale University, where he also directs student productions. His publications include co-editing *The Arts of Performance in Elizabethan and Early Stuart Drama* (1991).

Stephen J. Bottoms is a Senior Lecturer in Theatre Studies at the University of Glasgow, Scotland. He is the author of *Playing Underground: A Critical History of the 1960s Off-Off Broadway Movement* (2004), *Albee: Who's Afraid of Virginia Woolf?* (2000), and *The Theatre of Sam Shepard* (1998). He also regularly directs for theatre.

Mark Evans Bryan is an Assistant Professor at Dennison University.

Peter Civetta is a doctoral candidate in Theatre Studies at Cornell University's Department of Theatre, Film, and Dance. He is completing his dissertation on the performance of preaching at four upstate New York Jewish, Muslim, and Christian congregations.

Jerry Dickey, Associate Professor of Theatre Arts at the University of Arizona, is the author of several essays and book chapters on Sophie Treadwell, as well as *Sophie Treadwell: A Research and Production Sourcebook* (1997).

Jill Dolan holds the Zachary T. Scott Family Chair in Drama at the University of Texas at Austin. She is the author of *The Feminist Spectator as Critic* (1988), *Presence and Desire* (1993), and *Geographies of Learning* (2001).

Harry J. Elam, Jr. is the Robert and Ruth Halperin University Fellow for Under-graduate Education, Professor of Drama, Director of Graduate Studies in Drama, Director of the Institute for Diversity in the Arts, and Director of the Committee on Black Performing Arts at Stanford University. He is author of *Taking It to the Streets: The Social Protest Theater of Luis Valdez and Amiri Baraka* and *The Past as Present in the Drama of August Wilson*, co-editor of *African American Performance and Theatre History: A Critical Reader*, and co-editor of *Colored Contradictions: An Anthology of Contemporary African American Drama*, *The Fire This Time: African American Plays for the New Millennium*, and *Black Cultural Traffic: Crossroads in Black Performance and Popular Culture*.

Mark Fearnow teaches theatre history and playwriting at Hanover College. He is the author of *Clare Booth Luce* (1995) and *The American Stage and the Great Depression* (1997).

Anne Fletcher is an Assistant Professor at Southern Illinois University, Carbondale. Her work has appeared in *Theatre History Studies*, *Theatre Journal*, and *Theatre Symposium*. Her book on Group Theatre designer Mordecai Gorelik is forthcoming.

Ehren Fordyce is an Assistant Professor of Drama at Stanford University, where he teaches directing and contemporary performance. He has written on the rise of the directing profession in Romantic Paris, as well as on contemporary artists such as the Wooster Group and Reza Abdoh. He has also translated dramas by Büchner and Maeterlinck, and poetry by writers ranging form Petrarch to Mallarmé.

J. Ellen Gainor is Professor of Theatre and Associate Dean of the Graduate School at Cornell University. She is the author of *Shaw's Daughters: Dramatic and Narrative Constructions of Gender* and *Susan Glaspell in Context: American Theater, Culture, and Politics, 1915–48*. She has edited the volumes *Imperialism and Theatre* and *Performing America: Cultural Nationalism in American Theater*. She is currently co-editing *The Complete Plays of Susan Glaspell*.

Janet V. Haedicke is Professor of English at the University of Louisiana at Monroe, where she holds the Tommy and Mary Barham Endowed Professorship. She has published numerous articles in such journals as *Modern Drama* and *American Drama*, both of which accorded her essays special recognition. She has contributed to both critical anthologies and reference volumes in drama. Co-editor of the *Tennessee Williams Literary Journal*, she also serves as President of the David Mamet Society.

Ann Haugo teaches in the School of Theatre at Illinois State University. Her publications on Native theatre have appeared in *American Indian Theatre: A Reader*, *The Cambridge Companion to Native American Literature*, and various journals.

David Krasner is an instructor in Theatre Studies, English, and African American Studies at Yale University, where he teaches dramatic literature, theatre history, acting, and directing. He is the author of several books on American drama, African American theatre, performance theory, and theatre history.

Daphne Lei is Assistant Professor of Drama at the University of California, Irvine. She has published works on premodern Chinese literature and drama, and Asian and Asian American theatre.

Julia Listengarten is Assistant Professor of Theatre at the University of Central Florida. She is the author of *Russian Tragifarce: Its Cultural and Political Roots* and a number of articles, and served professionally as a director, translator, and production dramaturge. Her translation of the Russian absurdist play *Christmas at theIvanovs'* premiered in New York City at Classic Stage Company in 1997 and was included in the anthology *Theater of the Avant-Garde, 1890–1950*. Her most recent article on cultural translation is included in the forthcoming volume of *Translation Perspectives*.

Felicia Hardison Londré, Curators' Professor of Theatre at the University of Missouri-Kansas City, is co-author of *The History of North American Theater: The United States, Canada, and Mexico from Pre-Columbian Times to the Present*.

Tiffany Ana Lopez is Associate Professor of English and Director of CASA – Chicana/o Arts and Social Action at the University of California, Riverside. She is editor of *Growing Up Chicana/o* (1993) and author of *The Alchemy of Blood: Violence as a Critical Discourse in U.S. Latina/o Writing*. She has published widely on prison drama and Maria Irene Fornes, and is a frequent contributor to Performing for Los Angeles Youth. She is currently working on a collection of essays about Latina/o writing and performance related to prison issues.

Brenda A. Murphy is Professor of English at the University of Connecticut. She is author of, among other books, *O'Neill: Long Day's Journey Into Night*, *Congressional Theatre: Dramatizing McCarthyism on Stage, Film, and Television*, *Miller: Death of a Salesman*, *Tennessee Williams and Elia Kazan: A Collaboration in the Theatre*, and editor of the *Cambridge Companion to American Women Playwrights* and *A Realist in the American Theatre: Drama Criticism of William Dean Howells*.

Christopher Olsen has published two articles, one on audience surveys in *New Theatre Quarterly*, and one on drama technique for teaching students with learning disabilities in *Interview Magazine*. He is currently working on a book about off-off-

Broadway in the 1970s. He is a theatre and speech professor at York College and Millerville University, both in Pennsylvania.

Linda Rohrer Paige teaches in the Department of Literature and Philosophy at Georgia Southern University. She is the co-editor of *Southern Women Playwrights: New Essays in Literary History and Criticism*, and editor of the journal *Studies in American Culture*.

Ann Pellegrini is Associate Professor of Religious Studies and Performance Studies at New York University. She is the author of *Performance Anxieties: Staging Psycho-analysis, Staging Race* (1997) and co-author of *Love the Sin: Sexual Regulation and the Limits of Religious Tolerance* (2003). Her co-edited volumes include *Queer Theory and the Jewish Question* (2003).

Gene A. Plunka is Professor of English at the University of Memphis, where he teaches courses on modern and contemporary drama. His books include *Peter Shaffer: Roles, Rites, and Rituals in the Theater* (1988), *The Rites of Passage of Jean Genet: The Art and Aesthetics of Risk Taking* (1992), *Antonin Artaud and the Modern Theater* (edited, 1994), *Jean-Claude van Itallie and the Off-Broadway Theater* (1999), and *The Black Comedy of John Guare* (2002). He is currently finishing a book about the theatre of Beth Henley.

Steven Price is Lecturer in English at the University of Wales, Bangor, where he teaches literature and film. He has published extensively on American, British, and European drama, and is associate editor of *The Year's Work in English Studies*. With William Tydeman, he is co-author of *Oscar Wilde: Salome*. He is currently completing a study of the screenplay as a textual genre.

June Schlueter, Charles A. Dana Professor of English, Lafayette College, is author or editor of *Metafictional Characters in Modern Drama*, *Arthur Miller*, *Feminist Rereadings of Modern American Drama*, *Modern American Drama: The Female Canon*, and *Dramatic Closure*.

Mike Sell is Associate Professor of English at Indiana University of Pennsylvania. He has a forthcoming book, *Avant-Garde Performance and the Limits of Criticism: The Connection, Happenings/Fluxus, the Black Arts Movement*. His essay, "Arthur Miller and the Drama of Liberalism," will be published in *Arthur Miller's America*, and he is currently editing *The Ed Bullins Reader*.

Rachel Shteir is Head of Dramaturgy at the Theatre School at DePaul University. She has taught at Yale, Carnegie Mellon, Tisch School of the Arts, Columbia, the National Theatre Institute, and Bates College. She has published widely in magazines and newspapers including the *New York Times*, *American Theatre*, and the *Nation*. *Grit, Glamour, and the Grind*, her book about the history of striptease, is forthcoming.

Molly Smith is Artistic Director of the Arena Stage in Washington, DC. She was the founder of the Perseverance Theatre in Juneau, Alaska, and directed over 50 productions for 19 years as its Artistic Director. In 2001, she was awarded an Honorary Doctorate of Fine Arts from American University, has served as judge for the Susan B. Blackburn Prize, and was named one of *Washingtonian Magazine*'s 100 Most Powerful Women.

Andrew Sofer is Assistant Professor of English at Boston College. He is the author of *The Stage Life of Props* (2003) as well as essays on Shakespeare, Kyd, Miller, Williams, Beckett, Pinter, and others. He has directed many new and classical plays.

Leslie A. Wade is an Associate Professor in the Louisiana State University Department of Theatre. He has published numerous articles on contemporary performance and is the author of *Sam Shepard and the American Theatre*.

Foreword

Molly Smith, Artistic Director of the Arena Stage

Theatre is a place of ritual, a place of wonder, a place we come together as a community to experience stories, to sit and really listen to another person's predicament, join in their pain and joy and agree or disagree with the choices they make in their lives.

In the same way we gather in stadiums and churches, we gather in theatres for the heat of connection. In America, there is certainly no shortage of heat. Arguably the most culturally and racially diverse country in the world, America is, as Mark Twain put it, a "loud, raucous, cacophony of voices." I believe the best American plays are like the mountains in Alaska – huge and dangerous and full of God. Audiences love to laugh, are desperate to feel, need to get angry, are driven to think – and through these American voices, which are brave, ugly, sweet, bitchy, sensual, and hot blooded, we bring the world into human scale and recognize our own humanity.

Over 50 years ago visionaries like Zelda Fichandler of Arena Stage in Washington, DC decided that wonderful theatre could happen outside of New York – indeed, that resident theatres could be born in all corners of America that would serve and sustain the individual passions and needs of each community. The resident theatre, not-for-profit movement was born. Theatres like the Guthrie in Minneapolis, the Alley Theatre in Texas, the Seattle Repertory Theatre, the Mark Taper Forum, and the Oregon Shakespeare Festival were created. Today more than 350 large theatres and a few thousand small theatres populate the landscape of America. But very few of these theatres focus on American plays. Why?

I think we have a chip on our shoulders about American writers. When I talk to my colleagues, they are always looking to England to see what's new instead of investigating our own backyard. Look at Broadway – huge numbers of plays come from Europe before the Tony Awards, with our own American writers desperately trying to get an off-Broadway house. There is something wrong with this picture.

What other country has so many diverse dramatic writers? Poetic writers like Langston Hughes, Tennessee Williams, Gertrude Stein, Nilo Cruz, Zora Neale

Hurston; musical writers like Lerner and Loewe, Kander and Ebb, Rogers and Hammerstein and Frank Loesser; master storytellers like Arthur Miller, David Mamet, Marsha Norman, August Wilson, Clifford Odets, Wendy Wasserstein, Edward Albee, Beth Henley, Eugene O'Neill, Sam Shepard; political writers like Tony Kushner, Neil LaBute, Paula Vogel, Lillian Hellman, David Henry Hwang, Suzan-Lori Parks. These authors are as varied as the American landscape, our writers reflecting our dynamic heritage.

Maybe our respect for European art over American art comes from America's history as an emerging nation when Europe and other parts of the world were in full flower. But America is now in full flower. Just as we have branded and proudly exported our homegrown democracy, shouldn't we brand, proudly produce, and export our homegrown American drama?

. . . yes I said yes I will Yes.

Acknowledgments

I want to thank my long-time friend and colleague Anne Fletcher of Southern Illinois University and Laura Muir of the Missouri Repertory Company for their valuable help in gathering together photos for this volume. Andrew McNeillie, Jennifer Hunt, and Brigitte Lee at Blackwell have been supportive throughout this process. Audrey Healey's single-handed help as the office assistant and business manager of the Yale University's Theatre Studies Program has been enormous. My wife, Lynda, has been my pillar of support. Most of all, I want to thank the contributors. It is their hard work, dedication, and knowledge that make this work not only possible but significant. If there are any shortcomings to this collection, they are mine, not theirs.

This book was published with the assistance of the Frederick W. Hilles Publication Fund of Yale University.

David Krasner

1
Introduction:
The Changing Perceptions
of American Drama

David Krasner

For too many critics and historians American drama is still American literature's unwanted bastard child, the offspring of the whore that is American theatre.

Susan Harris Smith (1997: 10)

Molly Smith maintains that her aim as director of the Arena Stage in Washington, DC is *"to produce huge plays about all that is passionate, exuberant, profound, deep and dangerous in the American spirit"* (2003: 45, emphasis in original). Yet, as she makes clear in the Foreword to this book, her goals are not completely shared by others; very few American theatres, on Broadway, off-Broadway, or regional theatres, emphasize American drama. Smith's jeremiad has a long history in American dramatic criticism. In fact, American drama has struggled since its inception with a reputation of inferiority. For instance, in 1889 drama critic Brander Matthews inveighed against what he called the "decline" of American drama. American drama, he lamented, was "shabby in structure and shambling in action," nor had its practitioners "taken the trouble to learn [their] trade" (1889: 930). In 1954 drama critic John Gassner wrote that, despite the "seed of a vigorous democratic art," the century preceding Eugene O'Neill found American playwrights "of no importance whatsoever to the world" (1954: 632). The sorry state of affairs appeared intractable. Drama critic Susan Harris Smith, in her book *American Drama: The Bastard Art*, described American drama as having "always suffered from a bad reputation" (1997: 23). The "widespread discrimination" of American drama, she contends, "is of long standing," representing "the sour leitmotif in American publishing, academic or commercial, highbrow or low, where drama in general is slighted to a great extent but American drama virtually is erased" (29–30). Today, however, perceptions are beginning to change.

This books seeks to examine the vitality and broad scope of American dramatic literature by focusing on as many twentieth-century American dramatists and dramas as possible. The anthology is meant for students, scholars, and practitioners of theatre and American literary history alike, assisting them in discovering a richer and wider perception of American drama than has heretofore been acknowledged. In order to reveal the range of American drama, we will illuminate the history of playwrights both well known and not so well known. Particular attention is given to the institutions in which the dramas have been performed (the theatres, venues, and directors who assisted the playwrights), dramaturgical analysis of the plays, background to the playwrights, and the relationship between dramatic literature and broader historical continuities and social transformations. The history of a national literature inescapably concerns itself with questions of national identity. Literary history is neither social nor political history, but an historical understanding of dramatic literature cannot be separated from cultural influences, political movements, and social change. Directly or indirectly, American drama reflects the American social milieu.

Subjects are arranged within three categories: time periods, popular playwrights, and themes. Chapters examine the timeframe of particular dramas, focus exclusively on major playwrights and their works, or shed light on thematic relationships between playwrights. Every attempt has been made to distribute the research broadly in an effort to weigh the significance of the plays and their importance to the history of American drama. The contributors attempt at every instance to provide proportional emphasis given the diversity of dramas.

A Companion to Twentieth-Century American Drama embodies the work of a generation of scholars who have collectively and to a large extent defined the field, as well as that of a new generation who have contributed wide-ranging and useful insights. The authors come from various branches of American intellectual traditions, including theatre, drama, and performance studies; literary and American studies departments; and comparative literature.

The importance of this work is difficult to overstate. American drama may lag behind; however, it is far from being the "bastard child" it was once considered. Indeed, American dramatic literature is beginning to secure its place as representative of American art and culture. By attending to the various historical traditions and influences of American drama, as well as analysis of plays themselves, this work provides an overview of American drama and its place in twentieth-century American literary tradition.

BIBLIOGRAPHY

Gassner, J. (1954). *Masters of the Drama*, 3rd ed. New York: Dover.
Matthews, B. (1889). "The Dramatic Outlook in America." *Harper's New Monthly Magazine* 78 (May): 924–30.
Smith, M. (2003). "The Once and Future Musical." *American Theatre* (December): 45–7.
Smith, S. H. (1997). *American Drama: The Bastard Art*. New York: Cambridge University Press.

2

American Drama, 1900–1915

Mark Evans Bryan

The drama of the modern United States before World War I was in many ways not a *modern* drama at all. In the years before the Little Theatre Movement gave rise to a generation of American playwrights who experimented with European realisms and anti-realisms, and the "new stagecraft" made metaphoric space of theatre production, American drama existed much as it had since the Civil War. Literary and theatrical modernism in Europe was a response to the changing circumstances of modern life. Though the American social and political landscape was transformed by the same cultural forces, the American drama of the first 15 years of the twentieth century reflected instead a theatrical business structure that resisted new forms and a literary culture that produced few new works of drama, however much a series of uniquely American responses to modernity occurred.

The spectacular 1899 premiere of *Ben-Hur* in New York City typified the American drama of the turn of the twentieth century. Adapted by William Young from the best-selling novel by Lew Wallace, the six-act religious melodrama was a popular and critical success and the grandest stage spectacle that New York audiences had yet seen. Incorporating eight horses and two chariots running at a gallop on massive treadmills, a moving cyclorama background painting, and wind machines, the climactic chariot race of *Ben-Hur* is far more representative of the American stage at the beginning of the twentieth century than, for instance, the Boston premiere, nine years before, of the realist drama *Margaret Fleming* (1890) by James A. Herne, arguably the first modernist American drama.

In his 1886 column on literature, William Dean Howells, the arbiter of American realism, praises the work of vaudevillian Edward Harrigan. In Harrigan's short comedies of working-class Irish and German immigrant life in New York, Howells discerns "the actual life of the city . . . from laborers in the street to the most powerful of the ward politicians." Harrigan, Howells observes, "writes, stages, and plays his pieces; he has his own theatre, and can risk his own plays in it, simply and cheaply" (Howells 1886: 315–16). The business of American theatre, Howells adds, places a conservative stranglehold on the development of the drama:

> there has been so little that is fresh, native, and true on the stage for so long that the managers might not know what to make of [an innovative] piece; and it is to the manager, not the public, that the playwright appeals. . . . It costs so much to "stage" a play in these days of a material theatre but no drama, that [a manager] can only risk giving the old rubbish in some novel disguise. . . . With the present expensiveness of setting, a failure is ruinous, and nothing really new can be risked. So much money has to be put into the frame of the picture that only the well-known chromo-effects in sentiment, character, and situation can be afforded in the picture. (315)

The transformation of the theatre industry reflected massive changes in American culture. The years before the turn of the century were characterized by rapid economic development and the growth of national industries. In the Progressive Era (ca. 1890–1900), limited-liability corporations became the norm in American business and antitrust legislation was passed to reign in the power of American enterprise. Scientific management transformed the practices of the urban factory. Market instability, immigration from Europe, and agricultural crises in the Midwest and South produced a surplus of unskilled workers in American cities. Before 1890, the economy had depended largely on capital goods, but after the deflation of the 1880s, American capitalists directed their investments toward consumer goods (ready-to-wear clothing, leisure items, household goods, etc.). For the first time, the production of such goods became dominant, as the small trading store transformed, for example, into the department store, moving from proprietary to corporate capitalism.

American theatre "business" responded to the centralizing and corporatizing strategies of new American industry. The difficulties of touring in the United States before the Civil War were demonstrated by limitations for elaborate productions to profit from more than local audiences in the major theatre centers. The innovation of the combination company, which allowed large-scale productions to tour in their entirety on the nation's growing rail routes, made the production of theatre a potentially profitable enterprise for national touring corporations. Large producing and booking agencies for drama and vaudeville emerged in the metropolitan Northeast; as a result, American dramatists produced new plays in large numbers from the 1880s to the 1920s as demand, and copyright protections, increased.[1] Auditoriums that accommodated touring productions replaced local stock companies, regional "local color" writing in the theatre disappeared, and the American theatrical world fell under the influence of a relatively small number of producers. By the time of the writing of Howells's 1886 column, combination-touring companies from New York City dominated the popular theatre in the East. A decade later, the most powerful of these producing cartels was founded: the Syndicate, a booking and producing monopoly effectively controlling the "legitimate" American stage until the early 1910s, when the rival Shubert organization wrested control of it with its own growing monopoly. "I tell you," the playwright Clyde Fitch once wrote, "there will never be *good* American dramatists till there are good American producers!" In the Syndicate, Fitch found producers; indeed, perhaps no dramatist benefited from the producing monopolies as much as he did. But even Fitch lamented the power of Syndicate producer Charles Frohman: "what a state it is, when there is only *one man* to whom one can offer a play and expect to have it in any 1/2 adequate way presented" (Fitch, *Letters* 1924: 117).

The career of Clyde Fitch exemplifies the changing role of the dramatist in the United States at the turn of the century. Though he was one of the most commercially successful playwrights in American history and a favorite of Frohman and the Syndicate, Fitch was also admired by figures in the theatre as disparate as the literary critic Howells, the anti-Syndicate producer and playwright David Belasco, and the playwright Rachel Crothers. Brander Matthews suggested that *The Truth* (1907), Fitch's serious comedy of manners about an upper-middle-class married couple besieged by the pathological honesty of one and the pathological dishonesty of the other, "bid fair to achieve the cosmopolitan popularity of Ibsen's 'Doll's House'" (1926: 43). Fitch encompassed both models of the American dramatist in the new twentieth century: the literate, professional writer, whose experience of the theatre was dominated by collegiate theatricals, the study of the classics, and, for some, the seminars of George Pierce Baker at Harvard; and the professional theatre artist, whose experience of the theatre began with professional theatre production and whose career in playwriting complemented a career as a director, producer, or performer. A graduate of Amherst College, a budding novelist, and a young playwright who had been invited to speak before George Pierce Baker's drama club at Harvard, Fitch had produced only three full-length plays before he began his long association with Charles Frohman in 1892.

Fitch's popular melodramas, plays such as *The Girl with the Green Eyes* (1902) and *The Woman in Case* (1905), were episodic dramas of vice, blackmail, and violence, with Syndicate-required happy endings (Meserve 1994: 164).[2] A deft and observant comic writer as well, his comedies ranged from the realistic detail of *The Truth* to *Captain Jinks of the Horse Marines* (1901), in which the title character, the clumsy and unsuccessful military character made popular in the song "Captain Jinks of the Horse Marines" (ca. 1868), wagers one thousand dollars that he can woo a beautiful opera singer. Falling in love with her instead, the bet becomes public and Jinks nearly loses his love. The play ends with the lovers together, a happy toast, and the singing of "Captain Jinks of the Horse Marines." The comedy mixes romantic farce with political commentary: although the "Captain Jinks" song was popular in military circles, the figure of "Captain Jinks" was utilized by anti-imperialists who opposed the Spanish–American War (1898) and the nationalist, expansionist policies of the United States. Prominent anti-imperialist Ernest Crosby published his satirical, anti-war novel, *Captain Jinks, Hero*, the following year.

The plays of Clyde Fitch portrayed a modern world; they explored urban life, the pathologies of modern culture, and the new social structures of the industrializing age. His characters, if lacking depth, had detail. Rachel Crothers praised the complexity and moral ambiguity of the central character in *The Truth*: "I think you've done the most difficult of things," wrote Crothers to Fitch, "given us all sides of a human being, and made her intensely appealing in spite of very grave faults – a very complex and interesting study.... It makes the commonplace element extremely dramatic" (Fitch, *Letters* 1924: 332). Fitch's melodramas of contemporary society bridge the gap between the tradition of American romantic melodrama and social realism. In a 1904 speech, Fitch calls for a "real melodrama" that portrays the "truth" of the urban condition:

> the incidents, the events of everyday life in a big city are more melodramatic than anything that was ever put upon the stage.... [It is] a daily life which is blood and iron mixed with soul and sentiment – melodrama of the ancients, pure and simple.... Realism is only simplicity and truth. (*Plays* 1930: xli–xlii)

Fitch's last play, however, illustrates the playwright's ambiguous distinction between "real melodrama and the false." *The City* (1910), "a modern play of American life," is a traditional melodrama that appropriates the hallmarks of stage realism (443). It is located in the morally ambiguous urban world of social realism, using naturalistic dialogue and suggesting the role of heredity in its characters' lives. But *The City* is not a story of "everyday life in a big city." The death of George Rand, Sr., the scion of a rural New York family and the victim of blackmail at the hand of the melodramatic villain, Hannock – a "drug fiend," convicted felon, and Rand's illegitimate son – prompts the Rand family to move from rural "Middleburg" to New York City (478). Years later, George Rand, Jr. has climbed the social ladder as a businessman and likely gubernatorial candidate, becoming wealthy and successful, though corrupt. Hannock secretly marries Cicely Rand, his half-sister, but when George learns of their liaison, he attempts to end it by divulging the secret of Hannock's parentage. Hannock murders Cicely but is prevented from shooting himself by his half-brother, though he threatens to destroy George's political career with the scandal. In the end, George decides to "make a clean breast of it all!... no matter what it costs," withdraw from public life, and repent for all his crimes of action and inaction, while beginning a new life (618).

Although structurally melodramatic, *The City* is a commentary on the city itself, the stultifying nature of rural life, and the transformation of American urban culture. Fitch's career coincided with perhaps the most significant changes in the geopolitics of American society. The pastoral American past collided with industrial, urban America; the rapid industrialization had repercussions throughout American culture (Trachtenberg 1982). American theatre audiences embraced entertainments that appealed to nostalgia for an oftentimes fictional past, a premodern American landscape expressed in melodrama, minstrelsy, and the entertainments of the increasingly popular vaudeville stage. Fitch, however, a modernist in spirit if not in execution, directed his final play to question idyllic versions of rural life and extolled the possibilities of the new urban century: "Don't blame the City," George Rand, Jr. implores after the death of his sister and the end of his political career: "It's not her fault! It's our own! What the City does is bring out what's strongest in us....*She* gives the man his opportunity" (627–8).

Many of the social melodramas that held the stage during the career of Clyde Fitch explore the temptations, dangers, and possibilities of the new city. The American tradition of social satire and domestic comedy, however, was equally successful in portraying modern urban life. Changing social mores and upper-class urban culture are at the center of *The New York Idea* by Langdon Mitchell, who had grown up in the closed social world that he satirized. Arthur Hobson Quinn included *The New York Idea* with *The Great Divide* by William Vaughn Moody, *Jeanne d'Arc* by Percy MacKaye, and Crothers's *The Three of Us*, all of which premiered during the 1906–7 season in New York, as "the advance guard of the new drama" (Quinn 1927, vol. 2: 4).

The New York Idea is a comedy of manners, an indictment of upper-middle-class American culture, and a drama of society and marriage, not unlike English sentimental comedies of the eighteenth century, but placed in the new context of the burgeoning American divorce culture. (The rate of divorce in the United States rose sharply between the end of the Civil War and the writing of *The New York Idea*. In 1880, less than one half of 1 percent of all marriages ended in divorce; by the beginning of World War I, that rate had climbed to over 10 percent.) On the eve of the wedding of Philip Phillmore, a divorced Manhattan judge, and Mrs. Cynthia Karslake, a divorced heiress, the lives of a small group of the New York social elite are thrown into disarray as they couple and uncouple, forming fleeting unions rooted in love, spite, or social pressure. Cynthia has agreed to marry Philip, despite her desire to be "a free woman," because "a divorcée has no place in society" (Mitchell 1956: 140). The "society" to which Cynthia refers is a closed social world. The characters are "persons of breeding" (a series of horse metaphors and sexual innuendo begins with this Act 1 utterance), who "winter in Cairo" and inherit millions of dollars (124–6), and who own famous racehorses and consider bankruptcy to be "the next thing to" death (136).

The New York Idea satirizes upper-class mores, but it also charts society and social space in the changing New York (one of several horses mentioned in the play, in fact, is named "Urbanity"). The play reflects the increasing divisions in the United States in 1906: between the wealthy and the working, as well as the urban and the rural. Indeed, when Philip's sister, Grace, complains that the nineteenth of May is "ridiculously late to be in town," she renders invisible the majority of the more than four million people in the city of New York in 1906. It is an echo of the descriptions of the city in the summer in Edith Wharton's novel *The House of Mirth* (1905), in which New York is described as "a dusty deserted city" or as simply "deserted" (Wharton 1984: 224, 250). (The stage adaptation of *The House of Mirth*, by Wharton and Clyde

Fitch, premiered one month before Mitchell's play.) *The New York Idea* – that "a woman should marry whenever she has a whim for a man" – indicates an uneasiness in the conservative elite in an age where civil unions no longer guaranteed the inheritance of fortune and status (202). "I feel as if we are all taking tea on the slope of a volcano!" observes the first Mrs. Phillmore, as the characters of *The New York Idea* teeter on the edge of their new century (145).

The melodramas of Edward Sheldon are more explicitly ideological, exploring urban life, corruption, and racism. A graduate of George Pierce Baker's Workshop 47 at Harvard, the first-of-its-kind workshop in dramatic writing in the United States, Sheldon wrote melodramas in the nineteenth-century tradition about twentieth-century social problems. *Salvation Nell* (1908) is a melodrama of the urban condition that follows Nell, a working-class woman, as her life is nearly destroyed by her criminal lover. Nell is, at root, a traditionally melodramatic woman in distress, but she is the central character of a play set in believably realistic working-class surroundings. *Salvation Nell* was produced by Harrison Grey Fiske, an admirer of Henrik Ibsen, in a production that Quinn hailed as "as realistic a picture of slum life as can be imagined" (1927, vol. 2: 86).

In *The Nigger* (1910), Sheldon combines melodrama and social critique. Produced by Winthrop Ames during the debut season of the New Theatre, *The Nigger* was both a reconstruction of the "tragic mulatto" melodramas of the mid-nineteenth century and a response to the political and business climate of early twentieth-century America.[3] Set among the corrupt business and political leaders of an unidentified state in the South, *The Nigger* follows Philip Morrow, a white racist governor controlled by a powerful business monopoly, a corrupt media, and the secret of his African heritage. But even as the play relies on traditional melodramatic devices, it is a commentary on the undermining of America's Reconstruction (ca. 1865–76, which attempted to "reconstruct" the South by, among other things, incorporating newly freed slaves into the social fabric of American life). In the play, however, law, society, and Morrow himself are dominated by the will of industry and Southern racism, which cannot overcome attempts at racial reconciliation. Government in the post-Reconstruction South, Sheldon's play observes, was subsumed by the darkest elements of modern society: the anti-democratic power of industry; the primitive backwardness of American regions not fully engaged in the urban, modern world; and the legacies of American chattel slavery, the root source of American market successes in the nineteenth century. Although *The Nigger* is indeed a racist drama (as its title suggests), it is in many ways the modern incarnation of a genre of racial melodrama popularized in such plays as Dion Boucicault's *The Octoroon* (1859) and Bartley Campbell's *The White Slave* (1881). The play is a rebuff to the post-Reconstruction literature of reconciliation that united Northern and Southern whites at the expense of African Americans. *The Nigger* repudiates the perception of the Civil War as a nonsectarian heroic struggle and the myths of the benevolence of the antebellum agrarian South that gained currency in the period onstage and in fiction (as in the novels of Winston Churchill and Thomas Dixon, and D. W. Griffith's 1915 film, *The Birth of a Nation*, based on Dixon's racist bestseller).[4]

The Boss (1911), Sheldon's realistic melodrama of American business, follows the marriage of Michael Regan and Emily Griswold, whom Regan acquires as the settlement of a business arrangement. Regan has "swindled and blackjacked and knifed his way" to near dominance of the city's shipping industry and threatens to devastate the Griswolds' grain business by using the local press to expose their illegal financial dealings. He exhorts his only daughter from James Griswold; she selflessly accedes to the agreement, although for Emily, their marriage is indeed a "deal": it "stops at the door of the church" (Sheldon 1953: 885, 896). Emily's brother, Donald, incites a general strike among Regan's labor. When he is nearly successful, Regan prepares to move the grain shipping contracts out of the city ("the major reason this city has for existing") and Donald is nearly killed by Regan's thugs. In a jail cell, awaiting prosecution for the attack on Donald Griswold, Regan repents out of love for Emily and, in turn, Emily decides that she loves Michael Regan: "I've never told you," she tells her husband, "because I never knew it until now" (885, 924).

Set in "one of the Eastern lake-ports," *The Boss* reflects the extraordinary changes in cities that grew as national transportation hubs between the West and the Atlantic coast in the nineteenth century (the "lake-port" city of Sheldon's native Chicago, for instance, expanded rapidly after the Civil War as a center for distributing agricultural products). The play portrays the rising power of ethnic "bosses" in Eastern cities (as Harrigan had done in his Mulligan plays) and recalls the period of widespread labor insurrection that proceeded the turn of the century. Although the play fails to portray a realistic representation of American labor, it does reflect the increasing power of the business elite in cities centered on single industries and the influence of the Catholic Church in working-class communities in the industrial East. However, despite its portrayal of labor militancy, *The Boss* is an essentially pro-business play, assigning power finally with Regan and not with Griswold or his loosely banded union.

The massive changes in the character of Eastern labor were only part of the transformation of modern life reflected in the dramas of the twentieth century's first 15 years. Americans in the final decade of the nineteenth century witnessed the closing of the Western frontier. Westward expansion had characterized the age, but the rapid growth of rail lines beyond the Mississippi River after the Civil War opened up millions of acres of new land and, by the close of the nineteenth century, the end of the frontier was in sight. Popular American literature and entertainment reflected romantic associations with the disappearing "wild" American West. The "Wild West" shows of P. T. Barnum and "Buffalo Bill" Cody delighted audiences in the East and frontier melodramas surged in popularity in the Gilded Age with the plays of Bartley Campbell, Joaquin Miller, and Frank Murdoch and continued into the early twentieth century in such melodramas as Augustus Thomas's *Arizona* (1899) and William C. de Mille's *Strongheart* (1905). The "western" historical romance novel conquered the popular fiction market and stage adaptations were numerous; the stage version of Owen Wister's *The Virginian*, the best-selling novel of 1902, for instance, ran for over 100 performances on Broadway in 1904 and was revived the following year.[5]

The closing of the frontier in 1890, observes historian Richard Slotkin, "provided the basis" for Frederick Jackson Turner's "frontier thesis" (1994: 532). Turner advanced his theory, linking the idea of the frontier to the development of American culture, in a paper delivered at a meeting of historians in 1893 at the World's Columbian Exposition in Chicago. Two years later, William Vaughn Moody, early American drama's most eloquent poet of the frontier in the American imagination, accepted a teaching position at the University of Chicago, built around the midway of the Columbian Exposition. Moody admired the work of European modernists Ibsen, Yeats, Shaw, and Maeterlinck, though he found some of Shaw's work "pigheaded" and the realist writings of Ibsen too romantic.[6] He detested the commercial theatre, calling the central offices of the Syndicate, "the den of Apollyon" (343) and Broadway, "a monster of great incalculability of taste, wont to eat alive a playwright a day" (299). "For five years," wrote Moody in 1904, "Frohman and his gang [the Syndicate] have been ramming fustian down the good people's throats... [with] their patched-up French farces, their pick-me-up Clydefitcheries" (188). But in 1906, *The Great Divide*, Moody's dark, metaphorical drama of American character, culture, and region, became one of the most popular plays in the United States.

The Great Divide is a drama of the frontier and Eastern society, but its narrative and themes have little in common with the frontier plays of the age. In a rustic cabin in Arizona, described by one of the characters as an "unholy place," a transplanted Eastern woman, Ruth Jordan, is left alone by her family and menaced by three rough villains (1995: 269). They break down the door, subdue Ruth, and taunt her while they prepare a game of chance to determine who will win the "sole and exclusive rights... to love and cherish on the premises" (274). Moody does not, however, provide the expected male hero to save her from sexual assault, a conventional action in the melodrama. Instead, Ruth bargains with one of her attackers. As they roll the dice to decide her fate, she "*looks wildly about, shrinking from* [Ghent], *then with sudden resolution speaks*": "Save me, and I will make it up to you!... Save me from these others, and from yourself, and I will pay you – with my life" (273–4). Stephen Ghent agrees to the contract, buying "free field" with Ruth from one desperado with a string of gold nuggets and besting the other in an off-stage pistol duel. When conscience precludes Ruth from shooting the now-wounded Ghent and from killing herself, either of which might have suited the melodrama, she pleads with him to be merciful and release her from her bond. But instead of attacking or escaping from the man who had, moments before, come to her home to rape her, Ruth bathes and bandages his wound and leaves with him in the night.

The Jordan family, the audience learns in the opening moments of *The Great Divide*, have come to Arizona from Boston to profit from local industry. But only Ruth appreciates the desert frontier. "I think I shall be punished for being so happy," she tells her sister-in-law. With the Jordan family came Winthrop Newbury, an educated Easterner, whom Ruth rejects because he is "finished" (269). She wants a mate who "isn't finished . . . a sublime abstraction – of the glorious unfulfilled – of the West – the Desert" (271). When her family discovers Ruth again, in Act 2, she is married to Ghent, living in another cabin, this one overlooking the silver mine that has made him wealthy. She both hates and loves her husband, describing him as two creatures, standing side by side: the Ghent who "heard [her] prayer to him . . . and led [her] out of a world of little codes and customs into a great new world," and the "hateful" Ghent, the man who purchased her life and forced himself on her, "the human beast that goes to its horrible pleasure as not even a wild animal will go" (287–8). Secretly, Ruth has purchased the very string of gold nuggets with which Ghent bought her in order to buy her freedom and the freedom of their unborn child, leaving Ghent and the West. When Ghent arrives in Ruth's Boston home six months later, he argues that his wedding to Ruth was a "Second Birth." Resolving to leave Ruth and their child, Ghent meets her one last time. He offers his love, describes his suffering, and releases her from their contract: "Done is done, and lost is lost, and smashed to hell is smashed to hell." But before he leaves, Ruth declares her love for him, blaming "an angry Heaven" for her compulsion to drive him away and "cleanse" herself "the only way [her] fathers knew – by wretchedness, by self-torture" (297).

The Great Divide rejects both the predestination of melodramatic constructs as well as the predestination of Calvinist New England Christianity. The eschatology of melodrama is overturned by Ghent, who enters the play as a theatrical reprobate, but becomes a kind of hero. Similarly, within the narrative, Ghent is allowed an opportunity for radical repentance, but instead he becomes the embodiment of an alternative to the "self-torture" of Ruth's ascetic Protestantism. Moody's play offers another version of Turner's "frontier thesis": the American West and "Almighty Nature" as a "God" for Americans in the modern world. Although the language in *The Great Divide* is often florid and its melodramatic touches (the duel and Ghent's secret patronage of the Jordan family through the guise of a distant uncle) are perhaps the reason it proved so popular, it embraces a modern conception of female sexuality and challenges the conservative dramaturgy of the nineteenth-century melodrama, creating particularly complex figures in Ghent and Ruth. The play also challenges the corporate, progressive image of the West in sources like Wister's *The Virginian*. Unfortunately, like the racism of *The Nigger* and the sexual politics of *The Boss*, Moody's play marginalizes Ruth and portrays Ghent's Western masculinity as the ideal, minimizing the specter of Ruth's probable rape as part of masculine vitality and, perhaps, suggesting a metaphor of conquest that advocates American imperialism.

Moody rejected an offer from the Syndicate to produce his next work. The poet and playwright, whose final work, *The Faith Healer* (1909), was a commercial failure, had long since decided to join with Broadway's "Independents": Lee Shubert and his growing organization; Henry Miller, who had produced *The Great Divide*; and E. H. Sotherne, the producer, classical actor, and former Frohman apprentice. Perhaps the most independent theatre artist in New York, however, was not among Moody's

select allies, former Syndicate producer David Belasco, whose own drama of the frontier, *The Girl of the Golden West* (1905), had delighted Broadway audiences the year before. Producer and playwright, Belasco exemplified his own dictum that a drama could only be written "with a thorough technical knowledge... of so complicated and treacherous an instrument of artistic expression as the stage" (1919: 41). His career is the model of the playwright as theatre professional. Having been a child actor in his native San Francisco, Belasco produced theatre in New York for the Frohman brothers and the Syndicate before, in 1902, he became an independent producer and playwright, bringing dozens of plays to the New York stage prior to 1930. He was a technical innovator, self-consciously realistic – sometimes naturalistic – in stage setting, and famous in his day for the uses of electric lighting effects in his productions.

"Both as a playwright and producer I am a realist," David Belasco once wrote, "but I do not believe in harrowing audiences unnecessarily" (52). Clyde Fitch struggled with the same distinction when he contrasted "real melodrama and the false." "With two thirds of the general public," Fitch argues in the essay, "'realism' means something ugly, or horrible, or puerile" (*Plays* 1930: xlii). Belasco was, however, an innovative realist producer. He was also a meticulous researcher and, at times, an advocate of stark naturalism on the stage. In 1913, while preparing to produce *The Man Inside*, by Roland Burnham Molineaux, Belasco "went down near the Tombs Prison at 2 A.M. to listen to the sounds in the vicinity" and hired a "Bowery denizen" to guide him "on a slumming tour among Chinese opium-joints" (Belasco 1919: 52–3). For the scenography of his 1909 production of *The Easiest Way*, by Eugene Walter, Belasco

> went to the meanest theatrical lodging-house [he] could find in the Tenderloin district and bought the entire interior of one of its most dilapidated rooms – patched furniture, threadbare carpet, tarnished and broken gas fixtures, tumble-down cupboards, dingy doors and window-casings, and even the faded paper on the walls. (77)

Indeed, Belasco's production of *The Easiest Way*, a sentimental melodrama with a psychologically complex central character, is a significant event in the history of realism on the American stage, yet the play itself is a melodrama of the urban condition.

Although David Belasco was a "realistic" producer-director well known for his detailed sets, his plays are romantic melodramas. Like Fitch, Belasco's great talent was for "appeal[ing] to the public's constantly changing taste" (44). *Madame Butterfly* (1900) and *The Darling of the Gods* (1902), for instance, two of the plays produced by the partnership of Belasco and John Luther Long, are romances set in Japan; they capitalize on the growing significance of Pacific Asia to the United States. *The Girl of the Golden West* (1905) is a frontier melodrama. *The Return of Peter Grimm* (1911), a melodrama of the supernatural, was a platform for Belasco's technical innovation. Peter Grimm's ghostly return in Act 2 was achieved by inverting the traditional solution; instead of creating a special light for the actor portraying Grimm, Belasco directed his technicians to light around him, illuminating the living and cloaking the dead in darkness. Belasco was ultimately the producer of brilliantly staged events, rather than writing plays, and few of his dramas were produced later in the twentieth century.

Quinn's "advance guard of the new drama" included Langdon Mitchell, Percy MacKaye, and William Vaughn Moody, three Harvard-educated dramatists. But it also included Rachel Crothers, an artist whose professional life resembled Belasco's more so than it did any of her classmates in the "advance guard" of 1906. She began her career as an actress and directed many of her plays over her 30 years on the American stage. She was a talented commercial writer, whose facility with popular melodrama was matched by the ideological currency of her feminism. Her dramas explored the changing opportunities for women at the beginning of the twentieth century. The women's movement of the early Progressive Era overthrew the Victorian "cult of true womanhood" and produced a generation of women for whom education and work outside the home became more available and socially acceptable. Crothers's plays challenged longstanding social barriers for women during the period of activism that led to the passage of the Nineteenth Amendment, which guaranteed women the right to vote, in 1919.

Rachel Crothers's first success was the frontier melodrama *The Three of Us* (1906), conventional except in its focus. Narratives of the frontier at the turn of the century tended to be paeans to an explicitly masculine vitality; as different as are *The Virginian* and *The Great Divide*, their male central figures are in many ways indistinguishable from one another. The protagonist of *The Three of Us*, however, is Rhy MacChesney, an unmarried woman and the maternal influence on two younger brothers. Crothers sets the fundamental conflicts of *The Three of Us*, which was a massive popular success on Broadway, in a social sphere. The villain, Berresford, threatens MacChesney's gold mine not with force but with immoral business and personal dealings. MacChesney protects her family and her gold mine from Berresford at the expense of her reputation and the play becomes an argument against the nineteenth-century conception of female honor. Although the narrative is unmistakably melodramatic and the conclusion is ultimately conservative, Crothers's subversion of the familiar form of the frontier melodrama points toward her dramas of the "double standard" for men and women, *A Man's World* (1910) and *He and She* (1911).

A Man's World, directed by Crothers and produced by the Shubert organization, ran for only 71 performances in 1910, but it incited a wide variety of popular responses and, famously, a play, Augustus Thomas's *As a Man Thinks* (1911), a masculinist and racist rebuttal of Crothers's implicit argument against the "double standard" in male and female social and sexual interactions.[7] *A Man's World* is nominally a domestic melodrama. Although it follows the life of its exceptional female protagonist – Frank Ware, a novelist and social activist, the mother of an adopted son, Kiddie, and the center of a "bohemian" household of artists in New York City – the parentage of Kiddie is the central question of the drama. Acts 2 and 3 are centered on a debate within the boarding house: Kiddie resembles Malcolm Gaskell, Frank's frequent companion, and Lione, who provides the play its title when she questions the efficacy even of attempts at gender equality, is convinced that Malcolm and Frank are the child's biological parents. The accusation prompts Frank to confront Malcolm, who admits to parenting the child but refuses responsibility.

Although *A Man's World* conforms to a melodramatic construct in its focus on the secret of a character's parentage, Crothers questions the underlying rationale for the device: the economic motivation for the historical oppression of women. In this way, the play – like Mitchell's *The New York Idea* and Thomas's *As a Man Thinks*, which includes a lengthy defense of the double standard as a means to insure inheritance – is a reflection of the renewed oppression of women in an age where social revolution endangered the ruling American business aristocracy as well as the rising managerial class.

He and She continues Crothers's challenge to the double standard, as it relates to familial responsibility, social roles, and art. Ann Herford, a sculptor, is awarded a prestigious commission that everyone, including her daughter and husband, assumed would go to her husband, Tom, also a sculptor. But over the course of the four months between Acts 1 and 2, Ann loses touch with her daughter, Millicent, who has remained at boarding school during the holidays, rather than be ignored. Alone and away from home, Millicent has fallen in love with the school's chauffeur and announces that she intends to marry him. Deciding that she has neglected her maternal responsibility, Ann begs Tom to take the commission and sacrifices her career as an artist to be with her daughter: "I'll hate you because you're doing it – and I'll hate myself because I gave it up – and I'll almost – hate – her. I know. . . . There isn't any choice, Tom – she's part of my body – part of my soul" (Crothers, *He and She* 1995: 335).

He and She, Brenda Murphy contends, is a "discussion play" (1999: 83). But although it is a play that is conspicuously about ideas, it is a realist drama of middle-class life in the United States and is, perhaps, more similar to the work of Ibsen and Chekhov than any play written for the commercial theatre in its time. But *He and She* was not a success when it was written. The play failed in a series of cities and did not premiere in New York until 1920, when a new drama had begun to emerge in the United States.

Notes

1. David Belasco wrote that new plays "pour down upon [the producer] in avalanches" (1919: 42). The 1891 International Copyright Treaty, which protected American works overseas, and the revision of the American copyright law in 1909 to include a broader definition of "art" and the author's "works" afforded American dramatists a greater degree of control over their own works in publication. Moody, however, suspected that the "barbaric laws" governing copyright might "exist in favor of Frohman,

Shubert, *et al.*, in order to provide them ampler forage upon the brains of men who are misguided enough to write plays" (*Letters* 1935: 372).

2. In his discussion of Fitch's play *The Girl with the Green Eyes*, Walter J. Meserve notes especially that this melodrama "ends happily." "The happy ending," writes Meserve, "was a requirement of the 'Syndicate School'" (Meserve 1994: 164). Indeed, such an ending is a generic characteristic of the melodrama, a conservative form that achieved tremendous popularity in the nineteenth century in Europe and the United States. By the turn of the twentieth century, the Syndicate controlled theatres throughout the eastern United States, monopolizing touring auditoriums in many cities. Seeking dramas that appealed to the broad audience it had acquired, the Syndicate favored melodramas that were, though ideally exciting and spectacular, not likely to offend audience tastes outside the urban centers of the mid-Atlantic.

3. The New Theatre, a precursor to the American Little Theatre Movement, was funded by a group of arts-minded patrons but associated with the commercial Shubert organization. *The Nigger* was the only American play in the first season.

4. Winston Churchill's *The Crisis* was one of the best-selling books of 1901. The historical romance novel was adapted to the stage by Churchill and produced in New York in 1902 and 1908. Thomas Dixon adapted his novels *The Leopard's Spots* (1902) and *The Clansman* (1906) into a single play, *The Clansman*, which premiered in 1906. A decade later, D. W. Griffith adapted the stage melodrama based on the two novels into his feature film epic, *The Birth of a Nation* (1915). Robert Sklar describes *The Birth of a Nation* as a drama of racist reconciliation: "For that was what his film was about: the creation of a new nation after years of struggle and division, a nation of Northern and Southern whites united 'in common defense of their Aryan birthright,' with vigilante riders of the Klan as their symbol" (1975: 58). Sklar's quote comes from a title card in the film. See also the "Civil War" plays of the turn of the cen-

tury such as Bronson Howard's *Shenandoah* (1888), Belasco's *The Heart of Maryland* (1895), William Gillette's *Secret Service* (1895), in which he starred through the first decade of the twentieth century, and Augustus Thomas's *The Copperhead* (1918).

5. Owen Wister, *The Virginian* (New York: Macmillan, 1902). The novel was adapted for the stage by producer Kirke La Shelle and Wister, the first cousin of playwright Langdon Mitchell, with whom he had once collaborated on an unpublished novel. The twentieth-century "Western," the "fable of conservative values, a cultural equivalent to incorporation," writes Trachtenberg, was "complete" in *The Virginian*. Wister transformed "the implicit egalitarianism of the earlier mode into an explicitly ruling-class vision": "Wister's great tale of the cowboy hero who wants at once the values of personal honor and worldly success, who is prepared to kill to defend both his own reputation and his employer's property, completes the cultural appropriation of the West.... Fusing elements of several vocational types in his cowboy figure, including that of 'foreman,' or superintendent, over the band of migrant laborers who performed the cowpunching and herding on the ranches and plains, Wister re-created the cowboy as a romantic knight of the plains...[affording] knightly deference to the aristocratic owner...[and, when necessary, killing] just as defense of private property justifies, indeed demands" (24–5). The novel is dedicated to Wister's friend, President Theodore Roosevelt, whose own *The Winning of the West* made use of the myth of the West, "convert[ing] the history of the Frontier into a myth of origins for the Progressive movement" (Slotkin 1994: 532).

6. Moody called Shaw "pigheaded" in a letter to his future wife (*Letters* 1935: 345). He called Maeterlinck "a great, sincere, prophetic soul." "I envy him," wrote Moody, "with that kind of envy which between men is the keenest variant of love" (209). And in another letter, from 1907, Moody wondered "how Ibsen ever got the name of a realist. A very debauchee of Romance. And that is really the hold he has over people" (341).

7. *As a Man Thinks*, directed by the author, ran for 128 performances in 1911. Although Thomas's play is clearly a sexist rebuttal to Crothers's condemnation of the "double standard" – at one point, in Act 3, *A Man's World* is referenced ("that woman dramatist with her play was right...It is 'a man's world'") and ridiculed ("it's a pretty wise world") – George Pierce Baker, in the introduction to his 1920 collection in which *As a Man Thinks* appears, neglects to refer to the source text in any way (Thomas 1920: 65).

BIBLIOGRAPHY

Belasco, D. (1919). *The Theatre Through Its Stage Door*. New York: Harper.

Bordman, G. (1994). *American Theatre: A Chronicle of Comedy and Drama, 1869–1914*. New York: Oxford University Press.

Crothers, R. (1985). *A Man's World*. In J. E. Barlow (ed.), *Plays by American Women, 1900–1930*. New York: Applause, 1–69. (Original work produced 1910.)

——(1995). *He and She*. In S. Watt and G. A. Richardson (eds.), *American Drama: Colonial to Contemporary*. Ft. Worth, TX: Harcourt Brace College, 301–35. (Original work produced 1911.)

Dickinson, T. H. (1915). *The Case of American Drama*. Boston: Houghton Mifflin.

Fitch, C. (1924). *Clyde Fitch and His Letters*, ed. M. J. Moses and V. Gerson. Boston: Little, Brown.

——(1930). *Plays by Clyde Fitch*, vol. 4, ed. M. J. Moses and V. Gerson. Boston: Little, Brown.

Grau, R. (1910). *The Businessman in the Amusement World*. New York: Broadway.

Hobsbawm, E. (1989). *The Age of Empire, 1875–1914*. New York: Vintage.

Howells, W. D. (1886). "Editor's Study." *Harper's New Monthly Magazine* 73: 314–19.

——(1893). *Criticism and Fiction*. New York: Harper.

Kern, S. (1983). *The Culture and Time and Space, 1880–1918*. Cambridge, MA: Harvard University Press.

Kolko, G. (1963). *The Triumph of Conservatism*. New York: Free Press of Glencoe.

Lears, T. J. J. (1983). *No Place of Grace: Antimodernism and the Transformation of American Culture, 1880–1920*. Chicago: University of Chicago Press.

Matthews, B. (1926). *Rip Van Winkle Goes to the Play and Other Essays on Plays and Players*. New York: Charles Scribner's Sons.

Meserve, W. J. (1994). *An Outline History of American Drama*, 2nd ed. New York: Feedback Theatrebooks and Prospero Press.

Mitchell, L. (1956). *The New York Idea*. In E. Bentley (ed.), *From the American Drama*. Garden City, NY: Doubleday. (Original work produced 1906.)

Moody, W. V. (1935). *Letters to Harriet*, ed. Percy MacKaye. Boston: Houghton Mifflin.

——(1995). *The Great Divide*. In S. Watt and G. A. Richardson (eds.), *American Drama: Colonial to Contemporary*. Ft. Worth, TX: Harcourt Brace College, 268–97. (Original work produced 1906.)

Moses, M. J. (1911). *The American Dramatist*. Boston: Little, Brown.

Murphy, B. (1987). *American Realism and American Drama, 1880–1940*. Cambridge: Cambridge University Press.

——(1999). "Feminism and the Marketplace: The Career of Rachel Crothers." In B. Murphy (ed.), *The Cambridge Companion to American Women Playwrights*. Cambridge: Cambridge University Press, 82–97.

Quinn, A. H. (1927). *A History of American Drama from the Civil War to the Present Day*, vols. 1 and 2. New York: Harper.

Richardson, G. A. (1993). *American Drama: From the Colonial Period Through World War I*. New York: Twayne.

Sheldon, E. (1953). *The Boss*. In A. H. Quinn (ed.), *Representative American Plays, from 1767 to the Present Day*, 7th ed. New York: Appleton-Century-Crofts.

Sklar, R. (1975). *Movie-Made America: A Cultural History of American Movies*. New York: Vintage.

Slotkin, R. (1994). *The Fatal Environment: The Myth of the Frontier in the Age of Industrialization, 1800–1890*. Norman: University of Oklahoma Press.

Smith, S. H. (1997). *American Drama: The Bastard Art*. Cambridge: Cambridge University Press.

Thomas, A. (1920). *As a Man Thinks*. In G. P. Baker (ed.), *Modern American Plays*. New York: Harcourt, Brace, and Howe.

Trachtenberg, A. (1982). *The Incorporation of America: Culture and Society in the Gilded Age*. New York: Hill and Wang.

Turner, F. J. (1920). *The Frontier in American History*. New York: Holt.

Wharton, E. (1984). *The House of Mirth*. New York: Bantam. (Original work published 1905.)

Wilmeth, D. B. and Bigsby, C. (eds.) (1999). *The Cambridge History of American Theatre, Volume 2: 1870–1945*. Cambridge: Cambridge University Press.

3

Ethnic Theatre in America

Rachel Shteir

Ethnic Theatre: Origins

Ethnic theatre must, first of all, be defined by its perimeters. To be ethnic is to be American, since we are all (notwithstanding Native Americans) originally from somewhere else. Moreover, ethnicity is fluid; from the first settlers arriving on these shores, becoming "American" could take as little as one generation. Thus, defining the history of ethnic theatre requires examining the first generation of theatres these cultures created. Furthermore, it necessitates tracing the development of these theatres, as ethnic groups arrived and faced different challenges. A related responsibility is to specify each ethnic group, avoiding conflating different ethnicities and reducing the category known as "American" to generic terms. Finally, telling the story involves looking closely at the intersection of race along with ethnicity.

Ethnic theatres existed from the late eighteenth century. For the first groups of settlers, such as the French in Louisiana and the Italians in San Francisco, theatre served two purposes: it created a social center and it conjured remembrances of homeland. More than generating new plays, these theatres, for the most part, produced classics such as Molière and Shakespeare. New plays and genres in the ethnic theatre increased during Jacksonian America (ca. 1820s and 1830s), as Irish and German immigrants poured into New York and other locales. These immigrants differed from earlier generations because they formed part of a new working class that demanded entertainment. These ethnic groups created a theatrical genre of "types," which became a central force inspiring generations of American plays. Unfortunately, these groups also provoked others to create mocking caricatures through ethnic stereotypes. The power of ethnic caricature – primarily the buffoon – was so great that it lasted for decades: whether the type was German, Irish, Jewish, or Chinese, the ethnic buffoon appeared in most varieties of ethnic theatres. The comic caricature was most prevalent in blackface minstrelsy, where the actor, mostly played by Irish actors at first, blacked up. "Blacking up" was a technique whereby actors applied burnt cork to their faces and performed condescending "imitations" of African Americans. By the 1920s, almost every great Jewish American comedian began blacking up in vaudeville and burlesque (Al Jolson, for example).

In addition to the minstrel actor, among the first ethnic types to appear in Jacksonian-era melodramas was the "noble savage," an imitation of Native Americans. Generally speaking, the male character died a tragic death at the hands of the white man. If female Native American characters appeared, they converted to Christianity. A turning point came in the play *Metamora* (1829), the first to feature a Native American character as the "hero." Written by John Augustus Stone, *Metamora* starred the well-known American actor Edwin Forrest, who drew large audiences for 40 years in the role. The play pitted Indians and Englishmen in a Manichean battle for supremacy. Stone created Metamora as kind, chivalric, brave, and gentle; however, the character was, according to the prevailing sentiments of the time, inferior to the white man intellectually. At the play's conclusion Metamora lies dying while cursing the white man, which caused many audiences at that time to hiss.

Still, it is worth pointing out that *Metamora* is no simple-minded defense of the Indian Removal Act of 1830, a law justifying theft of Native American land and wholesale destruction of their civilization. Stone makes it clear that Metamora is betrayed by the white men's cruelty and greed rather than by his alleged savagery. However, because Forrest (made famous for his performance of Davy Crockett) performed Metamora, some scholars have observed that Metamora was subconsciously linked with American folk heroes such as Crockett, as well as other roles Forrest played: the "Yankee" character appearing in James H. Hackett's *Jonathan in England* (1828) and Charles Matthew's *A Trip to America* (1824), for example. Even as Stone presented Metamora as a caricature, Forrest's heroic performance in the role, and Forrest's association with the heroic Davy Crockett and "Yankee character," assuaged to some degree the debasing representation of Native Americans.

As waves of immigrants came to America during the antebellum years, ethnic theatres emerged for each group. These included Italian American, Swedish American, Irish American, Ukrainian American, Norwegian American, German American, Mexican American, especially in the American West and Southwest, and Chinese Americans in California. Indeed, ethnic theatre was, for the most part, regional. San Francisco's North Beach, for instance, turned into a center for Italian Americans. Los Angeles became home to Mexican American theatres. German Americans brought plays by Schiller and Goethe with them to New York. Some ethnic theatres toured across the country, seeking their local constituency. As each culture entered the United States, it brought its own folk-flavored dramas, performing plays that appealed to its sensibilities, concerns, and dilemmas. Still, nationwide the Irish ethnic group dominated theatre practice.

Beginning in the 1840s, Irish immigrants came in large numbers to America. Their departure from Ireland was largely owing to the potato famine. This group provided a clear picture of how definitions of ethnicity and race become conflated in the American theatre. During the decade, Irish performers continued to dominate blackface minstrelsy. But in contrast to the 1830s, when the Irish had been the butt of many "Irish" jokes in minstrelsy, Irishmen impersonated slaves more regularly in "Jim Crow" song and dance numbers as "the happy" Negro. In the 1840s, the Irishman E. P. Christy introduced the distinctive characteristics to the minstrel show's format. It was not until 1865 that the African American performer Charles Hicks became one of the first black men to produce a successful minstrel show, replacing whites in blackface.

While conflicting definitions of who could be American – which class and ethnicity – appeared in minstrelsy and melodrama, offstage a series of riots made it clear how important these definitions were. In 1849, the Astor Place Riot dramatized a fight between two actors: the American Edwin Forrest and the British William Macready. Forrest believed Macready had slandered him; as a result, he enlisted the "Bowery B'hoy" – slang for Irish American roughnecks – to disrupt the British actor's performance at the Astor Place Opera House. The National Guard was called in and 22 people were killed. The riot dramatized the tension between two opposing factions: one, elite and British, the other, "native" and *vox populi*. The Astor Place Riot revealed the fact that a class division had existed in America and that, as theatre historian David Grimsted put it, "one theatre was no longer enough to appeal to all classes" (1968: 219).

The staging of Harriet Beecher Stowe's 500-page novel of social justice, *Uncle Tom's Cabin*, adapted by white producer George L. Aiken in 1853 (one of among several adaptations), demonstrates how ethnic and racial identities can become closely intertwined. Even more than *Metamora* (with its conflation of Native American character and white popular actor), *Uncle Tom's Cabin* demonstrates how ethnic caricatures evolve into a more complicated social representation: in the plot, evil white characters exist alongside noble African American characters, and vice versa. But, likewise *Metamora*, the solution to social injustice resides less in changing the social system – slavery – than in the hands of one heroic, white individual. The play results in noble death: George, a slave, runs away to Canada, but ultimately he, like all good slaves in the era's fiction, dies nobly.

The collision of blackface minstrelsy's performance traditions and *Uncle Tom's Cabin* illustrates how the subject of a play made the intersection of race and ethnicity volatile. Whereas minstrelsy essentially presented comic entertainment, in *Uncle Tom's Cabin* the subject of slavery was so controversial that Irish actor G. C. Germon feared he would damage his career if he portrayed the lead role of the runaway slave, Uncle Tom. Many other theatres of the mid-nineteenth century (especially those in the comic tradition) used diction or dialect to divide ethnic identity from "American" identity. While the white characters spoke elevated English, the slaves replied in "slave dialectic."

After the Civil War, rising immigration created an emphasis on realism. As waves of new immigrants arrived, immigrant actors brought with them greater understanding of their lives to the stage; new plays portrayed new circumstances of immigrant life. Stage villains based on ethnic caricature still existed, such as the Jew in plays like

John Brougham's *Lottery* (1868) or Charles Townsend's *The Jail Bird* (1893). However, performers such as Edward Harrigan, who began his career by depicting Irish stereotypes in blackface minstrelsy, started his own stock company to broaden the way the Irish were portrayed.

Harrigan's most famous play, *The Mulligan Guard Ball* (1879), demonstrated this new interest in verisimilitude, albeit one still grounded in stock ideas of how each ethnicity behaved. In *The Mulligan Guard Ball*, Harrigan, influenced by Emile Zola's efforts to create naturalistic drama in France, tried to provide Americans with an indigenous drama that reflected their everyday experiences. According to one critic, "what Dickens was to London . . . and Zola to Paris, Mr. Harrigan is to New York" (qtd. in Moody 1966: 535). Harrigan's biographer, theatre scholar Richard Moody, remarks that Harrigan's characters were ordinary people, such as "grocery men, butchers, barbers, dock workers, river rats, undertakers, pawnbrokers, tailors" (35).

At the end of the nineteenth century, Irish and German plays burlesqued their own ethnic experiences. Ultimately during this era and into the twentieth century, different ethnic theatres and stereotypes were being assimilated into forms of popular entertainment. This was part of a movement striving to unite the populace as "Americans." Still, many ethnic theatres also continued to produce their plays apart from the mainstream. Some plays continued to reveal anxiety about the immigrant's role in America. Charles M. Hoyt's *A Trip to Chinatown* (1892) relays a fantasy of excluding various ethnicities from the mainstream. The plot features upper-class San Francisco characters "slumming" in Chinatown.

Popular culture appeared to be more inclusive, at least where race was concerned. In burlesque, some white producers were allowing black performers to speak for themselves, albeit with limitations. In 1890, for example, Sam T. Jack produced the first black "girlie" show, *The Creole Show*. A few years later, Will Marion Cooke, Paul Laurence Dunbar, and Jesse A. Shipp produced *In Dahomey* (1902–5) for the Williams and Walker Company. The musical takes the audience on a trip to a place where African Americans were treated like royalty. The cast was entirely African American.

The rise of vaudeville both diluted and popularized the Irish, German, and blackface caricatures created during the nineteenth century. In his book *The Voice of the City*, Robert Snyder observed that vaudeville offered something for everyone. This hardly meant that vaudeville presented every ethnicity equally; in fact, many of the old stereotypes remained. Rather, performers dropped some of their ethnic "markers," as Snyder puts it, creating instead the path from "ethnic origins to national stardom that would become so important in vaudeville" (Snyder 1989: 48; see also Gilbert 1963: 62).

Yiddish Theatre: The First Generation

In his book *Tenement Songs*, Mark Slobin lists three characteristics that epitomize ethnic theatres of the late nineteenth century: first, they draw from common melodramas,

Shakespeare, and plays about immigration, as well as invent plays about nostalgia and crises about their own experience; second, their plays describe their difficulties, as well as the constant change as generations of immigrants become assimilated and decide that they only want American theatre; and third, the plays primarily reveal happy endings. Despite these shared commonalities, in the Jewish ghetto in New York, the Yiddish theatre can be considered a special case, owing to the fact that the most prominent form of ethnic theatre in the last decade of the nineteenth century was Yiddish theatre. This "fact" has to do in part with numbers. In the 1870s, 40,000 Jewish immigrants came to America, a relatively small number compared to other groups. However, motivated by political unrest in Russia, the number of Jews immigrating increased tenfold in the next decades. In the 1880s, 200,000 arrived, followed by 300,000 in the 1890s and over a million in the following decade. Additionally, the strength of the Yiddish theatre rests on many other factors, including the intermingling of theatre and theatrical sensibility, which was deeply embedded in Jewish cultural roots.

The tradition of mixing trash and high art, what is termed in Yiddish as *shund*, became a Yiddish, and then an American, tradition. Notwithstanding the significance of theatre from Germans, Irish, and Chinese (Asian) roots, Jewish immigrants brought the most experienced theatrical tradition from Europe, creating a highly theatrical "style." While Chinese immigrants in America produced profoundly important theatrical styles (mostly on the West Coast), the Yiddish style eventually took hold in, and influenced, a realistic style prevalent in America. Another reason why the Yiddish theatre became prominent is because, during the last decades of the nineteenth century, a strong critical tradition in the Yiddish-language newspapers arose combined with an intense interest in the mainstream press. The press reported the theatrical events of the day, adding to the common interest in theatre as a form of social expression and literary criticism.

Journalists and critics in the mainstream and Yiddish press criticized the theatre's vulgarity. Perhaps because of vociferous pressure for assimilation, the newspaper remarks carried heft. Many critics, seeking highbrow approval, displayed a form of anti-Semitism as much as embarking on class warfare against what they perceived as "trashy" or lowbrow theatre. Even into the 1970s, the prejudice against theatricality remained a code for being "too Jewish" among Jewish intelligentsia. In *World of Our Fathers*, for example, Irving Howe writes that "the Yiddish theatre was always uneasy" in part because it focused on comedy more than the playwrights' literary virtuosity and socially acceptable "drama" (1976: 429). Still, Howe compares the Yiddish theatre's exuberance to that of *commedia dell'arte* and the Elizabethan theatre (420).

In its organizational efforts, the Yiddish theatre demonstrated a depth and breadth elsewhere unseen. Founded in 1902, the Hebrew Actors Union is the oldest actors' union in the world, predating Actors Equity and the White Rats, the vaudeville union, by several years. Still, early Yiddish theatre focused more on *shund* than literary culture. *Shund*, a burlesque potpourri, threw together pieces of every theatrical genre for maximum effect. It drew from melodrama, song, and popular culture. Critics often describe playwrights of this generation as "baking" or "building" plays. The two most important "bakers" of this generation were Joseph Latteiner (1853–1935) and Moyshe Hurwitz (1844–1910). Latteiner arrived in New York in 1883 and wrote over 80 plays, many of them domestic melodramas. He never met a genre he failed to like: he would steal a subplot here, add a farcical element there, in order to keep his audience interested. Among his most famous plays is *David's Violin* (1897). It is the story of two brothers, Tevye, a rich philistine, the other a *schlemiel* (pathetic loser). The play, a domestic love story, offers the message that music has the power to heal. *David's Violin* is also the first Yiddish play to present the Jewish entertainer as a charismatic figure that *The Jazz Singer* would later accomplish in the mid-1920s. Although *David's Violin* is written in *daytsmerish*, the "elevated" stage Yiddish evolved by that first generation of immigrants, it is also "baked" – full of vaudeville stage business and comic subplots (Slobin 1996: 88).

During the height of the Yiddish theatre, music helped to create its distinct flavor and uniqueness. By the 1890s, few if any Yiddish theatre productions occurred without songs. Early on, a school for Yiddish acting listed in its curriculum acting, diction, and the study of musical instrument and dance. But Latteiner's plays were not about music alone. Although they offered something for everyone, they also catered to working-class audiences' emotional needs. Set in Romania, another well-known play by Latteiner, *The Jewish Heart* (1908), is both a parable about Jewish identity and a variation on the Cain and Abel myth. Yankel, a Jewish art student, wins a prize for his work. Pleased, he also has to contend with the fact that his mother has another son, Victor, who happens to be both his arch-rival in art school and an anti-Semite. In love with a non-Jewish girl, Yankel, because of laws against intermarriage, needs his mother's signature to marry. The mother ultimately refuses when Victor brandishes a gun. After the incident, Yankel plans to immigrate to America. At that moment, Victor threatens to kill him. The revolver accidentally goes off and Victor dies. To save Yankel, the mother takes blame for the murder. Yankel eventually marries, and the mother, albeit under arrest, attends the wedding in the final scene. However, her grief and suffering – owing to her "Jewish heart" – are so intense they cause her to die.

As scholars point out, the "Jewish heart" play is not merely a simple tragedy. Latteiner interpolates comic scenes with a tragic plot. Sentimental characters, such as Yankel, speak *daytsmerish*, whereas the clown vaudeville characters in the comic sections of the play speak idiomatic, debased Yiddish. But the unifying factor is "the Jewish heart" and what happens to it when Jews search for identity in a hostile environment. The play expresses guilt that the characters have abandoned the old country, but it also shows the importance of self-actualization, justifying the decision to immigrate to the new world at a time when pogroms were destroying Jewish lives.

Latteiner's playwriting rival, "Professor" Moyshe Hurwitz, arrived in New York in 1886 and went on to write over 100 comedies and melodramas. He also staged "newspaper" dramas, plays dramatizing some sensational event from the press, similar to what the Living Newspapers accomplished in the 1930s. Hurwitz would some-times have his characters break into dialogue lifted from other plays; for instance, in the middle of one of his domestic comedies, a husband and wife recite a Yiddish prose version of *Othello*. In the 1870s, competition between Latteiner and Hurwitz kept things lively in the New York's Jewish Lower East Side. More importantly, their rivalry demonstrated how the first generation of Yiddish-language playwrights struggled with the issues of originality and copying. Sometimes the copies imposed Jewish themes on non-Jewish material so forcefully that the old idea surfaced in new garb. A popular theme was persecution of the Jews. Perhaps to distance the action and provide perspective, plays of persecution were often set during the Spanish Inquisition. For instance, Pinkhes Thomashekvsky's *The Lonely Cedar Valley, or the Jews under the Inquisition* (1883), Shaykevitsch's *The Spanish Inquisition* (1886), Hurwitz's *Don Joseph Abravanel*, Weissman's *Don Isaac Abravanel or Judith the Second* (1887), Sharkansky's *Kol Nidre, or, the Secret Jews in Madrid* (1896), and the actor Jacob Adler's *The King of Spain and the Jews* (1899) examine the theme of the wandering Jew in a Spanish milieu.

Poet and lyricist, the Russian-born Abraham Goldfaden (1840–1908), known as the "father of modern Yiddish drama," ushered Yiddish drama into the halls of literature. After founding his first theatre company in Romania in 1876, Goldfaden immigrated to America, where he struggled to prove that Yiddish theatre could be universally appealing and spring from specific folkloric sources as well. Goldfaden saw his plays as both enlightening the public and broadening Yiddish culture. Many of his plays are farce comedies returning to the same old world theme: the Hasidim (an extremely devout religious sect) and their narrow-mindedness where romance is concerned.

Goldfaden's plays evince dramatic and early instances of the Yiddish theatre's use of "doubling" both as comic device and a way to expose the romantic freedoms available in the new world. In his *The Grandmother and the Granddaughter, or Basye the do-gooder* (1877), the grandmother makes an arranged match, but her daughter loves someone else. A supernatural power promises the ailing grandmother that she will see the granddaughter before she dies. *Shmendrick* (1880) also agitates against the tyranny of arranged marriages. The title character is, as Nahma Sandrow puts it, a "Jewish Jerry Lewis" (1977: 48). In this play, the clever bride manages to dupe the antagonist so that she can marry her sweetheart. In *The Two Kuni Lemels* (1897), the two title characters are a foolish yeshiva boy and a sly con artist. The former frightens the girl who is his arranged bride: he is half blind, lame, as well as a stammerer. Fortunately, the bride's true love saves the day by impersonating Kuni Lemel, who undergoes a kind of identity crisis.

Some of Goldfaden's early works were influenced by European theatre theories, such as the Duke of Saxe Meiningen's crowd scenes. Goldfaden added elements of "shtick" comedy (comic routines). For example, in *The Witch* (1882), his first play performed in New York, there are old-world fairy tales, which attack superstition; Mirele's wicked stepmother consults a witch to scare the girl into running away from home, but a good-natured peddler foils her plan. With an operatic bravado, Goldfaden sets the second act in an Eastern European market.

During the late nineteenth and early twentieth centuries, the institution of Yiddish theatre had begun to change, not only in its dramaturgy but also in its approach to acting. In the early days, male actors played all of the roles; by the 1870s, women joined, although, as in all theatre, the profession of actress continued to be taboo. The political climate changed in Russia as well. Uprisings created a crackdown; the tsar banned Yiddish theatre in 1883 and Goldfaden began to change the focus of his dramaturgy. Now, instead of writing about the older generation's limitations, Goldfaden began to criticize the younger generation's foolishness. In *The Capricious Bride* (1877), he pokes fun at young people. A girl rejects a kind, older widow, and marries a fortune hunter who woos her with romantic lines. She changes her name from Hannele to Carolina and kills herself. Along with the rise of Zionism, Goldfaden's plays not only are based on mythological and biblical sources, but also address allegorical levels concerning Israel and Zionism. In this polemic mode, two of the most important were *The Sacrifice of Isaac* (1877) and *Bar Kokhba* (1883), the story of a small band of Jews who rebel against the Roman Empire. Set in 1370, the play begins as the high priest makes a speech about the practicality of obeying the Romans. But Bar Kokhba, the hero, insists on revolt. Bar Kokhba and his lover Dina give impassioned speeches from prison and fight a lion in the coliseum. In the end, the Jews lose, although Goldfaden makes the point that this is because of one man's pride, not a people's weakness.

Shulamis, or the Daughter of Jerusalem (1880), an opera set in ancient times, is also an allegory of the Jewish people's longing for a homeland and the necessity of keeping the faith in difficult times. Absalom rescues Shulamis from a well in the desert. They fall in love and vow to be faithful forever. But Absalom continues on to Jerusalem and forgets about Shulamis. He marries another woman and they have children. Because he has promised himself to Shulamis, the children die. Absalom remembers this and finds his way back to Shulamis. From the 1890s onward, Goldfaden became increasingly pro-Zionist. He wrote a number of Zionist plays, including his last, *Ben Ami* (1907), in which the hero begins as a European aristocrat but ends happily as a farmer in Palestine.

Jacob Gordin (1853–1909) was as influential as Goldfaden, and his competitor in many ways. Gordin dabbled in a variety of occupations before he immigrated to America in 1890. He wrote between 30 and 60 plays; he was both a critic and a reformer, nourishing artistic ambitions for the Yiddish stage. Whereas Goldfaden had focused on creating a Yiddish theatre, Gordin sought to turn the Yiddish theatre into an "art" theatre equivalent to European and modernist traditions. Gordin attempted this transformation in several ways; he hewed to the ideal of realism then in currency in the works of Chekhov, Ibsen, and Strindberg; he adapted more Shakespeare than any other Yiddish writer; and he insisted on the importance of the writer who valued actors.

Gordin is impressive for fighting a constant battle against *shund*. Although some of his plays do employ clownish characters and operatic intrusions, Gordin's first artistic success, *Siberia* (1891), was a realistic drama that used the American "rags to riches" story and catered to the specific brand of immigrant nostalgia for the old country. In *Siberia*, a refugee escapes from prison, starts a new life, becomes wealthy, and flourishes until a business colleague tells the police his true identity, forcing him into exile again. *Siberia* may have been the first play of the Yiddish theatre to eschew music and dancing. However, during the rehearsal process, the actors danced and sang, as was the custom. With the support of one of his actors, the Yiddish star Jacob Adler, Gordin fought the rest of his cast and prevailed against tradition. The play, unfortunately, was received so poorly that Adler had to resort to a curtain speech to make the audience stop booing and hissing.

Still, Gordin made a significant impact. Another of his realistic dramas, *The Pogrom in Russia* (1892), proved successful. Gordin, fleeing from Goldfaden's "Jewishness" and wounded by accusations of "anti-Semitism" in the Yiddish press, was inspired to turn to Shakespeare. At first Gordin's Shakespeare adaptations created a negative reaction for the same reason his realistic plays did: they were not theatrical – *shund*-like – enough. Ultimately, the plays resonated with the public. The focus on the Jewish family in America caught on with his audience: *The Jewish King Lear* (1892) and *The Jewish Queen Lear: Mirele Efros* (1898) describe the tension between children's assimilation and parents' alienation in ways that the audiences found meaningful.

The most important theme at end of the century would be the rage to adapt Shakespeare. Bardophilia was hardly unique; other theatrical cultures had been adapting Shakespeare since the eighteenth century. However, when the Yiddish theatre bent Shakespeare's plays to their own concerns, critics often accused it of bowdlerizing the Bard. In 1892, the same year that Gordin wrote *The Pogrom in Russia*, he adapted Shakespeare's play into *The Jewish King Lear*, with Adler in the title role. Six years later, he wrote *The Jewish Queen Lear*, which was also known by its Yiddish name, *Mirele Efros*. There are stories in Jewish folklore about how Yiddish audiences, having seen Gordin's Lears, preferred his version over Shakespeare. *The Jewish King Lear* has been described as being about the binding together of "antagonistic" generations (Prager 1996: 506). In the play, which opened in October 1892 at the Union Theatre, Lear is David Masheles, a wealthy Jewish businessman who has decided to divide his estate among three grown daughters and move with his wife to Palestine. In Act 2, Masheles's daughters abuse him. Act 3 ends happily as parents and children reconcile. The play was performed in colloquial Yiddish, not the elevated *daytsmerish*. The happy ending was required because it spoke to the social upheaval that naturally emerged as Jewish children were put into the parental position of guiding their own parents into the ways of the new world.

On the whole, Bardophilia was an attempt to fuse the process of turning the Yiddish theatre into both a particular and a universal cultural event. During the 1890s and 1900s, Shakespeare adaptations surged, making the Yiddish adaptations a part of mainstream fashion. Boris Thomashevsky's *The Yeshiva Boy* (1899) was promoted as the Yiddish Hamlet. When Mikhl Goldberg adapted *King Lear* at the People's Theatre in 1903 for Thomashevsky, he pared down the roles for the supporting actors, turning the focus of the play on an individual. Gordin himself continued to adapt. In 1894, two years after *The Jewish King Lear*, he wrote *The Lithuanian Brothers*, a "Jewish" *Romeo and Juliet*, although it was not advertised as such. Indeed, many of these adaptations were just domestic dramas with Shakespeare's name added.

Because it reverses genders, Jacob Gordin's sequel to *The Jewish King Lear*, *The Jewish Queen Lear*, is a radical departure from the original. The play opens in the middle of preparations for a wedding of Yosele Efros, the older of two sons of the wealthy widow Mirele Efros, and a poor beauty. The vulgarity of the poor beauty's parents leads Efros to break off the wedding. In a plot similar to Chekhov's *Three Sisters*, the poor beauty alienates the noble Mirele Efros, whose sons also grow alienated as the play unfolds. Unlike Shakespeare's version or even Gordin's *Lear*, there is little conflict between Mirele and her children. Rather it is the in-laws who provide the conflict. *Mirele Efros* paid homage to the strength of the mother in the Jewish ghetto – a popular theme in ethnic dramas – and at the same time, expressed anxiety about the emergence of the New Woman.

Other gender adaptations of Shakespeare (and lesser-known classics) into the Yiddish theatre reveal similar stories about the Jewish woman's shifting role in America. The Yiddish theatre's relationship with the famous actress Sarah Bernhardt deserves consideration, because it suggests ambivalence on the part of the Yiddish theatre movement. Bernhardt's Judaism was well known, yet many in the Jewish press scorned her presence. The historian Harley Erdman reminds us that Bernhardt played the role of "*La Belle Juive*," the dangerous, erotic Jewess who would become a force during her career. When Bernhardt played Hamlet in New York, some contemporary critics characterized her acting as freakish or farcical, in part because Bernhardt did not pretend to be a man. But two plays Bernhardt starred in, Sardou's *Fedora* (1882) and Octave Mirbeau's *Les Mauvais Bergers* (1897), endured on the Yiddish stage only because the great Jewish actress was associated with them.

It is also worth discussing the Yiddish theatre's adaptations of *The Merchant of Venice* since they reveal shifting definitions of Judaism. Joel Berkowitz contends that the staging of *Merchant* was nothing less than an investigation of "the Jew's position in a Gentile world" (1996: 172). In the mid-nineteenth century, some Irish American actors had played the role sympathetically, but historian William Winters describes Edmund Booth's version as "a fierce Jew, animated by hatred and greed," and John Brougham portrayed him as an exotic villain (1893: 60). In late nineteenth-and early twentieth-century Yiddish theatre, adaptations of *The Merchant of Venice* focused sympathetically on Shylock. *Shylock* (1901), Jacob Adler's famously bowdlerized version, humanizes him by eliminating the lovers' subplot. Without the lovers, the play stresses anti-Semitism (since there is no romance for him to thwart, Shylock is much less of a villain). On Broadway, Adler performed the role in Yiddish with an American cast to mixed reviews. Rudolph Schildkraut, the famous German Jewish actor, performed a similar version of the role in New York in 1911.

The Decline of the Golden Age

A famous anecdote about the second generation in the Yiddish theatre follows that a young playwright (fill in the name) goes to a theatre on the Lower East Side (known as the Jewish section of Manhattan) to hawk his play. Is it a comedy? We don't do comedies here, is the reply. Is it a drama? We don't do dramas here. We don't do plays by *yolds*, the manager said, using the term describing "greenhorns." It was, as the joke implies, hard for a young playwright with literary aspirations to succeed on the Yiddish stage. Yet some, influenced by modernist writing and theatrical traditions of Europe and Russia, managed to have their plays produced, albeit in sometimes bowdlerized states. Others found their own non-professional companies.

During the early twentieth century Gordin continued to tackle "social" issues through adapting the classics. *The Jewish Sappho* (1900) is about a young woman struggling to live by her own rules. His *God, Man, and Devil* (1900), a Jewish, melodramatic version of Goethe's *Faust*, warns of money's corrupting effect. From its prologue in heaven to its epilogue featuring a chorus of angels, *God, Man, and Devil* tells the story of a pious Torah scribe and weaver transformed by Satan into a dishonest factory owner who destroys the religious fabric of his community. But *God, Man, and Devil* is not merely a morality play; the Torah scribe brings himself down through his own excessive pride and ambition.

Another playwright of this generation, Leon Kobrin (1872–1946), wrote melodramatic-realistic pieces including *The Big Jew* (1911), *The Blind Musician, a Yiddish Othello* (1912), *The Lady Next Door* (1915), and a dramatization of his novel, *The Child of Nature*. More than focusing on the tension between the old and the new, Kobrin wrote about themes that obsessed many in his generation: the tension in intermarriage and the loneliness and spiritual and romantic emptiness experienced by Jews living in Russian shtetls. In *Yankl Boyla, or The Child of Nature* (1912), Yankl's father, on his deathbed, tries to get Yankl to promise not to marry the Russian girl he loves. In Act 2, when Yankl learns that she is pregnant, he kills himself.

In the years before World War I, the most vital aspect of the Yiddish theatre was the creation of the Yiddish Art Theatre, the Artef, and the Folksbiene Theatre, which Gordin founded in the 1890s. These theatres helped insure that some of the plays written in the 1880s would endure. Additionally, the rise of the director as a profession – ultimately a more important force than the playwright – provided the late nineteenth-century plays with a longer shelf life. Despite the rise in "art" theatres, a new wave of immigrants in 1905 desired *shund* over highbrow plays. Still, "literary" playwrights at the time strove toward naturalism, tales of the struggle of the Jewish proletariat, symbolist pieces, and religious allegories.

Influenced by symbolism as well as naturalism, Polish-born Peretz Hirschbein (1852–1915) arrived in America in 1911. His plays were largely produced after World War I. Many of these – such as *The Haunted Inn* (1919) – dealt with the Jews' domestic problems in the old world and some critics compared him to the Irish dramatist Sean O'Casey. *In the Dark*, *The Idle Inn* (1913), *Farvorfen Vinkel* (1918), and *The Blacksmith's Daughter* (1915) were praised by mainstream critics, including Carl Van Vechten, for their "folk" atmosphere (Goldberg 1916: 179). Hirschbein's most famous play was *Green Fields* (1916), part of a trilogy about comic life in the countryside, and homage to young love and the pastoral life.

Hirschbein's protégé, David Pinsky (1872–1959), arrived in New York in 1899, and studied literature at Columbia University. He is in some ways the most modern of all the Yiddish writers. His early plays include *Isaac Sheftl* (1899), about a peasant with artistic sensibilities whose impoverished environment has let him develop only enough to be a hack. Ultimately, he destroys his machines and himself. Other plays, such as *The Zwei Family* (1904), tell the story of a bourgeois Jewish family's fears as a pogrom roils. The patriarch of the family acts with dignity and confronts different members of the community in order to urge them to confront "what it means to be a Jew." Pinsky also wrote historical full-length plays and one-acts including *The Mute Messiah* (1914), which used biblical allegory. Although each of these plays concerns topical issues relevant to the Jewish community, Pinsky aspired to reach a wider public.

This is most easily observed in his comedy. *Yankel the Smith* (1910) features the comic Smith of the title who desires not only his own wife, but his neighbor's wife as well. The play ends happily, with Yankel content to be with just one woman. *Gavri and the Women* (1909), *Solomon Molchi* (1932), and several other one-act plays were all plays about the Jewish individual struggling to live in American society. One of Pinsky's most ambitious attempts was *The Treasure* (1920, produced by the Theatre Guild). Like Gordin's *God, Man, and the Devil*, *The Treasure*, which takes place in a village in the old country, examines money's power. Set in a Yiddish cemetery, the fourth act brings the play to a realization that the search for money literally wakes the dead.

A play from the Yiddish theatre that struck both universal and Yiddish notes was *The Melting Pot* (1908), by Israel Zangwill (1864–1926), a British Jew, Zionist, and reformer. The play champions race amalgamation. The violin-playing hero, David Quixano, comes to live with his grandfather and uncle in America. David marries Vera, a Russian immigrant and (we learn as the play unfolds) the daughter of the man who ordered the pogrom that killed his own parents. When David discovers this, he renounces Vera; the baron hands David a gun and asks to be shot. But David chooses his violin over violence. The play ends happily as the couple stands on the rooftop looking out on New York. Dedicated to Theodore Roosevelt, *The Melting Pot* imagines that all ethnic peoples will abandon their ethnic qualities as they intermarry in America. Roosevelt admired the play, as did much of the press, although some criticized it for its crude structure.

Yiddish writers of this era wrote folk comedies and symbolic dramas about Jewish suffering in the new world. The implicit question residing in many of these works is whether what had been gained in America was worth the loss of old world values. Ossip Dymov (1878–1959) examined this question in many plays, including the satire *Slaves of the People* (1918), whose subject was the Yiddish theatre itself. Another writer, dwelling on the glories of "folk" and the old country as well as the difficulties of living in New York, was the dramatist and short story writer Sholom Aleichem (1859–1916). Aleichem arrived in America in 1914, but died two years later. His most successful plays were in the comic-pastoral tradition, but he also wrote darker comedies such as *It's Hard to Be a Jew*, in which a Jew and a non-Jew trade places. Set in Russia, the play is a cautionary tale dealing with a Jew who acts too much like a non-Jew and, along the way, is arrested. A lighter look at Yiddish culture emerged in *Tevye the Dairyman*, which later became the Broadway musical *Fiddler on the Roof* in 1964.

Born in Poland, the playwright, novelist, and essayist Sholom Asch (1880–1957) arrived in New York shortly before World War I. Asch's nickname, after the famous French author, was "the Jewish Maupassant." His first play, published as a Yiddish novel, *With the Stream* (1904), was popular. His plays were performed on the Russian, Polish, and German stage. Asch's best-known plays are *God of Vengeance* (1907), *Mary* (1917), and *The Way to Oneself* (1914). The last two plays engaged the Zionist question, but Asch was as fascinated by the question of how the sacred and the profane intersect.

Maurice Schwartz, the artistic director of the Yiddish Art Theatre, adapted some of Asch's short stories for the stage. But Asch's play *The God of Vengeance*, first produced by Max Reinhardt in Germany in 1910, captured the tension between American and Yiddish culture after World War I. *The God of Vengeance*, a tragedy about a girl who has a lesbian relationship with a prostitute because of her parents' corrupt occupation as brothel-keepers, opened on Broadway in 1923 to community outrage and censorship. Some contemporary writers compared it to George Bernard Shaw's *Mrs. Warren's Profession*. The play expressed quite a different theme. Like many earlier Yiddish plays, it absorbed the tension between worldliness and piety and connected the destruction of the former to the rise of the latter. Furthermore, because the play represented a lesbian relationship on the American stage, it epitomized the Jewish community's anxiety in regard to outside perceptions.

As a result of its controversial subject matter, *God of Vengeance* had far-reaching consequences. Using section 1140A of the penal code, the police shut down the play, put the famous Yiddish actor Rudolph Schildekraut (who played the father) in jail, and fined him $200 (a considerable sum at the time). In the eyes of the purity campaigners, the controversy over *God of Vengeance* established the need for more stringent measures to censure salacious plays on Broadway and paved the way for the "Padlock Law," which allowed the License Commissioner and the District Attorney to shut theatres for as long as a year.

Written in 1914, S. Ansky's *The Dybbuk* dealt with possession in another way. The play concerns demonic possession as a passion that can remain in someone even through death. In 1922, Maurice Schwartz chose it for the first season of his Yiddish Art Theatre in New York. *The Dybbuk* illustrates the triumph of the supernatural over corruption and selfishness. As a melodrama, *The Dybbuk* revealed how, when true love is thwarted, an evil spirit can overtake a person's body and become more real than the events around them. After Leah's beloved, the impoverished rabbinical student Chonen, dies, her father wants Leah to marry a wealthy but moribund businessman. When she visits Chonen's grave, their spirits merge. Despite the community's efforts to rid the bride of Chonen's spirit (Dybbuk), Leah dies in Act 3 and the two lovers are united in death.

Some critics felt that *The Dybbuk* represented an advance in Yiddish dramaturgy. The play appeared to eliminate, once and for all, the stereotype of *shund*, offering instead a tragedy of universal proportions. Indeed, many in the Yiddish press celebrated *The Dybbuk* as one of the ways in which the Yiddish theatre could tell a story for the community and maintain universal appeal as well. But when the play was produced in New York in the 1925–6 season, a season that was also marked by an increase in sexual content on the Broadway stage, the reaction was mixed. The *New York Times* reviewer Alexander Woollcott characterized the play as "creepy," while Gilbert Seldes likened it to a fable and thus found it to be unrealistic and uninteresting (qtd. in Lifson 1970: 103).

By the late 1920s, the Yiddish theatre declined. More common were multi-ethnic comedies revealing America's wish for everyone to be equal; of these, the most famous was *Abie's Irish Rose*. Written in 1922 by Anne Nichols, this comedy presented the message that love conquers all, including, and especially, ethnic and religious barriers. Actors crossed ethnic lines to create the array of stereotypes represented in the play. *Abie's Irish Rose* contrasts first-generation immigrant identities with the Americanized second generation. It also revolves around a Jewish–Catholic romance. At the same time, some of the writers of the Harlem Renaissance were beginning to deal with questions of amalgamation. The poet and playwright Jean Toomer (1894–1967) wrote *Balo* (1922), a play in which the characters simply go about their everyday lives. The play dealt with the persistence of racial and ethnic tensions and the dominance of ethnic prejudice and racial inequality, as opposed to how these tensions could be resolved through love with a "fairytale" ending. If everyone managed this, with the exception of a few isolated instances, it is no great surprise that by the late 1920s, ethnic theatres began to decline, as there were no new immigrants to refresh them.

Founded as a Jewish workers' theatre in 1925, the early productions of the Artef would go on to influence the Workers' Theatre and the playwright Clifford Odets. The Artef introduced the techniques of the Russian avant-garde director Vsevelod Meyerhold as well as a socialist consciousness to America. But their work was uneven. *The Third Parade* (written in 1924, produced in 1933) by Charles R. Walker and Paul Peters offered a documentary panorama of the main events of the Bonus March – in 1924, the government had promised all veterans a "bonus," but with the Depression's arrival, the bonus never materialized. In 1932, James Ford, the Communist Party's candidate for vice president, suggested that veterans march in protest on Washington. Writing under the pen name Harold Edgar, Harold Clurman reviewed this production, observing that it needed realism. What Clurman meant by this was not dramaturgy but the actors' ethnicity. Clurman noted that "pale faced Artef actors" created an unreal image on stage (qtd. in Nahshon 1998: 203).

By the early 1930s, the Yiddish theatre, like many other ethnic theatres, continued to decline. In 1935, under the auspices of the Works Project Administration (WPA), the Federal Theatre Project resuscitated some ethnic theatres in order to employ actors and generate theatre. The WPA included a German theatre, a Yiddish theatre, and an African American theatre. However, ethnic theatre must have appeared museum-like to the Depression-era audiences clamoring for political change. During the Depression, the proletariats were, for the most part, attempting to unite as workers rather than as "ethnics." The Prolet-Bühne and the Workers Laboratory Theatre emerged as laboratories to create new work about class injustice. Langston Hughes's *The Scottsboro Boys*, about nine black men being tried for raping a white woman, was gaining root in America. In the Group Theatre, Clifford Odets wrote *Waiting for Lefty* (1935). The idea of what ethnic theatre could be and do — and what it meant to be an American — had already begun to change.

Bibliography

Adler, J. (1999). *Jacob Adler: A Life on The Stage*, trans. Lulla Rosenfeld. New York: Alfred A. Knopf.
Berkowitz, J. (1996). "A True Jewish Jew: Three Yiddish Shylocks." *Theatre Survey* 37, 1 (May): 75–81.
——(1999). "The Tallis or the Cross, Reviving Goldfaden at the Yiddish Art Theatre: 1924–26." *Journal of Jewish Studies* 50, 1.
——(2002). *Shakespeare on the American Yiddish Stage*. Iowa: University of Iowa Press.
——(ed.) (2003). *Yiddish Theatre, New Approaches*. New York: Littman.
Cerniglia, K. (2001). "Becoming American, A Critical History of Ethnicity in Popular Theatre." Dissertation, University of Washington.
Distler, P. A. (1963). "The Rise and Fall of Racial Comics in American Vaudeville." Dissertation, Tulane University.
Dorman, J. H. (1992). "Ethnic Cultures of the Mind: The Harrigan-Hart Mosaic." *American Studies* 5, 33: 21–40.
Erdman, H. (1997). *Staging the Jew: The Performance of an American Ethnicity 1860–1920*. New Brunswick, NJ: Rutgers University Press.
——(1999). "Jewish Anxiety in 'Days of Judgment': Community Conflict, Anti-Semitism, and the God of Vengeance Obscenity Case." *Theatre Survey* 40, 1: 51–74.
Gilbert, D. (1963). *American Vaudeville, Its Life and Times*. New York: Dover.
Goldberg, I. (ed.) (1916). *Six Plays of the Yiddish Theatre*. Boston: J. W. Luce.
Goldman, E. (1987). *The Social Significance of Modern Drama*. New York: Applause.
Grimsted, D. (1968). *Melodrama Unveiled*. Berkeley: University of California Press.
Howe, I. (1976). *World of Our Fathers: The Journey of the East European Jews to America and the Life they Found and Made*. New York: Schiffman.
Kanellos, N. (ed.) (1983). *Mexican American Theatre: Then and Now*. Houston: Arte Público.
Kraus, J. (1999). "How the Melting Pot Stirred America: The Reception of Zangwill's Play and Theatre's Role in the American Immigration Experience." *Meleus* 24, 3 (Fall): 3–19.
Landis, J. C. (ed.) (1986). *Three Great Jewish Plays*. New York: Applause.
Leuchs, F. (1928). *The Early German Theatre in New York: 1840–1872*. New York: AMS Press.
Lifson, D. S. (1970). *The Yiddish Theatre in America*. New York: T. Yoseloff.

Moody, R. (ed.) (1966). *Dramas from the American Theatre 1762–1909*. Cleveland: World Publishing.

Nahshon, E. (1998). *Yiddish Proletarian Theatre: The Art and Politics of the Artef*. Westport, CT: Greenwood.

Prager, L. (1996). "Of Parents and Children, Jacob Gordin's *The Jewish King Lear*." *American Quarterly* 18: 506–16.

Sandrow, N. (ed.) (1970). *God, Man, and Devil and other Yiddish Plays*, Syracuse, NY: University of Syracuse Press.

—— (1977). *Vagabond Stars: A World History of Yiddish Theatre*. New York: Harper and Row.

Schwartz-Sellers, M. (1983). *Ethnic Theatre in America*. Westport, CT: Greenwood.

Shumsky, N. L. (1974). "The Melting Pot, Ethnic Tensions Onstage." Dissertation, Temple University.

Slobin, M. (1982). *Tenement Songs: The Popular Music of Jewish Immigrants*. Urbana: University of Illinois Press.

—— (1986). "Some Intersections of Jews, Music, and Theatre." In Sarah Blacher Cohn (ed.), *From Hester Street to Hollywood*. Bloomington: Indiana University Press.

—— (ed.) (1996). *Yiddish Theatre in America*. New York: Garland.

Snyder, R. (1989). *The Voice of the City: Vaudeville and Popular Culture in New York*. New York: Oxford University Press.

Szuberla, G. (1995). "Zangwill's The Melting Pot Plays Chicago." *Meleus* 20: 3–20.

Warnke, N. (1996). "Immigrant Popular Culture as Contested Sphere: Yiddish Music Halls, the Yiddish Press, and the Processes of Americanization, 1900–1910." *Theatre Journal* 48, 3: 321–35.

Winters, W. (1893). *The Life and Art of Edwin Booth*. New York and London: Macmillan.

Zangwill, I. (1930). *The Melting Pot*. New York: Macmillan.

4
Susan Glaspell and Sophie Treadwell: Staging Feminism and Modernism, 1915–1941

J. Ellen Gainor and Jerry Dickey

The longstanding ideological separation of the commercial and avant-garde theatre in the United States has prompted the creation of two distinct historical narratives – chronologically parallel stories of the stage with little overlap of characters, theme, or methodology. Moreover, the critical privileging of the avant-garde, long identified with high culture, and the simultaneous dismissal of popular art forms, has only recently given way to more nuanced analyses of American cultural production of all kinds. Thus we have only lately realized that throughout the twentieth century, insurgent artists challenged this theatrical boundary through their efforts to bring the innovations of the avant-garde to audiences accustomed to the conventions of Broadway. Their goal was not to collapse these distinctions, but rather to prove the viability in multiple venues of aesthetically, intellectually, and politically challenging theatre. The remarkable similarities in the lives and careers of two modernist playwrights, Susan Glaspell and Sophie Treadwell, have rarely been noted, precisely because of this trope of separation, which connects Glaspell to the experimental theatre tradition and Treadwell to the commercial stage. Yet their stories provide an unprecedented scholarly opportunity to examine how artists in the early decades of the twentieth century struggled to stage dramas that strove to redefine who could attain theatrical production and what kinds of theatre would speak to American audiences. While Glaspell worked within the context of the burgeoning Little Theatre Movement early in her career, and only sought commercial production of her work once she was an established playwright, Treadwell always set her sights on Broadway. Their mutual engagements in modernism, feminism, and progressive politics inform their dramaturgy, yet these same commitments ultimately damned them commercially and critically. Thus their stories provide early evidence of issues of access and reception that still profoundly affect the professional theatre today.

Susan Glaspell

Susan Glaspell's lifetime (1876–1948), like Sophie Treadwell's (1885–1970), coincides closely with the rise of modernism in Europe and its arrival and development in the United States. Their biographies, moreover, epitomize the personal and professional tensions within American society that mark the transition from Victorian notions of women's roles to early twentieth-century efforts to reject the "separate spheres" ideology that lingered so tenaciously, prompting signal domestic, social, and political revolts in the modern period. Glaspell's 14 plays, written between 1915 and 1944, similarly reflect both stylistically and topically the stresses endemic to an era of upheaval and redefinition; Glaspell intuited the unrivaled potential of theatre to represent the struggles of her community and nation to define and embody these new realities.

Glaspell grew up in Davenport, Iowa, at that time a community more conducive than many other Midwestern locales to fostering creativity and progressive thought. As a teenager, Glaspell started writing for a local newspaper, focusing on society news. Glaspell and Treadwell convinced their families to let them join the still small ranks of women with college education. After graduating from Drake University with a degree in philosophy, Glaspell accepted a post as a reporter for the *Des Moines Daily News*. Like Treadwell, Glaspell found the profession of journalism comparatively receptive to women, and both writers developed keen observational and descriptive skills through this work that would later prove highly useful for their dramaturgy. Glaspell's coverage of the Hossack murder trial in 1900–1 provided the foundation for her best-known drama, *Trifles* (1916), and its short story counterpart, "A Jury of Her Peers" (1917). Glaspell soon determined, however, that she wanted to return to Davenport to pursue a creative writing career. She began to place her short stories in such national magazines as *Ladies' Home Journal*, *Booklovers*, and *Harper's*, among others. These stories reflect Glaspell's keen understanding of American fiction, drawing on the "local color" tradition but also displaying her prescient sensitivity to small-town hypocrisy and social and moral conservatism. In 1909 she published her first novel, *The Glory of the Conquered*, which features an artist heroine struggling to integrate and balance her professional and personal goals. The themes of her early stories and novels, especially *Fidelity* (1913), with its narrative of extra-marital love, would soon migrate to her playwriting. Her dramas expand the concerns of her early fiction by developing stronger connections between her characters' lives and their political convictions; the plays also document a wider geographical understanding of American regionalism as well as the dynamic relationship between community identity and personal behavior.

Glaspell and her husband, George Cram ("Jig") Cook, who had begun to feel increasingly at odds with Midwestern conventionality, determined to move east to the more radical and bohemian environs of Greenwich Village. Their relocation occurred at a pivotal moment when artists, intellectuals, and political activists coalesced to form what essayist Randolph Bourne would soon call the "beloved community" of like-minded individuals dedicated to reenvisioning America (1956: 284). As historian Christine Stansell observes, the bohemians embraced the concept of modernism, creating

> the first full-bodied alternative to an established cultural elite.... They developed an unrivaled vision of feminism – with its powers to recast men's and women's lives – as a critical ingredient of modern culture.... They injected into politics of the left a new cultural dimension, as well as psychological identifications between working-class and middle-class people.... They made Greenwich Village into a beacon of American possibility in the new age. (2000: 3)

Glaspell and Cook would soon become leading figures in the community as the co-founders of the Provincetown Players, a company dedicated to the development of new voices for the American theatre. Explicitly rejecting the commercialism of Broadway, the Players embraced the ideology of the Little Theatre Movement, working to foster drama that reflected their engagement with their community as well as with modernism.

In the summer of 1915, while vacationing with other Villagers on Cape Cod, Cook convinced Glaspell that they should stage a one-act play, *Suppressed Desires*, which they had written together the previous winter. Their friend Neith Boyce had also written a short play, *Constancy*, and they determined that they would produce the two pieces in a private performance for their circle. That evening prompted the creation of the Players the following summer and led to the subsequent expansion of their endeavors in New York for six legendary seasons. Perhaps best known for launching the career of Eugene O'Neill, the Players presented between 1915 and 1922 the creative work of an astounding array of American artists, including Djuna Barnes, Floyd Dell, Edna Ferber, Mina Loy, John Reed, Wallace Stevens, Edna St. Vincent Millay, William Carlos Williams, and William Zorach, among many others.[1] They embraced the spirit of experimentation that informed the visual and literary artistry of their bohemian colleagues; their Village stage became a crucible for a modern American theatre that strove to integrate social critique and the avant-garde.

For Glaspell, the summer of 1916 proved a professional turning point, as Cook insisted she write a play to sustain the momentum of their productions. Although she had initially planned to use the material for a story, she crafted her memory of the Hossack trial into the one-act *Trifles*, the drama that catalyzed her playwriting career. Glaspell wrote nine other pieces for the Players in a burst of creativity that evidences her mastery of the one-act form, her transition to full-length dramas, and her deployment of a panoply of dialogic, scenic, interpersonal, and topical innovations. Glaspell's dramaturgy not only reflects the tenets of American modernism, but also anticipates thematic and stylistic advances associated with the high modernist tradition that frequently ignored or discredited theatrical artistry. Her plays exhibit a close engagement with radical movements of the time, including the campaigns to protect free speech, to secure women's access to birth control, and to establish greater equality between the sexes. Bracketed by World Wars I and II, her dramaturgy mirrors the nation's preoccupation with these conflicts and their aftermaths – politically, socially, and culturally.

In a rare published interview, conducted soon after the opening of her most stylistically and thematically adventurous play, *The Verge* (1921), Glaspell remarked: "Of course I am interested in all progressive movements, whether feminist, social, or economic . . . but I can take no very active part other than through my writing" (Rohe 1921: 4). Glaspell reveals here that she saw her writing as political activism, and that she consciously chose to focus her energies on developing material for a platform that she believed could have the power to effect real, substantive change.[2] Glaspell's dramaturgy, however, never embraced the techniques of agit-prop that would later become so closely associated with political theatre. Rather, she explored a range of dramatic modes in her effort to create works of stylistic and thematic cohesion – works whose form and content would work together for the greatest audience impact.

One of the hallmarks of Glaspell's playwriting is her ability to represent truthfully the perspectives of all of her characters. While her commitment to feminism informs every play she wrote,[3] she is also careful to construct a balanced dramatic environment through which we come to understand fully the women's lives she depicts and the contexts for their choices and actions. *Trifles* exemplifies this dramatic strategy through its juxtaposition of male and female processes of ratiocination. It dramatizes the aftermath of the death of John Wright and the arrest of his wife Minnie on suspicion of his murder. A small group of characters arrive at the Wright home: three men whose goal is to reconstruct the crime and discover the evidence needed for the prosecution, and two women who are to gather some personal items to bring to Mrs. Wright in jail. Glaspell sets up a series of oppositions between the men and the women to illustrate her prescient understanding of a number of phenomena later codified by feminist theory, including the social construction of gender, women's bonding and identification against the patriarchy, and legal inequities between men and women in patriarchal society. As the male sheriff, the county prosecutor, and the neighbor who discovered Wright's body focus their investigation on the offstage bedroom where the crime occurred and the surrounding area, the wives of the sheriff and neighbor remain in the onstage kitchen, coming to know the absent Minnie through empathic association of the hardships of her daily life with their own. The men dismiss the significance of this domestic environment ("Nothing here but kitchen things" [Glaspell 1920: 8]) and criticize Minnie's work therein, which prompts the neighbor's wife to even stronger identification:

County Attorney:	Not much of a housekeeper, would you say, ladies?
Mrs. Hale:	(*Stiffly*.) There's a great deal of work to be done on a farm.
County Attorney:	To be sure. And yet . . . I know there are some Dickinson country farmhouses which do not have such roller towels. . . .
Mrs. Hale:	Those towels get dirty awful quick. Men's hands aren't always as clean as they might be. (9–10)

In the men's absence, the women, functioning as amateur detectives, discover evidence they believe could be used to establish Minnie's guilt – one of the "trifles" that the men have overlooked because of their preconceptions about the inconsequentiality of women's lives and actions. The women choose to become the "jury of her peers,"[4] which the United States legal system denied Minnie through its exclusion of women from judicial service; instead, they work to insure Minnie's release by concealing the crucial evidence that the men could have used against her.

Lauded for decades as an exemplar of the one-act form, *Trifles* and its short-story counterpart later became foundational texts in the development of Anglo-American feminist theory. Scholars saw in Glaspell's work not only her resistance to traditional notions of gender identity, but also her calculated reversal of viewpoint – her audiences see events through the women's eyes instead of with the traditional male perspective. By placing women characters at the center of her play (literally bringing them in from the margins in the opening scene) and displacing the men, by focusing on women's daily activities rather than the men's work, and by setting her action in the kitchen rather than in a male-dominated environment, Glaspell disrupts long-held notions of what constitutes a "good" drama. Moreover, these choices reveal her conscious participation in the evolution of a modern American theatre – one that appropriated conventions from Europe such as naturalism, realism, expressionism, and symbolism, but combined and deployed them to create a uniquely American stage.

Building on the interpersonal dynamics she had begun to explore in *Trifles*, Glaspell zeroed in on the nuances of women's close relationships with other women in contrast to those with men in her first full-length play, *Bernice* (1919). Like *Trifles*, *Bernice* features Glaspell's signature device of the "absent center" – a character we never see but around whom the action revolves. Like John Wright, Bernice has died before the action begins, but different questions about the death – and ones central to the issue of gendered relationships – define this drama. Bernice has convinced the family caretaker, Abbie, to tell her husband, the unfaithful novelist Craig, that she has committed suicide. But her dear friend Margaret, a political activist, cannot believe Bernice would have taken her own life. Abbie privately tells her that Bernice indeed died of natural causes but wanted her husband to think she killed herself for him – the gesture of belonging and dependence Bernice may not have been able to offer him in life, but understood he needed to retain from her death. Margaret, who has loved Bernice for her vivacity and self-sufficiency, comes to appreciate why her friend wanted different memories of herself to remain behind: one, the quiet, but almost melodramatic image of the stereotypically wronged wife, the other, that of an independent, generous woman who perceives and fulfills others' most fundamental needs and desires. As in *Trifles*, Glaspell guides us to these realizations through women's eyes and women's grappling with evolving notions of female identity and commitment.

Glaspell may well have drawn on the conflicted lives of many women in her bohemian circle to generate this drama. As Christine Stansell and other feminist historians of the era have noted, the Villagers' espousal of sexual equality rarely translated into true parity, in that men felt free to follow their desires, while women often had to fulfill maternal or other domestic responsibilities and may also have experienced greater conflict with lingering Victorian ideals of womanliness. Treadwell's play *Machinal* (1928) poignantly captures this sexual *zeitgeist* through its depiction of stifling social and familial pressures on women. Yet the era also saw the notable growth of women's organizations that provided their members opportunities to observe other women's lives, to foster mutual understanding, and to support causes of shared concern. Both Glaspell and Treadwell participated in this movement; Glaspell's membership in the Heterodoxy Club, a woman's discussion group whose members included many of the leading artists, intellectuals, activists, and professionals of the time, may have provided her with an unprecedented opportunity to witness both women's profound ties to each other and their struggles to fulfill their potential in male-dominated arenas.

Glaspell's deep engagement with feminist issues and with other women's activism came increasingly to dominate her work for the Players, amid generalized Village concerns with World War I, with growing social and economic inequities in the United States, and with the relationship between art and politics. Following on the heels of the two *Masses* trials,[5] she risked arrest and prosecution under the Espionage and Sedition Acts of 1917–18 for her play *Inheritors* (1920), which overtly challenged the growing jingoism of the postwar period. Through her central character Madeline Fejevary Morton, a young woman who evolves from a carefree co-ed to a committed spokesperson for democracy, free speech, and the rights of colonized peoples, Glaspell articulates her grave misgivings about the future of her country. She exposes how the government manipulates core national values of liberty and equality, part of the "inheritance" we share as Americans. Moreover, Madeline emerges as a role model for activists, as she refuses to compromise her beliefs or resort to feminine equivocation to evade the serious legal repercussions of her actions.

The play opens with an historical prologue demonstrating how the commitment to democratic values that has prompted revolutions at home and abroad must continue to be instilled for the future, especially through higher education. In this play, as does Treadwell in her later piece *Hope for a Harvest*, Glaspell links ideology to the agricultural foundation of the nation, crafting metaphors from farming ethics and the cyclical patterns of nature. The rest of *Inheritors* occurs in the present, on the anniversary of the founding of Morton College. The institution hopes to secure state funding for its operations, but the Senator who visits campus to assess its suitability expresses concerns about whether all the faculty reflect the "one-hundred-percent American" spirit the Senator – and by extension the government – requires: beliefs, we learn, that mirror his own jingoism and prejudice, disguised as patriotism (1921: 47). In the midst of the celebration, a dispute erupts between some Hindu students who oppose British imperialism in their home country and some of the American students who refuse to recognize the parallels to their own history in the Indians' anti-colonial struggle. Madeline, the "inheritor" of her family's commitment to democracy, sides with the foreign students and is arrested for attacking the police who try to quell their protest. In one of the most vivid and moving scenes in all of Glaspell's plays, we see Madeline measure out the dimensions of the prison cell of her friend Fred Jordan, jailed for his stance as a conscientious objector to World War I. Madeline steps inside this space and becomes "all the people who are in those cells" (119). Her refusal to recant her opposition to the suppression of free speech will, Glaspell implies, soon lead to Madeline's incarceration as well. Yet Madeline's heroic commitment to democratic ideals also prompts us to see in her resolve hope for the future. In this compelling and important political drama, set in the heartland of America, Glaspell pointedly uses the stage as vehicle to effect social change.

Glaspell also uses this heartland setting, but in a more comic vein, in *Chains of Dew* (1922), which dramatizes the spread of the campaign for birth control across the United States. She avoids the tones of stridency and militancy that informed much of the campaign's early rhetoric, favoring a more balanced representation of perspectives that ultimately serves to expose the hypocrisy of those who opposed the movement.[6] Her Villager heroine Nora Powers, who works for the campaign, cannot believe the ultra-conservative depiction of the Midwest presented by Seymore Standish, a married poet with artistic ties to New York, with whom she is romantically involved. Nora decides to visit his home in Bluff City to help found a birth control league for the Midwest. Glaspell thus pits the radical bohemian culture of her own community against the conservatism of her birthplace, using this regional tension to undergird the drama's political and artistic conflicts.

The birth control movement, in tandem with the suffrage campaign, was seen by opponents as only of concern to women and as rupturing the fabric of traditional domestic and civil life. Seymore explains the movement to his wife: "I mean a group of women banded together to keep other women from having children. Going to men and trying to change the laws so women can be told how not to have children. Isn't it dreadful, Dotty?" (1922: 2.1.4). Dotty, whom Nora befriends and selects as the first president for the league, feels torn between her understanding of the liberating potential the movement promises for all women and her commitment to Seymore, who needs to be the familial patriarch. Dotty ultimately resigns herself to the status quo, but her sacrifice stands as a poignant lesson for Glaspell's audience, who can see in Dotty's decision the questionable value of the "chains of dew" that bind us all.

Glaspell's choice of the birth control movement as the focus of her comedy highlighted a problem central to modern life. Identifying a political issue that resonated deeply with the changing personal and social climates of the time, Glaspell strove, as she had since *Suppressed Desires*, to make the Players' stage a locus for both the humorous exposé of her culture's foibles and the more serious study of the demons that haunted modern life. Quite early in her playwriting career, Glaspell began to employ innovative stylistic devices, now closely identified with literary modernism, to capture the emotional and psychic alienation of her female characters struggling most assertively against patriarchal society. In her influential essay "Modernism and Gender," Marianne DeKoven, drawing on the work of other critics, summarizes some of modernism's most salient features, which include "aesthetic self-consciousness..., juxtaposition, or montage (I would add fragmentation)... dehumanization and the demise of subjectivity conceived as unified...[and a] breaking away from familiar functions of language and conventions of form" (1999: 175).

In *The Verge*, Glaspell anticipates such landmark modernist novels as Virginia Woolf's *Mrs. Dalloway* (1925), for example, by establishing a connection between female hysteria and male shell shock in the aftermath of the war. She links style to character, consciously separating the high-modernist poetic language, scenic environment, and motifs associated with her protagonist Claire Archer from the quotidian realism with which Glaspell depicts those around her.[7] Drawing on multiple senses of a "verge," Glaspell constructs her drama around transitions and contrasts. Claire is a woman on the verge of insanity. Her social and familial behavior teeters on the edge of propriety. Her horticultural experiments bring plants to their biological limits, thrusting them toward an evolution into new species. And Glaspell's dramaturgical form echoes this indeterminacy: the play appears at times to be on the brink of farce; at other moments it mirrors a Strindbergian development from problem play to expressionism and symbolism.[8]

Claire, an unconventional woman married to a rather conventional man, attempts to find outlets for her creativity and intellect through botanical experimentation. Glaspell intertwines and juxtaposes Claire's floricultural work with her human interactions, particularly with the men in her life. But Claire's growing dissatisfaction with interpersonal relationships and disillusionment with her scientific work coalesce in her mental breakdown and the destruction of what she has cared for most. Claire refuses to relinquish the power to create and to destroy in her roles as artist and scientist, but also fears containment, exclaiming: "We need not be held in forms molded for us. There is outness – and otherness.... You think life can't break up, and go outside what it was?" (1922b: 19–20). The vision of new life Claire imagines also reflects the revolutionary force of modernism itself, with its upheavals in theatrical, literary, artistic, and other forms that rejected the stasis and torpor the bohemians believed inhered in dominant modes of cultural expression. Yet Glaspell's enigmatic conclusion to the play, which refused trad-itional narrative closure and denied audiences clear signs as to how to interpret Claire or her actions, also resonated with the modern era's ambivalence about what lay ahead.

Glaspell's Pulitzer Prize-winning drama, *Alison's House* (1930), takes up these modern concerns by looking back to their origins in the *fin de siècle* atmosphere of transition to the twentieth century. Set on New Year's Eve, 1899, the play chronicles the living legacy of Alison Stanhope, a poet loosely modeled on Emily Dickinson, whose death 18 years earlier renders her another of Glaspell's major absent center characters. During the course of the play, Alison's descendants discover her previously unknown love poems, the publication of which could enhance her artistic standing, but could also further tarnish the family's already dubious reputation. Glaspell uses this conflict to debate the question of who controls a figure who has become a cultural icon, to explore issues of morality and social convention, and to examine the value of art and artists in American society.

Alison's House again reflects Glaspell's keen sensitivity to the relationship of form to content. Precisely because of her interest in exploring the roots of modernism, Glaspell conceived her drama as a prototypical well-made play. She hearkened back to the theatrical form that gave way to the innovations of the twentieth-century stage both to emphasize the historicity of her narrative and to highlight the tension between the old and the new that informs the play's characterizations, themes, and style. Writing in the postwar, post-crash United States climate, Glaspell analyzes the national values around family and community that were quickly becoming part of a nostalgic sense of our recent past; yet the ideology reflected in these codes also may have seemed precarious to those contemplating the country's future.

Glaspell's faith in the importance of theatre in American society and to American culture never wavered, despite her renewed focus on fiction later in her career. When she and Cook left New York in 1922 to fulfill his life-long ambition of communing with Greek civilization, her connection with her theatre and her community was severed. Yet she strategically rebuilt some theatrical ties after Cook's unexpected death in 1924 and her return to the States. Her work with actress Eva Le Gallienne and the Civic Repertory Theatre, which staged a revival of *Inheritors* in 1927 and the premiere of *Alison's House*, proved fortuitous for the revivification of Glaspell's dramatic career and underscored Glaspell's ongoing com-mitment to other women artists and to a modern theatre willing to take risks. Glaspell's directorship of the Midwest Play Bureau of the Federal Theatre Project from 1936 to 1938 similarly reflected her engagement with theatre striving for national importance. The title of her last play, *Springs Eternal* (1944), perfectly exemplifies the ambivalence that defined her career, with its unspoken, ongoing "hope," in the face of the nation's political and cultural conservatism, for genuine equality, freedom, and peace.

Plate 1. Eva Le Gallienne in *Alison's House*, by Susan Glaspell, original production, Civic Repertory Theatre, 1930. Courtesy of the Burns Mantle Collection, Museum of the City of New York.

Sophie Treadwell

Born in 1885, Sophie Treadwell spent a large portion of her formative years on a 150-acre ranch near Stockton, California. Her grandparents had homesteaded the ranch beginning in 1850, and it is from them that she derived her identity as a pioneering, self-sufficient westerner. Treadwell's first sustained exposure to her subsequent dual career fields of theatre and journalism came while attending the University of California at Berkeley. There, she regularly performed with the drama club, began writing plays and short stories, and served as a campus correspondent for the *San Francisco Examiner*. Like Glaspell's early work, these fictional and dramatic writings relied heavily on local color while establishing the broad thematic concerns over gender relations that would resurface throughout her career.

After a brief venture performing in vaudeville following her college years, Treadwell obtained a secretarial position typing the memoirs of the famed actress Helena Modjeska at her home in Tustin, California. Later, Treadwell would speak rhapsodically of her months with Modjeska, from whom she received acting coaching and advice for marketing newly written playscripts. It was Modjeska who instilled in Treadwell the notion that compromise was ruinous to true artistic endeavor. To facilitate her success as a dramatist, Modjeska encouraged Treadwell to submit her plays under a male pseudonym in order to be given initial serious consideration and to make only cosmetic changes to scripts upon demand by producers. Treadwell followed this latter piece of advice throughout her playwriting career to mixed and sometimes disastrous results.

Returning to San Francisco in 1908, Treadwell was hired as a journalist for the *San Francisco Bulletin*, where she fused her interests in theatre and journalism. She interviewed noted performers and used her acting talents for occasional undercover reporting, most notably as a disguised, homeless prostitute in an acclaimed 18-part serial, "An Outcast at the Christian Door" (1914). A subsequent serial became the basis for her first produced play, *Sympathy* (1915), a short character sketch presented as part of a vaudeville bill in San Francisco. Treadwell had married noted *Bulletin* sports writer William O. McGeehan in 1910, but their marriage appeared to suffer from Treadwell's increasing celebrity status as a journalist. Late in 1914, McGeehan accepted a position with the *New York Evening Journal*, while Treadwell chose to continue her work for the *Bulletin*, including four months in France as a US-accredited foreign war correspondent during World War I. But, disappointed with having been denied access to the front lines, Treadwell returned to the United States in the fall of 1915 and settled with McGeehan in New York.

New York City in the latter half of the 1910s and early 1920s offered Treadwell an infusion of new ideas and likeminded associates in the venues of modernism and feminism. Shortly after her move to New York, Treadwell befriended Walter and Louise Arensberg, whose apartment on West 67th Street near Central Park served as the locale for one of New York's most influential modernist salons. The Arensbergs' apartment housed at the time one of America's finest collections of modern art, and between 1915 and 1920 it would serve "as a virtual open house for an international group of artists and writers, many of whom had sought refuge in this country from Europe's war-torn shores" (Naumann 1980: 3). France was particularly well represented in this loosely knit group of European and American artists and intellectuals, several of whom also maintained a visible presence in the Greenwich Village circle frequented by Glaspell. The Arensberg group included the likes of Francis Picabia, Henri-Pierre Roché, Albert Gleizes, William Carlos Williams, Wallace Stevens, Alfred Kreymborg, Djuna Barnes, Mina Loy, Man Ray, Beatrice Wood, Isadora Duncan, and Marcel Duchamp. Historian Robert M. Crunden asserts that it was at the salon's late night gatherings after dinner and the theatre that "Europe and America not only met and intermingled, but cross-fertilized: sexually, obscenely, mechanically, comically, interdisciplinarily, linguistically, and even artistically" (1993: 409). The effect of this encounter with modernist artists is plainly evident in several of Treadwell's one-act plays of this period, especially *John Doane* (ca. 1915–18), *To Him Who Waits* (ca. 1915–18), and *The Eye of the Beholder* (1919). Collectively, these one-acts explore nonrealistic devices such as the interior monologue, musical underscoring, symbolist suggestion, and the use of multiple onstage personas for a central character. At the core of the beliefs held by Treadwell and the artists at the Arensbergs' salon was a shared demand for "the new in life and art: new forms, new sexual values, new freedoms unhindered by old rules" (Crunden 1993: xii).

It is within this modernist demand for new forms and structures that feminist ideals flourished. During the prewar years, New York had been the center of the suffrage movement, and Treadwell had traveled there from San Francisco to join with the Lucy Stone League to deliver a petition in favor of suffrage to the New York Legislature. This League continued the legacy of the numerous women's clubs and organizations that emerged at the turn of the century by promoting women's education and public engagement. Under the leadership of Ruth Hale, the Lucy Stone League encouraged married women to retain their maiden names and take up separate residences from their husbands in order to maintain an autonomous identity, both practices which Treadwell adopted on her move to New York.

Such activism led to newfound sexual freedoms, especially those originating in openly discussed pre- and extra-marital relations, as well as in the previously taboo subject of birth control. Treadwell's passionate relationship with the western painter Maynard Dixon from 1916 to 1920, while never flaunted, was certainly no secret to McGeehan. In these respects, Treadwell typified the enlightened New Woman in America, a figure around whom she centered such later plays as *You Can't Have Everything* (1925), *Ladies Leave* (1929), and *Three* (1936). *Ladies Leave*, the only of these three to be produced, dramatizes the moral and sexual redefinition of Zizi Powers, the young wife of a conservative editor of a popular ladies magazine. Inspired by lectures from a visiting psychologist from Vienna, Zizi takes a lover before ultimately rejecting the selfish demands of both him and her husband and leaving for a life of her own in Europe. Treadwell believed passionately in the progressive advances in sexual equality and woman's independence. Yet, unlike *Ladies Leave*, many of her plays often reveal ambivalence about the actualization of such equality.

In fact, Treadwell's use of traditional and popular dramatic forms for her first two plays produced on Broadway overshadowed such gender concerns. Her first production, an adventure story of banditry and romance in Mexico called

Gringo (1922), employed the thrilling spectacle, local color, and plot contrivances of turn-of-the-century melodrama. The second, *O Nightingale* (1925), depicts a naive Midwestern girl aspiring to an acting career in New York in the format of a standard, boy-meets-girl sentimental comedy. There was little, then, in these first two Broadway efforts to prepare critics or audiences for her next play, the 1928 expressionist drama *Machinal*, a play that uniquely merged modernist dramatic form with feminist content.

Treadwell based *Machinal* in part on the 1927 trial and execution of Long Island housewife Ruth Snyder for the murder of her husband, a trial that Treadwell attended but did not cover in any official journalistic capacity. Told through a series of nine disjointed episodes, the play chronicles the journey of an office stenographer initially named only as the Young Woman. The various business and domestic locales of the play's first half contribute equally to the Young Woman's sense of a claustrophobic, "mechanical, nerve nagging" existence. Treadwell punctuates the dialogue of the characters by extensive offstage voices ("Characters in the Background Heard, but Unseen"), as well as off-and onstage sounds of mechanized, urban life (office machines, a radio, riveting from a construction site, etc.). The dialogue itself ranges from the telegraphic, staccato "rhythm of our common city speech" to lengthy monologues in which the racing thoughts of the neurasthenic Young Woman explode in stream-of-consciousness desperation (Treadwell 1993: xi–xii). In *Machinal*, Treadwell's use of such expressionist devices captured perfectly the modernist obsessions with the urban cityscape and the new psychology of the subconscious.

In *Machinal*, everyone from the Young Woman's co-workers to her dependent mother urges her to escape the stresses of the urban workplace by accepting an offer of leisurely marriage from her boss, a boorish but wealthy corporate vice president. But the first part of the play ends with the Young Woman's realization that her acceptance of this undesired marriage and the subsequent birth of a daughter has resulted not in liberation but in an even more stifling form of domestic entrapment. In the previously cited essay "Modernism and Gender," DeKoven states that the "radical implications of the social-cultural changes feminism advocated produced in modernist writing an unprecedented preoccupation with gender, both thematically and formally." Male modernists, DeKoven claims, expressed both a fascination and misogynist "fear of women's new power," resulting in an "irresolvable ambivalence toward powerful femininity." DeKoven goes on to assert insightfully that female modernist writers shared a similar ambivalence, but not due to the prospect of cultural change forged by newly empowered women. Instead, DeKoven contends that "the female Modernists generally feared punishment for desiring that change" (1999: 174–5).

The second part of *Machinal* dramatizes such a fear and demonstrates Treadwell's shared concern with the work of other female modernists. However, it is worth noting that the female modernists most typically cited by DeKoven and other literary critics are fiction writers, such as Charlotte Perkins Gilman, Kate Chopin, or Virginia Woolf. Discussion of allied dramatists, such as Treadwell and Glaspell, is too often absent. In the play's second half, the Young Woman has a brief but passionate affair

Plate 2. Clark Gable and Zita Johann in *Machinal*, by Sophie Treadwell, photo by Vandamm, original production. Courtesy of the Billy Rose Theatre Collection, New York Public Library for the Performing Arts, Astor, Lenox and Tilden Foundation.

with an American adventurer named Richard Roe, murders her crass husband, receives a conviction in a court of law, and ultimately departs by force from her prison cell en route to her execution. But along the way, Treadwell emphasizes the Young Woman's empowerment through sexual liberation in the affair with Roe. After making love for the first time in Roe's basement apartment, Treadwell provides a stage direction that shows the Young Woman at peace for the first time in the play: "She looks toward him, then throws her head slowly back, lifts her right arm – this gesture that is in so many statues of women – Volupte" (51). This moment of sexual liberation proves emblematic of the Young Woman's desire for the same sort of unencumbered freedom enjoyed by her male lover, as it was his stories of adventures in Mexico, including his murderous and unpunished escape from bandits, that first stimulated her attractions.

In addition, it is not until this second part of the play that we learn the actual name of the Young Woman – Helen Jones. She achieves her true identity only through personal rebellion against society's constraints on gendered behavior. Furthermore, Treadwell's choice of a commonplace name reflects her intent to write about "an ordinary young woman, any woman" (xi). Helen is not the enlightened, socially aware New Woman found in plays like *Ladies Leave*, women that Treadwell typically identifies by distinctly uncommon names – Zelda, Zizi, Kit. Like Glaspell's *Trifles*, *Machinal* derives its force in part from the implication that autonomy remains the right and within the power of "any woman," not solely the intellectual or political activist.

Yet Treadwell also implies that Helen's freedom cannot last. The play realizes the fear of punishment for such empowerment in swift, unrelenting episodes of society's retribution. In the courtroom scene following the husband's murder, the all-male judge, jury, bailiff, and messenger boys proceed in words and movements that are "routine – mechanical. Each is going through the motions of his own game" (60). Even her ex-lover, Roe, betrays Helen with a damning affidavit against her. Throughout the scene only Helen's actions are presented with sympathy, lacking the mechanical rigidity of all around her. Treadwell emphasizes the devastating effect of society's retaliation when, after her clumsy confession prompts raucous courtroom laughter, Helen "begins to moan – suddenly – as though the realization of the enormity of her isolation had just come upon her. It is the sound of desolation, of agony, of human woe" (76). Although Treadwell's final prison scene depicts the defeat and impending death of Helen, it also conveys her continued resistance. In the midst of preparations for her execution, Helen prefers defiance to passive acceptance of her punishment: "Oh my God am I never to be let alone! Always to have to submit – to submit! No more – not now – I'm going to die – I won't submit! Not now!" (79). Thus, while Treadwell displays the fear of punishment described by DeKoven, she also attempts to dissuade such fear by providing a lasting image of female resistance.

Treadwell returned time and again to this basic theme and form in various versions of a later play titled *For Saxophone* (1933–41). While some of the particulars of *Machinal*'s plot have been changed, the basic premise and gender concerns remain. Treadwell, however, more radically develops her use of modernist dramatic devices. Crunden notes that although American modernists borrowed techniques from their European counterparts, "in two areas [they] had exports of their own," most notably in techniques influenced from film and jazz (1993: xiv). *For Saxophone* remains one of the earliest attempts to adapt these methods for the American stage. Treadwell's play creates stage equivalents for such film techniques as crosscuts, long shots and close-ups, rapid cutting and montage. She intended the play for near-continuous under-scoring, primarily by saxophone, in order to approximate jazz's improvisation, spontaneity, and disruptions in rhythm and time. Longtime collaborator and friend Robert Edmond Jones conveyed to Treadwell his belief that this play contained "the germ of a new dramatic idiom" (qtd. in Wynn 1982: 175). As with *Machinal*, Treadwell once again employs modernist techniques in portraying the punishment in the form of death enacted on the newly empowered female protagonist. Unlike *Machinal*, though, the extreme form of the techniques employed made *For Saxophone* virtually unmarket-able with commercial theatre producers of the time.[9]

Taken together with Glaspell's *The Outside* and *The Verge*, however, these two plays by Treadwell form a select body of drama that utilizes experimental modernist forms to illuminate women's experience. Ronald Wainscott contends that Glaspell and Treadwell uniquely adapted the expressionist techniques that were in vogue on the American stage during the 1920s. Glaspell and Treadwell, Wainscott observes, "harnessed a strident and painful form and style, usually reserved for male protag-onists, to explicate a very different kind of inhumanity and isolation for their women protagonists suffering in a confusing and inhospitable postwar world" (1997: 140).

The decade of the 1930s proved a troubling one for Treadwell on both personal and professional fronts. She experienced increasing difficulty marketing her plays, and even those that she produced herself were met with indifferent or hostile critical response. Her trip to the Soviet Union in 1933 to participate in Alexander Tairov's production of *Machinal* resulted in a deep disillusionment over the difference between the ideals and the actualities of socialism. Within a year of her return, both her husband and mother died. After a lengthy voyage to Egypt and the Far East, she returned in 1937 to the family ranch near Stockton that she had now inherited. Thus, the arc of Treadwell's life and career bears a striking resemblance to that of Glaspell's. Both women began in rural settings writing works of local color, moved to urban centers for intellectual and artistic stimulation, and returned after the death of their husbands to the type of rural environment that shaped their early lives. In returning to Stockton, Treadwell sought to revive the agricultural productivity of the now-neglected land, and in doing so she hoped to create "the kind of life I longed to have around me – the simple, healthy, cheerful American farm life I had once known" (Treadwell 1941). What she discovered, though, contributed to an element of conservatism in her life and work, a conservatism born from awareness that the increasing presence of corporate business had radically altered this farm life she once knew.

In his study *Making America Corporate, 1870–1920*, Olivier Zunz convincingly argues that by the middle of the twentieth century, "the corporate reorganization of American society was a fait accompli" (1990: 1). Zunz explains the rapidity with which corporate bureaucracies and practices transformed the American farmscape, ultimately including that of the ranching West: "As it turned out, developing a high yield, mechanized agriculture required the concerted effort of only one generation" (151). After investing several years modernizing the farm, Treadwell realized that the absence of a supportive community had led to her failure as an independent farmer. Her response to this newfound isolation was the play and novel, *Hope for a Harvest*.

The play version, especially, reveals Treadwell's growing conservatism, most notably in its plea for Americans to return to an earlier work ethic and sense of mutual community cooperation. In this play, a family farm in Treadwell's same San Joachim Valley has been parceled off for sale, and the combination of the high cost of labor and low market prices driven down by conglomerate farmers results in fruit that remains unpicked and left to rot. The farm's owner, a bigoted and embittered man named Elliott Martin, must reevaluate his attitudes in response to his cousin, Lotta Thatcher, who recently returned to the farm seeking spiritual renewal after the death of her husband in war-ravaged Paris. Lotta eventually brokers a land-use pact for the family to cooperate with a neighboring Italian farmer, thus initiating the reversal of the farm's decline. As presented by the Theatre Guild, *Harvest* met with enthusiastic responses in Guild subscription cities such as New Haven, Boston, Washington, DC, Pittsburgh, and Baltimore. When the play transferred to New York in November of 1941, however, critics dismissed the play's didacticism and naive solution to a complex problem. This response prompted Treadwell to conclude that the New York intellectual and journalistic circles she once inhabited now seemed separated from the sensibilities of the American public and their memory of an agrarian or community-driven existence. "But thousands of Americans," Treadwell argued, "seem to recognize my play – even New York Americans. Not first-night New York Americans – they did not recognize it at all" (Treadwell 1941). *Harvest* closed after a disappointing run of 38 performances.

The dismissal of *Hope for a Harvest* by New York critics and literati proved the watershed in an increasing number of failures for Treadwell in the commercial Broadway theatre. During the previous two decades, Treadwell fought numerous battles on behalf of the artistic integrity of the dramatist: she brought a lawsuit against John Barrymore in 1924 for plagiarism of her play about Edgar Allan Poe;[10] she turned to producing her own works on Broadway in 1925 only after her comedy *O Nightingale* was suspended in limbo during a contract option to producer George C. Tyler, a not infrequent condition for playwrights resulting from Broadway's "stagger system" of play production;[11] and in an appeal through the Union of Soviet Authors, she became the first US dramatist to receive royalty payments for a play produced in the USSR. In her 1925 lecture entitled "Producing a Play," Treadwell outlined for students of the American Laboratory Theatre her dissatisfactions with Broadway play production practices. At the core of her discontent remained the relegation of the dramatist to a secondary, supporting figure, as evidenced by such practices as a rushed, standard four-week rehearsal period, demands for overnight revisions, the rampant use of play doctors, and an unwillingness for directors or producers to discuss the play's thematic content. After World War II, Treadwell devoted less and less attention to marketing her plays for Broadway, and her presence in the New York theatre scene virtually ended. She spent the next 25 years of her life writing fiction and largely revising earlier plays while restlessly searching for the type of community she had hoped to find in Stockton. She occupied residences in Newtown, Connecticut, Vienna, Mexico, Spain, and finally Tucson, Arizona, where she died in 1970.

In retrospect, it seems odd that Broadway remained the venue of choice for Treadwell, that she did not take advantage of the burgeoning Little Theatre Movement, as did Susan Glaspell. As noted earlier, such little theatres proved more hospitable to experiments in dramatic form and content than did Broadway. But Treadwell always envisioned herself as not only succeeding on a large, national platform like Broadway, but also using her success to reform this platform. Since the entrenchment of the Theatrical Syndicate and the Shubert Brothers at the turn of the century, play production in New York had evolved into a corporate enterprise that often overwhelmed the individual artist, much as corporate farming impeded the success of the independent farmer. Treadwell's mentor, Helena Modjeska, had often led the charge against such theatrical conglomeration, and her friends from the Arensbergs' modernist salon similarly rejected the notion of artistic compromise or commercialization in their pursuit of new forms. Yet after a while, Treadwell's insistence on marketing controversial or innovative material to Broadway producers baffled even her closest friends. Unlike other women playwright-producers of the first half of the twentieth century, such as Rachel Crothers, Treadwell remained unwilling to alter her later plays for critical acclaim or popular appeal. But in doing so, she obtained one sparkling achievement in the theatre – the once near forgotten but now canonized *Machinal*.

Full critical recognition of the work of Sophie Treadwell and Susan Glaspell remains hampered by the lack of comprehensive collections of their writing. Only two of Treadwell's 39 plays have ever been published, and the vast majority of her writings remain accessible only at the University of Arizona Library Special Collections. Although more of Glaspell's work has appeared in print, two of her plays remain available only in manuscript form and several of her other plays are no longer in publication. The final chapter on Glaspell's and Treadwell's contributions to modernism and feminism cannot be written until their unpublished writings become more readily available for wider critical assessment.

Notes

1. For a history of this theatre, see Sarlós (1982).
2. Many members of the Players also wrote for the radical Village newspaper *The Masses*, whose editors and contributors shared a conviction that their efforts could effect genuine social reform. For a discussion of *The Masses*, see O'Neill (1966).
3. It is important to understand Glaspell's feminism in relation to its cultural context and historical moment. See Gainor (2001), especially the Afterword.
4. Glaspell used this title for the 1917 short story version of this narrative.

5. For an analysis of the *Masses* trials, see O'Neill (1966).

6. For a history of the birth control movement in America, see Gordon (1990).

7. For another cogent discussion of *The Verge* and high modernism, see Makowsky (1999).

8. This discussion of *The Verge* borrows directly from my analysis of the play in Gainor (2001).

9. *For Saxophone* still has never been produced. For a more detailed discussion of expressionist techniques in *Machinal* and *For Saxophone*, see Dickey (1999).

10. Treadwell's play was eventually produced on Broadway in 1936 under the title *Plumes in the Dust*.

11. For a detailed discussion of the stagger system, see Reed (1935).

BIBLIOGRAPHY

Bourne, R. (1956). "Trans-National America." In R. Bourne, *History of a Literary Radical and Other Papers*, ed. Van Wyck Brooks. New York: S. A. Russell, 260–84.

Crunden, R. M. (1993). *American Salons: Encounters with European Modernism, 1885–1917*. New York: Oxford University Press.

DeKoven, M. (1999). "Modernism and Gender." In Michael Levenson (ed.), *The Cambridge Companion to Modernism*. Cambridge: Cambridge University Press, 174–93.

Dickey, J. (1999). "Sophie Treadwell: The Expressionist Moment." In Brenda Murphy (ed.), *The Cambridge Companion to American Women Playwrights*. Cambridge: Cambridge University Press, 66–81.

Gainor, J. E. (2001). *Susan Glaspell in Context: American Theater, Culture, and Politics, 1915–48*. Ann Arbor: University of Michigan Press.

Glaspell, S. (1920). *Trifles*. In *Plays*. Boston: Small, Maynard, 1–30.

——(1921). *Inheritors*. Boston: Small, Maynard.

——(1922a). *Chains of Dew*. Unpublished manuscript. Library of Congress.

——(1922b). *The Verge*. Boston: Small, Maynard.

Gordon, L. (1990). *Woman's Body, Woman's Right: Birth Control in America*, rev. ed. New York: Penguin.

Makowsky, V. (1999). "Susan Glaspell and Modernism." In Brenda Murphy (ed.), *The Cambridge Companion to American Women Playwrights*. Cambridge: Cambridge University Press, 49–65.

Naumann, F. (1980). "Walter Conrad Arensberg: Poet, Patron, and Participant in the New York Avant-Garde, 1915–20." *Philadelphia Museum of Art Bulletin* 76: 1–32.

O'Neill, W. (ed.) (1966). *Echoes of Revolt: The Masses, 1911–1917*. Chicago: Quadrangle.

Reed, J. V. (1935). *The Curtain Falls*. New York: Harcourt, Brace.

Rohe, A. (1921). "The Story of Susan Glaspell." *Morning Telegraph* (December 18), 2: 4.

Sarlós, R. K. (1982). *Jig Cook and the Provincetown Players: Theatre in Ferment*. Amherst: University of Massachusetts Press.

Stansell, C. (2000). *American Moderns: Bohemian New York and the Creation of a New Century*. New York: Metropolitan.

Treadwell, S. (1941). "I Remembered A Big White House." *New York Herald Tribune* (December 14). Clipping, Billy Rose Theatre Collection, New York Public Library for the Performing Arts.

——(1993). *Machinal*. London: Nick Hern.

Wainscott, R. H. (1997). *The Emergence of the Modern American Theater, 1914–1929*. New Haven, CT: Yale University Press.

Wynn, N. E. (1982). "Sophie Treadwell: The Career of a Twentieth-Century American Feminist Playwright." Dissertation, City University of New York.

Zunz, O. (1990). *Making America Corporate, 1870–1920*. Chicago: University of Chicago Press.

5

American Experimentalism, American Expressionism, and Early O'Neill

Deanna M. Toten Beard

"Isn't it, after all, pretty stupid, to demand that art deal only with the obvious realities of the world," wrote theatre and art critic Sheldon Cheney in 1921, "when there are so many realms of emotion, of imagination, of cosmic experience, which the artist is better fitted, spiritually, to explore and interpret to us than anyone else" (60). During the 1910s and 1920s, Cheney was one of America's strongest advocates for a modernist native drama, but being neither playwright, director, nor producer, he could do little more than cheer on the movement. This he did with aplomb as creator and editor of the influential *Theatre Arts Magazine*. Cheney and other pro-modernist advocates stood like tower guards, keenly watching for signs of an emerging modern drama in America. They celebrated any American dramatic experiment which shrugged off stage literalism and stale imitation, even when the play in question had to be praised with numerous caveats. The pro-modernists were so rabid for change that we might expect them to have bickered about when success had actually been achieved – that is, when a play had arrived which seemed to be both fully American and fully modern. In fact, critical consensus was reached in the spring of 1922. The play that by contemporary standards ushered in modern American drama was Eugene O'Neill's expressionist phenomenon, *The Hairy Ape*.

In many ways, early enthusiasts for *The Hairy Ape* were correct. Following the success of the play, the American theatre enjoyed a "vogue of Expressionism" that lasted until the Depression and which still resurfaces today (Wainscott 1997: 91). Furthermore, scholars continue to invoke *The Hairy Ape* as the exemplar of American expressionism, the country's first modern drama. However, the long-held belief that the American expressionism of Eugene O'Neill heralded the arrival of a modern American drama has also perpetuated the notion that all "new art" drama of the 1910s was mere rehearsal for the real modernism of the 1920s. This critical construct is based on the model of O'Neill's own dramaturgy but it is not consistent with the work of other experimental writers during the 1910s. O'Neill's writing in the 1910s shows how the playwright worked through techniques and themes that will emerge in his mature plays, both expressionistic and realistic. But the 1910s also witnessed an independent brand of experimentalism whose style would be eclipsed by both American expressionism and Eugene O'Neill.

Mainstream American theatre in the 1910s mostly featured light comedies and melodramas characterized by a kind of pseudo-realism in dialogue and scenic require-ments. Plays of the harsher and less palatable movement of European realism found an audience in America through the work of bold individual artists and the Little Theatre Movement. There were, however, a handful of plays in the 1910s that sought to escape the presentation – or imitation – of material reality on stage. These plays experimented with dreams, nightmares, hallucinations, the psychological, and the illogical. Such plays were also the province of little theatres in America, though, unlike European and European-inspired realist dramas, this kind of experimental drama did not belong to any self-conscious movement of writing. Critics have failed to group these plays into a neat category (as in the case with Martin Esslin's grouping, "Theatre of the Absurd," for example). As a result, these plays have been ignored or dismissed in the development of American drama. In order to investigate their shared artistic goals and means, I will group these plays under the hypothetical rubric (or genre) "American experimentalism." The following discussion will examine American experimentalism of the 1910s, the better-known American expressionism of the 1920s, and the relationship of Eugene O'Neill to both forms of drama.

American experimentalist plays were interested in stage poetry, but they were not verse drama; America's attempts at a native verse drama never took hold. The poetry of these dramatic experiments was a modern lyricism characterized by rhythm, image, and anxiety. American experimentalist plays emphasized the fantastic but they did not feature magical creatures. Magic had already been used as a plot device in other American plays, specifically Percy MacKaye's *The Scarecrow* (1908). However, a play about a demonic character bringing a scarecrow to life fails to belong to the same spirit of experimentalism because the witchcraft, though fictional, occurs as "real" and material in the play – all of the other characters interact with the scarecrow. In American experimentalist plays the focus is on making overt to the audience things that are hidden and spiritual in the world of the play.

Perhaps the earliest American experimentalist drama is Eleanor Gates's *The Poor Little Rich Girl* (1913). The play frames an extended hallucination scene with a sentimental and melodramatic plot: a governess, tutors, and a team of servants are raising the child of wealthy parents in a lavish city home. Little Gwendolyn wants for nothing, but her parents' materialism has deprived the girl of the simple pleasures she requires most: time with her family, time in the country, and time with other children. To get a night away from the nursery, Gwendolyn's nurse accidentally offers her too much sleeping medication. What follows is Gwendolyn's drug-induced nightmare featuring her childish images of the mysterious adult world she only hears about. Characters in the hallucination include "The Woman with the Bee in Her Bonnet" (Gwendolyn's mother), "The Man Who is Made of Money" (her father), "The Two-Faced Thing" (her nurse), and "The Snake in the Grass" (her governess). Gwendolyn's anxiety over her parents' priorities is resolved in the nightmare, and when she is revived she discovers that her frightened parents have decided to moderate their ambitious lifestyle and enjoy a lengthy family vacation in the country.

The Poor Little Rich Girl enjoyed moderate success with Broadway audiences, enduring for an admirable 160 performances. At the time, some critics considered Gates's play important simply for being an experimental drama written by an American. In 1916, drama critic George Jean Nathan wrote in a preface to the first published edition of *The Poor Little Rich Girl*:

> As against the not unhollow symbolic strut and gasconade of such over-paeaned pieces as let us for example say "The Blue Bird" of Maeterlinck, so simple and unaffected a bit of stage writing as this – of school dramatic intrinsically the same – cajoles the more honest heart and satisfies more plausibly and fully those of us whose thumbs are ever being pulled professionally for a native stage less smeared with the snobberies of empty, albeit high-sounding, nomenclature from overseas. (Gates 1916: vi)

While anyone familiar with Nathan might be shocked that he honored Gates's thin and overly sentimental drama with a glowing preface, the xenophobia of his comments shows that his real purpose was to promote native drama in general. In contrast, Arthur Hopkins, who directed *The Poor Little Rich Girl*, may have been attracted to the play because it provided a rare chance to produce not simply an American drama, but an American experimental drama. Such opportunities to explore non-realism on stage were few in 1913, but more were forthcoming.

Alice Gerstenberg's one-act *Overtones*, written in 1913 and produced by the Washington Square Players in 1915, provides a superb example of American experimentalism. *Overtones* explores the psychological conflict of Harriet and Margaret. Margaret, recently returned from Europe, has come for tea to the home of the wealthy Harriet. As a girl, Harriet dated an artistic boy from her hometown. When she realized that his plans for a career in the arts would mean a life of struggle, Harriet stopped seeing him and subsequently married a rich businessman. The aspiring artist then married Harriet's childhood friend, Margaret, and the couple moved to Europe to pursue his painting career. Now, Margaret and her husband are desperate for money, and secretly hope that Harriet will order a portrait. Harriet pines for her lost love and wants to commission a portrait as a means of spending time with him. The short play depicts each woman trying tactfully to obtain what she wants without revealing her motives.

Complicating this predicament, in an emotionally charged scene, is the presence of Hetty and Maggie, Harriet and Margaret's "primitive" selves or alter egos. Hetty and Maggie bicker with one another and side-coach their "cultured" selves.

Gerstenberg's stage directions provide concrete ideas for how this dual reality should be staged:

> HARRIET's gown is a light, "jealous" green. Her counterpart, HETTY, wears a gown of the same design but in a darker shade. MARGARET wears a gown of lavender chiffon while her counterpart, MAGGIE, wears a gown of the same design in purple, a purple scarf veiling her face. Chiffon is used to give a sheer effect, suggesting a possibility of primitive and cultured selves merging into one woman. The primitive and cultured selves never come into actual physical contact but try to sustain the impression of mental conflict. HARRIET never sees HETTY, never talks to her but rather thinks aloud looking into space. HETTY, however, looks at HARRIET, talks intently and shadows her continually. (Gerstenberg 1916: 59)

Gerstenberg creates a mechanism for externalizing psychological conflict. Psychology, specifically Freudian psychoanalysis, was popular in America during the period, a fact that contributed to the success of *Overtones*. Freudian thought received a comic treatment by Susan Glaspell and George Cram Cook's *Suppressed Desires* (1915) (see chapter 4) and would have an earnest airing in some American expressionist plays, in particular *Roger Bloomer* (1923).

Gerstenberg also provides detailed stage directions for how the externalization of psychology should sound in *Overtones*: "The voices of the cultured women are affected and lingering, the voices of the primitive impulsive and more or less staccato" (59). As we will see, patterning of sound will also be an early interest of O'Neill's and featured extensively in American expressionism. Just prior to the production of *Overtones*, Gerstenberg had stage success with her version of *Alice in Wonderland* (1915), an experience which may explain both her interest in the fantastic and her ability to imagine visually and aurally how a non-realistic atmosphere might be realized on stage. Theodore Dreiser, also a writer of experimental plays during the time, would prove much less familiar with, or less interested in, the physical limitations of theatrical production.

Dreiser is better known as a novelist than a playwright, but his 1916 collection *Plays of the Natural and Supernatural* features several excellent examples of American experimentalist drama. His most noteworthy early play is the one-act *Laughing Gas*, the story of a physician undergoing surgery for a neck abscess. Because it is a minor procedure, the surgeon and his physician patient agree to use nitrous oxide – "laughing gas" – instead of ether. Immediately upon going under the influence of the anesthesia, the physician becomes aware of metaphysical realities surrounding him. He is visited by "Shadows" from the first, second, third, and fourth astral planes. He speaks with the character of nitrous oxide, called "Demyaphon," and the power of physics, "Alcephoran." Perhaps the most abstract of the characters listed in the dramatis personae is "The Rhythm of the Universe" whose only lines in the play are the repetition of "Om." The physician's bizarre experiences escalate as his surgical team runs out of the oxygen needed to keep him alive. The metaphysical characters confront him with the dark meaninglessness of human life, as if to convince him to accept death. Yet, the physician rallies his strength and pulls through his surgery, awakening with a raucous laugh that surprises even the medical professionals who are accustomed to the effects of laughing gas.

Judging by Dreiser's cinematic, novelistic, and frequently unimaginable stage directions, the playwright may have intended his supernatural plays to be closet dramas or motion picture scenarios rather than stage plays. For example, Dreiser comments about physical sensations and thought processes in the stage directions: "The fumes of the gas reach his brain. A warm, delightful stupor overcomes him. He imagines he is moving his forefinger, but he is not" (Dreiser 2000: 40). Some of Dreiser's images require the sort of close-up realism we now associate with film: "He takes up a scalpel and makes an incision one and one-half inches long by one-half inch deep" (42). At other times, Dreiser writes directions that are as impossible as "The operating table sweeps on at limitless speed" (42). Similarly unstageable is Dreiser's supernatural one-act *In the Dark*, whose brief action sprawls over several blocks of a tenement neighborhood, in a train yard, and in the squalid apartment of an "Eye-talian" immigrant. Dreiser's *The Blue Sphere* moves quickly from a speaker on a distant train, to a mother in her kitchen, to her husband at work, and to a neighbor in the street. The location shifts from a line in one location to a line in the next, with no stage directions to explain how these changes can be presented on stage. The play also features images of fleeting memories:

Mrs. Delavan: (*A vision of the church door at Clarendon, a small town thirty miles away, and of herself entering it in this very dress, and Nate Saulsby passing her and looking at her admiringly, filling her eyes.*) That was such a pretty dress. It had such nice frilled collars and cuffs. I wonder how Nate is doing now. He was a nice, handsome, clever boy. (34–5).

Like *Laughing Gas*, the action of *The Blue Sphere* and *In the Dark* features spirits that sweep through the landscape, hover overhead, and pass through solid matter. Still, as some scholars use such evidence to argue that Dreiser's non-realistic one-acts were conceived as motion pictures, it is important to remember that there was a recent precedent for successfully showing ghosts on stage, for example, David Belasco's *The Return of Peter Grimm* in 1911.

Modern poet Edna St. Vincent Millay also explored the possibilities of the non-realistic stage, producing three plays with the Provincetown Players. The most enduring of her dramas is *Aria da Capo*, a *commedia dell'arte*-style one-act play first presented in December 1919. The non-realism in *Aria da Capo* stems from a meta-theatricality created by one set of characters in the play – Pierrot and Columbine of a traditional Harlequinade – being interrupted by characters eager to perform their own scene – two shepherds in a pastoral verse drama. Millay's anti-war critique can be observed in the shepherds' little play about a petty fight over land and natural resources. Her message is reinforced during the play's final moments. After the shepherd characters kill each other on stage because of their border dispute, the director – an authoritative classical figure called Cothurnus – orders Pierrot and Columbine back to perform again the frothy love scene which started *Aria da Capo*; the phrase *da capo* in music means "from the beginning." When they balk at the possibility of play-acting with dead bodies on stage, Cothurnus says, "Pull down the tablecloth on the other side and hide them from the house, and play the farce. The audience will forget" (Millay 1994: 720). Written in late 1919, during a time when America attempted to return to normalcy after World War I, Millay's message of sweeping corpses under the table would have been clear to her audience.

Other plays in the period also explore the theatricality and meta-theatricality of *commedia* characters. Alfred Kreymborg's *Lima Beans* (1916), for example, features a Pierrot-type husband and Columbine-type wife in a poetic comedy (it was also presented by the Provincetown Players). Unlike the playfulness seen in fellow-poet Kreymborg's play, Millay's dramatization of her anti-war message is more akin to non-realistic experimental drama. There is no logical explanation offered for why the shepherds' murders work. The "poison" one concocts to kill the other is made from black confetti, and before the second shepherd dies from this poison he strangles the first with flimsy crepe paper streamers. *Aria da Capo* fails to show actors carried away to the point that they actually conduct "stage fighting" too viciously and hurt each other. Rather, Millay creates a world in which the innocuous elements of the stage supernaturally possess the ability to kill, seemingly because Thyrsis and Corydon merely wish it so. The shepherds' desire to harm each other is made physically real in an illogical way. These examples demonstrate two very different tactics for staging the metaphysical. In *The Poor Little Rich Girl* and *Laughing Gas*, the distortion is explained medically, whereas *Overtones* and *Aria da Capo* simultaneously depict the natural and supernatural without any attempt to portray plausibility.

Eugene O'Neill's experiments in dramaturgy in the 1910s did not focus on dreams or the supernatural. Yet, like other writers, he was interested in avoiding realism and pseudo-realism that dominated mainstream American theatre at the time. A look at two of O'Neill's early one-acts, *Bound East for Cardiff* and *The Moon of the Caribbees*, is useful for investigating the particular quality of O'Neill's own dramatic experimentation. They are both sea plays, and their setting is similar to two of O'Neill's other short pieces taking place on the fictional British tramp steamer, the SS *Glencairn*.

Bound East for Cardiff was written in 1914, though it would not be performed until July 1916 when the Provincetown Players staged it on Cape Cod. The one-act has received significant attention for being associated both with the beginning of O'Neill's career and the founding of one of America's most important twentieth-century theatres. The play takes place in the forecastle of the Glencairn on a foggy night, while seamen pass their off-duty time sleeping, trading stories, playing music, and insulting each other. The mood this night is disturbed because one man lies dying in bed. Yank is sick owing to a bad fall from the deck into the hold. The men are all frightened by the nearness of death, especially Yank's friend Driscoll. Yank is resigned to dying, though his greatest fear is that he will be left when Driscoll goes on duty, dying alone in the forecastle to the sound of the other men snoring. Driscoll tries to comfort his friend by recalling an accident at sea in which the two men survived together after drifting in a lifeboat for days. Suddenly Yank starts to complain about a mist filling the room: "Must be my eyes gettin' weak, I guess" (O'Neill 2001: 29). As he struggles with his last few breaths, Yank tells Driscoll that he sees a pretty lady dressed in black. With that Yank dies, just as a seaman enters to announce that the fog has lifted. The play's final image is Driscoll kneeling in prayer in front of Yank's bunk.

If *Bound East for Cardiff* were a typical American experimentalist play, the lady in black whom Yank sees as he dies would have been seen by the audience as well. In *Cardiff*, O'Neill examines an idea based on character rather than plot. He is uninterested in creating the metaphysical image physical; instead, he is determined to manifest mood on stage. This notion of mood is frequently accomplished through innovative use of patterned sound. O'Neill's stage directions are replete with sounds: live accordion music underscoring a sailor's storytelling, the ship's whistle calling men to watch, bells announcing the time, men snoring in their bunks, and long periods of silence. Furthermore, the play, like all the plays that use the *Glencairn* as their setting, is richly imbued with a variety of working-class dialects: Irish, Scottish, Cockney, Swedish, and American, which add to the cacophony of mood.

O'Neill's technique of elevating character over plot is illustrated by another sea play, *The Moon of the Caribbees* (1917). Set again on the *Glencairn* as the ship moors one night off the West Indies, *The Moon of the Caribbees* begins with the seamen waiting on deck for the arrival of island girls and rum. While they wait, they bicker, trade stories, and sing. The women arrive and the party moves indoors to hide the illegal drinking. Smitty and The Donkeyman, however, stay alone on deck. The stage directions refer to gloomy "Negro" music coming from shore and the muffled clamor of the party behind closed doors. Smitty is a melancholy, thoughtful man, haunted by "mem'ries." The Donkeyman wonders why Smitty came to sea when he "ain't made for it" (12). His guess is that Smitty had woman problems: "An' she said she threw you over 'cause you was drunk; an' you said you was drunk 'cause she threw you over" (13). When the party spills out onto the deck, the stage is flooded with loud talking, laughing, accordion music, and abandoned dancing. The drunken men quickly turn to fighting and one receives a superficial knife wound. The brawl attracts the attention of the mate who quickly discovers the rum and orders the women off the ship. In the final moments of the play, Smitty is alone on stage with his memories and the night's stillness. The sounds of the music drift in gently from shore "like the mood of the moonlight made audible" (18).

The dramatic structure of *The Moon of the Caribbees* meanders and stalls, thereby avoiding a climax characteristic of traditional, Aristotelian drama. The play's organization is best described as musical or poetic rather than plot-centered, though its lyricism is brooding. The melancholy of the overly intellectual Smitty is communicated through the sorrowful music off-stage and the gloom of a party heard from behind closed doors. Smitty's self-made isolation is expressed more strongly than anything else in the play. We, like The Donkeyman, are made to wonder what has happened in Smitty's past to motivate him to seek a life at sea. Both *The Moon of the Caribbees* and *Bound East for Cardiff* demonstrate O'Neill's ability to create complex characters economically (with little or no dialogue) and a strong sense of place, traits that will continue to define his writing. These early plays also show O'Neill's growing interest in a complex stage poetry of sound and image which would specifically characterize his two major expressionist plays: *The Emperor Jones* (1920) and *The Hairy Ape* (1922).

The Emperor Jones opened at the Provincetown Players' small Playwright's Theatre in November 1920 and the show later moved to Broadway. In eight scenes, the play traces the fall of Pullman porter Brutus Jones's brief reign as "emperor" of a fictitious island in the West Indies. Charles Gilpin originated the title role, the first modern black character to be played on Broadway by an African American actor. Jeffrey H. Richards has pointed out that discussions of *The Emperor Jones* usually focus more on details of the original production than on the text itself (O'Neill 2001: xxxv–xxxvii). Indeed, the play's original success was largely due to the novelty of its leading actor, the visual impact created by director George Cram Cook and designer Cleon Throck-morton, and the innovative use of drumming to underscore the action of the play. This drumming begins during the first scene:

> From the distant hills comes the faint, steady thump of a tom-tom, low and vibrating. It starts at a rate exactly corresponding to normal pulse beat – 72 to the minute – and continues at a gradually accelerating rate from this point uninterruptedly to the very end of the play. (275)

The majority of the play is the protagonist's extended nightmarish vision as he flees through the jungles of the island. Jones's experience in the jungle is not presented as a dream or visit from the supernatural, but as a fugue state witnessed by the audience.

Since the premiere of *The Emperor Jones*, critics have enjoyed pointing out its similarities with German expressionist drama. Expressionism in literature, theatre, or visual art is generally defined as the external manifestation of an internal condition. Several years prior to American writers exploring the concept, German playwrights Oskar Kokoschka, Ernst Toller, and Georg Kaiser borrowed the principle of expressionism from painting. German expressionist drama strives to communicate the emotional experience of a single person through the exterior elements of people and things. The emotions communicated are nearly always painful. This desire to "express" strong emotional states is typically seen in exaggerated language and distorted visual representations. The typical German expressionist plot focuses on a central anti-heroic character as he journeys from one place to another. The German term describing expressionism's episodic plot structure is *stationen*, Stations of the Cross. Indeed, self-conscious reference to Christian symbolism is a common feature of

German expressionism, particularly the association of the protagonist to a sacrificial figure. Thematically, most German expressionist plays also share notions of mechanized, modernized society as dangerous to the souls of common men.

O'Neill, like other American playwrights, would deny having been influenced by German expressionism; given the anti-German climate in America during and immediately following World War I, it was certainly risky to align oneself publicly with anything German. In the case of *Emperor Jones*, there are undoubtedly parallels to German expressionism, but it is also evident that O'Neill modeled his emerging expressionism on his own earlier dramaturgy. The bells, accordion playing, snoring, and "Negro" music found in his earlier one-acts demonstrate O'Neill's keen sense of sound in performance, which we see amplified not only in the drumming of *The Emperor Jones* but also in its footfalls, wind, gunshots, and shrieks. Likewise, both his experimental and expressionist plays use a variety of strong dialects and long, lyrical monologues.

There are also interesting devices for O'Neill to have imitated in various home-grown American experimentalist plays. Gerstenberg's *Overtones*, for example, physicalizes its characters' psychological conflict just as O'Neill manifests Brutus Jones's psychotic paranoia in physical terms. The allegorization of "The Rhythm of the Universe" as a character in the nitrous oxide hallucination of Dreiser's *Laughing Gas* is certainly no stranger than in Jones's vision of "little formless fears," which the stage directions say are "black, shapeless, only their glittering little eyes can be seen. If they have any describable form at all it is that of a grubworm about the size of a creeping child" (279). *The Emperor Jones* is frequently characterized as the first American expressionist play; perhaps it is also the last American experimentalist play. In *The Hairy Ape*, however, O'Neill would break more distinctly from the American non-realism of the 1910s.

The Hairy Ape premiered in March 1922 in a production directed by James Light with assistance from Arthur Hopkins. The play is organized into eight scenes, as was *The Emperor Jones*, but here the structure is more symmetrical: the first four scenes are set on an ocean liner, above and below deck, and the second four take place in New York City. O'Neill's protagonist, the Hairy Ape himself, is Yank, a fireman on an ocean liner (while this name is repeated from the *Glencairn* plays, as are several other names, there is no suggested connection between the characters). Yank's journey in *The Hairy Ape* is from found to lost; at the beginning of the play he makes this statement about his place in the world, the world below deck:

> Everything else dat makes de woild move, somep'n makes it move. It can't move witout somep'n else, see? Den yuh get down to me. I'm at de bottom, get me! Dere ain't nothin' foither. I'm de end! I'm de start! I start somep'n and de woild moves! It – dat's me! – de new dat's moiderin' de old! I'm de ting in coal dat makes it boin; I'm steam and oil for de engines; I'm de ting in noise dat makes yuh hear it; I'm smoke and express trains and steamers and factory whistles; I'm de ting in gold dat makes it money! And I'm what makes iron into steel! (365)

Yank takes his identity from his place in mechanized society, but this sense of self is a form of oppression imposed on him by his station in life. When his worldview is challenged, however, Yank's philosophy fails him like a house of straw unable to withstand any threatening wind.

Above deck is the soft, privileged class represented by Mildred Douglas, whose father is the president of Nazareth Steel and chairman of the board of directors of the ship line. Mildred is fascinated by the working class and wants to be taken below to see the stokers whose labor powers the ocean liner. When Mildred enters the stokehole she immediately sees Yank, filthy from work and shouting in rage at the demands of engineers. Yank sees her, too, and because of her white dress he believes she is a ghost. For an instant neither can speak; then Mildred whimpers, "Oh, the filthy beast!" (373). The moment hurls Yank into an existential crisis. From then on he will not eat, sleep, or wash; instead he just sits alone in the pose of Rodin's "The Thinker." A shipmate tells Yank that Mildred's expression was as if she had seen a hairy ape who had escaped from the zoo, a description that haunts Yank. O'Neill appears to believe that the phrase "hairy ape" carries currency with seamen; when two *Glencairn* sailors get into an argument in *The Moon of the Caribbees*, they also hurl the same insult at each other. The term even appears as the title of a lost short story O'Neill wrote around 1917, the protagonist of which was also a stoker.

Yank decides he must avenge himself against Mildred for her misguided sense of superiority over him. On shore in New York City on a Sunday morning, Yank and Long, a fellow stoker, go to Fifth Avenue to look for Mildred. While there, Long shows Yank posh storefronts prominently displaying expensive merchandise; he wants Yank to understand Mildred's insult as a condition of the class structure. "I wants to awaken yer bloody clarss consciousness," says Long. "Then yer'll see its 'er clarss yer've got to fight, not 'er alone" (380). Just then, the smart set spills out of their churches. The stage directions call for these characters to move like "gaudy marionettes, yet with something of the relentless horror of Frankensteins in their detached, mechanical unawareness" (381). In the original production, costume designer Blanche Hays masked the Fifth Avenue socialites, further dehumanizing their appearance. The masking choice supported O'Neill's expressionist goal of visually manifesting Yank's perception of these characters, and which likely inspired O'Neill's more developed work with masks in *The Great God Brown* (1926). When one of the socialites comments on a display of monkey fur in a shop, Yank takes it as a personal insult and becomes violent. He hits a man rushing for the bus and the police descend upon Yank with clubs. They remove him to prison. The next scene reveals Yank seated like "The Thinker" in a set of jail cells which "disappear in the dark background as if they ran on, numberless, into infinity" (383). Yank touches the prison bars and says, "Steel," acknowledging the irony of being trapped by the modern machine that had once defined him (384).

In prison, Yank is convinced by a fellow inmate that his real enemy is the capitalism represented by Mildred's father. Scene 7 depicts Yank's search for a new identity at the meeting hall of the Industrial Workers of the World (the "Wobblies").

But when Yank offers his services for the group to help "blow tings up" (390), they suspect that he is a plain-clothes policeman and throw him out. Yank's journey ends in scene 8 with a visit to the zoo. Onstage we observe several cages, reminiscent of the prison cells in scene 6, one of which contains a large gorilla posed like "The Thinker." Alone with the gorilla, Yank confesses, "She wasn't wise dat I was in a cage, too – worser'n yours – sure – a damn sight – 'cause you got some chanct to bust loose – but me –" (393). Yank envies the gorilla's ability to avoid thinking and examining his place in the world. He also pities the gorilla for being stared at and judged as inferior by spectators. Suddenly, Yank pulls a tool from under his coat and jimmies open the gorilla cage. The loose animal embraces Yank in a deadly hug, breaking his ribs and squeezing the air out of his lungs. Yank dies as O'Neill's final stage direction suggests that, "perhaps, the Hairy Ape at last belongs" (395).

As in the earlier plays, O'Neill experiments with sound in *The Hairy Ape*, using interesting repetitions, choral lines, and choreographed cacophony. For example, Yank's shipmates frequently repeat a word that he has shouted, such as "T'ink" or "Love," and each time O'Neill offers almost the same stage direction: "The chorused word has a brazen, metallic quality as if their throats were phonograph horns. It is followed by a general uproar of hard, barking laughter" (360). The patterned sound in *The Hairy Ape* also extends beyond music and language to include harsh mechanical noise. For example, O'Neill describes a "tumult of noise" as the firemen work in the fiery stokehole: "This clash of sounds stuns one's ears with its rending dissonance. But there is order in it, rhythm, a mechanical regulated recurrence, a tempo" (370). The strongest aural element of *The Hairy Ape* is Yank's exaggerated dialect and expansive monologues.

Indeed, everything about *The Hairy Ape* is excessive – the heavy dialects, the filth of the stokehold, the whiteness of Mildred's dress, the soulless automatons on Fifth Avenue, the brutal strength of the gorilla – and every element supports Yank's subjective view of the world as a dangerous place. There is a painful social reality to Yank's dilemma of modern identity, yet O'Neill dons his crisis in poetic rhythm without realistic plausibility. Despite O'Neill's cultural reference to the Wobblies and Marxist thought, *The Hairy Ape* is neither agit-prop nor even political theatre. Through the contrast of Mildred and Yank, O'Neill demonstrates the problems created by the class system in the lives of both the working class and the leisure class, but the drama avoids didactic, Marxian solutions. O'Neill's interests are emotional, even spiritual, and less political. Like Kaiser in *From Morn to Midnight*, O'Neill shows that the smoothly working surface of mechanized society is built on the assumption that all the cogs will turn in their designated place. A worker who recognizes himself as a cog and steps out of the wheel is a threat to the machine; he is also a man without a place, and O'Neill is interested in the fate of that alienated individual. *The Hairy Ape* combines social problems, recognizable human beings, a search for truth, and theatrical poetry. This basic formula for American expressionism was then explored successfully by other plays of the 1920s, such as *The Adding Machine* and *Roger Bloomer*.

Elmer Rice offers credit to Dreiser's *Plays of the Natural and Supernatural* for inspiring his one expressionist play, *The Adding Machine* (1923), though other obvious influences are German expressionism and O'Neill. *The Adding Machine* dramatizes the descent of a clerical worker not unlike the Cashier in *From Morn to Midnight* (1912; produced in New York in 1922). Rice's protagonist, Mr. Zero, is a hen-pecked, sex-starved, neurotic accountant. On the twenty-fifth anniversary of his employment, Zero is told an adding machine is replacing him. He subsequently kills his boss and is executed for the murder. *The Adding Machine*, however, does not end with Zero's death. The last three scenes take place in the afterlife: first at his gravesite, then in the Elysian Fields, and finally in a purgatorial office where Zero returns to his job of accounting, this time on an adding machine. There he works for another 25 years, hoping for release or reward after his efforts. Instead he is told that he must return to earth to be born again and live out the same servile life he has lived ever since his soul was new.

Like O'Neill, Rice finds innovative uses for sound in *The Adding Machine*. When Zero is fired, Rice describes the stage revolving wildly and flooding with theatrical sound effects: "the wind, the waves, the galloping horses, the locomotive whistle, the sleigh bells, the automotive siren, the glass-crash.... The noise is deafening, maddening, unendurable. Suddenly it culminates in a terrific peal of thunder" (30). These chaotic visual and aural effects serve to express Zero's shock at losing his place in life. Rice also uses sound as a means of simultaneously depicting thought and reality, the same effect Gerstenberg was after in *Overtones*. For example, the conversation between Zero and his co-worker Daisy is little more than numbers punctuated by complaints:

> Aw, don't be givin' me so many orders. Sixty cents. Twenty-four cents. Seventy-five cents. A dollar fifty. Two fifty. One fifty. One fifty. Two fifty. I don't have to take it from you and what's more I won't. (10)

Once Rice establishes this pattern of repetition, he adds confessional lines from both Zero and Daisy that the other cannot hear – with the litany of numbers beating a tattoo under the dialogue like the tom-tom in *The Emperor Jones*. Yet another example of Rice's poetic use of sound is the mysterious off-stage noise of "a sharp clicking such as is made by the operation of the keys and levers of an adding machine" (35). Only Zero hears the sound, a ghostly reminder of the adding machine which took away his livelihood and to which he is enslaved in the afterlife.

Zero is Rice's modern American Everyman: "A waste product. A slave to a contraption of steel and iron. The animal's instincts, but none of his strength and skill. The animal's appetites, but not his unashamed indulgence of them" (138). He is as ignoble a dramatic hero as Brutus Jones or Yank. We know him to be voyeuristic, adulterous, cowardly, petty, and racist. Ronald H. Wainscott has observed that expressionism's "vogue in the United States bears a direct relationship to anxiety over the Great War and reflects growing cynicism with commercialism in American society" (1997: 92). John Howard Lawson's *Roger Bloomer*, an expressionist play of psychology and masculinity, likewise examines modern America's ruthless underbelly.

The minimalist, even stark, look called for in the stage directions for *Roger Bloomer* (1923) probably made it seem even more non-realistic to its original audiences than it appears today in the context of other American expressionist dramas. Throughout the play, which traces Roger Bloomer's Freudian search for identity and love, various locations are created simply and fluidly through the use of spare pieces of furniture, curtains, and lights. Eighteen-year-old Roger lives with his parents, owners of the largest department store in Excelsior, Iowa. Roger's father wants him to go to college so he can take up the family business. To this end Mr. Bloomer tries to orchestrate a friendship between Roger and an older boy, a Yale student named Eugene. Eugene's conversation turns to girls and sex, which reveals Roger's inexperience and embarrasses him. Roger retreats to his room and we see the first in a series of typically expressionistic stage moments in the play. Roger is in a ray of light, surrounded all around by darkness. At the edge of the light can be seen a purple curtain with black line drawings of monsters. Roger addresses the curtain as he speaks openly for the first time in the play. In his soliloquy he struggles with the desire "to see, to know, to touch life, to lay both hands upon it as if it were a woman, crush it to me with my fingers in the warm flesh lovingly" (Lawson 1946: 233). When Roger finally pulls back the curtain, however, it reveals only shelves of books, a reflection of his father's push for the young man to find his manhood through a college education.

Roger throws off his father's plans for his future by running off to New York in pursuit of Louise, a former clerk at Mr. Bloomer's department store. Louise takes the hungry and unemployed Roger under her wing in the big city and tries to help him obtain an executive job at the business where she is a secretary. Roger's interview at Louise's office calls for another forceful moment of expressionist staging. Onstage are five small office cubicles placed in a row, each identically furnished with a desk, a green light, a telephone, and a man busily shuffling papers. The door of each office opens into the next, creating a chain of impersonal "modern" workspaces. The men in these offices move impersonally and chorally like automatons. As Louise ushers Roger into his job interview, they pass through each office. The interview scene between Roger and Mr. Rumsey is punctuated with choreographed movement in the five small offices on stage: "In each of the five offices bells ring. Simultaneously, five men pull telephones toward them on adjustable arms" (255).

When Roger does not get the job, he becomes despondent about the cruelty of the city and drinks a bottle of rat poison. This image of the city as antagonist – in particular New York City – is a theme *Roger Bloomer* shares with *The Hairy Ape*. Unlike Yank, however, Freudian mother issues haunt Roger; he associates sinister maternalism with New York, calling it his "granite mother" (269). This theme of impersonal city life continues throughout the play, as does a fascination with money, sex, and love. Roger recovers from his suicide attempt, but the lack of money causes Roger and Louise to suffer. When Louise tries to solve this problem by stealing $3,000 worth of bonds from her office, Roger reprimands her and compels her to sneak back into work that night to return the bonds. There she finds her boss Mr. Rumsey still in the office and he surprises her with a friendly – though utterly passionless – offer of marriage. She refuses and Rumsey flies into a terror, grabbing her shoulders violently, destroying his desk, and firing Louise. Louise's spirit is broken by these events. She cries out for freedom, an unattainable freedom fraught with Freudian psychology of women as incomplete men. "I'd cut my hair off," Louise cries, "put on trousers and be a man, then you and I would go to sail the sea" (278–9). Louise's voice suddenly begins to weaken; she has taken poison and dies. Imprisoned as a material witness to her death, Roger is haunted by a nightmare of city and home, sex and death, lover and mother. Lawson's choice to stage a dream is more akin to American experimentalism than American expressionism. After all, Roger is "really" asleep and dreaming, making him more like the doctor in *Laughing Gas* than Brutus Jones.

Lawson writes that the dream should be played like "a very rapid ballet, with accompaniment of words half chanted. Playing time is extremely short, for it is done at great speed, like a piece of very exciting music" (285). Throughout, the dream is marked by Freudian symbolism. At one point, Roger stands in a ray of bright white light holding a long sword that flashes as he swings it. When a streetwalker tries to entice Roger, he stabs her with his long sword: "It sticks through her belly and with a ghostly smile she starts to wriggle on it. She is doing an Oriental dance, crooning lasciviously" (291). Roger pulls the sword out of her body, and it becomes a writhing green snake in his hand. Moments later during the same section of the nightmare, Roger unveils a shrouded figure to discover that it is his mother. Finally, Roger is saved from attack in the dream by the mystical arrival of Louise. Radiant and powerful, Louise counsels Roger, "I've given you yourself, take it" (295). She leaves him with a brief blessing: "A man's luck, Roger" (295). The nightmare ends with these words. Roger awakes and, with his jail cell unlocked, walks freely from prison.

Louise in *Roger Bloomer* and Daisy in *The Adding Machine* each have their own crisis in the play, enabling the audience to consider the impact of modernization on female identity. Such considerations are brief, however, because these women are unable to exist independent of men. Daisy commits suicide because she cannot live without her secret love, Mr. Zero, and Louise kills herself because she cannot live the life she wants as a woman. Louise's death is redemptive, however, because it frees Roger to live his life freely and independently. Resurrected and luminous, Louise is a Christ-figure sacrificed so that Roger can avoid suffering the death required of him as the expressionist hero. Mildred in *The Hairy Ape* is on the other end of the spectrum from Louise; we never see her again after the moment she and Yank meet in the stokehole. Mildred's horror at seeing Yank is perhaps as devastating to her, but O'Neill does not pursue that thread. Mildred is only an agent of change on Yank, not a subject herself.

The sexual politics of American expressionism are complicated further by two major plays by female playwrights featuring strong women as the expressionist heroes: Susan Glaspell's *The Verge* (1921) and Sophie Treadwell's *Machinal* (1928) (see chapter 4). The Provincetown Players staged Glaspell's play after *The Emperor Jones* and before *The Hairy Ape*. As Wainscott has noted, Glaspell's expressionism probably had a significant influence on O'Neill. Treadwell's *Machinal* is arguably the finest example of American expressionist drama. One of the greatest elements of *Machinal* is Treadwell's rich stage poetry of choreographed human and mechanical sound. Like *Roger Bloomer*, *Machinal* features a modern office girl proposed to by her rich boss. Treadwell's young woman accepts, however, and becomes the expressionist hero who must suffer loss of identity and die. The original production of *Machinal* was directed by Arthur Hopkins, who 15 years earlier had brought to the stage the first American experimentalist play, *The Poor Little Rich Girl*.

American expressionism had run its course by the time of the stock market crash of 1929. The social and economic climate of the 1930s had little tolerance for expressionism's brand of modernist stridency and aestheticism. Yet American expressionism was never an art estranged from the real world; its goal was to be immersed so deeply in the problems of modernity that it would transcend the mask of physical reality. American expressionism was a highpoint of dramatic literature in the 1920s and for this reason it has received great scholarly attention over the last several decades. Less attended to, however, are the experimental American plays which preceded the movement, usually seen as just that: plays preceding the designation of "Modern American Drama." We can observe, for example, the categories provided by Gerald Bordman in his 1995 *American Theatre: A Chronicle of Comedy and Drama, 1914–1930*, where he calls the period 1919–28 "The Great Act," to which the preceding teens were a "Prologue." O'Neill's expressionism adds to this critical myopia because if hindsight declares it the first Modern American Drama, then permission is tacitly granted to dismiss experimentalist plays. Indeed, Walter J. Meserve claims in his seminal work, *An Outline History of American Drama*: "In American drama, O'Neill found almost nothing to imitate" (1994: 227). A review of the bold works of American experimentalism in the 1910s reveals that this is simply not the case.

BIBLIOGRAPHY

Bordman, G. (1995). *American Theatre: A Chronicle of Comedy and Drama, 1914–1930*. New York: Oxford University Press.
Cheney, S. (1921). "Expressionism: Art's Latest Revolution." *Shadowland* 51 (October): 59–61.
Dreiser, T. (2000). *The Collected Plays of Theodore Dreiser*, ed. Keith Newlin and Frederic E. Rusch. Albany, NY: Whitson.
Gates, E. (1916). *The Poor Little Rich Girl*. New York: Samuel French.
Gerstenberg, A. (1916). *Overtones. Washington Square Plays*. Garden City, NY: Doubleday, Page, 55–82.
Lawson, J. H. (1946). *Roger Bloomer*. In A. R. Fulton (ed.), *Drama and Theatre Illustrated by Seven Modern Plays*. New York: Henry Holt, 210–95.
Mantle, B. and Sherwood, G. P. (eds.) (1933). *The Best Plays of 1909–1919*. New York: Dodd, Mead.
Meserve, W. J. (1994). *An Outline History of American Drama*, 2nd ed. New York: Feedback Theatrebooks and Prospero Press.
Millay, E. St. Vincent (1994). *Aria da Capo*. In John Gassner (ed.), *Twenty-Five Best Plays of the Modern American Theatre: Early Series*. New York: Crown, 712–20.

O'Neill, E. (2001). *Early Plays*, ed. Jeffrey H. Richards. New York: Penguin.

Rice, E. L. (1923). *The Adding Machine*. New York: Samuel French.

Sarlós, R. K. (1982). *Jig Cook and the Provincetown Players: Theatre in Ferment*. Amherst: University of Massachusetts Press.

Valgemae, M. (1972). *Accelerated Grimace: Expressionism in the American Drama of the 1920s*. Carbondale: Southern Illinois University Press.

Wainscott, R. H. (1997). *The Emergence of the Modern American Theater, 1914–1929*. New Haven, CT: Yale University Press.

6

Many-Faceted Mirror: Drama as Reflection of Uneasy Modernity in the 1920s

Felicia Hardison Londré

Examining the American drama of the 1920s is a daunting prospect, certainly because of the sheer number of new plays (more than in any other single decade of the twentieth century), but also because of the cultural complexities with which playwrights – like most Americans – were grappling during the decade. My preliminary working title for this chapter, "Shock and Schlock," was intended to encompass plays that skirted unmentionable subjects (sex before marriage and abortion, for example) as well as sentimental pieces that reaffirmed traditional values. However, the shock-versus-schlock paradigm appeared simplistic in the course of reading over 130 plays that I hoped would be representative of the 1,181 or so new American plays produced during the 1920s.[1]

In an era when an evening's outing to the theatre served roughly the same entertainment function as today's viewing of television situation comedies, the bulk of staged drama was bound to be disposable fare. "Schlock" may be the correct term when compared to works by Tennessee Williams or Edward Albee, but for a reader attempting total immersion in her grandmother's formative decade, the dramatic trifles cannot be lightly dismissed. Each 1920s play was a surprise package, and I became greedy to read – to consume! – as many plays as possible. Most rewarding were the original Samuel French editions published in the 1920s, because they included production photographs that were omitted from subsequent editions, presumably to avoid making the plays seem dated. The many play texts that survive in single-play editions from major publishers like Boni and Liveright, Brentano's, Alfred A. Knopf, Little, Brown, E. P. Dutton, Harper and Brothers, Longmans, Green, G. P. Putnam, and Thomas Seltzer testify to a vast play-reading public. The Little Theatre Movement that swept the country in the late 1910s and throughout the 1920s can be credited for the publication of a plethora of innocuous family comedies that had limited runs on Broadway but found avid audiences in the hinterland. In addition, the parallel growth of college dramatic workshops contributed to some of the many innovations in drama.

My selection of plays representing a cross-section of the decade began with the decision to read every play nominated for a Pulitzer Prize from the 1919–20 season to the 1929–30 season: a total of 64 plays.[2] This would establish a benchmark of dramatic and theatrical value as discerned in its own time. These plays stimulated other choices. For example, a reading of Zoë Akins's *Déclassée* (1919) set me on track to discover her subsequent 1920s plays. Another rationale for play selection was suggested by names of lesser-known authors that kept reappearing season after season. Although plays by writers like Martin Brown, Wilson Collison, Barry Conners, Frank Craven, Martin Flavin, Aaron Hoffman, William Hurlbut, Vincent Lawrence, Adelaide Matthews and Martha Stanley, Samuel Shipman, and Gladys Unger have neither held the stage nor entered the literary canon, they enjoyed popularity in the 1920s, and it seemed reasonable to examine a sampling of their works. The more plays I read, the more I felt that it was hardly enough to encompass the era, and that this appreciation of the decade could only be one person's very limited attempt to meet the decade in drama on its own terms.

Themes and Subjects

As behaviors, habits, expressed attitudes, and conventions emerged from the decade, there appeared noticeable consistencies. The recurring themes were not necessarily clichés, although dramatic clichés do abound. In numerous plays, for example, the father wants to read his newspaper in peace, but the family distracts him; or, the hometown girl is petulant because she cannot possibly be as attractive as those French girls her soldier-boyfriend must have observed during the war. Other tropes: Having a choice of two suitors for marriage, the young woman inevitably flouts her parents' preference. The young man with a future is studying architecture. A professor is not a good catch for a marriageable girl. The pent-up frustration of the married woman finds vicarious release through her children's social life or by tyrannizing her husband. Sophisticates, married or single, gather in the living room for ritual cocktail shaking. The piano frequently figures at the moment of truth in a relationship. There is grassroots cynicism about the law and the judicial system. These and many more are examples of the tropes that appeared in 1920s dramatic literature.

A majority of the themes during the time can be tied to larger issues and trends in American life. Having sent American troops in 1917 to fight – for the first time in Europe – "to make the world safe for democracy," the United States found itself regarded as a world power. But the immediate postwar period brought disillusionment; Americans faced inflation, strikes, Bolshevism ("the Red menace"), anarchist propaganda, and unemployment. In spite of the ensuing cynicism, Warren G. Harding's laissez-faire presidency launched a period of sustained prosperity, fueled by Henry Ford's successful methods of mass production. "The business of America is business," President Calvin Coolidge remarked in 1925, and indeed business was venerated as the foundation for the nationwide spending spree. Advertising, radio, motion pictures, and mass production of consumer goods contributed toward homogenization of the American public. Tabloid and yellow journalism promoted interest in celebrities, sports figures, murder trials, and Freudian psychology. Top stories of the decade included Lindbergh's 1927 trans-Atlantic solo flight and the infamous miscarriage of justice known as the Sacco–Vanzetti case. The Harlem Renaissance cast a spotlight on African American culture, though lynchings continued in the South. Women not only began to vote in 1920, but they smoked and went to college. Speakeasies, jazz, and motorcars gave rise to "flaming youth." Prohibition and bootlegging turned middle-class citizens into lawbreakers and created a colorful gangster class. However, the "roaring twenties," sometimes referred to as the Jazz Age of "the lost generation," halted abruptly with the stock market crash known as "Black Tuesday" (October 29, 1929).

Far and away the dominant concern of the decade – the subject that figures in virtually every play – is money, debt, and the business of getting rich. Closely related are explorations of the role of the businessman in American life, the nature of marriage as impacted by money, the bootlegging phenomenon, class consciousness, urban stress, and obsession with the motorcar as status symbol. Plays prior to the mid-decade often contain a few lines of grumbling dialogue about the pesky new income tax. The frenzy of Florida real estate speculation that peaked in 1925 serves as dramatic shorthand to flag a character as a fool soon to be parted from his money. The tacit assumption of most American drama of the 1920s is that middle-class Americans dream of marrying into wealth or tapping into a get-rich-quick scheme. Exposure of these false values is standard dramatic fare, in which the sympathetic character defies convention by seeking romantic love or choosing a simplified lifestyle built on a foundation of hard work. The character of Raphael Lord in S. N. Behrman's play *Meteor* (1929) acknowledges the contradictory attitudes: "Do you despise money? Why, this is the most commercial time in the history of the world. Money-technique is the essence of the age and I shall be a master of it! Despise money! Why, that's intellectual snobbery" (Behrman 1930: 28). In Channing Pollock's expressionist play *Mr. Moneypenny* (1928), Murphy (the custodian in the Day-and-Night Bank) upholds family values and resists the dream of easy money, while Jones, the night manager, takes the cynical view: "Coin . . . the only thing that counts! The only thing anybody gives a damn for!"

Murphy: Money don't buy happiness.
Jones: The hell it don't! Having things . . . that's happiness! All the things other people have, and a lot of things other people can't get! Look around you! We're all running the same way, and everybody but dubs has got to keep up with the parade! (Pollock 1928: 15)

Jones sells his soul to the Mephistophelean Mr. Moneypenny, but luckily his son-in-law – who is merely a professor – observes that moderation is the key to money issues: "I'm not talking about what people do *without* money; I'm talking about what they do *with* it. These people, of all kinds and classes, who have transformed life from a splendid striving into a greedy struggle" (158). Progress from rags to riches to a chastened happy medium may be observed as the dramatic arc in various plays.

The second great area of decade-long concern might be called the role and capabilities of women. This topic branches in various directions: the flapper who matures, the stenographer who marries the boss and leaves the workforce in order to keep house, the domineering wife or mother who focuses her social skills on clubs and committees, the under-appreciated woman who sacrifices herself for her family, the woman whose primary motive is to keep up appearances, the woman who becomes ill or goes mad thinking she is not good enough for the man she loves, the woman of ill repute, and, occasionally, a self-possessed woman who counters adversity with integrity, grace, and even humor. Women's issues are often linked with marriage. Wives, husbands, and their marriageable children question institutions dominated by money matters and devoid of the expected bliss. Why should a woman spend her days washing dishes when she has just as good a head for business as a man? Why should a man support a wife when coming home from work means being subjected to her nagging and whining about money? These questions are explored in both a comic and serious vein in plays like William Anthony McGuire's *Six-Cylinder Love* (1921), Arthur Richman's *Ambush* (1922), Maxwell Anderson's *Saturday's Children* (1927), and Marc Connelly and George S. Kaufman's *To the Ladies* (1921). In Gilbert Emery's *The Hero* (1921), Hester yearns for "things that give women a chance to look outside their own little dooryards – I don't know – to *be* something. Something that counts more in the world –" (231).

Two charming suburban homes are mortgaged and lost in McGuire's *Six-Cylinder Love*, because the husband accedes to his wife's desire for a motorcar. The expensive car attracts socially superior parasites and drains the finances first of the Burton family (for Mrs. Burton the car is a status symbol) and then of the Sterlings (for Mrs. Sterling the car offers freedom of movement). Before selling the car to their newlywed neighbors, the Burtons learn from the smart set some gossip about the Sterlings: "Well, before they were married she was a stenographer." "No!" "Yes. Actually prestidigitated for a living, and the worse of it is she seems proud of it, told it herself" (McGuire 1921: 1.13). By Act 2 the highball-swilling freeloaders have turned their backs on the bankrupt Burtons and already disrupted the Sterlings' quiet domesticity. The pretentious Margaret tells Marilyn Sterling: "cooking isn't part of the domestic bargain any more." Marilyn comments: "Oh, I don't mind the cooking so much, but I won't wash dirty dishes. . . . Especially when it's so easy to drive to the country club, or into town, or to go to one of the roadhouses. I hate housework anyway" (2.6). When the jazzy lifestyle jeopardizes Gilbert Sterling's job, he tells Marilyn: "Ever since you married me you've accepted my support. I've paid for your living, your clothes, your luxuries. I've even furnished a dancing partner for you.

And what have you ever done? Nothing!" (2.38). Forced to move to a cheap apartment building in the city, both Mrs. Burton and Mrs. Sterling learn the joys of housekeeping. Harmony is restored, but without the motorcar.

A vision of domestic bliss – usually involving a house and garden, like that lost by the Sterlings – drives the romantic inclinations of sympathetic young characters in innumerable plays. Living in a cottage and raising chickens is found to be the ideal existence in Rachel Crothers's *Nice People* (1921) and Kaufman and Connelly's *Beggar on Horseback* (1924). A white house with a garden is invoked in plays from Behrman's *Meteor* to Mae West's *Sex* (1926), and even poor downtrodden Sophie in Elmer Rice's *The Subway* (1929) dreams of a rose-covered cottage.

The possibility or threat of divorce looms in many a play. It drives the farcical complications in Adelaide Matthews and Martha Stanley's *Puppy Love* (1926). The ramifications of divorce are sometimes discussed at length, as in Philip Barry's *Paris Bound* (1927). In George Kelly's *Behold, the Bridegroom* (1927), Miss Lyle says: "I will *not* become one of those caricatures of women – that I'm running into all over the world. Disillusioned and divorced, and married and divorced again – like a lot of horrible monkeys" (100). There is even a subcategory of plays hinging on the implication that two couples would be better off exchanging spouses.

Whether tied to the changing place of women in American life or in a category of its own, sex emerges as the catalyst for dramatic action. Freudian psychology is bandied about in dramatic dialogue, even in featherweight material like *The Poor Nut* (1925) by J. C. and Elliot Nugent. According to John Gassner,

> an Oedipus complex, a regression to childhood, a slight case of sex inversion, a hypertrophied maternal instinct, or an undernourished or overfed libido was apt to win a nod or an embrace from playwrights and their public. . . . War was waged within the theatre, as it was waged in books, against "Puritanism." . . . [T]he thread of the "new" psychology and morality ran through the content of dramatic composition (1949: xxiv)

Confusion about sexual mores is part of the problem for the title character and the young woman who attracts his interest in John Howard Lawson's *Roger Bloomer* (1923) (see chapter 5). The prison doctor in *The Criminal Code* (1929) by Martin Flavin diagnoses a prisoner's declining morale and health in terms of sexual deprivation. Similarly, the doctor in *Rain* (1922) by John Colton and Clemence Randolph recognizes that Reverend Davidson's dreams about "the mountains of Nebraska" are possibly indicative of fantasizing about "a woman's breasts," and that the Davidsons' marriage – "entirely a contract of the spirit" – could be a case in which "indiscriminate denial often forces outlets – the true character of which would surprise us" (Colton and Randolph 1923: 217–22). Inhibitions and repressions are not merely talked about, but also boldly cast off. The double standard is dealt a mortal blow; adultery can be forgiven, even when it is the wife or fiancée who strays. Still, the last bastion of the unsullied reputation is that of the young unmarried girl. In Crothers's *Nice People*,

Teddy's father disinherits her because she refuses to save her reputation by marrying a man she does not love; the appearance of compromised honor concerns him more than the fact of her innocence. In Preston Sturges's *Strictly Dishonorable* (1929), Isabelle has read a book on psychoanalysis and is ready to be deflowered, but fortunately the man behaves honorably. At the end of George Abbot and Ann Preston Bridgers's *Coquette* (1927), Norma pays with her life for the one night she went too far with the man she loves.

Adult subject matter, handled so obliquely early in the decade that an adolescent theatregoer might remain oblivious to its implications, is treated more overtly as the decade progresses, as theatre practitioners test the limits – and, as satirically noted in George S. Kaufman's 1925 play, *The Butter and Egg Man*, the market value – of censorship. Eugene O'Neill's *Anna Christie* (1921), *Rain*, and *Sex* all portray a fallen woman redeemed by the promise of marriage to a man who knows her past, but it is *Sex*'s in-your-face sexuality with a comic twist that earned its author, Mae West, a ten-day prison sentence. Nor did West pull any punches in her plays of homosexual content, *The Drag, A Homosexual Comedy in Three Acts* (1927), and *The Pleasure Man, A Comedy Drama* (1928). Although *The Captive* by Edouard Bourdet (a controversial Parisian play about lesbians) reached Broadway in translation in 1926, most American dramatists other than Mae West remained reluctant to treat gay and lesbian relationships onstage. In Zoë Akins's *Daddy's Gone A-Hunting* (1921) and Sidney Howard's *Lucky Sam McCarver* (1925), homosexuality as a possible interpretation is so ambiguously written into the play that it appears left up to the actors' interpretation to determine its sexual content. In Akins's play, for example, Oscar enters from the studio where Julien sleeps, no longer sharing his wife's bed; Oscar "looks as though he had just dressed" (Akins 1923: 140). The two men discuss Julien's quasi-alienated wife Edith and Oscar's parasite Olga. Julien then comments: "We'd better not mess things up around here. Edith prepared breakfast at ten – and again at one – called us each time and each time we said we were getting up –" (143). The most shocking dramatic subject is perhaps the termination of a pregnancy, not to mention the child-murder in Eugene O'Neill's *Desire Under the Elms* (1924) (see chapter 10). While the words "pregnant" and "abortion" are never used explicitly, the subjects are unmistakable in O'Neill's *Strange Interlude* (1928) and Sidney Howard's *Ned McCobb's Daughter* (1926).

Generational conflict is a corollary of the new behavioral codes. Flaming youth, associated with the decadence of jazz, represents the extreme, but even well-bred young people manifest attitudes that make their elders uncomfortable. In *Nice People*, Aunt Margaret, whose son lies dead in France, comments to her wealthy brother-in-law about her niece's friends:

> If they were common little upstarts and parvenus it would be easy to understand. But nice people! What are their parents thinking of? Can't they see what it's going to do to future generations? . . . I've been here three days and I haven't heard her, nor any of her friends, say a single word or express a thought about anything on earth but their clothes

and their motors and themselves. They all talk alike, think alike, dress alike, sound alike. And the drinking! Your house is a bar. It pours out – at all hours. (Crothers 1924: 99, 101)

Similar sentiments are expressed in Avery Hopwood and David Gray's 1924 play, *The Best People*:

Grafton: . . . Every one of these girls wants to be mistaken for a fast woman; every one of these damned unmannerly boys is headed for being a Bolshevik or a rowdy. They have no respect for religion, family, tradition. They have no social standards. They'll dine with anybody who'll buy them a cocktail! I tell you, they're all going straight to the dogs!
Lenox: No. They're tired of form and convention, that's all. It's a revolt against all that false delicacy and hypocrisy of fifty years ago when you called a leg a limb. (Hopwood and Gray 1928: 29)

The beleaguered father in Arthur Richman's *Ambush* (1922) tries to hold the line for old-fashioned decency, but his wife defends their daughter:

Harriet: I don't blame her. Young people are young people – if she feels like having such things, let her have 'em.
Walter: You shouldn't come between us in a case like this, Harriet. Can't you see my reason? Can't you see the vulgarity of pretending to be what you aren't? (Richman 1922: 21).

As both Lenox and Walter imply, hypocrisy is often a defining factor in the dramatic depiction of the excesses of flaming youth.

In retrospect, the 1920s are most readily characterized by Prohibition, which was in effect from 1919 to 1933, and dramas vividly reflect its impact. Characters looking for a good time are always motoring out to roadhouses, speakeasies, or carrying hidden flasks. The bootlegger lives in an apartment upstairs in Gilbert Emery's *Tarnish* (1923), or provides a kid a lift on the road in Matthews and Stanley's *Puppy Love*, or sweet-talks a girl in *Ned McCobb's Daughter*, or bribes the Feds in various plays. Cocktails or highballs or champagne emerge as upwardly mobile middle-class status symbols or high society indulgences. Important action is built around cocktail drinking in Frank Craven's *The First Year* (1920), Vincent Lawrence's *In Love With Love* (1923), Jesse Lynch Williams's *Why Not?* (1922), and Gladys Unger's *Two Girls Wanted* (1926). The cocktail scene of *In a Garden* (1925) by Philip Barry is replete with innuendo. When a young man calls upon a girl at her home, he often banters with her father about Prohibition. In Barry Conners's *Applesauce* (1925), Bill takes out a new silver pocket flask, "a little private amendment to the Eighteenth Amendment." He makes a gift of the flask to Hazel's Pa, "because you are one of the few choice spirits in the town who really appreciate choice spirits" (28). Bootleg liquor secreted in the middle-class home takes a toll on uptight characters in *Puppy Love* and

Martin Flavin's *Broken Dishes* (1929). Alcoholism fells many a playboy, while "drunken scenes" find a place in both comedy and tragedy. The widespread flouting of the Eighteenth Amendment at all levels of society is undoubtedly a strong contributing factor to a pervasive cynical attitude about the law.

Numerous plays suggest that the law regularly sides with people of wealth or political power. The Judge in Sturges's *Strictly Dishonorable* repeatedly fixes sticky situations with the police for his friends. Even in a silly haunted-house farce like Adelaide Matthews and Martha Stanley's *The Wasp's Nest* (1927), the honest young man is on the verge of losing everything to the crooked trustee, because "I'm sure it isn't fair and square – but it's legal. There's a difference" (21). Similarly, in Zoë Akins's *Greatness* (1922), Tillerton finds himself trapped in an unfair situation, "and there's nothing on earth to do but pay them. There's nothing sentimental about that. It's very legal" (203).

The sensational and well-publicized trials of the 1920s inspire topical plays like Sophie Treadwell's *Machinal* (1928) (see chapter 4) and Maurine Watkins's *Chicago* (1926). Trial scenes, always good drama, occur with some frequency, and even extend to mock trials like that of the hobos in a boxcar in Maxwell Anderson's *Outside Looking In* (1925), as well as expressionistic trial scenes in Elmer Rice's *The Adding Machine* (1923) and Kaufman and Connelly's *Beggar on Horseback*. Sensationalizing journalism exacerbates such fraught situations, while the decision-making characters seemingly always must consider the impact of a news story on an upcoming election. Ben Hecht and Charles MacArthur's *The Front Page* (1928), *Chicago*, and Bartlett Cormack's *The Racket* (1927) are all by former newspapermen and draw upon actual people, places, and events in gangster-ridden Chicago. Aggressive reporters hound characters in several others, while news headlines comprise the dialogue of certain characters in Elmer Rice's *Subway* (1929). The power of the press drives characters in comedies like Kaufman and Connelly's *Merton of the Movies* (1922) and in serious dramas like *Meteor*. At the end of John Howard Lawson's *Processional* (1925) the journalist Phillpotts buys the newsboy's extra editions, tears them into confetti, and throws it around, saying: "there's where the news belongs!" (218).

The major flashpoint for questions of social justice in the drama of the 1920s is the 1921 trial and 1927 execution of Nicola Sacco and Bartolomeo Vanzetti, two Italian-born anarchists widely believed to be innocent of the murder charge on which they were convicted. The miscarriage of justice is variously attributed to police incompetence and possible frame-ups, fears of radical infiltration of labor unions, political corruption, and American xenophobia. Closely based upon the Sacco–Vanzetti case, Maxwell Anderson and Harold Hickerson's *Gods of the Lightning* (1928) exudes anger in its vivid depictions of coerced witnesses and skewed evidence perpetrated by an anti-labor politico-judiciary establishment. Prison dramas at the end of the decade, notably John Wexley's *The Last Mile* (1930) and *The Criminal Code*, indicate the need for prison reform and reconsideration of the death sentence. On the whole, however, 1920s plays dealing with social issues are not as prevalent nor – apart from works by Maxwell Anderson, John Howard Lawson, and a few less-known dramatists – as

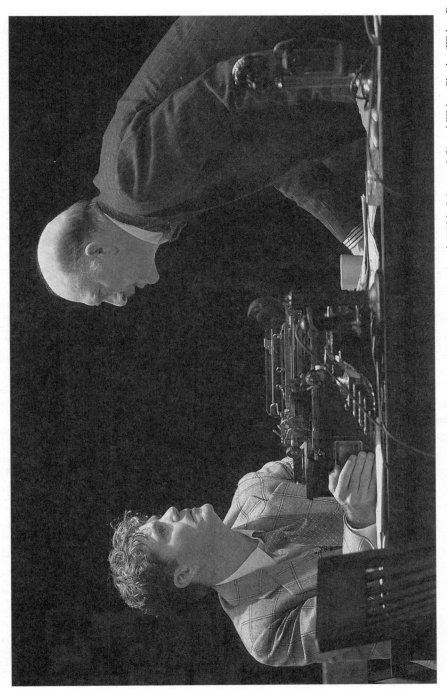

Plate 3. The Front Page, by Ben Hecht and Charles MacArthur, Missouri Repertory Theatre. Dan Snook (Hildy Johnson, left) and Walter Charles (Walter Burns), photo by Dan Ipock. Courtesy of the Missouri Repertory Theatre.

focused as the agit-prop drama of the 1930s. Ethics and values – often reduced to platitudes – take precedence over specific topics of social concern. Even the aftershock of American involvement in the Great War, whether or not one believes that it made "the world safe for democracy," perhaps finds some closure in Maxwell Anderson's *What Price Glory* (1924, with Laurence Stallings). Whatever social outrage finds dramatic expression in any of these plays usually leads back to the dominant subject of the decade – money – and its related concerns: who has it, whether it was ethically gained, how it is used, how difficult it is for the ordinary guy or girl to make a living, and the deadening urban grind for those at the bottom of the financial ladder.

Labor's pressure for restrictions on immigration led to passage by Congress of the Emergency Quota Act in May 1921. While one finds dramatic situations depicting American fear or resentment of foreigners (*Rain, Processional*), the subject rarely becomes the direct focus of socially conscious drama. Mixed ethnicities – notably Irish, Jewish, Italian, and African American – do come together incidentally in working-class settings, prisons, and hobo camps. But the foreigner or first-generation American is just as often a source of comedy, enjoyed for the entertainment value of stage dialects.

The juxtaposition of Jewish and Irish elements occurs in lots of plays both before and after Anne Nichols's *Abie's Irish Rose* (1922). For example, the "Kanuck" (French Canadian) Jenny in *Ned McCobb's Daughter* provides an opinion based upon her experience with both Irish and Jewish men:

> I hed all kinds in my day. Micks and Poles and Portugee boys and a Swede – a couple of Swedes – and plenty of Americans and one Jew. Micks is all right and hunky dory when things is goin' good, and when things ain't so good, Micks is terrible. You never know *where* you are with a Mick. Before you come in here, I was thinkin' over all the fellers I ever went with, and the only one I'd like t' see now's that Jewish boy. He wasn't no good on a party and he couldn't dance fer sour apples, but I took sick once, while I was goin' with him, and believe me, he was *there*. (Howard 1931: 45)

Elmer Rice's *Street Scene* (1929) shows a romantic attraction between Rose Maurrant (Moran in the original program's cast list) and Sam Kaplan, but keeps them apart. In Aaron Hoffman's *Two Blocks Away* (1921), the Jewish shoe repairman Nate Pommerantz optimistically lends his last money to his deadbeat Irish neighbor Mrs. Finnegan, who thanks him: "Ten thousand blessings on you, Nate Pommerantz – you're the salt of the earth. Sure it's a big mistake was made when you wasn't born a son of Erin." Nate replies: "I am a son of Aaron. Aaron, that was my father's name" (30). Apart from the Jewish–Irish juxtaposition, characters flagged as Jewish tend to appear as successful businessmen, as in *Déclassée*, Owen Davis's *The Detour* (1921), *Abie's Irish Rose*; as agents in plays about show business, as in Martin Flavin's *Lady of the Rose* (1925), Kaufman's *The Butter and Egg Man*, Kaufman and Edna Ferber's *The Royal Family* (1927); and as artists and scholars in Samson

Raphaelson's *The Jazz Singer* (1925), Mercedes de Acosta's *Jacob Slovak* (1927), and Rice's *Street Scene*.

Tony in Sidney Howard's *They Knew What They Wanted* (1924), who employs a Chinese man and sees an Irish priest, and the speakeasy denizens of *Strictly Dishonorable*, best represent Italian Americans. Diamond Louie in *The Front Page* is "sleek, bejeweled, and sinister to everybody but the caballeros of the pressroom, who knew him when he ran a fruit stand" (Hecht and MacArthur 2002: 76). Tom D'Amoro in *The Last Mile* is "the dago that croaked that cop" (Wexley 1930: 16). In *Gods of the Lightning*, the Italian anarchists Sacco and Vanzetti are transformed into the stage characters Macready (the one who gets the love interest) and Capraro, with a surrounding cast of various ethnicities, notably Jewish and Russian. Asian characters appear most often in melodrama. Comic foreigners are frequently Eastern Europeans, like the Bulgarian count in Zoë Akins's *The Texas Nightingale* (1922, a.k.a. *Greatness*), or the Bohemian acrobats in *Déclassée*.

While household servants are more often Irish than black, African Americans increasingly appear as full-fledged characters over the years, especially with the growing interest in folk drama. Eugene O'Neill paves the way with leading roles to be performed by black actors in *The Emperor Jones* (1920) (see chapter 5) and *All God's Chillun Got Wings* (1924), followed by other white authors writing on black subjects: Paul Green, DuBose and Dorothy Heyward, and culminating in Marc Connelly's *The Green Pastures* (1930). Mose, "a gentle-looking negro, middle-aged," is instrumental in aiding the escape of the young couple in Anderson's *Outside Looking In*, as well as having the curtain line (Anderson 1928: 112). However, there is the occasional shock of lines that now sound racist. Stimulated by Harlem Renaissance performances and W. E. B. Du Bois's Krigwa Playwriting Contest, African Americans begin writing for the theatre in unprecedented numbers. With the notable exception of Garland Anderson's *Appearances* (1925), few non-musical works by blacks make it to the New York stage in the 1920s, yet many one-act and full-length plays by Willis Richardson, Langston Hughes, Zora Neale Hurston, Georgia Douglas Johnson, Eulalie Spence, May Miller, and Marita Bonner hold lasting literary interest (see chapter 7 for plays of the Harlem Renaissance).

France is evoked more than any other country. In the decade's early years it is the place where American soldiers fought, learned about life, were wounded or died, with examples from the following plays: O'Neill's *Diff'rent* (1920), *The Hero, Nice People*, Channing Pollock's *The Fool* (1922), *Abie's Irish Rose*, Owen Davis's *Icebound* (1923), Hatcher Hughes's *Hell Bent fer Heaven* (1923), and Lee Wilson Dodd's *The Changelings* (1923). In later years France is the place to go for a honeymoon or a divorce, or an escape from a sticky situation at home, as exemplified in plays that opened in 1925 or after: Donald Ogden Stewart's *Rebound* (1930), *Paris Bound*, and *Behold, the Bridegroom*. French morals are perceived as a challenge to American innocence. For example, in Frank Craven's *Spite Corner* (1922), Ann reports on the "hussy clothes" being sold in a new rival dress shop: "She's brazen – calls herself Madame Florence and not a sign of a wedding ring." "Maybe she's French" (39). Characters sprinkle their speech with

French or faux French words. French food is discussed in Porter Emerson Browne's *The Bad Man* (1920): "Say, do they have clams in France?" "Only mussels." "They eat mussels. And frogs and hosses and cheese with bugs in it" (6). In Marc Connelly's 1926 play *The Wisdom Tooth*, three men speculate about the coming business expansion as soon as Congress gets the tax problems settled: "If they can get France and them other countries to pay up, I guess we'll be sittin' pretty in a year or two." "They'll never come through." "Oh, France'll come out of it all right, I guess." "Sure. Only I wouldn't lend her another nickel" (89).

Apart from France, few other European destinations get specific mention, usually Switzerland or Italy. Act 3 of Howard's *Lucky Sam McCarver* is set in a palazzo in Venice. Plays set in England are less frequent than one might expect, once one has expunged from consideration the many Broadway productions that originated in London. English characters appear occasionally in American-authored plays; some of them are effete, but some have the strength of character to transform themselves into quasi-Americans. Another exotic locale of choice in American plays is Mexico or along the Mexican border; *The Bad Man* and Sophie Treadwell's *Gringo* (1922) are among the better known of these. The latter half of the decade sees a fad for tropical Asian climes, the South Seas.

Religion merits mention in the drama with some regularity, if only to be dismissed, in the manner of Howard's strong-principled eponymous *Ned McCobb's Daughter*: "Never could keep my mind on religion when I hed anythin' important t' think 'bout" (59). Similarly lukewarm attitudes are expressed in McGuire's *Six-Cylinder Love*, when Sterling attempts to reassure his boss: "if there's one thing that we over-indulge in, it's church. You can over-do religion, you know." The boss replies: "Well, religion never hurts a man, that is, if he understands the idea of it" (2.15). The Bible frequently appears as a stage property, and is invoked or quoted by characters ranging from the well intentioned to the disreputable. Religious fanaticism drives the action in *Hell Bent fer Heaven*. Intolerant Puritanism takes a toll on quite a few characters. The minister's widow in A. E. Thomas's *Only 38* (1921) gradually frees herself of acquired repressions. Rufe Pryor in *Hell Bent fer Heaven*, the Ku Klux Klan figures in *Processional*, Reverend Davidson in *Rain*, and many others invoke Christian principles but behave otherwise. Religion cloaks sexuality in the highly charged *Bride of the Lamb* (1926) by William Hurlbut. Samson Raphaelson's emotionally wrenching *The Jazz Singer* and Channing Pollock's heavy-handed *The Fool* represent sympathetic treatments of the religious impulse in productions that made it to Broadway. Mercedes de Acosta wrote two devoutly religious plays in the 1920s, *Jehanne d'Arc* and *The Mother of Christ*, but neither reached the American professional stage. Prayers are uttered in a number of plays like Paul Green's *The Field God* (1927). Rabbi and priest work smoothly together in Nichols's *Abie's Irish Rose*. The Catholic priest in Wexley's *The Last Mile* is treated reverently, but the evangelist gets short shrift.

Broadway tends to serve as shorthand for the antithesis of religion and family values, and the "Broadway style" means flashily vulgar. Indeed, the opposition between religion and showbiz lies at the core of Raphaelson's *The Jazz Singer*. In

James Forbes's *The Famous Mrs. Fair* (1919), the simple charm of 18-year-old Sylvia is transformed by association with the Broadway crowd into the look of a rouged modern "cutie" with a "freakish" hat from Francine's, who "makes for all the smart chorus girls" (263); she becomes a pawn of the unscrupulous Gillette and narrowly escapes a disastrous marriage to him. "Chorus girl" is often used to imply a gold-digger or someone with cheap values and poor taste, but in Hopwood and Gray's *The Best People* it is the soft-spoken chorus girl Alice who refuses to marry the wealthy Bertie until he gives up his drinking. Broadway – or some show business offshoot – is the subject and setting of many plays of the decade. Especially vibrant in their depiction of seedy glamour and jazzy lingo are the backstage comedy dramas of George Abbott and Philip Dunning's *Broadway* (1926), Arthur Hopkins and George Manker Watters's *Burlesque* (1927), and West's *The Pleasure Man*, all of which provide glimpses of dressing room chatter and stage routines. *Burlesque* actually incorporates eight full-stage burlesque acts as seen by the audience, even as the story progresses, culminating in Bonnie and Skid's complete reconciliation during their soft-shoe number. We observe the business of the producer and out-of-town tryouts in Kaufman's *The Butter and Egg Man*, Tin Pan Alley in Kaufman and Ring Lardner's *June Moon* (1929), a nightclub in Howard's *Lucky Sam McCarver*, and a send-up of the Barrymores in Kaufman and Ferber's *The Royal Family*.

Amateur theatricals make for wonderful comedy in George Kelly's *The Torch-Bearers* (1922) and serve as backdrop for a murder mystery in Elmer Rice and Philip Barry's *Cock Robin* (1928). Young women like Sadie Cohen in *Processional* dream of careers on the stage, though their talent is not discernible. Perhaps the funniest scene in Barry Conners's *Hell's Bells* (1925, a.k.a. *Fool's Gold*) is that of Gladys demonstrating the talents that her professor says will make her a star; she "registers her emotions" by striking successive poses denoting Pleasure, Anger, and Joy. Similarly, in J. C. Nugent's *Kempy* (1922), the self-deluding Ruth performs her "pantomimic expressions." Characters discussing the motion picture they have just seen can also be a source of comedy; one of the best and longest sustained dialogue sequences occurs in *Broken Dishes*. The interminable, after-dinner recounting of a motion picture scenario to piano accompaniment is a hilarious set piece in George S. Kaufman and Marc Connelly's *Dulcy* (1921). In addition, their *Merton of the Movies* takes us to Hollywood for an inside look at the silent movie business.

The decade's drama is marked by other recurring constructs that can be briefly summarized. The aviator embodies escape and romantic idealism in Eugene O'Neill's *Strange Interlude* (1928) and Martin Flavin's *Children of the Moon* (1923). In Philip Barry's *You and I* (1923), *The Detour*, *The Torch-Bearers*, *Kempy*, *Dulcy*, Patterson McNutt and Anne Morrison's *Pigs* (1924), *Daddy's Gone A-Hunting*, *The Butter and Egg Man*, and others, a would-be artist gets a real opportunity and discovers the limits of his or her unremarkable talent. In George Kelly's *Craig's Wife* (1925), *Mr. Money-penny*, *The Poor Nut*, and *The Changelings*, someone expresses the opinion that a professor makes a poor catch for a marriageable girl. But in plays of college life – like *The Poor Nut* and *Only 38* – romance comes to the professor. Consciousness of correct speech occupies dialogue sequences in dozens of plays: young people criticize their father's use of "ain't" in Frank Craven's *New Brooms* (1924) and Barry Conners's *The Patsy* (1925); the eponymous character in *The Famous Mrs. Fair* picked up some slang in the trenches, and the upwardly mobile *Lucky Sam McCarver* learns to correct his own grammar.

Men who are successful in their business frequently come home to querulous wives and children; Booth Tarkington's *Clarence* (1919) is the most tenderly whimsical of the many such plays. A frequent plot device is the man – husband or son – who learns to be manly in his relationship with an overbearing woman; examples include *Craig's Wife*, *The Patsy*, Owen Davis's *Easy Come, Easy Go* (1925), *Broken Dishes*, and many others. In plays like Owen Davis's *The Nervous Wreck* (1923), *The Wisdom Tooth*, and *Merton of the Movies*, the man is an innocent fool, as is the 12-year-old daughter of a drunkard in Hurlbut's *Bride of the Lamb*. Even more prevalent than the naive simpleton is the person of integrity who is victimized, often by insensitive and selfish relatives: *Icebound*, George Kelly's *Daisy Mayme* (1926), Zona Gale's *Miss Lulu Bett* (1920), *The First Man*, *The Patsy*, Philip Barry's *The Youngest* (1924), *Ambush*, *Six-Cylinder Love*, *Children of the Moon*, *The Butter and Egg Man*, to name a few. For the housewife of limited horizons, greed or yearning for status tends to be subsumed in obsession with her home furnishings; *Craig's Wife* is merely the most extreme example of this widespread tendency.

Genres

Categorizing the plays of the decade by genre reveals the overwhelming popularity of comedy and farce, both risqué and wholesome. Comedies might be roughly divided into romantic comedies and family comedies, with a good deal of overlap. Gangsters, crooks, burglars, and bootleggers intrude into a surprising number of comedies, and often win sympathy. Melodrama comes in variations like "comedy melodrama" or "mystery melodrama." There is exotic melodrama like the lurid Far Eastern tale of Mother God Damn's vengeance in John Colton's *The Shanghai Gesture* (1926). Murder mysteries and haunted-house plays set on the East Coast in modern times also appear regularly. Domestic drama or tragedy holds a significant place, heralded by O'Neill's 1920 breakthrough drama *Beyond the Horizon* (see chapter 10). Freudian sex drama is a subcategory, best exemplified by Sidney Howard's *The Silver Cord* (1926). Folk drama becomes increasingly visible, even prestigious, as exemplified by Owen Davis's stated intention to draw upon the folk life of northern New England with his parlor drama *Icebound*. Jewish and African American ethnicities move beyond the comic stereotype to serious treatments, the comedy of stock devices exemplified by *Abie's Irish Rose*, the more substantial work notably by *The Jazz Singer*, Dorothy and DuBose Heyward's *Porgy* (1927), and Paul Green's *In Abraham's Bosom* (1926), among many others. Regional local color pervades plays ranging from the Carolina Mountains in *Hell Bent fer Heaven* and Lula Vollmer's *Sun-Up* (1923) to Western ranchlands in *The*

Nervous Wreck and *The Bad Man*. Sometimes the regional flavor is embodied in characters like the two Arizona prospectors in *Hell's Bells* (a.k.a. *Fool's Gold*). Midwestern states like Missouri, Iowa, and Nebraska are usually regarded as *ultima Thule* by urban Easterners, but wholesome family comedies like *Pigs* and *Broken Dishes* – undoubtedly destined for the little theatre market – are set in small Midwestern towns. With a few exceptions, historical costume dramas tend to be imports or adaptations from foreign sources.

Finally, in terms of genre, there are the decade's great experiments in dramatic form and technique. Beginning with O'Neill's *The Emperor Jones* in 1920, expressionism attracts serious dramatists, even if only, in some cases, such as *The Wisdom Tooth* and *In Abraham's Bosom*, as a fantasy sequence within a realistic play. Elmer Rice's *The Adding Machine* in 1923 demonstrates the effectiveness of expressionism in conveying the stress of modern urban life (see chapter 5). Expressionist drama peaks at the end of the decade, with Sophie Treadwell's *Machinal*, Dawn Powell's *Women at Four O' Clock* (1928), *Mr. Moneypenny*, Marita Bonner's *The Purple Flower* (1927), O'Neill's *Dynamo* (1929), and Rice's *The Subway*. Often allied or overlapping with expressionist drama are plays inspired by social issues. The proletarian protest of Lawson's *Processional* utilizes a variety of blatantly theatrical techniques, including vaudeville and expressionism. One can see the influence of expressionism on the scenic conception of some late 1920s realistic drama like Flavin's *The Criminal Code*, in which episodic glimpses of prison life use startling effects of sound and lighting to contribute to the effect of dehumanization of the inmates. The use of masks and the disturbing merging of identities in O'Neill's *The Great God Brown* (1926) spawned e. e. cummings's *him* (1928), which manages both to satirize O'Neill's experiments and to blaze its own avant-garde trail.

Dramaturgy

The standard format for a commercial play in the 1920s shows little change from previous decades, even to the extent that some plays are still written in four acts. Most now have three acts, allowing two intermissions. The action is continuous within an act; a break in time occurs only in instances when one of the acts has two scenes, or occasionally when a brief dimming of the lights indicates a passage of time. The average cast size is between eight and 15 characters. Yet there are exceptions: two couples comprise the cast of Samson Raphaelson's *Young Love* (1928), and S. N. Behrman's *The Second Man* (1927) requires only two men, two women, and an extra.

Rachel Crothers articulates a thoughtful approach to the playwright's craft in her lecture of April 20, 1928, at the University of Pennsylvania, in a series of presentations by eminent dramatists orchestrated by Arthur Hobson Quinn, chair of the Department of English. Her views certainly apply to good dramatic writing in any era, but she serves ably as spokesperson for the dramaturgy espoused by most dramatists of her own day. After emphasizing the need to advance the story through climactic build, Crothers adds:

> Inevitability, I believe, is the greatest quality in playwriting, not surprise and invention. They are very fine indeed in farce and the mystery play but not in drama. Inevitability is a true and psychological result coming out of the natures of the characters as they act and react upon each other under the given conditions. (1967: 123–4)

Crothers calls for acts that are closely knit together, avoiding expository dialogue about what happened between the acts. The smaller units within an act – scenes, speeches, and sentences – should all build to climax. "Each can only carry so much – its own beat. A little too long and the effect of the whole is hurt" (124). She cautions against overworking the duologue; the two-character scene should be held in reserve for when there is a "natural demand for a more intimate scene" (124). Crothers reiterates several times in her lecture the importance of holding something back, not overloading the action or the dialogue: "never fixed sets of characters saying all the author wants to say and coming to a complete stop in order to let the next set come on and say the next things" (125). *Rain* is noted as "a fine example of the simplicity of great construction and the growth of tense, deep drama coming out of the characteristics of two people . . . without one unnecessary stroke" (125).

Crothers upholds realism as "the highest form of dramatic writing. I believe that the most imaginative, poetic, or mystical drama is most powerfully written in realism." She welcomes new forms like expressionism and constructivism as long as they grow "out of the understanding of human nature and the skill of depicting human nature" (125–6). While work whose prime purpose is experimental fails to yield a great play, such innovations are stimulating to the real artist. "Out of the revolutionary period the theatre has just gone through, the sound dramatist has come into a freer, looser, more sketchy and swiftly moving style. He knows now it is better writing to merely suggest – to awaken the imagination of the audience and make them feel and see through that – than to tell them all there is to be told about everything and thereby stop their imagination" (126). She even credits the experimental work for "the brilliant treatment of the play *Broadway*. It moves swiftly from scene to scene in the same set. The variety of entrances, the steps, the upper levels are there, but they are there because they belong to the place – natural and necessary parts of it. As to the writing: "one scene flows into the other with a pace and rhythm that are electrical – many threads weaving in and out on that quick shuttle, never becoming entangled or confused – while we watch the tapestry woven swiftly before our eyes" (127).

Similarly, John Gassner observes in the American drama a "realistic bias even in stylized theatre." He cites Rice's *The Adding Machine* as an example of that, noting that American playwrights gravitate to expressionism as opposed to Maeterlinck-inspired quasi-mystical symbolism, because expressionism tempers its symbolist elements with naturalism (1961: x). It is appropriate here to signal a healthy cross-influence of European drama on the American drama, beginning with the founding of the Theatre Guild in 1919.

Dialogue

One of the joys of reading 1920s plays is the discovery of words like "yegg" (one who lives outside the law) and "flivver" (jalopy), and phrases like "be the goat" (get taken). *Sex*, *Broadway*, and *The Front Page* are especially good for peppy slang and snappy turns of phrase. On just one page of *Sex*, for example, we find: "I'm class, babe," "I'll plant you under the daisies," "you croaked a guy," and "you wouldn't dare squawk" (West 1997: 38). In *Broadway*: "Cheese it." "Look out, the dick." "Gee, the way these gangsters pop each other off. Well, I guess it's nothing but a lucky break kept me from occupying the slab right next to him." "Razzin' me, eh? All right, after tonight you gotta struggle along without me. How do you like them grapes?" (qtd. in Gassner 1949: 243, 247). Scarcely has the action begun in *The Front Page* when a reporter delivers the great line: "Is it true, Madame, that you were the victim of a Peeping Tom?" (Hecht and MacArthur 2002: 58). For sophisticated banter, no writer comes close to Philip Barry, although Booth Tarkington's *Clarence* and Jesse Lynch Williams's *Why Not?* have passages to savor. Zoë Akins's dialogue is often delicious. Zona Gale demonstrates a good ear for Midwestern speech. On the whole, however, mainstream dramatic dialogue of the era is not noteworthy for its economy or stylishness.

It is the expressionists who contribute most to a sense of poetry in speech for the stage. *Processional* achieves some compelling rhythms and images: "Ain't that the cat's knuckles? Ninety years a' drums arattlin', he's seen wars an' deaths an' the makin' a' the states an' yet he won't die." "[T]here's men marchin' men in a sweat an' their flag is the black smoke in the sky, 'cause they dig coal from the ground" (Lawson 1925: 14). e. e. cummings's *him* is an exercise in style, with scenic metaphors to reify the verbal variety. When Eugene intones his epic of industrialization to Sophie in scene 6 of *The Subway*, interspersed by her moans, it functions rhythmically and imagistically as a Love-Death.

During the 1920s, dramatists revel in writing dialect. They have no compunctions about using phonetic spelling to indicate regional speech or other oddities of pronunciation, including the suggestion of a lower social order. Even the leading actress might be given thick dialect, as exemplified by Ned McCobb's daughter Carrie in Sidney Howard's play: "Seems like there ain't nuthin' matters in this world but jest money. Church-goin' don't matter, nor keepin' house, nor the children bein' sick, nor nuthin'. Jest money" (Howard 1931: 49). Such use of phonetic spelling "to represent the ways in which words are spoken by the people of a particular locality" is sanctioned by George Pierce Baker himself (1919: 340). Use of dialect to convey ethnicity is also widespread, from the early 1920s plays of O'Neill to the late 1920s prison dramas that bring together characters of disparate ethnic origin.

In terms of naturalistic stage language, Laurence Stallings and Maxwell Anderson's *What Price Glory* (1924) stands as a watershed play for its recreation of the crudeness and profanity of soldiers' speech to match the violence of their war experience. John Gassner comments on "the growing frankness of the stage."

> Before the twenties the theatre had found it necessary to wage a battle for this prerogative.... That the victory over censorship was worth winning, that it resulted not in license for sensation-mongering but in freedom for significant drama, the theatre soon proved conclusively by the use it made of its liberty.... [W]hen the censors take the field they invariably confuse art with immorality – and for the very good reason that art cuts deeply while licentious trash only titillates. (1949: xi)

No doubt the victory over censorship encompassed subject matter and even stage business, but language, as the most concrete element of the drama, must be considered the crucial battlefield.

Theatricality

A number of productions won critical accolades for the opulence of their scenery and costumes: O'Neill's *Marco Millions* (1930), Colton's *The Shanghai Gesture*, Edward Sheldon and Charles MacArthur's *Lulu Belle* (1926). Thunder and lightning, trap doors, sliding panels, shadow projections, and crashing sounds operate to suspenseful effect in mysteries like Avery Hopwood and Mary Roberts Rinehart's *The Bat* (1920), John Willard's *The Cat and the Canary* (1922), and Matthews and Stanley's *The Wasp's Nest*. Another element of theatricality that demands recognition is the stage's reflection of the 1920s mania for motorcars. In most plays, it suffices to include a dialogue passage in which the characters make arrangements for their cars or their chauffeurs, or they tell about the drive they have just taken, a source of comedy in *Dulcy* and Connelly and Kaufman's *To the Ladies*. The wealthy in fact negotiate which of their cars the various family members will use this evening in *The Best People* and *Nice People*. Flappers and jazzbos are regularly associated with joyriding. Car salesmen, chauffeurs, and mechanics often appear as incidental characters. The mild-mannered eponymous Clarence amazes the family with his ability to drive and repair a car. The effect of the car on the rural lifestyle is shown in *The Detour*. Automobile collisions affect the course of the action in George Kelly's *The Show-Off* (1924) and McGuire's *Six-Cylinder Love*.

A few plays go beyond mere talk about cars and actually bring them on stage. Act 1 of *The Nervous Wreck* features two full-sized cars on stage, both of which move. After the flivver (a Ford) is driven off, a smaller version of the car is seen crossing the stage on an incline further back, and then a still smaller model travels even further upstage as if disappearing into the distance. Act 2 of *Puppy Love* is set in the family's garage. The father of the family has taken the wheel, comes crashing through the garage wall, and sits dazed in the car with a section of picket fence around his neck. The Samuel French editions of both of these family comedies include appendices with simplified versions of the scene, enabling little theatres to produce the plays without the major outlay to create the moving-car effects. One is tempted to speculate that it is the impossibility of writing the moving car out of the script for amateur production that kept the more important McGuire's *Six-Cylinder Love* from publication. In Act 1 of *Six-Cylinder Love* the car magnificently occupies center stage in the Burtons' back yard – until the car salesman sees a way of meeting the new neighbors to sell them the car. He demonstrates its power by crashing it through the fence that separates their back yards.

Other aspects of theatricality are evident, especially in expressionist plays like *Mr. Moneypenny*, *Machinal*, and *Subway*, with their staccato sequences and nightmare effects underscored by lurid sounds. Moneypenny's appearances are always accompanied by the sound of jingling coins. Industrial sounds underscore the characters' urban stress. And always there is jazz music to accompany the frenetic dancing and the swigging from flasks. As Crothers and Gassner note, American expressionism is most effective when set in a realistic framework. Thus we meet Brutus Jones of *The Emperor Jones*, Yank of *The Hairy Ape* (1922), Reuben of *Dynamo* (all by O'Neill), Roger of *Roger Bloomer*, Abraham McCranie of *In Abraham's Bosom*, and Neil McRae of *Beggar on Horseback* as psychologically motivated characters in recognizable circumstances before they take us into fantastic realms of the imagination.

Rachel Crothers speaks of theatricality in her 1928 address: "*Porgy* I consider the most important contribution to the theatre this season, both in writing and production. . . . The symbolism in *Porgy* is an integral part of the play – not superimposed for style's sake. Do you remember the reaching out of the long arms and fingers of fear and superstition and their shadows on the wall? The pace – the verve – the rhythm – color; tremendous – new – vibrating" (1967: 128).

Conclusion

The 1920s mark Eugene O'Neill's extraordinary rise to prominence along with general recognition that the United States had at last produced a dramatist of international stature. The decade also brought him his first three Pulitzer Prizes as well as four other nominations. George S. Kaufman took second place with six nominations, all but one of which were written with collaborators. Meanwhile, Maxwell Anderson gained a solid enough foothold with his social problem plays of the 1920s (tallying five Pulitzer Prize nominations) that he stood ready to blossom with his great verse dramas of the 1930s and after. Philip Barry, George Kelly, Sidney Howard, and Elmer Rice all earned recognition in the 1920s with plays that still hold a place in the repertoire. Of this group, Kelly probably fares less well than the others today, largely due to his lack of economy, especially in his somewhat ponderous dialogue, a problem that can be only partially blamed on the mundane lower-middle-class milieu of most of his plays. Stylistically, Philip Barry leads the pack with sharp, witty dialogue and poignant characterizations. Sidney Howard's slowly uncoiling dramas of character continue to fascinate, at least on the page. Elmer Rice holds his own with the expressionist play *The Adding Machine* as well as his realistic play, *Street Scene*.

Women dramatists had found audiences to equal those of men in earlier decades. The 1920s consolidated the reputations of some of those, notably Zoë Akins, Rachel Crothers, Susan Glaspell, and Sophie Treadwell. A new arrival on the 1920s scene was journalist Zona Gale, who actually won the Pulitzer Prize. Many established women playwrights continued finding audiences for plays that made no pretension to art: Katharine Clugston, Edith Ellis, Clare Kummer, Kate McLaurin, Adelaide Matthews, Martha Stanley, Gertrude Purcell, Zelda Sears, and Gladys Unger. Rida Johnson Young, a prolific dramatist and librettist in the 1910s, steadily supplied delightful work until her death of cancer in 1926. Others failed to live up to their earlier promise: Alice Brown, Eleanor Gates, Harriet Ford, and Margaret Mayo. Channing Pollock earned two Pulitzer Prize nominations for writing that seems turgid and heavy-handedly earnest in promoting his social agenda. As far as neglected dramatists whose work perhaps merits a second look, one might signal Gilbert Emery for serious drama and Barry Conners for comedy, particularly the hilarious *Hell's Bells*.

While one might challenge the choice of a winner of the Pulitzer Prize over some other nominated (or non-nominated) plays as representative of the decade, posterity has probably allowed the genuinely outstanding plays to find their way into the canon of American classics. The well-known plays rightly continue to engage us by their sheer artistry. Then, too, their status might in some measure arise from transcendence of the broad patterns described here. It could be argued that I took the low road, proceeding on the assumption that it is the vast network of plays in supporting roles that truly reveal the story of the decade and the people who lived it. On that note, it seems appropriate to permit Rachel Crothers the last word:

> The stage reflects life, it doesn't invent it. . . . The change of codes, morals, and manners that we find now shocking in the theatre, could not be there and would not be tolerated if it were not already a pervading thing in the world. The theatre is made up of all of us. Everything we are and do and think and believe gets into the theatre – it is the mirror of life. (1967: 133)

NOTES

1. My count is approximate, as I tried to exclude both musicals and dramatizations based upon foreign sources, yet occasional exceptions emerge. John Colton and Clemence Ran-

dolph's *Rain*, for example, must be considered an American product even though a story by W. Somerset Maugham serves as its basis. I also included *Beggar on Horseback* as an

American play despite its being inspired by a German-language source.

2. Surprisingly, three of the 64 Pulitzer Prize-nominated plays apparently were not published: *Six-Cylinder Love*, Maxwell Anderson's *Gypsy* (1929), and Edgar Selwyn and Edmond Goulding's *Dancing Mothers* (1924). Typescripts of the first two can be found in the Billy Rose Theatre Collection of the New York Public Library for the Performing Arts at Lincoln Center.

BIBLIOGRAPHY

Akins, Z. (1923). *Déclassée, Daddy's Gone A-Hunting, and Greatness – A Comedy*. New York: Boni and Liveright.

Anderson, M. (1928). *Outside Looking In*. In Maxwell Anderson and Harold Hickerson, *Gods of the Lightning*; Maxwell Anderson, *Outside Looking In*, based on "Beggars of Life" by Jim Tully. New York: Longmans, Green.

Baker, G. P. (1919). *Dramatic Technique*. Boston: Houghton Mifflin.

Behrman, S. N. (1930). *Meteor*. New York: Brentano's.

Bordman, G. (1995). *American Theatre: A Chronicle of Comedy and Drama, 1914–1930*. New York: Oxford University Press.

Bronner, E. J. (1980). *The Encyclopedia of the American Theatre, 1900–1975*. San Diego: A. S. Barnes.

Browne, P. E. (1926). *The Bad Man*. New York: Samuel French.

Colton, J. and Randolph, C. (1923). *Rain*. New York: Liveright.

Connelly, M. (1927). *The Wisdom Tooth*. New York: Samuel French.

Conners, B. (1926). *Applesauce*. New York: Samuel French.

Craven, F. (1923). *Spite Corner*. New York: Samuel French.

Crothers, R. (1924). *Expressing Willie, Nice People, 39 East: Three Plays by Rachel Crothers*. New York: Brentano's.

——(1967). "The Construction of a Play." Lectures delivered at the University of Pennsylvania on the Mask and Wig Foundation. In *The Art of Playwriting*. Freeport, NY: Books for Libraries Press, 115–34. (Originally published by the University of Pennsylvania Press, 1928.)

Emery, G. (1923). *The Hero*. In Arthur Hobson Quinn (ed.), *Contemporary American Plays*. New York: Charles Scribner's Sons.

Forbes, J. (1920). *The Famous Mrs. Fair and Other Plays by James Forbes*, with Introduction by Walter Prichard Eaton. New York: George H. Doran.

Gassner, J. (ed.) (1949). *Twenty-Five Best Plays of the Modern American Theatre: Early Series*. New York: Crown.

——(1961). *Best American Plays, 1918–1958: Supplementary Volume*. New York: Crown.

Hecht, B. and MacArthur, C. (2002). *The Front Page*. In George W. Hilton (ed.), *The Front Page: From Theater to Reality*. Hanover, NH: Smith and Kraus.

Hoffman, A. (1925). *Two Blocks Away*. New York: Samuel French.

Hopwood, A. and Gray, D. (1928). *The Best People*. New York: Samuel French.

Howard, S. (1931). *Ned McCobb's Daughter*. New York: Samuel French.

Kelly, G. (1928). *Behold, the Bridegroom*. Boston: Little, Brown.

Krutch, J. W. (1939). *The American Drama since 1918: An Informal History*. New York: Random House.

Lawson, J. H. (1925). *Processional: A Jazz Symphony of American Life in Four Acts*. New York: Thomas Seltzer.

McGuire, W. A. (1921). *Six-Cylinder Love*. Typescript. Billy Rose Theatre Collection. New York Public Library for the Performing Arts, Lincoln Center.

Mantle, B. (ed.). *The Best Plays of 1919–1920, 1920–1921, 1921–1922, 1922–1923, 1923–1924, 1924–1925, 1925–1926, 1926–1927, 1927–1928, 1928–1929, 1929–1930.* Boston: Small, Maynard (original editions); New York: Dodd, Mead (reprints).

Matthews, A. and Stanley, M. (1929). *The Wasp's Nest.* New York: Samuel French.

Pollock, C. (1928). *Mr. Moneypenny.* New York: Brentano's.

Rice, E. (1965). *Elmer Rice: Three Plays.* New York: Hill and Wang.

Richman, A. (1922). *Ambush.* New York: Duffield.

Wainscott, R. H. (1997). *The Emergence of the Modern American Theater, 1914–1929.* New Haven, CT: Yale University Press.

West, M. (1997). *Three Plays by Mae West*, ed. Lillian Schlissel. New York: Routledge.

Wexley, J. (1930). *The Last Mile.* New York: Samuel French.

7

Playwrights and Plays of the Harlem Renaissance

Annemarie Bean

I sit with Shakespeare and he winces not.
W. E. B. Du Bois, The Souls of Black Folk (1903)

Humanity Through Drama

The gestation of non-comedic and non-musical drama during the Harlem Renaissance (1917–35) was conceived in two early arenas at the turn of the century: the pageant and the folk play. Both of these areas continued to receive attention during the Harlem Renaissance, and new forms of drama were added, including those based on social issues such as birth control and lynching, and plays dealing with history. Additionally, there are a few examples of expressionist-style dramas, written primarily by Marita Bonner. All four – pageant, folk, social issue, and history – directly respond to W. E. B. Du Bois's call in 1903 to create "art of the black folk [that] compels recognition," in order to be rated as "human." Du Bois's point is crucial: Harlem Renaissance drama was written by playwrights under extensive pressure to provide full-bodied portrayals of black life to black and white audiences. Northern blacks knew little about rural Southern life; the Great Migration from the South fed the Northern cities with young, rural blacks whose lack of refinement was an anathema to some Northern blacks. African Americans were appalled by the 1896 Supreme Court *Plessy* v. *Ferguson* decision, in which, in the words of dissenting Justice John Marshall Harlan, a "condition of legal inferiority" was formally assigned to black people. Beyond the usual threats to playwrights of most eras and generations – poverty, social stigmas – African American playwrights of the Harlem Renaissance had to establish the very *humanness* of themselves, as well as their subjects.

The majority of plays to be discussed in this section were rarely, if ever, produced as full professional performances. This fact does not mean that these plays were written without the intention of performance; rather, the issue of production is a commentary on the complicated position of drama in the African American community during the years 1917–35. The presence of African Americans in the realm of American popular entertainment and theatre, either through mimesis (blackface minstrelsy) or as performers, had been established since the early years of the American Republic, often as servant or comic characters in farces. During the 1820s, two parallel experiences forever destined a split between the popular and the serious in African American theatre. One was the establishment of the Africa Grove Theatre, on the corner of Bleecker and Mercer Streets in lower Manhattan. Primarily a tea-garden that served liquor, the Africa Grove also featured the works of Shakespeare performed by the African Company, and introduced the talents of West Indian actor and producer James Hewlett. After the Africa Grove was closed down in 1824 (by white theatre managers threatened by the competition), Thomas Dartmouth Rice (ca. late 1820s) blackened his face and began his highly popular singing and dancing routine, establishing the minstrel tradition known as "Jim Crow." The popular entertainment aspects of African American theatre were reclaimed after the end of the Civil War with the touring sensations of the Hyers Sisters, Sissieretta Jones, and many other African American minstrel troupes. By the turn of the century, composers, lyricists, and performers such as James Reese Europe, Will Marion Cook, James Weldon Johnson, J. Rosamond Johnson, Bob Cole, George Walker, Aida Overton Walker, and Bert Williams were creating African American musical revues, with titles that ran the geographical gamut from *Trip to Coontown* (1898–1901) to *Abyssinia* (1902–5). By far the most successful of these musical endeavors was Eubie Blake and Noble Sissle's *Shuffle Along* (1921), which opened at the Cort Theatre on 63rd Street (far from Broadway, but Broadway, nonetheless), ran for 504 performances, and then expanded to include three touring companies.

Within the African American community, several responses surfaced for the inclusion of drama as a serious artistic form to be practiced and nurtured. Initially, the barrier to be broken down was to have black actors portray black roles written by white playwrights. Black actors were cast in three one-act folk dramas written by white playwright Ridgely Torrence in 1917 (known as *Three Plays for a Negro Theatre*), and Eugene O'Neill's expressionistic play *Emperor Jones* in 1920. Nevertheless, even though Charles S. Gilpin, and, in 1924, Paul Robeson, starred in *Emperor Jones*, the black community neither wholeheartedly embraced O'Neill's characterization of Brutus Jones nor entirely supported Gilpin and Robeson's participation in the role. As Robeson recounted in an essay written for *Opportunity*, the African American periodical sponsored by the National Urban League, the black community saw his roles in *Emperor Jones* and O'Neill's other "black play," *All God's Chillun Got Wings* (1924), as stepping-stones to the portrayal of a heroic figure (*Opportunity*, December 1924: 368–70). O'Neill and Torrence wrote supposedly black dialect that was difficult to decipher for actors and audience and embarrassingly similar to blackface minstrelsy and its misrepresentations. Additionally, O'Neill liberally used the term "nigger" throughout *Emperor Jones*, which Gilpin attempted to change to "Negro" or "colored." Debates in *Opportunity* and its National Association for the

Advancement of Colored People (NAACP) counterpart, *Crisis*, discussed white playwrights' and novelists' right to use the word (Carl Van Vechten's 1926 book *Nigger Heaven*, in particular). The contradiction was that, while African Americans were beginning to write themselves into plays and experiment with playwriting styles that eschewed race as the primary theme, white playwrights were still dehumanizing characters in their quest for "authenticity." In addition to debates about stereotypical characterizations, African Americans were denied seating in white-owned theatres. Some exceptions were made for the so-called "better class" of people, but on the whole segregation was entrenched. In the December 1927 issue of the *Messenger*, Gustavus Adolphus Steward decried the segregation of theatre spaces, calling for African Americans to "overcrowd the Jim Crow sections," causing theatre owners to see a profit in offering more and better seats to black patrons. In his March 1928 response to the issue in the *Messenger*, black playwright Randolph Edmonds contended that the solution lay in the "wholesale rejection" of a segregated seat by the "better class," and a movement to establish equal rights for all American citizens.

Middle-class African American acceptance of drama as literature was greatly helped by the playwriting contests sponsored each year in the periodicals *Crisis* and *Opportunity*. Beginning in 1924 and funded by Amy Spingarn, the *Crisis* prizes in literature and art were awarded annually. The editor of *Opportunity*, Charles S. Johnson, also arranged an annual literary contest in 1925, which culminated in a dinner with publishers and writers. The dramas of the first-, second-, and third-place winners were guaranteed publication. Frequently it was on the printed page that black readers were able to observe race portrayals through dramatic literature.

Role of Dramatic Art in the Harlem Renaissance

There has been a plenitude of critical commentary published during and after the Harlem Renaissance on the role of dramatic art. Samuel A. Hay has raised the interesting argument that most plays written in the twentieth century by and about African Americans are based on one of two dramatic theories. The theories, the first espoused by Alain Locke (1886–1954) and the second by W. E. B. Du Bois (1868–1963), were noted in several publications, including *Crisis* (Du Bois was its editor) and the anthology *The New Negro* (1925, edited by Locke). Du Bois's "school of theatre," Hay observes, is one of protest against racism and propaganda, showing people "as they actually were but also as they wished to be" (1994: 3). Locke, according to Hay, found Du Bois's theatre "indigestible," lacking artistic basis or merit. Hay identifies "Locke's Art-Theatre" as one of "ordinary folk – dressed up with poetry, music, and dance" (5). Extending Hay's analysis, the role of dramatic art in the Harlem Renaissance was highly nuanced. Plays written just prior to and during the Renaissance experimented with form, structure, and content. What seems clear is that, in the early stages of the period (ca. 1917–25), the pageant and the folk play were the dominant forms, keeping with Du Bois's often quoted statement in the program for the Krigwa Players Little Negro Theatre (1925), and reprinted in *Crisis* (July 1926):

> The plays of a real Negro theatre must be: *One: About us.* That is, they must have plots which reveal Negro life as it is. *Two: By us.* That is, they must be written by Negro authors who understand from birth and continual association just what it means to be a Negro today. *Three: For us.* That is, the theatre must cater primarily to Negro audiences and be supported and sustained by their entertainment and approval. *Fourth: Near us.* The theatre must be in a Negro neighborhood near the mass of ordinary Negro people. Only in this way can a real folk play movement of American Negroes be built up. (134)

Du Bois's assertions situated the "real Negro theatre" along the lines of the Little Theatre Movement in America. Emerging in Europe in the 1880s and brought to the United States in the early teens of the twentieth century, little theatres were "established from a love of drama, not from love of gain" (Mackay 1917: 1). The Little Theatre Movement in America influenced the rise of American regional theatres and ethnically identified theatres. Du Bois was prescient in realizing that the Little Theatre Movement might best serve black theatre of the Harlem Renaissance. By 1926, Du Bois describes his platform for drama in greater detail:

> Thus all art is propaganda and ever must be, despite the wailing of the purists. I stand in utter shamelessness and say that whatever art I have for writing has been used always for propaganda for gaining the right of black folk to love and enjoy. I do not care a damn for any art that is not used for propaganda. But I do care when propaganda is confined to one side while the other is stripped and silent. ("Criteria of Negro Art," *Crisis,* October: 292)

This speech (given at the Chicago Conference of the NAACP) was written in response to the writers Du Bois had identified in the past as "purists," Alain Locke and Langston Hughes. As Hughes writes in the *Nation* in 1926, for the African American artist who chooses to develop his creative art as an individual, rather than as part of a political platform, or to please a white patron, "The road . . . is most certainly rocky and the mountain high" ("The Negro Artist and the Racial Mountain," June 23: 692).

Du Bois recognized the value of "stress[ing] Beauty – all Beauty" in art (*Crisis,* May 1925: 8). However, Du Bois's aesthetic focus, while acknowledging the need to "stress Beauty," understood that the political climate was dire. Locke and Hughes attempted to mandate "beauty" convincingly. In 1922, Locke published his "Steps Toward the Negro Theatre," in which he maintains that the Howard Players, under the leadership of Montgomery Gregory at Howard University, represent the required training in aesthetics needed to produce fine art. By 1925, Gregory described these requirements in Locke's anthology *The New Negro*: "national Negro Theater where the Negro playwright, musician, actor, dancer, and artist in concert shall fashion a drama that will merit respect and admiration" (159). Begun as a College Dramatic Club in 1909 by Ernest Everett Just, the Howard Players evolved into a full dramatic department in 1947, with exceptional drama teachers such as Anne Cooke, Owen Dodson, and James Butcher. In 1920–1, the Howard Players produced plays by white playwrights, including classical works, as well as supporting original plays. The Washington, DC area was also a playwriting haven from 1926 to 1936, due to the S Street Salon, a literary group founded by the poet and playwright Georgia Douglas Johnson. Several playwrights took part in Johnson's S Street Salon, including Hughes, Locke, Randolph Edmonds, Willis Richardson, Marita Bonner, Angelina Weld Grimké, Zora Neale Hurston, and Mary Burrill. Over the years, the Howard Players would produce works by local black playwrights, and many playwrights experienced its program. Two other black theatres, the Lafayette Players in Harlem and the Ethiopian Art Theatre in Chicago, were both successful albeit relatively short-lived. In spirit and practice, the Howard Players may be the closest to a black national theatre inspired by the Harlem Renaissance.

Pageant

Processional, spectacular, and festival-like, the theatrical form of the pageant was revived throughout Europe and the United States in the early part of the twentieth century. The chief reason had to do with surges in immigration and emigration, and the resultant trend of nationalism (ethnic and cultural identification). In the African American community, pageants restored a history lost in the recesses of slavery and its aftermath. The form of the pageant encouraged mass participation and inclusiveness, and facilitated a national black identity through black-identified music, song, and dance:

> A pageant is a great Folk Play, with a series of scenes, and processions of persons in costumes of various periods, representing historic events. These scenes and actions are accompanied by music, dramatic incidents and the grouping and massing of color. In the pageant all classes and ages take part. It is a great human festival and may be of singular beauty and lasting impression. (Du Bois 1986: 161)

The most well-known pageant from the pre-Renaissance period is *The Star of Ethiopia* (a.k.a. *The People of Peoples and Their Gifts to Men*, 1911), written by Du Bois as a fundraising mechanism for a struggling NAACP in its first few years. According to David Krasner, *The Star of Ethiopia* was directly connected with the late nineteenth-century African American movement of Ethiopianism, which sought a postcolonial Africa rooted in Christianity (2002: 87–9). A precursor to Black Nationalist movements, Ethiopianism looked to Africa for cultural roots and to Christianity for a connection between African Americans and Africans. *The Star of Ethiopia*, which begins in 50,000 BCE and ends in the present time, personifies Africa in the form of Ethiopia, daughter of Shango, the Yoruba thunder god. A costly production,

Star grew from 350 to 1,300 performers, and was staged in New York City (1913), Washington, DC (1915), Philadelphia (1916), and Los Angeles (1925), with audiences numbering over 10,000 each time.

Pageants continued to be staged throughout the Harlem Renaissance, primarily at schools and colleges. In his *Plays and Pageants from the Life of the Negro* (1930), African American playwright Willis Richardson includes four pageants: *Two Races* (1930) by Inez M. Burke, *Out of the Dark* (1924) by Dorothy C. Guinn, *The Light of the Women* (1930) by Frances Gunner, and *Ethiopia at the Bar of Justice* (1924) by Edward J. McCoo. Given their intended majesty and regalia, the playscripts for these pageants are streamlined, revealing their educational intention. These four pageants and Du Bois's *Star* lack plots. They are instead based on the parade of allegorical and historical figures, which are intertwined in the performance. For example, the 12-minute *Two Races* has characters listed as "Sam, a Negro boy"; "Gilbert, a white boy"; "Spirit of Negro Progress"; and "Uncle Sam." The names of the Talkers (essentially a chorus) are "Adventure, Invention, Bravery, Oratory, Poetry, Music." Young schoolgirls likely vied for the choice part of the Spirit of Negro Progress with her elaborate costume of white robe and crown.

Two Races begins with two boys playing marbles. Gilbert shows a book to his friend, Sam, documenting "all the music, invention, art, and business that *my* people, *my* forefathers, have done." Sam replies, "Don't you think my people helped a little?" Gilbert notes, "Well, it isn't in these books." The Spirit of Negro Progress then allows for Sam to educate Gilbert; in the end, she tells Sam to "Stick to your school training, have a purpose in life, and add to the glorious achievements of the Negro Race" (302). *Out of the Dark* features appearances by poet Phillis Wheatley, mathematician Benjamin Bannaker, abolitionists Frederick Douglass and Sojourner Truth, founder of the Tuskegee Institute Booker T. Washington, and folk hero Uncle Remus. The pageant begins with the "Rape of a Continent" and ends, as noted in its synopsis, at the beginning, with a rousing rendition of the Negro National Anthem (also known as the Hymn of the Race), "Lift Every Voice and Sing." *Out of the Dark* also details the dance and music of the pageant. The music includes songs from blackface minstrelsy shows, "Old Black Joe" and "Sewanee River," as well as Felix Mendelssohn's "Spring Song" and the spiritual "Swing Low, Sweet Chariot." The last two pageants, *The Light of the Women* and *Ethiopia at the Bar of Justice*, equate pride in African American heritage with the elevation of Ethiopia. In these pageants, Ethiopia is always portrayed as a black woman dressed regally. At the end of *Ethiopia at the Bar of Justice*, Ethiopia and Justice marry, with Leniency and Oppression marching ahead of them down the aisle, all to the strains of "The Star Spangled Banner."

Folk Play

The use of the folk play in the Harlem Renaissance emerged from the larger American folk drama movement, which itself was influenced by the national tour of the Dublin-based Abbey Theatre Players in 1911. The Irish nationalist Abbey Players toured works by Irish playwrights, performed in a naturalistic acting style, and set in simple, domestic settings. Their work inspired several white American playwrights – Paul Green, Marc Connelly, Ridgely Torrence, DuBose Heyward, and Eugene O'Neill – to try their hand at depicting black life. Torrence's *Three Plays for a Negro Theatre* opened in 1917 at the Garden Theatre in Madison Square Garden in New York to critical acclaim by white and black critics. Some of the commentary in the black press focused on the performances of the actors, especially Alexander Rogers and Jesse Shipp. But mostly critics lauded the plays' existence, casting, and the effect of their combined presence on the audience. Typical were the comments by the *New York Globe* drama critic Louis Sherwin: "I was strangely moved by this performance. I felt as if I were witnessing by far the most significant effort of self-expression I had seen for a long time anywhere" (*Crisis*, June 1917: 81).

The success of *Three Plays for a Negro Theatre* established public interest in folk dramatizations of African American life. Indeed, interest had grown during the latter part of the nineteenth century, due to the hundreds of versions of the *Uncle Tom's Cabin* melodramas touring the country. Two play anthologies, *Plays and Pageants from the Life of the Negro*, edited by Willis Richardson, and *Six Plays for a Negro Theatre* (1934), by Randolph Edmonds, compiled the finest African American folk drama written during the Harlem Renaissance. Inspired by observing the play *Rachel* (written by the African American woman playwright Angelina Weld Grimké in 1916), Richardson had his first one-act plays produced by the Howard Players, but it was his *The Chip Woman's Fortune* (1923) that was most notable. *Chip Woman* was produced by the Ethiopian Art Players of Chicago, who brought their production to New York in 1923. It became the first drama by a black playwright on Broadway.

Richardson's four extant Harlem Renaissance-era folk plays – *The Chip Woman's Fortune, The Broken Banjo* (1925), *Compromise* (1925), and *The Idle Head* (1929) – were a direct response to what he perceived as the misguided interpretations of black life as written by Torrence and other white playwrights (O'Neill, Heyward, Connelly, and Green) who were inspired to write black folk drama. Leslie Catherine Sanders summarizes Richardson's goals in these plays:

> Richardson's folk plays thus consider the impact of various resolutions to problems black people encounter in their daily living. He never evokes pity for his characters; indeed, one of the recurrent criticisms of his work has been that he fails to make his characters adequately sympathetic. The effect of his dispassionate attitude is to allow his audience likewise to evaluate dispassionately the rightness of a character's choice or action. Richardson's impulse is always didactic. (1988: 30)

Chip Woman locates the contemporary Harlem Renaissance family on the edge of two eras, the African-based past and modern present. The Green family has purchased a Victrola as their own luxury, and they have also welcomed into their home Aunt Nancy, the chip woman of the story. Aunt Nancy uses herbs to heal the ill Liza Green, and in the process teaches Liza's daughter Emma wisdom. Silas, the patriarch, desperate for a means to keep up financially, finds Aunt Nancy's "fortune" buried in the back yard. She is keeping it for her son, Jim, who is scheduled to get out of jail after he has served time for beating a man who harmed his girlfriend. Jim arrives just in time, in the middle of the awkward situation, and happily gives half the money to the Green family.

The play addresses several themes constant in Richardson's work. First, the folk character of Aunt Nancy is seen as a valuable mentor to the Green family; her gentle teaching is needed in the harried world of the Greens. Aunt Nancy also addresses black bourgeoisie's tendencies toward wealth gain and judgmental morality. Silas speaks unkindly of men with jail records, but Aunt Nancy marks this as an indication of inequality. Silas wants to take all of Aunt Nancy's money; Jim, her son, is willing to give half of it to the Greens. Hypocritical bourgeois black and white values are condemned in *Chip Woman*, while the community and its outreach to the poor are applauded.

Randolph Edmonds's influence on theatre of the Harlem Renaissance was in developing training in the performance and writing of black theatre on college campuses. Educated at Oberlin College and Columbia University, Edmonds received a Rockefeller grant to study at the Yale School of Drama, as well as in London and Dublin. As a professor at Morgan College in Baltimore in 1930, Edmonds worked with four other traditional black colleges and universities in the area – Howard University, Hampton Institute, Virginia State College, and Virginia Union – to form the Negro Intercollegiate Dramatic Association (NIDA). Edmonds became Director of Drama at Dillard University, and then moved to Florida A & M University, where he continued to work in little theatre. NIDA inspired other collegiate dramatic associations to form. In 1936, he developed the Southern Association of Dramatic and Speech Arts, and then the National Association of Dramatic and Speech Arts. The plays Edmonds included in *Six Plays for a Negro Theatre* are specifically geared for production by college groups. Like Robeson and Du Bois, Edmonds thought that black theatre should appeal to the universal humanity of all beings. As a playwright and producer of black theatre, Edmonds's artistic choices were geared toward educating a relatively uneducated audience (at least, in theatre). He wanted audiences to become more accepting and, hopefully, more critically demanding. He defined these elements in the Preface as: "worthwhile themes, sharply drawn conflict, positive characters, and a melodramatic plot" (1934: 7).

One drama in *Six Plays*, titled *Old Man Pete*, provides contrasts and similarities to Richardson's *The Chip Woman's Fortune* in terms of their dramatizations of the worlds between the nineteenth-century African America and the twentieth. In *Old Man Pete*, an old couple sell their farm in Virginia and journey to Harlem to live with their children. When they arrive, the urban children have lives that are not conducive to having an old rural couple around. Pete and his wife Mandy speak in dialect, go to church often, and parade around the house in nothing but their underwear. After being insulted by Vivian, their son John's wife, they set out to leave New York on the coldest night of the year. Unable to find the train station, they freeze to death in Central Park, with Pete hallucinating about feeding pigs. It is a pitiful story. Edmonds literally taps into a "coldness" he sensed in the community toward anything or anyone rural by the middle-class urbanites. The characterizations of Pete and Mandy are complex as well. The religious couple discuss the value of the sermon they attended, contrasting other black plays that highlight the materialism of churchgoers. While Pete and Mandy speak in dialect, their children do not; as a result, the chiding by the young people's friends of their parents' accents embarrasses them. *Old Man Pete* ends tragically, and, in this tragedy, Edmonds credits the lack of communication between family members, not race, as the culprit.

Social Issue

The social issue plays of the Harlem Renaissance dramatize debates and protests generated in the African American community. They generally describe lynching, motherhood, religion, and miscegenation. Some of the plays cover more than one issue. Generally, plays speaking on the ill effects of poverty concern working-class and rural people; plays grappling with racism often portray middle-class characters. This trend reflects American drama of the period. The audiences for these dramas were frequently assumed to be middle class, black and white. Therefore, social issue playwrights appeal to audiences (and readers, in the case of those plays written for *Crisis* and *Opportunity* playwriting contests) with a standardized progression of associations and emotions: poverty–working class/rural–pity and racism–middle-class indignation.

For example, the earliest social issue play, *Rachel* (1916) by Angelina Weld Grimké, was written in response to the release of D. W. Griffith's film *Birth of a Nation* (1915) promoting white unity. Sponsored by the NAACP, *Rachel* has been called the organization's "first attempt to use the stage for race propaganda" (Hatch and Shine 1974). The playwright's father, Archibald Grimké, was executive director of the NAACP, and her great-aunt, Angelina Grimké Weld, was a well-known white abolitionist and suffragist. In 1916, Grimké's English teaching position at Dunbar High School in Washington, DC put her in close contact with other black poets and writers, including Mary Burrill. These young women writers may have been models for the protagonist of Grimké's *Rachel*. Beyond the propagandistic aspects of *Rachel*, the play provides a detailed perspective on the effects of a racist society on young African American women, particularly on their desire to become mothers. Set in Washington, DC, Rachel and her family have come "Upsouth" for a better life and to escape a past which includes the dual lynching of her father and brother. Though Rachel and her brother Tom are educated, they cannot find a job. Their mother, in poor health, must continue to make a living as a seamstress. The family has become part of an urban servant class. Rachel denies the love of John Strong because she cannot fathom giving birth to victims of racism. Ultimately, *Rachel* speaks an activist message in the form of a melodrama: she chooses "childlessness" over victimization.

As the writer of the first social issue play of the Harlem Renaissance, Grimké raises several themes that would continue in other social issue plays of the period: the Great Migration of Southern blacks to the North, lynching campaigns, and pervasive poverty. Other plays deal with intra-community conflicts, including color bias, miscegenation, and church hypocrisy. Georgia Douglas Johnson's play *Plumes* (1927) has been often anthologized. It concerns the complicated decision by a poor, rural black woman, Charity Brown, not to have her ill daughter operated on. Johnson's lynching dramas, *A Sunday Morning in the South* (1925), *Safe* (ca. 1929), and *Blue-Eyed Black Boy* (ca. 1930), were submitted to the Federal Theatre Project for production, but none was produced. *Blue-Eyed Black Boy* and another of Johnson's plays, *Blue Blood* (1926), examine miscegenation between white men of power and rural black women in the post-Reconstruction period. *Blue Blood* was produced in New York, featuring the acting of the poet and playwright May Miller. The play was also part of an evening of one-acts produced by the Howard Players, indicating its significance at the time.

Stories of miscegenation were central to the fictionalization and dramatization of black life in the nineteenth century. In the twentieth century, African American playwrights examined relationships between blacks and whites during the Harlem Renaissance. Following the tradition of white authors, black playwrights continued to view acts of miscegenation as doomed, however much love is involved. Myrtle Smith Livingston's *For Unborn Children* (1926) and Langston Hughes's *Mulatto* (1935) are prime examples. Hughes's *Mulatto* was produced on Broadway almost entirely without his knowledge or participation (he was in Russia and Asia at the time). It was the first full-length play by an African American produced on Broadway, the second being Lorraine Hansberry's *A Raisin in the Sun* (1959, with its title drawn from a Hughes poem). *Mulatto*'s central story concerns a son, one of three children of a black servant and a white plantation owner. *Mulatto*, however, was altered by its white producer; it included a rape scene of the mixed-race daughter. There are several key aspects of the play that are inventive. First, the plantation owner, Colonel Thomas Norwood, is actually a developed, three-dimensional character. Second, the mulatto character (the son, Bert) is male. Frequently the literary and dramatic stories of the "tragic mulatto" are female. Hughes describes Bert as much like his father, and because Norwood is a character in the play, the audience can make this uncomfortable comparison visually. At the same time, the close contact between the two makes the tragic result of their relationship all the more poignant.

Zora Neale Hurston spent most of her early life during the Harlem Renaissance in the theatre and in academia. Encouraged by May Miller to study at Howard University with Alain Locke, Hurston then enrolled in Barnard College, becoming the first African American to obtain a degree at the school in 1928. A trained anthropologist and collector of folklore, Hurston's plays feature the locations and speech of rural blacks. *Color Struck* (1925), winner of second place in the *Opportunity* awards, exposes color bias within the black community, a theme Georgia Douglas Johnson explores as well. The play opens in a "Jim Crow" railway car with couples on their way to a cakewalk contest. In the character descriptions, Hurston is very specific about the darkness and lightness of each character. "Black" Emmaline is with "light brown-skinned" John, and she believes he is interested in "mulatto" Effie. Emmaline's self-hatred continues long after John leaves her life, and when he returns, she allows her "very white" ill daughter to die. Despite its difficult subject matter, Hurston's writing in *Color Struck* and in her collaboration with Langston Hughes, *Mule Bone* (ca. 1930), featured playful, humorous, and realistic interactions between African Americans.

In 1919, Mary Burrill published two social issue plays, *They That Sit in Darkness* and *Aftermath*, in periodicals (*They That Sit in Darkness* was revised in 1930, becoming *Unto Third and Fourth Generations*). Burrill, a lifelong teacher and director who spent the majority of her career at Dunbar High School in Washington, DC, was a colleague of Angelina Weld Grimké and a mentor to Willis Richardson and May Miller. *They That Sit in Darkness* promotes free access to birth control as its message. In the play a bright young woman, Lindy, has received a scholarship to Tuskegee Institute. She is unable to go because her mother, worn out by having too many children, dies. *Aftermath* tells the story of a black soldier's distinguished military service in World War I. The themes of lynching and black military participation are explored by other playwrights, including Alice Dunbar-Nelson in *Mine Eyes Have Seen* (1918). Upon arriving home, John discovers his father has been lynched as the result of complaining about the price of cotton. At the end of the play, John takes his army-issued pistols to seek revenge, stating, "This ain't no time fu' preachers or prayers! You mean to tell me I mus' let them w'ite devils send me miles erway to suffer an' be shot up fu' the freedom of people I ain't nevah seen, while they're burnin' an' killin' my folks here at home! To Hell with 'em!" (65–6). John's recognition of racial inequity was influenced by the race riots of the summer of 1919, where returning black soldiers were attacked and sometimes killed by angry white mobs.

Another example of social issue plays are those dealing with church hypocrisy. What is significant about the plays of this genre is that they avoid racial struggles; instead, they concern class. Three of Willis Richardson's 1920s plays – *The Deacon's Awakening* (1920), *A Pillar of the Church* (1929), and *The Peacock's Feather* (ca. 1925) – critique religious conservatism practiced by domineering fathers in these family dramas. Ruth Gaines-Shelton's *The Church Fight* (another second-prize winner in *Crisis*, 1925), is rare in that it is a comedy. The characters level a trumped-up "charge" against their clergyman, Pastor Procrastinator, and cannot resolve their conflicts over him. These church hypocrisy plays are also an opportunity for playwrights to confront some of their chief detractors in the black community. The social issue plays have a sense of immediacy to them, which may have been more poignant had they been produced more often.

History

The history plays of the Harlem Renaissance were a creative extension of the pageants. These plays were written to educate black audiences to their history, and white audiences to African diasporic history. It is significant that many of the history plays draw upon international and historical figures that are not always American. This reflected a growing trend among black intellectuals to extend heroic models to include those of the Caribbean and Africa. In 1935, May Miller and Willis Richardson published *Negro History in Thirteen Plays*. Miller, part of Georgia Douglas Johnson's S Street Salon, graduate of Howard University, and daughter of Kelly Miller, an influential writer, sociologist, and dean at Howard, contributed three works: *Sojourner Truth*, *Samory*, and *Harriet Tubman*. Johnson contributed the plays *William and Ellen Craft* and *Frederick Douglass*. In these historical dramas, the mythology surrounding black heroes is developed for younger audiences, such as Miller's students at Frederick Douglass High School in Baltimore.

Shirley Graham's *Tom-Tom* (1932) situates her drama in related worlds: Africa, a Southern plantation, the Middle Passage, and Harlem. In the 1920s, Graham studied at the Sorbonne in Paris, engaging many West Africans. Based on her experience and her father's residency in Monrovia, Liberia, at the time, Graham wrote the three-act opera *Tom-Tom*. It premiered in the "Theatre of Nations" program in Cleveland in 1932, starring Jules Bledsoe at the Voodoo Man. *Tom-Tom* can be read as an operatic play exploring the cross-Atlantic experience in an explicitly historically connected way.

Expressionist Style

Marita Bonner sets the time for her one-act, *The Purple Flower* (1928), as "The Middle-of-Things-as-They-are (Which means the End-of-Things for some of the characters and the Beginning-of-Things for others)" (30). From this description, her reading audience knew that Bonner's style was experimental and expressionistic. Raised in the Boston area, Bonner was educated at Brookline High School and Radcliffe College. Unable to room at Radcliffe, which banned all black students from living on campus (following Harvard's rule), Bonner lived at home, while simultaneously teaching at a nearby high school. She continued teaching in the Washington, DC area, where she became influenced by Johnson's S Street Salon. It was during these years, 1925–8, that Bonner penned *The Pot Maker: A Play to be Read* (1927), *The Purple Flower*, and *Exit, an Illusion* (1928). Fluent in German, and a comparative literature major at Radcliffe, Bonner possibly studied the work of German philosophers Hegel and Marx, as well as expressionist playwrights such as Georg Kaiser and Ernst Toller. Primarily centered on a conflict between the modern and the traditional, expressionist plays were episodic and utopian. By 1924, the expressionist movement declined in

Germany, defeated by worsening economic conditions. However, Bonner and a few other American playwrights, including Eugene O'Neill, continued the development of expressionism. *The Pot Maker* and *Exit, an Illusion* are different in setting (*The Pot Maker* has a domestic setting and *Exit* an urban one), but both of these plays have as their conflict a black man's decision about his light-skinned girlfriend. *The Purple Flower* sets up a battle between the "Us's" and the "White Devils" over the "purple Flower-of-Life-At-Its-Fullest." With allegorically named characters and fight between not only white and black but also (traditional) black and (revolutionary) black, *The Purple Flower* is the most experimental play extant from the Harlem Renaissance.

Conclusion

Being a woman – you can wait. . . . Motionless on the outside. But on the inside?
> Bonner (1925: 64)

A reader of this chapter may have noticed that the participation of black women playwrights of the Harlem Renaissance dwarfs that of black men playwrights. It is an interesting conundrum. In actuality, because of the difficulty in publishing plays during the Renaissance, it is somewhat inaccurate to base conclusions on extant materials. Nevertheless, it appears that in the area of writing plays, women playwrights dominated as winners of the *Crisis* and *Opportunity* contests. The majority of playwrights in the Renaissance were not professional writers but professional educators (Langston Hughes and Zora Neale Hurston are exceptions). African American women in particular were educators in secondary schools (Grimké, Burrill, Miller), and on the college and university level, men were the theatre educators or were produced primarily by colleges (Gregory, Locke, Edmonds, Richardson). In the end, it is the melding of education and dramatic training on the campuses of traditionally black colleges and universities such as Howard and Atlanta University that continued the nurturing of African American plays and playwrights. From Langston Hughes's *Mulatto* to Lorraine Hansberry's *Raisin in the Sun*, there were no dramas written by an African American on Broadway. Black theatre created by blacks and exploring the works by black and white playwrights flourished in areas removed from the Great White Way.

Bibliography

Aiken, G. L. and Howard, G. C. (1994). *Uncle Tom's Cabin*, ed. Thomas Riis. New York: Garland.
Bonner, M. (1925). "On Being Young – a Woman – and Colored." *Crisis* (December). Reprinted in Joyce Flynn (ed.), *Frye Street and Environs: The Collected Works of Marita Bonner*. Boston: Beacon Press (1987), 3–8.
——(1987a). *Exit, An Illusion*. In Joyce Flynn (ed.), *Frye Street and Environs: The Collected Works of Marita Bonner*. Boston: Beacon Press, 47–56.

Bonner, M. (1987b). *The Pot Maker: A Play to Be Read*. In Joyce Flynn (ed.), *Frye Street and Environs: The Collected Works of Marita Bonner*. Boston: Beacon Press, 17–29.

——(1987c). *The Purple Flower*. In Joyce Flynn (ed.), *Frye Street and Environs: The Collected Works of Marita Bonner*. Boston: Beacon Press, 30–46.

Boyd, L. (1994/5). "The Folk, the Blues, and the Problems of *Mule Bone*." *Langston Hughes Review* 13, 1 (Fall/Spring): 33–44.

Burke, I. M. (1993). *Two Races: A Pageant*. In Willis Richardson (ed.), *Plays and Pageants from the Life of the Negro*. Jackson: University Press of Mississippi, 295–302.

Burrill, M. (1989a). *Aftermath*. In Kathy Perkins (ed.), *Black Female Playwrights: An Anthology of Plays Before 1950*. Bloomington: Indiana University Press, 57–66.

——(1989b). *They That Sit in Darkness*. In Kathy Perkins (ed.), *Black Female Playwrights: An Anthology of Plays Before 1950*. Bloomington: Indiana University Press, 67–74.

Chick, N. (1994/5). "Marita Bonner's Revolutionary Purple Flowers: Challenging the Symbol of White Womanhood." *Langston Hughes Review* 13, 1 (Fall/Spring): 21–32.

Du Bois, W. E. B. (1986). *The Star of Ethiopia: A Pageant*. In Herbert Aptheker (ed.), *Pamphlets and Leaflets*. White Plains, NY: Kraus-Thomson, 151–209.

——(1999). *The Souls of Black Folk*. New York: W. W. Norton.

Edmonds, R. (1934). *Six Plays for a Negro Theatre*. Boston: Walter H. Baker.

Graham, S. (1991). *Tom-Tom*. In Leo Hamalian and James V. Hatch (eds.), *The Roots of African American Drama: An Anthology of Early Plays, 1858–1938*. Detroit: Wayne State University Press, 238–86.

Grimké, A. W. (1974). *Rachel*. In James V. Hatch and Ted Shine (eds.), *Black Theatre U.S.A.: Forty-Five Plays by Black Americans, 1847–1974*. New York: Free Press, 139–72.

Guinn, D. C. (1993). *Out of the Dark: A Pageant*. In Willis Richardson (ed.), *Plays and Pageants from the Life of the Negro*. Jackson: University Press of Mississippi, 306–30.

Gunner, F. (1993). *The Light of the Women*. In Willis Richardson (ed.), *Plays and Pageants from the Life of the Negro*. Jackson: University Press of Mississippi, 333–42.

Hansberry, L. (1966). *A Raisin in the Sun*. New York: New American Library.

Hatch, J. V. (1993). *Sorrow Is The Only Faithful One: The Life of Owen Dodson*. Urbana: University of Illinois Press.

——(1999). "Theatre in Historically Black Colleges: A Survey of 100 Years." In Annemarie Bean (ed.), *A Sourcebook of African-American Performance: Plays, People, Movements*. London: Routledge, 150–64.

——and Shine, T. (eds.) (1974). *Black Theatre U.S.A.: Forty-Five Plays by Black Americans, 1847–1974*. New York: Free Press.

Hay, S. A. (1994). *African American Theatre: An Historical and Critical Analysis*. New York: Cambridge University Press.

Hughes, L. (1963). *Mulatto*. In Webster Smalley (ed.), *Five Plays by Langston Hughes*. Bloomington: Indiana University Press, 1–35.

Hurston, Z. N. (1989). *Color Struck*. In Kathy Perkins (ed.), *Black Female Playwrights: An Anthology of Plays Before 1950*. Bloomington: Indiana University Press, 89–102.

——and Hughes, L. (1991). *Mule Bone*. New York: Harper Perennial.

Johnson, G. D. (1989a). *A Sunday Morning in the South*. In Kathy Perkins (ed.), *Black Female Playwrights: An Anthology of Plays Before 1950*. Bloomington: Indiana University Press, 31–7.

——(1989b). *Blue Blood*. In Kathy Perkins (ed.), *Black Female Playwrights: An Anthology of Plays Before 1950*. Bloomington: Indiana University Press, 38–46.

——(1989c). *Blue-Eyed Black Boy*. In Kathy Perkins (ed.), *Black Female Playwrights: An Anthology of Plays Before 1950*. Bloomington: Indiana University Press, 47–51.

——(1989d). *Plumes*. In Kathy Perkins (ed.), *Black Female Playwrights: An Anthology of Plays Before 1950*. Bloomington: Indiana University Press, 24–30.

Krasner, D. (2002). *A Beautiful Pageant: African American Theatre, Drama and Performance in the Harlem Renaissance, 1910–1927*. New York: Palgrave.

Livingston, M. S. (1974). *For Unborn Children*. In James V. Hatch and Ted Shine (eds.), *Black Theatre U.S.A.: Forty-Five Plays by Black Americans, 1847–1974*. New York: Free Press, 184–87.

Locke, A. (ed.) (1992). *The New Negro: Voices of the Harlem Renaissance*. New York: Athenaeum.

McCoo, E. J. (1993). *Ethiopia at the Bar of Justice*. Willis Richardson (ed.), *Plays and Pageants from the Life of the Negro*. Jackson: University Press of Mississippi, 345–73.

Mackay, C. D. (1917). *The Little Theatre in the United States*. New York: Henry Holt.

O'Neill, E. (1940). *All God's Chillun Got Wings*. In *Nine Plays*. New York: Garden City.

——(1995). *Anna Christie/The Emperor Jones/The Hairy Ape*. New York: Vintage.

Perkins, K. and Stephens, J. L. (1998). *Strange Fruit: Plays on Lynching by American Women*. Bloomington: Indiana University Press.

Peterson, B. L., Jr. (1980). "Willis Richardson: Pioneer Playwright." In Errol Hill (ed.), *The Theatre of Black Americans: A Collection of Critical Essays*. New York: Applause, 113–25.

Plum, J. (1995). "Accounting for the Audience in Historical Reconstruction: Martin Jones's Production of Langston Hughes's *Mulatto*." *Theatre Survey* 36, 1 (May): 5–19.

Richardson, W. (1920). *The Deacon's Awakening*. *Crisis* (November): 10–15.

——(ca. 1925). *The Peacock's Feather*. Hatch-Billops Collection, New York.

——(1927). *The Broken Banjo*. In Alain Locke and Montgomery Gregory (eds.), *Plays of Negro Life*. New York: Harper, 301–20.

——(1996). *A Pillar of the Church*. In James V. Hatch and Leo Hamalian (eds.), *Lost Plays of the Harlem Renaissance, 1920–1940*. Detroit: Wayne State University Press, 32–44.

——(1974). *The Idle Head*. In James V. Hatch and Ted Shine (eds.), *Black Theater U.S.A.: Forty-Five Plays by Black Americans, 1847–1974*. New York: Free Press, 234–40.

——(1991). *The Chip Woman's Fortune*. In Leo Hamalian and James V. Hatch (eds.), *The Roots of African American Drama: An Anthology of Early Plays, 1858–1938*. Detroit: Wayne State University Press, 164–85.

——(1992). *Compromise*. In Alain Locke (ed.), *The New Negro: Voices of the Harlem Renaissance*. New York: Athenaeum, 168–95.

——(1993). *Plays and Pageants from the Life of the Negro*. Jackson: University Press of Mississippi.

Sanders, L. C. (1988). *The Development of Black Theater in America: From Shadows to Selves*. Baton Rouge: Louisiana State University Press.

Storm, W. (1993). "Reactions of a 'Highly-Strung Girl': Psychology and Dramatic Representation in Angelina W. Grimké's *Rachel*." *African American Review* 27, 3: 461–71.

Torrence, R. (1917). *Granny Maumee, The Rider of Dreams, Simon the Cyrenian: Three Plays for a Negro Theater*. New York: Macmillan.

8

Reading Across the 1930s

Anne Fletcher

Introduction

Bounded on one end by the stock market crash and on the other by World War II, American drama of the 1930s provided variety in terms of both the form and content. Over 1,500 plays, ranging in temperament from *The Children's Hour* to *You Can't Take It With You*, premiered in New York City between 1930 and 1939, with over 275 plays having runs of more than 100 performances. Producing agencies ranged from the Broadway ad hoc producer to organizations such as the venerated Theatre Guild, the Group Theatre, and the government-funded Federal Theatre Project, with the Theatre Union representing the most leftist perspective. Playwrights Maxwell Anderson, S. N. Behrman, Sidney Howard, Elmer Rice, and Robert Sherwood banded together to produce as the Playwrights' Company. The musical revue, exemplified by George White's *Scandals*, Earl Carroll's *Vanities*, the New Faces series, and the Ziegfeld Follies, still flourished, and Gilbert and Sullivan operettas were the most produced during the decade, with over 50 productions.

Criticism of the period generally takes a binary approach, reducing the dramatic literature to a conflict between the political dramas of the Depression on the one hand, and the ubiquitous drawing room comedies and musical theatre on the other. The decade's economic pattern exhibits the "boom" and "bust" of Marxist thought, but the plays of the period cannot be so neatly categorized.[1] Viewed against events of the decade (especially the Depression and the coming war) and considered through the lens of contemporary criticism, the dramatic literature of the 1930s reverberates with sociopolitical commentary. However, examined with a nod toward twenty-first-century pluralism, many of the plays reinforce unflattering and offensive stereotypes.

Examining which plays ultimately gained entrance into the "dramatic canon" provides insights into the period's social scene. As with most epochs, the topical pieces of the 1930s remain on the periphery, the most politicized pieces are resurrected only when similar sociopolitical conditions arise, and an examination of the lost plays of the period proves as edifying as an exploration of the commonly canonized dramatic literature. In this chapter predominantly plays produced in the New York theatre will be examined. An excursion into the theatre of the "hinterlands" would necessitate including more popular entertainment forms, such as Chautauquas or Toby shows, for example. Playwrights whose careers flourished earlier or later, and who are addressed in other chapters (Eugene O'Neill, for example), are also omitted.

A frequent barometer by which the alleged quality of dramatic literature is measured is an award such as the Pulitzer Prize or the New York Drama Critics' Circle. A quick survey of the decade's Pulitzer Prize-winning plays reveals the fallacy of this kind of measure. In 1935, Zoë Akins's *The Old Maid* won over more enduring plays, such as Clifford Odets's *Awake and Sing* and Lillian Hellman's *The Children's Hour* – a reminder of how awards say as much about awards themselves as they do about recipients. The Pulitzer Prize in drama was established for the purpose of recognizing each year excellence in a play by an American author, preferably original in its source and dealing with "American life." Sometimes an acerbic tongue was rewarded, as in the cases of George S. Kaufman and Morrie Ryskind's *Of Thee I Sing* and Maxwell Anderson's *Both Your Houses*. But it was not until a probing playwright like Lillian Hellman, whose plays hinted at alternative lifestyles, received recognition for her daring efforts that the Pulitzer began to acknowledge challenging dramas.[2] By and large, the Pulitzer Prize, until very recently, has reflected traditional American "values," such as "family traditions." A listing of the Pulitzer Prize winners of the 1930s, interspersed with selected "losers," follows. The so-called losers, as this chapter will demonstrate, emerged as some of the most popular and representative plays of the decade.

Year	*Pulitzer Prize*	*Also produced*
1930	*The Green Pastures* by Marc Connelly	
1931	*Alison's House* by Susan Glaspell	*Elizabeth the Queen* by Maxwell Anderson; *Once in a Lifetime* by George S. Kaufman and Moss Hart
1932	*Of Thee I Sing* by George S. Kaufman, Morrie Ryskind, and Ira Gershwin	*Mourning Becomes Electra* by Eugene O'Neill
1933	*Both Your Houses* by Maxwell Anderson	
1934	*Men in White* by Sidney Kingsley	*Mary of Scotland* by Maxwell Anderson; *Tobacco Road* by Jack Kirkland
1935	*The Old Maid* by Zoë Akins	*The Children's Hour* by Lillian Hellman; *Awake and Sing* by Clifford Odets; *Merrily We Roll Along* by George S. Kaufman and Moss Hart

1936	*Idiot's Delight* by Robert E. Sherwood	*Winterset* by Maxwell Anderson; *Porgy and Bess* by George and Ira Gershwin and DuBose Heyward
1937	*You Can't Take It With You* by Moss Hart and George S. Kaufman	*The Women* by Clare Booth Luce
1938	*Our Town* by Thornton Wilder	*Of Mice and Men* by John Steinbeck; *Golden Boy* by Clifford Odets
1939	*Abe Lincoln in Illinois* by Robert S. Sherwood	*The Little Foxes* by Lillian Hellman; *The Philadelphia Story* by Philip Barry

Playwrights who produced fewer scripts, or were writers by avocation rather than by vocation, provide valuable insights into the cultural apparatus of the decade. Among these may be counted Robert Ardrey, *Thunder Rock* (1939), Albert Bein, *Little Ol' Boy* (1933) and *Let Freedom Ring* (1935), Albert Maltz, *The Black Pit* (1935), George Sklar (with Maltz), *Merry-Go-Round* (1932) and *Peace on Earth* (1933), and John Wexley, *Steel* (1931) and *They Shall Not Die* (1934). Dramatists who offered valuable insights into their cultures and their worlds are Paul and Clare Clifton, Hallie Flanagan and Lucille Clifton, in plays such as *1931* and *Can You Hear Their Voices?* (1931). Others, prolific in their time, are more remembered for non-dramatic accomplishments, such as Sam Spewack (librettist for *Kiss Me Kate*) and Sidney Howard (screenwriter for *Gone With the Wind*). Frequently, "star" actors rather than dramatic merit immortalize plays. Among examples were *Alison's House*, featuring the star Eva Le Gallienne (see chapter 4), *The Old Maid*, in which the lead role was performed by another star, Helen Mencken, and even works by playwrights S. N. Behrman or Robert Sherwood that frequently featured the American acting duo known as the Lunts (Alfred Lunt and Lynn Fontane held the Broadway stage for more than 35 years) can be classified as star vehicles.

The Great Depression no doubt defined the American 1930s. The playwrights analyzed here have been selected based on the manner in which they examined, confronted, or seemingly ignored the cultural milieu of their time. Nevertheless, one obstacle in analyzing American drama of the 1930s stems from the common definition of "drama" that demands a cohesive written script. The most flagrant examples of exclusion due to the privileging of the printed page are the Federal Theatre Project plays such as the "swing" *Mikado*, as well as productions by Orson Welles such as his "voodoo" *Macbeth* and *The Cradle Will Rock*. The 1930s is a decade in which dramatic literature is infused with mixed genres and experimentation. Subtle references to the texts of serious dramas grace the pages of comedies, and technical innovations of political plays appear, especially in the works of George S. Kaufman and S. N. Behrman. Kaufman and Edna Ferber's *Stage Door* (1936) boasts a politically inclined character, replete with "set speeches" (monologues addressed to the audience that advance a political cause). Kaufman and Moss Hart even poke fun at the pedagogical production elements of the Federal Theatre Project in *I'd Rather Be*

Right! While the converse – leftist writers imitating or satirizing mainstream playwrights – is not as frequent, Flanagan and Clifton, for example, mimic the setting and dialogue of the drawing room comedy in the socialite scenes of their *Can You Hear Their Voices?*

Despite the left-wing tendency of several dramatists, as well as their experimentation in form, dramas of the 1930s for the most part reinforce American values. The plays reaffirm a staunch belief in capitalism as the most effective business structure and exhibit a renewed belief in the American Dream that hard work yields success, that the good are rewarded, and that the boy will get the girl in the end. By the end of the decade, through the use of an "historical drama," Robert Sherwood's *Abe Lincoln in Illinois* (1938) reflects the nation's newfound patriotism, and Elmer Rice's *American Landscape* (1938) portrays the contemporary temperament with the inclusion of characters from Americana. The threat of World War II rapidly overshadowed the poverty of the Depression, compelling America's theatrical community to mobilize against a clear-cut enemy – the Nazi regime.

Kaufman and his Collaborators: More than Senior Class Plays

Critics frequently attribute the popularity of comedy to the audience's desire for "escape." This notion of escapism is narrow, since many of the comedies and musical revues of the 1930s emphasized cultural circumstances and Depression-era conditions. Their confrontation with the Depression is sometimes obscured because upper-class characters frequent these plays. The affluent suffer afflictions as well, most pointedly experiencing a general malaise and sense of meaninglessness that is exhibited in a number of Kaufman's characters and in Behrman's works.

Perhaps more so than any other American playwright (notwithstanding the musical comedy teams Rodgers and Hart, and Rodgers and Hammerstein), George S. Kaufman is known as a great collaborator. Famous as part of the Kaufman and Hart team, he also worked with Edna Ferber, Alexander Woollcott, and Morrie Ryskind. Classic farce characters inhabit Kaufman's works, and in his comedies the typical "reunification" model occurs (lovers work out their problems in the end). The comedies end in celebrations, mostly marriages between ingénues and juvenile leads. Kaufman's adroit use of satire and his underlying concern for the human condition are often overlooked. He was also one of the pioneers of simultaneous dialogue in the American theatre, as evidenced earlier in his career by *Beggar on Horseback* (1924, with Marc Connelly). In *Merrily We Roll Along* (1934), the inspiration of Stephen Sondheim's 1981 musical, Kaufman and Hart experimented with time, beginning the plot in the present and moving the dramatic action backwards throughout the subsequent scenes.

Of Thee I Sing bears the distinctions of being the first musical to win the Pulitzer Prize (awarded for the book and lyrics, not the music) and the first to be published and disseminated for sale to the public. Produced in 1932, the play is a lighthearted satire of the American political system, and "safe" political drama for its time, when, despite the Depression, the country had faith in President Franklin Roosevelt. In its lampoon of campaigns and elections, *Of Thee I Sing* cleverly twists American myths and well-known clichés ("Mom's apple pie" becomes muffins, for example). The musical *Let 'Em Eat Cake* (1933) followed, but was a less successful sequel.

Kaufman's social commentary is evident in *Dinner at Eight* (1932) and *Stage Door*. Both plays depict the frivolity of the upper class and the effects of the Depression on out-of-work actors. *You Can't Take It With You* continues to win the hearts of its audiences and captured the Pulitzer Prize. Beneath the farcical surface of this play, described as "Menandrian" owing to its imitation of the ancient Greek comic playwright Menander (Mason 1988: 48), lies a message America required for morale boosting: the character of Grandpa stresses the American icons of rugged individualism, Yankee ingenuity, and freedom of choice. Similarly, Sheridan Whiteside, in *The Man Who Came to Dinner* (1939), despite his crusty veneer, loves Christmas and harkens back to "the larger-than-life heroes of American folklore" as well (Mason 1988: 57). The cynic in us is free to reassess these figures as fictive, while the romantic in us wants to believe these distinctly "American values" to be true. Thus, George S. Kaufman stands as the comic playwright of the decade whose work is less culture-bound and remains playable and remarkably open to reinterpretation, as witnessed by its successful revivals.

Left Out: Lawson and the Political Left

The exclusion of John Howard Lawson from the canon of American dramatic literature is ironic because, in addition to being well produced in the 1920s and 1930s, his textbook, *The Technique of Playwriting*, was utilized in playwriting classes for decades. Lawson's inconsistent performance was the result of his philosophical struggles and his rhetoric. Excoriated by Broadway critics and leftists alike, Lawson continuously tinkered with dramatic form. Throughout the decade he increasingly and stridently supported Communism and his participation as one of the "Hollywood Ten" – marked as a Communist and blacklisted from commercial venues – is well documented. In his realistic play, *Success Story* (1932), the drama concerns the economic rise of Sol Ginsberg from his impoverished beginnings on New York's Lower East Side to the presidency of a prominent advertising firm. Once a radical youth, Ginsberg jettisons his altruism and adopts a cruel capitalist philosophy. He tramples everyone in his path, blackmailing his way to the top and usurping the presidency of the company from a man who showed him kindness when he was young.

Gentlewoman (1934) is similar to *Success Story* in its melodramatic structure and its ideological confusion. It appears to be written in the drawing room mode but underneath the polished veneer resides a teeming class conflict of proletariat heroics versus upward mobility. Lawson asserts that the play "ostensibly tells the story of a love affair between a wealthy woman and a bohemian writer with radical tendencies, but it is really an examination of the nature of personal and political commitment"

Plate 4.   Success Story by John Howard Lawson, original Broadway production, set by Mordecai Gorelik, photo by Vandamm. Courtesy of the Mordecai Gorelik Collection, Morris Library, Southern Illinois University, Carbondale.

(qtd. in Smith 1990: 163–4). The play's protagonist, Gwyn Ballantine, a woman of taste and breeding, remains aloof until Rudy Flannagan (an autobiographical Lawson of sorts) seduces her. Flannagan spouts radical ideology but is, at root, shallow. The dramatic theme is grounded in the class conflict between these two characters. Despite Lawson's textual references to collective farming, breadlines, a radical meeting, stevedores, the farmers' league, and even Gwyn's final speech about walking "towards a red horizon," the play fails to present a clear and coherent ideology. The Marxist insertions are inorganic, shoehorned into the play's seamless realism in a way that Sidney Kingsley's advocacy of socialized medicine in *Men in White* (1933), for example, is not.

Critics reviled Lawson's *The Pure in Heart* (1934) with more justification than *Gentlewoman*. Sam Smiley's interpretation of the play's structure and ideology is generous; he remarks that the events of the play "build to a climactic scene in which the socioeconomic system can be blamed for the error of the individuals." However, even Smiley admits that the characters in *The Pure in Heart* "are unbelievable" (1972: 176), with the implausible plot centering on the rags-to-riches rise of Annabel Sparks, a post-adolescent would-be actress. Lawson takes the theatre as his metaphor for life, with all its falsity. In the space of one short week, Annabel charms her way into the chorus of a

Plate 5.   Dorothy Hall as Annabel Sparks in *The Pure in Heart*, by John Howard Lawson, original
Broadway production. Courtesy of the John Howard Lawson Collection, Morris Library, Southern Illinois
University at Carbondale.

musical; has an affair with its director; climbs into bed with its philandering
producer; is fired; persuades a donor to finance her acting lessons; and gives it all
up because she falls in "love at first sight" with the producer's gangster brother.

   There are similarities in plot between Lawson's plays and Kaufman's or S. N
Behrman's works (the suicidal husband to the "star" in *Merrily We Roll Along*, the

theatrical metaphor of *Stage Door*, and the lovers ripped apart by opposing ideologies in Behrman's *Biography*). Kaufman and Behrman, however, created artfully constructed plays with sociopolitical undertones, while Lawson attempted to inundate his plays with ideological baggage. As a result, Lawson sacrificed dramatic tension for political expediency and failed to achieve sustained success.

Liberalism and Democracy: Behrman and Sherwood

Two important playwrights of the period, S. N. Behrman and Robert Sherwood, demonstrate dramaturgical and thematic consistency. Like Lawson's works of the 1930s, their plays are generally realistic, each employing techniques of melodrama. Unlike Lawson, however, they also endow their dramas with humor and even "hokum." Behrman is most often associated with "high comedy," enjoying comparisons with George Bernard Shaw. However, to dismiss Behrman's work simply as comedy of manners fails to acknowledge his complexity as a playwright, for he is a social commentator *par excellence*. Behrman rejected propaganda plays *per se* as heavy-handed, believing that "enduring playwrights have been neutral" (qtd. in Gross 1992: 9). He focused instead on liberalism, populating his dramas with characters at odds with their origins, confused in their ideologies, and disenchanted with materialism. Behrman may be credited with introducing the Marxist character to the American stage in his creation of Sergei Voloschyn in *Brief Moment* (1931) (see Reed 1975: 57). Several of Behrman's scripts subvert the traditional comic structure of the lovers' conflict before the final curtain. His work is marked by the juxtaposition of comic and tragic elements.

That the American Pulitzer Prize was awarded to Robert Sherwood for *Idiot's Delight* (1936) is somewhat ironic, given that the play is set in Europe, satirizes pre-World War II political beliefs and practices, and is pacifistic (and therefore anti-American) in nature. The play epitomizes Sherwood's use of comic form to convey serious subject matter. (This was also true of *Reunion in Vienna*, ostensibly a farce about deposed royalty, with a Preface that explicates its message.) *Idiot's Delight* illustrates Sherwood's anguish across the decade, as prewar tensions mounted (expressed in his diaries, prefaces, and other personal writing). Set at a chalet in the former Austria, *Idiot's Delight* is peopled with a phony Russian princess who accompanies a distributor of poison gas; an aging vaudeville performer traveling with a troupe of stereotypical showgirls (during the 1930s the "aging vaudevillian character" emerges as an American icon); a pair of English newlyweds; Austrians affected by Italy's takeover; fascist soldiers; and a revolutionary who is eventually executed. There is an Italian air base on the property abutting the chalet. Sherwood deftly juxtaposes song, dance, and frivolous showgirls with the hard realities of war. All the characters are stranded at this location, bombing is imminent, no trains are allowed to depart, and no one is allowed to cross European borders. The play ends with the vaudevillian and the "princess" at the piano, drinking champagne while bombs fall and windows crash; they begin to sing "Onward Christian Soldiers" as the curtain falls. The play is reminiscent of G. B. Shaw's *Major Barbara* and *Heartbreak House*, and anticipates Arthur Miller's grappling with the morality of manufacturing for war in his 1947 play *All My Sons* (see chapter 14).

The Petrified Forest (1935) is perhaps Sherwood's most durable drama; in this play he blends idea and dramatic action within the context of an extended metaphor. The play's protagonist, Alan Squier, wanders into a Western truck stop. There he meets the proprietor's daughter, a young girl who dreams of leaving for France. An idealist, self-described as "part of a vanishing race . . . the intellectuals," Squier decides to leave her the money necessary for the trip. To this end, in a gangster raid on the establishment, he persuades someone to shoot him. The "petrified forest" symbolizes the death of the gentile past, and, as in other Sherwood plays, we observe the symbolic demise of American culture in the guise of the protagonists. Sherwood shifts gears with *Abe Lincoln in Illinois*, though the play is still enriched with moral ambiguity. The play considers the young Abe Lincoln's anguish over potential war, which reflected, and indirectly commented on, Franklin Delano Roosevelt's concerns about the coming world conflict. Sherwood would begin the decade of the 1940s with his justification of war in *There Shall Be No Night*. The hallmark of Sherwood's writing is an innate grasp of the builds and beats required of strong dramaturgy. He insightfully expressed this notion himself, acknowledging that he always began his plays with great ideas, but inevitably ended "merely" with good "entertainment."[3]

Balancing Act: Odets and Socialism

Clifford Odets's *Waiting for Lefty* (1935) falls neatly at the decade's halfway mark and aptly reflects the cultural moment. It is a polemic play advocating workers' rights. However, Odets's realistic "family" dramas are more representative of his corpus. *Awake and Sing* (1935), *Paradise Lost* (1935), *Golden Boy* (1937), *Rocket to the Moon* (1938), and *Night Music* (1940) reflect the despair of the Depression, hope for America's future, and faith in American youth. The playwright's enduring strength lies in his ability to craft New Yorkese dialogue, and create characters concomitant with the beliefs of his audience. Sentimental they may be, but Odets's plays encourage audience identification with protagonists who seek solace from their discouraging economic, social, and political conditions, aspiring to "awake and sing" – individually and collectively. Like Lawson, Odets's characters present contradictory political ideologies. However, in contrast to Lawson, Odets is able to separate his political bewilderment and naiveté from his dramatic form. His plays are dyed-in-the-wool social realism with melodramatic overtones, and include the structural foundations of the nineteenth-century "well-made plays." His plays frequently conclude with a "call to action," the benchmark of Marxist drama, and several incorporate the martyrdom of some characters. However, Odets's failure to support his unalloyed Marxism becomes apparent in his rhetoric, where sometimes his characters send mixed messages. Still, his characters are rooted in their recognizable (often Jewish) urban, lower middle

Plate 6. *Golden Boy*, by Clifford Odets, original Broadway production. Left to right: Frances Farmer (Lorna), Elia Kazan (Joe), Roman Bohnen (Moody), and Art Smith (Tokio). Courtesy of the Mordecai Gorelik Collection, Morris Library, Southern Illinois University, Carbondale.

class, and his plays frequently depict familiar family struggles. Sometimes Odets stretches the plausibility of his verisimilitude; characters appear exaggerated. Yet the poetry of his plays compensates for these shortcomings. We can forgive a son's surprising decision to hand his inheritance over to his mother in *Awake and Sing*. We can overlook the improbability of a youth being equally talented as a violinist and as a boxer in *Golden Boy*; we can accept the likelihood of a couple producing one child with a terminal illness, another who is shot in a botched heist, and yet another who obsessively plays the piano in *Paradise Lost*, all because the characters populating Odets's plays are multifaceted, poetic, and engaging. He creates characters who stand in for their sociopolitical stations in life, depicting them with such definitive passion and lyricism that their inconsistencies can be overlooked. Odets's characters are sympathetic, three-dimensional human beings, warts and all. Of the American playwrights of the 1930s, Odets produced a psychological realism that set a trend in American drama for years to come.

It is somewhat surprising that the most enduring workers' theatre drama of the decade is his *Waiting for Lefty*, given the fact that Odets lacked prior experience in writing propaganda. The story of Odets's personal struggle with commitment, his brief membership in the Communist Party, and its repercussions is well documented (see Himmelstein 1963; Smith 1990). His political ambiguity enabled him to craft a play that retains its inherent dramatic applicability while the more specific proletariat plays of the period fail to rise above the topical. His short drama has pathos and suspense, with "good" versus "evil" characters populating *Waiting for Lefty*. Centering *Waiting for Lefty* on a taxi drivers' strike, Odets applied the most successful conventions of agit-prop to his mosaic, updating the nineteenth-century melodramatic "well-made play" scheme to fit a new century's concerns. He balanced the stories of individuals with the collective spirit of the country in 1935, blending the personal with the political in an original way. *Waiting for Lefty* capitalized on the communal spirit and left-wing politics of the Depression era, offering an emotional outlet for audiences hungry for "relevant" theatre. The play transitions smoothly from vignette to vignette in a manner Odets claims to have derived from the distinctly American form of popular entertainment, the minstrel show (see Miller 1991: 82). *Waiting for Lefty* is also specifically American in its focus on the middle class and their fears during the economic crisis. Harold Cantor goes so far as to dub Clifford Odets a "middle-class poetic playwright" (2000: 10). The combination of *Waiting for Lefty*'s lyricism, political commitment, eccentric personalities, hybrid dramatic structure, forceful emotions, and representation of the era's politics justifies the play's recognition as an enduring American drama.

Social, political, and personal indecision, confusion, or sheer helplessness comprised America's zeitgeist of the 1930s. Clifford Odets's works reflected the ambiguity of the nation. This successful playwright of the 1930s never won a Pulitzer Prize and failed to produce another play after *The Flowering Peach* (1954). Odets's playwriting career was more of a trajectory than a crest. He rode the wave of the Depression into the Popular Front (the broad social movement that advanced progressive causes), but he beached abruptly. At the time of his death in 1963, Clifford Odets was hailed as a "writer of promise," proof that his rise to prominence had perhaps too neatly coincided with the decade of the 1930s.

Backwards and Forwards: Rice and Hellman

Remembered most as an American expressionist for the plays *The Adding Machine* (1923) and *The Subway* (1929), or photographic naturalism in *Street Scene* (1929), Elmer Rice serves as the surprising "poster child" for the dramaturgy of the 1930s. The epitome of the politically engaged playwright, Rice is perhaps the decade's most flagrant example of the writer in search of a medium for his message. His playwriting career spanned an astonishing half-century, from *On Trial* in 1914 to *Court of Last Resort* in 1965.

As the Depression worsened, the efficacy of democracy was questioned, and Rice explored the consequences of its potential demise. Like Behrman, Elmer Rice was influenced by George Bernard Shaw. He challenged the evils of American capitalism and the frailty of the American judicial system. Like several other playwrights, he visited the textile mills of North Carolina and the Soviet Union to fuel his political intent. An activist, a champion of the underdog, and a moralist, Rice advocated William Foster's radical political campaign in 1932, provided financial support for the Theatre Union, financed productions of his own polemic dramas, and resigned from the Federal Theatre Project as a result of the 1936 political crisis, culminating in the Ethiopia debacle. While his plays of the decade have their shortcomings, they are interesting examples of the era's attendant social problems.

Rice's *We, the People* (1933), *Judgment Day* (1934), *Between Two Worlds* (1934), and *American Landscape* (1938) trace the sociopolitical issues of the decade. Although *We, the People* predates Clifford Odets's political works, it is similar in its depiction of the consequences of the Depression on honest working-class Americans. In this play, Rice operates in a realistic vein and melodramatic framework. The Davis family, with its patriarch a successful factory foreman and its children educated, represents the middle class. Jobs are lost, educations truncated, and the bank in which the family's savings account is held goes "bust." The Collins family exemplifies the Midwestern farmers, drawn to drink or compelled to escape. The doomed romance between Helen Davis and Bert Collins unites the families and portrays the fallen dreams of many American couples of the Depression forced to postpone marriage or seek abortions because of financial dilemma. Unfortunately, as with most of Rice's plays of the decade, he overstates his case and utilizes melodramatic conventions. *Judgment Day*, for instance, dramatizes the Reichstag Trial and displays many of the same problems as Rice's other didactic works, such as turgid structure and employing mechanical devices that include the testimony of a tearful child, melodramatic curtain endings, coincidence, and the play's static court documentation, leading one to believe that the play is perhaps better read than staged. *Between Two Worlds* is another heavy-handed allegory that focuses on the conflict between the "old" and "new" world orders. Set on an ocean liner, the play chronicles the unlikely romance between a Russian director and a young American woman. With *American Landscape*, crafted as fantasy, Rice paints an exceedingly broad landscape. Historical personages (Harriet Beecher Stowe, for example) mingle with family members as the shoe factory owner contemplates selling out to big business. One daughter unites with a union representative to save the factory, while the other daughter's husband quits a lucrative position as a Hollywood writer to return to home and hearth. Rice characteristically mixes melodrama with fiery exhortative speeches, resulting in audience confusion. Still, the play exemplifies the end of the decade's economic shifts, fear of war, and national pride. Rice would never regain the dramatic stride he exhibited in the 1920s. His plays of the 1930s, however, merit reassessment as records of the cultural moment, typifying the politically committed artist's plight. Divergent in dramatic form, his plays share a deep concern for American life. Moralistic in tone, Rice's polemic dramas illustrate his sense of justice and, in fact, his patriotism.

Lillian Hellman shared Rice's burgeoning mid-decade political commitment. While she hardly fits the profile typifying leftist political writer, her 1930s plays address socioeconomic concerns. For instance, her play *Days to Come* (1936) is, in Christopher Bigsby's words, "Hellman's strike play" (1982: 277). It is a problematic drama that careens out of control in its attempt to manage too many subplots. *Days to Come* is derivative of Odets. Like Odets, Hellman generalizes the themes of the Depression, but unlike Odets her play is stilted and didactic. However, Hellman emerges with her own voice in her play *The Little Foxes* (1939) (along with her other plays, *The Autumn Garden* and *The Watch on the Rhine*), which assails the evils of wealth and the power of capitalism. It is with these political plays couched as family dramas that Hellman secures her place in American dramatic literature. *The Little Foxes* focuses on personal greed. However, she did not conceive the play as centered on the class issue, as many 1930s plays did, nor did she intend the family in the play, the Hubbards, to be taken altogether seriously. Although Hellman consciously employed the conventional dramaturgical structure and utilized elements of melodrama, she considered herself to be writing, in her words, a "dramatic comedy" (*New York Sun*, December 16, 1949, qtd. in Lederer 1979: 39).

The Little Foxes (the title of the play is taken from the Song of Solomon 2: 15) displays the tactics of siblings trying to outwit each other in a moneymaking scheme. Regina, the play's "villain," thinks nothing of withholding her husband's heart medicine and watching him struggle to reach for it, fall, and die. Her nephew, a lower-level bank employee, steals Regina's husband's investment bonds and gives them to her brothers to invest in the cotton mill, "cutting her out." Regina and her brother Ben make a sport of "out-foxing" each other, as their dimwitted brother, Oscar, plays straight man to their antics.

While *The Little Foxes* is often produced, Hellman's *The Children's Hour*, with its lesbianism and its focus on the damage a rumor can cause, is perhaps Hellman's best-known play. It, too, follows the well-made play convention, with a clear beginning, middle, and end, and a bracelet as the play's "clue." Mary, a boarding school student, accuses her teachers of lesbianism and blackmails her friend. She tells her grand-mother of her suspicions, and all the girls' parents withdraw their children from school, leaving Karen and Martha, the two teachers, to face the consequences. In light of the accusations, Karen's fiancé questions her sexual preferences. She releases him from their bond, and Martha, uncertain now of her sexual orientation, commits suicide. The typical well-made play's *scène à faire*, with the grandmother appearing to recant, is clichéd and somewhat outdated. Still, *The Children's Hour* sustains audience interest, retaining its topical relevance throughout the century.

Feminism and the 1930s: *The Women*

As the political issues of women's rights came to the forefront, Lillian Hellman towers above the other female dramatists of the decade.[4] However, Hellman avoided the categorization of either "female" or "Southern" playwright. As the feminist movement progressed, Hellman focused on women's rights as related to economics, saying: "I think it all comes down to whether you can support yourself as well as a man can" (qtd. in Horn 1998: 19). In contrast to Hellman and despite her social upbringing, Clare Booth Luce became a champion of the women's movement. Best known for her play *The Women* (1936, although she penned at least 18 other plays), the wealthy Luce was a prominent Republican, was named ambassador to two countries, and became a television personality, appearing on shows hosted by conservative social critic William F. Buckley. Her wit and caustic tongue were evident in her interviews as well as in her dramas.

   The Women tells the tale of adultery on the Upper West Side of New York City in the 1930s. While Luce claimed this story of money, manicurists, massages, haute couture, divorces in Reno, and "cat fights" was intended to criticize a small strata of American society, it was also meant to satirize the rich. The unflattering depictions of women made the play fair fodder for the feminist cause. Luce was a writer who took risks – in style and in subject matter, satirizing her own social class – but her plays of the 1930s were misunderstood. In *Kiss the Boys Good-bye* (1938), for example, set in an elite Connecticut residence, Luce utilizes the circuitous and charming tactics of the typical Southern belle to stand in for fascism. Her "political subtext" in this and other plays went largely unnoticed by playgoers and critics (Fearnow 1997: 72). Unfortu-nately, apart from *The Women*, Luce's dramatic writings are largely ignored. After the 1930s, she turned her attention to politics.

Anomaly of the Decade: Anderson's Poetic Dramas

The dramatist Maxwell Anderson argued passionately for the efficacy of the poetic drama and the legitimacy of the historical drama as a window into contemporary events. Nonetheless, it was for *Both Your Houses* (1933), a prose political lampoon, that he won the Pulitzer Prize. *Elizabeth the Queen* (1930) and *Mary of Scotland* (1933) are often revived but are not frequently examined for their relevance to the milieu of the 1930s. They are pertinent to a discussion of the decade, though, as are his *Valley Forge* (1934) and *Feast of Ortolans* (1937), for Anderson continually critiqued the contemporary forces of economics and politics within a historical framework. Like so many others, he ended the decade defending democracy. Gerald Rabkin believes that Anderson utilized "history as myth" and moved across the decade to employ "history as prophecy" (1964: 277). In *Winterset* (1935), Anderson's second response to the still fairly recent Sacco–Vanzetti case, the playwright's poetry, theory of tragedy, and ideas coalesce. *Winterset* stands apart from the "docudramas" in that, like Anderson's period dramas, it is a poetic interpretation of past events.

Because of his refusal to trust any ideology, the term "anarchist" is often used to describe Anderson. Anderson also considered the paradox of a pessimistic outlook (that action is futile) with the significance of commitment. His vast knowledge of history and philosophy was often an obstacle to his writing; he labored to create tragedies that complied with his ideals and conformed to particular philosophies, cluttering his plays with ideological baggage. Still, he was likely the most literary of the decade's playwrights, and his legacy will remain intact owing to his verse plays on British royalty.

American Myths: *Tobacco Road* and *Our Town*

Consideration of Jack Kirkland's play *Tobacco Road* (1934, based on the novel by Erskine Caldwell, a landmark drama of American theatre) generally divides along two lines. Some praise the script's documentary tone, considering it an almost naturalistic depiction of Southern poverty in the Depression; others find the play offensive for perpetuating Southern stereotypes. Some even consider the play's grotesque elements and its comedic bent (Fearnow 1997). The drama, somewhat clichéd by current standards, tells the tale of the effects of the Depression on a dysfunctional "Georgia cracker" family, the Lesters. The father, Jeeter, seems to have avoided working a "lick" in his life. The son, Dude, has no respect for his parents and willingly marries a self-proclaimed "preacher woman" in order to obtain a car. One daughter, Pearl, is married but refuses to let her husband touch her; her husband, in turn, pets her hair-lipped sister in view of the entire family. The mother, who has borne 17 children, announces that Pearl, her favorite, is the product of an affair. "Grandmother Lester" is beaten, taunted, and abused by the rest of the family. Jeeter learns that a bank will soon foreclose on the property and he will be forced to leave. He decides to force Pearl to return to her husband, who in turn will pay him a weekly wage and thus secure his home. A struggle ensues, Pearl runs away, and Dude, who has proven himself an unfit driver with several incidents recounted throughout the play, runs over his own mother.

Plate 7. *Tobacco Road*, by Jack Kirkland (adapted from the book by Erskine Caldwell), directed by Blair E. Beasley, Jr., Winthrop University. Courtesy of Anne Fletcher.

Incredibly popular in its initial run and tour, followed by a successful film version, *Tobacco Road* expresses the tensions of the decade. In its open display of seething sexuality, the play is shocking, while in its exaggeration of sex (as evidenced by the family comically trying to reach the window to peer in on Dude's conjugal sex) the play suggests a farce. However, the violence, cruelty, selfishness, and poverty forced upon its characters take the play into the realm of the socially conscious – the kind of play that can assuage its well-to-do audience of "survivor guilt" during the

Depression. The combination of genres in the drama – comic, tragic, social commentary – explains its broad appeal while also creating uncomfortable stereotypes to later generations.

Criticism of Thornton Wilder's *Our Town* (1938), likewise *Tobacco Road*, divides along several lines of thought: praise of Wilder for his spiritual optimism, his ability to make us recall universal truths, and his minimalist stage conventions; condemnation of his insensitivity toward those marginalized by race, ethnicity, gender, or religion; and misinterpretation of the play as intentionally nostalgic in its ability to make us yearn for traditional "American values." The first evaluation comes closest to Wilder's intentions (published in his letters and essays on dramaturgy). The second inspired the late twentieth-century avant-garde production company the Wooster Group to produce the play in 1981, underscoring its prejudices. The last evaluation is perhaps the most prevalent. Scholars, theatre critics, and even notable playwright Arthur Miller and critic Harold Clurman find the play overly sentimental (Bunge 1999: 353). Others, like playwright Lanford Wilson, find Wilder cynical (ibid., 349). Nancy Bunge offers an alternative reading, one that emphasizes the rigidity of the characters in the play, their refusal to take risks, and their desire to do little more than remain in Grover's Corners, the location of the play. She remarks that the parents of the village and their negative comments to their children fail to foster independence and self-confidence. Like *The Long Christmas Dinner* (1931) and *The Happy Journey from Camden to Trenton* (1931) before it, *Our Town* is deceptive in its apparent simplicity. Although it contains rituals and rites of passage, *Our Town* is not inherently religious; the play, in fact, can be viewed as spiritual similar to Japanese Noh plays (see Londraville 1999).

Utilizing pantomime and other theatrical conventions, *Our Town* depicts everyday activities in Grover's Corners, New Hampshire, following the dawn of the twentieth century. It is divided into three acts, entitled "Daily Routine," "Love and Marriage," and "Death," tracing the life rhythms of the townspeople. Time and space are malleable in the world of the play, and Wilder deliberately exaggerates the small New Hampshire village as a representation of universal context. Still, the daily activities observed in Act 1 take on vital importance in retrospect as the protagonist, Emily, returns from the dead to relive one day. While Wilder might be said to have a tragic vision, his best-known character, the Stage Manager who serves as a kind of narrator, affirms, "Something is eternal." Emily asks the rhetorical question, "Do any human beings ever realize life while they live it – every, every minute?" Given the arduous decade of the 1930s, *Our Town* balances faith with existential alienation, and enjoins us to remain alive in the moment and to practice mindfulness of others.

Docudramas of the 1930s: Stormbirds of the Working Class

Polemical plays, most especially those of the 1930s, must be evaluated cautiously regarding their efficacy. Their topicality prevents most didactic plays from enduring, thereby obstructing their entrance into the dramatic canon. However, read against other artifacts and events of the decade, they are intriguing. *Waiting for Lefty*, discussed earlier, is the most produced and most frequently anthologized because of its generality and its humanity. A number of other protest plays were written on the heels of the initial Scottsboro trials, where nine African Americans were falsely accused of raping two white women aboard an Alabama train. Among them were Langston Hughes's *Scottsboro Limited* (1931), John Wexley's *They Shall Not Die* (1934), and Denis Donoghue's melodrama *Legal Murder* (1934). The German-speaking workers' theatre, the Prolet-Bühne, staged a mass recitation treatment of the case called, simply, *Scottsboro*. Of these plays, only *They Shall Not Die* and *Legal Murder* (both cast in the mode of social realism/melodrama) appeared on Broadway. All of them consider the "real-life" incident and depict Communism as a panacea for the economic strife of the Depression. Hughes's poetic version is imbued with blues idioms, extending itself beyond the theatrical crudity of the Prolet-Bühne's stylized presentation. Wexley's drama is realistic in form, but his rhetoric echoes the stridency of *Scottsboro* and the symbolic *Scottsboro Limited*. His protagonist employs the "set speeches" common to many propaganda plays, emphasized by the title lines at the play's conclusion. All of the Scottsboro plays incorporate the characteristic "call to action" and martyrdom that appear in many Marxist-based political dramas of the 1930s.

Michael Denning's book *The Cultural Front* (1997) examines the rise of the Congress of Industrial Organizations (CIO) with the state of the arts across the 1930s. His assertions about the period are applicable to an analysis of many of the plays dealing with conflicts between workers and "management." The Theatre Union selected its scripts based almost exclusively on their potential relevance to working-class audiences. In addition, they launched a group sale drive commensurate with this selection process. Dockworkers, textile workers, coal miners, steelworkers, and automotive workers provided the subject matter of the plays. For instance, Paul Peters and George Sklar's *Stevedore* (1934) takes as its inspiration the circumstances of black dockworkers in New Orleans. The script, though melodramatic, is built on socialist realism, meeting the demands of Marxist dramaturgy through its deployment of the martyrdom of the protagonist and the "call to action" of its final scene. But it also follows a "folk" tradition of quotidian language and clichés, and in doing so, Peters and Sklar's dialogue inadvertently promotes African American stereotypic dialect. Nevertheless, the original production was lauded for its realistic illustration of New Orleans life. Like many left-wing writers of the 1930s, Peters immersed himself in the workers' milieu. Witnessing an incident of racism in a textile mill influenced his writing of *Stevedore*.

Socialist politics and theatre intermingled during the decade, not the least of which was due to the Depression. The burgeoning workers' theatre movement boasted some 400 theatre companies by mid-decade. The 1929 Gastonia, North Carolina, textile workers' strike became the subject of several workers' theatre plays of the 1930s. Textile workers were foregrounded in a number of plays, including Albert Bein's *Let*

Freedom Ring (1935), depicting the forced migration of North Carolina mountain people to the textile mill in town. Structured as social realism, within a melodramatic frame, Bein provides a graphic illustration of the environment and its effect on one particular family. Albert Maltz's *Black Pit* (1935) is arranged similarly and illustrates the plight of the coal miner. He creates in the worker/management conflict a unique twist when he portrays a "scab" as his sympathetic protagonist. John Wexley's *Steel* (1931, revived in 1937), the first play staged by the International Ladies Garment Workers Union's Labor Stage, focuses on organizing effects among steelworkers. Its production neatly coincides with "real-life" union organizing in western Pennsylvania (see Hyman 1997: 93).

Taking its title from a strike song and centered on a sit-down strike at an automotive plant, John Howard Lawson's *Marching Song* (1937) is the playwright's last attempt to mix ideology with dramaturgy. The play employs a collective as its protagonist follows the typical Marxist path from indecision and fear to political commitment and martyrdom. *Marching Song* typifies the workers' theatre qualities of militancy and victimization.

Approaching War: *The Time of Your Life*

William Saroyan's *The Time of Your Life* (1939) was emblematic of prewar America.[5] It was awarded both the Pulitzer Prize and the New York Drama Critics' Circle Award in 1940. However, Saroyan refused the monetary award because he believed art and capitalism should remain separate. The drama combines the detachment of comedy and the engagement of tragedy through the inhabitants of a honky-tonk bar in San Francisco. The pivotal character is Joe, a benevolent fixture at the bar and a *raisonneur* of sorts, who can also be interpreted as a Christ figure. While the drama moves chronologically in time, with the arc of the play concerning Joe, the story frequently veers off in multiple directions, revealing the dreams of its other individual characters. Saroyan's theme of life (and work) and the way in which his characters respond to this theme are reminiscent of the Russian dramatist Anton Chekhov's lyricism. It is also reminiscent of Chekhov in its ability to undercut sentimentality with humor. Still, *The Time of Your Life* is decidedly American in its ambiance and focus. Saroyan prefaced his play with an explicit "Credo," providing detailed stage directions that confirm his deliberate use of American myth, and incorporating lines that allude to the Great Depression and impending war. The play simultaneously exalts and critiques American myths and values: Joe is independently wealthy but reveals he made his money at the expense of others. Willie, who plays pinball incessantly, delivers a key speech about the American work ethic, and the pinball machine itself symbolizes America's "strike it rich" mentality. A Kit Carson figure blends fact and fiction, culminating in his narration of how he murdered the fascist figure, Blick. Tom and Kitty, the prostitute, play out the latter's fantasy of growing up to marry a doctor. All the while Saroyan's optimism, derived from his unabashed success in the

1930s, permeates the play, resulting in a work of depth and texture that remains open to interpretation.

Conclusion

The dramatic literature of the 1930s reached an apex mid-decade that paralleled world politics and economics. However, over time agit-prop dramas dwindled, owing to socialist realism's obsolescence as a dramatic form. At the close of the decade, with the threat of war, any drama that defended the country against outside threats became accepted. The 1930s rarely fulfilled the American theatregoing public's desire for "character" over propaganda. The caricatures of the polemic dramas failed to endure, and the collective protagonists of the workers' theatre dramas, while they played on the audience's predictable emotional response, avoided the American spirit of individuality and the need for plot-driven dramas. Americans could rally around the political left and even embrace Communism only while damage to their economic foundation seemed irreparable and only, if under these circumstances, they could still adhere to myths of pursuing the "American Dream." Many of the dramas of the 1930s, even the comedies, became quaint in their depiction of altruism over private desire. Viewed in retrospect, the plays of the 1930s reveal much about the decade often referred to as "turbulent" and about enduring "American values" as they are interrogated and reinterpreted by playwrights across the decade.

NOTES

1. Malcolm Himmelstein's *Drama was a Weapon* (1963), for example – long considered a seminal work in the field of 1930s political drama – exaggerates the efficacy of the theatre as a vehicle for social change and exhibits a rampant paranoia regarding the Communist Party.
2. The New York Drama Critics' Circle was formed because Pulitzer committee members refused to attend *The Children's Hour* (Lederer 1979: 23).
3. Sherwood made this self-deprecating remark to a journalist from the *Herald Tribune*. It has

been quoted in Brown (1962) and in Fearnow (1997: 62).
4. Apart from Hellman and Clare Booth Luce, Rachel Crothers, and Sophie Treadwell, whose works were more prominent in the 1920s, none of the *more than a hundred female playwrights* produced in the 1930s resurfaces for academic or production purposes.
5. The play takes its inspiration from Ecclesiastes.

BIBLIOGRAPHY

Balakian, N. (1998). *The World of William Saroyan*. Cranbury, NJ: Associated University Presses.

Bigsby, C. W. E. (1982). *A Critical Introduction to Twentieth-Century American Drama, Volume 1: 1900–1940*. New York: Cambridge University Press.

Brown, J. M. (1962). *The Worlds of Robert Sherwood: Mirror to His Times, 1896–1939*. New York: Harper and Row.

Bunge, N. (1999). "The Social Realism of *Our Town*: A Study in Misunderstanding." In Martin Joseph Blank, Dalma Hunyadi Brunauer, and David Garrett Izzo (eds.), *Thornton Wilder: New Essays*. West Cornwall, CT: Locust Hill Press, 349–64.

Cantor, H. (2000). *Clifford Odets: Playwright-Poet*. Lanham, MD: Scarecrow Press.

Demastes, W. W. (1996). *Realism and the American Dramatic Tradition*. Tuscaloosa: University of Alabama Press.

Denning, M. (1997). *The Cultural Front*. New York: Verso.

Duffy, S. (1992). *The Political Left in the American Theatre of the 1930s: A Bibliographic Sourcebook*. Metuchen, NJ: Scarecrow Press.

——(1996). *American Labor On Stage: Dramatic Interpretations of the Steel and Textile Industries in the 1930s*. Westport, CT: Greenwood.

Fearnow, M. (1995). *Clare Boothe Luce: A Research and Production Sourcebook*. Westport, CT: Greenwood.

——(1997). *The American Stage and the Great Depression*. New York: Cambridge University Press.

Goldstein, M. (1974). *The Political Stage: American Drama and Theatre in the Great Depression*. New York: Oxford University Press.

Gross, R. F. (1992). *S. N. Behrman: A Research and Production Sourcebook*. Westport, CT: Greenwood.

Himmelstein, M. (1963). *Drama was a Weapon: The Left-Wing Theatre in New York, 1929–1941*. New Brunswick, NJ: Rutgers University Press.

Horn, B. L. (1998). *Lillian Hellman: A Research and Production Sourcebook*. Westport, CT: Greenwood.

Hyman, C. A. (1997). *Staging Strikes: Workers' Theatre and the American Labor Movement*. Philadelphia: Temple University Press.

Keyishian, H. (1995). *Critical Essays on William Saroyan*. New York: G. K. Hall.

Lederer, K. (1979). *Lillian Hellman*. Boston: Twayne.

Londraville, R. (1999). "*Our Town*: An American Noh of the Ghosts." In Martin Joseph Blank, Dalma Hunyadi Brunauer, and David Garrett Izzo (eds.), *Thornton Wilder: New Essays*. West Cornwall, CT: Locust Hill Press, 365–78.

Mason, J. D. (1988). *Wise-Cracks: The Farces of George S. Kaufman*. Ann Arbor: UMI Research Press.

Meserve, W. J. (1970). *Robert E. Sherwood: Reluctant Moralist*. New York: Pegasus.

Miller, G. (ed.) (1991). *Critical Essays on Clifford Odets*. Boston: G. K. Hall.

Miller, J. Y. and Frazer, W. L. (1991). *American Drama Between the Wars: A Critical History*. Boston: Twayne.

Palmieri, A. F. R. (1980). *Elmer Rice: A Playwright's Vision of America*. Cranbury, NJ: Associated University Presses.

Rabkin, G. (1964). *Drama and Commitment: Politics in the American Theatre of the Thirties*. Bloomington: Indiana University Press.

Reed, K. T. (1975). *S. N Behrman*. Boston: Twayne.

Smiley, S. (1972). *The Drama of Attack: Didactic Plays of the American Depression*. Columbia, MO: University of Missouri Press.

Smith, W. (1990). *Real Life Drama: The Group Theatre and America, 1931–1940*. New York: Alfred A. Knopf.

Williams, J. (1974). *Stage Left*. New York: Charles Scribner's Sons.

9
Famous Unknowns:
The Dramas of Djuna Barnes
and Gertrude Stein

Sarah Bay-Cheng

I am the most famous unknown of the century!
                    Djuna Barnes, letter to Natalie Barney (May 31, 1963)

I always wanted to be historical . . .
                    Gertrude Stein, "A Message from Gertrude Stein" (1946)

When Djuna Barnes complained to Natalie Barney that she was "the most famous unknown of the century," she expressed not only regret at the lack of critical attention to her work, but also the central paradox of her dramatic writing. While Barnes craved the critical and popular attention of her male modernist contemporaries, such as T. S. Eliot and James Joyce, she was also an intensely private person who talked little about her life in general and even less about her unorthodox childhood. Yet, throughout her writing, her plays in particular, Barnes frequently draws from her life experience. Her parody of the expatriate lesbian community in Paris, *Ladies Almanack* (1928), is based directly on Barnes's circle of friends. Both of her major novels, *Ryder* (1928) and *Nightwood* (1936), are loosely based on different periods from her life. The first is an anguished portrayal of her family, and the second a deeply personal, though stylistically dense, rendering of her eight-year relationship with fellow expatriate and artist Thelma Wood. Though written in a highly abstruse style, *Nightwood* was clear enough for Wood to "hit Barnes in the mouth, knock her down twice, and throw a cup of tea at her when the novel was read aloud" (Herring 1995: 165).

Indeed, so visible appears the source material for much of Barnes's writing that her biographers have repeatedly turned to her fiction and drama for evidence of the events in her life. One central event biographers often attempt to unveil, and one that recurs throughout her writing, is the traumatic, perhaps violent, loss of Djuna Barnes's virginity. Djuna Barnes's father, Wald Barnes, was an avowed polygamist who lived with his legal wife and Djuna's mother and his mistress, as well as both women's respective children. His advocacy of sexual freedom extended to his daughter as well. One biographer suggests two possible scenarios regarding Djuna Barnes's violation: that her father raped her, which she allegedly told George Barker; or that he conspired to have "an Englishman three times her age" rape her (Herring 1995: 53). Both accounts of the event in Herring's study come from second-hand sources. Importantly, however, Herring favors the latter story, in part because that is the scene vividly recounted in Barnes's *The Antiphon*.

While critics have rightly warned against reading Barnes's work as exclusively autobiographical, the weight of her own history is inescapable in her drama, particularly the themes of familial abuse and sexual violence. Though hardly memory plays, Barnes's drama constantly looks to the past, using archaic language and classical form to render events that seem to be based on her own history. Barnes presents the actions of her plays as one remembers the past, frequently inverting narrative time, so that events unfold in reverse, with the effect visible before its cause. Action in the plays is limited; characters do little more than talk and they are most often contained (sometimes trapped) in a single room. Barnes thus creates highly volatile, intimate dramas in which the only action is interpersonal conflict that cannot be resolved. But while biography dominates the subject matter for her plays, Barnes is clearly ambivalent about its theatrical portrayal. She published only one of her three full-length plays (all of them about highly dysfunctional families) and while she wrote over a dozen plays with the Provincetown Players between 1916 and 1923, her last and best play, *The Antiphon*, was not published until 1958, more than 20 years after her second (unpublished) full-length play, *Biography of Julie von Bartmann* (1924).

Furthermore, the language of Barnes's drama appears to obscure the plot and characters intentionally. Unlike Gertrude Stein, whose experiments with avant-garde drama steadily became clearer, Barnes's dramatic writing became consistently more convoluted and archaic. Critics of *The Antiphon* have interpreted the dense style of Barnes's language in this play as an attempt to reveal and disguise the disturbing events of her past simultaneously. As Louis F. Kannenstine rightly observes of *The Antiphon*, "the language surely stands as a barrier to ready comprehension of much of the play's action and motives" (1977: 141). But if Barnes was so uneasy about the theatrical portrayal of events from her past, why did she consistently feature them in her drama, and why did she devote so much time to this endeavor in her final play?

One possible explanation is that Barnes wrote closet drama, plays intended for a solitary and sophisticated reader rather than a viewing public. The modernist writers, many of whom followed in the tradition of the romantic poets (fancying themselves disciples of Shakespeare), wrote numerous plays, only a handful of which were ever staged. Indeed, such dramas are, in the words of Arnold P. Hinchliffe, "verbally indulgent...dramatic poems rather than drama (1977: 127). In a closet drama written for a lone reader, rather than a mass audience, the personal events of Barnes's play would be protected from the scrutiny of the public. In his study of modernist drama, Martin Puchner argues quite convincingly that modernist drama was in fact anti-theatrical, precisely because it resisted public performance (2002: 11). Djuna Barnes, who wrote that she liked her "human experience served up with a little Silence and Restraint" (1931: 34), might very well have shared this modernist anti-theatricalism. Yet Barnes was associated with the American theatre for nearly her entire career. Her career in journalism covered numerous interviews with popular theatre figures, including Lillian Russell, David Belasco, and Rachel Crothers, and she wrote regular theatre and film reviews. She was a member of the Provincetown Players, with whom she wrote a dozen short plays and produced three: *Three from the Earth* (1919), *Kurzy of the Sea* (1920), and *An Irish Triangle* (1920). While in Paris during the 1920s, Barnes not only became acquainted with the city's numerous literary salons, she also regularly attended the theatre and wrote two full-length plays (both unpublished), *Ann Portuguise* (1920) and *Biography of Julie von Bartmann* (1924). When she returned to the United States in 1929, she worked as a regular columnist for *Theater Guild Magazine*, publishing dozens of articles and reviews between 1929 and 1931.

Rather than casting Barnes as a closet dramatist, it seems more likely that Barnes wrote with theatrical ambivalence. Alternately enthralled and terrified by public performance, Barnes wrote drama that both confuses and compels its audience. Startling acts of violence punctuate otherwise verbose plays, but she derives dramatic power precisely from this contrast. This ambivalence of theatrical viewing lies at the heart of Barnes's drama and informs her most significant dramatic choices. The negotiation between the private and the public – the solitary experience and public displays – ultimately universalizes the content of her plays. Although Barnes seems to have written from her own experience, her plays are neither self-indulgent nor narcissistic. Instead, Barnes uses the motifs of familial betrayal and sexual violence to articulate the broader concerns of a modern era, characterized by a loss of religious faith and moral certitude and traumatized by the technological devastation of two World Wars.

In her attempt to articulate the radical shift of modernity, Barnes not only creates tension between the private and the public, she also repeatedly brings the past into conflict with the present. From the beginning, Barnes's plays present scenarios in which the characters seem preoccupied with the past. Central characters frequently reminisce about the past, or attempt to resolve past conflict. In one of her most striking examples of historical obsession, Barnes's *Madame Collects Herself* (1918) depicts Madame Zolbo, who remembers past lovers (and literally re-members herself) by grafting parts of them onto her own body. As a character, Zolbo both embodies and criticizes the theatre, as she enacts her past in public performance by grafting various pieces from real people (her biography) onto her body. The creation of a female character enhanced by male parts, and set in a male-owned place of feminine refinement, a beauty salon, indicates not only Barnes's awareness of the delicate line between private creation and public performance, but also that this division frequently cuts through a female body.

The performance of the female body is a frequent motif throughout Barnes's dramas, often presenting women as self-consciously theatrical. Her protagonists are quite consciously the object of a gaze, both from the characters in the plays and from the audience. Moreover, the more comfortable women seem to be with their visibility, the more they are punished. In *Three from the Earth*, for example, the central character Kate is described as dressed "in a rather seductive fashion" with "an air of one used to adulation and the pleasure of exerting her will" (Barnes 1995b [1919]: 70) and is clearly meant to be viewed. The play opens with the arrival of three brothers (those from the earth, or the soil), who have come to claim the love letters sent by their father to Kate, his former mistress. However, when asked why they have arrived, they first answer, "we wanted to see how you walked, and sat down, and crossed your legs" (72). Indeed, both women mentioned in the play – Kate and the sons' deceased mother – have theatrical pasts. The mother is described as a prostitute who "was on the stage – she danced as they say, and she sang" (74), while Kate's theatrical experience is remembered (and visualized) through a photograph of amateur performance as the Madonna in "Crown of Thorns." In an ironic twist, Barnes thus casts the prostitute as mother, while the seductive adulteress plays the Madonna.

The play opens just as Kate is preparing to marry a Supreme Court judge, a union that will presumably give her legal and financial legitimacy. But before she can escape to her new life, she is confronted violently by her past. Although she surrenders the letters and the theatrical photograph, the sons are dissatisfied. In the closing moments of the play, the eldest son attacks Kate, kissing her on the mouth. When she protests: "Not that way! Not that way!" the second son James replies, "That's the way you bore him!" and the curtain falls (80). This final burst of violence not only offers the only real action in the play, it also raises the question of Kate's identity. Is she the mother of the sons, or have they simply recast her in the moment of attack? Joan Retallack has criticized these early plays both for their lack of dramatic action and their ambiguity. "The plays begin and end with the characters locked and isolated in little mysteries that fail to fascinate us" (1991: 48). But it is not the "little mysteries" that Barnes dramatizes. Rather, she is deeply aware of the tension of feminine performance and the threat of the past. Nothing appears to happen in *Three from the Earth* because Kate cannot rightly *do* anything. She is there to be looked at and to perform, but not to act. She has little control over how she will be viewed and, if the final aggression is any indication, she fails in her attempt to evade the revenge of the sons. Her identity is less a mystery for the audience to unravel than it is a perception of the sons who have decided to project both the Madonna and whore onto the body of Kate. Importantly, she does not choose this role, but rather is cast in it, one that specifically prohibits any action.

This inability to act characterizes many of Barnes's protagonists, particularly those of her ironically titled play *The Dove* (written 1923, published 1929). The title character is a young woman clothed all in white and described both as a dove and as a deer. Her appearance, however, is deceptive. Known only as "The Dove," she lives with two sisters, Amelia and Vera Burgson, in a pseudo-romantic triangle and she seems at first to be a submissive sexual pet for the sisters. Vera suggests otherwise: "Amelia called you the Dove, I'd never have thought of it. It's just like Amelia to call the most dangerous thing she ever knew the 'Dove'" (1995c [1929]: 157). Indeed, the Dove seems to be dangerous. Throughout the play, she polishes a sword, attempts to strangle Vera, and near the play's conclusion she deliberately and viciously bites Amelia on the breast. In a blatant analogy between sex and violence, Barnes surrounds her characters with both sexual paraphernalia (described as French novel and pin-up girls) and firearms. In the opening stage directions, Barnes describes the setting as "garish, dealing heavily in reds and pinks" with "firearms everywhere. Many groups of swords, ancient and modern, are secured to the wall. A pistol or two lie in chairs, etc." (149).

But like the tranquility and weakness of the Dove herself, Vera admits that the sexual and violent paraphernalia are empty props: Vera acknowledges that both sisters are virgins who "collect knives and pistols, but we only shoot our buttons off with the guns and cut our darning cotton with the knives" (150). In Vera's mind, it is the Dove who makes the weapons dangerous: "when you're out of this room all these weapons might be a lot of butter knives or pop guns, but let you come in . . . It becomes an arsenal" (157). Despite the peacefulness of her name, the Dove (more so than the weapons and sex items) emerges as the greatest threat of the play and, as such, she is the play's only casualty. In the final moments, Amelia rants almost incoherently to the Dove – "I hate the chimneys on the houses, I hate the doorways, I hate you, I hate Vera, but most of all I hate my red heels!" (161) – and then attempts to take the sword from the Dove. When Amelia misses and grabs the Dove's hand instead, the Dove "*Slowly . . . bares Amelia's left shoulder and breast, and leaning down, sets her teeth in.*" The Dove then exits, shouts "For the house of Burgson!" (161), and a gunshot is heard. Amelia exits and returns carrying Carpaccio's painting, *Two Venetian Women* (ca. 1495), with a visible bullet hole. In the final line of the play Amelia simply states, "*This* is obscene" (161).

The ultimate fate of the Dove remains unknown. She may have shot merely the painting, or she may have also shot herself. Critics (Larabee, Dalton) have debated the Dove's fate but Barnes's purpose here is not to articulate a final answer, but rather to critique the very nature of representation of female sexuality on the stage. Drawn from her experience as a theatre critic, Barnes writes with an awareness of women on stage as objects to be viewed (perhaps erroneously at times), sexualized, and dismissed. The Dove has no real name because she is not, in truth, a real person. Rather, she is a character that Amelia and Vera have created in their sexual fantasies drawn from French libertine novels, pin-ups, and Italian songs. Barnes reinforces the Dove's role as object by positioning her among numerous visual representations of women in the play. The Dove is compared to "Parisienne bathing girl's pictures" that Amelia pricks with pins, and her presence on stage is replaced by a (damaged) painting of two women. Like the images on the postcards and in the painting, the Dove exists largely to be looked at, full of potential that only the viewer can determine. Whether the

Dove dies or reinvents herself at the end is irrelevant. The Dove is simply a creation, like the women in the Carpaccio painting, and thus has no real agency or identity.

Not coincidentally, Carpaccio's painting is notable for its two different interpretations, through its respective titles, *Two Venetian Women* (the original) and *The Courtesans* (renamed by Ludwig and Molmenti, 1907). Art historian Vittorio Sgarbi suggests that the painting has been misjudged because of its alluring (but inaccurate) second title. He claims that the painting in its original position, next to the banal *Hunting on the Lagoon* (ca. 1495), provides "little credence to the facile romantic interpretations that influenced the enthusiastic opinions of Ruskin and other celebrated writers, such as Proust and D'Annunzio" (1994: 100). Like the misnamed and misinterpreted painting, the Dove is a blank screen on which the sisters, and, by extension, the audience, project their own fantasies. Does the Dove live or die? Is she the victim or the aggressor? By leaving this final decision to the viewer, Barnes ultimately makes the Dove *our* creation, thereby presenting and attacking the role of women on stage as constructed figures.

Though biography influenced Barnes's plays, the events from her past serve this larger critical purpose. Nowhere is this more prevalent than in her final and best play, *The Antiphon* (1958). Begun as early as 1937, *The Antiphon* brings together many of the themes that Barnes's shorter dramas explore individually. As noted by nearly every critic of the play, the plot of *The Antiphon* is a reworking of Barnes's own abuse at the hands of her father. Biographers like Philip Herring and Andrew Field have looked to this play for evidence of Barnes's early life. But critically, the play has also been considered in relation to the history of theatre as well, as a rejection of contemporary theatre in the 1930s and 1940s (Kannenstine 1977) and as a critique of Shakespeare's *The Tempest* (DeSalvo 1991). Beyond simply responding to contemporary theatre, or a specific dramatist, this play is noteworthy because it attacks representation itself.

The plot of *The Antiphon* is stark in its simplicity. The eldest son of the Burley Hobbs family, Jeremy, orchestrates a family reunion in which the various family members – widow Augusta, uncle Jonathan, brothers Dudley and Elisha, and daughter Miranda – return to confront the abuse of their father, Titus, particularly his role in the brutal rape of daughter Miranda. Jeremy's motives for the reunion are unclear, but he seems intent on forcing his family, most especially his mother, to confront this rape scene. In the play's painful climax, Jeremy enters holding a dollhouse that he calls a "beast-box, doll's house" (Barnes 2000 [1958]: 144). Looking into the dollhouse, Augusta "sees" the rape recounted by Jeremy: "The girl, damned, with her instep up-side-down, / Dragging rape-blood behind her, like the snail. / Whimpering 'Glory, glory!,'" to which Miranda herself adds: "Howling 'Glory, Glory!' for the god / In the cinders of that blasphemy. / And beneath her, in a lower room, / Her father rubbing down his hands" (150).

Much has been made of this scene as a revisiting of Barnes's own sexual violation. Biographers have used it as evidence of her father's abuse and her mother's complicity in the attack. Jeremy tells his mother, "You made yourself a *madam* by submission ... So I say between you both you made / Of that doll's *abattoir* a babe's *bordel* [*sic*]" (151). While the veracity of the theatrical recounting of Barnes's life is debatable (although there is ample evidence to suggest it is a somewhat accurate portrayal), more compelling is the way in which the event is represented in the drama, especially its position within the dollhouse. Barnes is no doubt capable of rendering sexual violence on stage. In the scene that directly precedes Jeremy's entrance with the dollhouse, Dudley and Elisha viciously attack their mother and sister. Dudley goads his brother to sodomize Miranda, "Slap her ears down. Stand her on four feet! / That'll set her up! I'd say that's one position / Of which she hasn't made the most in twenty years" (138). The brutal scene contains the most direct action in the play and, according to the brief and pointed stage directions, covers most of the stage. However, the critical moment of the play is not this attack scene. Instead of representing Miranda's rape on stage, Barnes miniaturizes the attack and displaces the event into the dollhouse in which the monstrous figure of Titus becomes, in the words of Augusta, "A little man soon cooled. A nothing!" (145). By forcing Augusta to look through the window of the dollhouse, Jeremy forces her to look at the past as if it occurs "onstage." Augusta assumes the position of the audience looking at the events through the proscenium frame. Like the mother, who silently turned away from her daughter's violation, the (presumably silent) audience of *The Antiphon* thus becomes complicit in the exploitation of Miranda.

A reading of the play as theatrical criticism is supported by numerous references to theatre and performance throughout the play. The opening stage directions specify that the play takes place among "all manner of stage costumes" and that Miranda wears "an elegant but rusty costume, obviously of the theater" (7). In their attack, Dudley and Elisha wear animal masks, "as if the playthings would make them anonymous" (136). When Augusta laments her painful history, Miranda advises her to "Blow less hard about the stage" (172), and in the opening, Jeremy talks explicitly to the audience, musing, "They say soliloquy is out of fashion" (23). Jeremy himself adopts a disguise throughout the play, acting as a coachman, "Jack Blow," but his disguise is readily transparent to Miranda, who states that "You talk too much, too much include, / Too much leave out" (17). Barnes's choice of character names also suggests the play's parallel to Shakespearean characters. Louise DeSalvo, for example, reads Miranda as a version of Prospero's daughter in *The Tempest*, a girl overwhelmingly controlled by her father. Yet naming the father Titus might also refer to another Shakespearean father, Titus Andronicus, whose violent self-interest submits his daughter to rape and mutilation at the hands of two brothers.

Literally, an antiphon is a response, but while it is possible to read *The Antiphon* as Barnes's response to the past, both her own and that of theatre history, the play is less concerned with the past as history than with the continuation of past horrors. Though set in 1939 and written in an anachronistic form, *The Antiphon* is intended to exist in the present. By using drama to articulate events of the play in a present performance, Barnes conflates time – the distant past, the recent past, and the present – to articulate Miranda's unending torment. Furthermore, by implicating the audience in a complicit viewing of her violation, Barnes condemns theatrical exploitation, extending from

Shakespeare to Ibsen (a possible source for the dollhouse). Like the hymn sung back and forth between the celebrant and the congregation, *The Antiphon* moves between Barnes's own past and the stage present, simultaneously revealing and concealing the events, theatricalizing and disguising her motives. Like the Dove, Barnes longs for an escape, but recognizes the impossibility of such release. She writes in *The Dove*, "I wish every man were beyond the reach of his own biography" (157), but demonstrates in *The Antiphon* that the past is inescapable. Barnes concludes that perhaps the best that can be achieved is to represent the past, while simultaneously condemning the very act of representation.

Although equally concerned with representation and performance, Gertrude Stein's dramas radically differ from those of Djuna Barnes and, indeed, nearly all of her American contemporaries. Although most literary modernists experimented with dramatic form, Stein deviated most extremely from recognizable dramatic structure, following not the verse dramas of high modernism but rather echoing the strange and unsettling performances staged by her European contemporaries in the avant-garde. Her early plays eliminated character, plot, and action completely, and her later, more developed works relied on repetition, fragmented characters, and non-linear, non-causal plot construction. Whereas Barnes looked to the past for both dramatic content and form, Stein resolutely embraced the future. She believed that in the wake of such radical concepts as the cinema, Einstein's theory of relativity, and the atomic bomb, the twentieth century had profoundly transformed the way people viewed the world. Her dramas attempted to incorporate the new perspectives of the modern age. As Stein wrote in 1938, "the twentieth century is a century which sees the earth as no one has ever seen it . . . and as everything destroys itself in the twentieth century and nothing continues, so then the twentieth century has a splendor which is its own" (1969 [1938]: 50).

Still, for all her innovation and radical treatment of language and structure, Stein did not ignore the past. On the contrary, Stein was obsessed with past events, particularly her own. Like Barnes and her publication of *Nightwood*, Stein gained widespread critical attention with a novel that documented life with her lesbian companion, *The Autobiography of Alice B. Toklas* (1933). Stein wrote two more conspicuous autobiographies, *Everybody's Autobiography* (1937) and *Wars I Have Seen* (1945), though like Barnes, these autobiographies frequently obscure events and Stein's own identity, even as they seek to represent her life. This type of autobiography encompasses her drama, in which she repeatedly complicates characters and actions in ways that seem to eliminate sense or meaning. Although Stein puts herself on stage in her final drama, *The Mother of Us All* (1945–6), her goal is not simply to recreate the past, nor to revisit her own history. Instead, Stein uses (and often distorts) past events in order to express the present. One need only consider her use of the phrase "continuous present" to realize that the distinction between the past and the present and the future is far less coherent than in Barnes's plays. As she wrote in 1934, "The business of Art as I tried to explain it . . . is to live in the actual present, that is the complete actual present, and to completely express that complete actual present" (1935: 104–5).

Stein's dramas attempt to articulate this "present" to an audience. Although she has often been either ignored as a playwright or considered instead a closet dramatist, her distortion of time, character, and action signifies her as likely America's first avant-garde playwright. Though rarely examined in the context of American theatre history, Stein's dramatic writings span over 30 years and include over 70 plays and two screenplays. Her *Four Saints in Three Acts* (written in 1927, published in 1932) was produced as an opera composed by Virgil Thomson on Broadway in 1934, and her *Lectures in America* (1935) argues that performance (both on stage and on screen) was central to Stein's experiments with language in poetry, prose, and fiction. While her dramas evolved over time, ranging from virtually unstageable early short works, *What Happened. A Five Act Play* (1913) and *I Like It to Be a Play* (1916), to an avant-garde adaptation of Faust, *Doctor Faustus Lights the Lights* (1938), to a simple melodrama, *Yes Is for a Very Young Man* (1944–5), Stein consistently drew from the events of her life to articulate the radical changes of the twentieth-century stage. Like Barnes, Stein recognized the importance of performance, and it is in her drama that her experiments with identity, time, and memory most vividly come to life.

Whereas Barnes uses the stage to return to a single, traumatic moment in the past, Stein treats memory with a lighter touch. Rather than recollect a major event, Stein draws on small, seemingly insignificant personal moments in her daily life. Most importantly, Stein's emphasis rarely focuses on the event itself or even on the characters experiencing it. Instead, she draws attention to the process of creating drama by writing plays in which dramatic representation bears little resemblance to reality. In other words, history and individual identity in Stein's plays, even when influenced by her own life, fail to refer to real events outside the play; the plays exist, rather, as fictional representations. Rather than Stein's life made visible to the audience, her dramas demonstrate her own self-consciously created *image* of the past. In a world that was becoming increasingly mechanized and mediated, Stein's drama recognized the prominence of the image over direct experience. As a result, she attempts to write drama in which the events of the past do not simply fall into a forgotten history, but rather remain continuously present in the minds of her audience.

Stein no doubt learned some of this from her avant-garde contemporaries in Paris and from the avant-garde films that pervaded Parisian culture during the 1920s. Although her dramatic works have rarely been considered a part of the avant-garde, Stein's dramatic structure follows many of the crucial elements of avant-garde performance in the early twentieth century, including the use of fragmentation, simultaneity, and the elimination of predictable character action and chronological progressive structure. Likewise Alfred Jarry's *Ubu Roi* (1896), arguably the first European avant-garde play, drew from his own boyhood to reinvent Shakespeare's *Macbeth* as a scathing critique of God, king, and predictable human psychology, Stein uses the events of her life to attack not only the realist and naturalist theatre of the late nineteenth century, but also the very notion of historical "truth." It is worth examining her plays as a radical redefinition of autobiography, along similar lines as her experiments with narration and memory in *The Autobiography of Alice B. Toklas*. Her use of autobiography and history in drama is not an attempt to come to terms with the events of the past, but rather an attempt to catapult the events of her present into an uncertain and unimagined future.

Stein's resistance to a fixed past is evident in her first play, *What Happened: A Five Act Play* (written in 1913, published in 1922). In it, Stein attempts to represent in pseudo-dramatic form the importance of representation over realism. Based on a dinner party Stein attended, the text of *What Happened* can hardly be called a play – there are no characters, no clear dialogue, and no actions – though it does represent an individual perspective. Small gestures and details of a party (dessert spoons, and turkey, and silences, to name a few) are woven into loosely formed paragraphs that Stein thought would "create the essence of what happened" (1935: 119). Claiming that anyone could tell stories, Stein dramatizes not the event itself but her own attempt to recreate it. In "Act Three" she equates a sense of isolation in the midst of a social gathering with the difficulty of rendering such a moment: "All alone with the best reception, all alone with more than the best reception, all alone with a paragraph and something that is worth something, worth almost anything" (1993 [1922]: 207–8). Alone at a party and alone with a paragraph, Stein attempts to record in language an experience that is not merely retold to a reader (or replayed for a viewer), but *reexperienced* by the observer. Tellingly, she distinguishes this attempt to record a moment from the fixed representation of photography, which she identifies as regrettable. At the conclusion of the play, Stein writes,

> A regret a single regret makes a doorway. What is a doorway, a door way is a photograph. What is a photograph a photograph is a sight and a sight is always a sight of something. Very likely there is a photograph that gives color if there is then there is that color that does not that does not change any more than it did when there was much more use for photography. (209)

This photographic "door way," or frame, fixes the event in time, making it permanently part of the past. Stein has little use for photography because it is finished and complete – the color does not change. Stein's paragraph relegates photography, a modern technology, to the past, a relic of a time "when there was much more use for photography," or in other words, when the world was capable of being captured in a fixed record.

Stein resists the permanent technology of photography precisely because it creates and stabilizes history, fixing it in the past, whereas Stein's language continually recreates and re-presents the event of the party. Though perhaps impossible to imagine onstage, Stein's earliest play teases an audience's expectation that a play might reveal something about a past event. Even the title itself, *What Happened*, mocks the audience's interest in the past, in verisimilitude, in the photographic record. One might read the title looking for an answer to her central question, "what happened." But rather than provide an answer, Stein simply responds, "a five act play." Each time the title is read, the joke repeats itself in a seemingly endless parody of theatrical expectation. Not unlike the famous "Who's on First?" routine (1945) by Bud Abbott and Lou Costello, Stein turns the past into an endlessly repeatable present (and pun). Thus, the past event ceases to exist, while the play (the artistic creation) continues in its present form, representing itself over and over again.

As Stein's dramatic works develop, she increasingly conflates the events of the past with the present. Her *Four Saints in Three Acts* (written in 1927, published in 1932) intersperses historical and religious figures from the past – Saints Therese, Ignatius, and Paul – with saints invented by Stein in the present, including Saint Settlement, Saint Electra, and Saint Plan. Again, Stein's title makes promises that her dramatic text fails to keep. There are many more than four saints throughout the play, and keeping track of the number of acts is nearly impossible. As she writes in Scene X (one of many such titled scenes), "Four Acts could be four acts could be when when four acts could be ten" (1998b [1932]: 31). Scenes repeat themselves (there are nine "Scene V"s) and ambiguous stage directions further complicate Stein's structure: "Repeat First Act" (16) and "Enact the end of an act" (17). Significantly, in *Four Saints in Three Acts*, Stein returns to her earlier interest in photography, explaining how photography might become more than simply a permanent record of the past. She bases the character of Saint Therese in part on a shop window display that she observed while walking in Paris. In the shop window (itself a frame), a young girl's process of becoming a nun is demonstrated in a sequence of photographs (Stein 1935: 130). In *Four Saints in Three Acts*, Stein describes Saint Therese's transformation thus: "Saint Therese could be photographed having been dressed like a lady and then they taking out her head changed her to a nun and a nun to a saint and a saint so" (17). Saint Therese, an icon from the past, consequently becomes an avant-garde construction – a picture in sequence, with each stage of the development from girl to nun simultaneously represented.

Stein explored the relationship between photography and time in a screenplay, *Film. Deux Sœurs Qui Ne Sont Pas Sœurs* (*Film. Two Sisters Who Are Not Sisters*, written in 1929, published in 1932). It was written only two years after *Four Saints in Three Acts* and similar in theme to her other dramatic writing of the period. The second of Stein's two attempts at cinematic writing, *Deux Sœurs* documents Stein and Toklas's acquisition of their first dog, Basket. In this short but cryptic screenplay, an "older washerwoman" finds and admires a photograph of two dogs. She is later joined by a young washerwoman, a young man, a young woman who "*est coiffée comme si elle venait d'avoir un prix dans un concours de beauté*" ("is made up as if she had just won a prize in a beauty contest") (Stein 1998a [1932]: 399), all of whom also admire the photograph. At the crucial moment of the screenplay, the photograph is taken by "two ladies" (presumably, the sisters who are not sisters), who drive away from the scene in their car. The dog returns in the final scene of the film as a live dog whizzing by in the car while carrying the original photograph in its mouth. The people still gathered on the street can only look, but Stein states that they do not understand anything (400).

Though based on events from her life, *Film* creates a complicated kind of auto-biography. Assuming that the screenplay would be filmed and projected (it never was), Stein creates a photographic record of an event that continues forever in the present. Her memory of her dog does not become a part of the past, even in its photographic form, but can be replayed, perhaps infinitely, in the present before an audience. The screenplay, thus, depicts both Stein's memory of an event and its creation as a work of art. Furthermore, this creation deviates from realistic representation by confusing perception and identity. We never learn who the two ladies are, or why they take the photograph. As the title directly states, the two sisters are not, in fact, sisters, and the emergence of the dog is never explained. In her notes on the film, Stein observed that the live dog on film was really no different from the photograph of the dogs on film. Both were photographs, even though the film created the illusion of movement for the live dog. By positioning herself in the cinematographic image, Stein draws attention to herself as a recognizable image and simultaneously attacks the notion that the audience can identify her.

But even as Stein continues to critique notions of representation in drama, her plays grow increasingly autobiographical. Like her autobiographies in which the narrator edges ever closer to Stein herself (from "Toklas" to "Everybody" to her final admission of "I" in *Wars I Have Seen*), Stein's dramas during the 1930s gradually admit identifiable and coherent characters into the text. While Saint Therese in *Four Saints* exists primarily as an icon to be fragmented (as in the sequence of photographs), the characters in *Listen to Me* (1936), and *Doctor Faustus Lights the Lights* (1938) emerge as individual people with specific problems to be solved. Indeed, it is not until her adaptation of the Faust myth in 1938 that one can discuss character objectives in Stein's drama. But in her two final plays – *Yes Is for a Very Young Man* (1944–5) and *The Mother of Us All* (written in 1945–6, published in 1949) – Stein writes what can only be called autobiographical drama. *Yes Is for a Very Young Man*, for example, quotes almost verbatim from *Wars I Have Seen*, and *The Mother of Us All* includes Stein and her collaborator, the composer Virgil Thomson, as characters. This final play, however, is perhaps Stein's most sophisticated challenge to the authority of autobiography and history. She makes this project explicit in the final speech of the play, when the central character, Susan B. Anthony, states, "We cannot retrace our steps, going forward may be the same as going backwards" (1975 [1949]: 87).

Ostensibly based on the life of nineteenth-century suffragette Susan B. Anthony, Stein's presence dominates *The Mother of Us All*. In addition to including both herself and Thomson as characters, Stein blends the character of Gertrude Stein with other characters in the play. For example, "All the characters" announce, "Daniel was my father's name, / My father's name was Daniel," to which the character Gertrude Stein repeats, "My father's name was Daniel" (53). Besides sharing fathers named Daniel, Susan B. Anthony's dramatic struggle for recognition echoes Stein's literary quest for recognition. Anne, a companion and secretary who accompanies Anthony, seems a clear parallel for Toklas. Franziska Gygax has argued that numerous names chosen for the play are taken from contemporary women writers or Stein's "literary foremothers" (1998: 53).

Still, for all the obvious parallels, Stein discourages a simplistic reading of the play as solely autobiography. Susan B. Anthony herself rejects the parallel when she (inaccurately) denies that her father's name was Daniel (54) and Gertrude Stein as a character disappears from the play before the end of the first scene. The rest of the play avoids focusing on "what is remembered" (the title of Toklas's autobiography in 1963), but instead stresses what is or will be forgotten. To reinforce this threat, one of the fictional characters, Isabel Wentworth, is casually forgotten early in the play. When Jo the Loiterer asks "has everybody forgotten Isabel Wentworth," Chris the Citizen replies, "Why shouldn't everybody forget Isabel Wentworth" (64), and even Anne admits that "We have forgotten we have forgotten Jenny Reefer, I don't even know who she is" (65). Similarly, at the play's conclusion, Henrietta M. (seen only three times during the play) returns to announce, "I have never been mentioned again" (84). All this forgetfulness clearly concerns Anthony, who in a private "interlude" with Anne pleads, "When this you see remember me" (59), a line that also ended Stein's earlier collection *Geography and Plays* (1922).

While the play itself seems to answer Anthony and Stein's concern for their historical legacy (after all, the play in performance brings back the memory of both Anthony and Stein), fear for the future ultimately dominates the structure of the play. Anthony's struggle to gain the vote progresses (successfully) forward; the play, however, seems stuck in time. The presence of characters from more than 100 years of American history discourages the notion of chronological progressive time. Moreover, their fantastical behavior and language eliminate historical accuracy. The past is thus haphazardly flung into the present, where figures from the past mix (somewhat oddly) with characters from the present. Anthony herself, though clearly looking to future progress, cannot help herself from continually thinking of the present as the past of the future. At the end of the play, Susan B. Anthony returns from the grave to witness both the passing of her laws and a statue erected in her memory. One would think that the statue would satisfy Anthony's concern for her legacy, but instead she has quite the opposite reaction: "here we are here, in marble and gold . . . But do I want what we have got, has it not gone . . . has it not gone because now it is had" (1975 [1949]: 87–8). Anthony rejects the statue because, like a photograph, she has become fixed in time. Similarly, success is not enough for Stein because critical or popular success can so readily become part of the forgettable past. Celebrity, like the statue and the photograph, too comfortably fixes the past in a cultural mind that forgets that which does not change. Stein's use of autobiography on stage is an attempt not to represent her life on stage, but rather to continuously *re*-present the dramatic struggle to be heard and, ultimately, to be remembered in the future present.

Given their radically different orientations to time and history, it is perhaps not surprising, then, that Barnes and Stein have had very different receptions of their dramatic work in the latter half of the twentieth century. Barnes, who spent much of her career in the theatre, has had virtually none of her plays staged, while Stein, who claimed to have stopped seeing theatre after childhood, has been regularly performed and adapted throughout the twentieth century. Though both grappled with being famous and unknown, it is Stein who has continued to be present in American theatre. Her reinventions of language and dramatic form ultimately succeeded in remaining in the present of American avant-garde theatre, precisely because she refused to become merely a part of the forgotten past. She remarked in 1945 that "remembering back is not only remembering but might be being" (1945: 11).

BIBLIOGRAPHY

Barnes, D. (1931). *The Playgoer's Almanac. Theater Guild Magazine* (January): 34.

——(1995a [1918]). *Madame Collects Herself.* In D. Messerli (ed.), *At the Root of the Stars: The Short Plays.* Los Angeles: Sun and Moon Press, 59–66.

——(1995b [1919]). *Three from the Earth.* In D. Messerli (ed.), *At the Root of the Stars: The Short Plays.* Los Angeles: Sun and Moon Press, 67–80.

——(1995c [1929]). *The Dove.* In D. Messerli (ed.), *At the Root of the Stars: The Short Plays.* Los Angeles: Sun and Moon Press, 145–61.

——(2000 [1958]). *The Antiphon.* Copenhagen: Green Integer.

Bay-Cheng, S. (2003). *Mama Dada: Gertrude Stein's Avant-Garde Theater.* New York: Routledge.

Benstock, S. (1986). *Women of the Left Bank: Paris, 1900–1940.* Austin: University of Texas Press.

Bowers, J. P. (1991). *"They Watch Me As They Watch This": Gertrude Stein's Metadrama.* Philadelphia: University of Pennsylvania Press.

Broe, M. L. (ed.) (1991). *Silence and Restraint: A Reevaluation of Djuna Barnes.* Carbondale: Southern Illinois University Press.

Clark, S. F. (2002). "Djuna Barnes: The Most Famous Unknown." In K. Marra and R. A. Schanke (eds.), *Staged Desire: Queer Readings in American Theater History.* Ann Arbor: University of Michigan Press, 105–25.

Dalton, A. B. (1993). "*'This* is Obscene': Female Voyeurism, Sexual Abuse, and Maternal Power in *The Dove.*" *Review of Contemporary Fiction* 13: 117–39.

De Koven, M. (1983). *A Different Language: Gertrude Stein's Experimental Writing.* Madison: University of Wisconsin Press.

DeSalvo, L. (1991). "'To Make her Mutton at Sixteen': Rape, Incest, and Child Abuse in *The Antiphon.*" In Mary Lynn Broe (ed.), *Silence and Restraint: A Reevaluation of Djuna Barnes.* Carbondale: Southern Illinois University Press, 300–15.

Dubnick, R. (1984). *The Structure of Obscurity: Stein, Language, and Cubism.* Urbana: University of Illinois Press.

Galvin, M. E. (1999). *Queer Poetics: Five Modernist Women Writers.* Westport, CT: Praeger.

Gygax, F. (1998). *Gender and Genre in Gertrude Stein.* Westport, CT: Greenwood.

Herring, P. (1995). *Djuna: The Life and Work of Djuna Barnes.* New York: Viking.

Hinchliffe, A. P. (1977). *Modern Verse Drama.* London: Methuen.

Hoffman, M. (1965). *The Development of Abstractionism in the Writing of Gertrude Stein.* Philadelphia: University of Pennsylvania Press.

Kannenstine, L. F. (1977). *The Art of Djuna Barnes: Duality and Damnation.* New York: New York University Press.

Larabee, A. (1991). "The Early Attic Stage of Djuna Barnes." In Mary Lynn Broe (ed.), *Silence and Restraint: A Reevaluation of Djuna Barnes.* Carbondale: Southern Illinois University Press, 37–44.

McCabe, S. (2001). "'Delight in Dislocation': The Cinematic Modernism of Stein, Chaplin, and Man Ray." *Modernism/Modernity* 8: 429–52.

Puchner, M. (2002). *Stage Fright: Modernism, Anti-Theatricality and Drama*. Baltimore: Johns Hopkins University Press.

Retallack, J. (1991). "The Early Plays of Djuna Barnes." In Mary Lynn Broe (ed.), *Silence and Restraint: A Reevaluation of Djuna Barnes*. Carbondale: Southern Illinois University Press, 46–52.

Sgarbi, V. (1994). *Carpaccio*, trans. J. Hyams. New York: Abbeville.

Stein, G. (1935). *Plays*. In *Lectures in America*. New York: Random House, 93–131.

——(1945). *Wars I Have Seen*. New York: Random House.

——(1967 [1940]). "What are Master-Pieces and Why are there so Few of Them." In P. Meyerowitz (ed.), *Writings and Lectures, 1909–1945*. London: Owen, 146–54.

——(1969 [1938]). *Picasso*. Boston: Beacon Press.

——(1975 [1949]). *The Mother of Us All*. In C. V. Vechten (ed.), *Last Operas and Plays*. New York: Random House, 52–88.

——(1993 [1922]). *What Happened. A Five Act Play*. In *Geography and Plays*. Madison: University of Wisconsin Press, 205–9.

——(1998a [1932]). *Film. Deux Sœurs Qui Ne Sont Pas Sœurs*. [*Film. Two Sisters Who Are Not Sisters*]. In *Operas and Plays*. Barrytown, NY: Station Hill Press, 399–400.

——(1998b [1932]). *Four Saints in Three Acts*. In *Operas and Plays*. Barrytown, NY: Station Hill Press, 11–47.

10

Eugene O'Neill: American Drama and American Modernism

David Krasner

Tragedy has the meaning the Greeks gave it.... It roused them to deeper spiritual understandings and released them from the petty greeds of everyday existence. When they saw a tragedy on the stage they felt their own hopeless hopes ennobled in art.... The point is that life in itself is nothing. It is the *dream* that keeps us fighting, willing – living!... A man wills his own defeat when he pursues the unattainable. But his *struggle* is his success!... Such a figure is necessarily tragic. But to me he is not depressing; he is exhilarating! He may be a failure in our materialistic sense. His treasures are in other kingdoms. Yet isn't he the most inspiring of all successes?

Eugene O'Neill, qtd. in Mullet (1922: 118, 120)

There are several reasons for the preeminence of Eugene O'Neill (1888–1953) as "the" twentieth-century American dramatist. His greatest works, *Long Day's Journey into Night* and *The Iceman Cometh* (written between 1939 and 1941), continue to be performed to this day. During his lifetime he received three Pulitzer Prizes for Drama – *Beyond the Horizon* in 1920, *Anna Christie* in 1921, *Strange Interlude* in 1928 – and a fourth, *Long Day's Journey into Night*, posthumously in 1956. In 1936 he became the only twentieth-century American dramatist awarded the Nobel Prize for Literature. He was prominent during the 1920s and 1930s, writing nearly 50 plays. He examined the use of masks onstage, explored inner monologues, developed an American brand of expressionism, and firmly established American dramatic realism.

O'Neill brought to the stage a richness of detail and psychological depth rarely seen before in American drama. His dialogue was sensitive to regional and ethnic vernacular, and his three-dimensional characterizations have rarely been equaled. Few playwrights in American theatre have made use of their personal life – family, experiences, and inadequacies – with similar candor. O'Neill's dramas explore his alcoholism, his life at sea, his father's disappointments, his mother's drug addiction, his brother's suicide by alcohol, and his own shortcomings. His plays probe the American Dream, race relations, class conflicts, sexuality, human aspirations, disappointment, alienation, psychoanalysis, and the American family with a thoroughness and intensity at a level his contemporaries could barely contemplate. He wrote about the wealthy and the underclass with equal perception. His plays investigate modern relationships and the human frailties they conceal. During the late 1910s and early 1920s, his dramas anchored the repertory of the Provincetown Players, the theatre company led by George Cram "Jig" Cook and Susan Glaspell, which helped establish a place for American experimental dramas. During the 1920s and 1930s O'Neill wrote Broadway melodramas that became the finest examples of American theatre of the period. His melodramas were atypical of the melodramas at the time, with their reliance on imminent catastrophe, vivid spectacle, graphic pyrotechnics, and a morally unambiguous landscape. Instead, his melodramas conveyed subtler intimacies, personal tragedies, and psychological complexities. Although his aims varied, O'Neill primarily sought to create a "modern American drama" that would, he hoped, rival the great works of European modernists such as Ibsen, Strindberg, and Shaw. The aim of this chapter is to examine selected O'Neill plays in light of their contribution to "modern American drama."

By "modern American drama" I mean a period (ca. 1910 to 1945) during which American playwrights sought to overturn nineteenth-century formal constraints (sexual prudery and intolerance), Victorian melodramas (clichéd notions of morality and emphasis on suspense), and outdated styles of performance (vocal bombast and stage gimmickry). In place of the bland moral certainty that characterized the nineteenth-century drama, American dramatists of the modern era examined human (often sexual) relationships with ruthless candor, portraying moral ambivalence that challenged the status quo. Invigorated by August Strindberg's theatre of psychological nuance and dream-like symbolism, O'Neill, as well as other playwrights, forged a new kind of drama.

"American modernism" in general began at the turn of the century and rose to prominence during mid-century. It is defined by liberal values associated with free love, free speech, and, to a certain degree, political anarchy. In addition, there was a rejection of sentimentality that had been characteristic of American provincialism; advocacy of the suffragette movement and women's rights; and commitment to uncovering the "truth" in the human condition. Modernism implied cosmopolitanism, reflecting an emergent urban life and its rising bohemianism (particularly New York City and its downtown artistic scene known as "Greenwich Village"). Modernism brought with it a sense of cultural leadership (the feeling that the participants were on the cutting edge of art and literature), and was marked by a determination to be politically and socially relevant to the working class. Along these lines, Christine Stansell, in her book *American Moderns: Bohemian New York and the Creation of a New Century*, writes:

In their determination to merge art and politics, the bohemians laid the groundwork for a liberal metropolitan elite committed as much to matters of cultural taste and innovation as to social reform. An attraction to modern, "revolutionary" and "political" art, jumbled together, would henceforth run through American culture, leading enlightened audiences and artists to advertise their solidarities with the "people" and see themselves, by virtue of the books they read, the art they admired, or the plays they attended, as subverting the status quo. (2000: 150)

What we encounter in O'Neill's plays are a powerful psychological engagement, a focus on human relations, a commitment to deeply personal and emotional experiences, an expression of ideas, and an emphasis on authenticity over facade, which are the hallmarks of modernism. In his dramas, he says, audiences "listen to ideas absolutely opposed to their ordinary habits of thought – and applaud these ideas." The appreciation of "ideas," O'Neill adds, is due to the fact that audiences

have been appealed to through their emotions... and our emotions are a better guide than our thoughts. Our emotions are instinctive. They are the result not only of our individual experiences but of the experiences of the whole human race, back through all the ages. They are the deep undercurrent, whereas our thoughts are often only the small individual surface reactions. Truth usually goes deep. So it reaches you through your emotions. (Qtd. in Mullett 1922: 34)

There was no unifying feature one can identify in modern American drama; if anything might define it, it was experimentation. To be a modern American dramatist was to be an experimenter, often examining the features of theatricality, how they worked to convey emotion. O'Neill's characters make use of masks (*The Great God Brown, All God's Chillun Got Wings*), talk directly to the audience and express their "true" feelings (*Strange Interlude*), explore class conflicts (*The Hairy Ape*), and address death, sexuality, guilt, and responsibility. Europeans – especially playwrights Ibsen and Strindberg, and Nietzsche's philosophy – informed modern American dramatists. O'Neill, for instance, reported seeing Ibsen's *Hedda Gabler* "ten successive nights" in his youth (*Letters* 1988b: 477) and made note of Strindberg and Nietzsche as having been influential (518). The Harlem Renaissance – the outpouring of African American literature, music, and drama during the 1920s (see chapter 7) – also influenced modern dramatists, prompting playwrights to write plays dealing with "Negro life": O'Neill's *The Dreamy Kid* in 1918 (produced in 1919), *The Emperor Jones* in 1920, and *All God's Chillun Got Wings* in 1924, for example. In addition, the concept of "primitivism" took hold around the same time. Primitivism – a rejection of technology and a desire to return humanity to its raw, "natural" state – worked, in many ways, to oppose Harlem Renaissance artists seeking to negate any association between African Americans and "primitiveness." Freudian and Jungian psychoanalysis, as well as Nietzsche's Dionysian philosophy of ritual and eternal recurrence, also played an important role in shaping O'Neill's plays. O'Neill often became immersed in the modernist movements of his time and applied them to his dramas, thereby ensuring his place as literary representative of modernism. Jordan Y. Miller and Winifred L. Frazer emphasize this point, noting that O'Neill's "constant experimentation in form and style" during the period between the two World Wars "puzzled, delighted, and infuriated critics and public alike, prompting more than one bewildered reviewer, racing to as many as four O'Neill openings within a single season, to cry 'Hold, enough!' in an effort to persuade this overenthusiastic artist to slow down, to determine just who he was, and above all, to find some consistent pattern for his artistry" (1997: 47).

Before O'Neill, American drama was largely either a European derivative of treacle melodrama or a hodgepodge of vaudeville, minstrelsy, and musicals. Few American plays were exported elsewhere; for the most part there was scant interest in America's sub-par dramas. In 1928, drama critic George Jean Nathan confirmed that "Until Eugene O'Neill appeared upon the scene, the American drama offered little for the mature European interest" (94) (few exceptions were Anna Cora Mowatt's 1845 comedy *Fashion; or, Life in New York*, and adaptations of *Uncle Tom's Cabin*, both enjoying success in London). O'Neill transformed American drama into an internationally respected art. To be sure, he borrowed from European ideas, especially classical Greek tragedy and the dramas of Ibsen and Strindberg, but his plays were fashioned into the substance of an American idiom.

O'Neill's youthful restlessness motivated him to abandon his father's moribund theatre world and his mother's rigid Catholicism. His father was the well-known matinee idol James O'Neill, who gained fame during the late nineteenth century portraying the leading role in the stage adaptation of *The Count of Monte Cristo*. While his father's success yielded him a small fortune, he felt trapped in his role for most of his career. Traveling with his father on tours, O'Neill learned the theatre from the ground up, but he rebelled against his father's tradition of bombastic acting and conventionality. His mother, Ella, a devout Irish Catholic, fell victim to a doctor's over-prescribing of morphine resulting in drug addiction. O'Neill's older brother, James, Jr., bright and charismatic, squandered his life as a Broadway ne'er-do-well and alcoholic. The O'Neill brothers shared a love-hate relationship with their father as well as a passionate and guilt-laden love for their mother. O'Neill loved his brother, but eventually recoiled from him owing to his brother's toxic jealousy and cynicism.

O'Neill dropped out of Princeton and sailed to Buenos Aires on a merchant ship in 1910; he also drifted from gold prospecting to sailing. In 1912 he entered a sanatorium with tuberculosis. During his hospitalization, he reached an epiphany and was, according to a biographer, "determined to become a dramatist" (Gelb and Gelb 1973: 195). He took part in George Pierce Baker's playwriting class at Harvard in 1914. With the help of his father, he published his first collection of one-act plays in 1916. One of the most significant events in his life came when he joined the Provincetown Players, a group of radicals seeking to establish an alternative theatre to Broadway's commercialism. From 1916 to 1920, O'Neill and Susan Glaspell became the Provincetown Players' most successful playwrights. He wrote numerous one-act and full-length plays for them, many of which reflected his life at sea, his sexual relationships, his experience at the sanatorium (*The Straw*), and his flirtation with socialism (*Thirst, Fog*). Four in particular, written during this period – *The Moon of the Caribbees*, *Bound East for Cardiff*, *The Long Voyage Home*, and *In the Zone* – fall into the category of O'Neill's sea plays (see chapter 5).

O'Neill's first Broadway success, *Beyond the Horizon* (1920), centers on the triangular relationship between two brothers, Robert and Andrew Mayo, and Ruth Atkins, a neighbor. At the beginning of this three-act play, Andrew (Andy) is in love with Ruth, while Robert confesses his desire for a world beyond the farm. Robert is bookish, frail, and poetic; Andy is sturdy and blunt. Andy is meant for the outdoor life, making him the logical heir to the family's farm. In the opening scene, Robert confesses to Ruth his love for a world "beyond the horizon." She is captivated by his eloquence and, while caught up in the moment, confesses her love of Robert. As a result, instead of Robert leaving the farm, Andy leaves, defeated and jealous. The rash decisions made by all three principals are catastrophic. Robert, in his ineptitude, tends the farm incompetently; Andy journeys to sea, but longs for Ruth and the farm; and Ruth grows cynical, realizing that it is Andy, not Robert, whom she truly loves. By the conclusion, Robert has fallen ill from overwork and melancholy, and Andy (having made a fortune in South America) returns to visit his dying brother. While melodramatic, *Beyond the Horizon* investigates O'Neill's fundamental themes: responsibility, guilt, redemption, impulsive desire, sibling rivalry, and the misplaced existential "dreamer." Andy is a pragmatic yet cynical survivor. Robert is a dreamer in a world that has little use for poets.

In 1920, O'Neill also wrote *The Emperor Jones*. It was an overnight success at the Provincetown Players, premiering on November 1 (it later transferred uptown to Broadway). It introduced a major African American actor, Charles Gilpin, in the leading role of Brutus Jones (later to be replaced by Paul Robeson, who performed the role in London). Travis Bogard observes that the "technical excitement of the play, with its drums, its sustained monologue, its rapidly shifting settings framed into a single desperate action were almost blinding in their virtuosity and in their assurance of important theatrical things to come. Not only the literate American drama, but the American theatre came of age with this play" (1988: 134). The play is O'Neill's first foray into expressionistic drama: divided into episodic scenes, it traces the mental deterioration of Brutus Jones. Jones is an African American con man who wrangles his way to rulership over "an island in the West Indies as yet not self-determined by white marines." Discovered to be a fraud, the people rise up and pursue him as a criminal. Jones eventually succumbs to madness and is killed.

The Hairy Ape (1922) is what O'Neill calls a "blend" of expressionism and naturalism (*Letters* 1988b: 445). It portrays Yank, a coal stoker who labors on a steamship, yet yearns for life "above." Yank is also a poet of sorts, expressing in rough language his physical prowess and lumpen-proletariat alienation. Because of his "ape-like" qualities, he is able to shovel coal at breakneck speed; because of Yank, the engines of the steamship (symbolizing modern machinery) possess an incessant rhythm. Yet he becomes lonely; spying women on the top deck, he seeks intimacy.

Yank is intelligent but uneducated, a brute with a mind whose life in the bowels of a steamship is an allegorical hell. His language, a mixture of Brooklyn dialect and working-class gusto, is filled with self-images of modern, industrial machismo. Yank's existential question, "Where do I fit in?" (*Letters* 1988b: 207), is a running motif for O'Neill's characters. In the bowels of the ship, Yank is a necessity. But up top and among the bourgeoisie, he is a mere cog. Like Robert Mayo and Brutus Jones, he is destroyed by his inefficacy in a world that has no use for him. These characters are driven by what one O'Neill biographer calls the author's own "questing spirit" as well as the feeling of "not 'belonging'" (Sheaffer 1968: 481). Yank may be the force behind technology, but once his usefulness expires, he is just an "ape" (in fact, he dies in a cage alongside a primate). In the play modern technology is found wanting; it is the hand of progress, but crushes the humanity it is meant to serve.

Anna Christie (1922) returns to the themes of the sea O'Neill had explored in his early one-acts at Provincetown. The three principal characters, Chris Christopherson, a Swedish bargeman, his daughter, Anna Christie, and Mat Burke, a ship's stoker, live along the wharf frequenting Johnny-the-Priest's bar. Christopherson has abandoned his daughter for a life at sea; when she finds him, she hides her past life as a prostitute. During the play Mat appears, surviving a near-drowning accident thanks to the help of Anna and her father. Mat and Anna fall in love; Mat, however, is made aware of Anna's past and is greatly disturbed. He must work through his traditional values in order to come to terms with their future. *Anna Christie* examines the conflicts of relationship that ensue, a theme O'Neill considers throughout his career. The play is significant for two other reasons: O'Neill refines his ongoing theme of the sea as a poetic metaphor, and, for the first time, he presents a strong female character. Anna is forceful, independent, and witty, able to hold her own in the rough-and-tumble world of prostitution and divvy bars. While the men in the play try to shelter her, she expresses her independence to both her father and her lover unabashedly:

> First thing is, I want to tell you two guys something. You was going on's if one of you had got to own me. But nobody owns me, see? – 'cepting myself. I'll do what I please and no man, I don't give a hoot who he is, can tell me what to do! I ain't asking either of you for a living. I can make it myself – one way or other. I'm my own boss. So put that in your pipe and smoke it! You and your orders! (*Plays* 1988a, vol. 1: 1007)

From the mid-to late 1920s to the early 1930s, O'Neill experimented with numerous dramatic ideas. He was concerned with relationships and the way character, or identity, formed. Influenced by August Strindberg's *The Father, Welded* (1923) examines the intensified love between Michael Cape, a writer, and Eleanor, an actress. Each is drawn to the other, yet their jealousies consume them. In their jealous rage they consider betrayal, only to find their desire for each other overwhelming. O'Neill's *Desire Under the Elms* (1924) also explores the extremity of passion, sin, and redemption. The triangular relationship in the play centers on Ephraim Cabot, his son Eben, and Abbie Putnam. Ephraim's wife has died; he has taken in her place a young and robust woman, Abbie, as his new wife. Ephraim's three sons, Eben as well as his two brothers Simeon and Peter, look upon the relationship with suspicion. However, Abbie and Eben fall in love and have a child. Guilt drives them both mad, with Abbie ultimately killing the child. Though he is innocent, Eben agrees to admit to the murder as well. His feelings of guilt motivate him to come to terms with his sins and betrayal of his father.

O'Neill continued to experiment throughout the 1920s, examining in particular the concept of masks. *All God's Chillun Got Wings* (1924), *The Great God Brown* (1926), *Marco Millions* (1928), and *Lazarus Laughed* (1928; see chapter 13) make use of stage masks in varying ways. In his essay "Memoranda on Masks," O'Neill refers to masks as the "freest solution of the modernist dramatist's problem as to how – with the greatest possible dramatic clarity and economy of means – he can express those profound hidden conflicts of the mind which the probings of psychology continue to disclose to us" (1932b: 65). Eugene M. Waith put it succinctly when he said that for O'Neill the "mask was a way of getting at the inner reality of character," yielding the "concealment and discovery" that enhances dramatic possibilities (1964: 30). Not only does *The Great God Brown* explore masks, it also focuses on the cynicism resulting from materialism. The play examines the relationship between college roommates William Brown and Dion Anthony, the former a conservative business-man and the latter a talented but self-destructive architect. Both love Margaret, with Dion marrying her. During the play, Dion's debauchery leads to his death. Brown assumes his identity by literally taking up his mask. In an essay titled "The Playwright Explains," O'Neill describes the character of Brown as representing "the visionless demi-god of our new materialistic myth – a Success – building his life of exterior things, inwardly empty and resourceless, an uncreative creature of superficial preordained social grooves, a by-product forced aside into the slack waters by the deep main current of life-desire" (1926: 1).

During the late 1920s, O'Neill turned his attention to an alternative "form" of masking. In *Strange Interlude* (1928), O'Neill's purpose was "to dramatize inner language by means of novelistic thought-asides" (Eisen 1994: 106). Characters function on two levels: on the surface they speak to each other through dialogue; on a deeper level, they speak monologues to the audience that express their internal thoughts, thoughts kept hidden from the other characters, somewhat like filmic "voiceovers" (Murphy 1999: 297). O'Neill explored new ideas emerging from the current psychology, using the surface language to "mask" or disguise the inner language of motivation and sexual desires. In the play, three men love one woman, Nina Leeds. Charles Marsden, an introverted professor, loves her platonically; Edmund Darrell, a doctor, has a physical passion for her; while Sam Evans, a plain, straightforward man, ends up marrying her and becoming a successful businessman. The play takes place over a 20-year period and unfolds in nine acts.

In *Mourning Becomes Electra* (1931), O'Neill explores Greek tragedy, attempting to modernize it. The play is based on Aeschylus's trilogy *The Oresteia* (though it is closer to Sophocles's *Electra* than to Aeschylus's plays). In a 1931 letter to drama critic

Brooks Atkinson, O'Neill wrote, "Greek criticism is as remote from us as the art it criticizes. What we need is a definition of Modern and not Classical Tragedy by which to guide our judgments" (*Letters* 1988b: 390). The play (a trilogy of three plays) examines a post-Civil War Northern family. In the first play, Brigadier General Ezra Mannon returns home only to be murdered by his wife, Christine, for his infidelity and her passion for another man. The remaining two plays concern the revenge of the daughter, Lavinia, and her brother, Orin. Revenge is the motivation, but guilt consumes the characters.

Following his attempt at comedy (*Ah Wilderness!* in 1933) and a play about Catholicism (*Days Without End* in 1934), from 1935 to 1939 O'Neill turned his attention to an 11-play cycle titled *A Tale of Possessions Self-Possessed*. Although never completed, the aim of the cycle was to portray two American families, "Hartford" and "Melody," depicting how they fall victim to corruption and greed (see Gallup 1998 and Bower 1992 for details). O'Neill called *A Touch of the Poet* "an Irish play," although "located in New England in 1828." It is, in his words, "the only one of the four cycle plays I had written which approached final form" (*Letters* 1988b: 546). However, only two plays have survived fully formed: *A Touch of the Poet* and *More Stately Mansions*.

From 1939 until the end of his writing career in 1943 (illness overcame him during the last decade of his life), O'Neill wrote four plays: *The Iceman Cometh, Long Day's Journey into Night, A Moon for the Misbegotten*, and the one-act *Hughie*. In a 1941 letter to his son, O'Neill wrote that *Long Day's Journey into Night* and *The Iceman Cometh* "will rank among the finest things I've ever done" (*Letters* 1988b: 517). All four were produced after World War II (*Long Day's Journey into Night* and *Hughie* posthumously), though none was enthusiastically received when it first appeared.

In *The Iceman Cometh* the large cast of characters presents a formidable challenge. But the details of each character and the complex relationships they create make this one of the most poignant plays in American drama. It takes place over 24 hours in Harry Hope's bar for down-and-outers in 1912. Events revolve around Harry's birthday; but the real excitement derives from the fact that every year, in honor of Hope's celebration, Theodore Hickman ("Hickey") arrives flush with cash and ready to "blow it" on the whores, losers, and drunkards who fill the bar (which is also a rooming house and an occasional whorehouse). Hickey's periodic appearances provide the high point for the bar regulars, because he spends money, knows how to have a good time, and drinks himself into a stupor. But he differs from the "regulars" in that, unlike them, he maintains a bourgeois life on the outside, complete with wife Evelyn, a steady salesman job, and temperance while working. Only with his friends at Harry Hope's bar does Hickey binge, eschewing his middle-class trappings and enjoying his bacchanal. However, something has changed.

Hickey arrives "on the wagon." He comes not to raise hell, swap stories, cheat on his wife, and drink. Instead, he has an objective: to strip away the "pipe dreams" from the bar's patrons. Hickey has "seen the light," ridding himself of any false pretense.

While he pays for the booze, food, and necessities for the party, he turns a bright light on their delusions. Hickey explains:

> The only reason I've quit [drinking] is – Well, I had the guts to face myself and throw overboard the damned lying pipe dream that'd been making me miserable, and do what I had to do for the happiness of all concerned – and then all at once I found I was at peace with myself and I didn't need booze anymore. That's all there was to it. (*Plays* 1988a, vol. 3: 609)

Hickey wants to promote redemption. Throughout the play he dismantles the "pipe dream," the false hope that someday these alcoholics might end their debauching and wend their way back to "respectability." Hickey is well equipped for this task; he is a superb salesman, a maestro of hawking, a mountebank who lives by charm, wit, and guile. But he comes with a hidden agenda, one that is slowly revealed as the play unfolds.

The bar's combustible chemistry of alcoholic losers and ill-assorted "pipe dreamers" oscillates between sentimental melancholy and volatility. The characters carry the illusion of someday resuming the careers they have squandered. From the beginning it is evident that the "pipe dream" is a boozy delusion; but O'Neill makes the point that these delusions are necessary "masks" worn by everyone, one way or another. The alcohol provides the defense needed to "hold the real at bay" (Bigsby 2000: 20), but the "pipe dream" provides the illusion that these characters have free will. The "pipe dream" mask, propped up by alcoholic brio, is worn to bolster self-confidence.

Hickey arrives and the first thing he does is chip away at their delusional masks. He is determined to make the bar patrons face the truth. Hickey, a drummer salesman, promises redemption – what he calls "peace" – if only they drop the "pipe dream." Hickey, however, has his own demons: he murdered his wife. After each incident of infidelity and carousing, Hickey returned to his wife Evelyn begging forgiveness. She forgives every time. The cycle of sin and forgiveness drives him mad; he finally breaks the cycle by murdering her. He can no longer tolerate his guilt. Hickey, knowing he will be caught and tried for the murder of his wife, also wants to plead insanity, and is using his performance of "sobering up" the bar regulars to demonstrate, and make the case for, his madness.

Hickey's performance, therefore, is both a deep investigation into the nature of guilt and irresponsibility driven to madness, and a "performance" of madness as well. Like Shakespeare's Hamlet, who feigns madness and is going mad simultaneously, Hickey moves from pretense to guilt and back to pretense. Like Hamlet, the ambiguity in Hickey's performance creates twin levels of perception. One of the main distinguishing features of modernism in American drama has been the unresolved and polarized extremes of values between actors "performing" the theatrical pretense and actors portraying the realistic actuality of their character's life. The combination of fakery and *verismo*, stylized theatrics (Hickey's sales pitch to convince everyone of his insanity) and realism (Stanislavskian authenticity) creates a duality in *Iceman*. The play is paradigmatic of the modernist simultaneity of "theatre as pretense" and the portrayal of psychological actuality.

The concept of the "pipe dream" also infuses the idea of performing with additional conflict. The outward presentation of a false notion that one can overcome fate and transform oneself is an illusion that parallels theatrical illusion. O'Neill's psychological biographer, Stephen A. Black, makes the point that the pipe dream in *Iceman Cometh* "is the development of the ego defenses that allows a person to live what is called ordinary life." The ego, Black contends, "functions to let us distinguish what is as we say *out there* from what is *in here*," thus confining the terrors of failure to our private world (1999: 428). But the defensiveness of the pipe dream is also an "act," an outward "mask" shared with the world. O'Neill was keen on using the notion of defense mechanisms as masking theatrical devices. Denial is a "dramatic action" requiring gesture, voice, movement, and conviction, all requirements for performance. The characters in Hope's bar are forced to confront their blustery denials; Hickey's insistence that they drop the pretense and face their demons unequivocally places their denials (their masks) in conflict with the "truth" as Hickey sees it.

But the play is about more than Hickey's guilt and desire for redemption, or realistic and non-realistic representation. Larry Slade, the philosopher drunk, and Don Parritt, the young radical who has betrayed the anarchist movement, are among the characters that, like Hickey and the rest, hide their deeper feelings. At the beginning of the play Parritt arrives seeking Larry (who he suspects is his father), in order to gain permission to commit suicide. As the play unfolds, we discover that Parritt turned in other radicals, including his own mother, to the police. He is now guilt-ridden. Parritt shares with Hickey a desire for peace. Parritt and Hickey experience parallel feelings shared by O'Neill and his older brother: Parritt and Hickey feel they have failed the women in their lives (Parritt his mother, Hickey his wife), while the O'Neill brothers shared mutual guilt over their own inadequacies toward their mother.

In *Hughie*, which takes place in a hotel lobby, Erie, the petty con artist, is "setting up" the night clerk for a scam in the same way that he "set up" the recently deceased Hughie (the prior night clerk). Using his wit, gift of gab, and salesmanship, Erie resembles O'Neill's older brother Jamie (as well as Hickey); Erie has bravado, guile, charm, and little else. O'Neill was often impressed by those, like his brother, who "put on the act": the blarney, the mountebank, the snake-oil salesman ready with a tall-tale and a glad hand. Within these characters are insecurity, fear of failure, and guilt. This dual characterization – charm on the outside, self-deprecation on the inside – epitomized many of O'Neill's characters.

A "play of old sorrow, written in tears and blood," *Long Day's Journey into Night* was offered to O'Neill's publisher, Bennet Cerf at Random House, with the understanding it would not be published until "twenty-five years after my death" (*Letters* 1988b: 575, 589), the motive here being painful truths concerning O'Neill's family (the play was produced in Stockholm in 1956, three years after O'Neill's death, by permission of O'Neill's wife and estate guardian, Carlotta). The play is set against a sunny morning (Act 1) and a hazy afternoon (Act 2); in Act 3 a thick fog descends, while in Act 4 nightfall encompasses the stage. By the end of the "long day's journey into night," the characters have been drinking and, in the case of their mother, doping heavily. The fog is symbolic, signifying the haze of inebriation, the spiritual descent into purgatory, and the aimless upheaval in the lives of the Tyrone family (a family mirroring O'Neill's own). In a 1940 letter to George Jean Nathan, O'Neill wrote that *Long Day's Journey into Night* is:

> The story of one day, 8 A.M. to midnight, in the life of a family of four – father, mother, and two sons – back in 1912, – a day in which things occur which evoke the whole past of the family and reveal every aspect of its interrelationships. A deeply tragic play, but without any violent tragic action. At the final curtain, there they still are, trapped within each other by the past, each guilty and at the same time innocent, scorning, loving, pitying each other, understanding and yet not understanding at all, forgiving but still doomed never to be able to forget. (*Letters* 1988b: 506–7)

This "confessional" play is O'Neill's mourning and homage to his self-destructive family. The plot is simple: the four main characters discover that the youngest son has consumption and must be sent to a sanatorium, and the mother, Mary Tyrone, has returned to her drug addiction. Throughout the course of the play the four characters confront the conflicts between responsibility to family and hedonism. Guilt arises stemming from selfishness and irresponsibility. James, the father, a successful actor trapped in a role, parsimoniously holds the family fortune. He invests in reckless land schemes for his own amusement but fails to provide well for his wife. Their home in Connecticut is comfortable but modest. We discover that James's penny-pinching caused him to hire a "quack" doctor for his pregnant wife. The "quack" over-prescribed morphine resulting in her addiction. Mary, caught up in her cycle of morphine, exits the stage frequently to shoot up in the attic (the others hear her nightly footsteps traipsing about in the attic, which has come to mean she is back on dope). Despite her efforts, she fails to conceal her condition. James, Jr., the older son and an alcoholic gadfly, frequents the company of Broadway show girls and whore-houses. His mother blames him for the death of their second (middle) child: Jamie, sick with a fever, was warned not to enter his younger brother's bedroom. Ignoring the warnings, he enters the room and infects his brother. The second son dies, and Mary never lets Jamie forget it (this event, as well as most of the play, reflected events in O'Neill's own life). By his mid-thirties, Jamie is racked with guilt and showing debilitation from debauchery. During Mary's difficult third pregnancy (where she became ill and addicted), Edmund (surrogate for O'Neill himself) is born. At the opening of the play, Edmund has returned home from a brief career as merchant sailor and newspaper reporter (like O'Neill himself). The reason for his return is a nagging cough, which turns out to be tuberculosis.

Plate 8. Long Day's Journey into Night, by Eugene O'Neill, Yale School of Drama. Jane Kaczmarek (Mary Tyrone) and Warren David Keith (Edmund), photo by Debra Spark.

The play deals with dependency, separation anxiety (Edmund must go away to the sanatorium, and Mary drifts into her morphine-induced inebriation), guilt, and redemption. Characters hurl accusations at each other for their shortcomings and irresponsibility; yet they remain bound together. According to Joel Phister, *Long Day's Journey into Night* epitomizes the "Irish tragic sense of determinism coupled with contemporary psychologists' pronouncements about familial determinism that partly sparks O'Neill's fascination with the 'can't help it' psychological resignation of the confessional Tyrones" (1995: 30). Looked at another way, O'Neill wanted to convey determinism in a modern idiom (destiny) that coincides with that found in Greek tragedy; characters are swept up by a fate that derails their free will, while audiences observe how the characters attempt to reverse the inevitable. In the play, O'Neill asserts that free will and the capacity to triumph over adversity are – in light of lingering human bonds, memory, and intractable destiny – largely illusions. The play is a melodrama, but it is far removed from the typical melodramatic assurances that a broken world can be repaired, if not by personal initiative then by redemptive insights. O'Neill's play, following the spirit of Nietzschean eternal recurrence, leaves us at the end where we began, in a tragic world that can be endured but never overcome.

Moon for the Misbegotten is O'Neill's final play. In contrast to the characters in *The Iceman Cometh* and *Long Day's Journey into Night*, "Josie and Tyrone are protected by no lasting illusions about themselves" (Falk 1982: 174). Josie, like Abbie in *Desire Under the Elms*, is a robust woman; but unlike Abbie, Josie is unable to find a mate. Her father hopes to capture their landlord, Jamie, for her. Jamie, like O'Neill's own brother and using the same character name (Jamie Tyrone) in *Long Day's Journey into Night*, is nearing the end of his self-destructive life. Jamie confesses to Josie that during his mother's funeral he sought out the companionship of a prostitute (mirroring the actual events of O'Neill's brother). This behavior, along with other feelings of self-deprecation, drives him to guilt-ridden suicide by alcohol. Jamie is motivated by what one critic calls the "compulsion to confess, to focus on haunting memories," even as the characters, and O'Neill himself, are "ashamed to acknowledge them" (Manheim 1982: 4).

> *Tyrone*:   You can take the truth, Josie – from me. Because you and I belong to the same club. We can kid the world but we can't fool ourselves, like most people, no matter what we do – nor escape ourselves no matter where we run away. Whether it's the bottom of a bottle, or a South Sea Island, we'd find our own ghosts there waiting to greet us. (*Plays* 1988a, vol. 3: 923)

Ghosts haunt O'Neill's characters. Yet his characters also seek "rebirth" and redemption, which yields "life its meaning" (Dubost 1997: 223). Emphasizing "confession" in his dramas, what Edward L. Shaughnessy calls his "Catholic sensibility" (2000: 79), O'Neill's plays are said to be "laid in an isolated, bizarre wasteland in which a few characters wander, lost and desolate, seeing someone to whom they can tell a story of a crime they have committed, and in making such confession find purgation" (Bogard 1988: xvi). Jamie Tyrone in *Moon for the Misbegotten* is eventually forgiven by Josie; the play's final lines demonstrate O'Neill's emphasis on purgation and redemption:

> *Josie*:   (*her face sad, tender and pitying – gently*). May you have your wish and die in your sleep soon, Jim, darling. May you rest forever in forgiveness and peace. (*She turns slowly and goes into the house*). (*Curtain*) (*Plays* 1988a, vol. 3: 946)

In his final full-length dramas – *Long Day's Journey into Night*, *The Iceman Cometh*, and *A Moon for the Misbegotten* – O'Neill exhibits a profound faith in language, in its ability to express, as well as mask, a character's angst and contradictions. In his characters' awkwardness, use of metaphor, and circumlocution, O'Neill deliberately attempts to portray the clumsy yet deeply felt desire for communication. Specifically, the glib veneer, as characterized by Hickey's "hail-fellow-well-met" persona, masks his painful awareness of lifelong disappointments. Mary Tyrone's denial of her drug addiction and her recriminating attacks on her family mask her painful disillusionment and cynicism. Jamie's attack on his brother in the final act of *Long Day's Journey into Night* is likewise revelatory of his noxious cynicism. By abusing his brother, Jamie drives him away in an effort to set him free. Attempting to "free" oneself of demons and inevitability is a recurring theme in O'Neill's dramas; Hickey experiences it, as do the Tyrone family in *Long Day's Journey into Night* and Jamie Tyrone in *Moon for the Misbegotten*. In his effort to "free" his brother, Jamie's cruelty in *Long Day's Journey into Night* is savage yet necessary, especially given Edmund's tuberculosis. The dual levels of reality – surface and depth – mesh together in all their awkwardness and revelation, revealing the struggle between free will and fate. As one critic put it, O'Neill wrote plays aiming to "reveal man's struggle – with its paradox of triumph in failure – against the mysterious force that shapes his existence and limits him" (Chabrowe 1976: xvi). Guilt and hope, crucifixion and resurrection, sin and redemption – the three sets of twin pillars that define Catholic ethos – are dialectically intertwined.

Denial is a major tactic of O'Neill's characters. The denials and the realities they disguise embody a powerful dramatic conceit, creating an intensity of emotion and a forceful expression of dramatic conflict. Audiences empathize with the characters as they struggle to maintain dignity within their fragile worlds. Characters seek the support of others, only to find that the support they crave is barely capable of shoring up anyone. Characters resist self-pity even as they acknowledge the pathetic conditions of their lives. This dramatic force – denial as an action pitted against reality – is O'Neill's realism at its most profound. Despite late twentieth-century criticisms of dramatic realism – that it somehow conceals contradictions, uncritically accepts determinates of history, and fixates on the middle class without acknowledging diversity – O'Neill's dramas, especially his later works, ideally express realism's enduring appeal. Besides O'Neill, few playwrights demonstrate such courage in the face of modern life's tragic conditions. The pathos of his characters is unequivocal, yet almost joyously expressed; in Nietzschean fashion, his characters rather than avert their eyes look straight into the abyss. His works no doubt depict "a journey into the subconscious" (Innes 1999: 141), and dramatize the "hidden phenomena" that attempt "to transcend the limitations imposed upon drama by the naturalistic demands for verisimilitude of appearances" (Törnqvist 1969: 254). Yet many of his plays engage in realism's demand for verisimilitude; his finest realistic dramas are couched in fidelity to real-world experiences. His own life is, in fact, grist for his creative mill. O'Neill absorbs the modern, romantic notion of the artist as self-observer depicted in a realistic setting. Joel Phister makes this very point clear when he describes O'Neill as "attuned to the cultural role of the modern artist as one who publicly symbolizes a romantic-psychological 'self'" (1995: 10). O'Neill's characters, like O'Neill himself, are haunted by past sins, seek sexual and emotional satisfaction, grope for human connections, and torture themselves in their search for happiness and redemption.

During the late twentieth and early twenty-first century, O'Neill's plays have enjoyed enormous success. Broadway revivals, such as *Hughie* with Al Pacino (1996); *The Iceman Cometh* with Kevin Spacey as Hickey (1999), also featuring Robert Sean Leonard as Parritt; *Moon for the Misbegotten* with Cherry Jones and Gabriel Byrne (2000); and *Long Day's Journey into Night* with Vanessa Redgrave (Mary), Brian Dennehy (James), Philip Seymour Hoffman (James, Jr.), and Robert Sean Leonard (Edmund) (2002), attest to O'Neill's enduring popularity. Not only have his exemplary realistic plays enjoyed success, his experimental plays, such as *The Emperor Jones* and *The Hairy Ape*, have also flourished in revivals by the avant-garde theatre company the Wooster Group during the mid-1990s. Revivals on Broadway, off-Broadway, regional theatres, and in translated performances around the world continue to attract audiences.

In 1925, O'Neill wrote a letter to theatre historian Arthur Hobson Quinn explaining his aims as a playwright:

> I'm always acutely conscious of the Force behind – (Fate, God, our biological past creating our present, whatever one calls it – Mystery, certainly) – and of the one eternal tragedy of Man in his glorious, self-destructive struggle to make the Force express him instead of being, as an animal is, an infinitesimal incident of expression. And my profound conviction is that this is the only subject worth writing about and that it is possible – or can be! – to develop a tragic expression in terms of transfigured modern values and symbols in the theatre which may to some degree bring home to members of a modern audience their ennobling identity with the tragic figures on the stage. (*Letters* 1988b: 195)

If one were to identify a flaw in O'Neill as a playwright, it would be his reliance on melodramatic excess. His plays are frequently overwrought. Yet he successfully transformed American melodrama from superficial conventions to moving examinations of human depth. Modernism requires "depth," and O'Neill provides it, using melodramatic conventions but shifting their emphasis. Rather than exploiting the one-dimensionality found in most melodramas and the razzle-dazzle of its stage effects, O'Neill sought to complicate melodrama's superficial morality, infusing it with contradictions, moral ambiguity, psychological depth, and human sorrow. According to Eric Bentley, if O'Neill "often failed to achieve tragedy, [he] succeeded as often in achieving melodrama" (1964: 214). Bentley adds elsewhere that O'Neill "undertook to free melodrama from what was cheap and tawdry and ineffective, and to write a melodrama that would be truly melodrama – a Monte Cristo raised to the nth power" (1987: 34). He was unrelentingly hard on his characters, but he was forgiving as well. His characters are caught in a conflict between Nietzschean live-for-the-moment and Catholicism's emphasis on responsibility and altruism. Hedonism and commitment – selfishness and selflessness – struggle within virtually all of his characters. Like most modernists, he saw heroism in these struggles, culling out the character's emotions and deepest fears. At his most successful, he was not merely one modern dramatist among many, but the predominant playwright of modern American drama.

BIBLIOGRAPHY

Bentley, E. (1964). *The Life of the Drama*. New York: Applause.
——(1987). "The Life and Hates of Eugene O'Neill." In *Thinking About the Playwright: Comments from Four Decades*. Evanston, IL: Northwestern University Press, 27–56.

Berlin, N. (1993). *O'Neill's Shakespeare*. Ann Arbor: University of Michigan Press.

Bigsby, C. W. E. (2000). *Modern American Drama, 1945–2000*. Cambridge: Cambridge University Press.

Black, S. A. (1999). *Eugene O'Neill: Beyond Mourning and Tragedy*. New Haven, CT: Yale University Press.

Bogard, T. (1988). *Contour of Time: The Plays of Eugene O'Neill*. New York: Oxford University Press.

Bowen, C. (1959). *The Curse of the Misbegotten: A Tale of the House of O'Neill*. New York: McGraw-Hill.

Bower, M. G. (1992). *Eugene O'Neill's Unfinished Threnody and Process of Invention in Four Cycle Plays*. Lewiston, NY: Edward Mellon.

Brietzke, Z. (2001). *The Aesthetics of Failure: Dynamic Structure in the Plays of Eugene O'Neill*. Jefferson, NC: McFarland.

Chabrowe, L. (1976). *Ritual and Pathos: The Theater of O'Neill*. Lewisburg, PA: Bucknell University Press.

Dubost, T. (1997). *Struggle, Defeat, or Rebirth: Eugene O'Neill's Vision of Humanity*. Jefferson, NC: McFarland.

Eisen, K. (1994). *The Inner Strength of Opposites: O'Neill's Novelistic Drama and the Melodramatic Imagination*. Athens: University of Georgia Press.

Falk, D. V. (1982). *Eugene O'Neill and the Tragic Tension*. New York: Gordian Press.

Fleche, A. (1997). *Mimetic Disillusion: Eugene O'Neill, Tennessee Williams, and U.S. Dramatic Realism*. Tuscaloosa: University of Alabama Press.

Gallup, D. C. (1998). *Eugene O'Neill and His Eleven-Play Cycle*. New Haven, CT: Yale University Press.

Gelb, A. and Gelb, B. (1973). *O'Neill*. New York: Harper and Row.

Hirsch, F. (1986). *Eugene O'Neill: Life, Work, and Criticism*. Fredericton, NB: York Press.

Innes, C. (1999). "Modernism in Drama." In Michael Levenson (ed.), *The Cambridge Companion to Modernism*. Cambridge: Cambridge University Press.

Houchin, J. H. (ed.) (1993). *The Critical Response to Eugene O'Neill*. Westport, CT: Greenwood.

Manheim, M. (1982). *Eugene O'Neill's New Language of Kinship*. Syracuse, NY: Syracuse University Press.

——(ed.) (1998). *The Cambridge Companion to Eugene O'Neill*. Cambridge: Cambridge University Press.

Miller, J. Y. and Frazer, W. L. (1997). *American Drama Between the Wars: A Critical History*. Boston: Twayne.

Mullett, M. B. (1922). "The Extraordinary Story of Eugene O'Neill." *American Magazine* 94, 5 (November): 34–6, 112, 114, 116, 118, 120.

Murphy, B. (1999). "Plays and Playwrights: 1915–1945." In D. B. Wilmeth and C. Bigsby (eds), *The Cambridge History of American Theatre*. Cambridge: Cambridge University Press, 289–342.

Nathan, G. J. (1928). "The American Prospect." *American Mercury* (October). Reprinted in Alan S. Downer (ed.), *American Drama and Its Critics: A Collection of Critical Essays*. Chicago: University of Chicago Press (1965), 78–115.

O'Neill, E. (1920). "A Letter from O'Neill." *New York Times*, April 11, Sec. 6: 2.

——(1921). "The Mail Bag." *New York Times*, December 18, Sec. 6: 1.

——(1924). "'All God's Chillun' Defended by O'Neill." *New York Times*, March 19: 19.

——(1926). "The Playwright Explains." *New York Times*, February 14, Sec. 6: 1.

——(1931). "O'Neill's Own Story of 'Electra' in the Making." *New York Herald Tribune*, November 8, Sec. 7: 2.

——(1932a). "O'Neill Says Soviet Stage Has Realized His Dream." *New York Herald Tribune*, June 19, Sec. 7: 2.

——(1932b). "Memoranda on Masks." *American Spectator* (November): 3. Reprinted in Toby Cole (ed.), *Playwrights on Playwriting*. New York: Hill and Wang (1961), 65–6.

——(1932c). "Second Thoughts." *American Spectator* (December): 2. Reprinted in Toby Cole (ed.), *Playwrights on Playwriting*. New York: Hill and Wang (1961), 67–9.

——(1933). "A Dramatist's Notebook." *American Spectator* (January): 2. Reprinted in Toby Cole (ed.), *Playwrights on Playwriting*. New York: Hill and Wang (1961), 69–71.

——(1988a). *O'Neill, Complete Plays, Volumes 1, 2, and 3*. New York: Modern Library.

O'Neill, E. (1988b). *Selected Letters of Eugene O'Neill*, ed. Travis Bogard and Jackson R. Bryer. New Haven, CT: Yale University Press.

Phister, J. (1995). *Staging Depth: Eugene O'Neill and the Politics of Psychological Discourse*. Chapel Hill: University of North Carolina Press.

Shaughnessy, E. L. (2000). *Down the Nights and Down the Days: Eugene O'Neill's Catholic Sensibility*. Notre Dame: University of Notre Dame Press.

Sheaffer, L. (1968). *O'Neill: Son and Playwright*. Boston: Little, Brown.

——(1990). *O'Neill: Son and Artist*. New York: Paragon.

Stansell, C. (2000). *American Moderns: Bohemian New York and the Creation of a New Century*. New York: Henry Holt.

Törnqvist, E. (1969). *A Drama of Souls*. New Haven, CT: Yale University Press.

Waith, E. M. (1964). "Eugene O'Neill: An Exercise in Unmasking." In John Gassner (ed.), *O'Neill: A Collection of Critical Essays*. Englewood Cliffs, NJ: Prentice-Hall, 29–41.

11

Fissures Beneath the Surface: Drama in the 1940s and 1950s

Thomas P. Adler

When, in his book *Leopards in the Temple*, Morris Dickstein remarks that, "On closer examination, postwar culture looks more edgy and unsettling than we once imagined, reflecting powerful and subversive social energies roiling beneath the placid surface of the Truman and Eisenhower years" (1999: 15), he is joining a chorus of recent social and cultural historians who have commented on the peculiarly bipolar or bifurcated nature of the American experience in the 1940s and 1950s. Already during the war years, the rightness of the moral stand against the forces of totalitarianism – the enemy without – that unified the nation exhibited its gritty subtext or dark underside – an enemy within – in racial segregation in both professional athletics and the armed services, in anti-Semitism, and in the internment camps into which Japanese Americans were herded. During the Truman years, the Marshall Plan that achieved economic reconstruction abroad was accompanied by a new wave of manifest destiny, a policing of the world by a nuclear power in the name of spreading democracy. At home, expansion and prosperity contributed to social dislocation as whites moved to the suburbs, leaving behind urban ghettos and sowing seeds for racial, class, and ethnic dissension, while the Kinsey reports that demystified the physiology and psychology of sex did little to bring about widespread acceptance of transgressive sexuality. The Eisenhower period, often too simplistically seen as a time of homogeneous belief in such traditional values as work, family, and religion, revealed its own fault lines in the regimentation and conformity of a reorganized economy that prized commodity consumption over production and loyalty over initiative, in the repression of just how inequitable and intolerant society was, and in a retrenchment of women's roles, resulting in feelings of anonymity and apathy, restlessness and psychic anxiety. If the Cold War mentality that generated paranoia and suspicion over the threat of Communism was used to justify forced loyalty oaths, blacklisting, witch-hunts, and even executions, more positive signs of the guarantee of civil rights could be seen in the outlawing of restrictive housing covenants and the end of segregated schools. Such is the background against which the playwrights of the period dramatize the war and its aftermath, relations between the sexes, the tension between the individual and society, and the realities of ethnic, sexual, and racial difference.

From Isolation to Intervention

Dickstein hypothesizes that perhaps the most telling clue to the time from 1945 on can be found in "its changing perspective on war, since the whole period was shadowed by memories of war and by Cold War fears of its recurrence in even more unspeakable forms" (1999: 40). Although Thornton Wilder's *The Skin of Our Teeth* (1942) does not mention World War II specifically, perhaps for that very reason it remains the most resonant play about war from this period. Featuring an allegorical family named the Antrobuses, Wilder's Pulitzer drama recounts human history in capsule form, in a wildly theatrical, surrealistic style, from the beginning of time on into the future, focusing on great catastrophic moments – the Ice Age, the Deluge, the War, any war – as natural and social history. In each case, the Antrobuses, because

Plate 9. *The Skin of Our Teeth*, by Thornton Wilder, Missouri Repertory Theatre. Left to right: Philip Christopher (Henry Antrobus), Robin Humphrey (Mrs. Antrobus), and Rebecca Engel-King (Dinosaur). Courtesy of the Missouri Repertory Theatre.

of natural disaster and/or human culpability, barely muddle through. Wilder replays the Cain and Abel story using the first murderer to represent the presence of evil in the world, the anarchic force that misuses freedom while refusing to exercise responsibility. He alludes as well to the invention of gunpowder, to the hedonistic pleasure principle that promotes aggression, and to the detrimental impact of totalitarianism. Ultimately, however, scientific and intellectual progress is possible, and humans can endure and prevail – provided that everyone pitches in and does their part.

By the time Robert E. Sherwood, who served Franklin Roosevelt as speechwriter and adviser, completed *There Shall Be No Night* (1941), his own isolationism (earlier he had been a pacifist) had given way to interventionism in response to the fascist and Nazi threat. *Night*, in fact, stands as unique in the annals of the stage for the way that it helped shape public opinion about America's entry into World War II. In a Finnish home on the eve of invasion, two men of science argue the limits of reason. While the German Dr. Ziemssen seeks to justify the Nazis' extermination of inferior races, the Nobel laureate Dr. Kaarlo Valkonen speaks about humankind's ability to discern an ethical dimension that will prevent their devolving into moral cretins. When right reason fails, then nations may have no choice but to take up arms. Maxwell Anderson's *Candle in the Wind* (1941), set in France in 1940, features a debate similar to Sherwood's between those who believe in the absolute autonomy of the state, however evil, and a coalition of democratic governments where minds are free. Although geographically America never became a theatre for battle, the war still invades the Washington drawing rooms in two Lillian Hellman plays, one portraying the choice to be involved, and the other looking at events that preceded the conflagration. *The Searching Wind* (1944), with its time shifts between the present, Italy in 1922, Berlin in 1923, and Paris in 1938, becomes a meditation on the moral failure of left-leaning intellectuals who fooled themselves about historical events – Victor Emmanuel's welcome of Mussolini into Rome; the early anti-Jewish pogroms; the Munich Pact – that they found easier to countenance and condone than to challenge. *Watch on the Rhine* (1941), among the most dramatically satisfying of these works, finds Fanny Farrelly playing hostess in her country estate to both an aristocratic German Nazi supporter and her son-in-law Kurt Muller, a freedom fighter in the anti-Nazi underground. Although Kurt disparages all violence as a moral sickness, he finds it necessary to kill the Nazi supporter to protect the lives of others. Fanny, shaken out of her complacency and guided by her late husband's conviction that an act of oppression committed anywhere affects everyone, everywhere, shows her mettle by financially supporting Kurt's cause. Works about America at war, even sincerely felt ones by well-established dramatists such as Anderson's *The Eve of St. Mark* (1942) and Moss Hart's *Winged Victory: The Air Force Play* (1943), tend to be little more than patriotic tracts. The subversion of sexual consummation, as husbands are torn from their wives, becomes a staple of these plays, elevating the shared pain of the women who must wait as an example of sacrifice for Americans at home.

Once the fighting ends, American playwrights feel able to examine patriotism more critically. Thomas Heggen and Joshua Logan's hit comedy *Mister Roberts* (1948) satirizes the fanatical commanding officer of a Navy cargo ship who is explicitly likened to the totalitarian leaders arrayed against America and its allies. But after Lt. Roberts successfully leads a rebellion against this petty tyrant, he requests transfer to combat duty, only to be killed while drinking coffee. By deromanticizing death in war, Heggen and Logan can, by implication, valorize all the seemingly unheroic acts of those who missed the chance to prove themselves in battle. Two other plays examine more serious excesses of zeal. Herman Wouk sets the 1954 adaptation of his novel *The Caine Mutiny Court Martial* within the framework of a courtroom melodrama. A Navy lawyer, Lt. Greenwald, is torn apart by his need to establish the mental incompetence of the obsessive disciplinarian Lt. Commander Queeg. Because he has been the victim of racial slurs himself, and because Queeg fought to save Jews like his mother, Greenwald insinuates that, in time of war, those in authority motivated by honorable ends are free to violate basic rights with impunity, and that all their orders must be carried out, even if wrong – similar to the rationalization that brings down the arrogant McLeod in Sidney Kingsley's *Detective Story* (1949). No such moral confusion mars Louis O. Coxe and Robert Chapman's 1951 adaptation of Herman Melville's *Billy Budd*, in which Captain Vere overturns the verdict of a court of ship's officers and condemns the innocent Billy to death. Against a background of mutinies on other vessels, Vere, though personally sympathetic to the scapegoat victim and knowing himself to be tragically wrong, still argues that conscience must be abrogated in favor of strict adherence to a code of military law.

Although Paul Osborn's dramatization of John Hersey's novel *A Bell for Adano* (1944) questions whether the military power that liberates differs substantially from the one that oppresses and is tinged (like John Patrick's *The Hasty Heart* of the following year) with an awareness of how, once back in the States, these soldiers united by a common enemy will inevitably divide again along race, class, and ethnic lines, by far the most damning critique of American colonialism comes a decade after Osborn in John Patrick's *The Teahouse of the August Moon*, adapted from Vern Sneider's novel and winner of the Pulitzer in 1954. The play's narrator, Sakini, who acts as interpreter for the occupation army, judges the current subjugation as only the most recent of a series perpetrated for more than six centuries – though any mention of the United States' dropping atomic and hydrogen bombs is noticeably missing. *Teahouse* documents the attempts of the American military to introduce technology, capitalism, and democratic rule into a culture more interested in beauty than utility. The rebel among the American soldiers, Capt. Fisby, renounces the geisha Lotus Blossom as wife because racial prejudice back home would insure her rejection, and he encourages the natives to construct an exquisitely simple teahouse as a site for their ritual ceremony, rather than the structure called for by the army manual. When the military conquerors order it dismantled, its destruction harkens back to the ax blows felling the trees at the end of Chekhov's *Cherry Orchard*. As Brechtian commentator, Sakini pointedly insists that any chance for coexistence between the two cultures is obliterated when an excess of missionary zeal requires that the natives become totally subservient to the cultural hegemony of the foreigners – a critique of America's interventionist policies that will surface again later in plays about the Vietnam War.

Three works from 1946, including Robert Anderson's *Come Marching Home* and Howard Lindsay and Russel Crouse's *State of the Union* – which introduces the metaphor that equates playing ball with playing politics to the American stage – provide a footnote to this group of plays. In Garson Kanin's *Born Yesterday*, the only one of the three (because of its proto-feminist heroine) still sometimes revived, Harry Brock, a scrap metal war profiteer whose political influence reaches into the halls of Congress, comes up against his spunky mistress Billie Dawn, who becomes educated at his insistence only to get the goods on his illegal financial dealings. Real empowerment resides in the knowledge that comes from the printed word and a free press, so much so that Brock, feeling threatened, destroys her books in an obvious allusion to the Nazi book burnings. A few years earlier, in the midst of the war, the genesis of some of the issues raised by these three plays was placed in historical context in Kingsley's *The Patriots* (1943), an imaginative reconstruction based on the letters of Alexander Hamilton, who argued the necessity for an aristocracy of wealth to rule the nation, and Thomas Jefferson, who believed in the common people and their ability to govern. It is his view that carries the day, if only by the skin of its teeth.

Staging the Sexes

William Inge, who had an almost unprecedented run of Broadway successes during the 1950s with a series of plays that scratched the veneer off Middle America, might be seen as the paradigmatic playwright of the period. And his Pulitzer Prize-winning *Picnic* (1953) encapsulates as well as any work – and sometimes in ways daring for its day – the fraught relations between the sexes during the postwar years, dramatizing many of the tensions that Betty Friedan would describe in *The Feminine Mystique* a decade after the play's appearance. Arguing that the mystique of the feminine, by valorizing passivity and nurturance, actually stunted women's potentialities for achieving self-development – just as Victorian culture had thwarted gratifying sexuality – Friedan argues that "women's failure to grow to complete identity has hampered rather than enriched her sexual fulfillment, virtually doomed her to be castrative to her husband and sons, and caused neuroses . . . equal to illnesses caused by sexual repression" (1985: 77). What marks and finally delimits the women in Inge's play is their nearly total subjugation to what might be called the curse of the romantic imagination. Flo Owens, who hopes to realize her unfulfilled dreams through two teenage daughters, tries to actualize the ideal of well-to-do domesticity fostered by serialized women's fiction and consumerism. Counter to this is the pull toward freedom and independence – symbolized by the train heard in the distance – with its equally unreal promise of happiness somewhere over the rainbow. Beautiful Madge, restless and narcissistic, hopes to be discovered by Hollywood, where the wandering derelict, Hal, is also headed. The arrival of this muscle-bound, swaggering jock, bare-chested or tee-shirted in the manner of Stanley Kowalski, sets all the neighbor women in a tizzy. Madge's decision to desert the putative security promised by her intellectual boyfriend Alan (whose appearance wearing an apron visually displaces the macho image that would typically confirm him as an appropriate husband), and follow Hal and the whistle, dismays her mother. Flo's neighbor, Helen Potts, whose mother had Helen's marriage annulled so that her only role would be as daughter/martyr, finds herself drawn to the antics of these youths, yet uneasy over her sexual attraction to Hal. Flo's boarder, the spinster schoolteacher Rosemary, who once put up a front of propriety by chiseling the genitals off the statue of a gladiator and objecting strenuously to books by the likes of D. H. Lawrence, masks her own sexual deprivation in an emasculating attitude that prevents her beau, Howard, from getting fresh with her.

Inge dramatizes the dynamics of these relationships in a ritual mating dance, a contest between the sexes in which traditional roles are temporarily thrown askew but that eventuates in a reconfirmation of the image of the woman as subservient to the man, even pleading to be allowed that unchallenging identity. As the dance begins, the partnerless Rosemary pairs off with the unpretty and awkward younger daughter Millie, but insists that she lead; moreover, she will not tolerate a parody of themselves when Hal and Howard imitate them in drag. In a pathetic attempt to recover her youth, jealous Rosemary later pulls Hal away from Millie, but finally turns on him and rips off his shirt when she realizes the impossibility of possessing him. In her desperation, Rosemary eventually pleads with the weak mama's boy, Howard, to take her as his wife and thus save her from a life of profligacy and one-night stands. Similar sexual frustration is rampant in Inge's first success, *Come Back, Little Sheba* (1950), in which Lola, thrown out by her possessive father after she got pregnant, left childless after she marries and the baby dies, and forbidden to work by her husband, spends her days sublimating unfulfilled needs by devouring candy, listening to soap operas, and eyeing both the husky milkman and Turk, the satyr-like, javelin-throwing lover of their boarder, Marie, who poses for her in his tracksuit. Inge clearly intends, of course, that Turk, like Hal in *Picnic*, will be the object of the gaze of gay males as well as of the females in the audience. Lola's husband, Doc, another mama's boy, gave up his dream of being a "real" doctor to become a chiropractor, suffered financial reverses, fell into alcoholism, and became physically abusive. Lola, who finds renewed contentment in keeping house when a chastened and repentant Doc returns, recounts her dream of watching, in fascination, Turk in Olympic competition. The referee, in the person of Lola's father, disqualifies Turk and gives the javelin to Doc, who throws it up in the air; but it fails ever to come down and penetrate the earth, which seems to presage Doc's emasculation. Now Lola, shorn of her dream of recapturing youth, and Doc, denied his drink, are locked together in mutual need.

Although readings of women as triumphant castrators held currency for a long time in Inge criticism, this character type's appearance is even more pronounced in another group of plays from the period. The almost archetypal work in this regard, as its title indicates, is Joseph Kramm's *The Shrike* (1952), which pits Jim Downs, a theatrical director until the war interrupted his career, against his shrewish wife, Ann, who had sacrificed her own career as an actress, and thus any possibility for cultivating "a room of [her] own," in order to be supportive of him. The criminal ward in city hospital where Jim is confined after a failed suicide attempt — inhabited by a too-perfect, textbook microcosm of races and nationalities — is a kind of Kafkaesque nightmare that Kramm equates with the army, with its rules and regimentation; with the theatre, as a place of pretense where masks and roles are assumed and then thrown off; and with a prison that keeps everyone under constant surveillance — as in Foucault's panopticon. (The sanatorium in Mary Chase's escapist farce *Harvey* [1945] is considerably more benign.) Jim chooses release into the conniving Ann's custody over continued incarceration, yet living under her control will be the most insidious imprisonment imaginable. This pattern of women seeking revenge by making their husbands dependent upon them appears in such other plays as Clifford Odets's *The Country Girl* (1950), in which Georgie, who like Ann gave up her career to marry, is jealous of her alcoholic husband Frank's comeback as an actor and tries to derail it; or in Michael Gazzo's *A Hatful of Rain* (1955), where the pregnant Celia distrusts her husband Johnny's promise to kick the drug habit he acquired after a war injury and calls the police to come and take him away.

Since Kitti Frings crafted the screenplay for *The Shrike*, it comes as no surprise that her skillful stage adaptation of Thomas Wolfe's massive novel, *Look Homeward, Angel*, in 1957 contains echoes of Ann Downs in the domineering wife and mother, Eliza Gant, who tries to deny man his art (whether it be sculpture or writing) and thus his life. Afraid to love because of the possibility of being hurt or disappointed, she makes the family home a workhouse for her offspring and, in turn, finds in the paying customers a surrogate family. In their Strindbergian battle of the sexes, her husband, the Falstaffian Gant, sees her as a vampirish bloodsucker. Both her sons, the dying Bert, whose consumption symbolizes his metaphorical drowning in her home, and the writer-in-the-making Eugene, plunged into a Whitmanesque verbal rapture by the sound of the train whistle that signals freedom, feel deserted by her and in need of substitute mothers. The serene-looking stone angel in his studio that Gant the unfulfilled artist has been trying unsuccessfully to copy comes to symbolize the difficult, transmutative process to which Eugene will need to subject his family's life if he is to transform it into something as elusive, yet transcendent, as art.

The men in these and several other plays from this period tend to be vulnerable, dissatisfied, and disillusioned creatures. Some realize they have failed to satisfy society's macho stereotypes, or are even unsure of their sexuality and so must prove their continued virility. Others are suffering from regret that what they have accomplished has fallen far short of what they had hoped and from the recognition that few, if any, choices still remain open to them. Still others are experiencing a more general sense of alienation and malaise, a feeling of disease or existential angst. Inge's two other major plays illustrate several of these motifs. The central story of the multi-plotted *Bus Stop* (1955), which explores the necessity of breaking down stereotypes about what constitutes manliness before love can be recognized and flourish, concerns

Bo Decker, a small-time rodeo cowboy, and Cherie, an exaggeratedly adorned night-club chanteuse, whom he has practically kidnapped for marriage on a ranch out West. On the surface, Bo plays the irresistible, experienced ladies' man, with whom one night of sex guarantees love everlasting; underneath, he is a pussycat, too tender-hearted even to go deer hunting. Yet to verbalize his true feelings and admit his lonesomeness would render him weak in the eyes of others. Subdued in a fistfight, he misjudges that Cherie would never want him again, when in reality she is tired of being commodified as a sex object and emerges as an early proponent of the softer, more respectful male. Because she does not demand that Bo conform to society's expectations, he is free to throw off his swagger and gently love her. The alcoholic Dr. Lyman, despite his own shortcomings, possesses considerable practical wisdom about how, in an age anxious about atomic cataclysm and survival that makes one put self first, true manliness understands that giving of self is not a lessening or an emptying out but a way of finding one's identity. In *The Dark at the Top of the Stairs* (1957), Inge again focuses on the insecurities that prevent individuals from forming intense bonds of communion. Set in an Oklahoma town during the oil boom of the 1920s, against the background of the transition from a cowboy/agrarian to a mercantile/industrial-ized economy – and thus for theatre audiences somewhat analogous to the post-World War II shift to a corporate/consumer society – the play treats in part the impact of social change on cultural stability and traditional institutions. The Flood family, because of Rubin's precarious livelihood as a traveling salesman of harnesses, a soon to be outmoded commodity, find themselves pushed farther to the fringes of the newly moneyed local society where being outside the group results in distrust and rejection. Because of prejudicial attitudes, however, not even money can guarantee admission to places like the country club that exclude some people such as the Jewish businessman from membership. Reluctant to marry because he saw it as restricting his freedom, Rubin has resorted to drinking and womanizing and, when his wife Cora rejects him sexually, to physical abusiveness. But losing his job in mid-career and recognizing the challenge in reeducating himself for another somewhat chasten him, allowing him to admit to Cora his feelings of inadequacy in a world where economic progress has left him behind and where the future and his place in it are unknown. The dark symbolizes, in part, that fear of the unknown. When Rubin stands naked at the top of the stairs (the audience sees only his feet) and beckons Cora to come, his nakedness suggests his acceptance of his vulnerability; now unafraid to reveal his weakness as well as his strength to Cora, he knows she will provide the reassurance of physical love and bolster his self-respect.

Laura Reynolds in Robert Anderson's *Tea and Sympathy* (1953) fulfills much this same role. When she married Bill, a housemaster at a New England boys' boarding school, she sensed his insecurities, yet believed that she could quiet his fears of latent homosexuality. Now among their charges is young Tom Lee, who, because of his walk and the way he wears his hair and his willingness to take female parts in school plays, is perceived as different by others, even by his father and Bill, since he refuses to be pigeonholed into the stereotype of the manly man. When he is discovered sunbathing nude with one of the teachers, suspicion that he is homosexual turns to persecution by others and uncertainty about himself that he tries to erase with an unsuccessful tryst with the town prostitute, followed by a failed suicide attempt. Laura, knowing that she has been unable to save Bill, finally overcomes her moral qualms and gives herself to Tom sexually, restoring his belief in his own manliness – though for many observers this confirmation of normative heterosexuality begs the deepest issue of Tom's sexual orientation. A number of critics have objected to the way that Anderson and other playwrights like him offer physical sexuality as redemptive, a panacea or too-easy cure for a person's ills, and such a charge is not totally ill-founded. In Paddy Chayefsky's *Middle of the Night* (1956), for instance, an older man who experiences mild depression over no longer being physically desired and a fear of impotence that temporarily becomes fact, is rejuvenated sexually by this love for a younger woman. But, at times, these same writers complicate this issue by adding a further dimension that has to do with the ethical imperative of setting aside traditional moral codes in order to respond compassionately to another's needs. In Anderson's *Silent Night, Lonely Night* (1959), for example, Katherine Johnson and John Sparrow, both married but temporarily alone and lonely, come together in an inn on Christmas Eve for a long night's confession of their domestic difficulties, culminating in a one-time sexual encounter before they each return to their spouse. To do this, Katherine must reject the guilt-fostering "shalt nots" of the God on a pendant given to her by her puritanical father for a situational ethic that endorses an affective morality and imparts a religious dimension to the act of love. A similar conflict occurs for Leona Samish in Arthur Laurents's *The Time of the Cuckoo* (1955), who goes to Venice carrying a whole trunkload of values and mores. There, her puritan guilt and sexual repression come up against the instinctive lust for life of Renato DiRossi, who believes that abstract moral notions of right and wrong must give way before a mutuality that makes life a little sweeter for the participants.

Individualism and Authority

In a 1960 essay entitled "The State of the Theater," Arthur Miller comments on what he considers the limitations of American playwriting during the late 1940s and early 1950s. "The plays of the forties, which began as an attempt to analyze the self in the world, are ending as a device to exclude the world.... [By the mid-1950s] the theater was retreating into an area of psychosexual romanticism, ... when great events both at home and abroad cried out for recognition and analytic inspection" (1996: 231–2). Miller's assertion would seem to have bearing on a considerable number of plays having to do with the individual's relationship with the self and with the society, many of which examine how one negotiates the terrain between the dictates of human conscience and some external authority. "The world" is still very much present in Lillian Hellman's darkly satiric *Another Part of the Forest* (1946), about a once genteel way of life being replaced by a more pragmatic and utilitarian business model that considers people negotiable commodities to be bartered for economic gain. The Hubbard's Southern Greek Revival mansion appears to be the seat of culture and learning in the 1880s, but devotion to the arts proves a thin veneer covering over venality and immorality; at the same time, Lionnet, the Bagtry family estate built on the institution of slavery, is falling into ruin because of the family's inability to adapt to a post-Civil War economy. The Hubbard patriarch profited during the war by running the blockade; his bourgeois sons now ride with the Klan and ruin him by swindling and blackmail, while they trade their ambitious sister, Regina, eventually with her consent, in a loveless marriage that will bring her husband's financial holdings into the family. In a pattern that resonates through the drama of the 1950s, the power of love is no challenge for the power of money.

Miller was not alone among commentators on American drama in decrying an inward turn from the social to the personal, where sexual problems seemed to override society's concerns. Robert Brustein, for example, decried the "aspirin fantasies" rather than the "radical surgery" doled out by many post-World War II stage realists, rebuking "the newer American playwrights who often confuse themselves with psychological counselors," and in whose works "you will generally find an object lesson about the diagnosis and treatment of romantic, emotional, family, or social disorders" (1965: 284). Among many examples indicative of this type of play about injured psyches and their healing is Laurents's *A Clearing in the Woods* (1957), a theatrically intricate stream-of-consciousness work that blends elements of fantasy and expressionism to dramatize its heroine Virginia's journey to psychological whole-ness, arrived at by confronting her three younger selves and the way each interacts with a man – father, teenage lover, husband. At each stage, Virginia coveted a life superior to and set apart from the ordinary. Dissatisfied with herself, she placed destructive expectations upon others; because she never really loved anyone, not even herself, she destroyed the men in her life. By becoming content with herself rather than pursuing a false image that never could be, she can accommodate rather than deny her former selves, and thus move with hope into the future. If the breakthrough here seems too easily won, it is perhaps more justly earned by the protagonist who moves safely from maternal control to marriage bed in Jane Bowles's delicate *In a Summer House* (1953). Another play featuring a woman curing her problems through caring for another is William Gibson's bittersweet comedy *Two for the Seesaw* (1958), in which the spunky and outspoken dance teacher named Gittel is willing to help the wimpy loser, Jerry, regain his self-confidence and return to his wife, learning in the process that she no longer needs to allow men to demean her just to keep herself from being lonely. A more substantial look at individuals coming into themselves occurs in Gibson's best-remembered play, *The Miracle Worker* (1959), based on the lives of Annie Sullivan and her renowned pupil, Helen Keller. Not just an uplifting examin-ation of how physical impairments can be overcome, the play explores the power of a love that dares to discipline and criticize, as well as the power of language – the biblical gift to name things – as a link between the self and the world outside. Helen (blind and able to make only barely articulate sounds) must be retaught language to express her thoughts and feelings. To accomplish this, Annie, initially greeted with skepticism because of her youth and lower immigrant social class, must exercise firmness without pity; only then can the teacher help shape the student and, in the process, achieve a reciprocal salvation.

The possibility for individuals to beat the odds and break through to begin creating not just new opportunities for themselves but a new world order pervades Clifford Odets's fanfare for the common (wo)man, *Night Music* (1940). In this Whitmanesque paean to America and its people, the older generation, represented by Rosenberger, keeps the younger from falling into disillusion by reminding them of their unlimited potential. Steve, fired from his job of transporting monkeys across the country to Hollywood and the movies, feels unwanted and inadequate, ready to explode because of his unfulfilling life. Faye, bored and unhappy, lonely and always struggling, is in rebellion against the living-but-partly-living lives of her materialistic parents. Rosenberger has great faith in youth's ability to change and make over the world – a faith that Faye finds confirmed in the always chipper night singing of her favorite animals, the crickets, and that Steve sees evidenced in the dream-dust-laden spaces at the World's Fair. If the sentimentalizing tendency evident in social protest plays from the 1930s still surfaces in Odets, two postwar plays whose titles significantly hint at or refer directly to the season of autumn are darker, proposing that possibilities only diminish with the passage of time, that opportunities for choices that might result in significant change have themselves been reduced or foreclosed by earlier decisions one has made. Inge's *A Loss of Roses* (1959) concerns a down-on-her-luck actress's attempt to discover stability and a renewed sense of self-worth. Long ago the victim of sexual abuse by her brother, and later of attempted sexual molestation by her father-in-law, Lila Green experiences a vague sense of having been somehow responsible for her own degradation because she was not tough enough, thereby inviting victimization. The deterministic pattern will be repeated, as she gives herself to a much younger man; after he goes back on his commitment to marry, she attempts suicide, and then enters a humiliating relationship with a manipulative man who will perform with her in blue movies and live sex acts. Innocence, once wrenched away, can never be regained, and the passage of time means aging and decay; to be a party to society's male-fashioned mystique of beauty and youth becomes a catch-22, condemning Lila to a life of exploitation. Hellman treats the issue of time and changes more subtly and philosophically in her Chekhovian play, *The Autumn Garden* (1951). Set in a boarding house along the Gulf Coast decorated with twin portraits of the owner painted 23 years apart and peopled mostly by middle-aged characters, often involved in sexual dalliances, who have difficulty reconciling desire with act, this drama's leitmotifs are regret, emptiness, waste, ennui, lost chances, and dashed dreams. One of the boarders, General Griggs, who out of compassion remains with his childlike wife in a loveless marriage, reflects soberly on the intersection between past decisions or indecisions and present options, explicitly voicing an existentialist perspective on how the succession of choices an individual must continually make finally creates, and thus determines, what one becomes, the content of one's character.

Brenda Murphy argues that, despite the widespread contention that American theatre "ignored the fundamental political issues" facing the nation between 1945 and 1960, there exists a "persistent subtext beneath the apparent self-absorption . . . in which political, social, and moral issues were engaged and debated with intensity and passion" (1999: 2–3). Because of this, even a whimsical comic vaudeville like Gore Vidal's *Visit to a Small Planet* (1957) could play upon Americans' fear of the Russians and issues of deterrence. Hellman called upon just such a sociopolitical subtext in 1952 in directing a revival of her 1934 play *The Children's Hour* so that the town's reaction to the suspected lesbian relationship of its heroines would reflect the malicious name calling and guilt-by-innuendo of the witch-hunts during the McCarthy era. Hellman also wrote two stage adaptations that bore directly on Cold War paranoia. Her adaptation of Emmanuel Robles's *Montserrat*, which she directed in 1949, centers on events during Simon Bolivar's 1812 insurrection against the Spanish occupation army in Venezuela. Montserrat must choose between his commitment to the cause and his responsibility to six people who have been rounded up – like the Jews during the Holocaust – and will be murdered because of his intransigence in supporting the liberator. One of the play's minor characters embodies a position that, given Hellman's blacklisting from Hollywood screenwriting for refusing to name names, seems prescient for the playwright herself when he insists upon an absolute zone of conscience he will not violate under pressure from any government. In *Scoundrel Time*, Hellman writes about her own appearance before the House committee in 1952, when she refused "to hurt innocent people . . . to save myself" and famously asserted, "I cannot and will not cut my conscience to serve this year's fashions" (1976: 93). In her 1955 adaptation of Jean Anouilh's *The Lark*, Hellman underscores the analogy between Joan of Arc and her inquisitors on the one hand and suspected Communists and the investigating committee on the other. The proto-feminist Joan embodies the absolute right, even duty, to disobey an established order that would thwart the minority in its midst. The only original American dramatic retelling of the popular story of the Maid of Orléans, Maxwell Anderson's *Joan of Lorraine* (1946), combines an emphasis on the tension between the directly inspired individual and the one who looks to institutionalized authority with a consideration of the related issue of scientific truth versus religious faith. Anderson employs the historical narrative of Joan as a play-within-the-play, framing it by the analogous story of Mary Grey, slated to perform in the title role. Just as Joan, true to her inner voices, felt compelled to challenge the Church, Mary uncompromisingly protests the validity of the new rendering the author and director are imposing upon the myth, vowing that she will even sacrifice acting Joan to remain true to her reading. Her interpretation is challenged by a more pragmatic viewpoint that concedes that some faith to live by is essential for every creature, but questions whether one system of belief is more defensible than any other.

The science versus religion conflict is faced most squarely by Jerome Lawrence and Robert E. Lee in *Inherit the Wind* (1955), based on the 1925 Scopes "monkey" trial, with Clarence Darrow for the defense and William Jennings Bryan for the prosecution, in the characters, respectively, of Henry Drummond and Matthew Brady. Ben Cates's decision to read to his high school science class a passage from Darwin's *Origin of Species* precipitates the conflict between faith and doubt, unity and pluralism, society's laws and the individual's rights, and the conservative South and more progressive North. Brady upholds the revealed truth of scripture, labeling all scientists agnostics and judging Darwin's theories false without having ever read him. The agile and flamboyant Drummond, on the other hand, asserts the power and sanctity of the human mind as it reasons for itself; there exists a plurality of truths, without any comforting abstract grid to arbitrarily plot the rightness and wrongness of every act. Although the jury selected for the conformity of their opinions pronounces Bert guilty, the judge proclaims a moral victory for him by assessing only a small fine to be appealed. Bert announces his intention to remain a pariah by continuing to oppose an unjust law – in yet another play that, coming after the House Un-American Activities Committee (HUAC) and McCarthy hearings, asserts the necessity for society to forsake its attempts to control thought.

If *Inherit the Wind* is the theatre's pivotal contribution during this period to the science and theology debate, the most enduring religious drama is not the St. Joan plays that trace her conflict with an earthly institution, but rather Archibald MacLeish's 1958 Pulitzer winner *J. B.*, which in retelling the Book of Job in modern dress pits humans directly against God. Here, the Everyman over whose soul God and Satan battle is a successful businessman seen celebrating Thanksgiving Day, the American feast that captures most forcibly the connection between spiritual election and material prosperity. He lives, however, not in an age of faith but the post-bomb nuclear age of anxiety, filled with imagery of dung heaps and cesspools that recall the modern wasteland of Beckettian absurdity. (When Clifford Odets retells the Noah story as Jewish family drama in *The Flowering Peach* [1954], he keeps the atomic age before audiences as well, with the Rood as an allegory of nuclear destruction.) As *J. B.* suffers loss after horrendous loss – for no other reason than that a capricious, irrational God decides to test a man who demands purpose and logic – the only avenue left for restoring meaning is, apparently, to demean himself by pleading guilty to a sin he did not commit. *J. B.*'s wife Sarah, however, enjoys an epiphany in finding a sprig of forsythia blooming in the ashes, which inspires her husband to forsake cynicism for a dynamic new faith in humanity. As in Chayefsky's *The Tenth Man* (1959), where the power of human love becomes contemporary man's religion in his search for definition and purpose, in *J. B.* the ultimate value resides in affective feelings that are here deified. So the final, somewhat sentimental image is of a paradise regained, as a new Adam and Eve set to work with restored confidence in the American ideal of self-reliance (see chapter 13).

Dramatizing Difference

In a 1960 essay defending his plays against the charge of "always plunging into sewers," Tennessee Williams looked back at his work over the past two decades, concluding: "I dare to suggest, from my POV [point of view], that the theater has made in our time its greatest artistic advance through the unlocking and lighting up and ventilation of the closets, attics, and basements of human behavior" (1978: 116–17). He might easily have been talking about two short plays from the early 1950s by William Inge. In *The Tiny Closet*, a fastidious middle-aged man, Mr. Newbold, insists upon his right to retain some private space and so forbids his landlady to unlock the door to his closet. But she and a neighbor lady, suspicious that any man so unnaturally prim must be involved in something illegal or seditious, break open the closet, only to discover his secret cache of elaborate women's hats. For this they brand him freakish and unnatural; by "outing" him, they undermine his self-esteem and curb his freedom to cross-dress. The conflation of what many people regarded as sexual perversion with suspicion of political subversion was, of course, rampant during the Cold War era; as Stephen Whitfield writes, "In an era that fixed so rigidly the distinction between Communist tyranny and the Free World, and which prescribed that men were men and women were housewives," only the "peril" of homosexuality could be "worse than Communism" (1991: 43). Although *Tiny Closet* might be Inge's response to HUAC, it offers a more generalized condemnation of the prejudice of all those who marginalize the "other." Inge exposes the pain of his own homosexuality most personally in *The Boy in the Basement*. Spencer Scranton, the mortician son of a prudish mother who has already reduced her invalid husband to an infantile state, can only express his homosexuality when he flees to the gay bars in the big city. When Joker, the young delivery boy whom Spencer desires chastely from afar, drowns during some horseplay on a picnic, Spencer must restrict his feelings of loss to the secrecy of the funeral home's basement preparation room, where he can delicately caress the dead boy's hands. For the closeted and lonely Spencer, Joker's funeral symbolically becomes his own.

An extended examination of religious bigotry and anti-Semitism among American fighting men occurs in Laurents's *Home of the Brave* (1945), where racist slurs against the Japanese enemy echo those directed at Pvt. Peter Coney. Laurents employs a heavily expressionistic form as Coney gradually relives the circumstances surrounding a psychosomatic paralysis. The victim of anti-Semitism from a young age when he suffered beatings by schoolmates for observing the Jewish holydays, Coney feels betrayed by his best buddy Finch – himself taunted for befriending Coney – when Finch just barely catches himself from uttering, albeit unthinkingly, a racist remark. Feeling somehow vindicated when Finch is shot, Coney's guilt causes paralysis. He only experiences a cure when another soldier, who has lost an arm and will be discriminated against for his disability, makes Coney realize that every soldier feels relief for surviving. Yet this argument that shared experience eradicates difference evades the problem of Jewishness: if acceptance into the American community demands hiding diversity, then a supposedly egalitarian society is rendered a sham. The culminating horror of anti-Semitism in the Holocaust finally reaches the American stage in Frances Goodrich and Albert Hackett's 1956 Pulitzer dramatization of *The Diary of Anne Frank*. Neither the original document nor the play itself centers, however, on the extermination camps; in fact, Goodrich and Hackett submerge the issue of race, only adding fuel to those who claim that Jewish denial and passivity in the face of evil actually made the victims complicit in their fate. The play testifies instead to the inability of any external force to imprison the mind and spirit, while demonstrating how inhuman conditions can lead to inhumane actions. Ultimately, however, this – like Carson McCullers's popular stage version of her novella *The Member of the Wedding* (1950) – is a coming-of-age or rite-of-passage play: Anne's extraordinary circumstances hasten her process of individuation and moral development as young woman and author. The narrator (Otto Frank) of the outer frame added to the stage version functions as a moral chorus, interpreting the inner narrator (Anne herself) and urging that the audience regard the work of art as capable of ameliorating the horror of the extermination camps. Faithful to the published *Diary*, it remains a play more of uplift than of outrage and anger.

Uplift is more legitimately won through the agency of anger in the only major work from this two-decade period by an African American dramatist, *A Raisin in the Sun* (1959), which catapulted Lorraine Hansberry to fame as the first black, only the fifth woman, and the youngest playwright ever to win the New York Drama Critics' Circle Award – though by no means was it the only notable work about the black experience during these years. In 1941, Paul Green collaborated with Richard Wright on the stage version of the latter's novel, *Native Son*; and in 1944, Abram Hill adapted Philip Yordan's *Anna Lucasta* for black, rather than the original Polish, characters. The most significant forerunner of Hansberry's work may well be Louis Peterson's *Take a Giant Step* (1953), whose young protagonist – ostracized by his ethnic buddies whose girlfriends refuse to be seen with a black man, and then suspended from school after being openly rebellious against a white history teacher who knows nothing about the role of African American soldiers in the Civil War – provides a prescient glimpse into the failure of integration and a prophetic early image of black separatism.

As the Younger family in *Raisin* argue over how to spend a $10,000 life insurance payment, "Mama" Lena, the dogged matriarch, acts as a catalyst for her adult children, determined they will embrace the rightness of certain moral values that she holds. Her refusal to countenance the word "nigger" and her insistence that no one is meant to be a servant indicate a nascent militancy that culminates in her decision to move from a black tenement into an all-white Chicago neighborhood – a revolutionary path that Hansberry considered analogous to Rosa Parks's refusal to move to the back of the bus that precipitated the Montgomery boycott. Mama's daughter Beneatha is searching for her identity as a mature adult by rebelling against her mother's orthodox Christianity in favor of a rational humanism; as a woman by choosing the non-traditional vocation of doctor; and as a black by rejecting her moneyed assimilationist boyfriend, donning native robes from Nigeria, and letting her hair go natural in an Afro. Mama's daughter-in-law Ruth, "other" (i.e., different) like all these women not only by race and gender but by social class as well, is exploited by the middle-and upper-class women for whom she works, and economic realities tempt her, to Mama's abhorrence, to consider aborting her child. Mama provides her son, Walter Lee, two weapons against his oppressed existence as chauffeur to the rich: the money that he sees as proof of having made it in America, and the moral courage and acuity capable of transforming him. After he is bilked out of the insurance money in a liquor store scam, Walter is willing to grovel like an Uncle Tom and take money from the neighborhood association to not move into their community. When Mama demands that if he disgraces himself it be in the presence of his son, he comes into his manhood by deciding to move into the house that his dead father earned. Still, their economic condition will be unchanged as they remain in subservient jobs and are likely to face, as Hansberry's own family did, bricks through windows. Thus *Raisin*, rather than naively support integration or allow its white audiences to applaud, and thus escape, protest directed against them, makes a more subversive statement – leading directly to the dramas that will respond to the social upheavals of the 1960s. It is, in fact, this group of plays dramatizing sexual, ethnic, and racial difference that, more than any other from the period of the 1940s and 1950s, looks forward to works at the end of the century more openly radical in both content and form by such diverse voices as Suzan-Lori Parks and Tony Kushner.

BIBLIOGRAPHY

Adler, T. P. (1994). *American Drama, 1940–1960: A Critical History*. New York: Twayne.

Bigsby, C. W. E. (1992). *Modern American Drama, 1945–1990*. Cambridge: Cambridge University Press.

Brustein, R. (1965). *Seasons of Discontent: Dramatic Opinions, 1959–1965*. New York: Simon and Schuster.

Clum, J. M. (1992). *Acting Gay: Male Homosexuality in Modern Drama*. New York: Columbia University Press.

Corder, R. J. (1997). *Homosexuality in Cold War America: Resistance and the Crisis of Masculinity*. Durham, NC: Duke University Press.

Dickstein, M. (1999). *Leopards in the Temple: The Transformation of American Fiction, 1945–1970*. Cambridge, MA: Harvard University Press.

Friedan, B. (1985). *The Feminine Mystique*. New York: Dell Laurel.

Hellman, L. (1976). *Scoundrel Time*. Boston: Little, Brown.

Miller, A. (1996). *The Theater Essays of Arthur Miller*, ed. Robert A. Martin and Steven R. Centola. New York: Da Capo.

Murphy, B. (1999). *Congressional Theatre: Dramatizing McCarthy on Stage, Film, and Television*. Cambridge: Cambridge University Press.

Sievers, D. W. (1955). *Freud on Broadway: A History of Psychoanalysis and the American Drama*. New York: Hermitage House.

Weales, G. (1962). *American Drama since World War II*. New York: Harcourt Brace.

Whitfield, S. J. (1991). *The Culture of the Cold War*. Baltimore: Johns Hopkins University Press.

Williams, T. (1978). *Where I Live: Selected Essays*, ed. Christine R. Day and Bob Woods. New York: New Directions.

12

Tennessee Williams

Brenda A. Murphy

Early Years

Most accounts of Tennessee Williams's career begin with *The Glass Menagerie* (1944; unless otherwise noted, the dates for plays refer to the first production), the playwright's first Broadway success, produced when he was 33 years old. If his earlier work is mentioned, it is generally to suggest that *Battle of Angels* (1940), which closed in Boston after only four performances, not even making it to New York, was an uncontrolled, youthful effort at the play that would become *Orpheus Descending* (1957) and the film *The Fugitive Kind* (1960). The plays Williams wrote during the 1930s, including the full-length *Fugitive Kind* (1937), not related to the film, *Spring Storm* (written 1937), and *Not About Nightingales* (1939), never published during Williams's lifetime, are generally dismissed as juvenilia. The recent publication of the 1930s plays by New Directions, however, has made it clear that the narrative of Williams's career that begins with *Glass Menagerie* is a distorted one, because it leaves out the years in which Williams was very much a playwright of the 1930s, influenced by the playwrights and the theatrical idiom of the decade and shaping his own works out of the hard times and the socially conscious theatre that nurtured him.

Fugitive Kind was written for The Mummers, the St. Louis theatre group that had staged Williams's protest play about a miners' strike, *Candles to the Sun* (1937). Set in an urban flophouse populated by society's derelicts – the homeless and jobless, the gangster, the yearning young woman with a "tough" exterior – *Fugitive Kind* also owes a great deal to the naturalistic drama of playwrights like Elmer Rice, Clifford Odets, and Sidney Kingsley, playwrights whose work Williams studied in his classes at the University of Missouri and the University of Iowa along with that of the modern Europeans. The characters and the central situation of *Fugitive Kind*, in which the heroine Glory is offered a chance to escape her confinement in the sordid establishment where she works by the gangster Terry, have their precursors in plays by the older American playwrights, as does the dialogue: "we're fugitives from *in*-justice, honey! We're runnin' away from stinkin' traps that people tried to catch us in!" (2001: 138). As Allean Hale notes, however, the play is also "a veritable index to [Williams's] later work as he tries out characters, situations, and themes he will develop in plays from as early as *Battle of Angels* [1940] to as late as *The Red Devil Battery Sign* [1975]" (xi). Most evident are Williams's pervasive themes of entrapment and escape and the notion of the "fugitive kind" itself, the people who live on the borders of society, always on the move, both searching for some indefinable fulfillment and fleeing a persecution by the majority that is sometimes imagined and sometimes real. The staging in *Fugitive Kind* exhibits an interest in lighting and visual symbolism and a juxtaposition of realism with expressionism that would develop into Williams's distinctive stage idiom in his later works.

Spring Storm was presented to Williams's playwriting professor at Iowa, E. P. Conkle, in response to an assignment to write an autobiographical play. The play, about four young people each of whom is in love with someone who loves someone else, contains several characters who foreshadow the figures in Williams's most significant work. Hertha, the spinster librarian, prefigures a number of desperate, "hysterical" or "neurasthenic," sexually dysfunctional women, who are based on Williams's sister Rose. Arthur, something of a self-portrait, is the painfully shy and isolated artist who was called a "sissy" in school. He says, "I want what I'm afraid of and I'm afraid of what I want so that I'm like a storm inside that can't break loose" (1999: 69), foreshadowing a number of tortured souls in the later plays. The plot involving Heavenly Critchfield, the young woman who transgresses the rules of her middle-class small-town Southern society by having sex with her boyfriend, Dick Miles, who embodies the "fugitive kind" in the play, might be seen as a prequel to the events involving Heavenly Finley and Chance Wayne in *Sweet Bird of Youth* (1959), where Williams examines the aftermath of the transgressive teenage love affair in much darker terms. In *Spring Storm*, the two women are left behind by the men when Arthur becomes "disgusted" by Hertha's frank expression of sexual desire for him and Dick goes off to work on the river, leaving Heavenly to become a "front porch girl," a well-bred spinster who has no chance to marry because she is considered "damaged goods" by the town.

The most important of the 1930s plays is *Not About Nightingales*, in which Williams frankly takes the conventions and issues of the left-wing theatre and makes them his own. In a course at Iowa that had emphasized the techniques of the Federal Theatre Project's Living Newspaper genre, Williams had written a short play based on a hunger strike at an Illinois prison. In 1938, when he read about the horrific incident at a prison in Holmesburg, Pennsylvania, during which 25 convicts who had staged a hunger strike were locked in a cell filled with steam and some of them were literally roasted alive, he decided to expand the earlier sketch to dramatize the Holmesburg incident. Allean Hale has noted the use of an announcer and captions for each scene as well as "shouted newspaper headlines, voices of broadcasters, sirens" (1998: xvii). All of these were techniques used to make the Living Newspapers, which were essentially dramatized documentaries, more exciting and engaging. Even more elemental is the conception of the drama itself as a series of episodes, some set in the warden's office, some in the cells, which are not always connected in a linear way. Williams combines realism with expressionism in a style that is reminiscent of O'Neill's *The Hairy Ape* (see chapters 5 and 10). The scene that begins the hunger strike employs expressionism to depict a growing animal force among the men in the same way that O'Neill uses it in depicting the stokehold: "*The chorus grows louder, more hysterical, becomes like the roaring of animals. As the yammering swells there is a clatter of tin cups ... each has a tin cup and plate with which he beats time to the chorus of the Chant led by Ollie, who stands, stage forward, in the spotlight*" (72).

Williams's technique also departs from that of the Living Newspapers in important ways, creating a theatrical idiom that is similar to Odets's embedding of realistic scenes to establish audience empathy in his seminal 1930s labor play, *Waiting for Lefty* (1935). Williams sets the group scenes among the prisoners off against a plot line that is centered on one sympathetic individual, Canary Jim, and concerns both a love story of sorts between Jim and Eva Crane, the secretary to the warden, and some character-istic Williams themes: the sense of entrapment or enclosure and the desperation for escape; the brutal, cruelly tyrannical relationship between the older "Boss Whalen," the warden, and the young prisoner; and the frustration of sexual desire. Biographi-cally, it is easy to see Tom Williams's frustration at being forced by his economic circumstances to live in the family home at the age of 27, believing he might never escape from under the thumb of his disapproving and authoritarian father and forced to work at a mind-numbing job in a shoe factory for the rest of his life. In the terms of the play, he transmutes this sense of oppression into a societal force. His romantic suggestion for dealing with it would fail to pass muster in any Marxist group, but it does suggest the developing line of his thought and his art: "They can tell us what to read, what to say, what to do – but they can't tell us what to *think*! And as long as man can think as he pleases he's never exactly locked up anywhere. He can think himself outside of all their walls and boundaries and make the world his place to live in" (1998: 38). The play ends with Jim's romantic gesture of escape, as he dives through the prison window into the ocean on the slim chance that he might be able to swim to safety on a passing ship.

The plays of the 1930s dramatize some of the deepest concerns of the young Williams, revealing a playwright well aware of both the literature and the theatrical techniques of the contemporary theatre (see chapter 8). But it is in *Battle of Angels* that he emerges as a distinctive voice in the American theatre, with his own subject matter and what was becoming a unique theatrical idiom. The play is set in the small-town South, and exposes the cruelties and brutalities that Williams saw as endemic to its social organization through a caricature and exaggeration of the minor characters that would become even greater in the revised version, *Orpheus Descending*. In the three major characters are the elements of what would become the most familiar Williams figures. Cassandra Whiteside, who has "snake-bitten ears," indicating a heightened sex drive, refers to herself as one of the fugitive kind, who have "too much passion" and "live on motion" (1971–92, vol. 1: 99, 97). Her opposite is Myra Torrance, the sexually repressed woman who *"verges on hysteria under slight strain"* (20) and is married to the brutal older man, Jabe. Into this mix comes Val Xavier, a figure who combines the elements of the fugitive kind with the power to create life-giving art and a sexual potency that is evident to every woman who sees him. Val, who is writing a book about "life," impregnates the hitherto "barren" Myra and is painted as Jesus by the visionary primitive artist, Vee Talbot. A heavy symbolism pervades the play, from Val's snakeskin jacket to the many references to birds, to the religious symbolism of the play, which takes place during Easter weekend, to the use of the Orpheus myth that would become the primary symbolic matrix for the later version, with Val figuring as Orpheus, Myra (Lady) as Eurydice, and Jabe as Hades. The violent fate of the fugitive, sexual artist Val foreshadows the destruction of many such figures in Williams's plays, as he is dragged away to be burned with a blowtorch after Jabe has shot Myra, completing the cycle of the Christ symbolism. Elements of other perennial Williams themes are also here, particularly the conflict between reality, symbolized visually by the "mercantile store...harsh and drab" and romantic illusion, symbolized by Myra's fancifully decorated confectionary "where she kept her dreams" (8), and the impossibility of ultimately meaningful human communication. As Val says, we are all sentenced to "solitary confinement inside our own skins" (50).

The Major Plays

While *Battle of Angels* did not make it to the Broadway stage until the revised version was produced in 1957, *The Glass Menagerie*, begun as a screenplay during Williams's short stint as a writer for MGM in 1943, was to become a major popular and critical success, running for 563 performances, and winning the New York Drama Critics' Circle Award. The play, set in St. Louis, where Williams lived from the age of 7, when his father moved the family away from his wife's family home in Clarkesdale, Mississippi, in order to take a management position in the shoe company he worked for, is Williams's most direct treatment of his family. The move from his grandfather's rectory in a Mississippi village to an anonymous brick apartment house in a Midwestern city proved traumatic for Tom Williams, his mother, a self-styled Southern belle, and his fragile sister Rose, his closest childhood companion, and the person he considered his anima or other half throughout his life. Earlier plays contained veiled treatments of Williams's father Cornelius, a distant, authoritarian figure who belittled his literary son, calling him "Miss Nancy," in such characters as Boss Whalen and Jabe Torrance. In *The Glass Menagerie*, Williams focused his attention on his mother and sister through the lens of guilt at having left them behind after he had escaped from St. Louis and the family, getting, as the character Tom puts it, "out of the coffin without removing one nail" (1971–92, vol. 1: 167), while his sister Rose lapsed into mental illness and was finally subjected to a lobotomy.

The theme of escape pervades the play: Tom's dream of escaping the coffin and joining the merchant marine; his mother Amanda's tales of her girlhood in a romanticized Blue Mountain; and his sister Laura's escape into her own private world of old phonograph records and her glass menagerie. It centers on Amanda's disastrous attempt to provide a future for Laura by introducing a "gentleman caller" into her life. In framing the action with commentary by Tom, Williams discovered the aesthetic of the "memory play": "Being a memory play, it is dimly lighted, it is sentimental, it is not realistic" (145). The play dramatizes Tom's subjective memory of the past. As such it is freed from the illusion of objectivity implied by theatrical realism and "can

Plate 10. *The Glass Menagerie*, by Tennessee Williams, Yale Repertory Theatre. Kali Rocha (Laura Wingfield), Jay Snyder (the Gentleman Caller), photo by T. Charles Erickson.

be presented with unusual freedom of convention" (131). With scenic designer Jo Mielziner, Williams found a way to represent the drawing of the audience into Tom's memory scenically by having his opening monologue to the audience delivered in front of a brick wall, which then became transparent, so that the audience could see Amanda and Laura through the wall, and then slowly ascended so that there was no fourth wall between the audience and the characters. The wall was brought down again at the end of the play, becoming blank again when the inside went dark on Tom's final line, "Blow out your candles, Laura – and so goodbye" (237).

Working in collaboration with Mielziner and other theatre artists, particularly director Elia Kazan, Williams was to refine his theatrical idiom constantly over the next 15 years, using it as an eloquent expression of the subjective vision of hard reality that he tried to represent on the stage. The first fruit of their collaboration was *A Streetcar Named Desire* (1947), for which Mielziner designed a fully transparent stage set that elaborated the visual image he had created for *Glass Menagerie*, producing an apartment for Stanley and Stella Kowalski that was literally penetrated by the French Quarter, and that became an eloquent visualization of the progress of Blanche DuBois's mind, from "hysteria" and "neurasthenia" to psychosis. To complete this process, Williams juxtaposed the expressionistic conventions with those of realism in more startling ways than he had done before. From the mildly subjective suggestion of the tender blue sky, "*which invests the scene with a kind of lyricism*," and the "*blue piano*" (1971–92, vol. 1: 243) that is the opening representation of the French Quarter, to a night "*filled with inhuman voices like cries in a jungle*" and "*shadows and lurid reflections*" moving "*sinuously as flames*" along the walls (399), the audience is brought into the increasingly frenzied state of Blanche's mind, hearing the remembered "Varsouviana" from the night of her husband's suicide that plagues her and seeing the woman who sells "*flores para los muertos*" ("flowers for the dead"). Although it does not always succeed in production, the theatrical text is meant to lead the audience into identification with Blanche's perception of this world, and of the danger that it poses for her, in the person of Stanley.

The conflict in *Streetcar* is seen by Blanche, another displaced Southern belle fighting for survival, as a battle between civilization and brutality, as she begs her sister Stella not to "*hang back with the brutes*," meaning Stanley. Blanche speaks for a world of "poetry and music . . . new light . . . tenderer feelings" (323). Stanley, "*the gaudy seed-bearer*," who is pervaded by "*animal joy in his being*" (264–5), sees the world in simpler terms. He wants what he feels is his due, which includes what property the Napoleonic Code says he has coming to him through his wife, and a sex life that is not hampered by an intrusive sister-in-law, who regards him as "swine." Stanley acts to strip Blanche of "imagination . . . and lies and conceit and tricks" (398), while Blanche desperately clings to the romantic illusions that have allowed her to evade the sordid realities of a life which has spun out of control, as she has engaged in compulsive drinking and promiscuity and finally lost her job because of an affair with a 17-year-old student.

Stanley destroys what Blanche thinks is her last chance at life with his friend Mitch by telling him about her past. He says he has to do this because he would "have that on my conscience the rest of my life if I knew all that stuff and let my best friend get caught" (366). At the end, Stanley rapes Blanche, saying "we've had this date with each other from the beginning" (402). He does this as an assertion of reality against Blanche's lies and illusions; but in the final scene he lies about the rape. Blanche is driven by his final brutality over the borderline into psychosis. After the chaotic moment of the rape, which climaxes the expressionistic effects in the play, the final scene of Blanche's removal to the state hospital is represented realistically, except for the return to the lyrical turquoise sky. In other words, with the perspective of Blanche removed, the life in the Quarter returns to normal, along with life in the Kowalski household, where Stella says she "couldn't believe [Blanche's] story and go on living with Stanley" (405). In Williams's view, the brute force of Stanley conquers the fragile Blanche every time. There is something to celebrate in the life force of the gaudy seed-bearer, who has produced a baby by the end of the play, but the tragedy is Blanche's, and perhaps American society's, when the cultural and aesthetic values that she embraces are destroyed along with her fragile spirit.

The conflict between Blanche and Stanley is an early formation of a fundamental dualism that Williams was to express in his plays throughout the period of his greatest work, between 1944 and 1961. It is most overtly dramatized in *Summer and Smoke* (1948), later revised as *Eccentricities of a Nightingale* (written 1951), which focuses on the body/soul dualism dramatized through the conflict between Dr. John Buchanan and Alma Winemiller, a minister's daughter. The play is set in a small Southern town, and Williams embodies the elemental conflict in the symbolic set, developed in collaboration with Mielziner, which consists of fragmentary suggestions of two "American Gothic" Victorian buildings: the realm of the soul, the rectory where Alma lives with her father and mother, and the realm of the body, the doctor's office where John grows up, eventually replacing his father as physician. Two visual symbols dominate the set: an anatomy chart that John eventually uses to confront Alma with her "human desires" (1971–92, vol. 2: 221) and the stone angel that occupies the space between the houses: "a symbolic figure (Eternity) brooding over the course of the play" (120).

During the play, Alma, one of Williams's "neurasthenic" women, overcomes her fear of her sexuality, partly through John's efforts as a physician, and confesses her desire for him. John, however, confesses to be "more afraid of your soul than you're afraid of my body" (222). During a reckless period of experimentation with a highly sexual "dark lady," Rosa Gonzalez, John descends into the underworld of the local casino, and his father is killed by Rosa's father. After this, John manages to find his soul, "an immaterial something – as thin as smoke" (244), by carrying on his father's research work and channeling his sexual desire into marriage with Nellie Ewell, a young woman who is, like Alma, a musician, but is also healthily sensual, embodying a balance between body and soul that John and Alma lack. The marriage provides a hopeful future for John, suggesting that there is a possibility of integrating the schism between the desires of the body and the needs of the soul. For Alma, however, a healthy integration remains impossible. Having overcome the repression of her sexual desire, she is unable to find a healthy way of satisfying it. The final scene depicts Alma picking up a traveling salesman in front of the stone angel and departing for the casino.

If *Summer and Smoke* presents Alma's fate in a tragic light, *The Rose Tattoo* (1950), dedicated to Williams's partner Frank Merlo, is a comic celebration of sexuality, a fabliau in dramatic form. (The fabliau is a comic or bawdy tale based on an incident from middle-class life; its characteristic theme is marital infidelity, and it often contains anti-clerical satire.) The play combines the simple, earthy humor of the folk tale with a symbolic scheme that is so heavily laid on that it becomes self-caricature. Williams dedicated the play "to Frank, in return for Sicily" (1971–92, vol. 2: 257), and its theatrical style, unique among his plays, reflects his sense of the vitality of the island's everyday life and its folk literature. It is a combination of realism in characterization and a fantastic, overblown comic aesthetic that reflects the wild carnival atmosphere of the fabliau.

The title refers to a tattoo that Rosario delle Rosa, the husband of the play's protagonist Serafina, had on his chest, a mark that magically appeared on her own breast when she realized she was pregnant with her son. When Serafina hears that Rosario has died, she is devastated by the loss of the husband she almost literally worshipped, cutting herself off from the world and denying her own very sensual nature as well as her daughter Rosa's blossoming sexuality. Serafina's sexuality is reawakened by Alvaro Mangiacavallo, a bumbling truck driver with the face of a clown whom she finds ridiculous, except that he has exactly the same physique as her dead husband. Alvaro proves to have a rose tattoo as well, and Serafina again feels the burning sensation of the rose tattoo on her breast after she makes love with him. She is able to free herself from her husband's memory and accept her sexuality after she finds out that her husband was having an affair with one of her customers, who had ordered a shirt made for him out of rose-colored silk. As a result, she stops opposing her daughter's love affair with a young sailor, and defies the censure of the neighboring women by openly admitting her relationship with Alvaro. In a carnivalesque scene embodying the comic spirit of integration, the women of the community end by participating in Serafina's symbolic gesture of conferring the rose-colored shirt that was meant for Rosario on Alvaro, passing it from hand to hand as they shout encouragement to him to come and join her. In broad symbolic language of the play, life overcomes death and Serafina gives up her widow's worship of Rosario's ashes and embraces sexual fulfillment with Alvaro.

The symbolism of *The Rose Tattoo* is exuberantly overstated, overblown and obvious, in keeping with the spirit of the play. Williams's next play, *Camino Real* (1953), developed from the 1948 one-act *Ten Blocks on the Camino Real*, has a similarly exaggerated symbolic scheme, but in the service of a much darker vision. Much like the new absurdist movement that was just beginning in Europe, Williams was working in a theatrical aesthetic based on a controlling metaphor, from which developed a non-realistic drama with its own aesthetic and its own rules of stage logic. In this case, the metaphor is that of the "Camino Real," which implies both "royal road" and "real road." Working through several versions, the final one not finished until after the New York production had closed following a disappointing run of 60 performances, Williams created a play that was framed by a scene in which Don Quixote falls asleep and dreams a "pageant," which will help him to determine who his next companion should be after Sancho Panza has left him. In the dream, Kilroy, the archetypal American GI of World War II, arrives in a strange place filled with refugees who are trying to get out. This is the Camino Real, closely modeled on the Casablanca of the 1942 film bearing the same name, which Williams knew well. The place is run with merciless absolutism by Gutman, who is modeled on the Sidney Greenstreet character, Señor Ferari, and peopled with a diverse collection of figures from history, literature, and popular culture, among them Lord Byron, Jacques Casanova, Marguerite Gautier (Camille), Proust's Baron de Charlus, and Esmeralda from *The Hunchback of Notre Dame*.

In the course of the play, the characters all try to escape from the Camino Real, with varying degrees of unsuccess, from the heroic Lord Byron, who ventures off into the "no man's land" beyond the place never to be heard from again, to Casanova and Camille, who miss the chance to escape on a plane called the "Fugitivo," to the Baron de Charlus, who is killed and carried off by mysterious "streetcleaners." After being stripped of his money and his champion boxer's belt and having his "sincere" love affair with Esmeralda thwarted by her mother the Gypsy, Kilroy is turned into a clown by Gutman and forced to tote baggage. He finally trades his heart, "pure gold and as big as the head of a baby" (1971–92, vol. 2: 580), for a pile of junk from the pawnshop in a last attempt to win Esmeralda away from her mother, but this proves impossible, and he finds himself "stewed, screwed and tattooed on the Camino Real" (587). It is then that Don Quixote wakes up and invites Kilroy to join him on his quest, with one piece of advice, "*Don't! Pity! Your! Self!*" (588). Kilroy's decision to go "*on* from – *here*" (589) exhibits the same romantic spirit that Williams gives to Lord Byron and Don Quixote. In other words, it is possible for the average Joe to change the sordid world of the Camino Real into the romantic quest of the Camino Real. Williams called *Camino Real* a plea for the wild of heart kept in cages, and his perennial affinity with the bohemian, the misfit, and the marginalized is expressed eloquently in this play.

His metaphorical allusions to the excesses of McCarthyism are also the closest he was to come to making a political statement in his drama during the 1950s, as Gutman has a man shot for uttering the dangerous word "Hermano" (brother) in the square and the Baron de Charlus is killed and hauled away by the streetcleaners for his homosexual activities. It was the issues related to homosexuality that were to preoccupy Williams throughout the latter half of the 1950s, while he was struggling with his own sexual identity, and the fate of the Baron de Charlus is an index of the anxiety that Williams felt as a gay man during the repressive 1950s. As a playwright whose success and livelihood depended on public acceptance not only of his work but of him personally, or at least his public persona, Williams had little choice but to remain a "closeted homosexual" as far as his public life was concerned, although he made no secret of his relationship with Frank Merlo in his private life. John Clum has written revealingly about the effect of the closet aesthetic on Williams's work, and it is particularly evident during this period when his anxieties came to a head, and the well-known psychoanalyst Dr. Lawrence Kubie, who tried to "cure" him of his homosexuality, treated him.

The aesthetics of the closet are most evident in *Cat on a Hot Tin Roof* (1955), with its theme of mendacity, and its focus on sexual dysfunction and guilt. In the play, Brick Pollitt has engaged in non-stop drinking and has refused to have sex with his wife Maggie since the suicide of his friend Skipper, who, it emerges in the course of the play, has killed himself because Brick hung up on him when Skipper tried to talk about his feelings for him. Like Blanche DuBois, Brick suffers from sexual dysfunction because of guilt stemming from the cruel rejection of a gay loved one – Blanche's husband Allan and Skipper. Williams makes it clear that Brick's failure is a failure of humanity through the reaction of Brick's father Big Daddy, a loud-talking, cigar-smoking, authoritarian patriarch who nonetheless is better able to accept Skipper's, and, he suspects, Brick's sexual identity, than Brick is. When Big Daddy hints that the relationship might have been more than a simple friendship, Brick, the "ass-aching puritan," becomes beside himself: "You think me an' Skipper did, did, did! – *sodomy*! – together?" (1971–92, vol. 3: 117); "You think that Skipper and me were a pair of dirty old men...ducking sissies? Queers?" (118). Big Daddy tries to counter Brick's homophobia with a broader perspective gained through his experience in the world, and especially working for the previous owners of his plantation, a gay couple named Jack Straw and Peter Ochello. He says he has always "lived with too much space around me to be infected by ideas of other people. One thing you can grow on a big place more important than cotton! – is *tolerance*! – I grown it" (120). When Brick finally admits that his last contact with Skipper was a long-distance call "in which he made a drunken confession to me and on which I hung up," Big Daddy responds that "we have tracked down the lie with which you're disgusted and which you are drinking to kill your disgust with." His disgust with mendacity, he tells Brick, "is disgust with yourself. *You!* – dug the grave of your friend and kicked him in it! – before you'd face the truth with him!" (124).

Brick responds to this challenge by countering that Big Daddy has given in to the mendacity of the medical establishment, accepting their lies about his cancer because he will not face the fact that he is dying. In the end, Big Daddy faces the truth, shouting, "CHRIST – DAMN – ALL LYING SONS OF – LYING BITCHES!" (128). Brick, however, is less courageous, and the trouble Williams had with finding a resolution to Brick's problems in the ending is perhaps an index of Williams's deep anxiety about the issue of the closet itself. Williams tried many different versions of the ending, and made so much of the fact that Elia Kazan persuaded him to revise it yet again for the Broadway production that he printed two versions of Act 3 when he published the play, neither of which presents a strong resolution to Brick's battle with mendacity or his relationship with Maggie.

Williams began his treatment with Dr. Kubie in 1957, and it is in *Suddenly Last Summer*, produced the following year, that he was to create his deepest and most powerful imaginative construction from his introspection about his sexual identity. The poet Sebastian Venable is perhaps the archetype of Williams's artist figures, embodying most fully the fundamental dualism that pervades his work. His name is an obvious reference to St. Sebastian, the martyr tied to a tree and shot with arrows, whose image is often associated with homosexuality in the arts. Sebastian is dead as the play begins, and his mother venerates his memory as that of a saint, who says, "my son was looking for God. I mean for a clear image of Him" (1971–92, vol. 3: 357). By his mother's account, Sebastian was an ascetic, who sought a life of pure spirituality. The dark side of Sebastian is depicted in sexual terms by his cousin Catherine, who says that he brought her with him on his travels to attract young men and boys, whom he talked about "as if they were – items on a menu"; he "was fed up with the dark ones and was famished for blonds" (375).

The imagery of devouring is brought to two horrifying climaxes in two versions of Sebastian's life narrated by Mrs. Venable and by Catherine. Sebastian's mother says that his search for God ended in the Encantadas, where he insisted on watching the Darwinian struggle as thousands of newly hatched sea-turtles made their dash for the sea and were attacked by sea birds, who dove down and turned them over "to expose their soft undersides, tearing the undersides open and rending and eating their flesh. Sebastian guessed that possibly only a hundredth of one percent of their number would escape to the sea" (356). After spending an entire day watching "that thing on the beach of the Encantadas," Sebastian came down and told his mother, "Well, now I've seen Him! – and he meant God" (357). The even more horrifying image comes in Catherine's description of Sebastian's death, when he is literally torn apart and devoured by a group of the boys he has been employing for sex in Cabeza de Lobo, "homeless young people that lived on the free beach like scavenger dogs, hungry children" (413). Catherine says that these children, "a flock of black plucked little birds," pursued Sebastian until they caught up with him in a frenzy; when she arrived at the place, she found they had "*devoured* parts of him. . . . Torn or cut parts of him away with their hands or knives . . . torn bits of him away and stuffed them into those gobbling fierce little empty black mouths of theirs" (422).

This image of cannibalism carries heavy symbolic freight for Williams. Not only does it refer back to Sebastian's dark image of divinity, but it also evokes the imagery of St. Sebastian and the deep mythic associations around the concept of ritual sacrifice. Is Sebastian a poet driven by the need to find God, or a sexual predator who meets a horrific fate that has some tragic justice for a man who treats other human beings "like items on a menu?" There is a tremendous sense of guilt conveyed in this imagery, at the same time that there is a plea for understanding of the artist's ultimate quest, the search for God. The nexus of guilt and religious ritual is similar to that in Williams's story, "Desire and the Black Masseur" (1946), which also juxtaposes cannibalism with the religious ritual of atonement. Williams would again return to it in *The Night of the Iguana*, another dramatic exploration of the seeming conflict between the physical and the spiritual that makes powerful use of metaphors for the human condition. Meanwhile, however, he revisited some of the unresolved issues in *Cat* with *Sweet Bird of Youth* (1959), his last theatrical collaboration with Elia Kazan and Jo Mielziner. There is no direct reference to homosexuality in the play, although the earliest drafts in the Williams collection at the Harry Ransom Humanities Research Center at the University of Texas in Austin show that the relationship between the Princess Kosmonopolis and Chance Wayne was originally intended to be that of two men.

As it eventually developed, *Sweet Bird* became a dramatization of the aftermath of the relationship between Heavenly and Richard of *Spring Storm*, now called Heavenly Finley and Chance Wayne. In this play, Heavenly, now in her twenties, is the daughter of the local political boss in a small town on the Gulf Coast. As a very young teenager, she had a love affair with Chance Wayne, who left town to try to become a success in Hollywood. In the years since, he has visited periodically, renewing his relationship with Heavenly, and finally, unbeknownst to him, has given Heavenly a venereal disease that has resulted in her having a hysterectomy. On Easter Sunday, Chance has come back to town in the employment of the Princess Kosmonopolis, an aging movie star called Alexandra del Lago, who is desperately trying to forget what she thinks was a disastrous attempt at a comeback through alcohol, drugs, and sex with Chance. He plans to impress the locals with her Cadillac and his access to luxury items, not realizing that Boss Finley and his son are making plans to have him castrated and kicked out of town. After failing at his attempts to blackmail the Princess, to regain Heavenly, and to regain the respect of the town, Chance is about to meet his fate as he refuses to go with the Princess as "part of her luggage."

Both Chance and the Princess are examples of the "fugitive kind," but there is a difference in the way they face life. For the Princess, life is essentially a performance, a work of art, and she has the capacity to absorb many a setback and still go on. After she finds out from a gossip columnist that her comeback performance is getting good reviews, she makes immediate plans to go to a spa for rehab, telling Chance: "we are two monsters, but with this difference between us. Out of the passion and torment of my existence I have created a thing that I can unveil, a sculpture, almost heroic, that I can unveil" (1971–92, vol. 4: 120). Chance, on the other hand, has come "back to the town you were born in, to a girl that won't see you because you put such rot in her body she had to be gutted" (120). While both characters embody a kind of carnal corruption, the Princess has the capacity to transcend through art, while Chance, lacking the talent, simply becomes an image of mortality. It is on that basis that his final speech is directed to the audience: "I don't ask for your pity, but just for your understanding – not even that – no. Just for your recognition of me in you, and the enemy, time, in us all" (124). In the figure of Chance, Williams universalizes the carnality, corruption, failure, and guilt that are evident in Brick and Sebastian as well, accepting them as part of the human condition and suggesting that the only hope of redemption comes from the transformative power of art.

The Night of the Iguana (1961) embodies a dramatic synthesis of the perennial issues that had driven Williams's playwriting through the previous 15 years. Set in a "Bohemian hotel" on a jungle-covered hilltop in Puerto Barrio, Mexico, the play is about the struggle of four souls in torment to find peace. A familiar dualism is embodied in the two main characters, different examples of the fugitive kind, the Rev. T. Lawrence Shannon, a minister who has been locked out of his church for preaching a sermon expressing his loss of faith in the traditional Christian God, which he calls "an angry, petulant old man" (1971–92, vol. 4: 303), and Hannah Jelkes, a saintly, androgynous New England spinster, who travels the world with her 97-year-old grandfather and makes her living selling watercolors. Completing the picture are Maxine Faulk, the owner of the hotel, a recent widow who seeks human contact in casual sexual encounters with her young employees, and Hannah's grandfather Nonno, the poet Jonathan Coffin, who has begged Hannah to bring him to the sea, "the cradle of life," as he tries to overcome his fear of his coming death.

The character who is most *in extremis* is Shannon, who has reached a nadir in his life and has brought the tour group of Baptist ladies he is leading to the hotel to try to get a grip on himself in order to go on. Shannon has a breakdown and undergoes what is literally a dark night of the soul, restrained in a hammock on the porch of the hotel, while Hannah tries to help him find the peace that she has found in dealing with her own tendency to hysteria and "blue devils." Hannah soothes Shannon with poppy-seed tea, and he calls her "Miss Thin-Standing-Up-Female-Buddha" (347). She tells Shannon that she has survived quite a battle with her own blue devils through "endurance" and "the tricks that panicky people use to outlast and outwit their panic." She has spent a good deal of time on her travels, not only around the world but also "subterranean travels, the . . . journeys that the spooked and bedeviled people are forced to take through the . . . *unlighted* sides of their natures" (353). She has found peace through various forms of human communication, some ephemeral, some enduring, like, most importantly, the "home" she has found traveling the world with Nonno, the "thing that two people have between them in which each can . . . well, nest – rest – live in, emotionally speaking" (356–7). Hannah points out to Shannon that much of his suffering is self-imposed, a dramatic attempt to "suffer and atone for the sins of himself and the world" that is really a "comparatively comfortable, almost voluptuous kind of crucifixion" (344). The dominant metaphor of the play is the iguana that is tied up below the verandah. It struggles all night, and is finally released by Shannon, after Hannah has helped to release him from his panic. Meanwhile, Nonno has composed his last poem, a threnody of acceptance of his own death. The end of the play is not a resolution but a kind of peaceful aftermath, pervaded by acceptance and endurance. Nonno dies peacefully, answering Hannah's prayer, "Oh, God, can't we stop now? Finally? Please let us. It's so quiet here, now" (375). Shannon decides to stay with Maxine, establishing the kind of "home" that Hannah talked about, and he recognizes that in cutting the iguana loose, he, like

Hannah, has performed "a little act of grace," so that "one of God's creatures could scramble home safe and free" (373).

The Later Plays

Iguana, which ran for 316 performances on Broadway and was made into a major film by John Huston, was Williams's last popular success. A number of factors combined at the beginning of the 1960s to put him at the mercy of his own self-described "blue devils." His relationship with Frank Merlo became increasingly troubled, ending with Merlo's death from cancer in 1963. His artistic relationship with Kazan broke down over Williams's increasing resentment of Kazan's role in the development of his plays, and they did not work together again after 1960, leaving Williams without a strong and trusted theatrical collaborator who would give him honest, constructive criticism of his scripts. Moreover, much like Shannon, Williams medicated his grief and his anxiety with increasing doses of prescription drugs and alcohol, so that he was to refer to the 1960s in his *Memoirs* (1975) as his "stoned decade." Nevertheless, he continued to write every day, as he always had, and, although the plays of the 1960s and 1970s lack the extraordinary craftsmanship of the earlier plays, they show Williams's startlingly creative imagination at work, and a more uninhibited sense of experimentation with the new forms and theatrical idioms that were emerging in the American theatre of the 1960s.

Williams's perennial themes remained central to his work in the period from 1963 until his death in 1983. Partly because of the increasingly hostile critical reception of his work, he was intensely focused on the artist and his place in the world. In *The Milk Train Doesn't Stop Here Anymore* (1963), he combined the themes of the fugitive artist/Orpheus figure with the acceptance of death in a play that, as Michael Paller and Allean Hale have pointed out, owes a great deal to the influence of Japanese Noh drama. Williams's stage directions also suggest that the play's eclectic idiom contains elements of Kabuki and classical Greek drama. In this play, Chris Flanders, a Christ-like artist figure reminiscent of Val Xavier, helps Mrs. Goforth to accept her inevitable death.

Perhaps the most personal of Williams's artist plays is the absurdist play *The Gnädiges Fräulein* (1966), based on the metaphor of predatory birds that is familiar from *Suddenly Last Summer*. The Gnädiges Fräulein is a former singer who has spiraled down through the levels of show business until she has ended up in a boarding house where she pays her rent by competing with the cocaloonies for the throwaway fish down at the docks. Every day, she does battle with the predatory birds, coming back bloodied with her fish. During the play, the birds peck out her eyes and hair, and tear off her clothes, leaving her naked and bloody. She sings a chant about having "cleverly intercepted a rather large mackerel thrown to the seal by catching this same rather large mackerel in her own lovely jaws!" (1971–92, vol. 7: 247), which becomes the hallmark of her act in show business. The image of the artist as trained seal, at the mercy of the critics who prey on her, is Williams's most overt expression of the desperation he felt during this period, as his craft began to fail and he felt that the critics had turned on him.

The image of the artist *in extremis* is also central to *In the Bar of a Tokyo Hotel* (1969), another Asian-influenced play that is about a painter who is being deserted by his wife as he desperately tries to pursue his art. Mark insists that "an artist has to lay his life on the line" (1971–92, vol. 7: 22), and he feels "as if I were crossing the frontier of a country I have no permission to enter . . . a new style of work can be stronger than you, but you learn to control it. It has to be controlled. You learn to control it" (19–21). His wife Miriam thinks he is mad, and plans to have him flown back to the States to be placed in the care of a "neuropathologist" while she continues her trip in Japan. The play reflects Williams's frame of mind at the end of the 1960s, as critics rejected his plays in increasingly stronger terms and he lost control of his life, and foreshadows his commitment by his younger brother Dakin later in 1969 to the psychiatric division of Barnes Hospital in St. Louis, where he underwent detoxification and other treatment.

After his hospital stay, Williams was able to regain control of his life, producing several significant plays during the 1970s and 1980s. Among them are *Crève Cœur* (1979) and *Vieux Carré* (1977), which return to realism as well as to the world of Williams's youth in St. Louis and New Orleans, and are reminiscent of the earlier plays in their rather tender treatment of displaced and marginalized characters like the frustrated spinster and the down-and-out denizens of a French Quarter rooming house. *Small Craft Warnings* (1972) is a similarly sympathetic treatment of the habitués of a California bar, each of whom is a social outcast for some reason, but each of whom finds some comfort and peace in the company of the others. *Something Cloudy, Something Clear* (1981) returns to Williams's early youth and his first gay love affair during a summer he spent in Provincetown when he was in his twenties. In his "ghost play," *Clothes for a Summer Hotel* (1980), Williams returned to the theme of the artist in his non-realistic play about Scott and Zelda Fitzgerald. Set in the asylum where Zelda was burned to death, the play again explores the conjunction of madness and creativity, and the destruction of the artist. The decades of the 1960s and 1970s also brought Williams's most overt political statements. In his novella *The Knightly Quest* (1966), he used the form of a dystopian satire to protest against the repression of freedom, and particularly the oppression of homosexuals, in the United States of the Cold War. In *The Red Devil Battery Sign* (Boston 1976), a powerful surrealistic and metaphorical play, he presents an apocalyptic vision of this repressive American society.

During his later years, Williams returned again and again to a play that he described as his most personal, and, for him, most significant. Variously called *The Two-Character Play* and *Outcry*, it was continuously revised and produced several times between 1967 and 1975, never successfully. A highly symbolic monodrama about the artist, the play makes use of the brother–sister dyad that pervaded Williams's imagination. In the play, brother and sister actors Felice and Clare have been abandoned by the rest of their theatrical troupe in a theatre on the road, and they decide, against Clare's protests, to put on Felice's play about the two of them. In the play-within-the-play, they are unable, despite their intentions and efforts, to leave the house where either their father shot their mother and then himself, or vice versa. After the performance is over – the play-within-the-play has no ending "in order to make a point about nothing really ending" (1971–92, vol. 5: 360). They are imprisoned in the theatre, and when Felice raises a revolver to shoot Clare, he is unable to do it. The play ends with brother and sister raising their hands to each other and slowly embracing. The symbolic import of the play touches the most essential elements in Williams's creative imagination, his conception of himself as an artist and his consciousness of the need for human connection. In a sense, *The Two-Character Play* tells the same story as *The Glass Menagerie*, and it ends the same way. The thing that tortured Williams, that he wanted so desperately to leave behind, his family, was the one thing he could not escape in his fugitive-kind wanderings. And for his art, this was a felicitous thing, for it was also the wellspring of his creativity and what compelled him to keep writing, until the day he died.

Bibliography

Arnott, C. M. (1985). *Tennessee Williams on File*. London: Methuen.

Clum, J. (1992). *Acting Gay: Male Homosexuality in Modern Drama*. New York: Columbia.

Crandell, G. (1996). *The Critical Response to Tennessee Williams*. Westport, CT: Greenwood.

Devlin, A. J. (ed.) (1986). *Conversations with Tennessee Williams*. Jackson: University Press of Mississippi.

——and Tischler, N. M. (eds.) (2000). *The Selected Letters of Tennessee Williams, Volume 1: 1920–1945*. New York: New Directions.

Hale, A. (1994). "Noh and Kabuki in the Drama of Tennessee Williams." *Text and Presentation* 15: 37–41.

Kolin, P. C. (ed.) (1998). *Tennessee Williams: A Guide to Research and Performance Information*. Westport, CT: Greenwood.

——(ed.) (2002). *The Undiscovered Country: The Later Plays of Tennessee Williams*. New York: Peter Lang.

Leverich, L. (1995). *Tom: The Unknown Tennessee Williams*. New York: Crown.

Martin, R. A. (ed.) (1997). *Critical Essays on Tennessee Williams*. New York: G. K. Hall.

Murphy, B. (1992). *Tennessee Williams and Elia Kazan: A Collaboration in the Theatre*. Cambridge: Cambridge University Press.

——(2002). "Tennessee Williams and Cold War Politics." In Barbara Ozieblo and Miriam López Rodriguez (eds.), *Staging a Cultural Paradigm: The Political and the Personal in American Drama*. Brussels: Peter Lang, 33–50.

Paller, M. (2002). "The Day On Which a Woman Dies: *The Milk Train Doesn't Stop Here Anymore* and No Theatre." In P. C. Kolin (ed.), *The Undiscovered Country: The Later Plays of Tennessee Williams*. New York: Peter Lang, 25–39.

Roudané, M. (1997). *The Cambridge Companion to Tennessee Williams*. Cambridge: Cambridge University Press.

Tharpe, J. (1977). *Tennessee Williams: A Tribute*. Jackson: University Press of Mississippi.

Williams, T. (1971–92). *The Theatre of Tennessee Williams*, 8 vols. New York: New Directions.

——(1975). *Memoirs*. New York: New Directions.

——(1978). *Where I Live: Selected Essays*. New York: New Directions.

—— (1985). *Collected Stories*. New York: New Directions.
—— (1998). *Not About Nightingales*, ed. Allean Hale. New York: New Directions.
—— (1999). *Spring Storm*, ed. Dan Isaac. New York: New Directions.
—— (2001). *Fugitive Kind*, ed. Allean Hale. New York: New Directions.

13

Expressing and Exploring Faith: Religious Drama in America

Peter Civetta

What exactly *is* religious drama? To approach this topic in twentieth-century America, we must first come to some understanding of what the term means. Does religious drama deal with spiritual themes, involve scriptural characters, or necessitate performance in a church? These questions yield a shifting tapestry of responses from across the century. Whether religious drama even exists in America has manifested debate. As Thomas Adler states, "the absence of a national religion and the strict separation of Church and State; the lack of a solid tradition of religious drama from the very beginning; the continuation of the puritan suspicion of things theatrical; the exaggerated emphasis on the commercial aspect of production" all indicate the lack of a real religious drama movement (1983: 139). Norman Fedder goes so far as to say, "What is religious theatre? Those of us in the field cringe at the question" (1980: 123). The problem stems from attempts to classify it as its own genre, and to locate religious drama as clearly distinct from other known groupings. Instead, religious drama appears amongst and between many different types of drama.

To discover the location of these sites in twentieth-century America, we need look no further than the elements listed by Adler. Religious drama in America, due to the absence of a national religion, appears through the plurality of the nation's religious practices; explores the meaning and limitations of the separation of Church and State; enjoys the freedom from prescriptive traditions such as the UK's and other religious states; contends with the ongoing puritanical anxiety between religion and theatre; and seeks its place within the parameters of a commercial marketplace. To encompass these many facets, religious drama needs to move away from genre classification altogether. Indeed, as stated by Harold Ehrensperger, "Religious drama is not a kind of drama, [religious drama] is a quality of drama" (1962: 67).

An overview of scholars who have researched in this area shows that finding a consistent definition of religious drama remains an elusive, almost illusory, task. Overall, two points of view emerge. One bloc dismisses the viability of the term religious drama, even finding forays into spirituality embarrassing. The other group depicts all theatre as inherently religious, owing to theatre's ritualistic origins. Fedder connects religious drama to the all-encompassing notion of "a value-centered endeavor" (1980: 124). He also establishes three categories – biblical, historical, and moral – utilizing the medieval mystery, miracle, and morality models. Along similar lines, George Kernodle systematically provides three approaches: to present biblical events in present-day idiom, to create miracle plays on historical subjects, or to dramatize a contemporary religious problem. However, Fedder and Kernodle's conceptions of religious drama are based upon assumptions of the content's universal recognition.

Playwright Jean-Claude van Itallie requires a ritualistic structure, stating, "the dramatic event itself is potentially an act of worship" (qtd. in Adler 1983: 154). Other definitions tie religious drama to explicitly religious topics, i.e., faith, divinity, ministers, etc., or require the play to portray actual scriptural characters or events. In the case of American Jewish drama, it must "explore specifically and emphatically some aspect of the American Jewish experience," i.e., it must make a cultural connection (Schiff 1996: xvii–xviii), while "the most important thing of all about drama for Christians is: that it partakes of the nature of incarnation" (Ehrensperger 1962: 70).

Harold Ehrensperger, one of the leading figures of the mid-century's engagement with religious drama, describes it as drama that "deals with characters, situations, and themes that are clarified . . . by man's relationship with his God, with himself, and with his fellow man because of the nature and meaning of his God" (68). The Religious Drama Project of the American Educational Theatre Association expanded this idea, stating, "It is not concerned exclusively with propaganda and/or edification." Rather, "religious drama is written, produced, and performed in a spirit of reverence and with concern for the enrichment of its participants, church, and community" (Ehrensperger 1962: 69). Still, this view limits religious drama to a particular faith community. The Religious Drama Workshop at Boston University in 1959 came up with the following definition: "A religious drama is any drama which allows man to discover or deepen his own relationship to the ultimate, or God" (ibid.). Wayne Rood expresses the theatrical means of such a discovery. "Good religious theatre is . . . likely to be questioning rather than answering, existential rather than systemic, and effective theology in the theater is likely to be implicit rather than explicit" (2000: 307).

Several themes emerge from these descriptions. First, in the vast majority of discussions, religious drama is almost synonymous with *Christian* drama. This chapter seeks to enlarge the conception of the term to include plays of other faiths and other spiritual traditions. Second, religious drama is linked with religious institutions. The specter of the "Church" looms large. This chapter seeks to break free of these institutional fetters, providing for personal expressions of faith as manifestations of religious drama. To engage this topic in a new way means to liberate it from many of the literalisms attached to it, locating religious drama according to categories

occurring both sequentially and concurrently. These categories will help to differentiate the plethora of potential religious drama in twentieth-century America.

The first category deals with the oldest notion of religious drama – theatre
performed primarily in/for/by a religious group. This definition includes chancel
drama as well as theatre produced, and often toured, by religious institutions. Most
prominent in the early part of the century, particularly in the 1920s and 1930s, this
type of drama currently enjoys a resurgence of interest. The second category focuses on
plays offering a critique of religious values, or, more commonly, religious institutions.
Often the product of mainstream commercial theatres, these plays speak to the
secular/religious conflict present in society. While this category dominated much of
religious drama from mid-century through the 1980s, it remains ever present. Finally,
there are dramas that explore or express religious or spiritual ideas or ideals. Not
necessarily tied to religious institutions or even directly referencing religion at all,
these plays focus on people's quest for and relationship to the Ultimate, whether
named as God or some other spiritual entity. These dramas, while present throughout
the century, come to prominence in the latter stages of the twentieth century. These
three categories – the Institutional, the Critical, and the Spiritual – contain powerful
examples of religious drama in twentieth-century America.

The Institutional Approach

In the 1920s, a series of primers was published for theatrical productions at American
churches. Not merely content to stage already existing plays, these churches commissioned and performed original works as a means of counteracting commercial theatre,
which was viewed as a "powerful rival." One primer, for instance, exclaims that if the
church fails to change, people will "seek their inspiration in other temples and will
worship at other shrines than those housed within our churches" (Alexander and
Goslin 1930: xix).

These churches turned to theatre for its potential to effectively disseminate religious ideology and build community bonding. Grace Sloan has observed: "There has
been a new emphasis upon community life and the development of a community
consciousness. Drama has provided a means for the expression of this consciousness"
(1926: 4). This sentiment was characteristic of the Little Theatre Movement during
the 1920s. The purpose of this church version remained twofold: to create powerful
theatrical events, and to foster an individual's relationship with her/his God and each
other. A Jewish theatrical primer provides an example: "For those who participate in
the dramatization, it provides unusual opportunities for emotional growth, social
adjustment and creative self-expression" (Citron 1956: 17). This religious drama
movement coincided with the Little Theatre Movement, emphasizing the faith of
the community, while simultaneously aspiring to create dynamic, professional-quality
production. (Every primer I surveyed emphasized simple production values: limited
use of makeup, lights, and costumes, anonymity of writers and performers – only the

characters and story matter – and even admonitions against being "too good.") Mary Hamlin is perhaps the most gifted of the playwrights of this period. Her play, *He Came Seeing* (1928), enjoyed wide popularity, even before becoming a part of the Riverside Church's Worship through their Drama series. This play explores the story of Jesus healing a man born blind. However, Jesus does not appear in the story. Instead, the play focuses on the social and political implications of the healing, presenting it in two distinct lights. First, the healing appears as a manifestation of God on earth. The blind man Joab, portrayed as weak and dependent before the healing, observes life as full of wonder and promise afterwards. Second, a religious leader, Hilkiah, warns the family that unless Joab denounces the healing and renounces Jesus, he faces excommunication. Fearing upheaval caused by the renegade healer, the religious institution responds harshly, as excommunication at that time carried more than religious significance. As Joab's mother explains, "if you're cast out of the Synagogue, there can't anybody give you fire or water. Nobody can speak to you" (185). *He Came Seeing* addresses the conflict found in living out religious beliefs in a sometimes unreceptive world. It voices the compelling powers of the hegemonic social order, where one's personal convictions may require subordination for the maintenance of the status quo. The play, as religious drama, seeks to fortify the congregation's need to stand firm in their beliefs within an increasingly secularized world.

In 1954 the University of Redlands in Nashville formed the Drama Trio, a small company designed to travel and perform Albert Johnson's play *Roger Williams and Mary* (1954). The play presents the prosecution of Roger Williams, leading to his formation of the religiously free state of Rhode Island. This drama extols the virtues of the separation of Church and State, dismissing the supremacy of a particular religious order over a pluralistic society. Williams takes a conscientious stand against the powerful Puritan majority, and the play's immense popularity stems from this point. Similar to Hamlin's message, the drama seeks to reinforce particularly fundamental or conservative believers who face cultural inhibitions to the full expression of their faith in the world. Intended originally as chancel drama, the play's popularity forced it toward larger venues including the Convention Hall in Atlantic City, where an audience of 10,000 from the American Baptist Convention gave the play a standing ovation in 1957. The play promotes faith over secular concerns, and it works as religious drama by reinforcing religious beliefs in the secular world.

Roger Williams and Mary serves as a harbinger of the use of drama by fundamental and evangelical churches. In fact, a major resurgence of what is dubbed here as "institutional approach drama" began in the late twentieth century. However, it remains difficult to analyze the works of these church/theatres. This is due to the fact that the majority of their scripts remain unpublished, and there is an underlying reticence to discuss and share these materials outside of their immediate groups. Nevertheless, much of this work that is available remains compelling. The Church of Latter Day Saints, for instance, produces pageants in huge outdoor amphitheatres, and not only in Utah. The *Hill Cumorah Pageant: America's Witness for Christ* (1988) in

Palmyra, New York, contains earthquakes, lightning, and a 37-foot erupting volcano. Performed since 1937, the show now takes place on seven different sound stages, all utilizing digital sound and high-tech lighting. Another example derives from Narro-Way Productions. Usually selling out a 3,000-seat amphitheatre that used to belong to the PTL ministry, this company stages large-scale Christian musicals. They currently have six different shows, including their original success *Two Thieves and a Savior* (1997). Many of these groups are touring companies, such as the Christian Adventist Theatre. They have five full-length plays in repertory, including a twelfth-century drama about the persecution of the Waldensians for distributing the Bible entitled *Lead Me On* (1996). Some companies, such as the Alden Christian Theatre Society (ACTS), produce a mixture of material from *The Crucible* and *Our Town* to their own original musical based on the biblical book Acts (1990). Theatres like these exist throughout the country and play to large and dedicated audiences.

The beginnings of American Jewish theatre trace back to the great Yiddish theatre of the early part of the century (see chapter 3). However, it becomes difficult to immediately equate this form with religious drama. Fedder highlights the problem:

> To call Yiddish and Hebrew theatre "religious" will, doubtless, raise strong objections among Jews who identify themselves ethnically, not religiously.... Yet most Yiddish plays reflect traditional Jewish life which was permeated with orthodox religious culture, and the fate of the state of Israel is very much a part of the historical experience of the Jewish people – and at the heart of the Jewish religion – which from the start emphasized peoplehood over theology. (1980: 126)

The added wrinkle of discerning Jewish religious drama comes from Jewish status as ethnic and cultural as much as religious or theological. Therefore, although numerous Jewish plays exist, few directly deal with aspects of faith. The first two-thirds of the century accentuate this point, as many emigrant Jews sought to assimilate to the greater American culture. The high level of intolerance and hostility faced by Jewish playwrights forced many to hide or abandon their faith publicly, further accenting the amazing contributions Jews have made to American theatre. Ellen Schiff observes that "intolerance probably accounts for the timidity or ambiguity with which some dramatists treated ethnicity, a practice that continued well into the 1960s. So, for example, transparently Jewish characters are named Jim Knight and Charlie Tyler in Samuel Shipman's *Cheaper to Marry*" (1996: xvi–xvii). Another example comes from Clifford Odets's *Awake and Sing* (1935) and its development from his earlier version entitled *I Got the Blues* (see chapter 8). In order to gain production with the Group Theatre, of which he was a member, Odets needed to strip away most of the explicit Jewish content of the play. In one case, he changed the character of Ralph's girlfriend from a shiksa to a "girl with no parents" (Schiff 1996: 219). Schiff believes Odets lost much of the richness of the characters through this transition (219–21). This type of treatment remains typical.

However, a newly revived and developing form, midrashic theatre, creates contemporary Jewish dramatic interpretations of sacred texts. The Institute for Contemporary Midrash's work focuses on bringing a woman's perspective to the Torah, exploring previously marginalized figures. Two of their shows are: Falon, Lowenstern, and Silberman-Brenner's *Herstory/Our Story*, about Sara, Leah, Miriam, and Yochevved, and Kaplan-Meyer and Spitzer's *10 Imaginings of Sarai and Hagar*, an interweaving of historical and emotional images. The work draws on the pivotal stories of the Jewish people: "The voices within the text call out to be heard again and again. . . . I see midrashic theatre as theatre that hopefully opens the heart to a spiritual place" (Deborah Baer Mozes, personal communication, 2003).

The Critical Approach

The atrocities of World War II left an indelible mark on the world of religion and religious drama. A broad skepticism permeated American culture as many people wondered aloud how God could permit the Holocaust. At the same time, developments in science debunked religious ideologies. The doctrine of creationism, for example, appeared insupportable by people reared on the facts of evolution. Religion became an anti-intellectual discourse. As a result, religious and biblical figures populated the stage, but with a radically different message than those dramatic characters found in the institutional approach. The critical approach focused on humanizing the larger-than-life figures, bringing them down to earth. In this environment, scriptural figures viewed "their haloes become dimmer, at times disappearing in the realistic presentation" (de los Reyes 1978: 1).

The most famous play of the critical approach, and perhaps the most well-known example of American religious drama, is Archibald MacLeish's 1958 Pulitzer Prize-winning *J. B.* In many ways a modern retelling of the biblical story of Job, MacLeish uses an intellectual examination, bringing critical faculties to bear upon "questions whose answers given previously seem to conflict with experience" (de los Reyes 1978: 66). MacLeish has stated that he chose the material due to its relevance. He felt he needed "an ancient structure on which to build a contemporary play and the 'Book of Job' was the only one that seemed to fit the modern situation. The drama of Job is his search for meaning behind his agony, and man today is searching for meaning behind his own" (MacLeish 1958b).

A millionaire New England banker, J. B. appears less devout than his biblical counterpart, but just as tied to a quid pro quo, justification theology expressed by J. B. early in the play – "God doesn't give all this for nothing: A good home, good food, Father, mother, brothers, sisters. We too have our part to play. If we do our part He does His" (1958a: 30). The story follows the systematic destruction of all he holds dear, including the increasingly horrific deaths of his children. In the God and Devil roles overseeing J. B.'s demise, MacLeish uses a pair of "broken-down" actors, Mr. Zuss and Mr. Nickles (3). These two characters argue about good and evil above a cheap, circus-like theatre, indicating MacLeish's critique of the biblical material. The play ruminates on the theme, "If God is God, He is not good, If God is good, He is not God" (11). MacLeish critiques the notion of God's responsibility for the good things one receives. If God does good, then consequently bad experiences must come from God as well, a notion J. B.'s wife Sarah cannot stomach. She exclaims moments before finally leaving J. B., "If God is just, our slaughtered children Stank with sin, were rotten with it!" (109). For her a God seeking such retribution is not a God worth worshipping: "I will not Let you sacrifice their deaths To make injustice justice and God good" (110). Renouncing traditional conceptions of religion, MacLeish opines that if the story of Job/J. B. really represents God's work, then the world should reject God.

MacLeish fills the void left by this callous God with a humanist outpouring of love. At the end of the play, Sarah reconciles with J. B.:

J. B.:   [God] does not love. He is.
Sarah: But we do. That's the wonder. (152)

As long as people can experience love, God becomes inconsequential. People can love and thus create a secular humanist religion, rejecting God's alleged passivity and that of religious institutions. MacLeish's blistering critique of mid-century theology works as religious drama not only because of its biblical themes, but also because of the guidance it offered to his audience. The critique addressed people both as rational beings and as those seeking to believe in something. They could use their intellect, but not succumb to existential despair.

Clifford Odets's last play, *The Flowering Peach* (1954), deals with the biblical story of Noah and the Flood, but turns it into a family drama analogous to the then current-day concerns about nuclear war and the obliteration of the human race. The play, populated with many stereotypical Jewish characters, centers around the conflict between Noah and his youngest son Japheth. A man of complete faith, Noah strictly follows the letter of the law laid down by God. His favorite son Japheth, however, questions the righteousness of a God that would kill so many innocents. He even refuses to enter the ark as the storm approaches, saying, "I'd rather die in protest" (Act 5, p. 67). Noah knocks Japheth unconscious and carries him on board; however, their conflict does not end, but rather shifts. Japheth seeks to build a rudder to steer the ark as well as other maintenance unauthorized by God. He pleads, "God had to pick human beings to help Him, didn't He? Now, if He doesn't like it that human beings act like human beings, He's out of luck!" (Act 6, p. 88). In the end, Noah relents to Japheth's enlightenment. Japheth's intellect and savvy come to dominate the play over the strictly faith-guided Noah. The play emphasizes self-determination rather than an over-reliance on God.

The best example of Jewish drama as critical approach emerges in Herb Gardner's 1991 *Conversations with My Father*. The play's protagonist Eddie fights with his Jewish identity, although primarily along cultural lines. After facing the horrors of the

October Pogrom before emigrating, Eddie fixates on his family's safety. To avoid violent discrimination, he changes their last name to Ross; still, he continues to raise his sons for their bar mitzvah. He states his precarious relationship with God as: "You treat God like you treat any dangerous looney – keep him calm and stay on his good side" (108). The religious critique is visible even in the writing itself: God as *him* not *Him*.

This tenuous relationship dissolves after the death of his son Joey in World War II. "I tell the Killer Bastard – get *this*, God, I ain't a Jew no more! Over, pal! Fifty years of bein' a Jew Loser; over, baby!" (165). Eddie refuses to attend a synagogue again and describes religion as a "criminal con" and a "sucker's game" (165). Eddie's wife, Gusta, represents the play's only religiously observant character. However, she remains a marginal figure to her son Charlie, who narrates the story. Her Jewish identification appears somewhat eccentric; she becomes a woman who refuses to learn English. She, and the religious aspects of Judaism, are marginalized and are therefore dominated by an assimilationist rejection of the faith. The play criticizes a reliance on God by showing it as foolhardy and stupid. God becomes merely another obstacle to survival in a difficult world.

Finally, a notable example of religious drama from faith traditions outside of Judeo-Christian religion is Bina Sharif's 1992 *My Ancestor's House*. The play details the frequently acrimonious relationships between adult siblings in Pakistan as they prepare for the eminent death of their mother. Bindia, who studied medicine and lives in America, causes the most stir. The resentments about her move and expectations about her subsequent life expose deep discontentment in their lives. Specifically, the weight of Islamic rules produces a stultifying effect on many in the family. It represents the societal constraints from which the women, in particular, cannot break free. As one sister laments, "Our religion, our parents, our Qur'an, our men, [have] weakened our soul" (269). As in all critical approach dramas, the institution of religion has ceased having a positive impact on the lives of the characters. However, non-religious alternatives have indirectly opened the way to a new type of religious drama.

The Spiritual Approach

As the century progressed, the weight of institutional critiques began to equal, and at times surpass, the institutional religions they sought to debunk. In addition, for all the advancements of science and technology, these progressive humanist institutions provided little if any substantive answers to life's metaphysical questions. Maxwell Anderson connected the genesis of a new religious drama movement back to the same post-World War II time period that facilitated the creation of most critical approach dramas. For Anderson and a handful of others, the lessons learned from the war moved these writers away from a reliance on science and technology. In his introduction to *Journey to Jerusalem*, Anderson writes, "We have pinned our hopes on civilization and progress by material change; we have put aside the ancient wisdom of the race as expressed by the prophets and the poets, and have thought, when we did not go so far as to say it, that there is no necessity for a morality based in religion" (1940: v). He goes on to say, almost creating a manifesto:

> if we are to believe in ourselves we must – and there is no way out of it – believe that there is a purpose and pattern in the universe, that man can contribute to this purpose and that every individual man has a sacred right to follow his own intuition toward that purpose in so far as his actions are compatible with the liberty and happiness of his neighbors. It should be every man's right and privilege to choose his own faith or work it out from his own flashes of revelation. But faith we must have. (vi)

Spiritual approach dramas typify this new sense of faith. Faith, in this context, need not necessarily align with mainstream religious institutions. Instead, faith may emphasize a journey or a revelation, but it normally reflects an embodied belief – a sense of living out one's faith in everyday life. Although many traditional theological teachings stress mental aspects of their faith over the physical, embodied belief is not innovative. Whether expressed through Cabalists in Judaism, Sufism in Islam, or Pentecostals in Christianity, a sense of a physical relationship to God has strong roots. Thomas Merton referred to prayer as breathing, exhibiting the visceral connection between faith and living. Religious drama's use of embodiment seeks to debunk the Cartesian mind–body split, embracing more holistic spiritual explorations. Spiritual dramas focus on faith and embodied belief as a means of expanding possible engagements with the Holy.

In Jewish drama, this focus means a new embrace of Jewish identity. The title character in James Sherman's 1985 comedy *The God of Isaac* wrestles with this identity within the turmoil of his new intermarriage and the impending Ku Klux Klan marches held in Skokie. Constantly interrupted by his mother in the audience, Isaac finally discovers that "The Bible doesn't say, 'The God of Abraham, Isaac, and Jacob.' It says, 'The God of Abraham, the God of Isaac, and the God of Jacob.' Each man must have his own relationship with God. Each man must find his own Judaism" (74). Religious belief manifests itself as an individual experience, a hallmark of Jewish belief infrequently expressed in drama.

The Tenth Man (1959), Paddy Chayefsky's American version of the classic Yiddish play *The Dybbuk* (see chapter 3), restores value to religion in a dismissive world. The story revolves around a group of old Jewish men attempting to organize the exorcism of a spirit (termed a Dybbuk in Hebrew) discovered in one of the characters' schizophrenic granddaughters. The play opens with the men attempting to have "morning prayer" services. Due to the Jewish custom requiring ten present to begin the service, known as a "Minyan," the sexton pulls a young stranger in off the street. Arthur enters the drama as one who has sought modern happiness and self-knowledge via psychoanalysis, becoming a workaholic, achieving perfect suburban family status, and binging on drugs and alcohol. He remains a lost soul until he deeply connects with the sick young woman. As he falls in love with her, he protests the oncoming anachronistic exorcism. However, once the ritual commences, Arthur becomes completely engrossed and participatory. When the Dybbuk is ordered out of the young woman's body, Arthur, rather than the girl, falls suddenly to the ground. The leading religious authority, the Cabalist, says, "He is possessed. He loves nothing. Love is an act of faith, and yours is a faithless generation" (172). The play ends with Arthur scooping up the girl and committing to their new relationship. Although not a conversion experience, the play denotes the increased significance of religion in a world previously dismissive of its value and values. The play's final line reads, "He still doesn't believe in God. He simply wants to love. And when you stop and think about it, gentlemen, is there any difference?" (187).

Two significant plays by Maxwell Anderson show the potential for religious crossover, as this Jewish playwright embraces Christian stories and characters. *Journey to Jerusalem* (1940) depicts the only biblical story of Jesus between his birth and ministry 30 years later. Anderson explores faith, belief, and inspiration through a very human boy, Jeshua, questioning his calling. In *Joan of Lorraine* (1946), the convention of a play within a play explores the tensions between living by faith or living by reason, seeking a way for them to coexist. The story centers around a production of a new play about Saint Joan, and the lead actress's problems with changes to the script. She states, "it seems to me the way the play is now it means that we all have to compromise and work with evil men – and that if you have faith it will come to nothing unless you get some of the forces of evil on your side" (35). As the performers debate this stand, each alternative to religious belief is rejected in kind. Each belief system relies on an individual's faith – faith in science is, as the play suggests, no different than faith in God. "Every faith looks ridiculous to those who don't have it. . . . But not one of us believes in anything more solid" (98). While not advocating a conventional religious view of the world, the play presents faith as a viable choice.

An early example of spiritual dramas comes from Eugene O'Neill's 1927 *Lazarus Laughed*. O'Neill explores what happens to Lazarus after Jesus has raised him from the dead. Using Nietzsche's theory of eternal recurrence, Lazarus perpetually laughs the laughter of God. This laughter expresses the joy always open to people as well as reminding how quickly religious experiences can become lost. While not favoring a specific religious view of life, O'Neill validates the importance of spiritual expression and formation. The play contains over 100 characters as members of different choruses, each portraying a "period of life." Each group holds seven different character "types" from the Simple, Ignorant to the Servile, Hypocritical, creating 49 combinations, each with distinct masks and costumes.

In contrast, Marc Connelly's Pulitzer Prize-winning *The Green Pastures* (1930) takes an almost anti-intellectual approach. The play explores biblical stories through the idiom of rural Southern blacks. Adapting Roark Bradford's stories *Ol' Man Adam an' His Chillun*, Connelly stages three key episodes of the Judeo-Christian story: the Creation and Fall, the Flood, and the Exodus from Egypt, as well as adding an invented tale foreshadowing Jesus. Despite the problems of racial stereotypes and condescension, the play expresses a beautiful and affirming belief system. The humor and theatricality of the play do not obscure the profound spiritual faith underneath it; in fact, the humor assists in conveying a new type of relationship.

The play begins with a heavenly fish fry attended by De Lawd. He decides his custard needs more firmament, so he "passes" a miracle. However, he makes too much, with no place to put it all. Thus creation occurs because of excess custard firmament needing a draining spot, with humans created as an additional experiment. However, humanity proves vexing to De Lawd as he tries repeatedly to keep people from sinning. In frustration he turns his back on humankind until he meets the invented character Hezdrel. Hezdrel leads a rag tag army to defend the Ark of the Covenant, facing almost certain destruction by Herod. Ironically, Hezdrel professes faith in De Lawd, without realizing De Lawd stands right in front of him disguised and has forsaken humanity. Hezdrel confidently calls upon the God of the prophet Hosea.

> *God*:   Ain't de God of Hosea de same Jehovah dat was de God of Moses?
> *Hezdrel*: (*contemptuously*) No. Dat ol' God of wrath and vengeance? We have de God dat
>   Hosea preached to us. He's de one God.
> *God*:   Who's he?
> *Hezdrel*: (*reverently*) De God of mercy. (166)

Hezdrel explains the change in God:

> I guess he lived wid man so much dat all he seen was de sins in man. Dat's what made him de God of wrath and vengeance. Co'se he made Hosea. An' Hosea never would a found what mercy was unless dere was a little of it in God, too. Anyway, he ain't a fearsome God no mo'. (167)

Interpreted as a simple anthropomorphization of God, a being we can relate to and enjoy, the play actually employs the progressive notion of co-creatorship. As co-creators, God and humans focus on their interrelationship. The world exists due to the continuous co-creation of God and humankind together, requiring a willing, empowered relationship for both parties. In this dynamic relationship God grows and develops along with humanity, as demonstrated by *The Green Pastures*. Hezdrel has a faith and a conviction that leads him to convert even De Lawd. This religious drama shows how people can empower themselves through their beliefs. Commitment leads to relationship that leads to co-creatorship. Although the play speaks in a very particular idiom, this truth transcends the limitations of ethnic dialect. One need not follow "De Lawd" to absorb the religious message fostered here.

A perfect end-of-the-century example of spiritual drama is Kristine Thatcher's *Emma's Child* (1997). This drama centers around a couple, Jean and Henry, adopting a baby after unsuccessful years of trying to have one of their own. The baby boy, Robin, is born with severe hydrocephalus, a disease where the baby's head is full of water and equal to the size of the rest of the body. Even though the adoption process is halted, Jean, desperate to mother a child, becomes attached to Robin, learning to care and hope for him. Through her persistence and love, he gradually begins to improve. However, Henry specifically requested only a healthy child, creating tension in their marriage. Before a decision on their future can occur, Robin dies suddenly. He stopped breathing and with the do-not-resuscitate order given by the birth mother, nothing can be done.

No clerical figures appear, yet this play demonstrates the ability to perform the functions of religion without needing its institutional trappings. In two particular instances, embodied belief supplants conventional religious involvement. The first occurs when Henry realizes the ultimatum to either adopt the sickly, dying child or face the breakup of his marriage. A confessed city-boy – "My definition of roughing it has always involved a screen door of some kind" (54) – Henry goes camping with an old friend Sam. In this crisis, Sam becomes his confessor and adviser, roles often held by clergy. As Henry revisits his recent harrowing cancer ordeal, he recognizes what still lies within his power. Quoting Keats, Henry says:

> I am content to follow to its source Every event in action or thought; Measure the lot; forgive myself the lot! When such as I cast out remorse So great a sweetness flows into the breast We must laugh and we must sing, We are blessed by everything, Everything we look upon is blest. (68–9)

The comfort and faith required to deal with his crisis come from the secular world, yet express a profound spiritual belief.

The most powerful scene comes after Jean discovers Robin has died. Together with Robin's caregivers, she performs an impromptu funeral in the hospital room. They dress him in his favorite clothes and place with him his treasured belongings. Each offers a eulogy, with only one consisting of a formal prayer to God, at the end of which Jean abstains from the "Amen." Her testimonial expresses her own faith, which she has acted out throughout the play. She says simply:

> I will blow kisses heavenward: shooting stars that will fall on your tummy, and your cheeks, and the soles of your feet. When you least expect them, they will rain down on you, and they will warm you, when you need warming, and they will make you laugh, when you feel alone, and they will remind you, when you need to remember. I will always love you, and I will always remember. (76–7)

Jean's words express the very core of spiritual drama's embodied belief. Her faith is not external to her or prescribed by outside experts of religion. She embodies the truth she feels; she lives the faith she knows. In this way, the play is sacramental, an outward and visible sign of an inward and spiritual grace. The play is about faith, commitment, and living life according to beliefs.

Mixed Messages

The examples of the three approaches conveyed above are neither rigid nor formalized. In some cases, dramas overlap categories. For example, Tony Kushner's two-part *Angels in America* does critique God and religion, but closer examination reveals a more complicated matter. As expressed by the Angel in *Perestroika*, " HE Left [. . .] And did not return. We do not know where HE has gone. He may *never*. . . . And bitter, cast-off, We wait, bewildered" (51). The state of the world, as this dialogue shows, evinces the lack of an all-powerful, controlling deity. Louis articulates a sentiment common throughout the plays: "I don't believe in God. [. . .] If there was a God He would've clobbered me by now. I'm the incontrovertible argument against the existence of a just God, or at least against His competence or attentiveness" (1993: 33).

However, in much the same way as spiritual drama, these plays do not completely dismiss God. In fact, religion and spirituality remain central themes, with many of the scenes making reference to organized religion or questions of faith. Whether it is God's protective ozone, the power of the Angel to sexually arouse, or the unseen blessing given to Prior after he rejects his prophethood, spiritual presence and procreative, metaphysical powers exist even within the plays' withering critique of institutional notions of God. Kushner's complex dynamic appears most vividly in the juxtaposition of Judaism and the Church of Latter Day Saints. The odd mix interweaving Mormons

Plate 11.   Angels in America, by Tony Kushner, directed by David Krasner, Southern Illinois University, Carbondale, Julie Esposito (Harper) and Justin DeGiacomo (Prior). Courtesy of David Krasner.

and Jews creates distinct ways of perceiving religion in the world. Mormonism aligns with the task of facing life's daily struggles, and religion's possible role in acerbating those struggles. Harper refers to herself as a "Jack Mormon. It means I'm flawed. Inferior Mormon product" because she falls short of the ideals of the faith (1994: 64). The play's Mormon characters struggle to live up to the heavy burden of "God's strictures, which are very . . . um . . . [. . .] strict" (1993: 53). Their faith represents an inflexible way of being in the world. These teachings put the characters at odds with their everyday experiences. Harper and Prior articulate this dilemma.

Prior: I'm a homosexual.
Harper: Oh! In my church we don't believe in homosexuals.
Prior: In my church we don't believe in Mormons.
Harper: What church do . . . oh! (*She laughs*). (1993: 32)

Judaism, on the other hand, aligns more with lifecycle or crisis events. *Millennium* opens with a Jewish funeral. In *Perestroika*, Louis recites Kaddish prayers (prayer for the dead) over the body of Roy Cohn, and in both plays questions concerning ultimate guilt or innocence appear through Jewish contexts and characters. In the end, both faiths portray life and religion as a struggle, whether internally, in the Mormon emphasis on dogma, or externally, in Judaism's emphasis on living actions. However, when Prior, neither Mormon nor Jewish, rejects his prophethood, the Rabbi he met at the beginning of the first play informs him, "You *should* struggle with the Almighty!" (1994: 138). The plays' spiritual nature understands this struggle as intrinsic to a relationship with God and the world. Religion need not provide explicit answers. As Hannah says, "An angel is just a belief, with wings and arms that can carry you. It's naught to be afraid of. If it lets you down, reject it. Seek for something new" (1994: 105). While *Angels in America* certainly critiques institutional religious practices, it still leaves itself open to spirituality, even if it is yet to be defined. Without advocating the secular humanism of *J. B.*, these plays admit an important role for spiritual faith. Kushner ends the plays with an empowered community still facing the perils of life; however, he has fortified them with "softness, compliance, forgiveness, grace" (1993: 100).

Some Musical Conclusions

One peculiar form of religious drama warrants a separate examination: the musical. From *Fiddler on the Roof* (1964) and *Joseph and His Amazing Technicolor Dreamcoat* (1982) to *Jesus Christ Superstar* (1971) and *Your Arms Are Too Short to Box with God* (1976), religion and musicals have made a surprisingly effective duo. The connection mainly consists of source/story material, particularly biblical. However, the connections can run to the music itself, as David Lewis claims: "there are distinctive threads of church music that weave through Andrew Lloyd Webber refrains, investing them with a subtle spiritual dimension, though he seems either unaware of the fact or unwilling to acknowledge it" (2002: 142). While many examples abound, two musicals in particular speak to the notions presented here.

In "Religious Experience as Musical," Joseph Swain discusses the distinction between musicals that use biblical or religious material and *Godspell* (1971), which he says works as a religious experience. The first simply requires a willing suspension of disbelief, treating the material in the same way one would handle Greek mythology. In contrast, creator John Michael Tebelak cites the intent of his project as "to weave God's spell over the audience" (Swain 2002: 295). To accomplish this goal, Tebelak transplants the ritual liturgy of the Episcopal Church's Easter Vigil service. The Liturgy of the Word portion of that service alternates scriptural readings from the Old Testament with psalms. In *Godspell* the readings come from story/scenes from Matthew's gospel with songs functioning as the psalms. Eleven of the 15 songs in the play come directly from psalm adaptations or from Matthew's gospel.

The play begins with a conversion intended to prefigure the experience of the audience. The "Prologue" starts with each cast member entering with a sweatshirt bearing the name of a famous western thinker: Socrates, Aquinas, Nietzsche, Sartre, etc. They each offer a philosophical summary statement, which begin to blend together creating an "ivory tower of Babel." A *shofar*, the ancient Jewish ram's horn, breaks through the cacophony. John the Baptist enters singing, "Prepare ye the way of the Lord," eventually assisting in the shedding of the sweatshirts. By the time the play formally opens, the entire cast, and hopefully the audience, has been transformed/ converted by the experience. Stephen Schwartz's music portrays Tebelak's intent by using contemplative, mantra-like prayer forms in such songs as "Day by Day." Although not created by/for/in a religious institution, it was created *through* and *as* a religious experience.

The second musical arrived in 1996, with an impact rarely seen by original musicals any more. *Rent*, in part owing to the tragic death of its author just as the play opened, became an overnight hit. Based on a general retelling of *La Bohème*, the play featured drag queens and drug addicts, and gave central prominence to AIDS. Driven by its loud rock score and concert atmosphere, younger audiences flocked to the show repeatedly, often sleeping outside the theatre to obtain rush tickets on the day of performance. Despite all this success, the play's religious context remains unexamined.

The play, capturing a new interest in alternative religions, embraces multiple ideologies. This amalgamation creates a perfect example of late twentieth-century spirituality, demonstrating practices based more on individual religious journeys over doctrinal institutional structures. The play's signature song "Seasons of Love" lists the many ways of categorizing and understanding this hectic and materialist world. The play offers an alternative: "How do you measure a year? How about love!" (Larson 1996, II: 1). Fittingly, the play's overall message comes during a Life Support Group meeting for people living with AIDS. The refrain, heard repeatedly throughout the show, carries the very Buddhist message, "Forget regret or life is yours to miss. No other road. No other way. No day but today" (Larson 1996, I: 13). Spirituality has blossomed expressly because it fills an unmet need. One member sings, "Look, I find some of what you teach suspect because I'm used to relying on intellect, but I try to open up to what I don't know because reason says I should have died three years ago" (ibid.). The mind, unable to satisfy life's deep questions, needs supplementing by a more embodied spiritual experience. This experience translated directly to many of the play's devotees. Exhibiting an extraordinary passion and physical commitment to a play, the audience for *Rent* demonstrates the commercial appeal for a show addressing religious yearnings. *Rent* filled a craving, a craving little noticed or responded to even today.

By relating to the spiritual beliefs of the times, the "qualities" of religious drama can influence and impact a wide variety of American drama. In fact, as theatre seeks to retain its relevance within an entertainment culture, religious approaches to drama offer increasingly appropriate ways of reaching an audience. Religious drama explores not only *what* people experience in the world, but also *how* they experience it. A major aspect of this potential lies with the increased expression of other faith traditions. As this country becomes more accustomed to other practices, and those people become more comfortable in their religious distinctiveness from mainstream culture, a broad spectrum of religious drama will present itself. Whether through traditional ideologies or inventive individual expressions, religious paths can provide meaning and hope. What more necessary gift can theatre give?

BIBLIOGRAPHY

Adler, T. P. (1983). "The Mystery of Things: The Varieties of Religious Experience in Modern American Drama." In James Redmond (ed.), *Themes in Drama*, 5. Cambridge: Cambridge University Press.

Alexander, R. C. and Goslin, O. P. (1930). *Worship Through Drama*. New York: Harper and Brothers.

Anderson, M. (1940). *Journey to Jerusalem*. Washington, DC: Anderson House.

——(1946). *Joan of Lorraine*. Washington, DC: Anderson House.

Chayefsky, P. (1994). *The Tenth Man*. In *The Collected Works of Paddy Chayefsky: The Stage Plays*. New York: Applause.

Citron, S. J. (ed.) (1956). *Dramatics the Year Round*. New York: United Synagogue Commission on Jewish Education.

Connelly, M. (1958). *The Green Pastures*. New York: Holt, Rinehart, and Winston.

——(1979). *The Green Pastures: The Screenplay*, ed. Thomas Cripp. Madison: University of Wisconsin Press.

De los Reyes, M. P. (1978). *The Biblical Theme in Modern Drama*. Quezon City: University of Philippines Press.

Ehrensperger, H. (1962). *Religious Drama: Ends and Means*. New York: Abingdon.

Fedder, N. J. (1980). "Beyond Absurdity and Sociopolitics: The Religious Theatre Movement in the Seventies." *Kansas Quarterly* 12, 4: 123–31.

Gardner, H. (1996). *Conversations with My Father*. In Ellen Schiff (ed.), *Fruitful and Multiplying: Nine Contemporary Plays from the American Jewish Repertoire*. New York: Mentor.

Hamlin, M. (1930). *He Came Seeing*. In Ryllis Clair Alexander and Omar Pancoast Goslin (eds.), *Worship Through Drama*. New York: Harper and Brothers.

Johnson, A. (1957). *Roger Williams and Mary*. New York: Friendship.

Kernodle, G. R. (1952). "Patterns of Belief in Contemporary Drama." In Stanley Romaine Hopper (ed.), *Spiritual Problems in Contemporary Literature*. New York: Harper and Brothers.

Kushner, T. (1993). *Angels in America Part One: Millennium Approaches*. New York: Theatre Communications Group.

——(1994). *Angels in America Part Two: Perestroika*. New York: Theatre Communications Group.

Larson, J. (1996). *Rent*. New York: Dreamworks Records.

Lewis, D. H. (2002). *Broadway Musicals: A Hundred-Year History*. Jefferson, NC: McFarland.

MacLeish, A. (1958a). *J. B*. Cambridge, MA: Riverside.

——(1958b). "Job and J. B." *Time*, December.

Odets, C. (1954). "*The Flowering Peach*; A Comedy." [n.p., 195-] 117 l. Typewritten manuscript.

O'Neill, E. (1927). *Lazarus Laughed*. New York: Boni and Liveright.

Rood, W. R. (2000). *Theater and Theology: Autobiography of an Unexpected Career*. Berkeley, CA: Wayne Rood.

Schiff, E. (ed.) (1995). *Awake and Singing: Seven Classic Plays from the American Jewish Repertoire*. New York: Mentor.

——(ed.) (1996). *Fruitful and Multiplying: Nine Contemporary Plays from the American Jewish Repertoire*. New York: Mentor.

Sharif, B. (1994). *My Ancestor's House*. In Kathy A. Perkins and Roberta Uno (eds.), *Contemporary Plays by Women of Color*. London: Routledge.

Sherman, J. (1995). *The God of Isaac*. New York: Samuel French.

Sloan, G. (1926). *Drama in Education: Theory and Technique*. Overton, NY: Century.

Swain, J. P. (2002). *The Broadway Musical: A Critical and Musical* Survey. Lanham, MD: Scarecrow.

Thatcher, K. (1997). *Emma's Child*. New York: Dramatist Play Service.

14

The American Jewishness
of Arthur Miller

Murray Biggs

To begin with an anecdote. I first met Arthur Miller, and his wife Inge Morath, in early May of 1970, when invited to lunch by the political cartoonist Robert Osborn and his wife at their house in northwestern Connecticut. It was a beautiful spring day; the atmosphere was relaxed and informal. The round table on the patio seated eight, and since I was supposed to know something about drama, I was seated next to the great man. A first-year assistant professor of English like myself could hardly resist the occasion of a lifetime to fire at the guest of honor such scintillating questions as "Are you Willy Loman?" But this gentle bear of a man with the commanding handshake, whom I had previously imagined as a shriveled neurotic, more Woody Allen than John Proctor, absolutely refused to discuss his work. All he would talk about was how to grow radishes in rural Connecticut. That insistence of his has stayed with me over the years as a dominant image of a playwright who, for all his idealism and occasional abstractness, not to mention his theatrical and political achievements around the globe, has never lost touch with the soil, and American soil at that.

Biography

Arthur Miller was born in Harlem, New York City, on October 17, 1915, the second of three children of an unlettered but prosperous clothing merchant and his wife. Both his parents were Polish Jews, though his mother was born in the United States. The boy was raised in Manhattan and later Brooklyn. A series of jobs intervened between high school and the University of Michigan, where Miller majored in English and started writing for the stage. Graduating from there in 1938, he first worked for the Federal Theatre Project before its closure by the government for its leftward leaning. After World War II, Miller came under scrutiny by another federal agency. In 1954 he was denied a passport to attend the Belgian premiere of *The

Crucible in Brussels, and two years later called before the House Un-American Activities Committee (HUAC), to which he refused to name names. Found guilty of contempt of Congress and given a suspended prison sentence, Miller had his conviction quashed by the United States court of appeals. In 1968 the playwright was a delegate to the Democratic National Convention in Chicago, and four years later in Miami. He remained courageously active in politics thereafter, both within and beyond his native country, especially (as president of PEN International) on behalf of fellow-writers subject to oppressive governments. At the same time, Miller never ceased to write, and not only plays. Sixty and more years of work include film and television scripts, radio pieces, an opera libretto, novels, short stories, essays, and memoirs.

On Miller himself the honors fell thicker and faster with the years: the New York Drama Critics' Circle Award (twice), two Emmy Awards, one Obie and three Tony Awards, a Pulitzer Prize for *Death of a Salesman* in 1949, the John F. Kennedy Lifetime Achievement Award, and in 2001 Japan's Praemium Imperiale Award for lifetime achievement in the arts; among many others. Most striking of all: Miller was still turning out plays well into his eighties, and finding himself more produced than ever, in New York, London, and around the world. Broadway alone hosted distinguished revivals of *All My Sons*, *A View from the Bridge*, *The Price*, *Death of a Salesman*, and *The Crucible* (heralded by the 1996 film, featuring the author's son-in-law, Daniel Day-Lewis). The Off-Broadway Signature Theatre devoted the whole of its 1997–8 season to productions of Miller's plays, both old and new.

This latter-day re-recognition of the country's premier living playwright followed a period in the 1970s and 1980s when Miller found himself something of a prophet without honor in his own land, although consistently admired abroad. There were two principal reasons for his fall from critical (though never popular) grace. The first was his playwriting style, which was perceived as traditionally realistic and therefore no longer compelling in a theatre bubbling with experiment. (In fact Miller was never simply a realist writer.) The second was his sometimes overt didacticism, which, linked with his activist politics, suggested to some that the message of his plays overwhelmed their artistic medium. But for Miller, the public life could never be kept out of the private, or shorn off from the artistic world of his plays.

The Price

At the height of his business, Arthur Miller's father employed several hundred workers, and a chauffeur. When the stock market burst in October 1929, the business collapsed with it, and the Miller family moved from Manhattan to humbler circumstances in Brooklyn. Arthur was just 14. His autobiography, *Timebends*, first published nearly 60 years later (1987), recalls this family trauma both vividly and succinctly:

"my father...had next to nothing" (1995: 31). But it was not until *The Price*, first staged in 1968, that Miller wrote a major play about the Depression, and even then its treatment was oblique. The work is about two brothers returning 16 years after their father's death (their mother having died over 20 years earlier) to the home they grew up in during the Depression years. The Manhattan brownstone attic in which they had been reduced to living (they too had employed a chauffeur) is stuffed to the rafters with old furniture and other family memorabilia. The older brother Walter, who moved away early and has made an outward success of his life, views the collection for the first time in a generation, and dismisses it as the "same old junk" (Miller 1981: 332).

Although the play is set in the present (1968), and despite the fact that much of the action is mediated by an aged Jewish furniture buyer casting an outside, ironic, and often comic eye on the brothers' trips down memory lane, the text uncovers the deeply buried and unresolved conflicts between them from 30 years before. Although Miller insists in his autobiography (13) that the brothers are not based on himself and his own brother Kermit, the first New York production of the play, in 1968, featured the Miller dining-room table. More significant, presumably, is the fact that the father in the play is described as, like the playwright's, "busted" by the Depression, from which he never recovered, spiritually; and the furniture itself is conceived as a metonym of the family that owned and used it. "How do you come to this?" asks the dealer, Solomon, surveying the household goods. "It was my family," Victor responds (315). "Looks a very nice family," the buyer concedes, looking it over (316). Solomon emphasizes the subjectivity of appraising "second-hand" furniture by equating its market value with how much outsiders are prepared to pay for it, which may be a lot less than its owners, bound to it by so many emotional ties, believe it is worth. "The whole thing is a viewpoint," he reflects. "It's a mental world" (325).

This "mental world" is the inner world of the play, the world recalled and gradually exposed by the brothers' meeting again after being estranged for most of their adult lives. It is no less than the world of their upbringing and, beyond that, the world they almost invisibly inherited from their parents. The playwright is sketchy about where those parents came from, but the father at least, whose last name was Franz, must have been ultimately German. Even the furniture, according to an early stage direction, has "a rich heaviness, something almost Germanic" about it (298). Although this is clearly not the play's major theme, it is tempting to go further and read both parents as Jewish, not only because Miller's were (though Polish rather than German), but also because the catalytic character of the play is so visibly and vibrantly Jewish that the furniture he comes to evaluate is felt not just as family but as family outcast from Europe – like him. Thus the fact that Victor's mother once gave her younger son fencing gauntlets for Christmas (346), like the fact that she "brought them from Paris," and her playing of the harp, may signify nothing more than her wish to assimilate the social mores of the upper-class Manhattanites around her. Indeed,

Victor's earlier allusion to items possibly bought in Europe by parents "who used to travel a great deal" (316) sounds like a euphemism to impress the appraiser. Solomon himself is invariably more direct. His belonging to a "whole family" of acrobats takes Victor off guard. "Funny – I never heard of a Jewish acrobat." Solomon's tough reply ("What's the matter with Jacob, he wasn't a wrestler? – wrestled with the Angel? Jews been acrobats since the beginning of the world," 319) seems to accuse Victor of denying his Jewishness. Later, Victor claims ignorance of an even better-known Jewish story, the Fall in Eden: "I never read the Bible" (329). By contrast, before Gregory Solomon first opens his mouth, the playwright prescribes his accent as "Russian-Yiddish," and his last name is clearly meant to recall its biblical antecedent. Indeed, he manifests the wisdom of the patriarch in his attempt to arbitrate between the brothers.

The American Clock

Miller confronted the Great Depression head on in *The American Clock*, fully staged for the first time in 1980. It is based both on Studs Terkel's oral history of the Depression, *Hard Times* (1970), and on the playwright's own adolescent memories. Although he subtitles the play "a vaudeville," which suggests a certain emotional detachment, it is clear that the Baum family resembles his own, and that the young Lee Baum is autobiographical. (In the first American production, the role of Rose Baum, based in part on Miller's mother, was played by the author's sister, Joan Copeland.) Like the Millers, the Baums live in Brooklyn. Their Jewishness is overt: not something to apologize for but rather to take for granted. Even the amateur fascist Kapush's "explosion" – "Ignorance, ignorance! People don't know facts. Greatest public library system in the entire world [in New York] and nobody goes in but Jews" – can be taken as a compliment (1989: 177). The "normal," lived Jewishness of the Baums and their extended family enables the author, among other things, to demonstrate that being Jewish is (to say the least) compatible with being American, since everyone is in the same sinking boat, and not just in New York. The opening stage direction specifies that "an impression of a surrounding vastness should be given, as though the whole country were really the setting" (106). The character Arthur A. Robertson, speaking chorally, widens the lens more graphically. "Nobody knows how many people are leaving their hometowns, their farms and cities, and hitting the road. Hundreds of thousands, maybe millions of internal refugees, Americans transformed into strangers" (135). Thus there are now refugees other than Eastern European, and not only strangers becoming Americans, but the reverse. Society's borders are collapsing on other than its Jewish margins, too. It is an Irish hobo, Callahan, who rescues the black Arkansas veteran, Banks (136); and it is another African American, the Louisiana café proprietor Isaac, who draws the conclusion: "the main thing about the Depression is that it finally hit the white people. 'Cause us folks never had nothin' else" (165).

Not that the economic experience of the Depression, shared as it was across race and class lines, cut off the possibility of scapegoating. Rather the opposite. Lee's boyhood friend Joe ruminates:

> I tell you I get the feeling every once in a while that some bright morning millions of people are going to come pouring out of the buildings and just...I don't know what...kill each other? Or only the Jews? (162)

This Jew scapegoats himself, and commits suicide.

Broken Glass

If fellow-Americans were not exactly killing Jews at this time, the Nazis were, or starting to. Miller approached this topic obliquely in a very late play, *Broken Glass* (1994), whose title alludes to the *Kristallnacht* of November 9–10, 1938, in which hoodlums smashed Jewish storefront windows in Berlin, and Hitler's fascist government confined Jews to ghettos and confiscated their goods. The play explores this event both metaphorically – "You don't realize how transparent you are," Margaret warns her husband; "You're a pane of glass, Harry" (1994: 48) – and as a racial experience that cannot be denied indefinitely. It is in fact both experience and memory, and both (the play argues) must be confronted. It is experience because the play is set in Brooklyn "in the last days of November, 1938," when the papers bring the news from Germany onto every American breakfast table; and it is memory because the play was written at a time, a half-century later, when most Americans (and others) were too young to have lived through the original persecutions even by report, *and* when attempts to deny them were gaining currency.

Broken Glass is a study of both those psychologies: the impulse to ignore what *is* happening, and the refusal to admit that it *did* happen. The play's whole thrust is in fact psychological at least as much as political. Dr. Hyman may be a regular general practitioner, who "barely know[s his] way around psychiatry" (20), but the Gellburg case, which preoccupies him, clearly calls for some fast learning.

Phillip and Sylvia Gellburg are joined by race and marriage, yet divided by both. He seeks to suppress his Jewishness, she to embrace it. He is sexually dysfunctional, she sexually unsatisfied. What Hyman diagnoses as her "hysterical paralysis" (13), with its source in her unconscious, is an effect of both these divisions. The playwright loses no time in setting up her husband's double denial. According to Christopher Bigsby, the play was originally titled *The Man in Black* (1997: 178). Even the opening stage direction has Gellburg "intense...in perfect stillness, legs crossed...in a black suit, black tie and shoes and white shirt" (7): an unpromising debut, especially opposite Margaret, the doctor's wife, who enters "lusty, energetic, carrying pruning shears," and whose laugh can be heard "all the way down the block" to the Gellburgs' house (8). Phillip has repeatedly to correct her understanding that his name is the

more commonly Jewish "Goldberg," and he claims Finnish, and therefore less
obviously Jewish, descent (8). The rest of the first scene offers a paradigm example
of an early encounter between analyst and patient in which the patient is reluctant
to acknowledge uncomfortable truths: here both his Jewishness and his sexual inadequacy. His questioner, by contrast, is almost brashly self-confident in both departments, cigar and all. (His last name, Hyman, is a kind of rebuke to Miller's
Salesman, Willy Loman.) Hyman is quite explicit about what is happening in Berlin
("forcing old men to scrub the sidewalks with toothbrushes," 11), but Gellburg
refuses to acknowledge it. He distinguishes himself from his wife, who is "very
upset about that" (11) and evidently annoys him when she talks about it. In fact
he goes on the offensive with Hyman and argues that German Jews, if they are
like German Jews in the United States, need taking down a peg, if not as much as
Russian or Polish Jews do. Publishing pictures of the Berlin persecutions, moreover,
may "put some fancy new ideas into these anti-Semites walking around New York
here" (16).

This version of "those Jews brought it on themselves" turns out to be explained, in
part, by Gellburg's job. He is head of the Mortgage Department of Brooklyn Guarantee
and Trust, "the largest lender east of the Mississippi" (15), and "the only Jew ever
worked for Brooklyn Guarantee in their whole history," going back to the 1890s (17).
Since, however, he does the firm's dirty work, foreclosing properties and dispossessing
their occupants, this distinction may not be as distinguished as it sounds. Indeed, when
Gellburg's eyes are finally opened, he rephrases his job description: "You got some lousy
rotten job to do, get Gellburg, send in the Yid" (68). For the time being, however, he
prefers to boast of his position. Why, he has even been sailing with his boss, winner of
the America's Cup, the ominously named Mr. Stanton Wylie Case.

Phillip is brought down to earth by two things. First is a spontaneous recollection,
"from the old country" of his parents, of a woman believed possessed by a Dybbuk: a
thought that reminds him of his wife's mysterious illness, and makes him wonder if a
rabbi might not "pray it out of her body" (19). Second is Hyman's use of Yiddish, and
the same Yiddish, twice: "*tuchas offen tisch*" (15, 19). Phillip is forced to translate it:
"get your ass on the table." Invisibly, his formal black-and-white attire, which makes
him look more "responsible" at work than, say, those uppity German Jews, can no
longer hide his identity, as a Jew or as a person.

It turns out later that Gellburg can be physically violent. He once slapped his wife
in the face with a steak (31). Another time he threw her up the stairs and cracked a
banister (32). Sylvia has internalized these memories so that they take root in her
unconscious and resurface in a dream that she has had every night since *Kristallnacht*,
in which she relives the photographs in the newspapers as one of the victims. Only her
abuser in the dream is her husband, which she rationalizes as because "he doesn't like
Jews" (55). She recognizes him in the dream by his face, of which he is evidently
ashamed. She asks him later: "What have you got against your face? A Jew can have a
Jewish face" (62).

But Phillip will have nothing Jewish about him except as a form of revenge: of beating the goyim at their own game. He is paranoid that his acquaintance with Allen Kershowitz will lose him his job with Brooklyn Guarantee (64). He votes Republican: "The Torah says a Jew has to be a Democrat?" (12). "You open your mouth," complains his sister-in-law Harriet, "and he gives you that Republican look down his nose and your brains dry up" (30). Overruling his wife, he urges his son on in the military: "I wanted people to see that a Jew doesn't have to be a lawyer or a doctor or a businessman.... For a Jewish boy, West Point is an honor.... He could be the first Jewish General in the United States Army" (24–5). The boy has already been spoken to, twice, by General MacArthur.

Thus Sylvia's own version of Jewishness had much to contend with even before Hitler's thugs went on the rampage. She reaches breaking point because not even her sister can respond to her feelings about Germany. "Why are you so interested in that?" Harriet asks. "What business of yours is that?" (23). And to Hyman she wonders: "I don't understand it, they're in *Germany*, how can she be so frightened, it's across the ocean, isn't it?" (30). Even Margaret Hyman, perceptive and compassionate as she is, questions the "sanity" of Sylvia's concern (48). Hyman himself, who studied medicine in Heidelberg because of "quotas on Jews" at American medical schools (12, 40), believes that, as the saying is, all this will pass; a nobler Germany will rediscover itself. His complaisance reinforces Sylvia's neurosis; and yet he is her only hope. He is the only one to understand that Sylvia "knows" something that the rest of them cannot or will not perceive. "It's like she's connected to some...some wire that goes half around the world, some truth that other people are blind to" (48).

Connectedness – the community of human experience as realized, for example, in the Depression (cf. *The American Clock*) – has always been a leitmotif of Miller's work. It is what makes him the most explicitly political major American playwright. It is characteristic of that ostrich-figure, Phillip Gellburg, that for him there is no Depression (31), just as there are no Jews. It is he, not Sylvia, who has the longest journey to travel in this play, and the work is optimistic to the extent that he goes the distance. In the last of 11 scenes, in bed after his heart attack and about to succumb to another, Gellburg finds his own unconscious and gives it voice:

> I...I want to tell you something; when I collapsed...it was like an explosion went off in my head, like a tremendous white light...It sounds funny but I felt a...happiness...that funny? (68)

The shock to his physical system, like the one to his wife's, releases deep memories, as for instance of walking down Orchard Street on the Lower East Side of Manhattan, looking for bargains among the tenement buildings stuffed with poor immigrants:

The street was full of pushcarts and men with long beards like a hundred years ago. It's funny, I felt so at home and happy there that day, a street full of Jews, one Moses after another.... I wish we could talk about the Jews. (69)

Which he does, realizing for the first time that "being a Jew is a full-time job" (70). But it can be experienced positively: "When the last Jew dies the light of the world will go out" (71). No doubt because, as even the anti-Semitic Kapush in *The American Clock* foresaw, there will be no more libraries.

Incident at Vichy

In 1964, 30 years before *Broken Glass*, Harold Clurman had directed the premiere of *Incident at Vichy* in New York. While this play recalls that "they were picking up Jews in Germany for years before the war" (Miller 1966: 17), that war is now in full swing. The scene is not Brooklyn in 1938 but Vichy France four years later. After their triumphal entry into Paris in June 1940, the Nazis occupied the northern half of France and the west coast and ran their zone directly. The south was officially "unoccupied" by the Germans until November 1942 (two months after the events of Miller's play), and until then controlled by a nominally French government in Vichy. From his earliest days as a writer, Miller had been exercised by issues of collaboration, both positive and negative. *The American Clock* demonstrates his belief in social rather than individual action to achieve the greatest good. But the Vichy regime exemplifies a more dangerous kind of collaboration: collaboration with, or appeasement of, a moral enemy, by the compromise of moral principles out of self-interest. The man who had all the luck, in Miller's play of that name (first produced in 1944), will not believe that he has earned it, morally speaking. In *All My Sons*, Joe Keller sacrifices all his country's sons for the sake of a quicker buck (1947); Willy Loman, in *Death of a Salesman*, cannot bear the consequences of a shabby double-dealing (1949); Eddie Carbone, in *A View from the Bridge*, performs the unthinkable, and rats on innocent relatives (1955); and John Proctor, in *The Crucible*, stands tall against the flow, and dies morally pure (1953).

Miller developed *Incident at Vichy* from a story told to him ten years earlier by his former psychoanalyst of a Jewish colleague he had known during the war in France who owed his life to the self-sacrifice of a non-Jew. The timing of Miller's writing also owed something to his witnessing the Nazi trials in Frankfurt in 1963–4, as well as to his marriage in 1962 to his third wife, the Austrian photographer Inge Morath. She was a non-Jew who had experienced the war in Europe, was forced to work in a German airplane factory, and who knew the Austrian prince on whom the play's von Berg is based (see Miller 1995: 538–9; 2000: 69–70).

Incident at Vichy, first performed in December 1964, is a long one-act play set in "a place of detention," where local Frenchmen suspected of being Jewish are being examined by a seamless partnership of French and German officials. One

Plate 12. All My Sons, by Arthur Miller, original Broadway production. Left to right: Arthur Kennedy (Chris Keller), Dudley Sadler (Frank Lubey), Lois Wheeler (Ann Deever), Beth Merrill (Kate Keller), Hope Cameron (Lydia Lubey), and Karl Malden (George Deever). Courtesy of the Mordecai Gorelik Collection, Morris Library, Southern Illinois University, Carbondale.

of those detained is neither French nor Jewish but an Austrian prince, arrested perhaps because he is foreign, although he also seems to be homosexual. In any event he is released, yet chooses to slip his white pass to a Jew, thus saving the other's life. He goes to his own death like the hero of *The Crucible*. (For all its remoteness from Vichy France, Miller's most famous play was written in the lingering shadow of the Holocaust, and can be said to align itself with its victims and the barbarous methods of their torture.) Von Berg, the outsider of *Incident at Vichy*, lover and patron of music, a nobleman protected by his wealth and family, has always been a romantic. The "spine" of this play, according to the author's note, is his "gradual awakening" (6) to the ugliest realities of the world around him, including the fact (though "beyond belief," according to Monceau, 30) that Harry Hyman also awoke to: that genuine lovers of good music or art like the Germans may also burn Jews. The counter-protagonist of *Vichy*, Leduc, reduces von Berg's naive ideals to nothing. Even the hope of "sharing," of a positive collaboration in, the suffering of the Nazis' victims is denied him, because such suffering has no "meaning" (45). The sturdy Leduc cannot even hold *himself* together: "He moves, deeply agitated, searching out a unity for his fragmented thoughts.... The total collapse of meaning is in his tone" (46). It is a purely existential moment. "What is left," von Berg had asked, "if one gives up one's ideals?" "*You* are left," is Leduc's comfortless response. "With or without ideals ... you are left" (45). Others have noted, and he himself has acknowledged, Miller's philosophical affinities with Sartre (see Miller 1996: 396–413; Sartre wrote the screenplay for the French film of *The Crucible*, titled *Les Sorcières de Salem*, in 1956). Leduc seems especially reminiscent of Jean in Sartre's play *Men Without Shadows* (*Morts sans sépulture*, 1946), which is itself set in a Vichy detention center guarded by French collaborators. Like Leduc, Jean is the one who deserves to get away.

In his note prefacing *Incident at Vichy*, the author debates the relative merits of realistic and metaphorical modes of producing his play, and leans toward metaphor, arguing for the work's "choral quality":

> It is not intended that the characterizations should exist for their own sakes, as in a realistic play, we shall never "know" them in that kind of detail, for these are people caught in an historical cul-de-sac, an emergency, when human beings reveal more or less what is relevant to the emergency and little more. (1966: 5)

In other words, the author is exploring both the essential humanity and the typical Jewishness of a group of representative individuals.

"Humanity" in the play is reduced to its barest bones. Will it even survive with any meaning? "What one used to conceive a human being to be," declares von Berg in a passionate outburst, "will have no room on this earth" (30). "There are no persons any more, don't you see that?" storms the conscience-stricken German major. "There will never be persons again" (41). "Persons" here are more than "individuals"; the very idea of personhood is defunct.

This is the context in which the Jews themselves, like their inquisitors, are seeking to define their essential Jewishness and to lose it as completely as they can. The text returns again and again, with an insistence like an instrument of torture itself, to the two superficial, physical signs of Jewishness supposed to be foolproof: circumcision, and the look of the face, especially the shape of the nose. (We may remember Phillip Gellburg's anxiety about his "Jewish face.") It is almost comical that the actor Monceau, perhaps unawares, was advertising his Jewishness to the Nazis by playing the huge-nosed Cyrano de Bergerac in occupied Paris. There is also the "Jewish" beard. The "Old Jew," deliberately never named and clearly meant to be symbolic, wears a beard reminiscent of those figures of Moses so fondly recalled by Phillip Gellburg on Orchard Street. Although Hoffman, the German "Professor" of racial anthropology, acknowledges that "a small proportion of gentiles" may be circumcised (32), and although there is some question whether Marchand "looks" Jewish (22–3) – "Jews are not a race," asserts Leduc, "they can look like anybody" (22) – these crumbs of hope and difference are swept aside by the "vulgar" simplicity of the Nazi killing machine.

The weakling Lebeau denies that he is "ashamed of being a Jew" (37), yet his indefinable "guilt" seems connected with his sense of himself as Jewish. He denounces the gospel of work, vaguely arguing the support of "the Bible" (12), yet seems not to realize that he is indirectly renouncing a large part of the history of his own people. He stumbles on the very word "Jewish," recognizing it as "inflammatory" (15), although in this respect he is not alone. Von Berg, who is not Jewish, "blunders" into using the term (16), and alienates the rest of the company, who are all, to a greater or lesser extent, in the process of denial. In fact denial is the principal subject of this play, as of *Broken Glass*. Miller starts forcing the issue early on, through the Gypsy. Even Lebeau calls for "some solidarity with Gypsies" (11), evidently innocent of the fact that the Nazis are ahead of him, having already classified the Gypsies in "the same category of the Racial Laws. Inferior" (16).

Like Harry Hyman, Leduc (his name suggesting "leader") is a doctor trained in Germany. Unlike Hyman, he is literally a psychoanalyst as well, with a degree from Vienna (18), and it is his probing that enables the others' passage from denial to knowledge, to accepting at least a measure of the truth of their situation. He forces Monceau, for example, to abandon "logic" and to recognize through his "feelings" the hidden motivation of his inconsistent behavior in Paris. "Your sub-conscious broke the logjam; despite yourself it forced you into the street and saved your life! Rely on what you know, not on what you think" (35). And it is partly through Leduc's skepticism about "logic" that, in a telling pre-echo of *Broken Glass*, von Berg realizes that the Nazis' ability to do the "inconceivably vile" is what "paralyzes the rest of us" (30). Its very banality is reflected in the mere "Incident" of Miller's title, which suggests that certain persons are merely incidental to the Nazi view of life. At the same time, however, the culminating "Incident" of the play provides a heroic counterpoint to the fascists' attempt to trivialize their victims.

"Rely on what you know." The knowing is all. Act 1 of *Broken Glass* ends with Hyman's realization that Sylvia "*knows* something! I don't know what it is, and she may not either – but I tell you it's real" (1994: 49). Whatever "it" is, Sylvia knows enough to wonder why, in 1938, the Jews in Germany "don't . . . run out of the country! What is the matter with those people?" (A question that came to haunt those trapped in Vichy four years later.) Sylvia continues, "screaming": "This is an *emergency*!" (cf. Miller's note on *Vichy*). "They are beating up little children! What if they kill those children! Where is Roosevelt! Where is England!" (59). Four years later it was no longer possible not to *know*. Von Berg's Austrian friends, presumably all gentiles, can choose to ignore the fate of his Jewish musicians (44), but for the Jews themselves, however they may try to postpone or reinterpret it, there can be no doubt of the awful reality. Bayard, the electrician with his feet on the ground, tries to convince the actor Monceau that things have gone beyond role-playing. "Look, chum, I'm telling you what I heard from people who know. . . . People who make it their business to know, you understand?" (17). Similarly, Leduc does not regard the furnaces as "only a rumor." "It should be known. I never heard of it before. It must be known" (44). Monceau's rebuke of Leduc's "Talmudic analysis" rings hollow. Like Phillip Gellburg, he blames another Jew for their plight. "I'll tell you what I think; I think it's people like you who brought this on us. People who give Jews a reputation for subversion" (39). Leduc is of course subversive; but that, as von Berg said of a related matter, "is exactly the point" (30).

Playing for Time

In 1980, Miller followed French (and other) Jews via the freight trains to the concentration camps and gas chambers. He adapted for television the memoir of Birkenau in Poland by Fania Fénelon (with Marcelle Routier), first published in French in 1976 as *Sursis pour l'Orchestre*, and translated into English by Judith Landry as *Playing for Time* (1977), the title also of Miller's screenplay and of a 1985 stage version. It is easy to see why the playwright was drawn to Fénelon's book. It confronts such issues as Jewish identity and the decision to suppress or acknowledge it; the duties of memory; and the ambiguous politics of music.

Birkenau, named (ironically) for its birch trees, was 2 miles west of Auschwitz. It was by far the largest camp in the Nazi system. More Jews died there than in any other, as well as 23,000 Gypsies. *Playing for Time* is primarily about the women's orchestra there, and its use as a strategy of survival that the English title tellingly suggests. Fénelon herself was an accomplished musician, and had made a name for herself in Paris as a café singer and pianist. She is the principal character of both the book and the screenplay. In the film, the first conversation we hear is between her and a younger woman, an overgrown child of 20 called Marianne, who idolizes her. They are on the train bound east. Marianne asks Fania if she is Jewish. "Half," the *chanteuse* responds. "I'm half too. Although it never meant anything to me." "Nor me," replies

Fania (Miller 1981: 451). Once in the camp, Fania is asked by a Polish worker, "How do I look, Jew-Crap?" Fania lets her have it: "I'm not Jew-Crap, I'm French" (458). But in the course of her Birkenau experience, Fania's pride in her Catholic half comes to seem trivial beside the need to assert her Jewishness.

One evening, for an audience including the camp commandant, Kramer, the women's supervisor, Mandel, and the infamous Dr. Mengele, Fania sings "Un bel di" from Puccini's *Madam Butterfly* in what the script describes as "an agonized and therefore extraordinarily moving way." She is enthusiastically applauded; even Mengele "appears... to have been deeply stirred." Fania cannot speak her thanks, but can only "nod... gratefully." She is "staring at the ultimate horror – their love for her music" (481). Harry Hyman and Prince von Berg had found it impossible to believe that a love of music and a willingness to perpetrate what became the Holocaust may exist in the same human sensibility; yet *Playing for Time* documents the fact. Von Berg spoke more wisely than he knew when he said of the Nazis that "their motives are musical and people are merely sounds they play" (Miller 1966: 30). It is said that musicians are the least political of artists, and even some of the Jews in the camp orchestra seem to be seduced by their own sweet sounds to the point where they become politically almost unconscious. Fania herself, in her "audition" for the ensemble, also with "Un bel di," "approaches the fabulous piano... like a dream." "In her face and voice, confident now and warm, are the ironic longings for the music's life-giving loveliness" (463): a phrase that memorably captures the sad fragility of music itself. Since, moreover, the audience of *Playing for Time* actually hears this music, like the Bach chaconne played in the distance by Charlotte ("a good violinist," 477), we too can be lulled by its power into suspending our political judgment.

But the Nazis' visible reaction to her art jolts Fénelon into a new awareness. It becomes a turning point for her, because it is at this moment that she chooses not just to accept but to proclaim her Jewishness.

> *Kramer*:   I must tell you, Mademoiselle Fénelon...
> *Fania*:   Excuse me, but my name is really not Fénelon. Fénelon was my mother's name.
> *Mandel*:   What is your name, then?
> *Fania*:   My father's name was Goldstein. I am Fania Goldstein. (481)

Such a declaration is beyond her protégée Marianne. She and Fania move in opposite directions. The weaker woman trades her body for official favors, and eventually becomes a "kapo," a prisoner working for the administration and armed with a truncheon. Miller defines such collaborators as "brutal, enjoying their power" (454). This kapo's final action, just before their liberation, is to flourish her club and "crack Fania to the floor of the car" in which they are being deported (527). Perhaps, after all, it was the sustaining power of music that enabled Fania to survive and write her book 30 years later. Marianne herself died of cancer "a few years after the war" (531).

But Fania had another gift, the gift of memory, to which both her book and Miller's rendering of it pay tribute. Each work keeps a particular memory alive for others. Early in Miller's script, Fania recognizes that endurance, survival itself, depends on a sense of direction, both past and future. "We must have an aim," she avows. "And I think the aim is to try to remember everything" (460). But there lies a paradox within this belief, since memory is entirely and deceptively individual. Indeed, Fania's gathering strength arises from her subjective consciousness and her willingness to stand by it. In a situation in which other human values have been destroyed, it is all that is left. Michou's Communism and Esther's proto-Zionism are alike shown to be inadequate and irrelevant solutions to the real problem. "*What* problem!" exclaims Esther, "anxiously, aggressively." "I don't see a problem!" The problem, as Fania patiently explains, is that a "murderer" like Mandel is nevertheless "human.... Like you. Like me. You don't think that's a problem?" (484).

Arthur Miller has always believed in collective solutions to society's diseases, yet his own humanism insists on the validity, indeed the prior necessity, of individual consciousness and responsibility. Elzvieta in *Playing for Time*, more deeply perceptive than Fania's ideological critics, "a rather aristocratic Pole" (and non-Jew), and – not least – "a very good violinist" (467), recognizes that Fania is "someone to trust." "Maybe it's that you have no ideology, you're satisfied just to be a person" (503). Being or becoming a person, and above all *remaining* a person, is no small achievement in the world beyond *Incident at Vichy*, a world in which even the resolute Fénelon falters: "Maybe it is too late for the whole human race," she muses (502). But Miller, no more than Fania herself, will let it go at despair. As he phrased it in an interview with Steven R. Centola in 1982, Fania's survival is "the survival of an alienated woman who knows she is alienated and has a vision of an unalienated world" (Miller 1996: 413). Even Mandel, in her eleventh-hour adoption of a Jewish child, is shown to be "a human being after all" (509), thus confirming Fania's intuition about the complexity of the human "problem." But more importantly, Miller the good socialist has to find solutions that may begin in individual awareness and responsibility but must eventually embrace the collective. He finds his signal moment near the end of *Playing for Time*. Mala and Edek "have been horribly beaten, can barely stand," and are brought to the gallows.

> The camera now turns out . . . picking up part of the immense crowd of prisoners forced to watch the executions. . . . This is a moment of such immense human import – for one after another, in defiance, they dare to bare their heads before the two doomed lovers and create a sea of shaven heads across a great space, while SS men and kapos club at them to cover themselves. (515)

After the Fall

After the Fall (1964) is Arthur Miller's most complex and difficult play. There are several reasons why it is not always easy to follow. First, it is Miller's most subjective work, being largely autobiographical. Second, "the action takes place in the mind, thought, and memory of Quentin" (Miller 1981: 127); it is therefore non-linear. Since mind and memory naturally jumble up temporal sequence, thoughts dart in and out of the protagonist's consciousness arbitrarily and unannounced. (Miller's actual auto-biography, *Timebends*, as its title suggests, unfolds with a similar disregard for chronology.) Third, as follows from the above, the play is unusually abstract. Indeed, Quentin himself is aware of the abstractness of his inner story. "I felt strangely abstract beside her." "She" is Maggie, a figure of the concrete: "she was just *there* — like a tree or a cat." From which he generalizes: "I saw that we are killing one another with abstractions" (181). There is a final difficulty with this text, which also springs from the first two. Miller brings all his past experience together in a mental heap: his parents and older brother, his childhood and the Depression, his and others' experi-ence of HUAC, his friendships and the loss of friends, his visit to a concentration camp, his three marriages.

Although the author's marriages, as represented in this play by (in chronological sequence) Louise, Maggie, and Holga, are not the subject of this chapter, they constitute the work's backbone, and should be briefly fleshed out. Miller's 1940 marriage to Mary Slattery ended in divorce in 1956. In the same year he married Marilyn Monroe; they were divorced in 1961, the year before her probable suicide. In 1963, the year after his wedding to Inge Morath, the playwright began to write *After the Fall*, which treats his final marriage with a hope that at the end of the century seemed to have been fully justified. It was Inge, too, who (like Holga in the play) introduced him to the concentration camp at Mauthausen, just outside Linz, in Austria (Miller 1995: 522–4).

After the Fall begins with a long description of the set that warns us of what to expect: rapid mental traverses that cannot be realized graphically. Vaguely "sculpted areas" create a "whole effect" that is "neolithic, a lavalike, supple geography in which, like pits and hollows found in lava, the scenes take place." "The effect . . . will be the surging, flitting, instantaneousness of a mind questing over its own surfaces and into its depths." The scene includes, however, one object (apart from a chair and a stairway) that is identifiable literally. "Rising above all, and dominating the stage, is the blasted stone tower of a German concentration camp. Its wide lookout windows are like eyes which at the moment seem blind and dark; bent reinforcing rods stick out of it like broken tentacles" (1981: 127).

It is easy for a mere reader of the play to forget that this ghoulishly expressionistic object hovers over the entire action. For an audience, it never goes away. Indeed, from time to time it lights up, to underscore a particular moment below it; and it can be cited metaphorically:

> *Quentin*: The view from here is rather pastoral; and the stone walls are warm in the sun, and quiet. I think . . . I may have imagined it more monstrous. Or bizarre. . . . I never thought the stones would look so ordinary. (142)

When Mickey confesses to his law partners that he was once a Communist, their faces become "stones. *The tower lights*," and Quentin draws the connection for the Listener, the audience: "Everything is one thing! You see?" His colleagues' refusal to accept Mickey's intellectual honesty (both as a former Communist and now in admitting it) is metaphorically illuminated by the symbolic beacon of truth. It is like the "tremendous white light" that finally dawns on Phillip Gellburg, endowing him with spiritual vision. "I could feel their backs turning on me," Mickey goes on. "It was horrible! As though – they would let me die" (160). That "as though" makes explicit Quentin's connection between their relatively trivial denial and the ultimate denial of not facing up to the Holocaust.

Such links occur only fleetingly in Quentin's mind. In fact the whole play can be read as a journey toward piecing together the fragments of individual and collective experience. Miller casts his dramatic persona as a lawyer, like Alfieri in *A View from the Bridge*, and like him a chorus figure, with direct access to the audience, which is invited to share, sympathize with, and tacitly help resolve his dilemma. A lawyer's job is to solve puzzles and make judgments. This play's puzzle is a recurring question: what has anything to do with anything else, and especially with a concentration camp? When Quentin/Miller's father learns of the death of his wife, named Rose as in *The American Clock* (Miller's actual mother had died in 1961), his grief

> didn't kill him either, with all his tears. I don't know what the hell I'm driving at! I – *He is caught by the bright tower*. I don't get the connection at the moment but . . . I visited a concentration camp in Germany. . . . *He has started toward the tower*. (136)

It is as if the father's need to be strong after his wife's death triggers an association in Quentin with (in this camp alone) "a minimum of two hundred thousand" other deaths which, however much more horrible, also need to be survived (137).

Needless to say, such slaughter cannot be survived without guilt, without a sense of complicity, however unwilling. Even Holga cannot entirely exonerate herself from the mass liquidation in her own country: "I didn't know. And now I don't know how I could not have known. I can't imagine not knowing, now" (141). Like her, Quentin feels that "something" in Mauthausen "touch[es his] shoulder like an accomplice" (157). "Who can be innocent again on this mountain of skulls? . . . My brothers died here . . . but my brothers built this place; our hearts have cut these stones!" (241). It is Fania Fénelon's recognition about Mandel: she is both monstrous and human.

Both *After the Fall* and *The Creation of the World and Other Business* (1972) suggest by their titles alone that Miller had grappled with at least the opening book of the Hebrew Bible. In fact he was obsessed throughout his work with the human species' loss of innocence, and the possibility of its reclamation, an enterprise not so much Jewish as transcendentally American. Occasionally throughout *After the Fall*, Quentin has a moment, if only a moment, of vision, a glimpse of moral resolution. At the end, he is able to sustain it.

> I wake each morning like a boy – even now, even now! I swear to you, there's something in me that could dare to love this world again. . . . Is the knowing all? To know, and even happily, that we meet unblessed; not in some garden of wax fruit and painted trees, that lie of Eden, but after, after the Fall, after many, many deaths. Is the knowing all? And the wish to kill is never killed, but with some gift of courage one may look into its face when it appears, and with a stroke of love – as to an idiot in the house – forgive it; again and again . . . forever? (241)

Or, as he has already realized, "a human being has to forgive himself" (237).

Quentin's final revelation is inspired by Holga/Inge, who has appeared on "the highest level" of the stage, where she "stands, unperturbed, resolute," waiting to draw him to her. The tower lights are "fierce, implacable" (240), like the vision itself. Quentin climbs up to it, "with his life following him" (242). It is a life that has learned the lessons of other Miller plays: embrace your Jewishness, remember the past, and find that "unseen web of connection" with others (166). Felice in this play has surgery on her nose to hide its telltale feature; Quentin (good for him) "liked her first nose better!" (133). Holga, who (like Inge) was submitted to forced labor by the Nazis, and might prefer to forget it, and worse, nevertheless bids bravely for memory: "One doesn't want to lose the past, even if it's dreadful" (138). Against this "looking before and after" (to borrow from Hamlet) is set Maggie's "now," which, charmingly seductive as it is, will not do to fashion moral stability. "I . . . was with two men . . . the same day," she confesses. "But I didn't realize it till that night. And I got very scared" (214).

Maggie, too, enables Quentin to figure out both the claims and the limits of connectedness. "You're not alone," he tries to reassure her (222), but in the end she is, as we all are. "I am a separate person!" Quentin had protested to Louise (168); and now, to Maggie, "we are all separate people" (233). He accepts responsibility for her life (238), but only up to a point, beyond which it is her own. To paraphrase Mickey (158), Maggie is no longer his rib. Quentin justly charges her with "setting [him] up for a murder. . . . But now I'm going away; so you're not my victim any more. It's just you, and your hand" (232–3). Quentin's "vision" here, his moral clarity in forgiving himself for Maggie's suicide, paves the way for his larger exoneration at the end. Yet his granting himself a future (with Holga) is conditional not only on his remembering and honoring the past, but also on his retaining even Maggie's truth: "it should all be one thing" (204). He himself had realized that "everything is one thing!" (160). No doubt he should not have been "one" with Louise to the extent of writing the paper that earned her an A (189); but his instinct was right. Her observation that Quentin "tend[s] to make relatives out of people" who are not his natural family ("your father, or your brother," 179–80) is crucially accurate. But where she reprimands, Miller – as always – applauds.

Conclusion

In his autobiography, Miller describes his upbringing in Manhattan and later Brooklyn as almost entirely devoid of anti-Semitism (Miller 1995: 24ff., 122). Part of this freedom was due to his father's insistence that Jews were essentially no different from other people: there were good and bad Jews, good and bad gentiles. "If ever any Jews should have melted into the proverbial pot, it was our family in the twenties" (62). By the late 1930s, Miller's perception of the place of Jews in the United States, and in the world, had inevitably changed. His novel *Focus*, published in 1945, tells a grim tale of anti-Semitism near the end of World War II in Brooklyn itself, where graffiti blast out such invectives as *"Kikes started WAR"* and *"Kill kikes kill ki"* (7). Looking back in 1984, Miller wrote that *Focus* "was written when a sensible person could wonder if such a right [as the right of Jews to exist] had reality at all" (Miller 2000: 206). In those years, and even later, Miller must have mused on the application to himself of his own insight: "the fear of the Jew is first of all the fear of his intelligence, which is mysterious and devilish and can embarrass and ensnare the unwary" (Miller 1995: 217). But Miller himself was never deterred by such fear. Like Gellburg once enlightened, Miller came to assert his Jewishness:

> I may have forgotten the little Hebrew I knew as a child. I never go to synagogue, and even find it troublesome to accurately remember which high holiday is which and what they signify, but something in me insists that there must continue to be Jews in the world or it will somehow end. (1995: xiv)

Miller even describes his "resistance to despair" in the face of the world's evils as having "something Jewish about it" (xv). Harold Bloom pinpoints Joe Keller, the protagonist of *All My Sons*, as "an ordinary man who wants to have a moderately good time, who wants his family never to suffer, and who lacks any imagination beyond the immediate: what is this except an authentic American Everyman" (Bloom 1987: 4)? Joe carries a German last name; he could also be Jewish. Yet he is, or has become, like the Old Yankee Pike in Odets's *Paradise Lost* (1935), "one hundred per cent American," as American as Williams's Stanley Kowalski (1947), who furiously resents his dismissal by the pretentiously "French" Blanche DuBois as only a dumb Polack:

> I am not a Polack. People from Poland are Poles, not Polacks. But what I am is a one hundred percent American, born and raised in the greatest country on earth and proud as hell of it, so don't ever call me a Polack. (Williams 1951: 110)

Bloom's nomination of Joe Keller as "an authentic American Everyman" belongs equally to the salesman Willy Loman, who (like Keller) is sadly obeisant to an ungrateful and unforgiving materialist American Dream. Each of them has made the grade as an American on the dream, but at an unacceptable price. They survive their guilt, but when forced to confront it and its consequences, they can endure it no longer and commit suicide. We do not know if either of them is Jewish, yet both could be; or rather, Jewish and American together, in an invisible ethnic compound that is itself characteristically American. Bloom, himself Jewish, concludes that

> Miller has caught an American kind of suffering that is also a universal mode of pain, quite possibly because his hidden paradigm for his American tragedy [*Death of a Salesman*] is an ancient Jewish one. Willy Loman is hardly a biblical figure, and he is not supposed to be Jewish, yet something crucial in him is Jewish, and the play does belong to that undefined entity we can call Jewish literature. . . . The only meaning of Willy Loman is the pain he suffers, and the pain his fate causes us to suffer. His tragedy makes sense only in the Freudian world of repression, which happens also to be the world of normative Jewish memory. (1987: 5)

John Proctor, the hero of the Salem witch-trials in *The Crucible*, is palpably not Jewish, yet he dies a martyr nonetheless, an innocent victim of tyranny. He is like Dr. Stockmann, the solitary and eponymous hero of Ibsen's *An Enemy of the People*, which Miller adapted for the American stage just two years before *The Crucible*. In *Timebends*, the author recalls Ibsen's "signature line" in that play: "He is strongest who is most alone" (1995: 314). Yet he goes on: "But the Jew in me shied from private salvation as something close to sin. One's truth must add its push to the evolution of public justice and mercy." Summing up Miller's work, Bloom regards him finally as "a passionate moralist, all but rabbinical in his ethical vision" (1987: 6). No American playwright of the twentieth century held more firmly to an ethical vision, or did more to exemplify the truth and its public push, in both his life and his work, than Arthur Miller.

BIBLIOGRAPHY

Bigsby, C. W. E. (1984). *A Critical Introduction to Twentieth-Century American Drama, Volume 2*. Cambridge: Cambridge University Press.
——(1987). *File on Miller*. London and New York: Methuen.
——(ed.) (1997). *The Cambridge Companion to Arthur Miller*. Cambridge: Cambridge University Press.
——(2000). *Modern American Drama, 1945–2000*. Cambridge: Cambridge University Press.
Bloom, H. (ed.) (1987). *Arthur Miller*. New York and Philadelphia: Chelsea House.
Fénelon, F., with Routier, M. (1977). *Playing for Time*, trans. Judith Landry. New York: Athenaeum.
Gussow, M. (2002). *Conversations with Miller*. New York: Applause.
Miller, A. (1945). *Focus*. New York: Reynal and Hitchcock.
——(1957). *Collected Plays*. New York: Viking.
——(1966). *Incident at Vichy*. New York: Dramatists Play Service.
——(1981). *Collected Plays, Volume 2*. New York: Viking.
——(1989). *The American Clock: A Vaudeville*. New York: Grove.
——(1994). *Broken Glass*. New York: Dramatists Play Service.
——(1995). *Timebends: A Life*. New York: Penguin. (Originally published 1987.)

Miller, A. (1996). *The Theater Essays* (revised and expanded), ed. Robert A. Martin and Steven R. Centola, foreword by the author. New York: Da Capo.

——(2000). *Echoes Down the Corridor*, ed. Steven R. Centola. New York: Penguin.

Roudané, M. C. (ed.) (1987). *Conversations with Arthur Miller.* Jackson: University Press of Mississippi.

Schlueter, J. and Flanagan, J. K. (1987). *Arthur Miller.* New York: Ungar.

Williams, T. (1951). *A Streetcar Named Desire.* New York: Signet.

15
Drama of the 1960s

Christopher Olsen

As the decade began, playwrights chose two primary creative paths, either to dissect the meaninglessness of everyday language (derived from the "absurdist" influence in Europe) or to develop the taut one-act with disparate characters confronting each other (Albee's *The Zoo Story* being a model). Playwrights were still writing realistic plays with linear plots but their perspective on familiar subjects was changing. They began to view honesty in politics, good race relations, and traditional family roles with increasing cynicism. Dramatists of this decade often created a consciousness in their plays that reflected rebellious nonconformity and "cynical dropout" characters. They also integrated satirical comedy in their perspectives, which frequently contributed to their plays' commercial successes.

Gore Vidal's *The Best Man* (1960) may not have been the most original political comedy to emerge from Broadway, but it heralded an era of political satire. Vidal, who remains a prolific writer of novels, wrote the play prior to John F. Kennedy's 1960 presidential campaign. The drama, which foreshadowed the beginning of the press's intense scrutiny of candidates' private lives, is set in the hotel suites of two political candidates running for office. These two adversaries from the same party, William Russell and Joe Cantwell, compete for their party's nomination. In the ensuing action, they threaten to expose each other with damaging personal information. However, Russell, a former Secretary of State and governor, refuses to submit to dirty politics, even though his adversary, a sitting senator, is all too willing to do whatever it takes to prevail. Ultimately, the "best man," who turns out to be a third candidate trailing both forerunners, becomes the party's nominee when Russell releases his voting block to this candidate. In doing so, Russell prevents Cantwell from exposing a damaging secret about his medical health. The play ran successfully on Broadway for a year and a half and presented a somber but humorous lesson in political malfeasance.

Satirizing the rigidity of American moral codes through the eyes of a rebellious outsider is the topic of Herb Gardner's first full-length play, *A Thousand Clowns* (1962). Murray Burns is an unemployed television writer specializing in children's programs. He has recently quit his latest job as head writer for "Chuckles the Chipmunk," a tired show with an aging, unfunny comedian as its star. Murray lives with his 12-year-old nephew, Nick, and is being pursued by the New York Bureau of Child Welfare. His unmarried sister has deserted Nick, leaving Murray to his care. Murray's cramped apartment and his continual unemployed status are grounds the Bureau uses for removing the child from his custody.

The realistic plot line is straightforward and somewhat clichéd, but what made this play successful in its time is Gardner's attractive anti-hero. Murray is a dropout from society, a link between the beat generation of the 1950s and the hippies of the 1960s. He makes his own rules and chooses to stick to his principles. Although he capitulates to a degree by becoming romantically involved with one of the social workers and promises to find a regular paying job to support Nick, Murray remains the clown who despises the world of provincial conformists. As the title suggests, most of society is made of foolish people who believe they are behaving responsibly and morally when in fact all they do is play by the rules. The real clown, however, knows better.

Murray Schisgal has sometimes been labeled a comic playwright with an absurdist streak. His plays are often tragicomedies reflecting dark humor and frustrating contradictions in modern, urban life. Like many European absurdist playwrights, he situates his dramas in nondescript settings such as grimy basements, colorless offices, and claustrophobic apartments. Schisgal features characters lacking direction in their lives and seeking to change their mundane and meaningless existence. The price of conformity and lack of meaningful interaction between humans are among Schisgal's favorite themes. Indeed, one of his one-act plays, *Fragments* (1967), begins with a destitute writer contemplating suicide in an apartment he shares with two child-hood friends. *The Basement* (1967) also revolves around the theme of isolation in which a research scientist decides to withdraw from society (and from his wife and brother) by working furiously alone in his own basement.

Schisgal's most famous plays include the two one-acts *The Typists* and *The Tiger* (1963), and *Luv* (1964), which was his only Broadway success. *The Typists* features two middle-class characters, Silvia and Paul, who meet as temporary typists in an office and reveal themselves as frustrated and lonely in their dead-end jobs. They talk of escape and fulfillment as they find themselves trapped in their claustrophobic environment, but their subsequent marriage to each other fails to provide them with the emotional freedom they both crave. *The Tiger* begins with the kidnapping of an educated woman by a man who feels he lacks sufficient education to realize his dreams of becoming a linguistics professor and to speak French fluently. The captor and captive eventually are attracted to each other and gingerly attempt to function together on a new emotional plateau.

Luv relies on physical humor and funny one-liners. Like Schisgal's other plays, it revolves around characters who are desperate and lost and who are destined to repeat the same mistakes of their past. The three-character play opens on a bridge where Harry Berlin, a self-indulgent, childish man who recites Dostoevsky, is about to commit suicide. A college friend, Milt Manville, stops him from carrying out his act and convinces him to start a new life. Milt's marriage has fallen apart and he is about to tell his wife, Ellen, that he wants a divorce so he can marry someone else. Ellen first declines the divorce but then changes her mind and marries Harry. By the end of the play, Milt and Ellen are back together and Harry again tries unsuccessfully to kill himself. Schisgal uses revolving action to suggest that nothing is ever really resolved in human affairs. As opposed to some European absurdists who use elite characters, Schisgal creates quotidian characters using colloquial language of urban America. Robert Anderson's *You Know I Can't Hear You When the Water's Running* (1967) is another comic satire made up of four one-act plays. Anderson's major stage successes were *Tea and Sympathy* (1953) and *I Never Sang for My Father* (1968), which explored controversial subjects such as homosexuality and suicide with greater depth than many other commercial playwrights of the period. The two most interesting plays of his quartet of one-acts are *The Shock of Recognition* and *I'll be Home for Christmas* (1967). The plot of the former revolves around a playwright who wants to innovate male nudity on Broadway. The play creates an absurd situation where the producer, playwright, and potentially nude actor discuss the "revolutionary" idea of justifying a male character's nudity onstage. Anderson satirizes everything from artistic inter-ference by producers to the hypocrisy of the implicit acceptance of female nudity without question. His satirical range extends to many areas of society's inability to talk frankly about sex. In the latter play, he examines a mid-life crisis in which a couple, Chuck and Edith Berringer, find it difficult to reconcile their discomfort with discussing the facts of life to their teenage children and their neuroses about their own sexual relationship. Anderson is effective at finding that breach between generations, particularly when it involves sexual intimacy and the inability to be able to confront it. He was part of a generation of playwrights who confronted sexual taboos in the repressive 1950s but only found an accepting audience in the more open ethos of the 1960s.

Slow Dance on the Killing Ground (1964) is part of the genre of plays about confrontation and misunderstanding between disparate characters in an urban envir-onment. In the case of William Hanley's play, it is set in a small convenience store in a district of warehouses and factories in Brooklyn where a street criminal and a lost college student seek refuge late in the evening. The play focuses on the relationship between the three characters as the criminal continually threatens the store owner. The three – an old German convenience store owner who survived the Holocaust, a young African American man on the run after committing a crime, and a college student who is seeking a physician to have an abortion – find themselves drawn to each other despite their vastly different personalities and backgrounds.

Hanley allows his characters to articulate their inner contradictions, which have caused each one great pain. Glas, a Holocaust survivor, is not in fact a Jew but a German Communist who married a Jewish woman. When they were sent to separate concentration camps, he was able to avoid incarceration by utilizing his profession as a railroad engineer. He was ordered to transport war materials for the Nazis and ended up ferrying prisoners to the death chambers. His family died in the camps yet he was able to survive. Randall is a clever young black man who grew up without parents. He never knew his father and his mother turned into a prostitute and virtually ignored him. He fancies himself as a kind of street philosopher yet he is also a petty thief and murderer. Rosie is an insecure college student who was caught having a sexual fling with a graduate student in her grandmother's attic. Several months later she found herself pregnant and alone and seeks to have an abortion. The plot, although somewhat contrived, has Randall seeking refuge from the police in the store. He threatens Glas initially but finds that the old man is sympathetic to his plight. Glas tries to help Rosie, who makes a wrong turn and finds herself lost in the warehouse area. Glas, however, is also running away from his "guilt" of escaping death in Nazi Germany while his family was murdered. All the characters are engaged in a "slow dance," filled with tension, bitterness, and regret, immersed in a quagmire without any means of escape.

Escape may lead to understanding, however, as depicted by Alice Childress in *Wine in the Wilderness* (1969). Childress had a long, prolific career as an African American writer of dramas and novels including *Trouble in Mind* (1954) and *Wedding Band: A Love/Hate Story in Black and White* (1966). *Wilderness* examines feminine identity in the black community through the character of Tomorrow Marie, an uneducated but determined 30-year-old woman living in Harlem in 1964. The play opens in the apartment of an artist, Bill Jameson, during a night of racial tensions. Jameson is proud of his African heritage and seeks to celebrate it on canvas. His current work is a triptych of the black woman: childhood, womanhood or "Mother Africa" (the "Wine in the Wilderness"), and the lost woman ("ignorant, unfeminine, coarse, rude"). Tomorrow Marie has lost her apartment to fire during the race riots and finds herself with her friend, a social worker named Cynthia, in Jameson's apartment. All the characters, including the "Oldtimer" and Cynthia's husband, Sonny-Man, represent different identities and attitudes within the black community. The characters' inter-action and stereotyping of each other reflect the fragmented nature of a black community accustomed to withstanding discrimination. Cynthia and Sonny-Man have tried to integrate into the white community unsuccessfully and Oldtimer has given up trying to improve his impoverished situation. However, it is Tomorrow who emerges as the symbol of the future for African Americans – a proud woman who pulls herself out of poverty and ignorance and teaches the others about self-respect and empowerment.

If Childress uses realism to reveal the consciousness of the African American female, Adrienne Kennedy uses surrealism and expressionism. Critics have associated Kennedy with European absurdists because the form of her plays is filled with symbols and repetitive language. She also has historical figures appear as part of dream-like sequences coming out from the mind of her central characters, often tortured black women. Her prolific output of plays includes *Funnyhouse of a Negro* (1964), *The Owl Answers* (1965), and *A Rat's Mass* (1966), and has continued into subsequent decades with such plays as *A Movie Star has to Star in Black and White* (1976) and *The Ohio State Murders* (1992). *Funnyhouse* begins with a character named

Sarah (or simply called "the negro") with a hangman's rope around her head and a face covered in blood. Sarah, who is about to commit suicide, is a young black woman who lives in a Harlem tenement and has a white Jewish boyfriend and a mother in a mental asylum. Her father, a revolutionary black activist, married her light-skinned mother and moved to Africa with his wife. As the marriage was breaking up, her father raped her mother and she was conceived. Subsequently, her father returned to New York and supposedly hung himself in his apartment. Sarah's character is presented through her other "selves" in a collage of distorted, historical figures: Patrice Lumumba, Christ, Queen Victoria, and the Duchess of Hapsburg. The selves, although diverse, often speak in unison and repeat the same lines in the fashion of a Greek chorus. The characters, however, are not presented in a realistic fashion. For example, Jesus is a cripple dressed in rags, Lumumba's head has blood oozing from it, and Queen Victoria and the Duchess of Hapsburg resemble each other, with exaggerated white complexions and Afro-style hair. As the play progresses to Sarah's inevitable suicide, Kennedy examines Sarah's fractured life and reveals that the obstacles of sexism and racism further hinder the search for a black woman's personal identity.

The Owl Answers is arranged in a dream-like sequence of interlocking scenes including a New York subway car, the Tower of London, and a Harlem hotel room in St. Peter's Church. "The Owl," Clara Passmore, is a 34-year-old schoolteacher in Savannah, Georgia, who is the child of "the Richest White Man in the Town" and his black servant. The Reverend Passmore and his white wife adopt Clara, but she is forbidden to attend his funeral. The play juxtaposes scenes from Clara's experiences visiting England, her father's country of origin, to hotel rooms, where she seduces black men she picks up in the subways. The characters transform themselves into other manifestations in Clara's mind; for example, her mother is called the "Bastard's Black Mother, The Reverend's Wife and Anne Boleyn." Other historical figures appear including Shakespeare, Chaucer, and William the Conqueror. Clara, who envisions herself as the Virgin Mary, eventually has a breakdown in a hotel room with her latest lover and changes into an owl. Kennedy's fragmentary style and her indictment of institutional racism and sexism did not make her very popular in the community of African American playwrights who espoused a realistic approach to their writings. Her postmodern approach to her subject matter, however, has greatly influenced playwrights from the next generation.

The Subject was Roses (1964) by Frank D. Gilroy resembles the typical American family drama where arguments take place in dining rooms or kitchens. Using a linear plot, Gilroy sets the play in the apartment of a Bronx couple welcoming their son back from World War II combat duty. Timmy Cleary has moved back in with his parents, John and Nettie, and hopes to begin a career as a writer. His father is embittered for not serving in the military and for taking on a tedious job in the coffee-importing business. What was supposed to be a joyous weekend reunion turns into a conflict among the trio. The marriage lacks intimacy, the son renounces the Catholicism of his parents, and the father reveals his bigotry and provincialism. The play was not an immediate success commercially but revealed the spare, taut dialogue of urban life that Gilroy used effectively as a Hollywood screenwriter.

Arthur Kopit and Edward Albee, it can be argued, were the most influential playwrights of the 1960s (for Albee, see chapter 16). Both were initially labeled "absurdists" when they started out, Albee with *The Zoo Story* (1959) and *The American Dream* (1961), and Kopit with *Oh, Dad, Poor Dad, Mamma's Hung You in the Closet and I'm Feelin' So Sad* (1960). Kopit scored a major success with this play, which demonstrates homage to European avant-garde writing in the tradition of Eugene Ionesco, Jean Genet, and Friedrich Dürrenmatt. The play is a fantasy about grotesque and strange characters trapped in their given identities. Much of absurdist writing revolves around characters recreating their lives over and over again. *Oh, Dad* features a family consisting of Madame Rosepettle, a woman of high breeding who travels the world with a piranha fish that feeds on cats, carnivorous Venus fly traps, and a dead husband nailed in a coffin. She is accompanied by her repressed, stuttering son, Jonathan, who reveals an almost Oedipal dependency on his mother. The setting is in a hotel suite in Havana and the plot follows Jonathan's efforts to break away from his domineering mother with the help of an amorous babysitter. The play features many farcical elements such as dead bodies falling out of coffins and scenes of physical seduction. As in many absurdist plays, the resolution never comes; in fact, the last line of the play has Madame Rosepettle asking the audience almost rhetorically, "What is the meaning of this?" (Kopit 1960: 89) after discovering her son's seducer dead on her bed. Kopit's indictment of American family values is revealed by Madame Rosepettle's off-handed remark: "Feelings are for animals, Monsieur. Words are the specialty of Man" (58).

Kopit developed his political perspective as the decade proceeded, and, like many playwrights, began to use episodic staging devices derivative of Brechtian methods. For example, *Indians* (1968), written in the midst of the anti-war and civil rights movements, features 13 episodic scenes covering over 40 years of American folklore. The play is about the dichotomy between the myth of the American West, as seen through American icons like Buffalo Bill and Wild Bill Hickok, and the reality of the brutal takeover of Indian land by American frontiersmen. Kopit juxtaposes two streams of consciousness in this play by presenting Buffalo Bill as the heroic frontiersman on the one hand, and as the conflicted Western star of the "Buffalo Bill Wild West Show" on the other. The scenes of the "Wild West Show" exaggerate his exploits and trivialize Indian chiefs, such as Geronimo and Sitting Bull. In one scene, a reporter, who has been writing about Buffalo Bill's legacy, arranges for the show to be presented in front of the American President and the First Lady. The show becomes a parody of frontier exploits (Wild Bill Hickok is featured as a cynical character who hates impersonating himself), and Buffalo Bill has problems remembering his lines and to whom he is speaking. The Indian characters end up creating stereotypical roles of themselves and getting lost in their improvised scripts. The play contrasts the myth of American frontiersmen taming the West and civilizing the native Indian population with the reality of heavy-handed legal maneuvering by the American government that led to the theft and exploitation of Indians' rights. At the end, Buffalo Bill is alone and is returned to a lifeless form in a glass case, along with Sitting Bull and other Indian artifacts. The myth of the American West has been preserved in museum-like fashion.

As American citizens became more politically polarized by the government's increasingly interventionist policies abroad as well as deteriorating race relations at home, playwrights borrowed idealistic beliefs and egalitarian messages from the present to illuminate historical events in the past. Recalling some of Arthur Miller's early plays, *Hogan's Goat* (1965) by William Alfred continues the tradition of exploring family confrontations in a particular ethnic urban setting. In this case, however, Alfred sets the play in the raucous era of Irish American politics in New York City of the 1890s. The protagonist is Matthew Stanton, a Brooklyn ward leader and aspirant to the office of mayor. His primary adversary is the sitting mayor, Edward Quinn, who is running for reelection. Written in verse with a strong dose of Irish dialect, Alfred creates a drama which falls somewhere between melodrama and Greek tragedy. The two politicians have loved the same woman, Agnes Hogan, who has a reputation for material and carnal excess and who is dying of consumption. Stanton's secret past is eventually uncovered, including his bigamy and his marriage to his present wife, Kathleen, outside the church. Stanton tries to cover up his personal indiscretions and put his life in order, only to discover that his actions claim more victims. The tension between the private man and the public leader in politics is endlessly fascinating and, as the title suggests, the strong leader turns into a weak follower – a goat.

Howard Sackler's *The Great White Hope* (1967) emulates much of Brecht's epic staging featuring a large cast, documentary-style "epic" scenes, musical numbers, and a political message. This play was unusual for the Broadway stage of the 1960s, which generally featured musicals, light comedies, and small-cast dramas. The timing of the play's opening, however, could not have been more fortuitous, since 1968 was a year of political violence and racial protest unparalleled in modern American history. Based on the story of Jack Johnson, who in 1908 became the first black heavyweight champion of the world, the play's ironic title describes the white community's attempts to reclaim the title with a white fighter. Sackler changes the name to Jefferson and traces the fighter's glory years in Australia and Europe to his fall from the top at the hands of a white fighter in Havana in 1915. Other than Jefferson and his Australian mistress, Eleanor, the other characters represent attitudes rather than personalities who provide a blueprint of society from many parts of the world of the early 1900s. Sackler also uses a chorus made up of members of an African American church who sing and comment on the bigotry represented in the narrative. In one scene, Jefferson is seen as an "Uncle Tom" figure performing like a circus animal, a cruel parody of the former champion. Sackler makes an important statement about the continuing American racism of the 1960s.

Barbara Gerson's *MacBird!* (1967) is a dark parody of Shakespeare's *Macbeth*, using American politics at the highest level as its backdrop. MacBird, the president-in-waiting (a surrogate for Lyndon Johnson), wants to usurp John Ken O'Dung

(John F. Kennedy), the present leader. He must foil his adversaries, including John's two brothers, Robert and Ted. Other characters featured include "Lady MacBird," "The Earl of Warren," and "Wayne of Morse." The play is written in a series of scenes using Shakespearean verse interwoven with contemporary prose. The play follows the Macbeth legend through the actions of MacBird who arranges for the assassination of his president and takes over the top job. He is eventually doomed by the predictions of the three witches: a student demonstrator, an African American follower of Mohammed, and a factory union worker. MacBird dies of a heart attack before Robert O'Dung, the brother of the slain president, can remove him. This play received considerable criticism because of its cynical look at the Kennedy myth and because many of its characters were still in government.

Paul Foster was one of the playwrights writing for Ellen Stewart's avant-garde Café La Mama in the early 1960s. Foster enjoyed the collective creative process and utilized Brechtian staging practices that incorporated strong political perspectives. Foster's greatest success was *Tom Paine* (1969), an ensemble piece about the historical figure who wrote such famous books as *The Rights of Man* and *The Age of Reason*. Paine, born a British subject, championed the American independence cause and risked his life to promote his egalitarian ideas. In the play, Paine is a divided individual with a real self and a reputation. The play follows Paine's life from convincing colonists of their rights to his audiences with Louis IV and George III. Foster's Paine is, moreover, a radical drunkard who is sailing to America for the first time to promote independence. He promotes revolution and confronts many obstacles, including narrow-minded bureaucrats, thieves, a chorus of "Greedies," and members of royalty. Actors play multiple roles and often use transformative techniques – a method borrowed from the 1960s Open Theatre that asks actors to "transform" from one character to another in front of the audience – to create images of war and destruction. The play is divided into an episodic structure and includes music, dancing, and scenes of sex and violence. The play found a receptive climate in 1968, one of the most violent years in American life, when assassinations and the Vietnam War dominated the headlines.

If many dramatists reveled in political commentary, Leonard Melfi mastered the intimate, one-act human encounter play, creating a confrontation between two disparate characters having a chance meeting. *Birdbath* (1965) is his most well-known play and features an encounter between a young struggling poet and a nervous troubled waitress at a New York cafeteria. Frankie Basta works as a cashier at the cafeteria and invites Velma Sparrow back to his apartment with an eye on seduction. Their encounter, however, reveals Frankie's need to validate his life (mostly through music and books) and Velma's uncontrollable tension due to a domineering mother. By the end, Frankie discovers that Velma has murdered her mother with a knife after being physically abused once too often. He puts her to bed and writes a poem comparing her to a dead bird without wings. Melfi is not a romantic but he is very sympathetic to the troubled souls in his plays. In this play, Melfi reveals a flair for bringing out idiosyncrasies in his wounded characters.

Tom Eyen's writing style fits into the 1960s dramatic tradition featuring characters searching for fame while living fragmented lives. His two most successful plays from the 1960s (one is part of a trilogy) are *The White Whore and the Bit Player* (1964) and *Why Hanna's Skirt Won't Stay Down* (1965). The "white whore" is in fact a woman in a sanatorium who is about to commit suicide because she believes she has destroyed her life by falsely representing herself. Her alter ego is a wisecracking nun who appears as a character and reveals her dual consciousness – how she saw herself originally (a nun) and how the world sees her now (a whore). The play has almost a vaudevillian feel to it as the characters interact using music and parody. It incorporates references to American pop icons such as Marilyn Monroe, whom the prostitute resembles (she is 36, blonde, and about to take an overdose of sleeping pills), and reveals the dichotomy between the fantasy and real roles American women are expected to play. In *Why Hanna's Skirt Won't Stay Down*, Eyen uses another disenfranchised woman (Hanna) as a symbol of the degrading image of women in American culture. The play opens with Hanna in the amusement park at Coney Island, standing on top of an air vent with her skirt flying up. The image of Marilyn Monroe in the film *Some Like it Hot* is recreated to suggest that Hanna, who works in a ticket booth in a movie theatre, has delusions of fame and romance. She meets a drifter named Arizona and the two have an affair, but are ultimately left to ruminate about the aspirations and dreams they are never to realize. To compound Hanna's problems of alienation, she has a sister, Sophie, who is almost her exact opposite. In Eyen's *Who Killed My Bald Sister Sophie?* (1968), Sophie is an Avon lady who attempts to live a simple life and not get carried away by her sister's delusions. However, her perfect marriage dissolves and her physical shortcomings (she has a bald spot on her head) compared to her sister are magnified. Eyen eventually turns all his main characters into frozen statues ("human impostors"), Hanna and Arizona at the end of *Hanna* and Sophie at the end of *Sophie*, cementing the idea that American culture is made up of too many impostors. Eyen evoked the values of middle-class America by depicting people from small towns who grew up after World War II and who found themselves caught up in the frenzied American culture of the 1960s.

Three authors most significantly influence the development of theatre and drama during the 1960s: Alan Kaprow, Michael Kirby, and Richard Kostelanetz. Kaprow introduced the concept of the "happening," a "hybridization" of materials, actions, words, and images designed to parallel modern life. Happenings were unrehearsed, spontaneous performances by non-professionals, creating an experience shared by audience members and performers alike (Kaprow 1966: 59–65). Kirby adds to the period's avant-garde by examining the influence of surrealism and abstract expressionism, where visual artists-turned-theatre practitioners created theatre pieces from various types of obsessive or psychic act. The productions of these forms were often dream-like in their execution (Kirby 1969: 97). Kirby also noted the development of environmental theatre, where the physical elements that surround the spectator become part of the performance (147). Finally, Kostelanetz observed that "the theatre of mixed means" seeks to synthesize the lines dividing different art forms and "pares the theatrical situation down to its absolute essentials" (Kostelanetz 1968: 283). Kostelanetz's description is probably the most identifiable terminology for experimental theatre of the 1960s, and the two theatre groups who best personified that impulse were the Open Theatre and the Living Theatre.

Megan Terry and Jean-Claude van Itallie were the leading playwrights-in-residence of the Open Theatre. Both wrote plays for the Open Theatre's Ensemble Company and incorporated transformative exercises that were integrated into the final scripted performances. "Transformation" defined an alternative approach to storytelling onstage. Instead of a plot line marked by a psychological progression and representing a fixed reality, transformation is image oriented, featuring simultaneous realities. A character can shift from a three-dimensional psychological character to an abstract organism, such as a machine or part of an unknown creature. A character might even turn into a historical figure or into an animal. The purpose of this constant shift of consciousness is to reveal the multiple realities human beings experience at any given moment.

Terry's dramas use transformation liberally, particularly in her *Calm Down Mother* (1965) and *Keep Tightly Closed on a Cool Dry Place* (1966). *Calm Down Mother* features three women who reenact multiple relationships between family members. A woman worries about her mother's terminal cancer and her father's alcoholism. An older prostitute schools her daughters in the art of surviving a violent pimp. A poor mother in a tenement argues with her daughters about how they should protect themselves from choosing irresponsible boyfriends. The play is a series of transformative scenes about the frustration women feel toward their given roles as procreators, protectors, and servants. *Keep Tightly Closed* is set in a prison cell where three men are incarcerated for the murder of the wife of one of them. Jaspers, a ruthless psychotic, hires Michaels, an insecure friend, to hire Gregory, a highly strung young man, to kill his wife. Although Gregory succeeds in killing Jaspers's wife, he is caught and implicates the others in the crime. The play explores the relationships among the three, using transformative scenes in which characters play multiple roles: performing vaudeville routines, playing drag queens and gangsters, and creating a "family" of a father and his two sons. The thrust of the plot is how Jaspers and Michaels try to coax a confession out of Gregory to admitting sole guilt.

Terry's most well-known play is *Viet Rock* (1966), described as a "folk war movie" (Terry 1966b: 19). Indeed, it has a cinematic feel with scenes interwoven in collage. Terry uses episodic structure with musical numbers. The play, which examines the media coverage of the Vietnam War, developed out of a workshop production at the Open Theatre. The actors play multiple parts including babies, soldiers, and inanimate objects. The play opens with a song and a reenactment of scenes and events of war as if children were playacting. The scene shifts abruptly to an army physical center, where several mothers have taken their draft-aged sons to enlist. Terry builds two simultaneous realities: the world of the recruits and the protestors against the war. The military point of view makes the stronger impression on the young soldiers. After a scene at a Senate hearing, where sympathetic and hostile witnesses testify on

America's involvement in Vietnam, the choice to win the war at any cost prevails. The second act involves scenes of war, including murder of civilians, mothers identifying their dead sons, and the omnipresent fantasy figure of "Hanoi Hannah" tempting naive American GIs. The play concludes when a bar filled with American soldiers is bombed and dead bodies are strewn all over the stage. This drama's cynical and ironic attitude about the American government's selling of the war foreshadowed later Hollywood films about Vietnam.

Van Itallie was less overtly political than Terry and was influenced more by European absurdist writers. He questioned the usefulness of language as a truthful communicator and criticized society for its commodification of individual experience. He embraced ideas emanating from Antonin Artaud's Theatre of Cruelty, including making attempts at shocking the audience in order to create catharsis and by using ritualistic energy as a vehicle for collective audience transformation. Furthermore, he wanted to create myths and strong poetic images onstage to highlight the contrast between an idealized world and banal reality (Plunka 1999: 43). Born in Belgium, he became a naturalized American citizen and came to prominence with his work with the Open Theatre in the mid-1960s. His trilogy of short plays under the collective name *America Hurrah* (1966) was hailed by some critics as influential as Edward Albee's *The Zoo Story*, written seven years earlier (Plunka 1999: 88). *Motel*, the earliest play of the trilogy, was originally entitled "The Savage God" and presents a microcosm of American society using three huge, distorted dolls. Not unlike the mascots who roam the sidelines of sports events today, the dolls with oversized heads represent the three characters onstage: a motel keeper and a young couple. The dolls are dressed in garish clothing and wear exaggerated wigs and makeup. The motel keeper's droning voice is piped in through a loudspeaker spewing out platitudes and alleged truisms. The "doll" couple make demands, write vulgar language all over the walls of their motel room, and destroy it completely before decapitating the motel keeper. Actors are inside the large dolls until the conclusion of the play. All of this takes place as screeching musak can be heard in the background over loudspeakers. The crude graffiti scrawl on the motel room's walls becomes the metaphor for the porous language of everyday American speech.

Both Terry and van Itallie worked on *The Serpent* (1968) at the Open Theatre, but it was van Itallie who claimed authorship when Terry withdrew. Critics have pointed out that *The Serpent* was one of the best examples of the successful techniques for collective creation so synonymous with theatre of the decade (Plunka 1999: 130). Van Itallie and his Open Theatre collaborators, notably the director Joe Chaikin, wanted to explore the Bible, using some of radical director Jerzy Grotowski's techniques for merging the inner soul of the actor with external transformative exercises. The script, however, grew as reenactments of the John F. Kennedy and Martin Luther King assassinations (the latter having just taken place as the script was being completed) were added.

The play, entitled a "ceremony " (van Itallie 1966: ii), features 13 scenes, beginning with an autopsy and ending with a "begetting" scene in which actors procreate, give birth, and grow old. In between, the Kennedy and King assassinations are reenacted, the stories of Eve and the serpent and Cain and Abel are created, and four female chorus members carry on a dialogue with the audience. In effect, *The Serpent* resembles Greek tragedy, although a major difference is the transformative actions of the performers. In addition to playing human characters, the actors transform into creatures, inanimate objects, and noise effects. For example, five male actors making up parts of the body create the serpent. Various actors play the voice of God when Adam and Eve are cast out of Eden. Actors who reenact not only the roles of lovers, babies, and old people but also the vocal accompaniment of their actions create the scenes of procreation and birth. Van Itallie shows how limited human beings are because they kill and destroy so indiscriminately. Characters do not necessarily physically die, but merely "empty out, in a kind of living death" (88). The play had strong reverberations during 1968, when the King and Kennedy assassinations, along with the rising death toll of Americans in Vietnam, dominated the headlines.

The Living Theatre's legacy began in the New York apartment of Julian Beck and Judith Malina, where they staged readings of poetic dramas in the 1940s. By the 1960s, they had moved to downtown New York (Fourteenth Street) where they staged their first commercial success: *The Connection* (1959), Jack Gelber's naturalistic portrait of drug addiction. Four years later, Malina staged Kenneth H. Brown's *The Brig* (1963), which is based on his experiences in an American Marine infantry unit. The play was set in 1957 in a prison controlled by Marines; it featured four guards and 11 prisoners living in repressive conditions. The guards represent different cultural and geographical backgrounds, as do the prisoners. The guards have names (Tepperman, Grace, The Warden, and Lintz), whereas a number and behavior patterns refer to the prisoners (i.e., "six, a rough-looking man of 34"). The play covers a single day in prison life and subjugates the prisoners (and audience) to acts of torture from merely demeaning to outright terrifying. One character, "six," refuses to be treated as a nondescript human being and demands that his rightful name be used. As a result, the guards exile him in chains to an insane asylum. Brown gives the audience a nightmare reminiscent of Antonin Artaud's Theatre of Cruelty, and Malina, his director, wrote about her insistence that the actors carry over the repressive discipline of the play into the rehearsal process (Brown 1963: 86). The play is in part based on a guidebook for Marines and turns into an allegory of brutality not only of the military, but also of American civilian life.

The Living Theatre spent considerable time abroad during the 1960s because of tax evasion problems, but they continued to create some of their signature productions while in exile. Unlike the combativeness of *The Brig*, these plays harkened back to Julian Beck and Judith Malina's belief that theatre is a place of inner experience where the ritual and poetic language can merge to transform audiences. In other words, the spectator participates in the ritual and emerges from the experience in a higher state of knowledge and self-understanding. Productions that reflected this philosophy liberally included *Mysteries and Smaller Pieces* (1964) and *Paradise Now* (1968). *Paradise Now* invited direct contribution from the audience by asking them to climb various philosophical "rungs" to reach a level of revolutionary non-violence (Biner 1972: 167–213). The eight rungs in the play have three states each: a Rite, a Vision, and an Action. The end of the play is not scripted because the audience participates and reaches different states at every production. Beck and Malina borrowed liberally from the philosophies of Cabalist and Tantric thought, which use the body to reveal attributes of God known as "*sefirot*," Hebrew inscriptions on the body. The play spans the journey from each successive rung beginning with the "Rite of Guerilla Theatre," and ending with the "Rite of I and Thous." Each Rite is accompanied by a Vision (in the first rung, "Death and Resurrection of the American Indian"; in the last, "Vision of Undoing the Myth of Eden") and an Action ("Acting out the violent forces of Law and Order," and walking out into the street surrounded by actors and audience colleagues). By the time the play/ritual is over, the audience and actors have bonded at some level and have carried out a series of actions.

Michael Kirby has observed that the revival of surrealism among visual artists of the 1950s carried over to theatre productions in the 1960s. Playwrights used dream sequences, juxtaposed scenes, and featured obsessive behavior as dramatic devices in their plays (Kirby 1969: 97). Rochelle Owens is certainly a surrealist in the sense that she juxtaposes ideas, words, and characters, locating them in situations that reveal their primal drives. She also works with symbols and situates many of her plays in historical settings such as fifteenth-century Constantinople (*Istanbul* [1965]), Africa (*Beclch* [1968]), and China during the Manchu dynasty (*He Wants Shih!* [1974]). She is interested in power that leads to violence, sex, and even transcendence, situating her characters in the fault line between the surface and the subconscious. *Futz* (1965), a one-act, is her most famous piece. The play recalls some of the work of the French surrealists such as Guillaume Apollinaire's *The Breasts of Teiresias*, in part because the scenes are short and seem to dissolve into each other in a kind of dream. *Futz*, however, does not take place in some exotic locale but rather in a rural American farm setting and in a local jail. The plot revolves around Cy Futz, a lonely farmer in a dysfunctional marriage who falls in love with his pig. His wife and family think he is crazy and have him locked up in jail. Futz meets a fellow prisoner, Oscar Loop, who has murdered a young girl whom he was trying to seduce. Both characters are uneducated with minimal emotional maturity, yet they both can articulate their primal needs. The play can be quite funny but underneath the pathetic situation is an indictment of American idealism. Cy Futz, a kind of American Gothic cartoon, is at the end murdered by his brother for his ignorance and inability to accept the morality of a cold, sanctimonious society.

The Beard (1965), by Michael McClure, is remembered more for its notoriety than its content. Yet it remains a compelling oddity that contributed to the eccentricities of 1960s theatre. Using a surrealistic approach, McClure successfully exposes the banality of mythologizing American icons. Opening originally at the Actors Workshop in San Francisco, the play features two American icons, Jean Harlow and Billy the Kid, who perform a literary duet in which the actors play the media creations of these two individuals. Harlow and Kid are chosen because of their symbolic qualities of sexual allure and brutal violence. The "stars" entertain the audience using their signature mythical roles to play out their sexual fantasies with each other. Billy the Kid is cast as the predator but Jean Harlow successfully parries his sexual advances with mocking statements about his lack of prowess. Their language is reduced to repetitive platitudes, vulgar one-liners used in a kind of ritual foreplay. The notoriety of this production derived from the final scene when the characters engage in simulated sexual intercourse. The play, however, reveals an early condemnation of disingenuous American mythmaking and owes a great deal to the conventions of the absurd movement where characters are trapped in designated roles conversing in meaningless language. A surrealistic style underscored by a satirical political perspective continued to be popular during the late 1960s, particularly in Greenwich Village. While most plays never made it beyond their initial productions, several of them moved to off-Broadway for lengthy runs. Julie Bovasso, a Greenwich Village playwright, who also acted and directed, wrote a kind of surrealistic farce, *Gloria and Esperanza* (1969), which featured herself in the leading role of Gloria. Gloria is a fantasy girlfriend of a struggling poet, Julius Esperanza, a kind of dominatrix who convinces him to elicit the help of a revolutionary named "the Black Prince." Julius feels trapped, both figuratively and literally, in a grungy basement apartment with machine gun fire and fighting taking place above. A war between various elements of society featuring soldiers, "guru" children, and abstract characters from the literary past, like an 8-foot chicken named "Solange," engage in a kind of warfare of ideas. Julius rightfully thinks he is going crazy and visits a psychiatrist, who ends up needing help more than his patient. The second act takes place in a madhouse where Julius and Gloria confront saints battling gladiators, and where Julius elicits the aid of the Black Prince to help him out of his mental quagmire. Eventually, the Black Prince creates a "revelation revue" featuring characters dressed up as religious figures performing various dance routines and ushering Julius into a new consciousness. The play, a satire of writers who see themselves as social revolutionaries, lampoons many onerous governmental institutions such as the US Post Office, the IRS, and the military.

Ronald Tavel was one of the original creators of the Theatre of the Ridiculous, which Charles Ludlam turned into the Ridiculous Theatre Company and made famous in the 1970s. Again, using a surrealistic and satirical approach to his material, Tavel takes stereotypical characters, particularly from the entertainment media, and has them spewing inane banalities at each other and at the audience. Sex roles are often juxtaposed, allowing the eccentric characters to exude cartoonish qualities. *Gorilla Queen* (1967) is Tavel's most well-known work that premiered at the Judson Poets Theatre in Greenwich Village. The production uses a 1930s motif and can best be described as a series of campy, vaudevillian sketches revolving around a loose theme. This satire is directed at the American public's lust for decadent entertainment at any cost and the story of *King Kong* is used as a backdrop. The principal character, "Queen Kong," features a male playing the female role. The play/revue follows the adventures of "Clyde Batty" and his search for Kong, only to meet a highly erudite creature with an affinity for Cartesian logic. She is also a kind of diva ("Venus in Furs") with a sadomasochistic flair for the double entendre. The skits include characters with names like "Brute," "Mais Oui," "Venus Fly Trap," and "Karma," accompanied by a chorus of "Glitz Jonas." Eventually, Clyde kills Kong and assumes her role "to give the audience what they want" in a not-too-convincing costume. The script, filled with rude asides and sexual innuendo, previewed some of the antics of Charles Ludlam's Ridiculous Theatre in the subsequent decade.

One cannot underestimate the impact of gay playwrights who wrote honestly about gay life and created complex characters. No play had more of an impact than *The Boys in the Band* (1968), one of off-Broadway's biggest hits not only because of its frank depiction of contemporary urban homosexual lifestyles, but also because of its witty dialogue. Mart Crowley's play centers on a birthday party given by an aspiring screenplay writer, Michael, for one of his friends. He has invited an assorted group of gay friends and acquaintances, including his current lover, his former college classmate, and a birthday present in the form of a "hired" escort named Cowboy. Crowley identifies everyone only by their first name, suggesting perhaps that his characters are representative of common behavior patterns within the gay community. The birthday party eventually includes a game where the guests must reveal their love for someone over the telephone. Although the play is slightly contrived and received some criticism from the gay community for its pessimistic depiction of homosexual relationships, it nevertheless made its effect by unleashing a more overt and frank examination of the homosexual community in contemporary American drama (see chapter 30).

Robert Patrick, another prominent gay playwright, came from the first generation of writers out of off-off-Broadway who congregated in such theatres as Caffé Cino, Café La Mama, and the Judson Poets Theatre. Patrick eventually moved to a theatre space in Greenwich Village, "The Old Reliable," and became essentially its principal playwright for several years. Patrick, a contemporary of Lanford Wilson's at the Caffé Cino, built a reputation as a kind of wordsmith prankster who experimented with dialogue and format. Like many New York playwrights of the time, the dialogue of European absurd playwrights as well as the lyrical realism of Albee and Wilson influenced him. He wrote many two-handed one-acts, some merely playful and others poignant. His most famous play, *Kennedy's Children* (1974), came much later in his career yet reflects many of the issues he brought out in his plays during the 1960s. In his first full-length play, *The Haunted Host* (1964), he examines the relationship between Jay, a gay writer, and Frank, a ghost who appears as his former suicidal lover. Jay taunts Frank, also an aspiring writer, for being uncommitted, yet Jay finds it difficult to integrate his own sexual needs for companionship with his artistic needs for solitude. Patrick experimented with overlapping dialogue in *Lights, Camera, Action* (1966), and with writing scenes from a love story in reverse order in *Still Love* (1966). Patrick's other big success in the 1960s, *I Came to New York to Write* (1969), is a series of scenes featuring the same setting of an apartment in New York over a period of 15 years. Each scene features a different pair of residents, couples who are engaged in some kind of personal conflict. The scenes are divided by years ranging from 1955 to 1969. Patrick developed a major talent for writing contemporary, realistic dialogue yet managed to instill his characters with a corresponding ability to articulate their fantasies. Many of his characters often embellish their lives with excursions into fantasy to lift themselves out of their drab existence.

Terrence McNally's writing career has spanned four decades and continues to bear fruit. He is certainly one of the leading American playwrights of the late twentieth century, not merely because of his considerable output, but also because he has tackled so many subject matters. He has written one-acts, adaptations of classics, biographical drama, plays with gay themes, and broad comedies. He is also an opera aficionado frequently incorporating references (such as character names) to operas and opera singers. His early work in the 1960s was greatly influenced by the Albee generation of American absurdists in that McNally wrote short one-acts with characters often on the brink of insanity. Frequently the characters are trapped in an untenable and confusing situation from which they cannot extricate themselves. *Next* (1967) is an interrogation of an overweight 40-year-old movie house manager who is being subjected to a physical exam for duty in the army reserves. *Sweet Eros* (1968) features a disturbed husband who pours out his thoughts to a naked female captive whom he plans to rape. *Noon* (1969) features a group of sexual swingers invited by the same person to a New York apartment for a "party." The host never shows up, so the characters reveal their true identities behind the roles their sexual fantasies call for. *And Things That Go Bump in the Night* (1966) was McNally's comic excursion into a dysfunctional family hiding in the basement of their home because of "threats" outside. These "threats" are never quite explained except that the family has an electric fence surrounding their home, which they turn on at night after curfew. The play evokes the nuclear hysteria in the early 1960s when communities built bunkers everywhere as shelter against a nuclear holocaust. The characters include a dying grandfather, a couple in their fifties, two teenagers, and a young friend of the family. The operatic references include the son's name (Sigfrid) and the occupation of his mother, Ruby, a former opera diva. Grandfather is a certified mental patient and a former actor. His son sits around vegetating, his grandson fancies himself a poet, and his granddaughter is a wisecracking, cynical 13-year-old. Sigfrid's friend, Clarence, joins them in the basement, clothed in a dress. The family sees him as an odd homosexual, but he thinks he is a squadron leader who plans to lead a demonstration as part of the "movement." Clarence befriends the family but is electrocuted by the fence as he tries to leave. The family remains trapped in their "mechanism," "pretending not to live," as Sigfrid points out (McNally 1972: 76). McNally has painted a devastating picture of the soullessness of American life as seen through one family's fantasy. Americans who define their existence by what the media tell them and by their excursions into literary fantasy are indeed trapped in their own hellhole.

The 1960s also featured many experimental theatre pieces, including innovative adaptations of classical works. Jerzy Grotowski's influence was immense and the taut one-act continued to be a favorite staple of playwrights. One cannot depart from the decade, however, without mentioning the influence of the musical *Hair*, which successfully combined rock music, episodic form, surrealism, and environmental "happening" staging that called for political action. *Hair* became a kind of anthem for disillusioned young Americans who rejected the Vietnam War, materialism, and racism. This theatre piece reflected most accurately how divided American generations were as the decade came to a close.

BIBLIOGRAPHY

Alfred, W. (1971). *Hogan's Goat*. In John Gassner (ed.), *Best American Plays, Sixth Series: 1963–1967*. New York: Crown, 137–84.

Anderson, R. (1971). *You Know I Can't Hear You When the Water's Running*. In John Gassner (ed.), *Best American Plays, Sixth Series: 1963–1967*. New York: Crown, 336–65.

Barranca, B. and Dasgupta, G. (eds.) (1981). *American Playwrights: A Critical Survey, Volume 1*. New York: Drama Book Specialists.

Biner, P. (1972). *The Living Theatre*. New York: Horizon.

Bovasso, J. (1972). *Gloria and Esperanza*. In Albert Poland and Bruce Mailman (eds.), *The Off-Off Broadway Book*. New York: Bobbs-Merrill, 317–51.

Brown, K. H. (1963). *The Brig*. New York: Hill and Wang.

Crowley, M. (1975). *Boys in the Band*. In Clive Barnes (ed.), *Best American Plays, Seventh Series: 1967–1973*. New York: Crown, 493–528.

Eyen, T. (1971). *Tom Eyen: Sarah B. Devine! and Other Plays*. In Michael Feingold (ed.), *The Winter Repertory*. New York: Winter House.

Fornes, M. I. (1987a). *Molly's Dream. Promenade and Other Plays*. New York: Performing Arts Journal Publications, 89–116.

——(1987b). *The Successful Life of 3. Promenade and Other Plays*. New York: Performing Arts Journal Publications, 47–65.

Foster, P. (1975). *Tom Paine*. In Clive Barnes (ed.), *Best American Plays, Seventh Series: 1967–1973*. New York: Crown, 393–423.

Gardner, H. (1963). *A Thousand Clowns*. In John Gassner (ed.), *Best American Plays, Fifth Series: 1957–1963*. New York: Crown, 419–58.

Gilroy, F. D. (1971). *The Subject was Roses*. In John Gassner (ed.), *Best American Plays, Sixth Series: 1963–1967*. New York: Crown, 567–94.

Hanley, W. (1971). *Slow Dance on the Killing Ground*. In John Gassner (ed.), *Best American Plays, Sixth Series: 1963–1967*. New York: Crown, 435–470.

Kaprow, A. (1966). "Manifesto." In Dick Higgins and Emmett Williams (eds.), *Manifestos*. New York: Something Else.

——(1993). *Essays on the Blurring of Art and Life*, ed. Jeff Kelley. Berkeley: University of California Press.

Kirby, M. (1969). *The Art of Time*. New York: Dutton.

Kopit, A. (1960). *Oh Dad, Poor Dad, Mamma's Hung You in the Closet and I'm Feelin' So Sad*. New York: Hill and Wang.

——(1969). *Indians*. New York: Hill and Wang.

Kostelanetz, R. (1968). *The Theatre of Mixed Means*. New York: Dial.

McClure, M. (1965). *The Beard*. New York: Grove Press.

McNally, T. (1969a). *Noon*. In *Morning, Noon and Night*. New York: Random House, 65–107.

——(1969b). *Sweet Eros, Next and Other Plays*. New York: Vantage Books, 77–96; 19–52.

McNally, T. (1972). *And Things That Go Bump in the Night*. In Albert Poland and Bruce Mailman (eds.), *The Off Off Broadway Book*. New York: Bobbs-Merrill, 44–81.

Melfi, L. (1967). *Encounters: Six One-Act Plays*. New York: Random House.

Owens, R. (1968). *Futz*. In William M. Hoffman (ed.), *New American Plays, Volume 2*. New York: Hill and Wang, 1–24.

Plunka, G. A. (1999). *Jean-Claude van Itallie and the Off-Broadway Theater*. Newark, NJ: University of Delaware Press.

Sackler, H. (1975). *The Great White Hope*. In Clive Barnes (ed.), *Best American Plays, Seventh Series: 1967–1973*. New York: Crown, 1–72.

Tavel, R. (1972). *Gorilla Queen*. In Albert Poland and Bruce Mailman (eds.), *The Off Off Broadway Book*. New York: Bobbs-Merrill, 199–230.

Terry, M. (1966a). *Calm Down Mother*. In Nick Orzel and Michael Smith (eds.), *Eight Plays from Off-Off Broadway*. New York: Bobbs-Merrill, 255–81.

——(1966b). *Viet Rock and Other Plays*. New York: Simon and Schuster.

Van Itallie, J.-C. (1966). *America Hurrah*. In Nick Orzel and Michael Smith (eds.), *Eight Plays from Off-Off Broadway*. New York: Bobbs-Merrill, 191–9.

Vidal, G. (1963). *The Best Man*. In John Gassner (ed.), *Best American Plays, Fifth Series: 1957–1963*. New York: Crown.

16

Fifteen-Love, Thirty-Love: Edward Albee

Steven Price

"People often ask me how long it takes me to write a play, and I tell them 'all of my life.'... With *Three Tall Women* I can pinpoint the instant I began writing it, for it coincides with my first awareness of consciousness" (Albee 1995c). With this, Edward Albee introduced the published text of the play that in the early 1990s returned him to a level of public and critical acclaim he had not enjoyed for approximately 30 years. It is a study, of sorts, of his adoptive mother at the ages of 92, 52, and 26, a cubist portrait into which Albee incorporates a young man who remains silent throughout, and represents the playwright himself at the time of his mother's dying. The brilliant *coup de théâtre* in the second act is to transform the elderly woman's assistant and lawyer into younger versions of herself, so that the youthful woman's optimistic innocence enters into an ironic dialogue with the older selves who have already experienced the future disappointments lying in wait.

Albee's preface plays similar games with time: the meaning of his earliest memory only becomes fully apparent with the completion of the play, while the play only becomes possible with the recuperation of the memory. That Albee recalls the event as occurring when he was no more than 3 months old may cast doubt on its accuracy, but this is less important than the double perspective, dramatized in *Three Tall Women*, that informs all such memories in which the child's experience is refracted through the consciousness of the adult.

In earlier plays Albee had frequently doubled characters of conspicuously different ages, like the Famous American Playwright and his younger counterpart in the playlet *Fam and Yam* (1960), or the two childless couples in *Who's Afraid of Virginia Woolf?* (1962). But *Three Tall Women* is the logical extension of the single character that appears to have several, separate lives, or can be young and old simultaneously. This distinctive figure is found from the beginning of Albee's career, and the playwright himself is the prime example. In 1960, *The Zoo Story*, his first produced play, seemed to many the creation of a dramatist who had arrived fully formed. The truth was different: he had been writing since childhood, and as he approached 30 was

beginning to fear that his literary efforts would come to naught. He was unknown –
even to himself, having been placed when he was two weeks old with an adoption
agency from which he was, in his word, "bought" by a wealthy couple, Reed and
Frances Albee (Gussow 2001: 22). On his thirtieth birthday he was to receive a sum of
money sufficiently large to secure independence from the emotionally detached
adoptive parents who, Albee felt, had treated him as little more than a disposable
commodity. These major, simultaneous changes in his economic and creative life,
together with the enormous blank of his biological parents, whom he never met and
about whom he knew nothing, contributed to "the myth of Albee, [which,] as
perpetuated by the playwright himself, is that he was born at the age of thirty"
(Gussow 2001: 18).

It is a myth that provides the basis of a paradigmatic story that underlies virtually
all of his work as a playwright; but that story should not be mistaken for Romantic
self-expression. There are Christian as well as autobiographical traces, while a pervasive parallel can be drawn with the lives of "wild children" such as Kaspar Hauser, the
nineteenth-century German foundling. This composite protagonist offers a way of
understanding some of the more problematic aspects of his plays, and of accounting
for the recurrence of certain patterns and structures throughout a body of work
characterized by a remarkable variety of form and an equally remarkable consistency
of theme.

The Zoo Story has been called "the most impressive debut ever made by an American
dramatist" (Bigsby 2000: 129). The play opens as Peter, a middle-aged stereotype of
Eisenhower-era, middle-class conformism, is suddenly confronted on his Central Park
bench by Jerry, a man in his thirties, whose opening lines immediately establish some
of the distinctive features of Albee's style: "I've been to the zoo. (PETER doesn't notice).
I said, I've been to the zoo. MISTER, I'VE BEEN TO THE ZOO!" (3). The startling effect is
produced by the absence of any of the introductory, phatic conventions ("hello,"
"excuse me") that ordinarily preface unprompted verbal communications with a
stranger. Jerry brings the shock of the new, breaking without warning into Peter's
too-settled existence, anticipating all of those figures in Albee's plays – babies,
adoptees, fictional creations, or foundlings – whose arrival in the present, like Albee's
on the New York stage, seems unencumbered by the past. For Jerry, the conventions
of polite conversation are of a piece with the social conservatism embodied in Peter –
Jerry reminds him that marriage "isn't a law, for God's sake" (5) – that forms a
carapace against the full, life-affirming, but potentially threatening participation in
the world that Jerry wants Peter to confront. The irony is that Jerry's withdrawal from
the world is even more profound, stuck as he is in a rooming-house whose inhabitants
live as if in cages, and unable to form a relationship even with the landlady's dog, the
subject of a lengthy monologue concerning his decision to "kill the dog with
kindness, and if that doesn't work...I'll just kill him" (16). Both strategies have
proved unsuccessful, but as a result Jerry has "learned that neither kindness nor
cruelty by themselves, independent of each other, creates any effect beyond themselves; and I have learned that the two, combined, together, at the same time, are the

teaching emotion" (21–2). Jerry takes on the role of preacher, using his encounter with Peter first in an attempt to convert him and then to transform himself into a martyr, initiating a fight over the bench and then impaling himself on the knife he has goaded Peter into holding. The slightly forced biblical analogy in the final moments is unmistakable, as the dying Jerry tells Peter that "I came unto you (*He laughs, so faintly*) and you have comforted me. Dear Peter" (30).

The warning Jerry brings would be articulated consistently on Albee's stage, often explicitly, as in *Fragments* (1993):

> I'm pretty sure – (*Pause.*) that there is a way to get through it – so long as you know there's doom right from the beginning; that there is a time, which is limited, and woe if you waste it; that there are no guarantees of anything – and that while we may not be responsible for everything that *does* happen to us, we certainly are for everything that *doesn't*; that since we're conscious, we have to be aware of both the awful futility of it and the amazing wonder. Participate, I suppose. (55)

Similar statements may be plucked from half-a-dozen plays from all stages of Albee's career, from *A Delicate Balance* to *Listening* and *Marriage Play*, while the first act of *Seascape* is largely an extended debate on a topic that forms the playwright's dominant theme, and which he has frequently addressed in interview:

> My concerns are the facts that we are too short-sighted, that we will not live on the precipice, that too many people prefer to go through this brief thing called life only half-alive, that too many people are going to end up with regret and bitterness at not having participated fully in their lives, that it's easier not to deal honorably with one another, that communication is a vitally important and dangerous matter. (Qtd. in Kolin 1988: 161)

The more oblique invocation of these ideas in *The Zoo Story* avoids the danger that an audience, especially one schooled in the American dramatic canon of representational realism, will recoil from the apparently undisguised expression of authorial intention.

That breaking of the realistic frame was one of the things that encouraged early critics to compare his work to that of Samuel Beckett, Jean Genet, and Eugene Ionesco, whose plays, like Albee's, were prominent off-Broadway and sometimes generalized as "the theatre of the absurd" (Esslin 1962). Ionesco's parody of middle-class cliché in *The Bald Prima Donna*, for example, is an undeniably important influence on Albee's *The Sandbox* (1960) and, especially, *The American Dream* (1961). But "the theatre of the absurd" label tended to collapse important distinctions into false universals, with the plays supposedly expressing a "human condition" as inescapable as original sin. Hence, there was the critical dismissal of *The Death of Bessie Smith* (1960) as a "purely realistic" and therefore "bad" play (Way 1967: 189, 200), because the shortcoming apparently emerged as an inevitable product of the play's realism.

More pertinent to Albee's oeuvre than the label of "absurd" are the contemporary American contexts of such plays as *The Zoo Story*. It stages not so much a confrontation as an attempted dialogue between the conservative affluence of the Eisenhower years, represented by Peter, and the libertarian, anti-authoritarian culture manifested variously in rock and roll, the screen personae of Marlon Brando and James Dean, and the writings and lifestyle of the beat poets. During a period when leading playwrights Arthur Miller, Eugene O'Neill, and Tennessee Williams were dormant or in decline, Broadway looked more atrophied and exclusively commercial than ever, while off-Broadway was the testing ground for new plays by Jack Gelber, Jack Richardson, and Albee. In *Zoo Story* Peter is a publisher, and there is a suppressed parable here about the frustrations of the artist in a commercialized market economy, which is metaphorically the subject of Herman Melville's *Bartleby the Scrivener*, an adaptation of which Albee was working on at about the same time.

That Albee was more than simply a voice of rebellion is indicated by the Broadway success of *Who's Afraid of Virginia Woolf?* Appropriately marrying some of the more realistic conventions of the well-made play to his iconoclastic sensibility, the drama remains arguably his finest work, a showcase of brilliant invective based around the feuding marriage of George, the failed academic, and Martha, the daughter of his college president. What connects them to the younger couple of Nick and Honey, whom Martha has induced to call for a late-night party, is childlessness. Honey has had a "hysterical pregnancy" (60), although George is convinced that she induces miscarriages, and the play concludes with the revelation that George and Martha's son is their invention. George pursues the motif of the imaginary child through his storytelling. Nick drunkenly tells George Honey's secret; George brings it into the open, in a coded but unmistakable allegory, to avenge Nick and Martha's mockery of his failed novel. That book introduces yet another fictional child: the 15-year-old boy who kills both of his parents, a story George has previously told Nick was true, and which George, according to Martha, had insisted to his father "isn't a novel at all…this is the truth…this really happened…TO ME!" (83). The conclusion of the play demonstrates that George and Martha's marriage has been built on a denial of their infertility, the frustrations of which have generated the spiteful anger that seems to underlie their set-piece invectives; however, this interpretation can be criticized as giving way to a positivist realization that the play charts George and Martha's progression from an initially sustaining, O'Neill-like "pipe dream" to a new phase in which their marriage will now be based on a painful but equally necessary freedom from illusion.

The enormous Broadway success of *Who's Afraid of Virginia Woolf?* followed with an adaptation of Carson McCullers's novella *The Ballad of the Sad Café* in 1963. The real problems with Albee's writing, however, began with *Tiny Alice* in 1964, in which Brother Julian, who has been sent to oversee an enormous donation Miss Alice wishes to make to the Church, is lured into marrying her and abjuring his faith before apparently discovering that he has really married Tiny Alice, who inhabits a giant model house of which the house in which the characters find themselves seems to be a replica. As if in response to Julian's demand that Alice/God reveal herself, lights come on in the model house, while at the same time exaggeratedly loud heartbeats are heard, raising the possibility that there is an infinity of houses within houses, in all of which the same events are happening simultaneously. The problem for both Julian (and the spectator) is that there is no possibility of maintaining what Agnes in *A Delicate Balance*, Albee's next original play, refers to as "the ability to view a situation objectively while I am in it" (81). It has been argued persuasively that this difficulty in making distinctions between houses, or Gods, marks *Tiny Alice* as another play about adoption: Julian is the object of a financial transaction that transfers him without his consent from one family (the Church) to another (Miss Alice's), and he "distinguishes between God the creator and the God that men have created, as the adopted child tries to separate the representations of his biological creators and the parents that men have arranged for him" (Glenn 1981: 261).

Albee again followed a controversial original work with an adaptation, this time of James Purdy's novel *Malcolm*. The play was a commercial and critical disaster when it was produced in early 1966, but its story of a child who is discovered on a park bench, soon to be passed around a series of characters buying and selling him before he dies from an excess of sexual intercourse, is consonant with Albee's dominant themes. The Pulitzer Prize awarded to *A Delicate Balance* (1966) looked like a belated apology for the fiasco over *Who's Afraid of Virginia Woolf?*, where the award was denied owing to opposition by some of the board members, one of whom dismissed *Virginia Woolf* as "a filthy play" (Gussow 2001: 189). *A Delicate Balance* begins a slow drift toward introspection, signaled in Edna's wistful remark that "the only skin you've ever known...is your own" (164). The basic situation gathers around Tobias's excessive hospitality to the intruders, Harry and Edna, who are supposedly his best friends yet bring with them an unknown "terror" and "plague" (161), and briefly threaten to take over the household. What makes the play unmistakably Albee's is the crisis confronting Julia. The surviving daughter of Tobias and Agnes – their son Teddy died in childhood – she is multiply divorced and approaching the age at which she will be unable to bear children of her own. Meanwhile she is haunted by fears that her parents will abandon her to Harry and Edna, who occupy her room and begin to take on the role of parents when Edna slaps her, describing it as "a godmother's duty" (116).

As with *Tiny Alice*, *A Delicate Balance* taps into the major currents in Albee's writing, and is the more effective for its understatement; but he was moving toward a solipsism that he would explore more fully in the death-watch drama *All Over* (1971), *Listening* (1975), which was initially a play for radio about a mental patient who appears autistic rather than insane, and a pair of two-handers about failing marriages, *Counting the Ways* (1976) and *Marriage Play* (1987). Christopher Bigsby's remark that "[t]here is a space between his characters which is literal as well as symbolic. Experience seems curiously intransitive" (2000: 133) is especially astute. However, the same could be said of Albee's *Box* and *Quotations from Chairman Mao Tse-Tung* (1968), a brilliant experiment in collage, which juxtaposes four different voices: Mao, the Long-Winded Lady, the Old Woman, and the voice of the cube-like structure, Box, which forms both a physical and a dramatic frame for *Mao*, since *Box* is to be played in different forms at the beginning and at the end of the piece. These figures do not interact at all on the stage; the meaning of the play instead coheres or fails to cohere in the unpredictable associations generated in the mind of the spectator.

Box-Mao-Box was Albee's last play of the 1960s. The new decade would see continued experimentation, but Albee's creativity was drifting. His best play of the 1970s is the Pulitzer Prize-winning *Seascape* (1975), which was initially planned as a companion piece, "Life," to the "Death" of *All Over*. In this most extreme and ambitious of Albee's many dramatizations of temporally distinct perspectives, the talking lizards, Leslie and Sarah, are close to the beginning of the evolutionary scale and therefore do not understand evolution itself. In attempting to explain evolution to them, Nancy and Charlie, the modern human couple who encounter the lizards on a beach, represent the whole of human history, their weary sophistication hinting that perhaps we are living at the end of time, an anxiety signaled by the planes that pass ominously overhead.

After *Seascape*, Albee found it increasingly difficult to find major theatres willing to stage his work, particularly in New York. If *Listening* and *Counting the Ways* showed his characters moving toward self-absorption, *The Lady from Dubuque* (1980) and *The Man Who Had Three Arms* (1982) were in different ways highly self-referential. The first of these plays returns to many of Albee's earlier ideas, including personalized, potentially aggressive games played at a late-night party (*Whose Afraid of Virginia Woolf?*), the knowledge that one of the characters is dying (*All Over*), and the ominous entry of mysterious strangers (*A Delicate Balance*). If *The Lady from Dubuque* provided some grounds for the view that Albee was beginning to repeat situations rather than develop them in new forms, *The Man Who Had Three Arms*, which followed a disastrous adaptation of *Lolita* (1981), was widely assumed to be an autobiographical rant about the playwright's own decline from critical favor. It is essentially a lecture given by the character "Himself," who had celebrity thrust upon him when he grew a third arm in the middle of his back, only for the public to return to indifference once the miraculous appendage began to disappear again. The arm was widely seen as a metaphor for the creativity that many felt had begun to desert Albee, but as he noted, Himself's success never had anything to do with ability. This being the case, however, the play is little more than an exposé of a culture of undeserved and disposable celebrity.

Aside from *Marriage Play*, the only new piece to appear before the end of the 1980s was *Finding the Sun* (1983), another reworking of familiar material, being set on a beach (*The Sandbox*, *Seascape*) with four pairs of characters of differing ages. Effective as it is in building a series of dramatic climaxes from a sequence of essentially static dialogues, it hardly prepared audiences for the extraordinary creative renaissance that began with *Three Tall Women* (first performed in 1991) and has continued with the ironically titled *The Play About the Baby* (1998) and *The Goat; or, Who Is Sylvia?* (2002), which bears comparison with his best work. This most recent play, like *Three Tall Women*, builds on ideas familiar to Albee into new and less familiar territory. A recurrent image in his plays has been the emotional relationships between men and animals: Jerry's murderous attempts to communicate with the dog in *The Zoo Story*, the sudden indifference displayed by a previously affectionate cat toward Tobias in *A Delicate Balance*, and the recognition by Nancy and Charlie in *Seascape* that their new lizard acquaintances are ancient evolutionary relatives. In *The Goat*, Martin's previously happy marriage falls apart when he admits to a sexual and, in his view, loving relationship with an animal. The first two scenes, in which Martin's long-time friend Ross discovers the secret and reveals it to Martin's wife Stevie, are black tragicomedy, offering one of Albee's most incisive dissections of marriage and the unpredictability of desire; the final scene, in which Martin tries to explain himself to his son, the ironically named Billy, ends in purest tragedy and a moment of Shepard-like hyperrealism, as Stevie drags in the body of the goat, whose throat she has cut.

Albee is, in a crude sense, a more repetitive playwright than his major contemporaries and near-contemporaries: he returns obsessively to particular images, patterns, structures, and ideas. It is necessary now to examine their meaning within his work as a whole, and in relation to a particular reading of American history that informs it. Mel Gussow's thorough and revealing biography traces innumerable references in the plays to Albee's own life; all that needs to be emphasized here is the formative experience of adoption, his complete ignorance of his biological parents, his unhappy experience of adoptive parents who displayed little warmth or affection, and his semi-serious creation of the myth of the man born at the age of 30. Likewise, the Christian allusions, while extensive, can be briefly summarized by noting the analogical connections with recurrent images in his work that need not have any explicitly Christian reference. There are connotations of the virgin birth in Albee's false babies, foundlings, and adoptees, figures that often become the preacher or martyred innocent. These sacrificial characters, whose life concludes with the image of crucifixion, prompted Bigsby to suggest that these endings "become almost the conventional ending to an Albee play" (1969: 89). Albee himself recalls leaving the Episcopalian Church at the age of 6 because "I was terribly upset about the idea of the Crucifixion" (qtd. in Kolin 1988: 133). Still more pervasive is the idea of resurrection. This is implicit in the adoption motif because the child is a new baby twice, to two different sets of parents in succession; but there are many more overt images of rebirth in his plays; for example in *The American Dream, Three Tall Women*, and in Albee's 1967 adaptation of Giles Cooper's *Everything in the Garden*, in which the murdered Jack returns to address the audience.

The Christian paradigm can only be extended so far, however, because Albee's plays explore the sexuality of a protagonist who is in any case usually a victim rather than a martyr. A more precise and illuminating parallel is suggested by a remark Albee made in 1965 concerning the overtly Christ-like Julian's experience in *Tiny Alice*: "I think the play started a couple of years ago when I read a small news item about someone in Germany who had been kept in a room within a room" (qtd. in Bigsby 1975: 100). Perhaps this was not a news item but the similar and very well-known story of Kaspar Hauser, which Albee may have known anyway: it is mentioned, for example, by Herman Melville, one of his favorite authors, in *Billy Budd*. In any case, Kaspar Hauser's life provides an intertextual, heuristic model for understanding the structures and gaps in plays that lack the integrated reality effect of the conventional American protagonist, yet which nonetheless have at their core the human drama described variously by Bigsby as "that expressed by Freud in *The Future of an Illusion*: 'man cannot remain a child for ever; he must venture at last into the hostile world. This may be called *education to reality'*" (1975: 151), and less sympathetically by Richard Schechner as "the game of the child who thinks he is being persecuted, who dreams up all kinds of outrages, and who concludes finally that his parents found him on the doorstep," leading Schechner to conclude that "Albee's characters, like the playwright himself, suffer from arrested development" (qtd. in Bigsby 1975: 63).

Kaspar Hauser was a youth aged about 15 who was found in the streets of Nuremberg in 1828. He knew few words, but after being taught to speak and write, described a life spent in a dark room, in which he would wake every morning to find bread and water. He does not seem to have realized that other people existed until shortly before he was released, when a man came to lead him to Nuremberg carrying letters of introduction that gave a seemingly false account of his life. He became instantly famous, a "wild child" or Rousseau-like innocent who, having grown up without culture or language, might demonstrate the state of "natural man." In 1829 he survived an attack from an unknown assailant, following which the Earl of Stanhope, a wealthy English aristocrat, acquired guardianship over him. Jeffrey Masson suggests that Stanhope was motivated by homosexual desire and may even have orchestrated a second attack in 1832 when the youth was lured to a park with the false promise of information about his mother, only to be stabbed by another mysterious stranger (1996: 17). Three days after this second unexplained assault, Kaspar Hauser died. In the opinion of many, he was a changeling as well as a foundling, a healthy baby of noble birth for whom a dying infant was substituted in a plot to alter the line of succession.

Whether or not Albee consciously drew on this tale, the recurrent characters and images that structure his plays present a similar story of a foundling, adoptee, innocence, dead child, and baby of miraculous birth (*The American Dream, Who's Afraid of Virginia Woolf?, Tiny Alice, Malcolm, A Delicate Balance, The Play About the Baby*). This figure usually enters the play as a youth aged around 15, yet it is still essentially a baby, sometimes searching for its parents (*Malcolm, Three Tall Women*), and knowing little about or unable to explain its past (*The American Dream, Who's Afraid of Virginia Woolf?, Tiny Alice, Malcolm*). Its early years are either unknown or are alluded to obliquely as a time of terrible violence. At the same time, the adoptee is a substitute for another child missing from the lives of the adoptive parents, who themselves are haunted either by infertility or by the death of their biological child. Almost without exception, Albee's plays revolve around a hollow center of loss and absence, most commonly expressed as the literal or metaphorical search for a missing parent or child.

Albee's characters are frequently not fully integrated human beings but incomplete, wanting another that would make them whole. The dismembered "bumble" of *The American Dream* recurs in different forms in many later plays: the growth and disappearance of an extra limb in *The Man Who Had Three Arms*, the division of A into three selves in *Three Tall Women*, as well as the disappearing acts performed on children in *Who's Afraid of Virginia Woolf?* and *The Play About the Baby*. There are also times when the figures on Albee's stage exchange roles, with Edna in *A Delicate Balance* briefly "becoming Agnes" (115), a metamorphosis anticipated in Agnes's announcement that according to a new book on psychiatry "the sexes are reversing, or coming to resemble each other too much" (57). More generally, the characters are often either absent from the stage altogether, denoted by a mere letter of the alphabet, or characterized as "Man" and "Woman."

The adult characters are at the mercy of a restless sexual desire that seems arbitrary and uncontrollable in its object-choices. This is surely what attracted Albee to *The Ballad of the Sad Café*, his adaptation of which retains almost verbatim McCullers's commentary on love:

> [Love] is a joint experience between two persons, but that fact does not mean that it is a similar experience to the two people involved. There are the lover and the beloved, but these two come from different countries. Often the beloved is only a stimulus for all the stored-up love which has lain quiet within the lover for a long time hitherto. [. . .] Now, the beloved can also be of any description: the most outlandish people can be the stimulus for love. (116)

Albee dilutes the play's strength by deferring this passage until close to the end; McCullers places it much earlier in the narrative, providing an interpretive frame for her tale about the love triangle of the giant, asexual Miss Amelia, her violent husband Marvin Macy, whose sexual advances she spurns on their wedding night, and Cousin Lymon, the hunchbacked dwarf who replaces Macy in Miss Amelia's life yet who ultimately sides with him when he returns to settle the score. While there are hints that Miss Amelia may fear sex and men because her mother died in childbirth, neither McCullers nor Albee makes any attempt to explain Macy's attraction to her, or Lymon's to Macy.

The sexuality of the child-protagonist is different, produced by the symbolic exchanges of the society into which it enters. The fragmentation of the self, its subjection to desire, and the sense that its existence is confirmed only by the mirroring effect of the presence or absence of another, has some connections with French psychoanalyst Jacques Lacan's notion of pre-linguistic stages of childhood that exist before entry into the symbolic stage (rules governing social order, kinships, and alliances). The pre-linguistic stages remain dormant throughout life, surfacing at times in the psychic arrangement of neurosis. In Albee's plays the social world, analogous to Lacan's symbolic order, reduces the character to an economic or sexual commodity that follows Lacan's "rules" of social alliances. These commodities are disposed of because they represent a threat once their usefulness and attractiveness have evaporated (e.g., *The American Dream*, *Tiny Alice*, *Malcolm*, *The Man Who Had Three Arms*, *The Play About the Baby*, *The Goat*). As Professor Cox tells Malcolm in *Malcolm*, "you want to give yourself to things" (9), before propelling him into a social vortex in which his portrait and body are bought and used by a succession of dysfunctional couples, and before he finally dies trying to satisfy the sexual demands of Melba. This is the horrific side to that "education to reality" demanded of the child. Albee's plays have a J. D. Salinger-like preoccupation with the innocence of children and the phoniness of adults, for just as Holden Caulfield in Salinger's *The Catcher in the Rye* suspects his teacher, Mr. Antolini, of being a sexual predator, so too is Malcolm the victim of another educator, Professor Cox. This sexualized teacher–pupil relationship indicates the power imbalance between adults and children.

As in *The Catcher in the Rye*, the "arrested development" that Schechner dismisses as a sign of authorial immaturity in fact represents a profound meditation on childhood and its transition into the contemporary adult world. If in Albee's mythic autobiography 30 is the new zero, the dangerous age for a character in the plays is around 15, when Kaspar Hauser emerged from obscurity. This is the age at which the protagonist of George's novel kills his parents; at which in *The Zoo Story* Jerry, whose parents are also dead, was homosexual "for a week and a half" (11); at which the eponymous hero of *Malcolm* is discovered; and at which Roger, in *Everything in the Garden*, comes home to discover that his mother is a prostitute, his father is exploding with anger, and they and their guests are about to murder one of the neighbors. Fifteen is the age of hormonal anarchy, above the age of puberty yet below the age of consent; but in Albee's unique constellation of child-characters the 15-year-old can also, like Kaspar Hauser, have the emotional and social skills of a young child with no history and little awareness of its own sexuality.

Albee has suggested that *The Lady from Dubuque* is about "the fact that our reality is determined by other people's view of it" (qtd. in Kolin 1988: 131). But the point may be extended to all his plays. *The Zoo Story* captures this perspective in Peter's unthinking deference to the conventions of corporate America, while *The American Dream* helpfully if rather crudely parodies a clichéd, middle-class, consumer-oriented discourse in which the Young Man feels quite at ease, describing himself as "Clean-cut, Midwest farm-boy type, almost insultingly good-looking in a typically American way" (115). Such preexisting discourses construct the babies, dead people, absentees, animals, or fictional characters who may be the center of attention yet literally cannot speak for themselves, and can therefore only be apprehended through the linguistic constructions of others. Conversely, these non-speaking figures contribute to those constructions. In *All Over* the dying man never speaks – in many productions he is not even seen – yet he makes his contribution to the problem of defining death and dying that constitutes virtually the whole action of the play. Death is signaled in the title, *All Over*, and is addressed from the outset, when the Mistress objects to the Wife's question "Is he dead?" by recalling a time when "he pointed out that the verb to be was not, to his mind, appropriate to a state of . . . non-being. That one cannot . . . *be* dead. He said his objection was a quirk – that the grammarians would scoff – but that one could be dying or have died . . . but could not . . . be . . . dead" (3–4). The language into which we are born continues to structure the experience of life even in its final moments, an idea Albee was to take much further in *Three Tall Women*.

Such anxieties lie behind much of the verbal prissiness of his characters who are often inappropriately obsessed with syntax and figurative language. A graphic example occurs in *The Goat*: while Billy is trying to come to terms with his father's sexual relationship with an animal, and with the potential breakup of his parents' marriage, Martin cannot help observing that he is mixing his metaphors (94). More broadly, Albee presents relationships in general and marriage in particular in terms of self-conscious, theatrical game playing, notably in *Who's Afraid of Virginia Woolf?* but also in *Counting the Ways* and *Marriage Play*, where the partners rehearse the process of separation and are acutely aware of the literary influences on their conversations about love. Accordingly, they doubt their essence, an anxiety dramatized once again by a perception of the self as double. As Jack says in *Marriage Play*, "I am aware that I am the object I am studying, that I am my own subject, or object" (21). For Samuel Beckett, such an "existence by proxy" (Harvey 1970: 247) expresses the sense of non-participation in one's own life; but for Albee, it is the opposite: "one has to survive always outside of one's time and outside of one's society. One must always be an outsider in order to participate" (qtd. in Roudané 1982: 41). What for Beckett is a condition of solipsistic nihilism is for Albee inseparable from his commitment to democratic, liberal politics, and to "a kind of more generalized political drama which realizes that it is the degree to which people are able to accept consciousness that justifies the degree to which they are permitted to participate in the consciousness that determines how they will govern themselves" (Wasserman 1983: 12).

It also has implications for the forms that drama will take, while producing two possible but perhaps contradictory interpretations of his plays. First, they are formal experimentations insisting that the real can and must be distinguished from illusion, and that it is possible to occupy a position of truth outside the language games that his characters so frequently play. This is implied in the revelation about George and Martha's fictive son at the end of *Who's Afraid of Virginia Woolf?*, or what is described in *The American Dream* as an attack on "the substitution of artificial values for real values" in American society (Kolin 1988: 9). In the latter play, as in *The Sandbox*, Grandma is a *raisonneur*, untainted by the discourse and values that hold the other characters in thrall. The separation of A into A, B, and C in *Three Tall Women* creates more subtle dramatic ironies: on the one hand the same character offers multiple perceptions of her life, but on the other, the older selves' retrospective knowledge of events that have not yet happened to the younger C suggests that a definitive account of C's experience, at least, may be constructed. In all of these plays a radically innovative form serves a more conventional, realistic movement toward insight and closure.

Second is that the multiple points of view contained in such characters are symptomatic of a broader architectural conception of perspective in both dialogue and stage space that resists the security of a fixed interpretation. This may account for Albee's interest in adaptation, which creates a second text that should stand independently of the original, and yet is always in an unspoken dialogue with the original. The use of narrators in the adaptations has been widely seen as a failure to translate into dramatic form the narrative passages of the source texts, but the awkwardness is deliberate. Asked why he chose to have a black narrator for *The Ballad of the Sad Café*, which would inevitably raise the question of Southern racism despite that issue's tangential relevance, he said: "I wanted the narrator to be removed from the remainder of the action of the play" (qtd. in Rutenberg 1969: 237). Alternatively, in his version of *Everything in the Garden*, Jack is a narrator as well as a character, even though there is no such device in Giles Cooper's original play. It is as if Albee wishes to present simultaneously the experiences of the actor on the stage and the spectator in the auditorium.

The most striking example of this structural conception of perspective is *Box*, the title of which refers variously to the large cube that is the only object on the stage during that play, to a voice within the play (and yet "*The* VOICE *should not come from the stage, but should seem to be coming from near by the spectator – from the back or the sides of the theatre*," 127), to a voice within *Mao*, and to the physical frame within which the action of *Mao* takes place. Box *is* the play, it *frames* the play, and it speaks *within* the play, while having an existence either independent of *Mao* or "enmeshed" with it (123). Like a building, *Box* cannot be observed in its totality from any single viewpoint. In writing of the pleasures of Louise Nevelson's work, Albee recalls an occasion when "I sat in the reconstruction of a room Mondrian had designed; imagine a Mondrian painting twenty by twenty feet; then imagine it a cube; then imagine yourself placed in the center of the cube. . . . I had been transformed from spectator to participant" (Albee 1980: 29).

Such remarks indicate that Albee's liberal, humanist politics can be expressed in a mode radically different to that of Arthur Miller, whose *Death of a Salesman* exemplifies the hybrid of realism and expressionism that has become dominant in the dramatic exploration of the consciousness of the American subject. Albee's dramatic forms suggest a different kind of liberalism from Miller's, along the lines that David Savran has proposed in regarding Miller as a "Cold War liberal" (1992: 25) rooted in the politics of masculinity and "false universals" (28), whereas Tennessee Williams's plays are found "at the impossible intersection of two incompatible and contradictory forms: the one linear, liberal, and realist, and the other, episodic, proto-socialist, and hallucinatory" (92). Savran's description of the distinctive structural aspects of Williams's writing is especially pertinent to Albee's work:

This habit of constructing plot upon a "guilty secret" that is never entirely divulged certainly encodes Williams's own "guilty secret" and the impossibility of its revelation during the 1940s and 1950s as anything other than an "ugly truth." Even more important, this practice acts both to ratify and subvert a psychoanalytical model of personality, for in the same gesture that directs the spectator's hermeneutical gaze toward the withheld secret, it seems to deny the primacy and intelligibility of that traumatic memory, both emphasizing and calling into question the determination of the present by a moment in the past. By so disrupting the relationship between past and present, Williams's plays tend to undermine the purely linear and irreversible temporal progression on which Miller's plays, and American realism in general, depends. (91–2)

Albee's plays also present an unknowable past, the disruption of linear structure, and the jamming of the interpretive apparatus of psychoanalysis; but in his case one cannot assume that the gaps in the past can be accounted for so easily. Albee's plays were first produced as Williams's plays was already in decline, by which time America was moving toward a more tolerant liberalism that made the keeping of such secrets a lesser priority, even if the times were not changing fast enough to cure some of Albee's critics of the belief that the more convincing the female character, the greater the likelihood of discovering that she was really a man, if only the author could be persuaded to let you look up her skirt.

Rarely is the past in Albee's best plays a stable, knowable place; often it is a Pinteresque arsenal of weapons to be used in the here and now, exemplified in *Who's Afraid of Virginia Woolf?* and embodied in Harry and Edna, who cannot provide any account of the terror they bring to Agnes and Tobias's house, in *A Delicate Balance*. The more conventional, expository treatment of the past elsewhere in that play marks the shift toward a more realistic style that would continue with *All Over*.

Genetic and biographical ties to a particular social and familial history hold the conventionally realistic character in place, and in the Ibsen model adapted by Miller the knowledge of these bonds reinforces the plot's compulsive examination of the past in order to explain the present. In Albee's most distinctive work, by contrast, the past is unrecoverable because it is either imaginary or nonexistent. Albee's foundlings and adoptees arrive in the world problematically severed from all roots, incarnations of an America mapped out in *Who's Afraid of Virginia Woolf?* by George, who is equally despairing of history and biology, of the impotence of the past and what he sees as the fascistic, genetically modified future to be ushered in by Nick's experiments in the laboratory. On this stage it is not the past but the present that compels attention: to the theatrical event being staged before one's eyes, as well as to the fictional story unfolding in the play.

The address to the audience also helps to establish Albee as a dramatist rooted in an American tradition. He has played a career-long role of American Jeremiah, demanding that attention be paid to the here and now; and his rhetorical strategies, eschatological moods, and visions of Armageddon "may be placed in the vein of the American literary tradition flowing from the seventeenth century," especially as Albee "casts his inquiries in aesthetic forms similar to those employed by seventeenth-century writers trying to express the Puritan purview" (Konkle 1997: 31–2). Albee tends to construct an America with a foreshortened history, beginning in 1776:

> We are supposed to be a revolutionary society. The reason for our existence, however, was an economic revolution, rather than a revolution for freedom as we all like to pretend. It was caused by an upper-middle class trying to get richer – like many revolutions. We've had a continuing revolution from the first one to the social revolution of 1932. If we've become static and stagnant, we may indeed have lost our value as a society. (Qtd. in Kolin 1988: 161)

Both a state of permanent revolution and a nation that has succumbed to consumption, Albee's America provides the context in which the formal contradictions between absurdism and the urge toward narrative revelation make oxymoronic sense. George and Martha are named after the first president and his wife, and the name of the institution of higher education at which George teaches, "New Carthage," is a comic-ironic indication of the fate that awaits them. *Who's Afraid of Virginia Woolf?*, which Albee has described as "an attempt to examine the success or failure of American revolutionary principles" (qtd. in Kolin 1988: 58), mines a contradiction in the metaphor of revolution itself, a term which encompasses both a radical break in history and mere circular repetition. The exploration of this contradiction on the American stage had only recently become possible. Albee feels that "[t]heater didn't get serious [in America] until around the end of the Second World War, with Tennessee Williams and the late O'Neill" (qtd. in Kolin 1988: 103), and it is with the late O'Neill, in particular, with plays such as *Hughie* and *The Iceman Cometh*, that a Beckett-like exploration of stasis enters the American stage. This is the context in which Albee's engagement with the aesthetically revolutionary European drama of the 1950s should be seen. Categorizing Albee under the rubric of "the theatre of the absurd" makes sense if, in light of Albee's plays, it questions the rational progression from cause to effect. The absurd is given to methods designed to break the causal chain: in place of plot development there is either chaos or a structure produced by poetic form and an intensification of the image. As a consequence it adopted an alternative approach to dramatic time, devoid of linear movement and replaced by repetition, catastrophe, or a gradual winding down. Albee was acutely aware that this represented a response to a new era ushered in by Hiroshima, after which "we developed the possibility of destroying ourselves totally and completely in a second" (qtd. in Kolin 1988: 36).

Images of apocalypse are to be found everywhere in Albee's plays, from *Box's* oblique, unsettling visions of dead babies and gathering flocks of birds, to Elizabeth's dream of nuclear war in *The Lady from Dubuque*, to the disappearance and reappearance of the sun in *Finding the Sun*. They bind the fear of nuclear Armageddon to the earliest expressions of American puritanism, a European-inflected exploration of stasis to a destabilizing narrative of manifest destiny, the end of time in an instantaneous nothing to the eschatological reading of history. The Armageddon images owe their force to an unspoken recognition of something terrible in the birth of the nation, in "a struggle motivated like any other by greed and passion and like any other without resolution short of the apocalypse" (Bercovitch 1975: 140–1). Albee owes much to dramatic forms that were prominent on the postwar European stage, but he has used them creatively to transform the dominant mode of American drama and to articulate a profoundly unsettling vision of the United States. Rarely does he express that vision directly. Instead it forms through the accumulated images of a dreadful, absent, or imaginary history, of the buying and selling of people, of a forthcoming catastrophe that can be averted only by fully conscious recognition of a terrible mistake made perhaps even before consciousness, whether that mistake is the creation of an enabling fiction or, as in *Seascape*, the beginnings of evolution itself. Albee's imaginary protagonist is a poetic, dramatic representation of an American history in which "Columbus was himself following a prototype devised long before, the idea of a Western land which was *terra incognita*, outside and beyond history, pregnant with new meanings for mankind," a land that "became the space exploration program of an expansive, intensely curious, entrepreneurial and often genocidal era of European adventuring": a land with an "imaginary history" (Ruland and Bradbury 1991: 14–15).

The foundling in Albee's plays is so often associated with a suppressed violent past that it carries echoes of this genocide, performed in the service of a materialistic ethos that is itself encapsulated in the fact that the adoptive baby is for sale. The fear is that this past is a signpost to the future glimpsed by *Box*, of "Seven hundred million babies dead in the time it takes, took, to knead the dough to make a proper loaf" (128). Such figures are the cousins of all those dead children to be found buried beneath the American stage. In *Long Day's Journey into Night* the Tyrones are forever tied to the past through their shared sense of guilt and mutual recrimination over the death of a baby to which O'Neill gave his own name, Eugene, just as the dead son of Agnes and Tobias in *A Delicate Balance* is named Teddy. Shepard's *Buried Child*, whose closing moments are perhaps recalled in those of *The Goat*, is the poetic masterpiece of this image, as Tilden carries in from the garden the corpse of a small child that may be the product of an incestuous union of Tilden and his mother, or the dead, *American Dream*-like mythic hero Ansel, or the murdered offspring of some other forbidden relationship. The body in the garden becomes a potent symbol of something rotten in Eden, just as African American playwrights August Wilson and Suzan-Lori Parks have used the archaeological metaphor of digging for bones in order to bring a suppressed national history to light. For this reason Albee's Americanization of *Everything in the Garden* gives Cooper's play a new, mythic resonance: Roger's comment that "Some people say we're *all* Jews. . . . The ten lost tribes" (176) is repeated verbatim from the original, but along with the hasty garden burial of the murdered Jack it casts ironic light on the mythic burden bestowed on America from the time of Columbus. That Jack returns from the dead in Albee's version suggests that this violent history cannot remain hidden forever: the past will out, and pay the present back with interest, like the hydra-headed mother of *Three Tall Women*, sprouting three new selves in the second act as if in vengeance for the death it suffered in the first, unobserved by the future playwright who sits beside her bed, convinced that she has finally been laid to rest.

BIBLIOGRAPHY

Albee, E. (1965a). *The Ballad of the Sad Café*. London: Cape.
——(1965b). *Who's Afraid of Virginia Woolf?* Harmondsworth: Penguin.
——(1967). *Malcolm*. London: Cape.
——(1968a). *A Delicate Balance*. London: Cape.

Albee, E. (1968b). *Everything in the Garden*. New York: Athenaeum.

——(1971). *Tiny Alice, Box and Quotations from Chairman Mao Tse-Tung*. Harmondsworth: Penguin.

——(1972). *All Over*. London: Cape.

——(1980). "Introduction." In *Louise Nevelson: Atmospheres and Environments*. New York: Clarkson N. Potter, 12–30.

——(1995a). *Fragments: A Sit-Around*. New York: Dramatists Play Service.

——(1995b). *Marriage Play*. New York: Dramatists Play Service.

——(1995c). *Three Tall Women*. Harmondsworth: Penguin.

——(1995d). *The Zoo Story and Other Plays* [*The Sandbox, The Death of Bessie Smith*, and *The American Dream*]. Harmondsworth: Penguin.

——(2003). *The Goat: or, Who Is Sylvia?* New York: Overlook Press.

Bercovitch, S. (1975). *The Puritan Origins of the American Self*. New Haven, CT: Yale University Press.

Bigsby, C. W. E. (1969). *Albee*. Edinburgh: Oliver and Boyd.

——(ed.) (1975). *Edward Albee: A Collection of Critical Essays*. Englewood Cliffs, NJ: Prentice-Hall.

——(2000). *Modern American Drama, 1945–2000*. Cambridge: Cambridge University Press.

Esslin, M. (1962). *The Theatre of the Absurd*. London: Eyre and Spottiswoode.

Glenn, J. (1981). "The Adoption Theme in Edward Albee's *Tiny Alice* and *The American Dream*." In Joseph T. Coltrera (ed.), *Lives, Events, and Other Players: Directions in Psychobiography*. New York: Aronson.

Gussow, M. (2001). *Edward Albee: A Singular Journey*. New York: Applause.

Harvey, L. (1970). *Samuel Beckett: Poet and Critic*. Princeton, NJ: Princeton University Press.

Kolin, P. C. (ed.) (1988). *Conversations with Edward Albee*. Jackson: University Press of Mississippi.

Konkle, L. (1997). "American Jeremiah: Edward Albee as Judgment Day Prophet in *The Lady from Dubuque*." *American Drama* 7, 1: 30–49.

Masson, J. M. (1996). *Lost Prince: The Unsolved Mystery of Kaspar Hauser*. New York: Free Press.

Roudané, M. C. (1982). "An Interview with Edward Albee." *Southern Humanities Review* 16: 29–44.

Ruland, R. and Bradbury, M. (1991). *From Puritanism to Postmodernism: A History of American Literature*. London: Routledge.

Rutenberg, M. E. (1969). *Edward Albee: Playwright in Protest*. New York: Drama Book Specialists.

Savran, D. (1992). *Communists, Cowboys, and Queers: The Politics of Masculinity in the Work of Arthur Miller and Tennessee Williams*. Minneapolis: University of Minnesota Press.

Wasserman, J. N. (1983). *Edward Albee: An Interview and Essays*. Houston: University of St. Thomas Press.

Way, B. (1967). "Albee and the Absurd: *The American Dream* and *The Zoo Story*." In John Russell Brown and Bernard Harris (eds.), *American Theatre*. London: Arnold, 189–208.

17

The Drama of the Black Arts Movement

Mike Sell

Decolonization, as we know, is a historical process: that is to say that it cannot be understood, it cannot become intelligible nor clear to itself except in the exact measure that we can discern the movements which give it historical form and content.

Frantz Fanon, "Concerning Violence" (1963: 36)

Fanon is clear on this point: study a movement that struggles against colonial power and you'll gain a more refined understanding of colonialism in general. The difficulty is also clear; Fanon tells us, in essence, that there can be no knowledge without struggle, a lesson he learned as a psychiatrist during the Algerian war for independence. Despite its global dimensions and aspirations, colonialism is always a situational form of cultural, economic, psychological, geographical, and political domination – as is any struggle against it. The challenge of anti-colonial theory is to link specific conflicts to broader contexts.

Drama and theatre are well suited to the representation of struggle. They can, at their best, produce credible, emotionally convincing, and aesthetically arresting links between the local (say, the specific dramatic situation or performance) and the global (the theme, the "universal," history). Not surprisingly, they were fundamental to the Black Arts Movement (BAM), a cultural nationalist movement that has waged an anti-colonial struggle in the United States and the Caribbean since 1965, though most expansively during its first decade. Described by Larry Neal in 1968 as the "aesthetic and spiritual sister to the Black Power concept" (1989: 62), it attempted to accomplish a traditional avant-garde goal: to change literature and, therefore, life. Hoyt Fuller confirms this: "The Black revolt is as palpable in letters as it is in the streets, and if it has not yet made its impact upon the Literary Establishment, then the nature of the revolt itself is the reason" (1972: 3). Inspired by Fanon, W. E. B. Du Bois, Amilcar Cabral, C. L. R. James, Kwame Nkrumah, Queen Audley Moore, John Henrik Clarke, Jomo Kenyatta, and, preeminently, Malcolm X; modeled after forward-looking cultural producers like John Coltrane, Ralph Ellison, Thelonious Monk, Richard Wright, Zora Neale Hurston, and Langston Hughes; and consciously sustaining a tradition dating back to William Wells Brown's African Grove Theatre of the 1820s, the movement attempted to create, both physically and conceptually, a "common spot out of the larger commonality of...national experience" (Baraka 1984: 297).

Errol Hill, one of many outstanding drama critics and theatre historians to emerge from this generation, writes, "Culture in this context becomes central to the struggle rather than peripheral. The arts become the means for reaching the public, and as a result the theatre, being the most public of the arts, finds itself in the forefront of the nationalist movement" (1980: 2). Ron Milner puts it more succinctly: "Black theater – go home!" (1972: 288). Of course, going home is never easy. In the case of the BAM, three distinct intellectual formations were brought together by playwrights and critics to link home to larger geopolitical demands: (1) engagement with the vital, inherently empowering, even revolutionary qualities of black folk culture; (2) application of diverse, radical theological systems to art and criticism; and (3) implementation of innovative, non-western forms of humanism.

A note about a key term before moving on. "Blackness" is a racial designation neither for the movement nor for this chapter; rather, it is a term that marks an ideological stance based in a specific cultural, economic, and political situation and a specific cultural, economic, and political response to that situation. Race is certainly a significant issue for the BAM, but it is best understood in the words of Lorraine Hansberry's Tshembe Matoseh from her play *Les Blancs* (1968): "I said racism is a device that, of itself, explains nothing...a device *is* a device, but...it also has consequences: once invented it takes on a life, a reality of its own" (1994: 92). "Blackness," in short, is a complex response to the history of this racist device, the designation given to anti-racist, anti-colonial struggle in the United States carried on by African American artists, audiences, and critics after the movement was initiated in 1965. Such a definition of blackness does not tie up all loose ends, and it should not. Though "merely" a device, for blackness to catalyze cultural, political, and economic change, it must possess the concreteness and procedural qualities of dramatic experience.

Seeking the Soul of Black Folk

Though an inheritance of Romanticism and the avant-garde tradition (as noted by Green and Poggioli), the commitment to folk culture was more directly the bequest of W. E. B. Du Bois and C. L. R. James's path-clearing sociological and historical studies, the Maoist revolution in China, the Négritude movement, and nascent folklore studies and creative ethnography programs of the 1950s and 1960s. It is no overestimation, then, to call this trend of the Black Arts a paradigm shift in African American arts and letters, as Houston Baker, Jr. has done.

It was Mao who emphasized as fundamental to the revolutionary struggle the role of language, aesthetic forms, and everyday experiences of the people.[1] But it was Malcolm X who laid out the issue in the distinctive tones of blackness:

> Our cultural revolution must be the means of bringing us closer to our African brothers and sisters. It must begin in the community and be based on community participation. Afro-Americans will be free to create only when they can depend on the Afro-American community for support and Afro-American artists must realize that they depend on the Afro-American for inspiration. (1970: 427)

Milner seconds Malcolm X: "[T]he further you go ... the more startlingly new and black the techniques become" (1972: 291). He argues that going home is an aesthetic movement, a psychic movement, and, just as importantly, a physical movement: "For this theater must be housed in, sustained and judged by, and be a useable projection of, and to, a black community" (ibid.).

The necessity of homeward movement — and the tragic, corrosively ironic consequences of avoiding it — is dramatized by Baraka in *Dutchman* (1964), a play that is rightfully considered the opening salvo of the BAM as *dramatic* movement. It is a sexy, scary, and still entertaining portrayal of public seduction, the power of stereotypes, and the uncanny relationship of sexual desire and racial identity. As was often the case, this dramatic text established a crucial ethical principle for the BAM: that statements about blackness are essentially meaningless, unless they are *for* and *near* blacks. Clay's oft-quoted monologue, during which he claims to be a member of the hallowed line of "blues people" just before a knife is plunged into his chest, bespeaks an aesthetic and attitudinal movement home to blackness. However, Baraka would have us understand that the claim to blackness is mere old-school absurdism because of Clay's audience and his place of performance: an anonymous, apathetic, multi-racial cluster of passengers aboard a subway.

The play's original production would have struck the Black Nationalist as itself absurd, since it was staged for a resolutely left-liberal, activist, but decidedly integrationist audience. In contrast, when produced on Harlem street corners the next year as part of the Black Arts Repertory Theatre/School's cultural outreach program, this Obie Award-winning play was deemed racist and just cause for the revocation of funds. The most corrosively ironic aspect of this revocation was that it was called by foundation administrators who had given Baraka the money precisely because of the acclaim the play had received at the Cherry Lane Theatre. Having gone home, Baraka's play became too black for comfort.

Dutchman translated Malcolm X's edict into terms that made sense for playwrights and theatre developers: art cannot be "black" except in "black" context. Both text and context must be nationalized. Milner's *Who's Got His Own* (1967) also illustrates the need for textual and institutional transformation. Concerning the former, the script tells the story of the widow, son, and daughter of an abusive factory janitor remembering, dismantling, and rebuilding the bonds that hold them together as family.

Formally within the mainstream of US domestic drama, at its peak just prior to the movement's start (think O'Neill, Miller, and Williams), the play confirms William Cook's assertion that black family dramas confront the necessity of "preserv[ing] values inherent in the Black experience" (1980: 180).[2] The values here are clearly in jeopardy. Tim Jr. is violent, an early-stage alcoholic, and dangerously in debt, while Clara has joined a female-only community after getting an abortion and has, perhaps, become a lesbian.[3] The crisis catalyzes transformation and self-recognition: the impact of racism on their lives and the relative validity of their father's struggle are recognized.

Who's Got His Own was also a significant institutional event. After hitting big at the American Place Theatre, it toured colleges and universities with the support of the New York State Council of the Arts, surprising given the play's message of violent action against racism and racists. It was the premiere production of the New Lafayette Theatre, and its publication in Milner and Woodie King's foundational *Black Drama Anthology* (1971) guaranteed that book – and its other contributors – a widespread readership. Both an exploration of black community and the catalyst for a new community of readers and theatregoers, Milner's play is a convincing response to Malcolm X's call for liberation through collaboration.

Kimberly Benston asserts that collaboration is a fundamental characteristic of black drama and theatre, which explores the shifting grounds between mimesis ("the representation of an action") and methexis ("communal helping-out of the action by all assembled") (1980: 62). Benston's mentor Neal seconds that emotion, describing drama as "inextricably linked to the Afro-American political dynamic [and] . . . perfectly consistent with Black America's contemporary demands" (1989: 33). "[P]otentially the most social of all of the arts," he continues, "it is an integral part of the socializing process" (ibid.). Black playwrights had to bring drama and dramaturgy into line with an array of theoretical demands and shifting performance situations, not least of which are the demands of the black audience. This explains why "theory and practice have rarely been as sensitive to each other as in the Black Arts Movement" (Benston 1980: 78). Benston further notes that the methectic qualities of black drama effectively served its "persistently ideological inquiry" as well as its "concern with the nucleus of the artistic transaction" between audience and event (71). These approaches ultimately "led to inquiries into the nature of the dramatic experience itself" (64).

A perfect example of such inquiry is William Wellington Mackey's *Requiem for Brother X* (1966). In *Requiem*, Mackey sunders setting and stage, enabling him to explore the intriguing territory shared by love and ideology. The script tells the story of an African American family in crisis following the assassination of Malcolm X. Younger brother Nate is a Black Nationalist on the hunt for Malcolm's killers while, unbeknownst to him, a woman is giving birth to his son in Nate's father's house. The stage shows a different kind of crisis. Divided into six areas, it doesn't in any way mimic the setting implied by the dialogue. Rather than blocking their movement in realistic fashion, Mackey gives each character a distinct degree of mobility and position: Matt, the oldest son, sits on a stool, never rising, on a platform at center stage. Martha, his wife, sits downstage left at floor level, like her husband never rising. Jude, the wheelchair-bound father "on the verge of senility," maneuvers around the left side of the stage (326). He shares space with his youngest child Bonita (for whom movement is optional, but unlimited), who attends to a "little white girl" giving birth to Nate's child. The labor is occurring on a platform above Jude and Bonita, out of reach of both (326). Punctuating the disjuncture of stage and set, a coffin with five lilies near the head "hangs from the flies," presumably representing the coffin of X, but also a more general condition of morbidity (326). We have here a clear division between the "scene" and the "seen." Mackey's play seems to synthesize the thematic and institutional demands of drama-for-the-people – and highlights the fact that any effort to create a revolutionary people's culture needs to consider carefully the medium of that culture.

The drama of going home was a full-time commitment for many playwrights, particularly Ed Bullins. Despite his consistent support for boundary-breakers like Mackey (and his own experiments, some of which we'll look at later), his best-known work and the work of participants in the workshop he led at the New Lafayette Theatre explored in fairly traditional fashion the tenuous commitments of neighbors, lovers, friends, and revolutionaries. Marked by a refusal to judge behavior or situation, by the desire to spark but not control debate and discussion, by a commitment to honest portrayal, and by a sly self-reflexivity (Bullins called it "natural" drama to distinguish it from the ideologically slanted tradition of naturalism), this veritable New Lafayette school of black playwriting enjoyed widespread appeal and high quality.

Three plays by workshop members are of particular interest in the context of the crises and opportunities of community transformation. J. E. "Sonny Jim" Gaines's *What If It Had Turned Up Heads?* (1972) is a story of love, desire, and alcoholism among three late middle-age down-and-outers running a bootleg liquor business from an almost Beckettian basement apartment. The tender reconciliation of Jacob and Jennie after she is raped and he beaten emphasizes the importance of shared pain and non-monetary relations – an explicit denunciation of the pimp mythos that put them all on the garbage heap in the first place. Martie Charles's *Black Cycle* (1971) is a touching presentation of a mother–daughter conflict that ironically dooms the younger to live the life the older barely managed to escape. Its hair-and-wig styling-shop setting is arresting and effective, enabling Charles to emphasize the economic, aesthetic, and community dimensions of the familial conflict with confidence. A specialist in cosmetic appearances, Vera relentlessly pushes her Jeannie to "succeed," and thus dooms her:

> I know what you thinkin', Sadie....I ain't got no further with Jeannie than you did with Carolyn. But I'd do it again, and again, and again even. 'Cause I rather foh her to turn up dead than to end up like Carolyn, repeatin' mah life all over. 'Cause it cain't be no different foh her than it was foh me, no sense in her living. (551)

Her friend Sadie, bristling at the comparison between their two daughters, clarifies things for her "friend": "Well, I guess she daid then. 'Cause damn sure ain't nothin' different 'bout her now. She out there in the streets like you and me when we was that age" (ibid.). Richard Wesley's *The Sirens* (1976) is also concerned with intergenerational conflict among women and the vicious cycle of prostitution. Wesley creates an elegant, incisive dramatic parallel between the private exchanges of young lovers and the illicit exchanges of johns and hookers. Sharing with *Black Cycle* a montage-style narrative approach, Wesley gets his audience thinking hard about the parallels between those "in love" and those in the trade. All these plays ask their viewers to consider what holds the community together and what chance the community has to survive the crises of progressive transformation.

Not a member of the Lafayette workshop, J. E. Franklin nevertheless lives in the same formal and thematic neighborhood. *Black Girl* (1971) dramatizes the relations among four generations of women left to fend for themselves by here-again-gone-again men. The resolution of their interpersonal crisis is credibly ambiguous and emotionally pleasing. The center of the piece is Billie Jean, the youngest daughter, a free spirit and promising dancer being almost literally crowded to death in a setting that demonstrates smart stage economy. Like the settings of Gaines's and Charles's plays, Franklin's features a space that isn't wholly public or private. Billie Jean's "room" is a "freak of architecture, sandwiched between the living room and the bathroom" (4). The grim regularity of violation that she must tolerate is driving her to self-destruction – that she dances at a local club seems merely a reflection of the open-door treatment of her puberty. Franklin turns the piece toward a positive conclusion, but takes us through the kind of harrowing emotional experience that can only be found in an overcrowded, economically desperate apartment.

Charles Fuller's Pulitzer Prize-winning *A Soldier's Play* (1982) is a defeatist but theatrically powerful exploration of the BAM theme of community-in-crisis.[4] This story of black-on-black violence in a segregated army squad stationed deep in the racist South during World War II exposes the deep fissures and embedded lies that maintain relationships of power between those with very different visions of culture and history. Of particular interest is the way the officer charged with investigating the murder communicates with all factions in the divided camp as he investigates the crime, from the liberal commander and his racist underlings to the diverse squadron of African American soldier/baseball players. This kind of fluency with the many languages of African America – purportedly modeled on Fuller's childhood friend Neal – is the playwright's effort to define the kind of agent who can achieve "intimacy with the people" in the name of social, political, and economic justice (Neal 1969: 55).

Fuller was not the first playwright to compose apparently "black" plays that, on closer examination, lack a clear commitment to anti-colonial struggle. The Negro Ensemble Company (NEC), which premiered Fuller's play, is rightfully recognized as one of the most important institutions in African American theatre history. Actor

Robert Hooks, producer Gerald S. Krone, and playwright Douglas Turner Ward founded the NEC in 1965 to promote theatrical professionalism, excellence, and craft. Those principles do not imply any particular commitment to blackness as I've defined it. In the literature of the BAM, one commonly finds the NEC characterized as selling out, as obsequious servants of a severely spooked liberal audience, and, worst of all, as traitors of the very community that had promoted the need for African American theatrical institutions. For many, the very location of the theatre, in Greenwich Village rather than Harlem, spoke for itself.

That said, the NEC's commitment to "just let . . . Blackness speak for itself" (archly quoted by Bullins in his opening comment to the first black theatre issue of the *Drama Review*) led to a number of dramatically excellent plays and productions by and about African Americans, including Ward's *Day of Absence* (1966), Lonne Elder III's *Ceremonies in Dark Old Men* (1965, NEC production 1969), Joseph Walker's *The River Niger* (1973), Leslie Lee's *The First Breeze of Summer* (1975), Philip Hayes Dean's *Sty of the Blind Pig* (1971), and *Home* (1979) by Samm-Art Williams. The NEC excelled at realism, particularly realism anchored in domestic dispute. Elder and Dean's plays are emblematic in this regard. Interestingly, both address the tension between commitment to family and commitment to community, a tension exacerbated by the clear need to strengthen and transform both.

Also exacerbated was tension between the BAM and the NEC by these plays; both feature characters that can be interpreted as directly (e.g., Elder's character Blue Haven, threatening representative of the ideologically dubious "Black Committee") or indirectly (Dean's nomadic blues player insinuating himself into the stultified relationship of mother and daughter) denigrating Black Nationalism. Such an interpretation isn't entirely unfounded, though it can obscure larger issues addressed by the plays and their generally critical stance toward the African American middle classes. Broad-stroke criticism of the NEC can also obscure works that, while not expressing any particular ideological commitment, present dramatic situations of great relevance to community and its role in anti-colonial struggle. Gus Edward's *The Offering* (1977), for example, explores what Eve Kosofsky Sedgwick has characterized as the "continuum between homosocial and homosexual" relationships. The exchange of women between Bob Tyrone, an aging ex-gangster, and Martin, an assassin and former protégé, is dramatically coherent and grounded in solidly anchored characters.

The tendency for home-going dramas such as those of Fuller, Elder, Dean, and Edwards to lack ideological precision was at least one of the reasons why agit-prop playwrights are a significant presence in the BAM dramatic archive. One in particular, truly the king of the one-act (called so by Kenneth Bowman 1999: 808), wrote scores of memorable pieces that accomplish the classic agit-prop goal of making abstract concepts visually and dramatically concrete. Ben Caldwell's *Riot Sale, or Dollar Psyche Fake Out* (1968) opens on a scene of chaotic crowd movement, strobe-lit so "the action seems static" (41). This gives way to a confrontation between blacks and the police. To get out of the standoff, the cops call in a special weapon.

Looming "in the vague lighting is a huge muzzle projecting from the black cavernous opening" of a newly arrived police vehicle. When fired, out comes money: "Apparently millions of dollars! Fives, tens! Twenties! Millions!" (ibid.). The play concludes: "Niggers now, they gather money in boxes and run towards home," while the officer laughs, "Look at the black bastards go after that money!" (42). *The Job* (1968) concludes with a jazz musician, described as "[o]ne of those 'black nationalist' characters" (45), clubbing a white employment officer to death with his saxophone – a clear manifestation of the power of black culture to destroy white bureaucracy. *Mission Accomplished* (1968) works a burlesque turn on the classic meeting of white colonizers and African kings. Here, nuns do a bump-and-grind that allows them to distract the king's guards while a priest sneaks up behind to club him unconscious with a crucifix.

Caldwell's pieces are examples of a new subgenre of agit-prop invented by the BAM, the revolutionary commercial, which takes the traditional goal of the genre – dramatic compression in the service of concrete imagery – to a new level. Designed to counteract the ubiquity of the white-controlled mass media, the revolutionary commercial moved fast and often focused on the dynamics of communication. Bullins's *Black Commercial #2* (1967) is a good example. It opens on two men trying their best to kill each other while a crowd, described as "the Black Chorus," chants, "KILL KILL KILL . . . THAT BLACK MATHAFUKKER!" As the fight intensifies, a young Black Man, "neatly dressed and speak[ing] softly," steps from the crowd and says, simply, "Brothers." "What you say, man?" asks one of the men. "Brothers." The two men then ask together, "Huh???" "Brothers." "You mean you think him and me is brothers?" "Brothers" (132–3). The chorus ("Intermittent voices, bewildered," but growing "more confident") begins to chant the young man's word as he disappears among them (133). The fighters "clasp hands and speak of their mutual plans for the future, working in unity" (134). The whole thing lasts about two minutes.

Gracefully completing a similarly compressed dramatic line, Marvin X's *The Black Bird* (*Al Tair Aswad*) (1969) emphasizes the need for personal contact, Afrocentric art, and the identification of the "big white lies" that oppress African Americans. A young black Muslim, after a round of basic instruction in the ideology of the Nation of Islam, tells two little girls the story of a black bird that almost loses its life for fear of leaving its cage. This dramatic revision of a favorite metaphor of Malcolm X's (the house slave rushing to put out the fire in his master's home) implicitly asserts, as Bettye I. Lattimer puts it, that young children's bonds to the community are threatened by "clowns, fairies, elves, and angels, as well as Peter Pan, Little Red Riding Hood, and that grand matriarch, Mother Goose" (qtd. in Hay 1994: 106). In this case, the revolutionary commercial functions as a concrete intervention against mass-mediated racism. If, as Guy Debord contends, commodity culture produces distance between alienated individuals, Marvin X and other playwrights exploring the drama of the black community were clearly devising ways to close that distance.

Radical Theology, Affect, Narrative

Many in the BAM would argue that the mass media's most invidious effect was spiritual. African American radical theology supplied a range of cosmological frameworks not only to fight that influence, but undermine the very western Enlightenment tradition. As James T. Stewart asserts, "[E]xisting white paradigms or models do not correspond to the realities of Black existence. It is imperative that we construct models with different basic assumptions. The dilemma of the 'negro' artist is that he makes assumptions based on the wrong models" (1968: 3). The Christian Church coalitions of Martin Luther King, Jr., the Honorable Elijah Muhammad's Nation of Islam, and the Kawaida system of Maulana (Ron Karenga's US organization) were perhaps the most significant seedbeds for such cosmic revisioning, though also important were Reverend Albert Clague's Shrine of the Black Madonna in Detroit, the cosmic music of Sun Ra, and the neo-Africanisms created in Baba Oserjiman Adefumi's Harlem Yoruba Temple and Jahnheinz Jahn's book *Muntu: An Outline of Neo-African Culture* (1961).[5] To those seeking alternative conceptions of spirit, other ways of experiencing the bonds between self and world – alternative ontologies, in short – theological drama and theatre were powerful tools.

One could spill much ink discussing religion and its impact on BAM drama; in fact, whole studies of black drama and theatre have been shaped by Afrocentric theological systems (e.g., Hay and Harrison).[6] Ritual drama, in particular, dominated the stages and periodicals of black theatre in the late 1960s, attracting the likes of Baraka (*Bloodrites* [1971]), Joseph Walker (*Ododo* [1971]), Marvin X (*The Resurrection of the Dead* [1969]), Paul Carter Harrison (*The Great MacDaddy* [1973]), and Adrienne Kennedy (*An Evening with Dead Essex* [1973]). Generally, such pieces blend boldly drawn dramatic structure, a range of presentational techniques (chanting, choral movement, song), multimedia, and, especially, the deeply affecting invocation of the texts, movements, cadences, intonations, and props of a range of religious performance traditions, including some fresh-minted. Reactions were extremely mixed, though one critic, reviewing the Lafayette's *a ritual to bind together and strengthen black people so that they can survive the long struggle to come* (1969), called it "an experience unlike any other I've had in the theatre: deeply moving, totally produced, and finally peaceful" ("Ritual" 1969: 5). The Kuumba Workshop in Chicago staged events organized around the familiar Protestant Christian sermon structure, but anchored it to a more secular black ethos by planting actors in the audience who quoted contemporary black writers in moments of semi-improvised "testifying." Hoyt Fuller reports that the audience reacted "with fervor," adding their own testimonials to the mix (qtd. in Hay 1994: 117). Newark's Spirit House staged chants and mini-rituals that Hay characterizes as "show[ing] African Americans in control of the world, as well as themselves" (116). Baraka saw them as engaging in linguistic innovation, too, "a kind of unconscious future language" that "recreate[s] that kind of emotional tone that exists in the Black church, but put a different content in it, a content that has to do with things which we can't completely understand yet" (qtd. in Hay 1994: 116).

The National Black Theatre of Harlem's *A Revival! Change! Love! Organize!* (1969) by Charles Russell and Barbara Ann Teer mixed cutting-edge environmental theatre techniques with a fairly conventional drama-of-the-street narrative: a heroin addict owes money to his dealer and, having lost it, meets up with the leader of the "Temple of Liberation," Toussaint, during his flight. Later, he is nabbed by his creditor, severely beaten, then revived by a group of faith healers and put on the path of righteous blackness. This fairly conventional, if presentationally staged narrative was punctuated by three participatory rituals: a voudon ceremony for the Yoruba goddess Oshun, a group consciousness-raising session concerning African American consumer- ism, and a Christian faith-healing ritual (see Harris 1980: 288–91). The juxtaposition of narrative drama and participatory activity – and their mutually reinforcing conclu- sions (the rituals all address Porky's tribulations) – is the key here. Three modes of storytelling are utilized in *A Revival!* (mythical, conversational, and dramatic), and with them three distinct experiences of theatrical time (cyclical, non-directive, and linear), all of which are drawn together at the evening's climax. Two distinct modes of audience participation are also at work: observation of action and participation in process.

This kind of careful blending of narrative structure with various kinds of methectic theatrical experience left a clear mark on subsequent dramatic works, as we see in August Wilson's *Joe Turner's Come and Gone* (1987) (see chapter 20). The cosmic scale of Herald Loomis's suffering is first revealed as the residents of the Holly boarding house "Juba down!," clapping hands, shuffling, and stomping around the kitchen table. Wilson asks that it "be as African as possible, with the performers working themselves up into a near frenzy" (1988: 52). The reunion of Herald with Martha at the end of the play is a more significant dramatic moment, but also an affectively intense one. While the residents look on in fear and awe, Martha recites the twenty- third Psalm and Herald, spitting hellfire, retells the tale of the mortal abuse of his spirit by the chain-gang leader Joe Turner. The moment gets two things done: First, it resolves the key dramatic tension, Herald's quest for his lost love. Second, it ratifies the prophecy of Bynum Walker, a "rootworker" who dreamt that he'd one day meet a "shining man." The dramatic and the prophetic dovetail.

Religion was not universally appreciated as a useful anti-colonial tool; in fact, many saw it as just the opposite. The Last Poets' *Epitaph to a Coagulated Trinity* turns an unblinking eye toward the Catholic Church's failure to declare slavery a sin in the 1600s. And though he was a leading voice in the ritual theatre movement, Baraka also explored the ways that religious consciousness and ritual structure could trap the unsuspecting. *Dutchman*, for example, pulls off a neat trick at its climax, when what had seemed to be an Aristotelian drama of fear-soaked seduction turns out to be a ritual murder. More precisely, it is Clay's failure to understand that he has stumbled into a ritual that leads to his murder.

Caldwell shows no sympathy for the theologically minded in his razor-honed satire *Prayer Meeting, or, The First Militant Minister* (1968). This play depicts a hilarious bit of subterfuge by a quick-on-his-feet burglar and a hopelessly gullible liberal preacher who mistakes the intruder for God. The burglar happens to be a nationalist and convinces the preacher to give up his non-violent ways and pick up a pistol. "The time has come," he intones as the lights fade. "The time has come" (594). Harry Elam, Jr. writes that Caldwell "invokes the sacred while deconstructing its associations with Christianity and realigning it within the context of Black nationalism" (qtd. in Bowman 1999: 808).

Bandung Humanism and Neocolonialism

The populist and cosmological perspectives of the BAM can't be considered separately from the geopolitical – the unity of blackness was always conceptualized by black artists in international terms. Thus, the third anti-colonialist trend that sparked the BAM: the Bandung humanist movement initiated at the Asian–African conference at Bandung, Indonesia, in April 1955. Defined by President Sukarno in his opening address as the common experience and detestation of colonialism, Bandung humanism would enable what we now call the "Third World" to conceptually and affectively unify.

The challenge of Bandung humanism is to link the specificity of local conditions and identities to more general, more abstractly conceptualized global contexts and issues – the philosopher's stone of unity-in-diversity. One of the first African American dramatists to take up Bandung's challenge was Lorraine Hansberry, whose *A Raisin in the Sun* (1959) should be read not only as a response to the Bandung imperative, but also as the apex of Hansberry's work with United States-based anti-colonialist organizations during the 1950s. Beneatha's story is particularly interesting; her dramatic conflict bridges the local and the global in both affective and aesthetic terms. Beneatha must choose between participation in the development of an African nation (as the spouse of African intellectual Asagai) or the purchase and defense of a suburban American home (and commitment to the nuclear American family). Affect is mirrored in aesthetics. As the romantic quandary intensifies, Beneatha's appearance transforms; she sports "natural" and the colorful cloth given her by Asagai virtually explodes in the tired apartment of the Youngers (see chapter 11 for more discussion of the play).

Anti-colonial rhetoric, Afrocentric costumes, and allusions to African political struggles pepper the BAM archive. However, explicit references to Africa and the Third World are not the only nor the most interesting evidence of Bandung humanist influences. Concern with the role of "neocolonialism," defined as the cultural and economic domination of a nation after the end of political and/or military domination, was also common – and tended to call into question the very dramatic and theatrical forms favored by Hansberry. Two aspects of American theatre and drama were of particular concern: the theatre as a way of seeing and drama as a structure of thought.

The theatre considered as a visual technique or "optic" that shapes perception was often the subject of dramatic inquiry. We've seen this in Mackey's *Requiem for Brother X*. In experientially intense, profoundly iconoclastic works such as *The Theme is Blackness* (1966) and *It Bees Dat Way* (1970), Ed Bullins also addressed theatrical vision, particularly the ironic distance enabled by spectatorship, the visual and performance codes that constitute stereotypes, and the reliance on vision to form concepts of self and other. *The Theme is Blackness* plunges its audience into complete darkness for 20 minutes, robbing the spectator of a basic prerogative – the ability to *see*. Doing so, Bullins challenges not only the perceptual foundations of the theatre, but the visual bias of the western Enlightenment itself.[7] Smashing that most precious of modern theatrical technologies – electrical light – he homogenizes his audience in a fashion not unlike that described by Fanon in *The Wretched of the Earth*: "Decoloniza-tion unifies...people by the radical decision to remove from it its heterogenei-ty.... The native intellectual takes part, in a sort of auto-da-fé, in the destruction of all his idols" (1963: 46–7).

It Bees Dat Way mounts an even riskier theatrical move. The audience (as in *Theme*, specified as "predominantly white") enters a space with no discernible difference between auditorium or stage, the sounds of a jazz quartet emanating from somewhere equally difficult to discern. The "single setting" consists of a street lamp that stands metonymically for a "Harlem street corner" (5). The drama here is supplied by a group of malevolent African Americans who enter the space with the audience (5). What Bullins gives us is both one of the most troubling acts of theatrical terror ever devised – not to mention produced (as it was in London in 1970). The six characters converse with and jostle the spectators, systematically pressing toward verbal and physical violence: "Whichever way the audience goes, the actors go counter to it or with it, whatever is most unlikely and threatening, even into physical abuse: scuf-fling, rape, strong-arming, and beating the audience" (6). On the one hand, *It Bees Dat Way* is the expression of a deep-seated rage and a commitment to violent revolutionary action not unlike that demonstrated in *Death List* (1971). On the other, it's a theatrically self-reflexive attack on the neocolonialist logic of avant-garde theatre. Bullins places among the most daring, most radically chic of white theatregoers the "usual suspects" of the drama of African American lumpen life that Bullins himself popularized.

Bullins is clearly concerned that his "natural" style of drama was being turned into just another fund of stereotypes for a new liberal audience. This wasn't a small or short-lived issue for those who had to balance the demands of style and revolutionary orthodoxy. Alice Childress's *Trouble in Mind* (1955) confronted a similar issue a decade and a half earlier. In this beautifully crafted, brutally ironic backstage play, a veteran African American actor finds herself at the end of her patience – and career. Cast in a supposedly progressive drama about the evils of lynching, she discovers very little in the way of progress. Refusing to continue the rehearsal, she confronts the patronizing director: "This ain't sayin' nothin', don't make sense. Talkin' 'bout the truth is anything I can believe...well, I don't believe this" (169). Wiletta's final stand ("I'm playin' a leadin' part and I want this script changed or else," 172) may mean the end of the production, but insures her a final wish: "to do somethin' real grand...in the theater...to stand forth at my best...to stand up here and do anything I want" (173).

Though Childress's target at first appears to be the vacuous liberal theatre of her time, a wider historical glance reveals something else in her scope. BAM playwrights believed that theatre had served as a material support for what Alexander Saxton has called a "half century of inurement to the uses of white supremacy" (qtd. in Lott 1995: 3). But the absence of overt signs of minstrelsy in plays such as those of Bullins and Childress doesn't mean the tradition wasn't present in other, less obvious ways. Much as Kwame Nkrumah identified the forms of domination that persisted after independence, black dramatists identified the forms of theatrical domination that persisted after the creation of independent black theatres. This work had to be subtle and, thus, should be considered a precursor to Eric Lott's justly celebrated exploration of the complex, subterranean cultural dynamics surrounding the minstrel tradition, *Love and Theft: Blackface Minstrelsy and the American Working Class* (1995). Contrary to Lott's dismissive treatment of the Black Arts generation, a closer reading of black drama reveals that artists and theorists often traversed the reticulated terrain of minstrelsy, colonial oppression, and the struggle for identity and public voice.

Baraka's *The Slave* (1964) and *Jello* (1970) are good examples. Contra Lott, Baraka doesn't portray minstrelsy as a simplistic tool of racist domination (Lott 1995: 7). Rather, he invokes and deploys blackface as an unstable form of disguise and a dangerous but empowering form of insight into the lower circles of racism. As he puts it in his difficult text "A Poem for Willie Best," blackface enables the wearer to be a "renegade / behind the mask. And even / the mask, a renegade / disguise" (1991a: 58). This kind of play with appearances is a specialty of theatre, of course, and Baraka knew it. Neal reports that one production of *The Slave* chose as the emblem of the black revolutionary army "a red-mouthed grinning field slave," demonstrating a "radical alter[ation]" in meaning and a "supreme act of freedom, available only to those who have liberated themselves psychically" (1989: 72).

Jello's send-up of the popular *The Jack Benny Program* transforms the put-upon, gravel-voiced Rochester played by Eddie Anderson into "Ratfester," described by Neal as "*blues people* smiling and shuffling while trying to figure out how to destroy the white thing...the Signifying Monkey, Shine, and Stackolee all rolled into one" (ibid.). Neal is sensitive to the fact that Baraka is condemning neither the Rochester character nor Anderson. To return to "Willie Best": "No one / will turn to that station again," but "All This should be / invested" (55). Neal sees Ratfester as a concrete manifestation of an unprecedented institutional and affective rupture: "There are no stereotypes anymore. . . . Behind the . . . shuffling porter loom visions of white throats being cut and cities burning" (ibid.).

Of course, the more direct move was still popular, as is clear in Doug Barnett's *Da Minstrel Show* (1969) or Douglas Turner Ward's classic *Day of Absence* (1966). The latter is among the best-known and loved BAM plays for the way it turns the theatrical tables on minstrelsy by having African American actors play white characters in "whiteface." Ward called it "a reverse minstrel show" (36). The sudden absence of African Americans in a small Southern town comically escalates into a national crisis. The absence of blacks on the narrative level is counter-balanced by the theatrical absence of white performers (it is an all-black cast). Ward launches a delightfully unsubtle volley at the theatrical history of racism, pulling in not only Rod Serling's *Twilight Zone*, but also, according to Kevin Sanders, the most utopian dimensions of the black radical tradition. It is one of a handful of really great BAM comedies, and though its humor alone recommends it, its dramatic linking of minstrelsy and patriotic fervor makes it especially topical for today's readers and theatregoers. "This is a red-white-and-blue play," he tells us. "Opening scenes stage-lit with white rays of morning, transforming to panic reds of afternoon, flowing into ominous blues of evening" (37). Patriotism in this play literally wears rose-colored spectacles – and seems incapable of seeing the African American.

OyamO's *The Breakout* (1969) does not at first appear to have anything to do with minstrelsy. Rather, it seems to be about two down-on-their-luck, egregiously smart-assed convicts. However, as the gags about feet size, derisive comments about sexual prowess, and endless malapropisms begin to accumulate, Slam and Feet start to resemble a more famous duo: Tambo and Bones. The liberal "Rev. J. P. Jackson," ensconced in a super-plush cell just across from Slam and Feet, at first seems merely the butt of conventional ideological jabs, but winds up the third in the classic minstrelsy trio: the interlocutor. OyamO plays a trick on his audience here, luring them into thinking that they are encountering "realistic" representations of the black lumpen classes, transparently obvious ideological positions, and yet another example of a "black" attack on its *bête noire*. Quite the contrary, read in the light of the anti-minstrelsy offensive, such dramatic conventions appear as nothing more than the bloodthirsty revenants of good old-fashioned white-supremacist hi-jinks. OyamO's play suggests that the wine of anti-colonial drama is easily contained in the bottles of neocolonialist power.

Ntozake Shange is not usually considered a BAM playwright, and this assumption has enabled scholars to overlook her fluency in the movement's fundamental concern with the necessity of creating sophisticated theatrical art to address the ways that racist perceptual structures embed in the theatrical arts. Her debut play *for colored girls who have considered suicide / when the rainbow is enuf* (1974) perfected the efforts of black playwrights to utilize the compositional principles of music and spoken-word poetry in order to challenge theatricalized assumptions about the African American voice and experience. *Spell #7*'s (1979) non-linear, presentational style takes place in a kind of haven of blackness, a lounge just off the "Great White Way" and set squarely beneath an enormous minstrel mask. Shange asks that the mask be visible as the audience enters, thus making clear that watching any representation of "black" life is always bracketed by Tambo and Bones: "The members of the audience must integrate this grotesque, larger-than-life misrepresentation of life into their pre-show chatter...the mask looms even larger in the darkness" when the house lights fade (7). The actors, when they first appear, are dressed in classic minstrel-show garb, and their decision to remove the mask is a thematically important moment. The audience should not be fooled into thinking that the masks are gone, however. Though the performers share their lives, their frustrations, their hopes in a spirit of courage and community, their concluding song, "colored & love it / love it being colored," is performed as the huge minstrel mask is lowered from the flies back into the light.

The troubling theatricality of blackness, particularly as it intersects with anti-female violence, is exposed in one scene of Sonia Sanchez's *Uh-Uh; But How Do It Free Us?* (1974). Skewering a sacred cow of Black Nationalism, five men dress a black prostitute in a fur coat and face paint, making her the "queen." Sanchez asks the performer to walk a delicate line: "She's obviously scared. But as she walks, she relaxes, and as she passes by the second time, her face changes and her body seems taller. She looks queenly, like a latter day Lady Day [Billie Holiday] looked on TV, nervous and unsure but queenly" (184). White Dude can't take the ambiguity: "Stop it. What is this sheeeet? Who she think she is anyway? If anyone's gon' be queen of the universe around here, it's gon' be me" (ibid.). He goes to the closet and dons a fur coat, shoes, wig, and earrings of his own. As could only be expected, violence punctuates the moment as White Dude punches his rival in the stomach and face and kicks her repeatedly as she lies on the floor. The point here is not merely to deflate the rhetoric of female praise in the movement (or bolster Sanchez's conservative racial-sexual politics), but to criticize the profit-seeking tendencies of the movement. Brother Man: "It's the 1970s, and don't ya forget it. The decade of the hustles. The hustlers.... We know who we are" (185).

BAM playwrights also concerned themselves with the neocolonial tendencies of western drama as narrative tradition. Mischievous play with the conventions of socially conscious western drama is found in Martie Charles's *Job Security* (1970). As was the case with Childress, OyamO, and Shange, Charles identifies and dramatically undermines assumptions not only *about* African Americans but about *theatre* about African Americans. Here, what appears to be a well-crafted but fairly conventional social reform play about a fiery young girl cast among a group of cynical, ineffectual teachers suddenly turns into an anarchic bit of *grand guignol* when the special ingredient in a boxful of candies is revealed. Suckering her audience into the most pathetic, self-serving forms of sympathy and pity, Charles suggests that they may be no different than the girl's patronizing teachers – and no less valid a target for criticism. They bite into the play's sugar-sweet narrative only to discover a serial-killer sensibility oozing from its center.

The drama of liberal progressivism was not the only Euro-American tradition to bear the brunt of black critique. The dramatic and theatrical traditions of absurdism, understood by many within the movement as the *sine qua non* of avant-gardism, are simultaneously utilized and critiqued by Sharon Stockard Martin in her stunning *The Moving Violation* (1979). Initially striking one as an anarchic and decidedly clever bit of dadaist play with dramatic conventions of character and narrative, it moves inexorably into a situation of horror and desperation reminiscent of some of Harold Pinter's later work. Not simply playing with the conventions of absurdism, Martin anchors the terrifying lack of fit between language and identity in a world of arbitrary violence and endlessly deferred mourning: a black world.

Many playwrights and critics refused to orient their work around those "white" forms at all, even if taking a critical stance toward them. Neal, for example, viewed Bullins's *We Righteous Bombers* (1968) as tied to an ineffectual tradition of social criticism plays, mired in western notions of individuality, and ultimately structured by Aristotelian principles despite its superficial play with Brechtian devices. Neal tried to educate his colleagues about the danger lurking within western conventions: "See what happens is that one of the hang-ups in terms of writing in the West is that we have inherited some forms that are dead, useless.... Now it's the job of the revolutionary artist to find out what forms in his culture are best used to express a certain kind of idea" ("Lafayette Theatre Reaction to Bombers" 1969: 19). Neal makes clear in other essays that the quest for non-western form and, as a consequence, the shaking off of neocolonial control of African Americans, would only be successful if the playwright explored indigenous people's cultural forms and non-western metaphysical systems.

Thus, the significance of music – both popular and avant-garde – on black playwriting and performance must be noted, particularly because it enabled the vital dynamic of tradition and innovation called for by cultural revolutionaries such as Nkrumah, Kenyatta, Mao, and Malcolm X. A touchstone of the BAM critical and dramatic archive, the blues, rhythm-and-blues, gospel music, and jazz were considered the "key," as Neal puts it, to expanding the movement's connections to local, national, and international currents (1968: 653). The connections are clear in Baraka's description of Sun Ra: "The Weirdness, Outness, Way Outness, Otherness was immediate. Some space metaphysical philosophical surrealistic bop funk. Some blue pyramid home nigger southern different color meaning hip shift. Ra. Sun Ra" (1995: 253).

Though, as Hay notes, Black Nationalist musicals were rare (1994: 112–13), exploration of such "different color meaning hip shift" was common. For example, Bullins utilizes music both thematically and structurally in many of his works and has been composing full-fledged musicals since the mid-1970s (e.g., *Home Boy* [1976], *High John da Conqueror* [1985], *Satchmo* [1981], *Hot Feet* [2003]). Bullins's experimentation with musical form reflects a long-term interest in the power of sound, rhythm, and oratorical force as well as his commitment to popular culture (e.g., *Black Commercial #2*). Music serves a number of roles in his work: grounding dramatic situations in particular historical and social contexts, as is the case with *In the Wine Time* (1968, where the sounds of gospel and rhythm-and-blues infuse the street-level drama with metaphysical implications); giving formal coherence to his notoriously non-linear dramas, particularly those that unfold in shifting social gatherings (e.g., *The Fabulous Miss Marie* [1971], *House Party* [1973], *The Pig Pen* [1970]); and unifying disparate lines of character or thematic development in almost operatic fashion. Music can be the familiar stuff of chord progressions and harmony for Bullins, but so can repeated lines of dialogue, a particular intonation of voice, or (as in *The Pig Pen*) a sound effect with no clear relationship to the dramatic narrative.

Baraka collaborated closely with Sun Ra and Archie Shepp on two works (*A Black Mass* [1967] and *Slave Ship* [1967]) and has attested to how much the former influenced his thinking in general. Commenting on the recently rereleased soundtrack for *A Black Mass*, Baraka writes that,

> [h]eard with the text of *The Black Mass*, both connect and extend each other with a dramatic gestalt of Myth-Science music, and the mythologized history deepens our emotional perception of what is being told. For me, re-heard with the benefit of study and another kind of thoughtfulness, it even projects a rationale that's more scientifically based, "search-lighting" some evasive facts of human history as well as projecting the premise which I have long held, that art is creation, and that we must oppose the "creation of what does not need to be created." (2003)

Music in *Slave Ship* serves both atmospheric and conceptual purposes; Shepp's use of traditional, noise, and avant-garde musical modes reinforces Baraka's point that there is no history: African Americans have yet to complete the Middle Passage. The play's structured use of improvisation marks an even more radical turn, which Jeff Schwartz characterizes as being "as close as any work to formally embodying Baraka's revolutionary Black Aesthetic, by fully incorporating the improvisational procedures of free jazz into theater." Germane to Schwartz's point, Leslie C. Sanders notes that Baraka views music as paradoxically radical: "When the musicians go back to the roots of experience for appropriate forms and place them in a modern context, the forms are changed and given new meanings. What is produced is radical both in the sense of departing from the mainstream and in the sense of returning to its roots" (1988: 130–1).

As Fanon defines it, the anti-colonial struggle must be grounded in tradition yet innovative in approach – or, as Baraka puts it in a profile of Sun Ra, "[t]he future is always here in the past" (1995: 255). This is where we should conclude: with the movement's most significant and paradoxical impact – and the source of its continuing relevance in our own times of fundamentalist violence. It would be grossly incorrect to assert that the movement no longer exists (in fact, it is as strong in some cities – e.g., Boston and Chicago – as it was in the 1960s and 1970s), or to ignore the continuing validity of its anti-colonial stance bolstered by the demand for independent cultural institutions.[8] But considering dramatic literature separate from such issues, one might argue that it is the challenge to western dramatic form inspired by African American music and its paradoxically radical vision of tradition and innovation that has had the most far-reaching impact on post-BAM African American theatrical arts, especially drama. The work of August Wilson and Adrienne Kennedy hardly needs commentary in this regard, and Thulani Davis's *X* (1986) and Aishah Rahman's *Unfinished Women Die in a No-Man's Land While a Bird Dies in a Gilded Cage* (1977) are just two instances of the kind of effective implementation of the black aesthetic in dramatic form called for by the Black Arts generation. Shange's *for colored girls* was, perhaps, the pivotal event in this cross-generational, relentlessly experimental, resolutely critical crossing of music and drama – and continues to stand as both model and a vital presence in the black canon. Too often, as Cedric Robinson has demonstrated, the continuity of the black radical tradition has been obscured in critical conflicts within the tradition (1983: 202ff.). Continuity is clear, however, not only in the work of Shange, Kennedy, Wilson, Davis, Rahman, and countless others, but also in the current surge of hip-hop musical theatre. Though yet to be tested by time, Will Power's *Flow* (2003), Rennie Harris's *Facing Mekka* (2000), and the workshops of Toni Blackman's Freestyle Union (1994–present) faithfully carry the tradition of path-seeking creation, historical revisionism, community consciousness, critical spirituality, and vanguard formal experimentation of "Black Arts Drama" (see McCarter 2003). The editors of the recent *Role Call* anthology identify the responsibility carried by this new generation as a necessary response to the Black Art Movement's call for social justice and transformative, turbulent African American creativity: "Who is present? / *Raise ya hands in the air!* / Who's here? / *Say it loud! I'm Black and I'm . . .* / Uh huh. / Thought so" (Medina, Bashir, and Lansana 2002: xviii).

NOTES

1. For the influence of Mao on the BAM, see Mullen (2002).

2. For more general discussion of family in US drama, see Scanlan (1978).

3. The fear of Clara's lesbianism, characterized by Neal as the consequence of attempting to emulate white, upper-class females and "a rejection of the body" (1989: 75), confirms Green's assertion that the Romantic roots of the folk metaphor often serve as a prop for misogyny.

4. For discussion of *A Soldier's Play*'s defeatist implications, see Baraka (1983).

5. Thanks to Katie Suwala for her diligent research on this subject as a member of the undergraduate BAM research group in the spring of 2003.

6. For a synoptic anthology devoted to ritual performance within the African diaspora, see Paul Carter Harrison, Victor Leo Walker II, and Gus Edwards (eds.), *Black Theatre: Ritual Performance in the African Diaspora* (Philadelphia: Temple University Press, 2002).

7. See Jay (1993) for the visual bias of the western philosophical tradition. My thanks to Sam Z. Hamilton for his research and thoughts on this issue.

8. As August Wilson made clear in his address to the 1997 National Black Theatre Festival. See Wilson (1997a, b).

BIBLIOGRAPHY

Baker, H., Jr. (1981). "Generational Shifts and the Recent Criticism of Afro-American Literature." *Black American Literature Forum* 15, 1 (Spring): 3–21.

Baraka, A. (LeRoi Jones) (1963). *Blues People: Negro Music in White America*. New York: William Morrow.

——(1970). *Jello*. Chicago: Third World Press.

——(1971). *Bloodrites*. In Woodie King and Ron Milner (eds.), *Black Drama Anthology*. New York: Meridian.

——(1983). "The Descent of Charlie Fuller into Pulitzerland and the Need for African-American Institutions." *Black American Literature Forum* 17, 2 (Summer): 51–4.

——(1984). *The Autobiography of LeRoi Jones*. Chicago: Lawrence Hill.

——(1991a). "A Poem for Willie Best." In William J. Harris (ed.), *The LeRoi Jones/Amiri Baraka Reader*. New York: Thunder's Mouth Press.

——(1991b). *Dutchman*. In William J. Harris (ed.), *The LeRoi Jones/Amiri Baraka Reader*. New York: Thunder's Mouth Press.

——(1995). "Jazzmen: Diz and Sun Ra." *African American Review* 29, 2 (Summer): 249–55.

——(1998). *A Black Mass. Four Revolutionary Plays*. New York: Marion Boyars.

——(2003). Liner Notes. *A Black Mass* by Amiri Baraka and the Sun Ra Myth-Science Arkestra. Forced Exposure, June 29; http://www.forcedexposure.com/artists/baraka.leroi.jones.and.the.sun.ra.myth.science.arkestra.amiri.html.

Benston, K. (1980). "The Aesthetic of Modern Black Drama: From Mimesis to Methexis." In Errol Hill (ed.), *The Theatre of Black Americans: A Collection of Critical Essays*. New York: Applause.

Bowman, K. (1999). "The Revolution Will Not Be Televised Nor Staged: An Interview with Ben Caldwell." *Callaloo* 22, 4 (Fall): 808–24.

Brustein, R. (1990). "Review of *The Piano Lesson*, by August Wilson." *New Republic*, May 21: 28–30.

Bullins, E. (1969). *In the Wine Time. Five Plays*. New York: Bobbs-Merrill.

——(1971). *Death List. Black Theatre* 5: 38–43.

——(1973a). *It Bees Dat Way*. In *The Theme is Blackness, "The Corner" and Other Plays*. New York: William Morrow.

——(1973b). *BlackCommercial #2*. In *The Theme is Blackness, "The Corner" and Other Plays*. New York: William Morrow.

——(1973c). *House Party*. Unpublished manuscript. The Ed Bullins Collection.

——(1973d). *The Pig Pen. Four Dynamite Plays*. New York: William Morrow.

——(1973e). *The Theme is Blackness, "The Corner" and Other Plays*. New York: William Morrow.

——(1974). *The Fabulous Miss Marie*. In Ed Bullins (ed.), *The New Lafayette Theatre Presents*. Garden City, NY: Anchor/Doubleday.

——(1976). *Home Boy*. Unpublished manuscript. The Ed Bullins Collection.

——(1981). *Satchmo: An American Musical Legend*. Unpublished manuscript. The Ed Bullins collection.

——(1993). *High John da Conqueror: The Musical*. In Ethel Pitts Walker (ed.), *New/Lost Plays by Ed Bullins*. Aiea, HI: That New Publishing Company.

Caldwell, B. (1968a). *The Job. Drama Review* 12, 4 (Summer): 43–68.

——(1968b). *Mission Accomplished. Drama Review* 12, 4 (Summer): 50–2.

——(1968c). *Prayer Meeting, or, The First Militant Minister*. In LeRoi Jones and Larry Neal (eds.), *Black Fire: An Anthology of Afro-American Writing*. New York: William Morrow.

——(1968d). *Riot Sale, or Dollar Psyche Fake Out. Drama Review* 12, 4 (Summer): 41–2.

Charles, M. (1971). *Black Cycle*. In Woodie King and Ron Milner (eds.), *Black Drama Anthology*. New York: Meridian.

Childress, A. (1971). *Trouble in Mind*. In Lindsay Patterson (comp.), *Black Theater: A 20th-Century Collection of the Work of Its Best Playwrights*. New York: Dodd, Mead.

Cook, W. (1980). "Mom, Dad, and God: Values in Black Theater." In Errol Hill (ed.), *The Theatre of Black Americans: A Collection of Critical Essays*. New York: Applause.

Davis, T. (1994). *X*. In Sydné Mahone (ed.), *Moon Marked and Touched by Sun: Plays by African-American Women*. New York: Theatre Communications Group.

Debord, G. (1995). *The Society of the Spectacle*, trans. Donald Nicholson-Smith. New York: Zone.

Fanon, F. (1963). *The Wretched of the Earth*, trans. Constance Farrington. New York: Grove Weidenfeld.

Franklin, J. E. (1971). *Black Girl*. Unpublished manuscript. Collection of author.

Fuller, C. (1981). *A Soldier's Play*. Garden City, NY: Doubleday.

Fuller, H. (1972). "Towards a Black Aesthetic." In Addison Gayle, Jr. (ed.), *The Black Aesthetic*. New York: Anchor.

Gaines, J. E. (1974). *What If It Had Turned Up Heads?* In Ed Bullins (ed.), *The New Lafayette Theatre Presents*. Garden City, NY: Anchor/Doubleday.

Gates, H. L., Jr. (2001). "The Chitlin Circuit." In Harry Elam, Jr. and David Krasner (eds.), *African American Performance and Theatre History: A Critical Reader*. New York: Oxford University Press.

Giovanni, N. (1979). "Our Detroit Conference." In *Black Feeling, Black Talk/Black Judgement*. New York: William Morrow.

Green, J. (1970). "Black Romanticism." In Toni Cade (ed.), *The Black Woman*. New York: Mentor.

Hansberry, L. (1994). *Les Blancs: The Collected Last Plays*, ed. Robert Nemiroff. New York: Vintage.

Harris, J. B. (1980). "The National Black Theatre: The Sun People of 125th Street." In Errol Hill (ed.), *The Theatre of Black Americans: A Collection of Critical Essays*. New York: Applause.

Harrison, P. C. (1974). "Introduction." In *Kuntu Drama: Plays of the African Continuum*. New York: Grove.

Hay, S. A. (1994). *African American Theatre: An Historical and Critical Analysis*. Cambridge: Cambridge University Press.

Hill, E. (1980). "Introduction." In Errol Hill (ed.), *The Theatre of Black Americans: A Collection of Critical Essays*. New York: Applause.

Jahn, J. (1961). *Muntu: An Outline of Neo-African Culture*. London: Faber and Faber.

Jay, M. (1993). *Downcast Eyes: The Denigration of Vision in Twentieth-Century French Thought*. Berkeley: University of California Press.

Kelley, R. D. G. (2002). *Freedom Dreams: The Black Radical Imagination*. Boston: Beacon Press.

Kennedy, A. (2001). *An Evening with Dead Essex*. In Werner Sollors (comp.), *The Adrienne Kennedy Reader*. Minneapolis: University of Minnesota Press.

"Lafayette Theatre Reaction to Bombers" (1969). *Black Theatre* 4: 15–26.

Lott, E. (1995). *Love and Theft: Blackface Minstrelsy and the American Working Class*. New York: Oxford University Press.

McCarter, J. (2003). "Hip-Hop and Musicals: Made for Each Other?" *New York Times*, June 8: AR 5, 8.

Mackey, W. W. (1971). *Requiem for Brother X*. In Woodie King and Ron Milner (eds.), *Black Drama Anthology*. New York: Meridian.

Malcolm X (1970). "The Organization of Afro-American Unity: For Human Rights and Dignity." In John H. Bracey, Jr., August Meier, and Elliott Rudwick (eds.), *Black Nationalism in America*. Indianapolis: Bobbs-Merrill.

Martin, S. S. (1981). *The Moving Violation*. In Eileen Joyce Ostrow (ed.), *Center Stage: An Anthology of 21 Contemporary Black-American Plays*. Oakland, CA: Sea Urchin Press.

Marvin X (Marvin Jackmon) (1969a). *The Black Bird*. In Ed Bullins (ed.), *New Plays from the Black Theatre*. New York: Bantam.

——(1969b). *The Resurrection of the Dead. Black Theatre* 3: 26–7.

Medina, T., Bashir, S. A., and Lansana, Q. A. (2002). "Call and Response." In Tony Medina, Samiya A. Bashir, and Quraysh Ali Lansana (eds.), *Role Call: A Generational Anthology of Social and Political Black Literature and Art*. Chicago: Third World Press.

Milner, R. (1971). *Who's Got His Own*. In Woodie King and Ron Milner (eds.), *Black Drama Anthology*. New York: Meridian.

——(1972). "Black Theater – Go Home!" In Addison Gayle, Jr. (ed.), *The Black Aesthetic*. New York: Anchor, 288–94.

Mullen, B. (2002). "Seeking Correspondence: Robert F. Williams, Detroit, and the Bandung Era." In Mike Sell (ed.), "Vectors of the Radical: Global Consciousness, Textual Exchange, and the 1960s." Special issue. *Works and Days* 20, 39–40: 189–216.

Neal, L. (1968). "And Shine Swam On." In LeRoi Jones and Larry Neal (eds.), *Black Fire: An Anthology of Afro-American Writing*. New York: William Morrow.

——(1969). "Any Day Now: Black Art and Black Liberation." *Ebony* 24 (August): 54–62.

——(1989). "The Black Arts Movement." In Michael Schwartz (ed.), *Visions of a Liberated Future*. New York: Thunder's Mouth Press.

OyamO (Charles Gordon) (1971). *The Breakout*. In Woodie King and Ron Milner (eds.), *Black Drama Anthology*. New York: Meridian.

Poggioli, R. (1968). *The Theory of the Avant-Garde*, trans. Gerald Fitzgerald. Cambridge, MA: Harvard University Press.

Rahman, A. (1984). *Unfinished Women Die in a No-Man's Land While a Bird Dies in a Gilded Cage*. New York: Drama Jazz House.

"Ritual." (1969). Review of *a ritual to bind together and strengthen black people so that they can survive the long struggle to come*, by Ed Bullins and the New Lafayette Players. *Bay State Banner* 4 (September): 5.

Robinson, C. J. (1983). *Black Marxism: The Making of the Black Radical Tradition*. London: Zed.

Sanchez, S. (1974). *Uh-Uh; But How Do It Free Us?* In Ed Bullins (ed.), *The New Lafayette Theatre Presents*. Garden City, NY: Anchor.

Sanders, K. (2003). "Yearning for Our Land: The Black Arts Movement's Artists' Role." Unpublished manuscript. Indiana University of Pennsylvania.

Sanders, L. C. (1988). *The Development of Black Theater in America: From Shadows to Selves*. Baton Rouge: Louisiana State University Press.

Scanlan, T. (1978). *Family, Drama, and American Dreams*. Westport, CT: Greenwood.

Schwartz, J. (2003). "Jazz as Literary Theory: Amiri Baraka's *Slave Ship*." June 29; http://www.geocities.com/jeff_l_schwartz/slaveship.html.

Sedgwick, E. K. (1985). *Between Men: English Literature and Male Homosocial Desire*. New York: Columbia University Press.

Sell, M. (2001). "The Black Arts Movement: Performance, Neo-Orality, and the Destruction of the 'White Thing.'" In Harry Elam, Jr. and David Krasner (eds.), *African American Performance and Theatre History: A Critical Reader*. New York: Oxford University Press.

Shange, N. (1975). *for colored girls who have considered suicide / when the rainbow is enuf*. New York: Scribner Poetry.

——(1981). *spell #7: geechee jibara quik magic trance manual for technologically stressed third world people. three pieces*. New York: St. Martin's.

Sobehart, L. A. and Harvith, J. (2003). "Pitt in the News." *Pitt Chronicle Online*, June 24; http://www.univ-relations.pitt.edu/media/pcc030203/inthenews.html.

Stewart, J. T. (1968). "The Development of the Black Revolutionary Artist." In LeRoi Jones and Larry Neal (eds.), *Black Fire: An Anthology of Afro-American Writing*. New York: William Morrow.

Walker, J. (1971). *Ododo*. In Woodie King and Ron Milner (eds.), *Black Drama Anthology*. New York: Meridian.

Ward, D. T. (1966). *Happy Ending and Day of Absence: Two Plays*. New York: Dramatists Play Service.

Wesley, R. (1981). *The Sirens*. In Eileen Joyce Ostrow (ed.), *Center Stage: An Anthology of 21 Contemporary Black-American Plays*. Oakland, CA: Sea Urchin Press.

Wilson, A. (1988). *Joe Turner's Come and Gone*. New York: Penguin.

——(1997a). "The Ground on Which I Stand." *Callaloo* 20, 3 (Summer): 493–503.

——(1997b). "National Black Theater Festival 1997." *Callaloo* 20, 3 (Summer): 483–92.

Young, R. J. C. (2001). *Postcolonialism: An Historical Introduction*. Malden, MA: Blackwell.

18

Sam Shepard and the American Sunset: Enchantment of the Mythic West

Leslie A. Wade

Sam Shepard ranks as one of America's most celebrated dramatists. He has written nearly 50 plays and has seen his work produced across the nation, in venues ranging from Greenwich Village coffee shops to regional professional and community theatres, from college campuses to commercial Broadway houses. His plays are regularly anthologized, and theatre professors teach Sam Shepard as a canonical American author. Outside of his stage work, he has achieved fame as an actor, writer, and director in the film industry. With a career that now spans nearly 40 years, Sam Shepard has gained the critical regard, media attention, and iconic status enjoyed by only a rare few in American theatre.

Throughout his career Shepard has amassed numerous grants, prizes, fellowships, and awards, including the Cannes *Palme d'Or* and the Pulitzer Prize. He has received abundant popular praise and critical adulation, revered by one scholar as "after all the most original and vital playwright of our age" (Rosen 1993: 1). While the assessment of Shepard's standing may evidence occasional hyperbole, there can be little doubt that he has spoken in a compelling way to American theatre audiences, and that his plays have found deep resonance in the nation's cultural imagination. Wynn Handman, artistic director of the American Place Theatre, once described Shepard as "a conduit that digs down into the American soil and what flows out of him is what we're all about" (qtd. in Kroll, Guthrie, and Huck 1985: 71).

This chapter both recounts and investigates Shepard's extraordinary success. It also speculates that the acclaim and popularity of his plays owe much to the strong evocations of America found in his works, images of the nation centrally informed by the history and mythology of the American West.[1] No other playwright has so consistently utilized Western locales, characters, and imagery for such wide and popular appeal. Given this strong regional inflection, however, Shepard's regard as an American writer invites questions of emphasis and empowerment. No doubt the

American experience has taken its form and complexion from a multitude of stories, struggles, and accomplishments, involving many regions, groups, and historical periods (that is, Shepard's America is not that of the twentieth-century immigrant experience). Shepard's work thus begs investigation as to why Shepard rose to fame in the time that he did, and why he has been regarded as the most American of our contemporary playwrights.

What follows is an examination of Shepard as a cultural phenomenon, one implicated in an ongoing cultural battle over the control and deployment of national identity and imagery. Benedict Anderson's influential work *Imagined Communities* (1983) explains how community bonds are created and secured, often enforced through imagined, arbitrary, or constructed belief systems. Simon During corroborates this view and underscores that nations have a "battery" of aesthetic forms and practices that function to consolidate group identity (1990: 138). Often embedded in national narratives are powerful ideological subtexts bearing upon rights, privileges, and measures of belonging. From the Vietnam era to the present – the span of Shepard's career – the United States has undergone a protracted culture war, a contest over the imagery and vision that defines the status of citizens and the nature of American community. This chapter situates Shepard in this context, and while this analysis touches upon the early stages of Shepard's career, it primarily focuses upon his work in the early 1980s, specifically his play *True West*, when Shepard's renown was nearing its peak. The essay explores how Shepard's work participated in the cultural contestation of this period in American history when the Western mythos (and its attendant ideology) was revived with great force and success.

Perhaps no other phenomenon in United States history has generated more storied events and characters than the settling of the West, and without question many have invoked and rallied around these narratives for inspiration and assurance. Western imagery has been ubiquitous in both literary and visual representations, from Buffalo Bill road shows to Louis L'Amour novels to Marlboro cigarette ads. Personalities such as Randolph Scott and John Wayne made careers of their cowboy images. While the mythos of the West has recently come under criticism and often censure – for example, Clint Eastwood's film *The Unforgiven* contests the nobility of the cowboy – imagery of the Wild West remains potent. Following the assault of 9/11, President George W. Bush evoked gunslinger rhetoric by identifying Osama bin Laden as an outlaw "wanted dead or alive." The president's frequent appearance in a cowboy hat works to assuage the fears of the nation, revealing the president as an American of courage, dependability, and resolve, attributes associated with the loner cowboy fighting evil.

The West has not only offered storytellers strong images and characters, it has often functioned as a powerful ideological device, a symbol of America (and the idea of America) itself. Ralph Waldo Emerson spoke of the West in enthusiastic, almost visionary terms, declaring: "the new yet unapproachable America I have found in the West" (qtd. in Bercovitch 1978: 183). The West is in part geography and topography, but perhaps more important is its symbolic dimension. While early settlers literally moved westward, from the Atlantic to the Pacific, the geographical phenomenon brought strong cultural effects. In his famous 1903 lecture, noted historian Frederick Jackson Turner emphasized the Western frontier as "the most rapid and effective line of Americanization" (1920: 3). In short, westward expansion acted as a great leveler, naturalizing the large numbers of immigrants coming into the United States. The West gained immense associative value, as a place and a state of being, which promised cherished rewards – freedom, opportunity, and the open range, where an individual could always begin anew. In addition, it has long possessed a powerful hold on the American imagination, one that has mandated the "manifest destiny" of exploration and settlement.

Recent history has, however, reevaluated the achievement of westward expansion. The darker features of the American West include the widespread slaughter of Native Americans, the despoiling of natural resources, and a lawlessness favoring the use of violence and might. The American West has consequently assumed a paradoxical status: inspiring some, troubling others. What bears emphasis is not just the actual or embellished history of the West, but rather how the West has been pressed into service, as a constellation of attitudes and outlooks affirming American exceptionalism and specific features (chiefly masculine) of an American character. In short, the West has been saddled with considerable ideological baggage. It has come to represent a range of values: industriousness, taciturn emotion, self-reliance, and individualism. However, the West also includes a problematic subset of contradictions; it has long encouraged a suspicion of government, education, and woman. Reflecting a fundamental national dispute between libertarian and communitarian positions, the West has privileged individualism and has thus triggered debate on a number of divisive issues, including gender, race, social obligation, and economic justice. Playwright Tony Kushner, author of *Angels in America*, has in fact assailed this view of American character, indicting individualism as a deleterious national trait, for which "Americans pay high prices" (1996: 149). In sum, the West on a basic level has become an ideological flashpoint and a focal point of contention between conflicting parties seeking control of the national dialogue.

Hailed as "the poet laureate of the American West" (Coe 1980: 122), Shepard developed an early understanding of the Western sensibility that involved a blending of actual experience and myth. Though born in Illinois, Shepard grew up on a ranch in Duarte, California, and had personal experience with the physical labor of ranching and raising livestock.[2] However, as Shepard himself would admit, much of his knowledge of the West came through movies and TV. His glamorized (and rather ahistorical) view of cowboy life was once disclosed in an interview in which he acknowledged his admiration for those 16- or 17-year-old "guys" who "took on this entire country, and didn't have any real rules. Just moving cattle from Texas to Kansas City, from the North to the South, or wherever it was" (qtd. in Chubb et al. 1981: 190). Shepard's teenage years were often difficult for the restless and combative youth, and he found inspiration and comfort in the Western code of freedom and self-direction. According to John Clum, this influence was profound, as Shepard "built his persona" upon the cowboy ideal (2002: 173).

One of the most fascinating aspects of Shepard's career concerns his progress from the Greenwich Village avant-garde in the 1960s to his status as media icon in the 1980s. While Shepard has always infused his plays with characters, language, energy, and emotion that bespeak the West, he has deployed these elements differently in the successive stages of his career, for various personal, creative, and rhetorical ends.

Eager to leave Duarte and the troubled relationship with his father, Shepard came to New York in his late teens and began playwriting in the early foment of the off-off-Broadway movement. He inaugurated his career with two one-act plays at Theatre Genesis, *The Rock Garden* and *Cowboys* (1964). In the later work, Shepard presents the anarchic antics of two youthful characters acting out the cowboy roles of "Mel" and "Clem" in a bleak, inhospitable urban realm. The meandering work highlights playfulness and energetic expenditure. What one chiefly sees in this and other of Shepard's early efforts is a restless adolescent energy and an exuberant defiance of authority.

In both his plays and his personal life, Shepard at this time sought space free from convention and patriarchal demands. His early years in Manhattan were in fact quite chaotic and impulsive. He indulged in the experimentation common to the time, in regards to both sex and drugs. Shepard recounts playing games of "cowboy and Indians" amid the midtown traffic. However, Shepard's activities, which included performing as a musician, threw him into the midst of a very vital and creative environment, and he became a part of the burgeoning counterculture scene, meeting experimental artists from a wide array of fields.

While Shepard's early plays channeled the personal angst of the young writer, they also spoke to the mood of the times, finding favor with the counterculture and making Shepard a celebrity of the avant-garde. Shepard frequently used Western motifs in these works. *The Holy Ghostly* (1969) and *Operation Sidewinder* (1970) both utilize Native American characters as counterpoints to establishment culture. Representing seekers and questioners, Western characters appear prominently in *Cowboy Mouth* (1971) and *Mad Dog Blues* (1971). Perhaps Shepard's most intriguing use of such material came in *The Unseen Hand* (1969), a piece with strong anti-authority themes, in which an old-time cowboy Blue Morphan is visited by gunslingers – Cisco and Sycamore – and the space freak Willie, who struggles to free himself from the mind-control of his planet's leaders.

In such works Shepard used Western motifs to celebrate freedom and to efface social constraints. In these plays cowboys act as embodiments of liberation. Embracing the attitudes of such works as Herbert Marcuse's *Eros and Civilization*, the youth culture welcomed transgressive art and its challenge to authority. Counterculture theatre contested establishment values and the patriarchal, corporate world – fostered by the conformist ethos of the 1950s – that grew into the bureaucratic establishment of the 1960s. It was this establishment that endorsed the war in Vietnam and sought the suppression of liberation politics.

While Shepard discovered that his high-energy, iconoclastic plays were welcomed by the counterculture and brought him renown, he did not share in the communal sensibility of the 1960s. His main interest was freedom and the defiance of restraint. He did not turn to Maoism or Marxism and did not embrace flower power. Shepard reveled in the liberation but found no group solidarity. In fact, Shepard soon grew exhausted and aggrieved with the counterculture scene and in 1971 relocated to England.

Following Shepard's off-off-Broadway adventure the playwright went into a period of retreat and introspection and sought to investigate who he was as an artist and as an individual. His stay in England proved pivotal for the writer, as the experience heightened his notion of cultural difference and illuminated his sense of his own American heritage. In London he wrote a number of important works, including *The Tooth of Crime* (1972), *Geography of a Horse Dreamer* (1974), and *Action* (1974). All of these works deal with dislocation and the attempt to find existential and cultural moorings. *Action* is set in an ambiguous frontier environment where survival is in doubt. *Geography of a Horse Dreamer* focuses upon a Wyoming sheep rancher, Cody, who has been kidnapped by London hoodlums; he is ultimately saved by the unexpected arrival of his Wild West brothers, who enter with six-guns blasting. Cody's fear of displacement and dispossession parallel the playwright's own outlook at the time, as he soon desired to return to the United States and its more familiar environment. Nonetheless, these years were highly influential in Shepard's career, as he not only advanced as a dramatic craftsman but experienced considerable reflection upon his American roots and his purpose as a writer.

When Shepard returned home, the United States was undergoing a profound self-examination that questioned its position in the world, its outlook and values, and its internal bonds of connection. Historians have described the 1970s as a time of cultural introspection following the turmoil of Vietnam and the cynicism of Watergate. One seismic change in these years concerned the issue of cultural identity, as many sought to explore definitions that diminished the importance of nationalist affiliation. During these years, characterized by one critic as "the decade of the ethnics" (Novak 1971: 70), the country witnessed an explosion of subgroup consciousness, as many looked to define themselves outside of nationalist categories. Various efforts in rights advocacy that had begun in the 1960s, such as the civil rights and women's liberation movements, spurred a general rise in cultural awareness, bringing increased attention and emphasis to identities based not on any concept of national affiliation but according to categories of race, gender, sexual preference, region, religion, and ethnicity. It was during these years that American culture, including the academy and the theatre, began to explore visions of a multicultural rather than an assimilationist America. In this era of identity politics, the metaphor of the melting pot gave way to images of the salad bowl, gumbo, and kaleidoscope.

Seen by some critics as evidence of a cultural unraveling, this challenge to national identity and its determination was accompanied by a host of political, social, and economic matters that highlighted a diminished sense of the nation's might, purpose, and self-regard. In addition to the ignominious retreat from Vietnam and the resignation of an American president, the country during the 1970s witnessed a severe recession attending the 1973 OPEC oil embargo. It also saw a steep decline in national economic productivity and experienced a jobless rate not seen since the end of World War II. In his book *The Lean Years* (1980), Richard Barnett described this time in terms of depletion and scarcity. As the decade neared its end, President Carter labored to rally the country from its dispirited mood, what Carter characterized as a "national malaise." However, the beleaguered state of the country was further exacerbated by the seizure of the United States embassy in Teheran, a protracted event that seemed to emblematize the incapacitated national condition.

If one views the 1980 election as a referendum on the direction of the country and a response to an assailed national identity, the election of Ronald Reagan signaled a new era in the life of the nation that would have profound political and social effect. The Reagan revolution brought a new attitude toward governmental social policy and a renewed vigor to American exceptionalism. The 1980s exhibited something of a backlash against the liberal social and political postures of prior years. In terms of policy, Reagan immediately sought to scale back the size of American government and the Great Society programs inaugurated in the Johnson administration. Reagan advocated massive tax cuts and limited governmental spending. Budget Director David Stockman explained this enterprise as a "frontal assault on the welfare state" (qtd. in Karp 1988: 129).

Aside from its policy stratagems and budgetary programs, the Reagan era revivified Western imagery and its frontier codes. Along with such imagery came postures and pronouncements that echoed a Western sensibility. While Carter had appeared as a bookish and ineffectual national leader, Reagan stood as a resolute and robust outdoorsman, an impression furthered by many publicity photos of Reagan riding his horse on his California ranch. Reagan advocated a rugged individualism and an open-range attitude to the market economy. His tough-minded rhetoric was often that of the gunslinger, and his willingness to flex American muscle was evidenced in international relations, particularly with the Soviet Union, Grenada, and Nicaragua.

Political writer Kevin Phillips explains Reagan's rise in popularity (and the valuation of Western imagery) not just in political but in demographic terms. The rise of Republican politics in the 1980s corresponded to population shifts attending the rise of the Sunbelt states of the South and Southwest. For Phillips, this demographic change accounted for a shift in cultural taste; interest shifted from the counterculture's Woodstock to Country and Western's Grand Old Opry (1981: xv). This transition in national sensibility privileged Western images and icons that in turn infiltrated many aspects of popular culture. In the mid-1980s the homespun Texas humor of *Greater Tuna* played widely in theatres across the nation. This time saw the rise of Willie Nelson's "Farm Aid" concerts and a number of save-the-farm films, including *Places in the Heart* and *Country*, a film that featured Shepard himself. Country music enjoyed a new cachet during this time, and many bars and dance halls welcomed the newest fad in honky-tonk entertainment: the mechanical bull.

Shepard's rise to popularity in the 1980s must be seen in light of this shift in national mood and the renewed valuation of the Western ethic. Several key aspects of Shepard's life and work in the 1970s prepared the way for what would become his ascent as a great American playwright. After his time in London, Shepard returned to California, leased a small ranch, and began participating in local rodeo events. He largely disregarded New York at this time and sought production in regional theatre, chiefly the Magic Theatre in San Francisco, which would serve as a home-base for the writer. During this time Shepard valued his frontier lifestyle; he once claimed, "If I'm at home anywhere it's in the West" (qtd. in Kakutani 1984: 2.1). The West proved a recurrent theme in the plays of this time; Rabbit, for example, the central figure in *Angel City*, hails from the West and appears as an earth-affirming shaman (opposed to the soulless movie moguls of Hollywood). Another frontier loner, Henry Hackamore in *Seduced*, explores psychic limits on the very edge of civilization. In these plays Shepard used aspects of the Western persona to investigate the inner life of the artist – his inspiration, solitude, and endurance. He, moreover, explored his own regional roots as a Westerner, at a time when the nation at large was questioning its origins and identities.

Shepard's plays in these years were, however, highly elliptical, and somewhat solipsistic, self-conscious attempts to investigate his own particular nature and practice as an artist. *Angel City* (1976), *Suicide in B-Flat* (1976), and *Seduced* (1978) all deal with elusive, creative characters, sequestered from communal attachment. Shepard subsequently expressed some dissatisfaction with the introspective and experimental nature of his plays and voiced his desire to write on a broader level, one more national in scope. Shepard declared that he had been "writing for ten years in an experimental maze – poking around, fishing in the dark" (qtd. in Allen 1988: 148). It is thus illuminating that Shepard turned to one of the most conventional forms of drama, the family play. In short, Shepard sought at this time a wider audience and the means to speak on a broader level of cultural conversation. In the next years Shepard would write a series of plays that secured his fame in the American theatre. In *Curse of the Starving Class* (1977), *Buried Child* (1978), *True West* (1980), *Fool for Love* (1983), and *A Lie of the Mind* (1985), Shepard explored the American family and in so doing exposed deep-rooted aspects of the national character. In these plays the West is not just a backdrop to the action but a state of mind and a complex of values that inform the conflict and emotional upheaval of Shepard's dramatic world.

It was thus during the early and mid-1980s that Shepard began to achieve the success and notoriety he never could have anticipated in his days as a Greenwich Village experimentalist. *Buried Child* was awarded the Pulitzer Prize for Drama in 1979, and the play was soon scheduled in seasons of regional and university theatres across the country. During this time Shepard also gained attention as a film actor, performing in a range of movies that included *Days of Heaven*, *Resurrection*, *Raggedy Man*, *Frances*, and *The Right Stuff*. His work in the last film earned him an Oscar nomination for best supporting actor. Certainly Shepard's star was in its ascent. The uncanny rise to fame was fueled by a powerful alignment of forces, including the maturing of the playwright, his visibility as a movie personality, and his wish to reach a wider audience. It also owed much to the desire of the American public, who recognized in Shepard a link with the country's powerful Western past.

True West did not rank as an immediate success for the playwright. The piece was first staged at the Magic Theatre but then experienced a troubled New York premiere, as personnel and artistic problems beset the production. The play did not enjoy great attention until revived in a production by Chicago's Steppenwolf Theatre starring

Plate 13. *True West*, by Sam Shepard, Missouri Repertory Theatre. Jim Birdsall (Lee) and Mark Robbins (Austin), photo by Keith Flannery. Courtesy of the Missouri Repertory Theatre.

John Malkovich and Gary Sinise that played in New York to popular and critical acclaim. *True West* has since arguably become Shepard's signature piece, the leanest, most pointed of his full-length works. Although it did not receive the Pulitzer (as did *Buried Child*), it remains the most revived Shepard play in American theatres. It is, moreover, a vital and popular piece in the contemporary repertory and in 2000 enjoyed a highly praised Broadway revival, starring Philip Seymour Hoffman and John C. Reilly. *True West* can be seen as an essential expression of Shepard's vision, exploring the core concerns of his career: masculinity, Western identity, and the individual's stance toward communal relations.

True West is fundamentally a drama of sibling rivalry, as two brothers (Lee and Austin) occupy their mother's home while she is away on a vacation. The relationship of the brothers is clearly an uneasy one, as each has chosen a radically different life path. Austin has gone the establishment route. Ivy League-educated, he has a wife and family and enjoys a successful career as a screenwriter. Lee, conversely, is a loner, homeless and unemployed. He is oftentimes a thief and inhabits the outskirts of civilization, living months at a time in the desert. Lee's arrival is unexpected, and Austin labors to appease his brother, to maintain civility and calm. In the course of the play's action, the two jockey for position, igniting a volatile male power dynamic.

The fundamental dramatic tension begins when Lee comes between Austin and the film producer, Saul, who has been considering backing a project written by Austin. Lee, in fact, diverts Austin's project and sells Saul his own pitch, that of a contemporary Western, one that would be true to life. The tension between the brothers escalates as Lee founders at the typewriter, unable to put his ideas into script-form, and works to enlist the aid (and skills) of Austin. This struggle produces numerous accusations and confessions, finally drawing the brothers into a strange intimacy: Lee will take Austin to the desert if he will help Lee complete the screenplay. This pact, and the peculiar closeness that the brothers experience, is disrupted by the mother's untimely return.

One of the key elements of *True West*'s dramatic world is its pervasive uncertainty. The brothers suffer from deep anxieties regarding the direction and meaning of their lives. Both have a longing for assurances, for confirmation. On one level the brothers' tentative condition stems from the profound lack of parental authority. As the ending of the play reveals, the mother figure is disconnected and delusional, believing that Picasso will be appearing at the local art museum. She proves herself completely unwilling and unable to quell the outbreak of violence at the play's conclusion. The father of the play (off-stage and unseen) also proves ineffective and withdrawn, having retreated to live in alcoholic isolation in the desert. One of the play's most moving moments comes when Austin tells Lee of visiting the father: "all he did was play Al Jolson records and spit at me" (39).

The parental dysfunction in the play signals a wider existential unease for the brothers, neither of whom feels comfortably situated in his life. Both confess a want of control and a strong desire for alternative possibilities. Lee tells of visiting a nearby neighborhood and secretly looking into the kitchen of an affluent home: "Like a paradise. . . . Warm yellow lights. Mexican tile all around. Copper pots hangin' over the stove. . . . Kinda' place you wish you sorta' grew up in, ya' know" (12). Lee recounts episodes of deprivation in his life as a drifter and later rails at his mother, "I'm tired of eatin' outa' my bare hands" (56). In contrast, Austin suffers the numbing effects of middle-class accumulation. Lee chides his brother over the comfort of his lifestyle and asks: "What's the toughest part? Deciding whether to jog or play tennis?" (25). In fact, as the play nears its end, Austin voices a readiness to renounce his lifestyle and to jettison his job and family. He begins to emulate his brother; he goes into the night and steals scores of toasters from his neighbors. He finally exclaims: "There's nothin' real down here, Lee! Least of all me" (49).

It is against this backdrop of drift and vacuity that Shepard deploys various motifs of the West. The title of the play references a Western-oriented pulp magazine of that name, a choice that may initially suggest an attitude toward the West that is more parody than endorsement. But the play's representations of the West are multiple and prismatic, and while the drama empties some motifs of value, others are revalidated.

On one level the play targets the present-day West, that of contemporary suburbia and the allure of Southern California. This is the version of American luxury popularized after World War II when ranch homes were proliferating and advertisers promoted the wonders of dishwashers, vacuum cleaners, and sundry appliances. It is telling that the bulk of the play's action occurs in the kitchen of the home (which is summarily destroyed). This sort of West is seen as enervating, choked by conformity and consumerism. Austin keeps thinking he is back in the 1950s and finds himself frightened by this world's lack of anything substantive: "Wandering down streets I thought I recognized that turn out to be replicas of streets I remember. . . . Streets I can't tell if I lived on or saw in a postcard" (49). Coupled with the suburbia image is another contemporary version of the West, represented by Saul, the Hollywood producer. Saul chiefly embodies the business aspect of the film industry, and when he reverses his commitment to Austin the audience understands that the producer operates less by ethical standards than expediency. Saul thus reveals the hollow promise of stardom and discloses the easy betrayal of relationships and ideals. Saul's West is that of tinsel and hype.

Shepard's dramatization becomes less schematic and more complicated when the West of American movies enters the play. On one level American movie making is derided as action-driven entertainment for the masses, as Lee echoes Saul, "Leave the films to the French" (28). This patronizing attitude colors Austin's comments on Lee's project, which involves a two-man chase scene across the Texas panhandle. Austin ridicules the contrivances of this plot and accuses Lee of being out of touch. According to Austin, the Western is a dead genre.

Despite Austin's pejorative assessment, the Western (and its contrivances) is not censured in the play but rather retains an evocative and efficacious power. Lee specifically recalls the film *Lonely Are the Brave*, starring Kirk Douglas, in which, as Lee notes, "the man dies for the love of his horse" (18). While this sequence plays as a comic moment, highlighting the sentimental manipulation of the film, the exchange is also somewhat poignant. Lee reminds Austin and Saul of the horse's screaming, the animal's execution, and the powerful sense of loss conveyed when Douglas closes his eyes. Given the fractious relationship of the brothers and the shady dealings of the movie producer, this moment introduces a note of solemnity, a nobility of feeling and action.

Clearly for Austin, his middle-class existence seems profoundly devoid of any ennobled activity or emotion. In *West of Everything*, Jane Thompkins suggests that the central appeal of the Western genre comes from its dramatization of the "fully saturated moment" in which the hero is put to an extreme test and consequently experiences a unity of thought and deed, self and environment (1992: 14). Lee's life in the desert is no noble adventure but the result of desperation and a deficiency of social skills. Still, his casual knowledge of the Mojave and the San Gabriels, along with his evocation of the Texas panhandle (and familiarity with goose-neck trailers), suggests an earthy vitality and a "saturated" kind of experience. This element is what Saul emphasizes when he tells Austin that he is backing his brother's project: "It has the ring of truth. . . . Something about the land" (35). Finally, it is this sort of experience, modeled in the Western, which tantalizes Austin when he confesses his willingness to surrender the comforts of his position and join Lee in a desert life.

Without question *True West* admits the hackneyed conventions of the West, how it has been propagated by pulp novels and B-movies. And many of Shepard's plays such as *Mad Dog Blues* have parodied Western imagery in postmodern pastiche. However, even as *True West* acknowledges and exposes the contrivances of the Western stereotypes, the play refuses to evacuate the Western ideal. Numerous critics have noted this aspect of Shepard's work and identify the strands of affirmation that operate amidst ironic citation. In his analysis of the cowboys in *The Unseen Hand*, David DeRose, for instance, writes that the figures embody "an authentic and potentially formidable force" (1992: 46). What is, perhaps, most vital to the brothers in *True West* (and to Shepard himself) is not so much the movie images or the cowboy trappings but the embedded values and codes of the West. Such codes model strength, competitive resolve, self-reliance, and assurance of purpose – in short, the Western displays the pattern for American manhood.

If one brings biographical matter to an analysis of the play, Shepard's interviews, personal attitudes, and particular behavior choices corroborate a valorization of the Western ethos. He has attempted to remain close to a frontier-like lifestyle and has for many years worked on raising and training horses. Shepard has participated in rodeo events and has admitted liking the danger of the event. He has also confessed to having at one time carried a handgun. And he has occasionally spoken from a kind of libertarian viewpoint, reproaching the "government" for bringing the demise of "horse culture" (qtd. in Sessums 1988: 78).

Shepard has also been party to his own mythology as he has often performed in frontier-ethic films. Indeed, Terrence Malick, director of *Days of Heaven*, cast Shepard for his looks and his horsemanship. His breakthrough performance as Sam Yeager in

The Right Stuff saw Shepard play a modern-day cowboy, a test pilot expanding the bounds of the next frontier. Critics have observed that Shepard recalls something of the John Ford Western classics, and his persona has invited comparison to Gary Cooper, John Wayne, and Audie Murphy.

The Western outlook seems deeply ingrained in Shepard's dramatic and personal vision. He has often described the process of playwriting in cowboy terms, likening it to taming a horse or performing in a rodeo. The imagery he employs in a 1983 interview is especially revealing: "I feel like there are territories within us that are totally unknown.... Huge, unknown territories.... If you don't enter those areas that are deeply mysterious and dangerous, then you're not doing anything so far as I can tell" (qtd. in Lippman 1983: 6). In sum, Shepard views the imagination as a kind of dangerous frontier, a territory to be explored and tamed by the venturesome artist/cowboy.

Much of the recent Shepard criticism has taken the playwright to task for his Western outlook and postures. Critics have focused on the subtextual ideologies of his plays and have examined how his understanding of the West evidences problematic aspects of masculinity and communal relations. In this light the cowboy appears as a decidedly asocial creature, out of step with the contemporary complexities of a pluralistic America. Among the troubling features of the Western hero and his code of masculinity is his insistence on dominance, mastery over himself, the environment, and those around him. *True West* on a fundamental level dramatizes the problematic aspect of a Western mentality, and the play's action finally leads to a violent assertion of dominance. Richard Slotkin has identified violence as a pernicious aspect of the Western outlook. In *Fatal Environment* (1985) he explains how the frontier not only tolerated but also glorified violence, as a necessary regenerative step in the conquest of a hostile environment.

Along with the affirmation of violence, the Western ethic privileges solitude over community, indicating a reluctance or fear of engaging with or yielding to any sort of "other." The solitary outlook fosters the rugged individualism that informs the cowboy sensibility. The outlook also contributes to sexist attitudes and fear of intimate involvement. As Carla McDonough observes, women reside "at the margins" in Shepard's plays (1995: 65). *True West* confirms this point. Austin's wife is mentioned but never seen; Lee attempts to call a woman in Bakersfield but cannot remember her last name; and the mother appears only as an incidental character. Shepard's view of gender has been criticized as antiquated, relegating women to a secondary status. His commitment to the Western ethic, finally, privileges a strong male outlook and devalues community and empathetic involvement.

The ending of *True West* is a despairing one. The buffoonish mother steps aside as Austin rails at his brother for reneging on their deal. He attempts to stop Lee from exiting, choking him with a phone cord, and throwing him to the floor. When Lee rises, he peers at Austin with murderous rage. The stage darkens and a bleached light – suggestive of desert moonlight – momentarily illuminates the brothers, indicating their psychic remove to the primal frontier.

The brothers in this play ultimately find nothing that would qualify as a "true" West. They are enchanted by its mythic promise of committed experience, independence, and mastery over self, others, and the environment. In reality, the allure leads only to violent self-assertion and isolation. If anything the ending of the play dramatizes the failure of the frontier mentality. The brothers savage the family home and finally cannot sustain their momentary cooperation and intimacy. Lee and Austin face off, as though in a duel – and in this realm, only one man can be left standing.

One would be incorrect to ascribe a cynical outlook to Shepard's play. *True West* is not simply postmodern parody, parading empty and often-repeated images of the West. The attitudes of the frontier energize the brothers and engender a longing for fullness and the vitality that the West has long offered Americans. And yet the drama provides no outright, uncomplicated endorsement of the West. It admits the clichés surrounding the myth. Still, it presents the ideal of the West as a worthy principle to uphold, the vestige of a former time that makes the present seem wanting in comparison. In this aspect Shepard's drama performs a kind of nationalistic service. Seamus Deane has written how nationalistic literatures frequently deride the present as fallen "from a state of bliss" into a "modern condition of alienation" (1993: 9). Such works glorify the past and encourage a reverential attitude toward idealized former times (and their particular ideological stances).

In this regard, one can understand Shepard's rise to popularity in the 1980s, specifically given that *True West*'s critique of contemporary America and its fascination with a more authentic Western past spoke to a broad hunger in the public imagination. Certainly the rise of Ronald Reagan during these years had much to do with a profound cultural nostalgia. Reagan championed the pioneer ethic of self-reliance, open markets, deregulation, and quick use of physical force. His persona spoke to a populace fatigued with national impotence on the global stage, economic insecurity, and protracted cultural battles over identity and belonging. For many the images and values of the West promised a return or an evocation of a better time in America, one in which the American character found its fullest realization.

If one views the 1980s in terms of a national culture war, with the control of symbol and ideology at stake, images of the West were upheld as images of the nation at large. In short, the West served as a synecdoche for America itself. Werner Sollors remarked that the 1970s had seen "the end of assimilationist hope" (1986: 20); it was during this time that the national consensus came under challenge and national categories of identity gave way to multicultural views and new stories of American experience. However, the Reagan era worked to reverse (or obscure) this change, fostering a kind of purification of memory. On one level the Reagan administration supported legislation unfriendly to minorities; it evinced resistance before the equal rights amendment and civil rights legislation. On another level, the Reagan outlook diminished the importance of those whose narratives did not accord with the American frontier story. Attention turned to an American image that predated the Vietnam War and the multicultural nation that followed. As a result, Sam Shepard's

Western-inflected dramas translated into fundamental American dramas (more so than, for instance, the plays of Adrienne Kennedy, Marsha Norman, or A. R. Gurney). It is telling that Shepard was grouped with certain iconic figures of American culture, such as Woody Guthrie and John Steinbeck, whose works represent a pioneer outlook and a white rural past. One may contend that Shepard's rising acclaim in the 1980s was not just the result of sustained personal creative effort, but that the images and outlooks dramatized in his plays (and by his image on screen) tapped into a potent bedrock of national imagery, reflecting the cultural nostalgia of the 1980s and its appetite for long-held attitudes toward American character and promise.

Given Shepard's renown as a cowboy playwright of high-testosterone drama, his shift in dramatic outlook following the writing of *True West* merits mention. In both *Fool for Love* and *A Lie of the Mind* the playwright attempted an analysis and critique of the male psyche and its inclination to violence. And following these works Shepard went into something of a professional hiatus, not producing another play for six years. When he emerged from this retreat in the early 1990s his work exhibited a suspicion of the frontier ethic that had long infused his vision.[3]

Spurred by his distaste with the public celebration of the 1991 Gulf War and its antiseptic satellite TV presentation, Shepard wrote *States of Shock* (1991), a stridently anti-war play that censures the valuation of aggression and conquest. He followed this one-act with the full-length piece *Simpatico* (1994), a play concerning duplicity in the horse-breeding business (the work drew only a lukewarm response from audiences and critics). In *Simpatico* Shepard again dealt with competing, dysfunctional males and the power of the Western ethos. He, however, introduced a new element into his writing seen in the character Simms, who retreats from revenge and models an attitude of acceptance and reconciliation. During the end of the twentieth century the playwright's output was limited, producing just two plays, *Eyes for Consuela* (1998) and *The Late Henry Moss* (2000), both of which continued Shepard's meditative turn and distance from machismo postures. However, Shepard's plays during the 1990s drew little popular favor or critical acclaim, and the writer's profile in the American theatre has traversed into eclipse. Shepard's reputation remains connected to his earlier plays, those fueled by aggression and the lure of Western manhood.

Just prior to the second Iraqi conflict, commentator Bill Moyers on an installment of his PBS series *Now* reproached those who flaunt images of the American flag for partisan purposes, claiming instead that the flag belonged to all citizens, regardless of their attitude toward the war. He summarily pinned a small flag to his lapel as a gesture of recuperation. Moyers's act signifies that the control and deployment of national imagery remains a vital, fervently contested issue. In fact, given early twenty-first century global threats and national insecurity, dispute over the management of national imagery may only intensify. It is thus not surprising that Western icons and outlooks have once again found new life. Despite Austin's assertion that the West is a "dead issue" (35), its ethic and imagery have returned in a powerful way to the cultural and political life of the United States. In the crisis and anxiety of the early twentieth-first century, President Bush has invoked the frontier outlook and adopted a cowboy tone and demeanor, often shown laboring on his Texas ranch (his contributors are accorded the honorary designations of "rangers" and "pioneers"). His administration has reintroduced many of the policies and postures of the Reagan era, espousing resolve and self-reliance. Shepard's later work cautions against this all-too-enthusiastic embrace of the Western ethos. As the nation heads into the future, the easy recollection of a nineteenth-century point of view begs scrutiny and question. It is safe to assume, however, that the American West will continue to energize its advocates and detractors, and to act as a touchstone in the national dialogue on American identity, values, and purpose.

NOTES

1. For a fuller and more detailed discussion of how these issues inform Shepard's career, see my book, *Sam Shepard and the American Theatre* (Westport, CT: Praeger, 1997).
2. For biographical information on Shepard, see Vivian Patraka and Marc Seigel, *Sam Shepard* (Boise, ID: Boise State University Press, 1985); Martin Tucker, *Sam Shepard* (New York: Continuum, 1992); Ellen Oumano, *Sam Shepard: The Life and Work of an American Dreamer* (New York: St. Martin's, 1986); and Don Shewey, *Sam Shepard* (New York: Dell, 1985).
3. For examination of Shepard's plays in the 1990s, see my essay, "*States of Shock, Simpatico,* and *Eyes for Consuela*: Shepard's Plays of the 1990s," in Matthew Roudané (ed.), *The Cambridge Companion to Sam Shepard* (Cambridge: Cambridge University Press, 2002).

BIBLIOGRAPHY

Allen, J. (1988). "The Man on the High Horse." *Esquire* (November): 141–4, 146, 148, 150–1.

Anderson, B. (1983). *Imagined Communities*. London: Verso.

Barnett, R. (1980). *The Lean Years*. New York: Simon and Schuster.

Bercovitch, S. (1978). *The American Jeremiad*. Madison: University of Wisconsin Press.

Chubb, K. and the editors of *Theatre Quarterly* (1981). "Metaphors, Mad Dogs, and Old Time Cowboys." In Bonnie Marranca (ed.), *American Dreams: The Imagination of Sam Shepard*. New York: Performing Arts Journal Publications, 187–209.

Clum, J. (2002). "The Classic Western and Sam Shepard's Family Sagas." In Matthew Roudané (ed.), *The Cambridge Companion to Sam Shepard*. Cambridge: Cambridge University Press, 171–88.

Coe, R. (1980). "Saga of Sam Shepard." *New York Times Magazine*, November 23: 56–9, 118, 120, 122, 124.

Deane, S. (1993). "Introduction." In Terry Eagleton, Frederic Jameson, and Edward W. Said, *Nationalism, Colonialism, and Literature*. Minneapolis: University of Minnesota Press.

DeRose, D. J. (1992). *Sam Shepard*. New York: Twayne.

During, S. (1990). "Literature: Nationalism's Other? The Case for Revision." In Homi K. Bhaba (ed.), *Nation and Narration*. New York: Routledge, 138–54.

Kakutani, M. (1984). "Myths, Dreams, Realities: Sam Shepard's America." *New York Times*, January 29, Sec. 2: 1, 26–8.

Karp, W. (1988). *Liberty Under Siege: American Politics, 1976–1988*. New York: Henry Holt.

Kroll, J., Guthrie, C., and Huck, J. (1985). "Who's That Tall Dark Stranger?" *Newsweek*, November 11: 68–74.

Kushner, T. (1996). "Afterword." In *Angels in America, Part Two: Perestroika*. New York: Theatre Communications Group.

Lippman, A. (1983). "Interview: A Conversation with Sam Shepard." *Harvard Advocate* 117, 1: 2–6, 44–6.

McDonough, C. J. (1995). "The Politics of Stage Space: Women and Male Identity in Sam Shepard's Family Plays." *Journal of Dramatic Theory and Criticism*, 9, 2: 65–83.

Marcuse, H. (1974). *Eros and Civilization*. Boston: Beacon Press.

Novak, M. (1971). *The Rise of the Unmeltable Ethnics*. New York: Macmillan.

Phillips, K. P. (1981). *Post-Conservative America*. New York: Random House.

Rosen, C. (1993). "Emotional Territory: An Interview with Sam Shepard." *Modern Drama* 36, 1: 1–11.

Savran, D. (1998). *Taking It Like a Man: White Masculinity, Masochism, and Contemporary American Culture*. Princeton, NJ: Princeton University Press.

Sessums, K. (1988). "Geography of a Horse Dreamer." *Interview* (September): 79–81, 85–6.

Shepard, S. (1986). *True West*. In *Seven Plays*. New York: Bantam Books.

Slotkin, R. (1985). *Fatal Environment*. New York: Athenaeum.

Sollors, W. (1986). *Beyond Ethnicity*. Oxford: Oxford University Press.

Thompkins, J. (1992). *West of Everything*. New York: Oxford University Press.

Turner, F. J. (1920). *The Frontier in American History*. New York: Henry Holt.

Williams, M. (1997). "Nowhere Man and the Twentieth-Century Cowboy: Images of Identity in Sam Shepard's *True West*." *Modern Drama* 40: 57–73.

19

Staging the Binary: Asian American Theatre in the Late Twentieth Century

Daphne Lei

The success of playwright David Henry Hwang's (b. 1957) *M. Butterfly* on Broadway in 1989 appears to have finally placed Asian American theatre on the United States theatrical map. Asian American theatre has emerged as one of the major components in constituting a multicultural curriculum, which can be said to be both a facsimile of diversity and an illusion of democracy and equality. Including *M. Butterfly* in the theatre curriculum is a symbolic gesture, a first step toward multiculturalism. Ironically, *M. Butterfly*, a story of love and deceit, gender bending, and the stereotyping of the Asian other known as "Orientalism," dramatizes the relationship between a French diplomat and a Chinese opera singer; it therefore, at least on the level of plot, concerns neither Americans nor Asian Americans. Why, then, is *M. Butterfly* considered an "Asian American" play? Perhaps because the author is one of the most important American playwrights of Asian descent, it can certainly be argued that authorship alone qualifies *M. Butterfly* as belonging within this ethnic genre. However, the general conception of *M. Butterfly* as a representative Asian American play challenges the definition of "Asian American theatre" and implies a blurring of distinctions between Asian and Asian American, and between white Europeans and white Americans. That is to say, the Chinese opera singer in the play represents "American-born Asian," while the white Europeans represent all of "white America." Taken together, the protagonists in Hwang's drama represent both halves of the binary Asian American. This conflation of representative figures acting as surrogates for the term "Asian American" also implies that, as a genre, Asian American theatre is reduced to a binary system of Asian versus American. No doubt numerous Asian American plays deal with the binary confrontation, but limiting the definition of the genre to this system alone also suggests a desire to regulate the genre that is still nascent and rather unstable. Certain questions can be raised: Does this desire for binaries come from within or without the Asian American theatre community? Does this binary system help to enrich the genre or rather stultify it by reducing its complexity to an either/or option that particularly contradicts the emergence of its complexity in light of multiculturalism and globalization?

In this chapter I examine several dramatic works that consider the struggle and survival in the binary system, and some other works that express the hope of eradicating the binary idea, creating instead a different and more complex description of "Asian American." I assert that the creation of the binary, and the subsequent efforts to cut against the grain of its simplifying representations, is an enlightened trajectory of Asian American theatre, one that has surfaced during the last decades of the twentieth century. After examining plays that reinforce the binary system, I consider whether the emphasis on binaries has contributed to making Asian American theatre an "ethnic" or "minority" theatre within American multicultural theatre. Although the distinction between binary and non-binary dramas is not strictly chronological, plays from the first period of Asian American drama's popularity tend to deal with the "either/or" choice (having to choose being either Asian or American, or having to position oneself on either side of the binary system), while later plays appear to embrace a different representation of identity, establishing an alternative "neither/nor" situation and implying an avoidance of ethnic positioning – whether by choice or by force.

Defining "Asian American" and Asian American Theatre

In her book *Performing Asian America: Race and Ethnicity on the Contemporary Stage*, Josephine Lee draws attention to African American scholar and social critic W. E. B. Du Bois and his well-known 1926 definition of "Negro theatre" (1997: 8) (see chapter 7). According to Du Bois, African American theatre is "about us," "by us," "for us," and "near us." Although this model was likely suitable for small-scale ethnic theatres during the early twentieth century, it presents difficulties in mid- to late twentieth-century dramas during what has been termed the age of globalization. Still, Du Bois's definition provokes imaginative configurations for Asian American theatre, raising the fundamental question: Who and what is "us," and who and what defines Asian American?

Asian Americans are most commonly identified as Americans of Asian ancestry. Nevertheless, further examination challenges this simplified definition. Is "ancestry" defined by birth or naturalized citizenry? Is citizenry described by birthright or is it citizenry established by permanent residency? Can long-time illegal residents qualify? What about recent legal immigrants to the United States, euphemistically termed "FOB," or "fresh off the boat" (which is also the title of a David Henry Hwang play to be discussed shortly)? These inquiries are important in Asian American theatre, no doubt because in many plays the representations of Asian American rely on the binary system: Asian vs. American, us vs. them. Several Asian American dramas defend the complexity of the "Asian" by asserting that Asians are more than merely Chinese and Japanese, that not all "Orientals" look alike, and that there is no "pan-Asian" overarching ethnicity. However, in some instances during the same dramas, the representation of "American" becomes a homogeneous ethnicity: white Americans symbolize power and authority and have therefore the status of "oppressor" and "enemy." The "us vs. them" ideology inevitably obviates the complexity for both groups. As a result, the struggle in the binary system and the concomitant search for an identity (either Asian or American) are among the most common themes in Asian American plays.

Identity formations within the binary system are not quite the notion of what Richard Schechner terms the "culture of choice." According to Schechner,

> people will wish to celebrate their cultural specificity, but increasingly that will be a choice rather than something into which you are simply born automatically... we will select what elements of what cultures we want to belong to, and most people will choose their parents' culture to promulgate, as it were – but that will be a conscious choice. (1996: 49)

In Asian American theatre, such cultural travelers described above are rare. Frequently the choice is predestined and involves a change of self-identity requiring a complex struggle. Let us examine the ways in which these binaries helped to establish an identity formation that has had positive and negative consequences.

Either/Or: Traditional Asian Virtues vs. American Individuality

The first large wave of immigration from Asia coincided with the mid-nineteenth-century gold rush. One and a half centuries later, Asian Americans, according to the 2000 United States Census, constitute 4.2 percent of the entire population. The need for labor in the San Francisco Bay area during the gold rush attracted many workers from Southern China. Working first in mines and later on railroads, early Chinese immigrants contributed enormously to the growth and development of the American West. However, after the exhaustion of gold and the completion of the transcontinental railroad in 1869, the excess laborers in the West led to anti-Chinese xenophobia, culminating in the Chinese Exclusion Act in 1882, the first immigration act targeting a specific nationality. The first theatrical representations of the "Asian American" were created under this political climate. For instance, "Ah Sin," a comic servant character sketched by Bret Harte and Mark Twain, surfaced onstage in the 1870s, complete with a queue, infantile smile, docile attitude, and hidden cunning nature.[1] The derogatory "Ah Sin" character introduces the "Chinaman" stereotype that later Asian American writers try to obliterate. Ironically, some of the negative qualities of this character also suggest some "traditional Asian virtues" that are applauded by Asian American communities but satirized by American writers. For the most part, however, Ah Sin represents clichés; for instance, his typical greeting revolves around his laundry business: "You wantee washee-washee? One dollar hap dozen – me plenty washee you" (45). The frugality of the Asian worker and immigrant, a quality that helped early arrivals survive in the harsh environment of California and the enforced economic restrictions imposed on Asian Americans, also inspired depictions of Asian Americans by racists as a "moral cancer" and an "unsolvable political problem" (46).

Early twentieth-century Asian American plays generally dramatize the struggle of the first Asian immigrants and their dependence on traditional Asian virtues for survival. Nostalgia for home and the frustrations of racial discrimination mark these early immigrants as more "Asian" than American. In these works, the Asian American question is an "either/or" binary: one is forced to make a choice between being "Asian," i.e., holding onto old-world values, or "American," embracing the new world. But the characters have no real choice beyond this binary. Moreover, these plays also reflect historical moments when anti-Asian sentiment ran high and Asian immigrants had little or no choice but to remain little more than "Asian." A double or hyphenated identity seems unthinkable for the first-generation immigrants. The play, *And the Soul Shall Dance* (1977) by Wakako Yamauchi (b. 1924), set in California in the 1930s, is a typical example of the "Asian" plays. The representations of *issei* ("first-generation" immigrants from Japan) parents and *nisei* ("second-generation") children in this play dramatize "traditional" Asian values as essential survival tools for Asian Americans.

Yamauchi, *nisei* Japanese American, grew up in a farming community in California's Imperial Valley. During World War II, her family, like many Japanese American families on the West Coast, was "relocated" to an internment camp. Her experience in the camp at Poston, Arizona, had a profound impact on her. As a teenager, she lost her father, met a lifelong writer friend Hisaye Yamamoto, and began experimenting with arts and writing. Her play *12-1-A* (1982) takes place in the camp in Poston, depicting some of her struggles, both personal and political, during her youth. *And the Soul Shall Dance* was originally a short story Yamauchi wrote and contributed to the pioneering Asian American literary anthology *Aiiieeeee!* (1974). Mako, who in 1965 founded East West Players, the first Asian American theatre company in the United States, was impressed by the story and urged the author to transform it into a drama. The East West Players eventually produced it in 1977. This first play by Yamauchi, based on her childhood experience in Imperial Valley, remains her best-known work and a benchmark of Asian American art and drama.

And the Soul Shall Dance follows the lives of two Japanese American farming families, the Muratas and the Okas. Times are burdensome: the farmers work diligently and yet remain poor. Oka invites the Murata family to use their bath, because Masako, the 11-year-old Murata girl, has accidentally burned down their own family bathhouse. As the play unfolds, the dark secrets of Emiko, the beautiful but emotionally fragile wife of Oka, gradually come to light. After the death of Oka's first wife, Emiko's sister, her parents force Emiko on him. A woman cultivated in tea ceremony and dance, but unfortunately "lost" in city life, Emiko is resented by Oka as "a second-hand woman" (150). Her sophisticated tastes and lost love create an unbearable life for her in the desert. Longing for her true love and the exquisite Japanese lifestyle, as well as resenting the hardships on the desolate farm and her husband's physical abuse, Emiko seeks to escape. Her drinking, smoking, singing, and dancing all seem improper and "crazy" to the farmers. She endures because she has a dream – to return to Japan and to find her lost love: "I must keep the dream alive. . . . The dream is all I live for. I am only in exile now. Because if I give in, all I've lived before . . . will mean nothing. . . . I would die" (152). Oka, however, ignores her homesickness, steals money she has been saving for ten years for her journey home, and uses the cash to bring his daughter Kiyoko by his first wife from Japan. Out of desperation, Emiko tries to sell her fine kimono to Hana, Murata's wife, but the latter cannot afford such luxury. At the end of the play, Masako sees Emiko in her best kimono, singing the title song and dancing deliriously into the desert.

And the Soul Shall Dance presents many characteristics of a typical first-generation Asian American play. Rather than being about "us," many of the first-generation plays are about "our parents." Homesickness and struggles in a foreign land have created hard conditions, while racial discrimination has thwarted their hope of ever becoming "American." For Japanese American farmers, the land of opportunity has become the land of despair. The predicament of early Japanese immigrant farmers is well expressed in *The Music Lesson* (1977), another play by Yamauchi set in the California farmland during the same period. Kaoru, an itinerant violinist from the city, inquires about the living situation in the farm. The dialogue with the farmer Nakamura illuminates (or dims?) the whole situation:

> Nakamura: Well, first you get some names together. Good names. You can use mine. Sponsors, you know? Then you go to a produce company – in Los Angeles – put on a good suit, talking big . . . how you going to make big money for them. Get in debt. Then you pay back after the harvest (*the futility of it occurs to him*). Then you borrow again next year. Then you pay back. If you can. Same thing next year. You never get the farm. The farm gets you (*he drinks from the bottle*).
>
> Kaoru: You never get the farm?
>
> Nakamura: 'S true. Orientals can't own land here. It's the law.
>
> Kaoru: The law? Then how is it that (you) . . .
>
> Nakamura: Well, I lease. If you have a son old enough you can buy land under his name. He's American citizen, you see? That's if you have enough money.
>
> Kaoru: I'll apply for citizenship, then.
>
> Nakamura: There's a law against that too. Orientals can't be citizens.
>
> Kaoru: We can't?
>
> Nakamura: That's the law. Didn't you know? (68)

The 1913 Alien Land Act prohibited immigrants from owning land, while the Immigration Act of 1924 forbade foreigners (i.e., Japanese) from becoming citizens. Like nomads, the immigrants were consigned to an eternally foreign status. They had left home, but hardship in the new land destroyed their hopes of building a permanent "American" home. They lived in isolation, working on the "transient" foreign land, enduring alienation and hoping their children would have a better life. In *And the Soul Shall Dance*, Hana, Murata's wife, embodies "traditional" Asian female virtues: she is hardworking, reserved, and understanding. When Emiko dances in front of the Muratas, everyone is startled. Hana, trying to defend her, says to her daughter:

> Emiko-san isn't crazy.... She had too much to drink tonight.... She can't adjust to this life. She can't get over the good times she had in Japan. Well, it's not easy... but one has to know when to bend... like the bamboo. When the winds blow, bamboo bends. You bend or crack. Remember that, Masako. (148)

To bend means to preserve a traditional Asian value of "endurance." In order to survive, one has to "bend" to be "Asian." Masako tells her mother about a book she has been reading dealing with the struggles of early settlers in the prairie. The early settlers came from the "East. Just like you and Papa came from Japan." Hana corrects her: "We came from far far East. That's different. White people are different from us.... White people among white people... that's different from Japanese among white people... we are nobody here" (153–4).

The family loves the land, but their powerlessness prevents *issei* farmers from assimilating into white American society and ultimately obtaining land. Poverty and frustration make the homeland even sweeter. Masako asks her mother:

	Do you want to go back to Japan, Mama?
Hana:	Everyone does.
Masako:	Do you, papa?
Murata:	I'll have to make some money first.
Masako:	I don't. Not me. Not Kiyoko. (148)

Although the generation gap is handled subtly in this play, the drama illuminates the major differences between the *issei* parents and the *nisei* children in their relationship with and attitudes toward the homeland. Members of the *issei* generation, whether it is the "bent" Hana, or the "cracked" Emiko, all experience nostalgia for the homeland. The *nisei* generation, however, has little or no particular association with their parents' home. Masako does not like Japanese hot baths or Japanese girlish giggles. She protests against her mother's "teachings" and does not want to go back to Japan.

The nostalgia, the dream of returning to the homeland, as well as the sadness and sorrows of the *issei* parents, typify the characters in the play as "Asian." The Asian parents transfer their dead dream to their children: they want the children to preserve Asian values; however, they simultaneously long for their children to assimilate into mainstream American white society. As a consequence, the second generation is required to absorb a hyphenated identity: "Asian-American." The hyphen provides the illusion of an identity that is equally divided into Asian and American, with the best facets from both sides. However, it also implies an identity that is only "half" American and suggests a certain "lack," or inadequacy.[2] This experience likely explains why a sufficient number of dramas that represent the voices of the second generation are rebelliously "un-Asian." Taken to the other end of the binary system, the *nisei* generation is surprisingly "American." Not only are they entirely assimilated into mainstream society, having largely forsaken their parents' value system, they additionally go to the extreme of adopting American racism, which plagued their parents and even themselves. In other words, the binary system is still at work: to be American is to be non-Asian, and the characters in these plays adapt this self-effacing attitude.

David Henry Hwang's 1979 play *FOB*, a play about "us," not about our parents, illustrates the conflicts inherent in being a second-generation Asian American. Set in the back room of a Chinese restaurant in Torrance, California, *FOB* tells how Steve, an FOB ("fresh off the boat," a new immigrant), pays a surprise visit to Grace, who immigrated to the United States when she was a child. This visit arouses jealousy in Dale, an ABC ("American-born Chinese"). Vying for Grace's attention, Dale wants to prove how much better he is than Steve – that is, how American he is:

> My parents – they don't know nothing about the world, about watching Benson at the Roxy, about ordering hors d'œuvres at Scandia's, downshifting onto the Ventura Freeway at midnight. They're yellow ghosts and they've tried to cage me up with Chinese-ness when all the time we were in America. (*Pause*) So, I've had to work real hard – real hard – to be myself. To not be a Chinese, a yellow, a slant, a gook. To be just a human being, like everyone else. (*Pause*) I've paid my dues. And that's why I am much better now. I'm making it, you know? I'm making it in America. (32)

"To be myself," or "to be just a human being," is to be anything other than Chinese. By despising the Chinese, adopting American racism toward "Orientals," and even going so far as to use words such as "gook," "slant," and "ghost" to refer to Chinese, Dale gains a kind of sadomasochistic pleasure. He cannot escape his yellowness; the only thing he can do is mock his own yellowness through proxies, the victimized FOBs, "the sworn enemies of all ABC" (6). At this moment, he is split into two selves, the Asian and the American. He embodies the binary system. Josephine Lee argues that this kind of split results from the character's existence under the pressure of capitalism (1997: 168). Indeed, all the success indicators in Dale's speech are linked to materialism. By siding with American capitalism and racism, Dale considers himself superior to the FOB Steve; by mocking Asian heritage and ethnicity as a collective body, Dale embraces American individualism – "to be just a human being, like everyone else." Within the binary system, Dale chooses to be American by violently erasing the Asian self.

The three characters represent different degrees of Asianness: while the FOB Steve and the ABC Dale lie at opposite ends of the spectrum, the Asian-born,

American-educated Grace falls between the extremes. Dale is a self-proclaimed "American," while Grace has experienced a typical assimilation crisis in her child-hood. She attempts to fit into American society by bleaching her hair and "hanging out" at the beach. Steve, on the other hand, represents the perpetual Asian FOB; he *is* the Chinese immigration history:

> I come here five times – I raise lifetime fortune five times. Five times, I first come here, you say to me I am illegal, you return me on boat to fathers and uncles with no gold, no treasure, no fortune, no rice. I only want to come to America – come to "Mountain of Gold." And I hate Mountain and I hate America and I hate you! (21)

While *And the Soul Shall Dance* presents images of bamboo and kimono, which are the reminders of *Asianness*, in *FOB* – though the play still makes use of stage props such as Chinese food and presenting a Chinese restaurant in the background – the Asianness is for the young characters rooted in *Asian American* culture. Steve incorporates, in Hwang's words, the persona of Gwan Gung, "God of warriors, writers and prostitutes!" (10). Grace, in contrast, embodies the characteristics of Fa Mu Lan (the woman warrior who goes to the battle in her father's place). Throughout the course of the play, constant verbal and physical fights occur in the style of Chinese martial arts and opera, with the striking of two pots to indicate the change of speaker. Gwan Gung and Fa Mu Lan, both legendary Chinese heroic figures, are popularized in Asian American literature and become the ultimate icons of Asian culture. In the brief introduction to the play, Hwang maintains that the source of these two figures is not in Chinese literature but in Maxine Hong Kingston's *The Woman Warrior* and Frank Chin's *Gee, Pop!* This is to assert that there is an "Asian American literary tradition," as Gwan Gung is the "adopted god of Chinese America" (3). As the exotic homeland of the immigrant parents is accessible only in stories, Asian American writers feel a need to create a new "Asia," an Asia in the new world, an Asia that constitutes part of the past of Asian America.[3]

The fact that *FOB* is a play requiring an all-Asian American cast makes the performance of "Asianness" more complicated. The different degrees of Asianness have to be expressed through performance of legendary Asian roles. Steve and Grace can transform into the "Asianness" gracefully, while Dale frequently appears to be clumsy and awkward, less Asian and thus more "American." Whether the representa-tion of the Asian is physical (*FOB*) or metaphorical (*And the Soul Shall Dance*), it further illustrates that both Asianness and Americanness are representational. Ethni-city is indeed a performance.[4] The positional choice within the binary system, whether voluntary or compulsory, reinforces the binary system.

Neither/Nor: The Non-Asian Non-American Limbo

Chickencoop Chinaman (1972) by Frank Chin (b. 1940) presents an alternative repre-sentation – neither the bent bamboo image of the traditional Asian, nor the racist and individualized image of the American, but rather a defiant image of the modern "Chinaman." Frank Chin, born in Berkeley, California, is a novelist, essayist, playwright, and the main editor of *Aiiieeeee!* He is often considered a kind of "loudmouth godfather" figure in Asian American literature. In the introduction of *Aiiieeeee!*, he describes white supremacy and racial stereotyping:

> The general function of any racial stereotype is to establish and preserve order between different elements of society, maintain the continuity and growth of Western civilization and enforce white supremacy with a minimum of effort, attention, and expense. The ideal racial stereotype is a low-maintenance engine of white supremacy whose efficiency increases with age, as it becomes authenticated and historically verified. (2002: xxvi–xxvii)

Destroying racial stereotypes is the first step to challenge the fake history constructed for Asian Americans. The early immigrants, in Chin's mind, like other frontier settlers, were heroic and masculine – they were an integral part of the Western history. However, racial discrimination and economic hardship contributed to an emasculating effect and castration anxiety for Chinese sojourners. Chin believes that this drive to emasculate, deeply rooted in racism, actually reflects the male anxiety of white America:

> White America is as securely indifferent about us as men as plantation owners were about their loyal house niggers. House niggers is what America has made of us, admiring us for being patient, submissive, aesthetic, passive, accommodating, essentially feminine in character – what whites call "Confuciusist," dreaming us up a goofy version of Chinese culture to preserve in becoming the white male's dream minority. Our white-dream identity being feminine, the carriers of our strength, the power of the race belongs to our women. The dream women of this dream minority naturally prefer white men to their own. (1998: 99–100)

The "white male's dream minority," the "assimilated Asian American," is a new stereotype for the American public. In the *US News and World Report* of December 26, 1966, Chinese Americans were praised as the trouble-free, self-helping, complaisant model minority: "At a time when it is being proposed that hundreds of billions be spent to uplift Negroes and other minorities, the nation's 300,000 Chinese-Americans are moving ahead on their own – with no help from anyone else." Moreover, low crime rates make Chinese districts "islands of peace and stability." Traditional Chinese notions of kinship and family values also save American taxpayers a lot of money, as "few Chinese-Americans are getting welfare handouts – or even want them" (6). Chin humorously sums up this ideology: "Blacks are a problem: badass. Chinese Americans are not a problem: kissass" (1998: 74).

Chin wants to combat both the early stereotypes such as "Ah Sin," the obedient and infantile Chinaman, and the later stereotypes of the model minority, the successful but complaisant Chinese American. *Chickencoop Chinaman* sets out to overthrow both images. The main plot involves Tam Lum, a writer and filmmaker, searching for the father of the former lightweight champion Ovatine Jack Dancer for a documentary film he is creating. Charlie Popcorn, a former boxing trainer who was mistaken for Ovatine's father, is now running a "pornie movie house." Tam visits "Blackjap" Kenji, his longtime Japanese American friend, Lee, a Eurasian woman, and her son Robbie. Kenji lives with Lee, but is not Robbie's father; Robbie's father Tom, a Chinese American "model minority," is despised by Tam for his assimilation. Tom is happy to be accepted: "We used to be kicked around, but that's history, brother. Today we have good jobs, good pay, and we're lucky. Americans are proud today we send more of our kids to college than any other race. We are accepted. We worked hard for it. I've made my peace" (Chin 1981: 59). Tam himself is not a good father, either: he is divorced from his Caucasian wife and has left his two children. "Chinamans do make lousy fathers. I know. I have one" (23). The absence of a positive father figure in the play expresses the predicament of the continuation of Chinese heritage, which further endangers Chinese masculinity.

Chinese masculinity seems unobtainable in this play: in Tam's memory, his father always wore underwear in the bath, for fear of white old ladies "peeking him through the keyhole" (16). Even the defiant Tam is called "willowy," with the implication that he seems "queer" (58–9). He is unable to save his marriage or keep his children; it is only in his dream that he successfully "gets" the girl – the fantasy woman Hong Kong Dream Girl.[5]

In a dream sequence concerning the Lone Ranger, the issue of Chinese ethnicity and masculinity is examined in considerable detail. Tam always thought that the Lone Ranger was Chinese: "he wore that mask to hide his Chinese eyes" (32). But his childhood hero turns out to be a broken-down white racist who thinks Chinese are "honorary white" – "legendary obeyers of the law, legendary humble, legendary passive" (37). The ironic comparison is an Asian-versioned Helen Keller (hear no evil, see no evil, speak no evil): "Helen Keller overcame her handicaps without riot! She overcame her handicaps without looting! She overcame her handicaps without violence! And you Chinks and Japs can too" (11).

Chin laments the lost heritage of Chinese heroes, defies the fake image of early Chinamen and Chinese Americans, and continues to fight white racism. The vision is often pessimistic and alienated. In a scene entitled "Limbo," Tam says: "Foong. Wind.... Lawk sur, rain... gum yut yit, hot today or gum yut lahng, cold today.... That's all we talked. Foong chur, lawk gun sur, yit, lahng, gum yut lahng, lawk gun sur, foong chur, gum yut yit" (51). The limited Chinese vocabulary can only convey superficial meaning, and loss of the "native tongue" further marks the "orphan" status of Chinese Americans. "As a people, we are pre-verbal, preliterate .... We are a people without a native tongue. To whites, we're all foreigners, still learning English.... And to Asians born to Asian culture – Asian by birth and experience and American by choice – our Chinese and Japanese is a fake" (xvii). He rejects either endurance of traditional Asian values or assimilation into the rubric – and binary system – of Asian American. His Chinese hero is neither Asian nor

Plate 14. *Chickencoop Chinaman*, by Frank Chin, directed by Pamela Wu. Noel Benora (Tam Lum) and Kristin Liu (Hong Kong Dream Girl), photo by Bob Hsiang. Courtesy of the Asian American Theatre Company.

American, but a rare species of modern-day Chinaman. This modern Chinaman is angry. Tom says to him: "I can call you 'Chinaman' and insult you, I can call you 'Chinese American' and insult you, 'Americanized Chinese' and insult you, 'Chinese' and insult you, 'American,' 'Chink,' 'jap,' 'Japanese,' 'White' and insult you, 'Black' and insult you. You're angry" (60). Tam resembles a trapped beast whose rage and fury are ultimately futile, like a Chinaman trapped in a chickencoop, whose angry "Buck Buck Bagaw" is unintelligible.

At the end of the play, Tam is alone, and maybe more alone than ever. Even his old friend Kenji is ready to move on.

> Kenji: I told you it's not funny, now, man. Nobody wants it anymore. You're too old to
>   be badmouthing everything, everything like you do. Nobody's gonna run with
>   that, man.
> Tam: Yeah, I'm a loner.
> Kenji: You wanta be a loner, you're a loner. You're a mean rogue, somewhere, out
>   there, ya know what I mean?
> Tam: Like a mad elephant, blowin his nose alone in the dark.
> Kenji: It isn't funny. (61)

Angry and lonely, orphaned and wounded: this is Frank Chin's image of the modern-day Chinaman. Refusing to choose within the binary system, yet nevertheless affected by the choices, this first stage of the "neither/nor" character is like a tragic hero, heroic but hopelessly defeated.

The orphan image and the neither/nor situation are expressed in another play, but with a more hopeful spin. In *Cleveland Raining* (1990), Sung Rno (b. 1967) portrays a Midwestern Korean immigrant family as "a family of leavers": "We leave Korea. Then we leave each other" (267). The first-generation parents have disappeared before the play starts, and now their children have to deal with painful memories, daily life, and their future. Mari, a failed pianist who also has rejected her medical studies, wants instead to be a "professional healer" (263). Her brother Jimmy Rodin, a failed artist who also has lost his job at a grocery store, considers himself a prophet. He wants to convert his Volkswagen into a boat in order to sail off on the day of apocalyptic flooding. The play is set in a kind of limbo state: the parents are gone, the children have left their professions, and the characters are working on sailing to the future; the entire action takes place in the garage where the sky blue Volkswagen is parked, and on the front porch it is neither indoors nor outdoors, but in a transitional space.

Mari, the youngest of the family, has vague memories of their mother, but still tries to find their father (who has just left) by driving up and down the interstate freeway. During one such search she witnesses a car accident, in which the biker woman Storm has accidentally killed her own grandmother. Storm, a woman with Asian looks, appears at the Kim family home looking for her missing motorcycle. She is also an orphan figure who has no knowledge of her origins, and her Granny is not her real grandmother. She even denies her ethnic heritage: "I'm not Korean. (*Pause*) Did you hear me? . . . Just leave me out of all this ethnic bullshit" (245). The only non-Asian character, Mick, is a mechanic who is convinced by Jimmy's vision and willing to work on the Volkswagen. Mick, a native Ohioan, has his own phobia: he cannot stand corn. He feels trapped in the Midwestern "corn country," "where flat is a color, and gray is a song" (244). He also understands the urgency to "leave." Jimmy and Mick work together on converting the car into a Noah's ark, and Jimmy comes to the conclusion that the new engine should run on "emotional loss." Jimmy explains: "it's all based on entropy. Harnessing the energy of emotional breakdown" (247).

Although three out of the four characters in this play are Asian American, "Asian-ness" is expressed only in a very superficial way. Jimmy is fired from his grocery store job because he considers a woman's request for bananas as a "racial slur" and thus starts a scene in the store. Mari objects: "Chink is a slur. Gook is a slur. *Banana* is . . . a fruit." Jimmy defends himself: "It means *assimilated*. That's a fucking slur, if I've ever heard one" (231). Jimmy is not happy with the "non-ethnic" behavior of Storm: "She's a fucking banana in a leather jacket!" (260). He lives on a strange diet: kimchee, rice, and beer. When Mari says kimchee is just like sauerkraut, Jimmy argues, "Sauerkraut is for a baseball game, on top of a hot dog. Kimchee is more . . . spiritual"; however, when Mari asks if he eats kimchee for its spirituality, he says: "I eat it because I'm lazy" (230–1). Jimmy is the character who has the most "ethnic" behavior, but the ethnicity issues are limited to two foods: bananas and kimchee. He objects to the image of the banana (assimilated Asian), but refuses to go for the deeper meaning of Asian spirituality (kimchee). He likes kimchee for its convenience, not for its ethnicity.

Cleveland Raining should be described not as an ethnic play but rather as a memory play of a dysfunctional family, or "a ghost family," akin to a "faded photograph. Black and white. Smudged. Grainy" (263). The play also depicts a family injured and in pain. Not only have the parents abandoned their children, but Jimmy, who has "a talent for hurting everybody around him, most of all himself" (250), also stepped on Mari's fingers intentionally to destroy her future as a pianist, and shot himself in the foot in a hunting trip. Mari deliberately tries to "reassemble" her broken home from her faded memories through such activities as looking for her lost father and her favorite childhood painting, a painting of cherries by her mother. However, Jimmy, who as the older brother has a clearer memory of the family past, does his best to destroy all memories. For instance, in an outing Mick tries to confront his own corn phobia by digging into a cornfield; in doing so, he actually discovers the cherry painting that Jimmy has buried. Jimmy finally reveals a note that the father has left them with: "Remember to forget" (267).

At this point, Mari has stopped searching for the past and is ready to move on. She can now appreciate Jimmy's vision and dream: "The Volkswagen. The flood, . . . that's the beauty of dreams. They're based on hope. They're based on maybe things changing from what they are today. From what they really are. You see yourself doing things you wouldn't do. You see a strange face. A car floating. Rain." She adds: "This family . . . it needs to be put to rest. . . . Now we need to do something new" (268). At the conclusion of the play, Mari and Storm leave together, while Jimmy and Mick get ready to "sail" away in the Volkswagen. Jimmy puts the cherry painting in the car engine, and the engine "roars to life, glowing with a surreal and bright light" (269). The painful past has been turned into energy for the future.

Sung Rno, who started as an aspiring physicist who also wrote poetry, often combines poetic language and scientific fantasy in his dramatic works. He represents one of several refreshing voices among a new generation of Asian American theatre.[6] Although the characters in *Cleveland Raining* are Asian Americans, the issues addressed are not exactly "Asian." No doubt limited stereotypical Asian references are used in the play, but the characters also have gone beyond the "Asian" issues. For example, references to kimchee and sauerkraut on hot dogs seem merely to provide a framework for the play, rather than developing and continuing identity issues or providing any internal dramatic tension. The frame, however, helps situate the play in the neither/nor Asian American state.

Both *Chickencoop Chinaman* and *Cleveland Raining* examine irresponsible Asian parents and their children in the neither/nor limbo state. Tam is angry, rejecting both his Asian parents and his assimilated Asian American peers, but his fury fails to provide him with a release from his "limbo" condition. We observe him consumed in his "Chinaman" concept: a wounded hero, a dying species, and a tragic loner. He is in mourning, but the mourning fails to present a solution. In *Cleveland Raining*, although painful memories and family secrets are gradually revealed throughout the play, the characters come to a new understanding. It remains a neither/nor limbo state: the past is "forgotten" but the future is not yet reached. The exit from this state is invisible, but at least the play provides hope; the dream has not come true, but there is potential and the remnants of a vision. The hopeful vision represents a new voice of the neither/nor Asian American theatre. Both Chin's violent rejection of the binary and Rno's use of the binary as mere frame suggest that Asian American theatre exists in a unique state: it is always on the move, always being negotiated and redefined.

Most ethnic theatres in the United States vie to fight vicious racial discrimination, but they also rely on such viciousness from "white America" for energy and inspiration. Many ethnic theatres have to come to terms with this paradox. Asian American theatre is no exception. Drawing on the examples considered in this chapter, it is evident that many Asian American dramas rely on the binary system: one has to choose a side, to be Asian or to be American, or one can reject both while still depending on both to position oneself in the fight. The tension between the binary choices is a consistent factor in the plays, whether between generations or within oneself. Neither the half-half of a hyphenated identity nor the harmonious fusion of the melting pot seems to be a popular topic. The idea that one can easily be both Asian and American without any identity struggle is as ridiculous as the formula promoted by an Education TV program that Frank Chin satirizes: "I'm Chinese because I like chow mein, and I'm American because I like spaghetti" (1998: 69–70). The chow mein/spaghetti image is nowhere near the identity that Asian Americans desire.

In the age of globalization, every day borders are being crossed and cultures are being exchanged, consolidated, and recreated. Tokenized Asianness or Americanness becomes ever more crucial to the survival of Asian American theatre as a distinctive genre. Returning to the issues presented by *M. Butterfly* and the possibility of challenging the definition of Asian American theatre, one might observe that the definition of this genre is even harder when Asian American theatre becomes multivocal, multi-ethnic, and multimedia. The early works are mostly full-length plays by second- and third-generation Chinese or Japanese American writers, but with the change of immigration patterns and other political factors, more writers of South and Southeast Asian descent have emerged, and mixed-raced writers (who also share Asian heritage) have also entered the Asian American arena. The definition of Asian American also has changed from "by birth" to including "naturalized" Asian Americans.[7] Various artistic forms have been experimented and diverse themes explored (very often, they have little to do with ethnicity). As an artistic development, Asian American theatre has probably reached its richest state; however, its inclusiveness has blurred its distinctive features as a unique genre and a unique voice that many early writers worked hard to create. As the definition of culture and ethnicity has become fluid, it is indeed difficult to maintain "Asian American theatre" as an ethnic theatre. Perhaps the best way is not to define it as an ethnic theatre. But, then, how can it be defined if not as ethnic? The either/or, neither/nor model might provide one way of encompassing this extensive body of dramas as a description of Asian American theatre. But rather than using the binary system as a detention camp to preserve a minority theatre or a public desire to regulate Asian American ethnicity, I suggest we use the binary system merely as a theoretical frame that can evolve onto the stage in which interlinked Asian and American ethnicities can be created, negotiated, and performed.

NOTES

1. See Harte and Twain (1876).
2. Judy Yung, for instance, rejects the hyphenated identity and prefers "Asian American." "Asian American" denotes an identity that is quintessentially American, but with Asian qualities. The word "Asian" becomes an adjective that modifies the noun American (see Yung 1995: xi).
3. Gwan Gung (or Guan Gong, Lord Guan) is the common title for Guan Yu, also known as Guan Yunchang (160?–219), a historical character from the period of Three Kingdoms (220–80). Details of his biography are given in *The Records of the Three Kingdoms* by Chen Shou (233–97) and are elaborated in the more famous novel *The Romance of the Three Kingdoms* by Luo Guanzhong (fl. 1330–1400). In the popular imagination, Gwan embodies bravery, loyalty, righteousness, and brotherhood. His stories are dramatized in various theatrical forms. He is also worshipped as a popular god, and his temples can be seen in many places in China and in the Chinese diaspora. "Imported" by early Chinese immigrants to the New World, Gwan Gung has now become the representative Chinese god in Asian America. Fa Mu Lan, or Hua Mulan, is a legendary character whose historical existence cannot be verified. The source of her story is a poem titled "The Ballad of Mulan," commonly dated to the period of the Northern and Southern dynasties (239–589). According to the poem, Mu Lan's aging father was drafted during wartime, but she volunteered to go in his place because she had no older brother who could take up such responsibility. Mu Lan disguised herself as a man and stayed in the army for 12 years. The Mu Lan story is retold in many different forms. In the United States, her

story has been popularized in Maxine Hong Kingston's *The Woman Warrior* (1975) and in the Disney animated movie *Mulan* (1998).

4. The issue of "ethnicity as performance" is complicated and definitely worth further discussion; however, because of the limited space, I suggest we consider some of the historical casting conventions as a starting point. How is the traditional "black-faced" Othello different from "black-faced" minstrel shows? How is the "yellow gook" Steve (played by an Asian actor) in *FOB* different from a yellow-faced Ah Sin (played by a white actor)? Is the Asian character played by an Asian actor (who might be from a different nationality) more "authentic" than the one played by a white actor?

5. I would like to express my gratitude toward the following people for obtaining plate 14:

Sal Guerena, Director of California Ethnic and Multicultural Archives at the University of California Santa Barbara, Wei Ming Dariotis, President of the Asian American Theatre Company (AATC), Sean Lim, Managing Artistic Director of AATC, and Pamela Wu, director of the 1998 AATC production of *Chickencoop Chinaman*.

6. For a general introduction to Sung Rno's work, see Lei (2002).

7. For instance, Josephine Lee (1998) urges people to continue looking at works by immigrants, both past and present, when approaching Asian American theatre. By challenging and redefining a stable or monolithic "American" identity, one can gain a better understanding of Asian American theatre.

BIBLIOGRAPHY

Chin, F. (1981). *Chickencoop Chinaman.* In Frank Chin, *Chickencoop Chinaman and The Year of Dragon: Two Plays by Frank Chin.* Seattle: University of Washington Press, 1–71.

—— (1998). "Confessions of a Chinatown Cowboy." In Frank Chin, *Bulletproof Buddhists and Other Plays.* Honolulu: University of Hawaii Press, 63–109.

——, Chan, J. P., Inada, L. F., and Wong, S. H. (eds.) (2002). "Introduction." In Frank Chin, Jeffery Paul Chan, Lawson Fusao Inada, and Shawn Hsu Wong (eds.), *Aiiieeeee!: An Anthology of Asian American Writers.* Washington, DC: Howard University Press.

Harte, B. and Twain, M. (1876). *Ah Sin.* Reprinted in Dave Williams (ed.), *The Chinese Other: 1850–1925.* New York: University Press of America (1997), 39–95.

Houston, V. H. (ed.) (1997). *The Politics of Life: Four Plays by Asian American Women.* Philadelphia: Temple University Press.

Hwang, D. H. (1990). *FOB.* In David Henry Hwang, *FOB and Other Plays.* New York: New American Library.

Lee, J. (1997). *Performing Asian America: Race and Ethnicity on the Contemporary Stage.* Philadelphia: Temple University Press.

—— (1998). "Between Immigration and Hyphenation. The Problems of Theorizing Asian American Theatre." *Journal of Dramatic Theory and Criticism* 8, 1 (Fall): 45–69.

Lei, D. (2002). "Sung Rno Biography." In Miles Xian Liu (ed.), *Asian American Playwrights: A Bio-Bibliographical Critical Sourcebook.* Westport, CT: Greenwood, 292–7.

Liu, M. X. (ed.) (2002). *Asian American Playwrights: A Bio-Bibliographical Critical Sourcebook.* Westport, CT: Greenwood.

McDonald, D. R. (1981). "Introduction." In Frank Chin, *Chickencoop Chinaman and The Year of Dragon: Two Plays by Frank Chin.* Seattle: University of Washington Press, ix–xxix.

Moy, J. S. (1993). *Marginal Sights: Staging the Chinese in America.* Iowa City: University of Iowa Press.

Nelson, B. (ed.) (1997). *Asian American Drama: Nine Plays from the Multiethnic Landscape.* New York: Applause.

Rno, S. J. (1997). *Cleveland Raining*. In Velina Hasu Houston (ed.), *But Still, Like Air, I'll Rise*. Philadelphia: Temple University Press.

Schechner, R. (1996). "Interculturalism and the Culture of Choice." In Patrice Pavis (ed.), *The Intercultural Performance Reader*. London: Routledge, 41–50.

Takaki, R. (1998). *Strangers from a Different Shore: A History of Asian Americans*. New York: Little, Brown.

US News and World Report (1966). "Success Story of One Minority Group in U.S," December 26. Reprinted in Amy Tachiki, Eddie Wong, Franklin Odo, and Buck Wong (eds.), *Roots: An Asian American Reader*. Los Angeles: Continental Graphics (1971), 6–9.

Yamauchi, W. (1990). *And the Soul Shall Dance*. In Misha Berson (ed.), *Between Worlds: Contemporary Asian-American Plays*. New York: Theatre Communications Group.

——(1993). *The Music Lesson*. In Roberta Uno (ed.), *Unbroken Thread: An Anthology of Plays by Asian American Women*. Amherst: University of Massachusetts Press, 53–104.

Yung, J. (1995). *Unbound Feet: A Social History of Chinese Women in San Francisco*. Berkeley: University of California Press.

20

August Wilson

Harry J. Elam, Jr.

With two Pulitzer Prizes, two Tony Awards, and numerous other accolades, August Wilson stands out as one of if not the most preeminent playwrights in the contemporary American theatre. Wilson's self-imposed dramatic project is to review African American history in the twentieth century by writing a play for each decade. With each work, he recreates and reevaluates the choices that blacks have made in the past by refracting them through the lens of the present. Wilson focuses on the experiences and daily lives of ordinary black people within particular historical circumstances. Carefully situating each play at critical junctures in African American history, Wilson explores the pain and perseverance, the determination and dignity in these black lives.

In his early playwriting career Wilson did write works that are not part of this cycle, such as *Recycle* (1973), *The Homecoming* (1976), *Black Bart and the Sacred Hills*, a musical satire (1977), *The Coldest Day of the Year* (1977), *How the Coyote Got His Special Power and Used It to Help the People* (1978), and *Fullerton Street* (1980). Most of these works were produced, but all remain unpublished. Thus, his recognition and renown as a playwright came as a result of and in conjunction with his twentieth-century cycle. Although not written in chronological order, Wilson has to date completed plays on the 1900s with *Gem of the Ocean*, 1910s with *Joe Turner's Come and Gone*, the 1920s with *Ma Rainey's Black Bottom*, the 1930s with *The Piano Lesson*, the 1940s with *Seven Guitars*, the 1950s with *Fences*, 1960s with *Two Trains Running*, 1970s with *Jitney*, and the 1980s with *King Hedley II*.

Gem of the Ocean, set in 1904, is Wilson's latest work. It premiered in April 2003 at the Goodman Theatre in Chicago. *Gem* focuses on Aunt Esther, a character as old as the black presence in America, and the action that transpires when Citizen Barlow arrives at her house in spiritual turmoil seeking sanctuary. While Wilson previously creates the off-stage character of Aunt Esther in *Two Trains Running* and *King Hedley II*, *Gem of the Ocean* marks the first appearance of this figure Wilson now believes is "the most significant person of the cycle. The characters, after all, are her children" (2002: 1). With the stated import of Aunt Esther to his historical project as a whole, it seems right and even offers a telling testimony to his creative processes that, at this juncture and in this play that marks the ultimate inception and near culmination of the cycle, Wilson has worked his way around to presenting Aunt Esther "in the flesh." This work, like all of Wilson's dramas to date save *Ma Rainey*, is set in Wilson's childhood home, the Hill district of Pittsburgh, Pennsylvania. As with the earlier plays, Wilson superbly blends blues music, poetic dialogue, and rich, complex characterizations together as he creates images of America's past from a decidedly African American perspective.

Critical to each play in Wilson's historical cycle is the concept that one must go backwards in order to move forward. Repeatedly, Wilson creates black characters who are displaced and disconnected from their history and from their individual identity, and are in search of spiritual resurrection and cultural reconnection. For these characters, past events have a commanding influence on their present dreams and aspirations. Their personal stories are inextricably linked to the history of African American struggle and survival in this country. Wilson's dramatic cycle demonstrates the impact of the past on the present. Ethics and aesthetics conjoin as the personal dynamics of his characters' lives have profound political consequences. He terms his project "a 400-year-old autobiography, which is the black experience" (qtd. in Shannon 1996: 179–80). As an African American "autobiography," Wilson's work links African American collective memory with Wilson's own memories and with his activist racial agenda. His family background and own life experiences are evident in this project.

Early Influences

August Wilson was born August Frederick Kittel on April 27, 1945. He was the fourth of six children. His father, Frederick Kittel, a German baker, rarely lived with the family. His mother, Daisy Wilson, worked as a cleaning woman and later married David Bedford, a black ex-convict and former high school football star. Wilson's troubled and troubling relationship with these two men figures in his plays and their depictions of masculinity and race. As signaled by his decision to change his surname from Kittel to his mother's surname, Wilson, August Wilson has never identified with his white father, but strictly with his African American heritage. According to Wilson, "I stand myself and my art squarely on the self-defining ground of the slave quarters, and find the ground to be hallowed and made fertile by the blood and bones of the men and women who can be described as warriors on the cultural battlefield that affirmed their self-worth" (1996a: 16). Wilson believes his identity as an African American artist is inherently linked to the legacy of African American struggle and survival.

Wilson learned an early lesson about integrity and survival in ninth grade, when a teacher accused him of plagiarizing a 25-page paper he had rigorously researched on Napoleon Bonaparte. The teacher, Mr. Biggs, put two grades on the paper, one an

"A+" he would receive if he proved that he completed this paper on his own without assistance. The other grade, an "F," was the grade the teacher believed he deserved for deceitfully claiming another's work as his own. Bruised by this false accusation, Wilson dropped out of school in 1960. While this injustice ended his formal education, it did not deter his thirst for knowledge. A voracious reader, Wilson spent considerable time in the public library devouring the books in the "Negro section." Reading the works of Ralph Ellison and James Baldwin, Wilson determined that he too wanted to be a writer. "Just the idea black people would write books. I wanted my book up there too" (qtd. in Freeman 1987: 49). His desire to be a writer motivated him to poetry first. In 1965 he helped to organize the Center Avenue Poets Theatre Workshop. That same year, at age 19, he moved out of his mother's house and rented a basement apartment in Pittsburgh's Hill district, "where he fraternized with a group of writers and painters" (qtd. in Shannon 1995: 17). He took on part-time odd jobs and would, whenever he had free time, write for hours. More importantly, he studied the characters and haunts of his neighborhood. He observed their vernacular, their "signifyin' games" and verbal boasts. Their language, style, and cultural politics would later become the stuff of his drama and an important source for his dramaturgy.

Wilson describes his poetry as largely "imitative." He found his own true voice as a dramatist as the decade of the 1960s drew to a close. Affected by the urgencies around black cultural nationalism of the late 1960s, Wilson, along with his friend Rob Penny, co-founded Pittsburgh's Black Horizon's Theatre, a revolutionary-inclined African American theatre. With his work at Black Horizon's, Wilson encountered one of the influences that continue to shape his dramas, the fiery playwright and poet Amiri Baraka (LeRoi Jones), the leading theatre practitioner of the black revolutionary theatre movement of the late 1960s and early 1970s (see chapter 17). Wilson maintains that Baraka's words and cultural politics inspired his own desire to use drama as a means to social ends.

In and around the same time, Wilson discovered three more influences: Jorge Luis Borges, Romare Bearden, and the blues. Argentinean short story writer Borges became significant to Wilson because of his ability to blend the metaphysical and the mystical within his complex plot lines. With his skillful use of narration, Borges mixes the fantastical and the spiritual as his characters follow difficult and convoluted pathways. Within plays such as *Fences*, *Joe Turner's Come and Gone*, *The Piano Lesson*, and *Gem of the Ocean*, Wilson's incorporation of the supernatural and metaphysical has been influenced by the writing of Borges.

Wilson discovered the work of fellow Pittsburgh native Romare Bearden in 1977, when his friend Charles Purdy purchased a copy of his collage, *The Prevalence of Ritual* (1964). Viewing this artwork had a profound effect on Wilson: "My response was visceral. I was looking at myself in ways I hadn't thought of before and have never ceased to think of since. In Bearden I found my artistic mentor and sought, and still aspire, to make my plays the equal of his canvases" (qtd. in Fishman 1994: 134). Bearden's collages *Millhands Lunch Bucket* (1978) and *The Piano Lesson* (1984) directly inspired Wilson's plays *Joe Turner* and *Piano Lesson*, respectively. Bearden's formula for collage, his use of found objects, and his blending of past and present are examples reflected in Wilson's pastiche style of playwriting and his interest in the impact of history upon present conditions. Within the artistry of both men, the metaphorical and ritualistic coexist with everyday experiences of African Americans. Unfortunately, the two men never met in Bearden's lifetime.

Despite the impact of Bearden, Borges, and Baraka on Wilson and his work, the most significant and most transformative of the four influences (referred to as the "4Bs" because all begin with the letter "B") is the blues. Twelve years prior to encountering Bearden in 1965, Wilson discovered the blues while listening to an old recording of Bessie Smith's "Nobody in Town Can Bake a Sweet Jellyroll Like Mine." This recording transformed his life and his cultural ideology. The blues become not only a guiding force in his writing, but also the foundation he discovers for African American expressive culture and for what Wilson believes is a distinctly African American way of "being" (1991: ix–x). According to Wilson, the cultural, social, political, and spiritual all interact within the blues. Forged in and from the economics of slavery as a method of mediating the pains and dehumanization of that experience, the blues are purposefully duplicitous, containing a matrix of meanings. The blues for Wilson continue to offer a methodology for negotiating the difficult spaces of African American existence and achieving African American survival.

Structurally, Wilson's "bluesology" acts as an aesthetic and cultural intervention disrupting the conventional frame of realism. Rather than plot or action, character and the lyrical music of the dialogue drive the plays. Wilson, a poet before he became a playwright, celebrates the poetic power contained in the speech of poor and uneducated peoples. Wilson allows his character to voice their history in the verbal equivalent of musical solos. For instance, Troy Maxson – an illiterate garbage man and central figure in *Fences* – fashions his identity and self-awareness through bold expressive tales. Like the ancient city of Troy, he is an epic force, impregnable and larger than life. Troy's stories, which serve to describe the African American experiences as well as his individual life, expand the realistic canvas of the play, reaching beyond the conventional temporal and spatial limits to reveal the inner presence of history impacting on an individual.

Ralph Ellison calls the blues a unique combination of the "tragic and the comic," of poetry and ritual (1964: 256). Wilson's plays embody this blues formula on a multitude of occasions. In each of the plays, Wilson's characters engage in a series of vernacular games, the dozens, and signifyin'. All these cultural activities are extensions of the blues or variations on a blues theme. Wilson sets his works in sites that enable such communal engagement, verbal jousting, and oral transmission of culture. For instance, he places the band interaction in *Ma Rainey* in the band room downstairs (in another area onstage), separated from the recording studio above (a separate stage area). The band room represents what Houston A. Baker terms a "blues matrix." Baker envisions the blues matrix as a "point of ceaseless input and output, a web of intersecting, crisscrossing impulses always in productive transit" (1984: 3). For Baker the prototypical site of the blues matrix is a railroad crossing, "the juncture of multidirectionality," and a place "betwixt and between" (7). Situated at the blues matrix, the blues singer transcends spatial and sociohistorical limitations. The band room as blues matrix is equally a site of power and potential. The band room is a space of unfinished business, where the band must rehearse its songs and await the arrival of Ma Rainey. It is a metaphorical space where the band members enact rituals and tales of survival that replicate the patterns of black experiences in America.

Along similar lines, Seth's boarding house in *Joe Turner's Come and Gone*, and Memphis's restaurant in *Two Trains Running*, the respective settings for these two dramas, are liminal spaces, blues matrixes, "betwixt and between" places. The boarding house serves as a way station for African Americans during the Great Migration from the South heading North to find work. Seth remarks: "word get out they need men to work in the mill and put in these road... and niggers drop everything and head North look for freedom" (1991: 209). The characters come to Seth's boarding house in search of a new life, a new sense of self, or as Wilson notes, "they search for ways to reconnect, to reassemble, to give clear and luminous meaning to the song" (203). Memphis's restaurant also functions as a way station for its regular customers. As the play opens the restaurant is threatened by the advent of urban renewal and the impending reality that it soon will be torn down. Its liminal (temporary) space is confirmed. The restaurant exists between its past glory and its uncertain future. Memphis laments: "At one time you couldn't get a set in here. Had the jukebox working and everything. Time somebody get up somebody sit down before they could get out the door" (1993: 309–10). The liminality of the spaces creates locations of great creative and destructive potential simultaneously. They are sites in which Wilson employs the "productive transit" of the blues, with its multi-directionality and cross-purposes.

Bolstered by the blues and other influences, Wilson set out to become a play-wright. At his friend Charles Purdy's instigation, he moved to St. Paul, Minnesota, in 1978 and wrote plays, including *Black Bart and the Sacred Hills*, for Purdy to direct with his company. In order to subsidize his income, Wilson also worked as a scriptwriter for the Science Museum of Minnesota. His career and his destiny changed forever in 1982, when he submitted an early draft of his play, *Ma Rainey's Black Bottom*, to the Eugene O'Neill Playwrights Workshop in Waterford, Connecticut. It was accepted (he had tried the previous year with *Fullerton Street*, but it was turned down). At the O'Neill, he met Lloyd Richards, the Director of the O'Neill Play-wrights Workshop as well as the Artistic Director of the Yale Drama School. Richards was also the first black director ever on Broadway, directing the production of Lorraine Hansberry's *A Raisin in the Sun* in 1959. Richards and Wilson began a friendship and collaboration that would lead to the production of six of Wilson's cycle plays at regional theatres across the country and on Broadway.

Ma Rainey's Black Bottom (1984), Wilson's first critically acclaimed play, and arguably the most musical of his plays to date, establishes a foundation for Wilson's blues theology that he examines with his later plays. In *Ma Rainey*, the significance of finding one's cultural and spiritual regeneration through the blues song plays out principally through the conflicting views of the title character, Ma Rainey, and the spirited young trumpet player, Levee. Levee fails to understand his relationship to the music, and never realizes his blues song. Ma Rainey, in contrast, recognizes that the blues can become both a self-accentuating song and a declaration of the collective, cultural memory of African Americans.

In *Ma Rainey*, as in Wilson's subsequent works, the dominant culture seeks to suppress, to control, and to commodify the black blues song. *Ma Rainey* opens with two white characters, Ma Rainey's manager, Irvin, and Sturdyvant, the recording studio owner and a producer of "race records," onstage. Together Irvin and Sturdyvant concoct their plan for the recording session and for capturing Ma Rainey's blues voice with a less than generous contract. Wilson juxtaposes Irvin and Sturdyvant's plan to commercialize Ma Rainey's blues song with Ma's own resolve to protect the integrity of herself and her music. Ma testifies to Wilson's contention that the blues are a uniquely black voice that whites' desire but cannot understand: "White folks don't understand about the blues. They hear it come out, but they don't know how it got there" (1991: 499).

Throughout his historical cycle of plays, Wilson replays this theme, as whites repeatedly attempt to seize or possess black music, the black blues song. Early in *The Piano Lesson*, when the protagonist, Boy Willie, inquires about potential buyers for the family's heirloom, a carved piano, his uncle Doaker tells him that there is a white man going around trying to buy up black people's musical instruments. Even more significantly, the ghost of the recently deceased white Southern landowner, Sutter, materializes in the Pittsburgh home of Doaker and Boy Willie's sister, Berniece, in an effort to reclaim the family's piano, the symbol of their African American struggle and survival. In *Joe Turner's Come and Gone*, the brooding central figure in the play, Herald Loomis, has lost his identity and his place in the world after being incarcerated by Joe Turner. The title character, Joe Turner, is an absent presence in the play. Mythologized in an old blues song, Joe Turne(y)r was the brother of a former governor of Tennessee who kept black men in servitude for seven years. (The actual twenty-ninth governor of Tennessee from 1893 to 1897 was Pete Turney as well as his brother Joe Turney. However, as related in the autobiography of W. C. Handy, the name was changed to Joe Turner in the blues song that black women sang to lament the abuse and capture of their husbands and loved ones.) These indentured black men functioned as a personal chain gang performing menial labor throughout the state. Through the action of the play, Wilson reveals that Joe Turner imprisoned Herald Loomis and other black men in an effort to capture their "song." In Wilson's plays, music and song act as metaphors for African American identity, spirit, and soul. Through the invisible presence and symbolic activities of off-stage white characters, Wilson suggests that the dominant culture has continually sought to subjugate African American human-ity and suppress the power and ability of African Americans to sing their song without looking over their shoulder.

Wilson's blues theology privileges the blues musician. He posits the blues musician as a potentially powerful site of black resistive agency. Too often, however, the musicians fail to realize the power they possess. As with any gift or power, the power of the blues musician exacts certain costs and expectations from the ones to whom it is given. Lyons in *Fences*, Jeremy in *Joe Turner's Come and Gone*, and Wining Boy in *The Piano Lesson*, for instance, all represent blues musicians who have misunderstood the spiritual force of the blues song and the cultural responsibility inherent in their ability to play the blues. As a result, they are exploited for their music and fall victim to those who wish to control their spirit and song. The band members in *Ma Rainey*, similarly, fail to realize fully the power and privilege of their music, their blues voice. Toledo, the piano player, chastises his fellow band members, "You lucky they [white people] let you be an entertainer. They ain't got to accept your way of entertaining. You lucky and don't even know it" (1991: 507). Still, it is on and through these musicians that Wilson positions himself as blues musician improvising on a theme. Toledo's declarations of the need for African Americans to recognize their connections to Africa represent an important element of Wilson's blues theology. Wilson believes that in order for African Americans to be able to sing their own song, to feel truly liberated in the American context, they must rediscover their "African-ness." Wilson puts it this way: "One of the things I'm trying to say in my writing is that we can never begin to make a contribution to the society except as Africans" (qtd. in Savran 1988: 296). Toledo, accordingly, reprimands the band and himself for not being African and for being imitation white men.

Ma Rainey, the title character based on the legendary blues singer Gertrude "Ma Rainey" Pridgett, recognizes the power of the music to move through her. "You don't sing to feel better. . . . You sing 'cause it's a way of understanding life" (1991: 499). Ma explains that singing the blues is not simply therapy but rather an engagement with a complex and enabling force that acts to understand and even to transform and to transcend life. Ma remains a fiercely independent woman throughout the action of the play. Recognizing that the purpose of the recording session is to record her voice and her music, Ma will not be objectified; instead, she uses her position as a desired musical commodity to legitimize her authority. She vociferously maintains that the band works for her, not the other way around. After the recording session, Ma exercises her blues voice in one final act of defiance. She delays signing the release forms that legally grant Irvin and Sturdyvant control over her recorded music. Through this act, she asserts the power of the blues singer to overcome material limitations. She retains her artistic autonomy and rebuts others who wish to claim her song.

Still, the play does not end with Ma's defiant exit from the recording studio, but escalates into tragedy in the band room below. The ending of *Ma Rainey*, in which one of the band members murders another, is a complex and confounding blues moment. It stands in stark contrast to endings of Wilson's later dramas such as *Fences*, *Joe Turner*, and *Piano Lesson*, in which characters reach moments of spiritual fulfillment, acknowledge their relationships to the African American past, and perform actions of self-actualization, self-determination, and collective communion. Present in the final scene of *Ma Rainey*, in contrast, is the ironic anguish of the blues wail. After being exploited by the white studio owner Sturdyvant, Levee transfers his anger and stabs Toledo, who unfortunately steps on his shoes. Levee's stabbing of Toledo, like all acts of black-on-black violence, strikes out against African American collectivity and cultural unity. The murder of Toledo represents a performance of tragic, unfulfilled promise, a loss of the black self that must be reclaimed through the triumph of the blues voice. The death of Toledo stands as a lesson that African Americans must learn from and that Wilson builds upon in his later plays.

Wilson claims that he started *Fences* (1986), his first Pulitzer Prize-winning play, with "the image of a man standing in his yard with a baby in his arms" (qtd. in DeVries 1987: 25). Beginning with this image, Wilson sought to subvert the dominant culture's representations of African American men as irresponsible, absentee fathers. Wilson creates Troy Maxson, a larger-than-life figure, who feels an overwhelming sense of duty and responsibility to his family. With an impenetrable resolve, he perceives familial values only from his perspective. Troy's self-involved concept of familial duty and responsibility prevents him from seeing the harm he causes, the pain his decisions inflict on other family members.

Through a series of retrospective stories performed by Troy, Wilson reveals Troy's victimization by and resentment of the forces of social and economic oppression. Wilson also uses these moments to disclose the influence that Troy's prior relationship with his father now exacts on his relationship with his own son Cory. Physically beaten by his father, Troy was forced to strike out on his own. During the course of the play, Cory must undergo a similar rite of passage. Repeating the family history, Cory physically confronts his father, is beaten by Troy, and forced to leave his father's house. The repetition of behavior patterns by father and son underscores Wilson's conviction that history plays an important role in determining contemporary identity. Only by literally confronting the embodiment of the past, one's father or "forefathers," can one gain entrance into the future or ascendancy into adulthood.

In the play's second act, Troy's adultery provides the catalyst that propels his wife, Rose, to reassess her position, to gain a greater self-awareness and to change. Rose blooms. Although Rose spiritually distances herself from Troy, she does not leave the marriage. Her final assessment of their marriage, delivered to her son Cory in the last scene, functions to reconcile father and son and emphasizes Rose's own resignation to "what life offered me in terms of being a woman" (1991: 190). At the close of *Fences*, Cory is able to accept the continued "presence" of his father in his life. This acceptance comes after Cory has returned home from the Marines and announces to Rose his intent to boycott his father's funeral. Wilson juxtaposes Cory's return with the entrance of a new character, Troy's 7-year-old daughter from his affair, Raynell (Cory's half-sister). Wilson uses Raynell as a critical element in his redemptive strategy. Raynell visually represents the inextricable connection between past and present. Not only is she the manifestation of Troy's past infidelities but the signifier of his redemption. Her appearance enables both the audience and Cory to understand better the importance of inheritance, the perpetuation and veneration of history. In addition, here as in other Wilson works the child, Raynell, symbolizes the hope for the family's future. Significantly, her entrance into the action occurs not just on the day of Troy's funeral, but in the year 1965, in the midst of the civil rights era, a period of intense struggle and new opportunity for African Americans.

To date, *Joe Turner's Come and Gone* (1987) remains August Wilson's most non-realistic, non-linear, and most ritualistic work. Rhythms, symbols, and spirituality propel this drama. The action does not evolve directly out of causal progression, but emerges disjointedly. As Paul Carter Harrison writes, "The play operates outside the logic of naturalism which can only serve to restrain the ritualistic passage of time and burden the potential enlargement of events with fixed expectations of cause and effect" (1991: 314). The events set this play within a world of liminality, betwixt and between. The year is 1911, a time on the cusp of the "Great Migration" from the South to North. The context of the environment allows Wilson to foreground the spiritual nature of the acts that take place within this space. The play as a whole operates as ritual conveying blessings on the audience as a gathered congregation. Wilson set the work in 1911 because of the palpable and direct relationship of African Americans at that time to their African roots. Within this work perhaps more visibly than his others, Wilson asserts the African in African American experience.

The central character, Herald Loomis, arrives at Seth's Pittsburgh boarding house spiritually and psychologically dislocated. He is in search of his wife, Martha, from whom he was separated some 11 years before when he was incarcerated for seven years by Joe Turner. Along with his daughter, Zonia, he has been on the road, moving for four years in search of Martha. For Loomis, paradoxically, the contradiction between his constant movement and the lack of movement within the direction of his life is most acute. Loomis realizes that his forward motion depends on retreating to the past and settling his unfinished business with his wife. His arrival at the boarding house, to the distress of its owner, Seth, interrupts the behavior and life of all the inhabitants.

While Loomis wears the pain of his alienation on his face, the scars run much deeper and are hidden behind his facade until Bynum goads his revelation through song. Bynum provokes him into revealing his servitude by singing the song "They Tell Me Joe Turner's Come and Gone." When Loomis hears the song, he reacts vehemently against it. The song has clear political and social implications, acting as a powerful medium for change. With the assistance of the mysterious and powerful Bynum, a conjure man and resident of the boarding house, Loomis comes to understand his search as a spiritual and practical quest to find his "song," a connection to a past lost while enslaved by Joe Turner. He journeys toward self-knowledge, spiritual and psychological liberation.

Hilary DeVries points out that "Loomis's search for his own past symbolizes the quest of an entire race" (1987: 25). Wilson believes that black Americans must rediscover "their song," their connection with their African heritage (qtd. in ibid.: 23). In the play's final scene, Loomis draws a knife and cuts his own chest, proceeding to bleed. He bleeds for himself, but he also symbolically bleeds for black America in search of its collective song. Unshackled from the painful psychological burdens of servitude, Loomis rediscovers his song, his identity, and shines. His personal

Plate 15. Joe Turner's Come and Gone, by August Wilson, Missouri Repertory Theatre. Left to right: Al White (Seth Holly), Adolphus Ward (Bynum Walker), Cheryl Lynn Bruce (Bertha Holly), and Larry Paulsen (Rutherford Selig), photo by Dan Ipock. Courtesy of the Missouri Repertory Theatre.

transcendence heralds the need for black Americans to regain their African past and reorient themselves in the future.

In his second Pulitzer Prize-winning play, *The Piano Lesson* (1990), as in his first Pulitzer Prize winner, *Fences*, August Wilson appropriates and expands the traditions of American family drama in order to examine issues of inheritance. At the center of the family conflict is a piano. According to Wilson, "The real issue is the piano, the legacy. How are you going to use it?" (qtd. in DeVries 1987: 25). As a symbol, the piano is complex and multileveled; its meanings are both personal and political. The sociohistory of the piano is inextricably linked to the sociohistory of the Charles family. Boy Willie Charles intends to sell the piano in order to buy land where his father worked as a sharecropper and his grandfather as a slave. His sister Berniece, on the other hand, believes that this piano, which her father gave his life to protect, must be kept in the family and can never be sold. The ideological separation of Boy Willie, the Southern brother, from Berniece, the Northern sister, becomes the site for a practical, spiritual, and ontological reconnection. On another level, in fact, the play is a ghost story concerned with the "real" threat represented by the ghost of the recently deceased white landowner, Sutter, who returns to haunt the family in his search for the piano. Ultimately Wilson suggests in *Piano Lesson*, as he does in his other works, that African American survival in the United States depends on the celebration of that spirit, that cultural memory that is particularly African.

Berniece, the sister who has migrated North, is a figure of conflict and contradiction. She both acknowledges and attempts to ignore the impact of the past on the present. Berniece controls the piano in *Piano Lesson*. It resides in her house and she is determined to keep it there. In her rational and persuasive arguments for keeping the piano, and thwarting Boy Willie's efforts to sell it, Berniece relies upon the history, the legacy of familial sacrifice, both maternal and paternal, that has carried the piano to its current resting place. For Berniece, selling the piano is a sacrilege that would desecrate her parents' memories. Their uncle, Doaker, explains that Berniece will not sell the piano because her father died over the possession of it. The piano, therefore, carried symbolic meaning to her. At the same time, however, Berniece seeks to avoid the memories of the past. She is fragmented and dislocated from her Southern roots and wants to maintain this dislocation. As a result, she neglects her duties as cultural progenitor. While Berniece keeps the piano, she avoids playing it. Her neglect of the piano and her unwillingness to confront the ghosts of her past threaten the current stability of the Charles family, allowing the ghost of Sutter to return and compete for the ownership of the piano and the possession of their "songs." It is this position that Wilson seeks to critique in *Piano Lesson*; as he says, "the question was, 'Can one acquire a sense of self-worth by denying one's past?'"(qtd. in Savran 1988: 24).

Only at the conclusion of the play, when Berniece returns to the piano, can the ghost of Sutter be exorcised. Berniece, drawn to the piano by the confrontation between Boy Willie and Sutter's ghost, plays a song that explicitly calls on the ancestral spirits for assistance. Wilson describes Berniece's offering to the ancestral spirits as *"an old urge to song that is both a commandment and a plea. With each repetition it gains strength. It is intended as an exorcism and a dressing for battle. A rustle of wind blowing across two continents"* (1990: 106). Inherent, then, in Berniece's calling on her ancestors is the African tradition of ancestral worship. Her act symbolically unites her with her ancestors in Africa. Berniece recognizes the importance of the ancestral spirits and the power of these "ghosts." This moment is significant in Wilson's preeminent project to recuperate the African-ness in African American experience.

As with his other historical dramas, August Wilson sets *Two Trains Running* (1992) in a time of transition, the year 1969, the final year of a decade that has come to symbolize resistance, irreverence, anarchy, and upheaval in America. During that time, African Americans turned from the peaceful non-violence of the civil rights movement to the revolutionary militancy of the Black Power Movement. Wilson locates *Two Trains Running* in a small Pittsburgh restaurant that is at once within as well as outside of the pressing urgencies of those times. The shop must be torn down as part of the process of urban renewal. Outside its confines, a funeral for the deceased Prophet Samuel and a rally for the slain black leader Malcolm X are held. Inside the shop, the background characters confront issues of identity and black power, gender and self-determination. The play is at once timely and timeless, operating within a specific historical context and at the same time commenting on contemporary African American culture. Wilson writes about the black idealism and cultural nationalism of the 1960s from the historical distance of the 1990s.

The plot of the play revolves around the regulars who frequent the restaurant and an interloper, Sterling, a young man recently released from prison who enters the restaurant early in the first act in search of direction. At issue in the play is the relationship between capitalism and spirituality. Set during the time when the rhetoric of Black Nationalism and 1960s paradigms of black liberation emerged, Wilson bemoans the lack of black investment in the black community. Holloway, a wizened old regular at Memphis's restaurant, reports, "That's all you got around here is niggers with somebody else's money in their pocket. And they don't do nothing but trade it off on each other, I got it today and you got it tomorrow. Until sooner or later as sure as the sun shine, somebody gonna take it and give it to the white man. Money go from you to me to you and then – bingo, it's gone" (1993: 33–4). Wilson argues that there is a linkage between black economics and spirituality. The spiritual center of the play is Aunt Esther, the off-stage mystic who at 349 years old is as old as the black presence in the United States. When spoken, her name, "Aunt Esther," sounds purposefully like the word "ancestor." Symbolically through her, Wilson links past to present and underscores the African in African American traditions. Although off-stage, she dispenses wisdom and advice. Then, in a manner not unlike African traditions for honoring river goddesses, she asks her visitors to pay tribute by throwing $20 into the river.

While Holloway, Sterling, and Memphis eventually honor Aunt Esther, Mr. West, another regular at the restaurant, does not. He refuses to throw his money away in this fashion. West, the owner of the local funeral parlor and the richest man in town, is spiritually moribund. He does not recognize the need for African American economic strategy connecting the acquisition of wealth to the maintenance of spiritual and social wellbeing within the black community. Wilson contrasts West with the character Hambone. Hambone's mental condition has deteriorated to where he can only repeat two phrases: "He gonna give me my ham!" "I want my ham!" (14). Nine and one half years before the play begins, Hambone painted a fence for the white butcher Lutz. Lutz explained to him that he would pay him a ham if he did a good job or a chicken if the job was just adequate. After completing the work and expecting a ham, Lutz offered Hambone only a chicken. Hambone refused to accept the chicken; he believes he deserved the ham. Every morning for nine and one half years he stands in front of Lutz's Meat Market and demands his ham. Lutz defers and repeats his offer of the chicken. Hambone, like Gabriel in *Fences* and Hedley in *Seven Guitars*, is another of Wilson's characters that have special powers and a unique understanding of the world. Holloway says of Hambone: "I say he might have more sense than me and you. Cause he ain't willing to accept whatever the white man throw at him" (30). Symbolically Hambone represents both the forgotten promise of 40 acres and a mule due to black people and the obsessed determination to obtain rightful payment – reparations – for slavery. When Hambone dies, West reveals that his body was scarred from head to toe. He literally wears the scars of slavery and is a monument to the black past.

In *Seven Guitars* (1995), Wilson's sixth play to reach Broadway, the blues inform both form and content. Wilson sets *Seven Guitars* in the 1940s. The play opens just after the funeral for the misguided bluesman Floyd Barton. The other characters gather in the backyard of Floyd's former girlfriend, Vera, to drink and commiserate. Floyd was a promising blues singer with a hit record to his credit. As the plot unfolds, the circumstances surrounding his death are revealed. The main action of the play concerns flashbacks to times when Barton was alive. Consequently, the real movement of the play has already occurred, back in the past, before the opening scene. The play literally progresses forward by going backward. Floyd "Schoolboy" Barton's story is reminiscent of the tragic myths and legends of larger-than-life black bluesmen. Floyd believes fiercely that his success depends on a new record deal with Mr. T. L. Hall, a white producer and agent. Mr. T. L. Hall, however, has exploited the illiterate Barton and the white-controlled record industry. Floyd's myopic, self-obsessed desire for fame and fortune in Chicago results in his betrayal of the redemptive power of the blues and values of community which the blues inspire. His capitulation to white hegemony is symbolized by his pawning his guitar, the instrument of his cultural potency. His demise is inevitable.

The West Indian Hedley rants and raves about black social action. He rages against the white power structure, but his cries go unheeded by the other characters. Wilson, however, wants the audience to recognize the truth, power, and prophesy in Hedley's words. Hedley's obsession, his singular focus, enables him to connect with the suppressed and oppressed African American song of freedom in ways "a normal or sane mind" can not. Throughout the play Floyd and Hedley play a game around a lyric to the song "I thought I heard Buddy Bolden say" or "Buddy Bolden's Blues." Bolden, a builder and part-time barber, cornet player, and bandleader in New Orleans, 1877–1931, has been called the first man of jazz, the "King" of New Orleans. Floyd and Hedley's disagreement over the lyric reflects back on the improvisational nature of the song and its oral transmission through time. It also symbolizes Floyd and Hedley's divergent ideologies. While Floyd imagines Bolden as a self-serving fellow musician demanding payment, Hedley envisions him as a redemptive figure bearing monetary gifts and offering salvation. Within the drama of *Seven Guitars* Wilson considers the cultural, social, and spiritual power of music and musicians. Art and ethics unite, and art can function as a force for social change.

In *Jitney*, concern over the proposed demolition of Becker's jitney cabstand becomes an occasion for Becker and his drivers to move to a new position of collective unity and resistance. Within the world of Becker's cab station, Wilson develops the particular histories and idiosyncrasies of the cab drivers. The stories of Youngblood's desire to buy a house, of Fielding's drinking problems, and Turnbo's overwhelming desire to be involved in everybody else's business, unfold. These riffs and antiphonal melodies are spaces within which the conflict of the play explodes and the characters clash. Youngblood reacts to Turnbo's insidious implications and unwanted involvement in his love life. Still, at the same time, the action also joins the characters together in an ensemble. The final scene of the play, the funeral for Becker and its aftermath, constitutes a moment where the characters harmonize in solemn communion. There is collective understanding of the need to work, to struggle together for the benefit of all.

Most centrally in *Jitney*, as in *Fences*, is a father–son conflict. The prodigal son, Booster, has returned from prison where he has served time for the murder of his white girlfriend and now comes to make peace with the father who never visited him in prison. The son reaches out to a father that neglected him in a time of particular need and misunderstanding, but his father cannot reach back. As each man expresses his own loss, his own particular sense of the past and perspectives on their relationship, each fails to communicate with the other or to achieve any reconciliation. Becker, still struggling with his own relation to the white power structure, cannot offer his son the forgiveness and love he desires.

Wilson does, however, move Booster and Becker to a new understanding of their own identity and their shared connections. The rapprochement they reach does not occur face to face and yet the communication is dialectic: they both learn lessons from each other as the father's spirit lives on in the son. Jolted by his reunion with his son, Becker decides that he can no longer wait on the future, but in 1977 must fight now for change against the forces of urban renewal. Becker determines to act for himself, to be his own man and not compromise his position and fight the ensuing urban renewal. Booster, too, evolves in his understanding of his father and his appreciation of his father's stature. After he learns of Becker's sudden death, Booster, the ex-con son, immediately turns to answering the telephone at the gypsy cab station and symbolically and defiantly assumes his father's position. Becker and Booster are able to forgive and let go even as they hold on to memory. The distance built up over 20 years of imprisonment dissolves. Tragically, this resolution comes without the opportunity to express their mutual forgiveness. The influence of the father still remains an indelible part of the son.

Internal ruptures are the focus for the apocalyptic vision of the African American community in the 1980s that Wilson imagines in *King Hedley II*. Wilson depicts a black wasteland devastated by black-on-black violence and crime. Significantly, Aunt Esther dies of grief in *King Hedley II*. Her black cat dies as well. Wilson perceives a black America during the 1980s in which community has been destroyed by systematic abandonment, internalized oppression, self-destructive violence, and, thus, is in need of spiritual and social regeneration.

Through the man/child title character of *King Hedley II*, Wilson reveals what happens to dreams deferred, to hopes unfulfilled, and to the power of the past unrealized in the present. Tragically, *King Hedley II* is a toxic combination of heredity and environment; the sins of the father are in fact reaped upon this son. His mother, Ruby, has named him after King Hedley, the man she slept with when young and pregnant by another man, and King, the son, naively believes Hedley to be his real father. Ruby has not told him differently. Consequently, the son lives in what he perceives to be his father's footsteps. While he possesses that same insurgent spirit that consumed Hedley in *Seven Guitars*, he is also a product of an urban environment that has thwarted his potential and stunted his revolutionary growth.

The end of *King Hedley II* is, then, the most tragically violent moment in a Wilson play to date. In an effort to save her son's life, Ruby accidentally shoots and kills King.

King's death is both an ending and a beginning. He falls on the grave of Aunt Esther's black cat and his blood seeps onto the grave, symbolically blessing the ground, enabling Aunt Esther to be reborn. King is now literally the chosen one who is sacrificed in order to prepare the way for the regeneration of the greater community, for the good of those who live on. The concluding moment of *King Hedley II* continues the Wilson trope of the redemptive power of madness as Stool Pigeon, in the face of seemingly insurmountable tragedy, calls out God and for God's renewal. "Thy Will! Not man's will! Thy Will! You wrote the Beginning and the End! Bring down the Fire!" (2003: 68). Standing over the body of the sacrificial King, Stool Pigeon sounds a chant that unites the Christian and African and he extols God to act. "The Conquering Lion of Judea! Our Bright and Morning Star! I want your best! See Him coming! We give you our Glory!" (69). As the lights conclude the play, Wilson asks that "*the sound of a cat's meow is heard.*" The sound of the cat signals the success of Stool Pigeon's efforts, of King's sacrifice; it trumpets the potential rebirth of Aunt Esther and thus renews hope for the African American future.

Even as Wilson works out plans for the final play in his cycle, his own life continues to link art and activism. Aligning himself with the African American history of struggle and survival as well as the black tradition of a functional art of protest, Wilson delivered a powerful call for a new black theatre movement at the Theatre Communications Group 1996 National Convention. Spurred on by the enthusiastic responses to this speech, Wilson helped to organize a National Black Theatre Summit at Golden Pond near Dartmouth College in March 1997. Over 300 black theatre scholars, theatre practitioners, economic entrepreneurs, and community activists joined to examine the future of black theatre. Significantly, the summit led to the creation of a new national black theatre organization, the African Grove Institute, named after the very first documented black theatre in this country, Mr. Brown's African Grove Company (1821–3). In his most recent one-man show entitled *How I Learned What I Learned*, first staged in May 2003 at the Seattle Repertory Theatre, Wilson performs his own history, a history that is at once figurative and real. As he recalls stories, people, and memories from his past, he situates himself in effect as a character within his African American cycle. Within this performance, Wilson understands his own life in terms of the pageant of African American history.

Bibliography

Baker, H. A. (1984). *Blues, Ideology, and Afro-American Literature: A Vernacular Theory.* Chicago: University of Chicago Press.

DeVries, H. (1987). "A Song in Search of Myself." *American Theatre*, January 25.

Ellison, R. (1964). "Blues People." In *The Shadow and The Act.* New York: Random House.

Fishman, J. (1994). "Romare Bearden and August Wilson." In Alan Nadel (ed.), *May All Your Fences Have Gates: Essays on the Drama of August Wilson.* Iowa City: University of Iowa Press.

Freeman, S. (1987). "A Voice from the Streets." *New York Times Magazine*, March 15.

Harrison, P. C. (1991). "August Wilson's Blues Poetics." In *Three Plays by August Wilson*. Pittsburgh: University of Pittsburgh Press.

Savran, D. (1988). "August Wilson." In *In Their Own Words*. New York: Theatre Communications Group.

Shannon, S. (1995). *The Dramatic Vision of August Wilson*. Washington, DC: Howard University Press.

——(1996). "August Wilson's Autobiography." In A. Singh et al. (eds.), *Memory and Cultural Politics*. Boston: Northeastern University Press.

Wilson, A. (1985). *Ma Rainey's Black Bottom*. New York: New American Library.

——(1987). *Fences*. New York: New American Library.

——(1988). *Joe Turner's Come and Gone*. New York: New American Library.

——(1990). *The Piano Lesson*. New York: Plume.

——(1991). *Three Plays* [*Ma Rainey's Black Bottom*, *Fences*, and *Joe Turner's Come and Gone*]. Pittsburgh: University of Pittsburgh Press.

——(1993). *Two Trains Running*. New York: New American Library.

——(1996a). "The Ground on Which I Stand." *American Theatre*: 16.

——(1996b). *Seven Guitars*. New York: Dutton.

——(2000). *Jitney*. Woodstock, NY: Overlook Press.

——(2002). "American Histories: Chasing Dreams and Nightmares; Sailing the Stream of Black Culture." *New York Times*, April 23, Sec. 2: 1.

——(2003). *King Hedley II*. In Harry J. Elam, Jr. and Robert Alexander (eds.), *The Fire This Time!* New York: Theatre Communications Group.

21

Native American Drama

Ann Haugo

During the last quarter of the twentieth century, important changes occurred for American Indian people and cultures in American theatre, both on stage and in scholarship. The Native Theatre Movement, which was begun in the early 1970s by Kiowa/Delaware playwright Hanay Geiogamah with the formation of the American Indian Theatre Ensemble, was sustained through the formation of several other companies in the next few years, most notably the 1974 founding of the Thunderbird Theatre company at Haskell Indian Nations University and the 1975 formation of Spiderwoman Theatre. As a result of these theatres, as well as others, there are now Native theatres throughout the United States and Canada, with dozens of playwrights from many different Native nations publishing and producing their works. This chapter will provide a survey of the Native Theatre Movement, shedding light on key artists, plays, and scholarly publications in the field.

Colonialism, Theatre, and American Indian Identity

During the 1960s and 1970s, examinations of American Indian drama would have focused on dramas written by non-Native authors about Native subjects. Plays like Arthur Kopit's *Indians* are examples, but his drama is hardly the first of its kind. Some of the most famous early American dramas, such as John Augustus Stone's *Metamora: or, The Last of the Wampanoags* in 1829 created Native characters (caricatures) in their dramas. In addition, some of the first theatre publications on American Indian subjects examined plays by non-Native authors. Eugene Jones's book *Native Americans as Shown on the Stage, 1753–1916* (1988) studies Indian "character types" by non-Native playwrights. The consequences of Jones's work inspired a series of scholarly books that examine the representation of Native Americans during the nineteenth and twentieth centuries. Don Wilmeth's 1989 article "Noble or Ruthless Savage? The

American Indian on Stage and in the Drama" also focuses on dramatic stereotypes of Indian men – the "noble savage" and "red villain," for instance – from early American drama to the plays of the late twentieth century. Wilmeth draws attention to Native playwrights, such as Monica Charles, Robert Shorty (Navajo), Bruce King (Oneida), and Hanay Geiogamah (Kiowa/Delaware), in the later portion of this article. He briefly discusses Geiogamah's plays *Body Indian* and *Foghorn*, noting that Geiogamah's characters "avoid, for the most part, the stereotypic image of the usual stage Indian, although he is not above using stereotypes for his own purposes" (2000: 146). Wilmeth closes his article by observing:

> The majority of plays about American Indians, certainly those that have gained some popularity or critical attention, have been written by white authors with little know-ledge of real Native Americans. For the most part plays with Indian characters have only created stereotypical Indians, dominated by the noble savage, the villainous red devil, and the Indian princess or pathetic maiden, with few of these types portrayed as real people having distinctive personalities. (150)

Wilmeth's statement still resonates. A few additional American Indian character-izations appearing to portray Native Americans "as real people having distinctive personalities" have surfaced onstage in the late twentieth century. Yet these produc-tions – Christopher Sergel's adaptation of *Black Elk Speaks*, or Robert Schenkkan's *The Kentucky Cycle*, for example – fail to escape the unfortunate shortcomings of American Indian representations on the stage. Perhaps the most egregious fault lies in the fact that these plays, as well as others, tend to depict American Indians in the past tense (as if they no longer exist) rather than as contemporary, living people with families, homes, jobs, and dreams.

An examination of Native theatre should acknowledge the inheritance of these misrepresentations in American theatre, because that inheritance establishes what I have referred to elsewhere as a particularly hostile representational context for Native playwrights and actors (Haugo 2004). The problem is hardly a theatrical one, but rather a problem endemic to American popular culture in general. The equivalent of minstrel shows, with their stereotypic depiction of African Americans, still occurs for Native America, most notably in the performances of sports team mascots like the Cleveland Indians' Chief Wahoo or the University of Illinois at Urbana-Champaign's Chief Illiniwek.[1] America cultivates the obsession with what Cherokee author Rayna Green has dubbed "Playing Indian": non-Native people pretending to be Indian. Green describes this desire to perform Indianness as "one of the oldest and most pervasive forms of American cultural expression," a practice having roots in the "establishment of a distinctive American culture," and implicated in the growth of American national identity (1988: 31). Philip Deloria's book *Playing Indian* (1998) also documents and explicates some of these performative traditions, such as the carnivalesque masquerade of the Boston Tea Party, the Tammany Society, the Boy Scouts, and the Grateful Dead.[2]

Postcolonial critics have noted that a colonizing culture tends to speak for the colonized, and in doing so tends to reinterpret the colonized people's identity. In America, this has meant defining Native cultures as "primitive," passing legislation that defines who can and cannot be recognized as Indian by the government, and replacing tribal groups' names. Thus, the Anishinabe became the "Chippewa" and the Ho-Chunk were given the name of "Winnebago." Colonial cultures obsessively control the identity of the colonized subject, and in a rather ironic way, the obsession is sometimes enacted in masquerade.[3]

African philosopher and psychiatrist Frantz Fanon has argued that the colonial project completes its final act of domination when the colonized people see themselves through the eyes of the colonizer. In America, following Fanon's assertion, if Native people accept misrepresentations on screen, stage, in the classroom, or in the sports arena, the American colonial project succeeds. However, resistance to these images and innuendoes emerges. While there are undoubtedly social and political problems in Native communities (as in all communities), Native people are far from a defeated Nation and still actively resist colonization. Native theatre is merely one of many venues through which the resistance happens. Some Native theatre artists resist consciously and overtly, in politically charged theatre creations that challenge stereo-typical, colonial policies and their aftermath. Other artists, whose work is not overtly political or confrontational, challenge ongoing colonialism indirectly; for example, some theatres employ Native languages, using the stage as a way to teach and preserve inherited languages that are endangered. Some Native theatres focus primarily on helping Native people recover from the effects of colonialism, aiding in the recovery of spiritual values and identities as indigenous people. One such play is *Strength of Indian Women* by Vera Manuel (Secwepemc and Ktunaxa), which draws on the stories of women who survive abuses of the residential school system in Canada. The play is frequently performed at conferences for survivors, providing a catalyst for dialogue about the experiences of being taken from their families, all too often physically and sexually abused, and taught to be ashamed of their Native identity and families. Some Native theatres draw on oral traditions, dramatizing trickster stories or creation stories. The importance of these works is political as well as aesthetic. Muriel Miguel of Spiderwoman Theatre notes that "just the fact that you're on stage telling these stories is political. Just the fact that you're there" (Haugo 2002: 227). In a society that would have eradicated their languages (and in some cases succeeded), taken their children, and eliminated as much Native culture as possible, the mere public act of claiming one's Native identity is a political act.

In an illuminating illustration of the power of Native theatre to resist colonial attitudes, Gloria Miguel of Spiderwoman Theatre stands onstage toward the end of the play *Winnetou's Snake Oil Show from Wigwam City*. Arms extended from her sides, she turns slightly so that the entire audience can see her. "See me. I'm talking, loving, hating, drinking too much, creating, performing, my stories, my songs, my dances, my ideas. Now, I telling you, step back, move aside, sit down, hold your breath, save your own culture. Discover your own spirituality." The other performers then join her, each speaking their own words of survival: "I'm alive. I'm not defeated." "My stories, my songs. My culture." "All our bones are not in museums. We are not defeated. We are still here" (262).

The Native American Theatre Ensemble

In the late 1960s, a literary movement began that scholars now refer to as the Native American Literary Renaissance. Its initial moments are marked by the 1968 publication of *House Made of Dawn*, a novel by Kiowa author N. Scott Momaday. That novel won the 1969 Pulitzer Prize for Literature, the first time that a Native American author won the prize. While Native Americans had been publishing literature since the eighteenth century, it took till the 1970s for a new level of attention to be paid to Native writers. Presses began programs specializing in Native literature; universities began teaching courses on Native literature; and Native writers were included in "survey" courses of American literature. Authors such as Momaday, James Welch (Blackfeet/Gros Ventre), Leslie Marmon Silko (Laguna Pueblo), Paula Gunn Allen (Laguna Pueblo), and others, observed their rising presence in the literary scene.

Parallel to the literary movement and certainly influencing it was the "Red Power Movement," the term used to describe the civil rights movement for American Indians. Organizations whose activities gave initial strength to the movement were the National Indian Youth Council (founded 1961), the Native American Rights Fund (1964), and the Indian Historical Society (1964), but the organization that became the best known in the Red Power Movement was AIM, the American Indian Movement, founded in Minneapolis in 1966. These new pan-Indian organizations fought for the improvement of American Indians' lives throughout the United States and Canada.[4]

It was during the activity of the Red Power Movement and the Native American Literary Renaissance that Hanay Geiogamah ventured to New York City to start an American Indian theatre company. American Indians had been working in the entertainment industry – theatre, film, and television – for decades, but few Native artists had creative control. The founding of the American Indian Theatre Ensemble (later known as the Native American Theatre Ensemble or NATE) marks a moment when Native theatre artists in this company and in other endeavors began to incorporate a greater degree of control over their own work by running companies, writing plays, and directing productions.

At the time a youth barely out of college, Geiogamah started examining the possibility of an American Indian theatre company in the summer of 1970. During the period there were plenty of models of minority theatres, but very few models of professional Native theatres. Geiogamah was aware of companies like Arthur Junaluska's American Indian Repertory Company, but very little information was available about them. The Institute of American Indian Arts in Santa Fe, New Mexico, had started a Native theatre training program, but it did not have a professional theatre company to coincide with the training school. As a result, it was to other minority theatres that Geiogamah turned for guidance, examining how theatres like El Teatro Campesino worked in its community, or how the theatres of the Black Arts Movement incorporated social, cultural, and identity issues in their works (see chapter 17 for more on the Black Arts Movement). From the outset, Geiogamah's vision for a Native theatre was not simply to bring Native artists together to do theatre, but to do theatre that would relate to the lives of the artists and the audiences, performing stories that came from Native cultures and examining issues relevant to Native audiences.

When Geiogamah met with National Endowment for the Arts representatives in Washington, DC, they recommended that he talk to people at New York City theatres that could serve as models for him, such as the New Lafayette, a black theatre in Harlem, or La Mama Experimental Theatre Club on New York's Lower East Side. Geiogamah began by contacting them, recalling that "they were intrigued, puzzled, happily bemused that here's an Indian person trying to do this" (personal interview, March 14, 2003). From those initial phone calls came in-person consultations with many of the most significant theatre leaders of off-Broadway. Geiogamah found himself traveling between Washington, DC, and New York City for most of that summer, making plans for the launch of the company. By the end of the summer, Ellen Stewart of La MaMa had become Geiogamah's staunchest advocate and adviser. Geiogamah credits both her and La MaMa Artistic Director Wilford Leach with helping him define the company's scope.

With Stewart, he worked out a one-year budget for a 16-person company that would be housed at La MaMa. The plan was to bring together a group of 10–12 actors, as well as designers, playwrights, a director, and possibly a choreographer and a musician/composer. According to Geiogamah, his plan from the outset was for a pan-tribal company, a company made up of artists from many different Native nations. Although some sources have since argued that the purpose of making the company pan-tribal was to deconstruct stereotypes, Geiogamah states that the purpose of making the company pan-tribal was based on the logistics of pulling a company together; if that conquers stereotypes, it is more an effect than a cause. Geiogamah remarks:

> Pan-tribal reality had very little, if anything, to do with countering stereotypes. Pan-tribal reality was that you couldn't get 12 Siouxs together to do theatre, 12 Navajos together to do it. At IAIA [Institute of American Indian Arts], they had people from all over. Pan-tribalism was politically prevalent at the time, not something we just invented, just part of our reality, that became the necessary ethos. The reality was that it was just about impossible to get one tribal unit together in a company, although I'm sure somebody would strongly disagree.
>
> Pan-tribalism lent itself to the social issues, the political issues. All tribes were impacted by poverty, by alcoholism, by loss of spiritual strength. The issues applied to everybody. At least in those days the plays could present a form that could be applicable

to all Indians. *Body Indian* is a pan-tribal play because the things it addresses applied at that time to everybody, not to just one tribe. (Personal interview, 2003)

Geiogamah had already been in contact with Lloyd Kiva New (Cherokee), who was then director of the Institute. About half of the theatre artists who Geiogamah would bring together in the American Indian Theatre Ensemble would be IAIA-trained artists.

The Institute had begun developing its theatre coursework in 1964 when New was art director. Drama instructor Rolland Meinholtz, music instructor Louis Ballard, and dance instructor Rosalie Jones all helped to build the theatre program. The theatre curriculum was well developed when New composed his "Credo for an American Indian Theatre" (1969), which outlined how an American Indian theatre, as a distinct form of American theatre, could be created. New was careful to point out that an American Indian theatre should grow from "the most sensitive approaches imaginable" to "the framework of Indian traditions." Ceremonies, powwow, and even dramatic representations of American Indian people were referred to by New as "raw material" (qtd. in "Traditional Elders' Circle"). An American Indian theatre would be a new form of American drama, one that would demand from its artists an emphasis on both rigorous training in Euro-American methods and knowledge of American Indian cultural traditions, combining these interpretive skills to bring cultural traditions to the stage.

Geiogamah's approach was not unlike New's: emphasizing training, drawing from indigenous traditions, and finding methods that would combine Euro-American and American Indian elements while remaining true to what was uniquely indigenous. The company first assembled together in New York City in March of 1972. They set their target date for an opening production as October of 1972 – providing seven months for a massive training program that Stewart and Geiogamah had conceived and to write and rehearse the material. They met their deadline and presented two pieces for their premiere performance in October 1972: *Body Indian* and *Na Haaz Zaan*. *Body Indian* is a short play that Geiogamah wrote for the opening. The play was eventually turned over to the company members to workshop the piece during their rehearsals; Geiogamah suggested changes that were significant to the play's success. They also presented *Na Haaz Zaan*, an adaptation of the Navajo creation story that company members Geraldine Keams, Robert Shorty, and Timothy Clashin had shaped and rehearsed with the help of Lee Breuer, director of Mabou Mines (Brown 2000 [1973]: 170–1; Geiogamah, personal interview, 2003).

Their premiere performance was reviewed positively, and NATE continued to perform regularly through 1976, including a tour to Europe, although some company members did depart for other opportunities. Three plays that Geiogamah wrote for the company – *Body Indian*, *Foghorn*, and *49* – were published in 1980, becoming the first collection of Native plays published by Native authors in either the United States or Canada. Several NATE members went on to form other companies and to have long careers in the performing arts, including Geiogamah himself. When asked what he felt NATE's greatest contributions had been, Geiogamah's answer is twofold. First, NATE demonstrated that it was possible to form and sustain an American Indian theatre, even with minimal funding. And second – what Geiogamah describes as NATE's primary legacy – NATE offered a model for establishing theatres in tribal communities, a goal that Geiogamah had in mind from the outset, and that he would pursue throughout his career. From New York City, NATE had relocated to Oklahoma. Following their success, several other companies formed in tribal communities or towns near reservation communities (Geiogamah, personal interview, 2003).

Spiderwoman Theatre

When Joseph Chaikin and Peter Feldman founded the Open Theatre in 1963 in New York City, one of their original company members was a 20-something modern dancer and choreographer, Muriel Miguel, who was raised in a Native family in New York City. Her mother was Rappahannock (American Indian) and her father was Kuna, an indigenous tribe from the San Blas Islands off the coast of Panama. An experimental artist, Miguel appeared in some of the edgiest performance of the time, including Megan Terry's *Viet Rock*, the first major play to protest the war in Vietnam (see chapter 15). By the first years of the 1970s, the feminist theatre movement had emerged partly out of the experimental theatres of the 1960s, and woman-focused theatres were surfacing in major cities around the country. In New York City, Miguel began to bring women together to perform their own stories, and by 1975 she had secured a grant to gather a company of five women, including her two sisters, Lisa Mayo and Gloria Miguel, as well as Lois Weaver and Brandy Penn. Mayo and Gloria Miguel also came from performance backgrounds. All three sisters had actually performed as children with their parents in "snake oil shows": performances for largely white audiences in which Native people played, quite literally, popular stereotypes. But as adults, each sister pursued different venues for professional performance training. Muriel Miguel had studied dance. Lisa Mayo was a classically trained mezzo-soprano who began studying acting for her work in opera, then began to focus more heavily on theatre performance, studying with master acting teachers Charles Nelson Reilly and Uta Hagen. Gloria Miguel majored in theatre at Oberlin College, where she had studied with Bill Irwin and others.

The original members named the company Spiderwoman Theatre after the Hopi goddess who taught her people to weave. Muriel Miguel's close friend Josephine Mofsie (Hopi) had performed with Miguel and Lois Weaver in an earlier performance about women's spirituality. Mofsie had told the Spiderwoman creation story while finger-weaving. Just a few months later, and before the new company premiered, Mofsie died tragically in a car accident; the company embraced the name of Spiderwoman to honor her work and her memory. The name also helped the company define and describe their process; the concept of "weaving" would become important in their method of performance creation. As a consequence of this style, Spiderwoman created their own performances, on their feet, without writing scripts. In programs, they described their "storyweaving" technique as "creating designs and weaving stories with words and movement."

> We work onstage as an ensemble, basing our productions on life experiences. We translate our personal stories, dreams and images into movement, and refine them into the essential threads of human experience. In seeking out, exploring, and weaving our own patterns, we reflect the human tapestry, the web of our common humanity. Finding, loving and transcending our own flaws, as in the flaw in the goddess's tapestry, provide the means for our spirits to find their way out, to be free. (Chinoy and Jenkins 1981: 303–4)

Spiderwoman Theatre's performances throughout the 1970s and into the 1980s were always about women's issues: exploring the effects of violence in women's lives, deconstructing popular images of women, satirizing popular ideas about sexuality, and so on. The company was multi-ethnic, and perhaps because of that, unlike most feminist theatres of the period, Spiderwoman's performances always investigated racial issues and racism. The company performed throughout the 1970s with a fairly elastic group, some members leaving, others joining (some for several years), and some working together for just one or two productions. The most significant member change occurred in 1980. The Spiderwoman group developed two separate performance pieces. The Mayo and Miguel sisters created *Sun, Moon, and Feather*, inspired by their childhood in the Red Hook section of Brooklyn. Weaver and Peggy Shaw developed *Split Britches*, a play about Weaver's female relatives in the Blue Ridge Mountains. The process of working independently convinced the two groups to make their way as separate companies. Weaver and Shaw left the company to form the lesbian company Split Britches, and Spiderwoman's core members were now the three Kuna-Rappahannock sisters from Brooklyn.[5]

It would be seamless, perhaps, to suggest that the transition in 1981 marks the moment when Spiderwoman "became" a Native theatre. The reasonable truth, however, is more complicated. As company members, the sisters had always contributed stories to Spiderwoman performances, and Native issues were part of Spiderwoman pieces from the beginning. Their first piece, *Women in Violence*, contains vignettes offered by every company member, including two scenes that were inspired by the Miguel sisters' personal experiences as part of the American Indian Movement. In the first scene, Muriel sits at a table with an unidentified (and in performance, invisible) man across from her. She flirts, makes jokes, and is suddenly and abruptly hit in the face twice. She protests, "Hey, I was just fooling," and she gets hit again. Through her protests, she gets hit again, and again, until finally she lands on the floor. She stands up and addresses him: "I know about genocide. I'm your mother, I'm your sister, I'm your cousin." When the unidentified man continues to assault her, she calls for the help of the other women who surround her, protect her from the abuse, and with her, face the audience, all repeating: "In a revolution, a woman is equal." The women move forward and describe being second-class citizens within their own civil rights movement. Following this, they merge to the words spoken at the 1973 occupation of Wounded Knee, South Dakota, by Wallace Black Elk, a Lakota elder and descendant of Nicholas Black Elk. Black Elk describes the tree of life of the Lakota, symbolically linking them with all other human beings, different branches growing from the same root.

As early as 1976, with the premiere of *Women in Violence*, Spiderwoman was performing stories within their works that came from a Native perspective and emphasized Native issues. Starting a feminist company with women from different backgrounds and different ethnicities meant that Miguel and the other women had to struggle with race issues, and as Native women, the sisters had to confront the mainstream face of feminism that often, if not always, ignored Native American issues. As Spiderwoman grew and as its membership changed, the philosophy of its feminism and its relationship to Native issues also evolved.

> So we started to define ourselves. We were not White people. We were women of color. We were women. And that is the reason why it eventually turned into a Native theater, because we had all these things happening to us. We didn't look like anyone else. We didn't look like the ones in our group, so we were pulled out because they wanted to take pictures of us. (Qtd. in Haugo 2002: 228)

According to Miguel, by the time the company performed *The Three Sisters from Here to There* (1982), a retelling of Chekhov's *The Three Sisters* in which the sisters' dreams are not of Moscow but of crossing the Brooklyn Bridge to Manhattan, all Spiderwoman pieces tended to deal heavily with racism, though not necessarily just from the perspective of Native people. Several members throughout its history had been women of color: Chicana, Asian American, and African American. During the 1980s, Spiderwoman's membership continued to shift, as did the emphasis of their productions. "We were changing. We kept adding more and more Indian-themed things." By the time the company developed *Winnetou's Snake Oil Show from Wigwam City* (1988), the focus was on Native politics, though always also from a feminist perspective. For this performance, they were joined by fellow Native performer Hortensia Colorado (Chichimec/Otomi), who helped to develop the performance and currently performs the piece with Spiderwoman whenever possible.

Winnetou's Snake Oil Show from Wigwam City premiered in Holland at the Stage Door Festival, with its United States premiere following in 1989 at New York's Theatre for the New City. The Traditional Elders' Circle had asked Spiderwoman to create a play that would address the increasing problem of spiritual exploitation: the "selling" of Native American spirituality. As early as 1980, the Traditional Elders' Circle issued a warning to Native and non-Native people to be vigilant, to inquire about the backgrounds of people who purported to be medicine people and to understand the seriousness of the problem. "These individuals are gathering non-Indian people as followers who believe they are receiving instructions of the original people. We, the

Elders and our representatives sitting in Council, give warning to these non-Indian followers that it is our understanding this is not a proper process, that the authority to carry these sacred objects is given by the people, and the purpose and procedure is specific to time and the needs of the people." The name that quickly attached itself to those practicing this spiritual fakery was "plastic shamans."

Winnetou's Snake Oil Show from Wigwam City examines plastic shamanism and Indian fakery more generally, calling into question centuries of stereotypes of American Indians that include the late twentieth-century trend to adopt Indian identity and spirituality, often in partial and questionable ways. The title and a good portion of the play refer to the German novel *Winnetou* by Karl May, a novel whose hero is the noble savage Winnetou. May wrote the novel without ever meeting a Native person or visiting the United States, and despite this, the novel was wildly popular and influenced what generations of Germans – and other Europeans – believed to be "real" about American Indians. In creating the performance, Spiderwoman's method was, as always, as much autobiographical as it was research oriented, delving into their own pasts, however painful that might be, recognizing their own and their family's part in the exploitation, and their responsibility to help curb it.

> We've been a part of that circus. We've been a part of sideshows. We've been in Wild West shows. When we did *Winnetou's Snake Oil Show*, all of that stuff came from our backgrounds. The whip. The sharpshooter. The horseback rider. . . . So we just kept on layering it. Like my nagahyde (a costume piece), when I said, "You know how many nagahydes I killed for this?" (laughter) Well, people think that that's the way you look. All of those old movies. That's the way they looked, with fake braids. (Qtd. in Haugo 2002: 227)

Spiderwoman created several other performances that drew on contemporary Native issues and the authors' experiences as Native women. *Reverb-ber-ber-rations* (1991) explored the gifts of spirituality. After critiquing exploitations of Native spirituality in *Winnetou*, Spiderwoman had stories to tell about their own spirituality, in a more positive sense about what it means to be spiritual Native women and to value that spirituality. *Power Pipes* (1992) brought the Colorado sisters back to work with Spiderwoman; both Elvira and Hortensia Colorado had worked with Spiderwoman previously, in between developing their own work. Also joining the company was Gloria's daughter Monique Mojica, a playwright and actor. In recreations of the play, Muriel's daughter, Murielle Borst (also a playwright and actor), joined the company. In 2001, the company began work on *Persistence of Memory*, a play reflecting on what Spiderwoman has accomplished and how it has influenced the future. In a revealing scene, the three sisters weave actions on stage with fractured, repeated phrases: "I understand now, but I didn't understand then," and "I understand. No, I don't understand." Gloria, in increments, begins to tell a story about her great-niece Josie, Muriel's granddaughter. As Gloria steps forward, she mimes holding a picture in one arm and speaks as Josie addressing her Auntie, asking her about the picture in which one child's brown face appears out of a sea of white children's faces in a classroom.

> "Is that you, Aunt Gloria?" Yes, that's me. Looking up at me she said, "Then you know how I feel." Our eyes met for a moment. Yes, Josie, I know how you feel. Three generations, three generations and that knowing feeling is still present. (14)

In the young Josie's recognition of her place and her ability at the age of six to articulate it to an Auntie, Spiderwoman assert their influence and hopes. As young girls themselves, they "didn't understand" how to value themselves as Native women, how to survive, intact, amid a sea of whiteness – in a classroom or in the world. For them, being proud, perhaps defiant, and certainly rooted in their identities as Native women, has been a process of becoming, a process sometimes painful and arduous. Gloria's final line bridges to a film clip of Josie singing the *Persistence of Memory* song: "She understands now" (15).

Likewise their other works, this Spiderwoman play emerged from the intersection of all aspects of the sisters' identities: gender, ethnicity, class, and sexuality. At the end of *Reverb-ber-ber-rations*, Muriel Miguel addresses the audience simply and directly, with words that speak to the healing power of performing their own stories, not simply for their generation, but for the next:

> I am an Indian woman.
> I am proud of the women that came before me.
> I am a woman with two daughters.
> I am a woman with a woman lover.
> I am a woman whose knowledge is the wisdom of the women in the family.
> I am here now.
> I say this now because to deny these events
> About me and my life
> Would be denying my children. (212)

The Canada Connection: Native Earth Performing Arts

In the fall of 1986, Muriel Miguel, Gloria Miguel, and Monique Mojica created three roles in the Toronto premiere of the play *The Rez Sisters* by Tomson Highway. A Cree playwright from Manitoba, Highway was then artistic director of a Native theatre company in Toronto titled Native Earth Performing Arts (NEPA). Native Earth had started in 1982 as a performance collective, and Mojica had been active in its development, including a stint as its artistic director. This was one of many times that the Spiderwoman sisters or other Native artists would cross the border – Canadian Native artists working in the United States or American Indian artists working in Canada. It is important to treat the two performance worlds as connected, since there is more cross-fertilization between the United States and Canada in Native theatre than in any other drama and theatre.

Rez Sisters went on to win the Dora Mavor Moore Award for Best New Play in Toronto's 1986–7 season, as well as the 1986 Floyd S. Chalmers Award for Outstanding Canadian Play. Other Native companies had been producing theatre as well. De-ba-jeh-mu-jig Theatre Group was founded on Manitoulin Island by Shirley Cheechoo (Cree) in 1984. Highway, in fact, had started writing *Rez Sisters* while serving as their artistic director. In 1974, a group of Native artists in Toronto had created the Association for Native Development in the Performing and Visual Arts (ANDPVA); recognizing early on the need to train Native people in the arts, they had also founded the Native Theatre School, which still operates and has trained many professional Native artists over the last quarter of the twentieth century. But the success of Native Earth's first scripted piece, *The Rez Sisters*, catapulted Native theatre into the Canadian spotlight and earned Highway and Native Earth international recognition. Native Earth continued to earn nominations for Dora Mavor Moore awards over the next few years, and then, with a co-production with Toronto's Theatre Passe Muraille in the spring of 1989, Highway and NEPA earned six Dora nominations and claimed four for *Dry Lips Oughta Move to Kapuskasing*, a sequel to *The Rez Sisters*.

It is important to note that mainstream success is only one measure of value in a minority theatre movement. Any narrative that privileges awards and mainstream recognition over the reception of Highway's plays by Native people should be suspect unless balanced by an analysis that included Native American reception. Geiogamah offers a lesson in how to evaluate Native plays:

> In judging an Indian play, readers and viewers should keep in mind that the most important function of the Indian dramatist is to communicate with his own people. The major questions are: Does the play speak effectively to Indians? Can Indians understand what is happening on stage? If there is a message, is it communicated clearly and effectively in Indian terms? Are the characters and dialogue culturally authentic? (2000: 163)

Geiogamah adds that even when all these parameters are met, a Native play can still be accessible to a non-Native audience. Highway's plays seem to be examples of Native plays that speak across a wide spectrum, to a Native audience yet still accessible to non-Native audiences (providing that mainstream recognition serves as an example of broad accessibility). Both plays, *Rez Sisters* and *Dry Lips*, draw on Cree and Ojibway traditions in their creation of the central trickster character, Nanabush, and both liberally draw on indigenous language in the writing. *Dry Lips* earned its share of controversy among Native people, as some women critics questioned its gender politics, but the arguments were not about the effectiveness of the representation of Cree or Ojibway cultures and characters onstage.[6]

In the same season that *Dry Lips* premiered, Native Earth began a festival of new plays called "Weesageechak Begins to Dance," a festival that continues to sponsor

Native dramas in the twentieth-first century. Festivals like this have become important in both the United States and Canada as a means for Native artists – accomplished
or new on the scene – to develop their work among other Native artists. In the United
States, the Native Voices Festival, started by Randy Reinholz and Jean Bruce Scott in
1994 at Illinois State University and now located at the Autry Museum of Western
History, offers a similar opportunity, and Native community venues like the American Indian Community House in New York City often serve as locales for workshop
performances.

Into the New Millennium

With the work of companies like NATE, Spiderwoman, and NEPA, and the development of new generations of artists at IAIA, Haskell's Thunderbird Theatre, and
Toronto's Native Theatre School, the Native Theatre Movement had taken root in
the 1970s and 1980s. By the 1990s, the movement was energized, with several
resident Native American companies throughout the United States and Canada, and
an increasing number of Native-authored plays in publication.

IAIA continued its theatre program in the early 1990s, with playwrights Bruce
King (Oneida) and William S. Yellow Robe, Jr. (Assiniboine) teaching in the Creative
Writing and Theatre programs, respectively. Under their instruction, students produced and wrote several plays, and for several consecutive years published their plays
in collections printed by the Institute. IAIA and Haskell Indian Nations University
fulfilled important roles throughout the last three decades of the twentieth century,
training Native theatre artists in all aspects of theatre. Both institutions, however,
survive on federal funding, and in 1996 Congress cut roughly one-third of IAIA's
budget, forcing the Institute to reduce its faculty from 27 instructors to 11. The
Performing Arts program, which had played such an important part in the Native
Theatre Movement since New and Rolland Meinholz's work, was cut, and both King
and Yellow Robe sought opportunities elsewhere.

Yellow Robe had studied under Meinholz at the University of Montana and
worked in regional theatres around the country, including as literary manager for
the Seattle Group Theatre. While several of his plays had been produced and
published in the 1980s and 1990s, a collection of his plays, *Where the Pavement
Ends*, was published in 2000. Many of the plays included in it had been produced
by the pan-tribal company he founded in Albuquerque in 1997, Wakiknabe, drawing
its name from an Assiniboine word meaning "we return home" and envisioning a
place for artists to gather, develop their craft, and share their talents ("Wakiknabe
Theater Company," n.d.).[7]

King had attended IAIA and studied under Meinholz as well, writing his first play,
To Catch a Never Dream, and publishing it in the late 1960s, before the founding of
NATE. He continued to write, and his play *Evening at the Warbonnet* became a popular
play for Native companies in the late 1990s. After putting his plays in the hands of a

non-Native, off-Broadway producer and finding himself less than pleased with the result, he decided it would be much better to "pilot my own ship," and still early in his career, King co-founded Indian Time Theatre in Buffalo, New York (qtd. in Rathbun 2000a: 316). Like Geiogamah, King saw the potential for theatre to bring Native communities together. Since the 1970s, King has developed several community-authored pieces in which he removed his name from the program. In a 1993 interview with *Native Playwrights' Newsletter* editor Paul Rathbun, King explained what it takes to create a community-based, Native theatre.

> To succeed, you have to find some equilibrium for those people to come together to work. Well, Shakespeare does not cut it. The reality is that I have to go by what's going to work in that community, and which everybody will agree to. Most of the time what they agree to comes out of the middle of them, where they can all invest their ideas and invest their opinions. They invest something that they have to say that affects them all, and that they agree on. Then it starts working. (2000a: 307).

The communities that King works together with might be a reservation community like the Menominee reservation in Wisconsin, or a group of urban teenagers, using theatre as a way to "change their interests from gang-banging to staying alive" (307) and creating performances from their lives, about substance abuse or other issues that affect their survival, for example.

Several other playwrights saw their work published and produced. E. Donald Two Rivers (Anishinabe) published *Briefcase Warriors* in 2001. Two volumes of Cherokee playwright Diane Glancy's plays appeared: *War Cries* in 1997 and *American Gypsy* in 2003. A prolific playwright, poet, and author, Glancy, like many other Native playwrights, tends to find it easier to publish her work than get it produced, and that is a significant challenge that playwrights are taking into the twentieth-first century. Yellow Robe and Two Rivers addressed the challenge in one way, by starting their own companies, but for many playwrights, founding a company is not an effective answer.[8]

Four important multi-author collections appeared in the last decade, all selecting a balance of work by playwrights relatively new on the scene as well as those who have figured importantly in the development of Native theatre. *Seventh Generation: An Anthology of Native American Plays* (1999), edited by Mimi Gisolfi D'aponte, was one of the first to appear. It contains plays by Native writers from the continental United States, Canada, and Hawaii, including arguably William S. Yellow Robe's most popular play, *The Independence of Eddie Rose*. In the same year, *Stories of Our Way: An Anthology of American Indian Plays* was co-edited by Hanay Geiogamah and Jaye T. Darby as part of a new initiative Geiogamah founded in 1997, Project HOOP (Honoring Our Origins and People through Native Theatre, Education, and Community Development). The anthology appears with a companion volume of essays and other resources, *American Indian Theater in Performance: A Reader* (2000), designed for use in college classrooms. Geiogamah's vision for a Native theatre in tribal communities was further advanced through Project HOOP, as one of the primary goals of the program was to develop theatre curriculums at tribal colleges, piloting the project at Sinte Gleska University on the Rosebud Reservation in South Dakota, and then partnering with Haskell Indian Nations University.

Darby co-edited another volume of plays published through Project HOOP, this volume with Stephanie Fitzgerald (Cree). *Keepers of the Morning Star: An Anthology of Native Women's Theater* (2003) collected eight plays and performance pieces by Native women from the United States and Canada, including some of the most innovative artists working today. Marie Clements's one-woman play *Urban Tattoo* was developed through Native Earth's Weesageechak Begins to Dance Festival in 1995 and grew through several supported workshops and festivals, including a tech-supported staged reading at the Native Voices Festival. A Vancouver-based Métis performer, Clements worked with some of the most influential artists in Canadian Native theatre, including Margo Kane (Cree/Saulteaux), founder and artistic director of Full Circle: First Nations Performance. Melding storytelling and biography with detailed multimedia presentations, *Urban Tattoo* tells the story of Rosemarie, a Métis girl displaced from her history and identity. Through her memories, encounters that she replays to herself, Rosemarie reconnects herself, her "memories getting caught on my skin," gathering tattoos as emblems as she does so, until in the final moments of the play she stands facing the audience, "tall":

> As if those tattoos had come from me.
> As if we had an understanding that in going past I know my place
> And in going forward I have I become bigger than you can
> Imagine.
> Amen.
> Ho. (Darby and Fitzgerald 2003: 228)

The most recent collection is a co-edited volume by Monique Mojica and Ric Knowles, the first multi-author collection of Native plays to be published in Canada by a large press. *Staging Coyote's Dream: An Anthology of First Nations Drama in English* (2003) presents plays by ten Native playwrights and companies from the United States and Canada, including Mojica's *Princess Pocahontas and the Blue Spots*, the first time that that play has been republished since its 1991 first publication. It contains Highway's previously unpublished work *Aria*, and works by Drew Hayden Taylor, Floyd Favel, and Daniel David Moses are also represented here. These latter three authors are arguably the most popular and influential Native playwrights working in Canada.

In the first years of the twenty-first century, we have seen what some artists and scholars have called an "explosion" of Native theatre. From few experiments in Native theatre before 1960, the United States and Canada now boast dozens, as well as dozens of working playwrights, actors, and other theatre professionals. Discussions within the Native theatre circle about how to find more production venues or funding to support new and exciting companies are evidence that the Movement is still underway and that there are undoubtedly more plays to write, stories to tell, and productions to mount. If the last 30 years of the twentieth century are evidence, the next century might prove to be even more exciting.

NOTES

1. See King and Springwood (2001) for a collection of writing on the mascot controversy.
2. See Bird (1996) and Huhndorf (2001) for more scholarship on the numerous manifestations of "playing Indian" in America.
3. A useful introduction to postcolonial studies with an excellent bibliography and references to primary sources is Ashcroft, Griffiths, and Tiffin (2000).
4. See Johnson, Nagel, and Champagne (1997) and Smith and Warrior (1997).
5. Several sources document Spiderwoman's history. See Canning (1996), Haugo (2002), and Schneider (1997).
6. See Baker (1991).
7. For more information about Yellow Robe's work, see Rathbun (2000b) and Pulitano (1998).
8. For further discussion on this issue, see "NAWPA Authors' Roundtable" (1999).

BIBLIOGRAPHY

Ashcroft, B., Griffiths, G., and Tiffin, H. (eds.) (2000). *Post-Colonial Studies: The Key Concepts*. New York: Routledge.

Baker, M. A. (1991). "Angry Enough to Spit, but with Dry Lips It Hurts More than You Know." *Canadian Theatre Review* 68 (Fall): 88–9.

Bird, S. E. (1996). *Dressing in Feathers: The Construction of the Indian in American Popular Culture*. Boulder, CO: Westview.

Brown, K. (2000). "The American Indian Theater Ensemble." In Hanay Geiogamah and Jaye T. Darby (eds.), *American Indian Theater in Performance: A Reader*. Los Angeles: UCLA American Indian Studies Center Press, 169–74.

Canning, C. (1996). *Feminist Theaters in the U.S.A.: Staging Women's Experience*. New York: Routledge.

Chinoy, H. K. and Jenkins, L. W. (eds.) (1981). *Women in American Theatre*. New York: Theatre Communications Group.

Darby, J. T. and Fitzgerald, S. (eds.) (2003). *Keepers of the Morning Star: An Anthology of Native Women's Theater*. Los Angeles: UCLA American Indian Studies Center Press.

Deloria, P. (1998). *Playing Indian*. New Haven, CT: Yale University Press.

Fanon, F. (1967). *Black Skin, White Masks*. New York: Grove.

Geiogamah, H. (2000). "The New American Indian Theater: An Introduction." In Hanay Geiogamah and Jaye T. Darby (eds.), *American Indian Theater in Performance: A Reader*. Los Angeles: UCLA American Indian Studies Center Press, 159–64.

——and Darby, J. T. (eds.) (1999). *Stories of Our Way: An Anthology of American Indian Plays*. Los Angeles: UCLA American Indian Studies Center Press.

——and Darby, J. T. (eds.) (2000). *American Indian Theater in Performance: A Reader*. Los Angeles: UCLA American Indian Studies Center Press.

Green, R. (1988). "The Tribe Called Wannabee: Playing Indian in American and Europe." *Folklore* 99, 1: 30–55.

Haugo, A. (2000). "'Circles upon Circles upon Circles': Native Women in Theater and Performance." In Hanay Geiogamah and Jaye T. Darby (eds.), *American Indian Theater in Performance: A Reader*. Los Angeles: UCLA American Indian Studies Center Press, 228–55.

—— (2002). "Weaving a Legacy: An Interview with Muriel Miguel of the Spiderwoman Theater." In Roberta Uno and Lucy Mae San Pablo Burns (eds.), *The Color of Theater: Race, Culture, and Contemporary Performance*. New York: Continuum, 218–34.

—— (2004). "American Indian Theatre." In Kenneth Roemer and Joy Porter (eds.), *The Cambridge Companion to Native American Literature*. Cambridge: Cambridge University Press.

Heath, S. A. (1995). "The Development of Native American Theatre Companies in the Continental United States." PhD dissertation, University of Colorado at Boulder.

Huhndorf, S. M. (2001). *Going Native: Indians in the American Cultural Imagination*. Ithaca, NY: Cornell University Press.

Johnson, T., Nagel, J., and Champagne, D. (eds.) (1997). *American Indian Activism: Alcatraz to the Longest Walk*. Urbana: University of Illinois Press.

Jones, E. F. (1988). *Native Americans as Shown on the Stage, 1753–1916*. Metuchen, NJ: Scarecrow Press.

King, B. (1999). *Evening at the Warbonnet*. In Hanay Geiogamah and Jaye T. Darby (eds.), *Stories of Our Way: An Anthology of American Indian Plays*. Los Angeles: UCLA American Indian Studies Center Press, 355–440.

King, C. R. and Springwood, C. F. (eds.) (2001). *Team Spirits: The Native American Mascot Controversy*. Lincoln, NE: Bison Books.

Manuel, V. (1998). *Strength of Indian Women*. In *Two Plays about Residential School*. Vancouver: Living Traditions Writers Group, 75–119.

Mojica, M. and Knowles, R. (eds.) (2003). *Staging Coyote's Dream: An Anthology of First Nations Drama in English*. Toronto: Playwrights Canada Press.

"NAWPA Authors' Roundtable" (1999). *Native American Women Playwrights' Archive*, March 19; staff. lib.muohio.edu/nawpa/roundtable.html.

New, L. K. (2000). "Credo for an American Indian Theatre." In Hanay Geiogamah and Jaye T. Darby (eds.), *American Indian Theater in Performance: A Reader*. Los Angeles: UCLA American Indian Studies Center Press, 3–4.

Preston, J. (1992). "Weesageechak Begins to Dance." *TDR* 36, 1: 135–59.

Pulitano, E. (1998). "Telling Stories through the Stage: A Conversation with William Yellow Robe." *Studies in American Indian Literatures* 10, 1: 19–44.

Rathbun, P. (2000a). "*Native Playwrights' Newsletter* Interview: Bruce King." In Hanay Geiogamah and Jaye T. Darby (eds.), *American Indian Theater in Performance: A Reader*. Los Angeles: UCLA American Indian Studies Center Press.

—— (2000b). "*Native Playwrights' Newsletter* Interview: William Yellow Robe, Jr." In Hanay Geiogamah and Jaye T. Darby (eds.), *American Indian Theater in Performance: A Reader*. Los Angeles: UCLA American Indian Studies Center Press.

Schneider, R. (1997). *The Explicit Body in Performance*. New York: Routledge.

Smith, P. C. and Warrior, R. A. (1997). *Like a Hurricane: The Indian Movement from Alcatraz to Wounded Knee*. New York: New Press.

Spiderwoman Theatre (1976). *Women in Violence*. Unpublished manuscript.

—— (1992). *Reverb-ber-ber-rations*. *Women and Performance: A Journal of Feminist Theory* 5, 2: 184–212.

—— (2003). *Winnetou's Snake Oil Show from Wigwam City*. In Jaye T. Darby and Stephanie Fitzgerald (eds.), *Keepers of the Morning Star: An Anthology of Native Women's Theater*. Los Angeles: UCLA American Indian Studies Center Press, 229–62.

—— (n.d.). *Persistence of Memory*. Unpublished manuscript.

Traditional Elders' Circle (1980). "Resolution of the Fifth Annual Meeting of the Traditional Elders' Circle." *Fourth World Documentation Project*, October 5; www.cwis.org/fwdp/Resolutions/Other/elders.txt (December 17, 2003).

"Wakiknabe Theater Company" (n.d.). American Theater website; www.americantheaterweb.com/TheaterDetail.asp?ID=1486 (September 15, 2003).

Wilmeth, D. B. (2000). "Noble or Ruthless Savage? The American Indian on Stage and in the Drama." In Hanay Geiogamah and Jaye T. Darby (eds.), *American Indian Theater in Performance: A Reader*. Los Angeles: UCLA American Indian Studies Center Press, 127–56.

22

John Guare and the Popular Culture Hype of Celebrity Status

Gene A. Plunka

John Guare poses the existentialist dilemma of how individuals in contemporary American society can maintain a sense of dignity and humanism despite a ubiquitous fraudulence that characterizes American culture. Artistic director of the Signature Theatre, James Houghton, has observed that Guare "reveals a wildly vivid imagination and insight into the struggle each of us has to make a difference and feel we belong. All his plays deal with the need for us to matter" (qtd. in Drukman 1999: 7). Guare's characters spend most of their time in fantasyland, either dreaming of an idyllic past or hoping for their big break in the future. The motif that runs throughout his plays is E. M. Forster's message, "only connect," which suggests a need to focus on establishing relationships with friends or loved ones – a means of maintaining dignity and reaffirming a spirit of humanism. Instead of connecting with others, Guare's protagonists immerse themselves in the myth of celebrity status and, by so doing, discover that their dreams are merely artificial. Despite the fact that Guare's protagonists often become prisoners of their own warped fantasies created by the media and the worship of popular culture, Guare has mixed feelings about the results, privately admiring individuals who pursue their imaginative dreams of a better (sometimes even utopian) way of life.

Guare acts as a sociologist who probes a troubled, conflicted, angst-ridden contemporary American society. Harold Clurman has stated, "What motivates him [Guare] is scorn for the fraudulence of our way of life" (1971: 285). Although the intrinsic value of human relationships may produce happiness, the cultural norms and values of society have instilled Americans with the notion that pleasure and satisfaction actually derive from money, beauty, and fame; this dichotomy of values between our need to connect and the media hype of glitz and glamour Guare views as fraudulent. The promised American Dream, depicted in pop culture through the media, equates success with fame and fortune. Guare's wife, Adele Chatfield-Taylor, notes that her husband is himself star-struck: "He thinks people wanting to be famous for fifteen minutes is the great engine of twentieth-century life" (qtd. in Friend 1992: 329). Our own lives are often nebulous and amorphous, fraught with failures and impediments to success; however, celebrities are seen as icons of an Edenic existence devoid of the banalities of everyday life. Guare's characters buy into the media hype that celebrity status is synonymous with the American Dream. In short, an individual's worth begins to be associated with celebrity status, while one's inner qualities and the ability to relate to others become subordinate. Daryl Chin astutely observes that "Guare's characters approach their lives as if the lyrics of pop songs, the melodramatic extremes of movies, and the complications of television sit-coms were the reality of their lives" (1991: 9). Instead of focusing on relationships in the present, Guare's characters, in an attempt to avoid humiliation, often try to emulate the rich and famous, ignoring the loved ones around them and thus ending up with a life that is passionless, love-starved, and spiritually bankrupt. Guare strips the veneer of modern American society to indicate its vacuity, where the very real dangers of the hype of commercialization and pop culture have reduced individuals to neurotic automatons searching for utopian dreams in a sterile world inundated with superficial facades.

Muzeeka (1967), Guare's playwriting debut on the New York stage, is concerned with the dilemma of whether we can find an identity in a society that turns us into conformists. The protagonist of the play, Jack Argue (Argue is an anagram of Guare while Jack is synonymous with John), is an idealist who endures a bland domestic relationship with his plain wife and a mundane professional life working for the Muzeeka Corporation, where he pipes the company's music into elevators, offices, and homes. Argue's drab home environment is spiced up with brief forays into the glamorous life found in *Playboy* and interludes with the prostitute Evelyn Landis. Argue's wife is having a baby, yet he apologizes to Evelyn for seeking comfort: "I'm sorry... I want to connect in some way" (1970: 64). Argue winds up in Vietnam and tells his buddy, the anony-Mass Number Two, that CBS Television will be covering their battle tomorrow. This alarms Number Two, who is under contract with NBC and will lose his rank if NBC discovers that CBS gets the film coverage. Number Two associates his role in the war with celebrity status and fears the loss of his stardom: "An educational network unit. I'm not fighting for no Channel Thirteen. I don't want to break contracts" (72).

Guare suggests that American society has become dehumanized, interested more in commercialization of celebrity than in the value of life. Argue and Number Two, both under contract to different television networks, have degenerated into automatons for commercial enterprises fighting not for the salvation of the spirit of democracy, but instead for celebrity status that might increase television ratings. Number Two even boasts to Argue, "I been on the cover of *Look* and that spread in the *Saturday Evening Post*. I have been in the *New York Times* and the *L.A. Times* and the *Daily News Sunday Colorado*" (75). During Argue's debacle in Vietnam, he is reunited with Evelyn Landis, who, in a takeoff of the archetypal songstress entertaining the troops, strips herself of army fatigues to reveal a bikini made of newspaper columns. As she rips clumps of newspaper off her body, Guare intimates that the media hype helps America subliminally to associate celebrity with godhead:

Timothy Leary
& Jesus Christ
Bonnie and Clyde
& Jesus Christ
Rocky & Romney
& Jesus Christ
Johnny Carson
& Jesus Christ
Television
& Jesus Christ
Eugene McCarthy
May be Jesus Christ. (82)

Guare implies that in a society that inculcates itself with blandness and superficiality, the media moguls have no trouble manipulating our consciousness.

In Guare's next play, *Cop-Out* (1968), realistic scenes depicting the relationship between an unnamed Policeman and a young female anti-war demonstrator alternate with the mythical Brett Arrow scenes, and having one actor play the roles of the Policeman and Arrow cements the connection between the two men and between reality and mythmaking. The peacenik carries a blank sign suggesting that her commitment to causes is nebulous, but once she establishes a relationship with the Policeman, we discover that her desire to connect with someone is actually her raison d'être. The Brett Arrow scenes reflect the Policeman's fantasy as "the world's toughest superstar" (1970: 12), glamorized by the Hollywood media as the charismatic, macho Sam Spade-like sleuth or a Mickey Spillane depiction of Mike Hammer. Decked out with two guns, the tough, cocky super-sleuth parades through a fantasy world of gorgeous women, sleazy underworld characters, and multiple disguises in pursuit of the murderous Mr. Big. The last segment of the play ties together the Arrow tale with the Policeman's otherwise bland life. After having a vasectomy, the Policeman winds up working at a tollbooth, hoping to get reassigned to more invigorating police work. He blames his demotion on his former girlfriend, who duped him into her radical behavior. When she begins picketing in front of him, he goes berserk, shooting her. He has "copped out" of his role to adopt the Brett Arrow fantasy life of celebrity ace detective. The glitz and glamour of the movies has become stronger than reality. Guare depicts the madness of contemporary American society in which myths, fabricated and embellished by the media, tend to overshadow reality.

The House of Blue Leaves (1971), Guare's first full-length play, is his most fully developed study of the dichotomy of the reality of our failed dreams in conflict with a powerful, glamorized media conception of celebrity that convinces us that fame and fortune are within our grasp. Guare set the play in Queens, New York, which suggested the magic of the American Dream – a residential community, unlike commercial Manhattan, where parents could raise their children in peace and aspire toward social mobility. In the "Introduction" to the play, Guare describes how Queens became the ideal setting for his play about vanquished dreams:

Queens was built in the twenties in that flush of optimism as a bedroom community for people on their way up who worked in Manhattan but wanted to pretend they had the better things in life until the inevitable break came and they could make the official move to the Scarsdales and the Ryes and the Greenwiches of their dreams, the pay-off that was the birthright of every American. Queens named its communities Forest Hills, Kew Gardens, Elmhurst, Woodside, Sunnyside, Jackson Heights, Corona, Astoria (after the Astors, of all people). The builders built the apartment houses in mock Tudor or Gothic or Colonial and then named them The Chateau, The El Dorado, Linsley Hall, the Alhambra. . . . And the lobbies had Chippendale furniture and Aztec fireplaces, and the elevators had roman numerals on the buttons. (1987b: 3–4)

The dichotomy between New York and Hollywood reflects Guare's vision of the gap between the real and the ideal, which was also depicted in *Landscape of the Body* (1977). In that play, Guare's protagonist, Betty Yearn, left New England, which represents the idyllic to Guare, to settle in Manhattan with her son Bert. She eventually is unable to establish meaningful relationships in what becomes a vast urban metropolis that is synonymous with the onerous, crippling, devastating, and violent effects of modern life that vanquish idealistic dreams.

Middle-aged Artie Shaughnessy epitomizes such a life in Queens where reality and fantasy are hopelessly intertwined. Although Artie prefers to fantasize, drab reality weighs heavily upon his life. Artie is a zookeeper by day; at night, he comes home to a different sort of zoo. His shabby apartment is filled with jungle animals, constantly reminding him that his domestic life more closely resembles a zoo than it does Hollywood. The six bolts required to lock the doors and the iron folding gate across the window suggest that Artie is virtually a caged animal, imprisoned in a wacky domestic life. He laments, "Work all day in a zoo. Come home to a zoo" (30).

Artie's family life is a big disappointment, a bitter pill to swallow for someone who has great aspirations. Much of the zookeeper's domestic menagerie consists of caring for his mentally ill wife, Bananas. When the animals in the zoo get testy, Artie is called in to calm them down. Similarly, when Bananas becomes hysterical (and her name implies that she has a tendency to do so), Artie forces tranquilizers down her throat. Artie constantly threatens to have her committed to an insane asylum. At the same time, he is saddled with an alienated and rebellious 18-year-old son who is AWOL from the US Army. However, Ronnie's sense of rebellion, demonstrated by a desire to kill the pope with a homemade bomb, is more than typical adolescent angst. Bananas's insanity and Ronnie's deeply rooted insecurity indicate that the Shaughnessy family is highly dysfunctional.

Artie refuses to recognize the reality of his dismal domestic life and instead dreams of committing his wife to a mental institution while he pursues his fantasy life as a successful songwriter. In hopes of fulfilling his dreams, Artie plays the piano on amateur nights at the El Dorado bar. He demands a spotlight and rapt audience attention while he sings what he believes will be "hits," such as "Where Is the Devil in Evelyn?" Artie's tunes often reflect the desperation in his quest for a better life: "I'm

Plate 16.   The House of Blue Leaves, by John Guare, Missouri Repertory Theatre. Left to right: Jim Birdsall (Artie), Vicki Oleson (Bunny), and Peggy Friesen (Bananas). Courtesy of the Missouri Repertory Theatre.

looking for Something, / I've searched every-where" (14). Yet the reality is that, as Artie readily acknowledges, "I'm too old to be a young talent!!!" (85). The brutal truth is that during his search for stardom at the El Dorado, Artie's audience is inattentive and unappreciative, and he is treated rather shabbily, forced to pay for his own beers. Even worse, Artie's Tin Pan Alley-type songs are not original creations, for most of his tunes are plagiarized versions of Irving Berlin's "White Christmas." His talent is part of his fantasy. Dissatisfied with his drab domestic life, Artie forms a relationship with his downstairs neighbor, Bunny Flingus, whose name suggests that the couple will enjoy a fling together. Although Artie has known Bunny for only two months, she plays upon his fantasy life in a way that Bananas does not. She reinforces Artie's fantasies of being rich and famous, insisting that his songs are classics and that he has talent that would thrive were he discovered by Hollywood moguls.

Artie is enamored with celebrities and with individuals who have been successful. He has bought into the myth of the American Dream to such a degree that he has become oblivious to people who are not rich and famous, and thus blind to the reality that life in Queens may be his fate. His living room is filled with pictures of movie stars – icons for Artie to worship. He is forever boasting of rubbing shoulders with the likes of his friend, Billy Einhorn, a big-shot Hollywood producer and director. Upon seeing Billy's friend, Corrinna, Artie says, "You call Billy and he sends stars. Stars!" (55). After Corrinna is killed in the bomb accident, Artie's reaction is predictably, "She could've been one of the big ones. A lady Biggie. Boy. Stardust. Handfuls of it. All over her" (73). Artie's dream is to have his wife committed to an insane asylum, elope with Bunny, and make good in Hollywood like his old friend Billy. Einhorn, the mythical unicorn, is Guare's subliminal hint that the American Dream is merely fantasy.

Artie views Pope Paul's visit to New York City to deliver a speech about peace to the United Nations as his chance to get close to a celebrity. Artie hopes that during the pope's procession down Queens Boulevard en route to Manhattan, His Holiness will bless his songs; the "superstar" will then provide enough impetus for Artie to make his own luck in Hollywood. While he watches the pope on television, which only serves to reinforce the pope's celebrity status, the zookeeper pleads, "Help me – help me – Your Holiness" (47). Artie's fantasy penetrates his unconscious when he dreams that Ronnie becomes the pope. Pope Ronnie picks Artie up in a limousine and takes him to Rome where the songwriter is canonized in fame and fortune as "a Saint of the Church and in charge of writing all the hymns for the Church. A hymn couldn't be played unless it was mine and the whole congregation sang 'Where Is the Devil in Evelyn?'" (28).

The time is exactly right for miracles to occur: the pope is coming to America, and Billy Einhorn, representing the glitter and glamour of celebrity-ridden California, is Artie's ticket out of the mire of Queens. However, Artie's dreams remain unfulfilled; the myth of fame and fortune leaves us disillusioned. Artie loses Bunny, who selfishly chooses to go to Hollywood with Billy, while the director tells his old "friend" that he is better off staying in Queens. The American Dream has been demythologized, reduced to nothing more than an illusion. During the denouement of the drama, the meaning of the title of the play can be discerned. Near the mental asylum in which Artie plans to have Bananas committed is a tree full of blue birds, which Artie erroneously assumes are blue leaves. When the birds fly away, the "tree" appears to have lost its leaves and thus becomes visibly barren. The illusion is fleeting; behind it resides the barren reality. Gautam Dasgupta contends that "Somewhat like the bluebirds resting on a tree, which Artie mistakenly takes to be a tree with blue leaves, the world is a mirage forever eluding one's grasp" (1981: 47). At the end of the play, when the stage is inundated with blue leaves, Artie's mockery is consummated.

Ronnie, like his father, has his own warped dreams of fame and fortune. At age 12, Ronnie auditioned to win the role of the "Ideal American Boy" to play Huckleberry Finn in a movie Billy Einhorn was producing. Billy's reaction to Ronnie's charades, which he expressed to Ronnie's parents as, "You never told me you had a mentally retarded child" (53), completely devastated the youngster. From that moment on, Ronnie was seen as a failure: "My father thinks I'm nothing. Billy. My sergeant. They laugh at me. You laughing at me?" (53). Ronnie, who hopes to regain his sense of self-respect while simultaneously showing spite for his father, muses about his "revenge": "Pop, I'm going to blow up the Pope and when *Time* interviews me tonight, I won't even mention you. I'll say I was an orphan" (67). In this perverse scenario, Ronnie plans to become famous, even if it means being notorious for one of the most heinous crimes of the century. Ronnie boasts that he will soon have celebrity status: "By tonight, I'll be on headlines all over the world. Cover of *Time. Life.* TV specials. (*He shows a picture of himself on the wall.*) I hope they use this picture of me – I look better with hair" (53). As the person who assassinates the pope, Ronnie realizes, "I'll be too big for any of you" (53). However, Guare's black comedy puts star-struck Ronnie in his rightful place. Ronnie's bomb misses the target and instead kills two nuns and Corrinna.

Like Artie and Ronnie, Bunny Flingus is shallow and selfish, lacking any spiritual empathy for anyone. Although she admits that she is "not good in bed" (24), her first name implies that she has had plenty of contact with men but no spiritual relationships with them; they are merely temporal "flings." Sex will always be unsatisfying to her because it is never accompanied by a loving relationship. To Bunny, Artie's marriage is simply an inconvenience, an obstacle to her own personal happiness. Her plans for Artie do not include his wife: "As soon as Bananas here is carted off, we'll step off that plane and Billy and you and I and Corrinna here will eat and dance and drink and love until the middle of the next full moon" (65). Her selfishness is also revealed in what she plans to say to the pope when he passes in his limousine: "Your Holiness, marry us – the hell with peace to the world – bring peace to us" (21). This comment is particularly unnerving when one realizes that the purpose of the pope's visit is to plead for world peace at the United Nations while the Vietnam War rages on and while Artie's son is about to be sent to fight in that war. At the end of the play, when Bunny gets her chance to go to California with Billy, she cruelly and selfishly leaves Artie behind. Moreover, Bunny's transience, her lack of identity, is reflected in the numerous flighty jobs that she has held. She has worked for a telephone company, Con Edison, a movie theatre, a law office, a lending library, a theatrical furniture store, a travel agency, a ski lodge, and the music department at Macy's – and this list consists of only the jobs we know about and does not include perhaps many others.

Bunny's values have been formed through the popular culture of gossip columns, television, and movie magazines. In short, the media have cultivated her belief that humans are worthless unless they possess the glamour of celebrities. She is more concerned about Sandra Dee losing her hair curlers the evening before her film debut than she is about establishing a purposeful spiritual connection with others. Like mainstream America, she has become "narcotized" to popular culture's influence. Bunny is also mesmerized by the notion of celebrity to the extent that it is of paramount importance in her life. Her dream is to marry Artie and live in Hollywood, the place where celebrity status is fully appreciated. Her vision is for Artie to win the Oscar for Best Song and to be presented with the award by none other than Greer Garson herself. Bunny treats Billy with reverence, as if he were the savior with the capacity to discover ordinary individuals for the movies, thus enshrining and ennobling them for eternity. When Artie hesitates calling his friend at two o'clock in the morning, Bunny indicates that she sees Billy not as an individual with feelings, but as an icon of fame and fortune who can never be bothered by such a minor intrusion as a telephone call: "In Hollywood! Come off it, he's probably not even in yet – they're out there frigging and frugging and swinging and eating and dancing. Since Georgina died, he's probably got a brace of nude starlets splashing in the pool" (36–7). Moreover, deaf movie starlet Corrinna Stroller, whose only claim to fame was the one B-movie that she made, is perceived by Bunny to be emulated as a success story: "Corrinna Stroller! Limos in the streets. Oh, Miss Stroller, I saw your one movie, *Warmonger*, but it is permanently enshrined in the Loew's of my heart" (55).

Bunny, decked out in binoculars and wearing two Brownie cameras on cords, wants to get a good spot on Queens Boulevard so she can get a glimpse of the ultimate celebrity, the pope himself. Bunny equates the pope's procession to a movie premiere: "They're stretched out in the gutter waiting for the sun to come out so they can start snapping pictures. I haven't seen so many people, Artie, so excited since the premiere of *Cleopatra*. It's that big" (18–19). Wearing an "I Love Paul" button on her coat, Bunny explains, "They ran out of 'Welcome Pope' buttons so I ran downstairs and got my leftover from when the Beatles were here!" (48). The pope and the Beatles are synonymous to Bunny as charismatic popular culture icons. When the pope is seen on television delivering a speech from Yankee Stadium later that day, he becomes further enshrined as a media celebrity, despite the fact that his underlying message is spiritual:

> We feel, too, that the entire American people is here present with its noblest and most characteristic traits: a people basing its conception of life on spiritual values, on a religious sense, on freedom, on loyalty, on work, on the respect of duty, on family affection, on generosity and courage. (71)

The irony is that for Bunny and for millions of Americans like her who are awestruck more by the pope's temporal majesty than by his plea for spiritual connection, his message falls on deaf ears.

Starved for love and victimized by her selfish husband who refuses to care for her, Bananas reaches out to touch the stars as well. Her conversations are replete with almost pathological adulation for the celebrities she occasionally mentions: Bob Hope, Cardinal Spellman, Jackie Kennedy, Johnny Carson, and Kate Smith. To Bananas, the pope has the same type of eminence, and she dreamily admits that he might provide the love, nurturance, and compassion missing in her life: "He'd take me in his arms and bless me" (36). In a pathetic scenario, Bananas runs to the television screen to kiss the pope's garments, hoping to come into contact with His Holiness so that her life can be changed for the better. Unfortunately, Bananas can only sigh, "The screen is so cold" (47). This image suggests that the meretricious media hype intended to make religious leaders as well as popular culture icons into celebrities is alluring yet essentially cold and disingenuous.

Artie calls on his old friend, Billy, to provide salvation. Upon first glance, Billy would seem to be the logical choice to help Artie, for he has made his fortune and ostensibly commands a certain amount of respect as a filmmaker in California, the place where fantasies are realized. However, when the veneer of celebrity is examined more closely, we find out that underneath lies artificiality. Billy's first film, *Conduct of Life*, was an artistic success and still is shown regularly in museums. In contrast, at the height of his success, Billy sold out his talent in favor of making sugarcoated commercial movies with Doris Day and Rock Hudson. Billy's name suggests the immaturity of adolescence has reneged on a chance to be a mature talent and opts instead for appealing to the frivolous and mundane tastes of the starry-eyed masses, including Artie himself. Billy's latest project is to move to Australia and make a film, which is unimaginatively to be titled *Kangaroo*. Artie views this movie as a success story similar to Billy's previous film, *Warmonger*, another mundane effort created with a title that would likely attract mass audiences.

Billy, the celebrity, is not merely superficial, he is also incapable of helping Artie. Billy demythologizes the notion of the American Dream of fame and fortune. Supposedly playing the role of a genuine success story for Artie, Billy instead argues that the songwriter has the best of all possible worlds at home in Queens with Bananas. Billy views his life as a sham compared to Artie's "success story": "You were always healthy. You married a wonderful little Italian girl. You have a son. Where am I?" (80). Rather than acting as a role model, Billy instead perceives his chance to replace his dead wife, Georgina, with the lively Bunny Flingus, who jumps at the opportunity to go to Australia with the movie producer and abandon Artie. Billy justifies the need for Artie to remain in Queens, deflating his friend's dreams:

> If ever I thought you and Bananas weren't here in Sunnyside, seeing my work, loving my work, I could never work again. You're my touch with reality. (*He goes to Bananas.*) Bananas, do you know what the greatest talent in the world is? To be an audience. Anybody can create. But to be an audience . . . be an audience. . . . (84)

Artie believed that Queens was unreal and that Hollywood was the ultimate reality. Billy demythologizes the dream by insisting that Queens is real and that the identity of the rich and famous depends on middle-class Americans who pay to see the stars. Guare indicates that Artie, who tried to use Billy to enhance his dreams of success, much in the same manner that he tried to avail himself of the pope, realizes that his fantasies have been naive.

Guare's next major play, *Rich and Famous* (1976), also examines the pitfalls of celebrity worship. Bing Ringling, the protagonist of the play, is a confused young man with a consuming desire to be a celebrity. Bing's first name reminds us of Bing Crosby who, in one national poll, was the most popular person in the United States during the 1940s; Ringling intimates the circus as icon for popular entertainment. The alliterative name also indicates a somewhat cartoonish figure. Indeed, when we first see Bing on stage, he appears to be rather clownish, wearing a rented tuxedo and clutching the script of his play destined, he hopes, for Broadway. He tells his friend Leanara that his life will be immortalized in musicals one day and enshrined in bookstores: "I went into that little all-night bookstore over there on the corner to see where I'll fit in and I'll be between Rimbaud and Rin Tin Tin" (1996: 154).

Somewhere between Rimbaud and Rin Tin Tin is exactly where his talents lie. His cultural tastes seem to be rather parochial. He admonishes Leanara for criticizing Chekhov because, despite the Russian playwright's attempts at drama, Bing says, "He tried" (153). Bing, who fears being stereotyped as the World's Oldest Living Promising Young Playwright, believes he has outdone Aeschylus, Brecht, Chekhov, Molière, Feydeau, and Racine by writing 843 plays. His latest play, a musical version of *Dante's Inferno*, appropriately titled *Spreaded Thin*, now playing on Lower Death Street way off-Broadway, is, he swears, his ticket to success. He is so confident about his talents that he has bought a pair of cufflinks in a magic store; they are imprinted with the letters "R" and "F," for "rich" and "famous." However, when Bing recites his favorite lines from his play, we realize that his dreams may be premature: "I ran down into the subway. In a panic. I'll go anywhere. Trains rush past me. E trains. F trains. As. GGs. RRs. Cs. Pursued by the entire alphabet" (154). Bing thus can be compared to Artie Shaughnessy, another dreamer who wants to "make it big" in the world of show business but cannot seem to escape the reality of his lack of talent.

Bing notices the face of his childhood friend, Tybalt Dunleavy, on a billboard overlooking Times Square. Tybalt has gone on to become a successful actor who is now starring in a new movie, *Gangland*, advertised on the billboard. Tybalt Dunleavy sounds like a name of someone who is rich and famous – which is everything Bing would love to be – since obviously children from the lower or working classes are rarely named Tybalt. The billboard dominates the stage action throughout the play, offering the subliminal message that Bing's alter ego overshadows everything the aspiring playwright does.

Tybalt is so impressed with the opening night of *Dante's Inferno* that he wants to star in his old friend's play. He hands Bing a note that reads, "God, *Gangland* played to five hundred million people in movie theaters and I envy you tonight playing to ninety-five live ones" (157). Just as Billy Einhorn, the celebrity who had it all, craves to be in his friend Artie's shoes, Tybalt is not happy with his existence and fantasizes about adopting Bing's persona. The implication is that our fantasies force us to anticipate the future, and even those who have reached the pinnacle of success must have their own dreams. In his drive for glory, Bing seeks out Tybalt at the Algonquin Hotel, hoping that the star's presence in his play will make the difference between failure and success. However, Bing's hopes of becoming famous are dashed when he reads the pitiful theatre reviews of his play. To make matters worse, Bing learns that Tybalt checked out of his hotel room, a sign, Bing muses, that after Tybalt read those horrid reviews, he wanted no part of a losing venture.

Bing seeks solace in the home of his collaborator, Anatol Torah, a sadomasochistic Jewish bisexual composer. Torah has proof that he once rubbed shoulders with celebrities, for in his apartment are signed photographs of Greta Garbo, Charlie Chaplin, Indira Gandhi, and Harry Truman. Bing is enthralled with Torah's music, admitting that he grew up listening to it. He is also encouraged by the fact that Torah has told him that reviews are meaningless – it is the work that counts; thus, Bing can ignore the harsh critical responses to his play. When we hear Torah sing his songs, we realize that they are all absurdly repetitive of Yiddish double talk: "Moloch Mosai, Mallaca Mazoy" (164). Likewise Artie Shaughnessy's songs, Torah's tunes all sound alike. He has no discernible taste, which is perhaps why he can praise Bing's work, especially his acolyte's latest endeavor, *The Odiad*, a musical version of *The Iliad* and *The Odyssey*.

Gradually, we realize that Torah fawns over Bing's work not because he has any artistic interest in it, but because he is sexually attracted to Bing. In short, his motives are selfish. Bing is so impressed with Torah, however, that he calls Leanara in order that the composer might sing one of his famous songs for her. During his telephone conversation, Bing learns that Leanara has just received a job offer to do a television series and is thus leaving town. There is no spiritual connection between Bing and his girlfriend; when she receives a better offer, particularly one that might lead to fame and fortune, she takes it. In this narcissistic society, relationships are abandoned in favor of hope that springs eternal. Torah's response to Leanara's departure is also selfish, for he can now have Bing for himself without competition: "Good! Get rid of the baggage. Artists and revolutionaries should never have families. Never have connections" (168).

To make *The Odiad* successful, Torah insists on casting Tybalt to play Ulysses. Torah worships celebrity and thus insists that it is Tybalt's star status that will determine the success of Bing's new play. Torah admits, "Tybalt Dunleavy wouldn't be too big for me, but he thinks he's bigger than me and that's what I want! That's what I need! Someone bigger than me!!!" (170). Torah well understands that Bing is awed by superstar status and thus tries to impress him with the story of how he met the penultimate celebrity:

> Jesus appeared in my room. In the dark. All lit up. Inner light. Looking great. I said, Jesus, what are you doing here? He said, I hope I haven't bothered you, but I just wanted to meet you once before you died. He, Jesus, wanted to meet me. I'm not even Christian. His light shown up the dark. Now that's big! (170)

Torah implies that if he fraternizes with Jesus, then he certainly is good enough for Tybalt Dunleavy. Torah then produces a contract that reveals that when Bing delivers Tybalt to him, his working relationship with Bing is over, and Tybalt becomes the new collaborator. In short, just as Leanara abandoned her friend once she had a better offer, Torah will do likewise.

While at an art gallery, Bing runs into his former school chum, Allison de Mears. Allison has heard about Bing's new musical and admires his talents. She admits that Bing inspires her: "I'll never be rich and famous like you are, but I can have a life. I'm so frightened. Give me courage. I want to thank you. What a wonderful bump-into" (175). Bing provides the impetus for Allison to divorce her rude husband, perhaps get a job working with emotionally disturbed children, or go to night school to advance.

Thus, the absurdity continues as we see that Allison idolizes Bing, who worships Anatol Torah, who fantasizes about Tybalt Dunleavy. Guare reveals that each chain in the link is nebulous and superficial.

Bing's visit to his parents indicates how much his mother and father have inculcated in him the notion that life is worth living only if one is rich and famous. Bing's father, in particular, is so enamored with celebrity status that he rhythmically inundates his conversations with the names of famous talents so as to make his own son aware, perhaps subliminally, of successful people:

Mom: Why don't you write?
Dad: Orville Wright! Wilbur Wright!
Mom: Call anytime of the day or night.
Dad: Dennis Day. Fuzzy McKnight.
Mom: Either one of us is always here in case you want to come home. Twenty-four hour devotions at the phone in case you want to call.
Dad: Alexander Graham Bell. (176)

Bing's parents expect that the budding playwright is proceeding up the ladder to the top of the show business world. Bing, however, realizes himself as a failure and instead returns to his parents to reconnect with self and relatives. Bing seeks to establish an identity free from the fantasies of his parents. His hints that his play might fail fall on deaf ears until he whips out the reviews of the play to reveal the truth. Bing's father is so upset at his son's ineptitude that he pulls out a gun and shoots at Bing. Bing's parents surmise that if Tybalt had been their son, their fantasies would have materialized. Seeking only to connect with someone, Bing is now rejected by his own parents.

The last segment of the play, Bing's encounter with Tybalt, his alter ego, is a tour de force. The scene takes place on top of Tybalt's billboard advertising *Gangland* in Times Square. Tybalt, clinging to his own image atop a scaffolding, tells Bing that a consortium headed by Norman Mailer has bought the rights to his death; he plans to jump off the billboard, committing suicide right in the middle of Times Square. Tybalt believes that his suicide will make him immortal, enshrining him forever in fame. Tybalt assumes that after he leaps to his death, a book will be made about his life, then a play followed by a movie, a stage musical, and ultimately a film musical. Tybalt hopes to reach the pinnacle of perfection in his profession: "I'll be bigger in death than I ever was in life" (186). Through Tybalt, Bing begins to see how artificial his dreams have been; Tybalt, the envy of everyone, is nothing more than vain and shallow. After Tybalt pitches himself off the scaffolding, the stage directions read, "*And Bing digs his hands into his eyes as if to dig out these old eyes. Tybalt is like the amputation of some terrible part of himself*" (187). Bing realizes that if being rich and famous means divorcing oneself from any sort of connection with others in order to enhance one's status as legend, then the dream must be superficial in the first place. In short, in a society where the dream to be rich and famous is paramount, we are often led down the wrong path, ignoring personal relationships in favor of fantasies.

Six Degrees of Separation (1990) is in addition concerned with establishing identity in an essentially fraudulent society. The play begins as a flashback in the plush New York apartment of waspy Upper East-siders Flan and Ouisa Kittredge, who are recovering from their previous evening's encounter with a young black man named Paul they invited to stay overnight. Paul took advantage of them by picking up a male prostitute on the street and inviting him back to the bedroom. Flan is an art dealer who specializes in buying from friends and then selling the paintings for much higher prices, even for millions of dollars, overseas. Flan and Ouisa are entertaining Geoffrey, a British South African businessman and art dealer who has made his fortune in gold mines. The Kittredges hope to wine and dine Geoffrey to get him to contribute $2 million to their purchase of a Cézanne, which will eventually be sold to Japanese collectors for $10 million.

Geoffrey is well liked by the Kittredges despite his pomposity. Asked why he remains in South Africa, Geoffrey replies, "One has to stay there to educate the black workers and we'll know we've been successful when they kill us" (1994: 10). To repay the favor of such a quaint evening's entertainment, Geoffrey invites the Kittredges to South Africa to show them the sights: "I'll take you on my plane into the Okavango Swamps" (12). Yet Flan and Ouisa are willing to tolerate Geoffrey's excesses because they are enamored with his wealth. Ouisa describes Geoffrey as "King Midas rich. Literally. Gold mines" (7). Although they mock Geoffrey for not having the price of a dinner, they realize that his $2 million is what counts. Ouisa acknowledges, "Rich people can do something for you even if you're not sure what it is you want them to do" (9). While they laugh at his jokes, Ouisa muses, "We weren't auditioning but I kept thinking Two million dollars two million dollars" (13). Flan and Ouisa are more concerned with the art of the deal than they are with the art. They are willing to prostitute themselves in order to get Geoffrey to commit to $2 million. Money is equated with value, but values are lost in the transaction. As John Peter suggested in his review of the London production of the play at the Royal Court Theatre, the artwork of the transaction becomes more significant than buying the art itself, distinguishing value from values (1992: 6). Through elegance and erudition, Flan and Ouisa have mastered the art of the deal but are oblivious to their hypocrisy; instead, they see themselves as charming and sophisticated socialites, but underneath shallowness lies at the core of their lives.

The art dealings are interrupted when Paul, a preppy African American male in his early twenties, is ushered into the apartment. Paul claims that he was mugged in nearby Central Park and that he is a school chum of the Kittredges' sons, Talbot and Woody, at Harvard. After the mugging, he remembered that the Kittredges' sons had given him their parents' address, and realizing that their apartment was across from Central Park, he sought solace there. Paul tells them that his father is actor Sidney Poitier, who is coming to New York to conduct auditions for a movie version of *Cats* that he plans to direct. To legitimize his story, Paul intimately recounts the details of Poitier's life, including the exact titles and dates of nine of his 42 films. Flan and Ouisa, awed by celebrity status, are thus intrigued by having the son of a movie star in their home. Flan woos Paul: "Tell us stories of movie stars tying up their children and being cruel" (25). During dinner, Paul displays his charming wit and personality. Flan and Ouisa are mesmerized by Paul's account of his childhood in Switzerland, his travels, and his overall literacy level. They insist that Paul stay overnight and even give him $50 as spending money upon agreement that he will maneuver to get them roles as extras in *Cats*. Geoffrey is so enamored with Paul that he envisions plans for a Black American Film Festival in South Africa, juried, of course, by Sidney Poitier. Flan and Ouisa, like Evelyn Landis in *Muzeeka*, begin to equate money and celebrity with godhead:

Flan: There is a God.
Ouisa: And his name is –
Flan: Geoffrey?
Ouisa: Sidney. (44)

Paul is eventually discovered to be a con artist who has duped several of the Kittredges' friends by being allowed to stay overnight in their homes while he abuses their hospitality. The Kittredges urge Paul to turn himself in to the police. Questioned about why he would bring a hustler back to the room after the Kittredges extended their hospitality and their trust to him, Paul responds, "I was so happy. I wanted to add sex to it. Don't you do that?" (108). Paul is implying that he values the experience – the vitality of meaningful contact with others. When Ouisa responds that she does not add sex to her marriage, this middle-aged sterility indicates the overt effects of the modern neurosis. Ouisa begins to accept Paul's individuality and chooses to defer going to an auction at Sotheby's in order to take Paul to the police where, she says, "They will treat you with dignity" (114). However, when Ouisa and Flan arrive to meet Paul, the police had already dragged him, kicking and screaming, into a squad car. Ouisa and Flan are helpless to bail Paul out because they do not even know his real name and thus cannot identify him for the authorities.

Six Degrees of Separation documents the pathology of middle-and upper-class modern urban life in the United States. Guare depicts a life of fatuity in which anecdote has replaced worthwhile experience. In his essay, "Radical Chic," Tom Wolfe described how wealthy Leonard Bernstein invited revolutionary members of the Black Panther party to soirées at his penthouse on Park Avenue. Attendees included celebrities from all walks of life who had a liberal penchant for ennobling the downtrodden. Full of guilt, the Bernsteins and their compatriots made a desperate effort to hire white servants for these "occasions" with the Panthers. The trend, endemic to the upper classes, is described as *"nostalgie de la boue,"* a romanticizing of "primitive souls" (1970: 32). Julie Salamon asserts that Paul becomes the perfect black man for the Kittredges to fetishize: Ivy League, polite, a celebrity, and the son of a man who himself is an anecdote, the barrier breaker of the 1950s and 1960s (1993: A14). Paul's upbringing in Europe, his polished education, and his fine ancestry make him less of a threat. He even admits, "I don't feel American. I don't even feel black" (30).

The Kittredges are not the only ones duped by Paul's celebrity status. Kitty and Larkin's encounter with Paul is reduced to the proud announcement: "We are going to be in the movie of *Cats*" (55). Dr. Fine, who also invited Paul into his home, is seduced by the lure of the movies: "And this kid's father – the bravery of his films – had given me a direction, a confidence" (64). Paul's con game also affects those who aspire to the values of radical chic. Trent Conway, who kept records of the lives of the rich and famous, worships Paul to the extent that the latter becomes a sex object and uses the MIT student to gain valuable information about the argot of the wealthy. Finally, Rick and Elizabeth, two star-struck artists who invited Paul into their loft with visions of performing Shakespeare and Chekhov all over the world, are conned by Paul's admission that his father is a millionaire. Paul entices Rick and Elizabeth to give him money by implying that their assistance will one day lead to their own stardom as celebrities:

> But I am going to give you the money to put on a showcase of any play you want and you'll be in it and agents will come see you and you'll be seen and you'll be started. And when you win your Oscars – both of you – you'll look in the camera and thank me. (88–9)

Although on the surface Guare explores the concept of radical chic, the leitmotif of the play involves the fragmentation of the psyche and our efforts to connect self with others in a society where we are constantly alienated. Ouisa mentions the spiritual connection that seemingly unites us all: "I read somewhere that everybody on this planet is separated by only six other people. Six degrees of separation" (81). However, one must find the right six people to make the connection. Most individuals in modern American society are alienated to the extent that separation and division have become the norm. Guare stated, "For me, the play is all about the Kandinsky" (qtd. in Campbell 1992: 19). The painting by Kandinsky is the image that opens and closes the play. The stage directions indicate, "*One side is geometric and somber. The other side is wild and vivid*" (4). Flan reduces the painting to "A burst of color asked to carry so much" (14). The Kandinsky represents color without structure, a condition that characterizes the lives of Ouisa and Flan. Ouisa realizes, "There is color in my life, but I'm not aware of any structure" (118). Color also becomes a metaphor for the race-based problems of separation inherent in the play. Furthermore, as Frank Rich observes, Ouisa and Flan are, like the Kandinsky, two-faced and double-sided (1990: 7). The spiritual needs of the psyche do not coincide with our superficial desire for celebrity. Ouisa sadly admits to her colleagues, who were also duped by Paul, "It seems the common thread linking us all is an overwhelming need to be in the movie of *Cats*" (68).

In *Six Degrees of Separation*, alienation and isolation are the norm rather than spiritual connection. Parents do not know their children, heterosexuals are alienated from homosexuals, whites are separated from blacks, and the wealthy do not understand the less fortunate. Guare depicts a bifurcated society in which the emotional and intellectual vitality of individual consciousness is reduced to fragmentation and a neurotic obsession with celebrity status. Individuals are divorced from each other, and thus families, classes, and races are also further divided. Thus, *Six Degrees of Separation* has much in common with his earlier play, *Bosoms and Neglect* (1979), which focuses on whether individuals in contemporary American society can connect with each other in some meaningful or spiritual way, despite the fact that neglect, indifference, and alienation reflect the norm in human relationships. In *Bosoms and Neglect*, a play based upon neglected relationships, Guare also examines how we seek refuge from the reality by immersing ourselves in self-centered fantasy lives.

This modern estrangement has allowed us to wear the mask of the con artist to hide our real feelings while taking advantage of others. Paul gains access to houses in order to find the family that he lacks; he is searching for an identity and yearns to be loved, wanted, and appreciated. He seeks contact in a society out of touch with the spiritual and with no passion for individuality. When Paul is asked what he wanted from the Kittredges, he states, "everlasting friendship" (99). However, Paul, like so many of us, is outwardly interested in rubbing shoulders with the rich and famous, and thus his envy of celebrity forces him to assume the guise of con artist. Similarly, Flan and Ouisa, whose children are alienated from them, reach out to Paul as the ideal son they would love to have as part of the family. On the surface, however, Ouisa and Flan are con artists just like Paul, only their scams involve Cézannes and Kandinskys. Their seduction of Geoffrey is a fine example of the con game fully at work. Like Paul, Flan and Ouisa have learned the art of the deal: figure out what the client wants and then deliver it.

Paul becomes the catalyst to help Ouisa understand how estranged modern society has become and how empty her own life is without the vitality of imagination. Paul laments the lack of passion in a society where habit, convenience, and style have replaced meaningful human communication. Paul tries to explain his existence to Ouisa and Flan: he is an effective con artist because he is merely mirroring American values, succumbing to the myth of the American Dream as we know it. This type of society, where human connections are fleeting and imagination is nonexistent, gets what it deserves: hustlers, con men, and impostors. Values are distorted: art is sold mainly for profit in private homes and in public at places like Sotheby's, *Cats* achieves theatrical prominence, and intimate experience is devalued in favor of cocktail-party anecdote. As David A. Zimmerman suggests, Paul becomes an art object for the Kittredges, "a thing they consume and trade at soirées and business meetings for their pleasure and their profit, a thing whose value hangs only on their interest in valorizing him" (1999: 120). Paul realizes that to connect with others, we must first come to grips with ourselves, our imaginations. Ouisa begins to understand the need to connect with others by using our imaginations to hold onto a purity of experience that may be alive, vibrant, and poignant rather than to substitute it for disposable anecdotal information.

Although the Kittredges are wealthy and seem to have everything to make them feel comfortable, they learn that material things do not suffice when there is no connection with self and others. Again, Guare demonstrates that the lives of the rich and famous are often spiritually hollow at the core – certainly nothing to emulate. Paul provided the Kittredges with the chance to connect emotionally with another human being. In a neurotic society where most people are two-faced like the Kandinsky and contact is fleeting, reduced primarily to disposable anecdotes, Ouisa desperately wants to hold onto the experience. As she explores the existential angst troubling her, Ouisa's dilemma concerns the modern identity in a fraudulent society: "But it was an experience. How do we *keep* the experience?" (118). In other words, how do we find the right six people in the chain that will lead to an authentic spiritual connection? Guare expects his audience to identify with Ouisa's epiphany and question the artificial values that we readily accept as fueling modern American society.

Guare's plays acknowledge that the individual must make meaningful connections with self and others, free both from the "narcotizing" power of commercialization that hypes the glitz and glamour of celebrity status and from our own superficial desires of fame and fortune. Individuals who become immersed in the popular culture hype of celebrity status will find themselves trapped in warped fantasies that others have created for them, and thus their lives will become artificial and superficial. When their outlandish dreams cannot be realized, individuals who have invested their lives in such superficial facades find themselves immersed in anomie and anguish. Guare has been successful because his plays touch nerves, affecting audiences viscerally as he explores the search for dignity amidst the neuroticism of modern American society.

BIBLIOGRAPHY

Campbell, J. (1992). "Radical Cheek." *Times Literary Supplement*, June 26: 19.

Chin, D. (1991). "From Popular to Pop: The Arts in/of Commerce." *Performing Arts Journal* 37: 5–20.

Clurman, H. (1971). "Theatre." *Nation* 1 (March): 285–6.

Dasgupta, G. (1981). "John Guare." In Bonnie Marranca and Gautam Dasgupta (eds.), *American Playwrights: A Critical Survey*, vol. 1. New York: Drama Book Specialists, 41–52.

Drukman, S. (1999). "In Guare's Art, Zero Degrees of Separation." *New York Times*, April 11, Sec. 2: 7, 24.

Friend, T. (1992). "The Guare Facts." *Vogue* (March): 327–9.

Guare, J. (1970). *Three Plays by John Guare: Cop-Out, Muzeeka, Home Fires*. New York: Grove.

——(1987a). *The House of Blue Leaves and Two Other Plays: Landscape of the Body and Bosoms and Neglect*. New York: Plume.

——(1987b). "Introduction." In *The House of Blue Leaves and Two Other Plays: Landscape of the Body and Bosoms and Neglect*. New York: Plume, 3–8.

——(1994). *Six Degrees of Separation*, 2nd ed. New York: Vintage.

——(1996). *Rich and Famous*. In *The War Against the Kitchen Sink*, vol. 1. Contemporary Playwrights Series. Lyme, NH: Smith and Kraus, 151–88.

Peter, J. (1992). "Reality Take Two." *Sunday Times*, June 21, Sec. 7: 6–7.

Rich, F. (1990). "A Guidebook to the Soul of a City in Confusion." *New York Times*, July 1, Sec. 2: 1, 7.

Salamon, J. (1993). "A Young Con Artist, Old Men on Ice, and a Weird Lady." *Wall Street Journal*, December 9: A14.

Wolfe, T. (1970). *Radical Chic and Mau-Mauing the Flak Catchers*. New York: Farrar, Straus, and Giroux.

Zimmerman, D. A. (1999). "Six Degrees of Distinction: Connection, Contagion, and the Aesthetics of Anything." *Arizona Quarterly* 55, 3: 106–33.

23

Writing Beyond Borders:
A Survey of US Latina/o Drama

Tiffany Ana Lopez

What language communicates to people who have already been put down is how society regards them; in their case, often with little respect. But a play provides a distance from which to view these sinister acts of language.

Miguel Algarin (in Algarin and Griffith 1997)

In the early 1980s when Maria Irene Fornes founded the Hispanic Playwrights Lab at INTAR (International Arts Relations) in New York City, her goal was to enrich the American theatre by fostering a new generation of writers. Historically, Latina/o dramatists have struggled to have their work recognized beyond festivals, development labs, second stages, and other potentially segregated spaces. Latina/o drama is now beginning to appear in the spotlight of a richly illuminated American stage, as evidenced by such distinctions as the 2003 Pulitzer Prize for Drama to Nilo Cruz (*Anna in the Tropics*), the numerous Tony Award nominations for John Leguizamo (*Sexaholix* and *Freak*), and the Signature Theatre Company's prestigious devotion of an entire season to Fornes's body of work, including the world premiere of *Letters from Cuba*, which garnered Obie Awards for both her writing and directing (1999–2000, see chapter 27). There have also been other signs of embrace from some of the most influential American stages: the Kennedy Center's attention to dynamic collaborative work by Sandra Munoz, Alma Cervantes, Marisela Norte, and Luis Alfaro (*Black Butterfly*); the Public Theatre's commission of work by Migdalia Cruz (*El Grito del Bronx*) and the play's continued support by INTAR in New York City; productions of fresh works by new voices such as Joe Hortua, Jorge Ignacio Cortinas, and Ricardo Bracho; and the support of projects by Elia Arce, Aya de Leon, Caridad "La Bruja" de la Luz, and others representing the cutting edge of Latina/o drama and performance.

I would like to thank Julian Felix and Zina Rodriguez for their notable research assistance, Tanya Gonzalez for her reading and feedback, and David Krasner for his endless support of this work.

In the formative years of the 1960s, foundational theatre companies such as El Teatro Campesino and the Puerto Rican Traveling Theatre Company defined themselves in response to cultural issues and the oppression of Latinas/os through painfully repeated stereotypes and narrowly conceived cultural performances. Working from the civil rights movements, regional and grassroots theatres were formed to promote social critique and cultural pride while advocating drama and theatre as absolutely integral to community building. As cultural conversations shifted and public and governmental support for the arts changed, Latina/o playwrights began to redefine themselves and their drama. At the end of the twentieth century, Latina/o dramatists write in response to an even more varied spectrum of cultural questions and concerns. The field has grown such that one now finds Latina/o dramatists creating parody and political satire in response to both the dominant culture and one's own culture (for example, the works of Carmelita Tropicana, Chicano Secret Service, Monica Palacios, and Marga Gomez). While Latina/o dramatic writing has become unmoored from strict political expectations, many playwrights remain steadfast in promoting their artistic vision as inextricably linked to matters of community building (for example, Cherrie Moraga, Migdalia Cruz, and Culture Clash). Contemporary audiences observe Latina/o drama through multiple registers.

Latinos comprise one of the largest and fastest-growing populations in the United States. United States Latina/o drama is comprised of writers whose works communicate a sense of culture, history, and aesthetic sensibility. Some writers freely categorize themselves as Latina/o dramatists, others refuse to be reductively categorized, and still others choose terms depending on audience and geographical, cultural, or political location. In addition to describing a genre of American theatre, Latina/o drama also denotes a distinct field, with its own history and contexts. For example, Cherrie Moraga's *The Hungry Woman: A Mexican Medea* corresponds to many other dramatic adaptations of the Medea story. Yet, it also draws on indigenous mythology, Mexican American legend, and Chicana/o folklore as well as feminist debates about sexuality and class.

Latina/o plays that deal with very specific geographical or cultural locations, such as Migdalia Cruz's *Miriam's Flowers* about a young Puerto Rican girl in the South Bronx, have received readings worldwide because of their powerful artistry and engagement with issues that cross cultures. Notably, Latina/o drama is characterized by what critics have termed some of the most vibrant writers for the American stage: Maria Irene Fornes, Jose Rivera, Nilo Cruz, John Leguizamo, Cherrie Moraga, Luis Alfaro, Migdalia Cruz, Oliver Mayer, Carmelita Tropicana, and Culture Clash, to name just a few. Yet, to date, with the exception of a handful of playwrights (Valdez, Fornes, Piñero, and Leguizamo), United States Latina/o drama is still neither widely read nor taught as part of a larger body of American dramatic writing. Most theatre departments lack trained specialists working in the field. With the exception of the early *actos* of El Teatro Campesino, Latina/o drama is rarely included in studies of Latina/o literature. Too often, the work falls in between disciplines. The reasons for this undoubtedly vary: from scholars being unaware of evolving and emerging voices,

to lack of easy access to performance texts. This is compounded by large publishers'
tendency only to print works with successful runs at mainstream theatres. These
factors impact what makes it into print and, subsequently, what shapes understanding
of the field. Anthologies, including the fairly recent *Out of the Fringe* (Svich and
Marrero 2000), *Puro Teatro* (Sandoval-Sanchez and Sternbach 2001), *Latino Plays from
South Coast Repertory* (Carillo and Gonzalez 2001), and *Corpus Delecti* (Fusco 2000),
have therefore been crucial to the circulation of plays.

Works that cross disciplines play a major role in increasing critical interest in
Latina/o drama. Scholarly books have broken new ground by both documenting and
interrogating the field. Pivotal works include Jorge Huerta's *Necessary Theater* (1989)
and *Chicano Drama: Performance, Society, and Myth* (2000), Diana Taylor's *The Archive
and the Repertoire: Performing Cultural Memory in the Americas* (2003), Taylor and Juan
Venegas's *Negotiating Performance: Gender, Sexuality, and Theatricality in Latin/o America*
(1994), Alberto Sandoval-Sanchez's *Jose, Can You See? Latinos On and Off Broadway*
(1999), Sandoval-Sanchez and Nancy Saporta Sternbach's *Stages of Life: Transcultural
Performance and Identity in U.S. Latina Theater* (2001), Yvonne Yarbro-Bejarano's *The
Wounded Heart: Writing on Cherrie Moraga* (2001), Yolanda Broyles-Gonzalez's *El
Teatro Campesino: Theater in the Chicano Movement* (1994), Alicia Arrizon's *Latina
Performance: Traversing the Stage* (1999), Jose Esteban Munoz's *Disidentifications: Queers
of Color and the Performance of Politics* (1999), and David Román's *Acts of Intervention:
Performance, Gay Culture, and AIDS* (1998). Such works make plays readily accessible
to a wide readership while also illustrating the very rich ways Latina/o drama fosters
critical engagement through its focus on issues central to the fields of literary, theatre,
performance, and cultural studies.

Yolanda Broyles-Gonzalez (1994) powerfully illustrates the way uncritical deployment of language and gender functioned in early writing about the Chicano theatre
troupe El Teatro Campesino to the point that, with little exception, the contributions
of women receded into the background. Broyles-Gonzalez describes the resulting
shortsightedness: "Within oral culture, performed words make sense only as communal creations and as part of a larger historical performance context. In the absence of
that greater communal performance context, only the great man – and not the
community – becomes identified with the written text" (1994: xiii). The critically
imperative term "Latina/o" is historically recent. In Spanish, the masculine ending (as
in Chican*o* or Latin*o*) is presumed to be all inclusive. Beginning in the 1980s, feminist
scholars began using the "a/o" split (in Chicana/o or Latina/o) to emphasize the
distinct and significant roles of women in cultural and creative production. The "a/
o" split purposefully signifies both female and male members. An important politics
drives this rhetorical move: women would no longer remain an invisible subgroup.
Contemporary scholarship necessarily explores matters of gender and sexuality in a
quest to cover accurately the broad spectrum of identity performance now reflected in
Latina/o dramatic work.

The term Latina/o combines those in the United States with roots in Mexican
American, Cuban American, Puerto Rican, Nuyorican, Dominican, Salvadoran, and

many other related cultures. Significantly, Latinas/os comprise a heterogeneous group with as many differences as commonalities. The spectrum of Latina/o identity in the United States is reflected by the diversity of regional theatres and their very different approaches to promoting Latina/o drama, developing artists, and cultivating Latina/o audiences: INTAR Hispanic American Arts Center (New York City), Bilingual Foundation for the Arts (Los Angeles), the Hispanic Playwrights Project at South Coast Repertory (Costa Mesa, California), the Latino Theatre Initiative at the Mark Taper Forum (Los Angeles), Teatro Sabor (San Francisco), El Centro Su Teatro (Denver), Guadalupe Cultural Arts Center (San Antonio, Texas), Repetorio Espanol (New York City), Teatro Luna (Chicago), Latino Experimental Fantastic Theatre (New York City), Teatro Avante (Miami), Teatro del Pueblo (St. Paul, Minnesota), Teatro Humanidad (Austin, Texas). Some writers eschew labels and other reductive identity markers. Others, such as Moraga, view the use of identity categories as strategic choices that enrich the writer and her community. They opt to employ the broader, more inclusive term "Latina" or "Latino" in situations that necessitate larger affiliations and use more specific terms, such as Chicana or lesbian, in other situations. Generally, "Latina/o" is preferred over "Hispanic," viewed by many politicized insiders as an oppressive term whose history is one of imposition from the United States government rather than one linked to a chosen identity politics.

Foundational Figures

In 1965 Luis Valdez founded El Teatro Campesino (ETC), "the farmworker's theatre," which employed short sketches called *actos* to dramatize the need for a farmworkers' union. This work quickly defined the burgeoning Chicana/o theatre movement as a network of grassroots teatros dedicated to educating audiences through performances that focus on urgent political issues. As Jorge Huerta explains, Valdez's plays "serve as historical documents and living examples of necessary theater; they are expressions of the Chicanos' continuing struggle for cultural, linguistic, economic, spiritual and political survival" (1989: 5). Valdez's first full-length play, *The Shrunken Head of Pancho Villa* (1964), was produced at San Jose State College in California. After his graduation, Valdez worked with the San Francisco Mime Troupe before founding ETC. Valdez's early works with ETC include the anti-war play *Dark Root of a Scream* (1967); the one-act *Bernabe* (1970); a Vietnam War *acto*, *Soladado Razo* (1970); and *La Gran Carpa de los Rasquachis* (1973). Among Valdez's single-authored plays are *Bandido!* (1982), *Corridos* (1983), and *I Don't Have to Show You No Stinking Badges* (1985). His signature play, *Zoot Suit*, was first co-produced by Teatro Campesino and the Center Theatre Group of Los Angeles at the Mark Taper Forum (1978), with its landmark Broadway production following in 1979. Based on the Zoot Suit "riots" and the 1942 trial of Henry Leyva and eight other youths in the notorious Sleepy Lagoon murder case in Los Angeles, the play employs interviews, court transcripts, archival research, and songs by Lalo Guerrero. Valdez explains his unprecedented desire to see

Zoot Suit produced on Broadway: "They won't take us seriously until we succeed on their turf, on their terms" (qtd. in Huerta 2000: 5). While some critics see Valdez's Broadway success as ushering in a new era of Chicana/o theatre that provides aspiring dramatists with "a totally different kind of professional production to invigorate and stimulate them" (Huerta 2000: 7), others, such as Yolanda Broyles-Gonzalez, observe the moment as representing an irreversible departure from the political focus that originally drove Chicana/o theatre because "the idea of selling the theatrical product becomes the chief consideration; all other considerations become secondary" (1994: 237). Valdez's career is further characterized by his insistent work across genres and venues that include mainstream theatre (*Zoot Suit*, 1978), television (*Los Vendidos*, *La Pastorela*), and film (*Zoot Suit*, 1982 and *La Bamba*, 1987).

Jorge Huerta's early collaborations with groundbreaking Chicano theatre companies such as El Teatro Campesino and El Teatro de la Esperanza, and his founding of pivotal organizations such as TENAZ (El Teatro Nacional de Aztlan/The National Theatre of Aztlan), make him a pioneer critic of Chicano teatro. In the early 1970s Huerta began documenting performances, placing them within a literary and social context that emphasized this body of work as a "necessary theater," an educational tool of community building (1989: 5). Such collaborative work between critics and playwrights continues to inform the field, as evidenced by dramatist Caridad Svich and scholar Maria Teresa Marrero's co-edited volume, *Out of the Fringe* (2000), David Román's edited collection *Downtown and Elsewhere: A Luis Alfaro Reader* (2004), Diana Taylor and Roselyn Costantino's *Holy Terrors: Latin American Women Perform* (2004), and the groundbreaking website for the Hemispheric Institute (hemi.nyu.edu), founded by Diana Taylor, which includes "web cuadernos," online curations of multimedia materials including photos, videos, texts, hyperlinks, bibliographies, and audio recordings.

Scholars have also been instrumental in creating new audiences for Latina/o theatre through efforts of programming and organization, such as Taylor's creation of the Hemispheric Institute of Performance and Politics, which hosts yearly and ongoing seminars, workshops, and symposia on shared performance practices in the Americas. Past presenters include Guillermo Gómez-Peña, Alina Troyano (a.k.a. Carmelita Tropicana), Marga Gomez, Nao Bustamante, Jesusa Rodriguez, Diana Raznovich, Astrid Hadad, Grupo Cultural Yuyachkani, and Marinela Boan and DanzAbierta. Huerta's promotion of the Consortium of Chicano Theatre Educators and Artists led to the group hosting the summer of 2002 Festival of Chicano Theatre Classics at the University of California, Los Angeles, under the direction of Jose Luis Valenzuela. This week-long event consisting of workshops and conversation among artists, directors, scholars, performers, and students included performances of many pivotal early works, such as El Teatro de la Esperanza's *La Victima* and *Guadalupe*, Carlos Morton's *Las Many Muertes de Danny Rosales*, and El Teatro Campesino's *La Gran Carpa de los Rasquachis*. These plays had not been staged for over 20 years. The festival also included more recent plays: the Latino Theatre Company's *August 29* and Chusma's *The Naco Show*. In addition to energizing conversation, the festival also generated controversy over the absence of women and gay and lesbian playwrights, most notably Cherrie Moraga, a foundational Chicana lesbian playwright whose work clearly stands in dialogue with the early Chicano movement plays and whose lengthy career embodies the spirit of teatro, albeit through redefining the terms of its cultural politics. Yvonne Yarbro-Bejarano explains that "The plays that form the canonical Chicano theater repertory tend to perpetuate the hierarchy based on gender, confining the representation of women within the polarized gender structure that theater reflects and reproduces" (2001: 24).

Moraga has been writing since the early 1980s. Her dramatic works include: *Giving Up the Ghost* (1984), *Shadow of a Man* (1989), *Heroes and Saints* (1989), *The Hungry Woman: A Mexican Medea* (1995), *Heart of the Earth: A Popul Vuh Story* (1994), *Watsonville: Some Place Not Here* (1996), and *Circle in the Dirt* (1995). Both *Shadow* and *Watsonville* won the Kennedy Center Fund for New American Plays Award, in 1991 and 1995, respectively; *Heroes and Saints* earned the Pen West Award for Drama in 1992; Moraga is also the recipient of a National Endowment for the Arts' Theatre Playwrights' Fellowship and a member of Theatre Communications Group. Her books of autobiographical writings, poetry, essays, and memoir include *Loving in the War Years* (1983), *The Last Generation* (1993), and *Waiting in the Wings: Portrait of a Queer Motherhood* (1997); she has also co-edited several influential anthologies: *This Bridge Called my Back* (1981), *Cuentos: Stories by Latinas* (1983), and *The Sexuality of Latinas* (1993). Notably, Moraga is one of the first openly Chicana lesbian writers. As a Chicana lesbian historically exiled from her own community, Moraga determinedly carves out a space for herself within Chicano culture by critically expanding definitions of Chicanismo. In their insistence that matters of sexuality and politics mutually inform one another, *Bridge* and *Loving* revolutionized Chicana criticism, Chicana/o theatre studies, and feminist theory. Alicia Arrizon notes the historical impact of this work: "Since the 1980s, as a result of Moraga's work, more emphasis has been given to the female body in this alternative space, and more direct questioning of sexuality has emerged" (1999: 76).

Moraga describes the evolution of her playwriting from her earlier work: "I did not come to the theater quickly. My plays grew out of that place where my poetry and autobiographical essays left off, a place where having told my own story as honestly as I was able [*Loving in the War Years*, 1983], a space opened up inside me inviting entrance for the first time for fictional characters to speak their own stories" (qtd. in Perkins and Uno 1996: 230). Moraga's poetry and essays often extend the questions and issues performed by her plays. Like Valdez, Moraga creates plays in the spirit of Chicano teatro to communicate a sense of political urgency. For example, her *Heroes and Saints* directly responds to Valdez's *The Shrunken Head of Pancho Villa* to further explore the relationship between issues of environmental and economic violence, gender and politics, and body and memory. Such works ask the audience to bear witness to social struggle and leave the theatre with a greater sense of responsibility about community building. She explains: "As any writer of any culture should, I try to write as specifically as possible of the complexities in our lives. In that the universality of the Chicano experience is found and the work becomes 'cross-cultural' in the deepest sense" (Perkins and Uno 1996: 231).

Like Moraga, Miguel Algarin also turned to theatre as a vehicle for social change. Algarin co-founded the Nuyorican Poets Café (established in 1973), a performance and cultural arts space in New York's East Village dedicated to entertaining and instructing while also documenting "the quest to understand." For Algarin, New York's Lower East Side/East Village, with its rich cultural mix of peoples, necessitated presentations that spoke to diverse communities. In her book *Boricua Literature*, Lisa Sanchez Gonzalez locates Algarin within a generation of writers of the Nuyorican Renaissance whose chief goals were "the construction, through literature, of Boricua cultural citizenship as an organic – and organically resistant – North American formation" (2001: 103). In her introduction to *Action: The Nuyorican Poets Café Theater Festival*, Lois Griffith describes Algarin's original focus to provide a place where he could nurture and display the talents of the "best of his neighborhood," most especially members of the underclass working to shape American culture (Algarin and Griffith 1997: xii). Following his motto "Truth first, then theater" (ibid.: xv), Algarin based one of his early plays, *The Murder of Pito* (1974), on a local police officer's killing of a young congero drumming in the subway. Much like Fornes's founding of the INTAR Hispanic Playwrights Lab to create a space that would foster new Latina/o playwrights and actresses, Algarin founded the Nuyorican Poets Café Theatre Festival "so that all actors of color could drop the bandanas wrapped around their heads, pull the razors out of their pockets and the knives from their jackets, and just act. At the Café they auditioned for roles that had substance, knowing they would not be stereotyped into the familiar urban guerilla war front image" (Algarin and Griffith 1997: xv). Algarin also participated in several dramatic collaborations, among them a play with Tato Laviera, *Olu Clemente*, which is a musical eulogy for Puerto Rican baseball player and activist Roberto Clemente (who died in a 1972 plane crash while bringing aid to Nicaraguan earthquake victims). Alberto Sandoval-Sanchez praises this work as belonging to a new era of Nuyorican plays driven by "compassion, pride, spirituality, hope and positive identity formation" that portray survival in the barrio as "a constant process of negotiation" (1999: 116). Perhaps Algarin's most noted collaboration is co-founding the Nuyorican Poets Café with the playwright Miguel Piñero.

Born in Puerto Rico and raised in New York City, Piñero wrote his signature play, *Short Eyes*, in the early 1970s (produced in 1972) while incarcerated in the notoriously violent Sing-Sing prison. There he participated in a prison repertory group known as "the Family." In his work, Piñero strove to reflect precisely what he witnessed and experienced in prison. Produced by Joseph Papp shortly after Piñero's release from prison, *Short Eyes* received immediate critical attention. Early reviews described mixed audience responses, from celebrations of its bold social critique of prisons to condemnations of its raw and explicit violence. Awards for this work include a New York Drama Critics' Circle Award as Best American Play of 1973–4, an Obie (the principal off-Broadway award), and six Tony nominations. Piñero also earned a 1973–4 Elizabeth Hull–Kate Warner Award from the Dramatists' Guild of New York. *Short Eyes* remains a powerful and relevant work as blacks and Latinos continue to comprise the majority of prisoners in the United States. Piñero's other published plays include *The Sun Always Shines for the Cool*, *Eulogy for a Small-Time Thief*, *A Midnight Moon at the Greasy Spoon*, and *Playland Blues*. Along with *Short Eyes*, these plays examine the lives of people pushed to the very margins of society.

In the early 1980s, Maria Irene Fornes created the Hispanic Playwrights Lab at INTAR in New York City to increase the number of Latina/o dramatists in the United States, to enhance artistic diversity, and to elevate the richness of different dramatic styles and voices. She viewed the Lab as an institutional intervention because at that moment, Hispanic playwrights, in her words, "have no one to look to and think 'Oh, I could be a playwright like so-and-so'" (qtd. in Osborn 1987: 47). In her workshops, Fornes artistically validates playwrights' existence not merely as Latina/o dramatists but as playwrights, period. Throughout her career, Fornes has focused on the most pressing political issues of a given moment. Though she writes about identity, she disavows identity politics and avoids the use of categories such as feminist, lesbian, or Latina. For her, preconceived notions of identity cripple playwrights by making them dependent on the expectations of others. In a recent tribute volume to her work, the wide range of participants from her workshops – Caridad Svich, Oliver Mayer, Kat Avila, Edit Villarreal, Migdalia Cruz, Otavio Solis, Luis Alfaro, Cherrie Moraga, Elaine Romero, Anne Garcia-Romero, Silvia Gonzalez S., Juliette Carillo, and Teresa Marrero, among dozens of others – credited her nearly strict attention to aesthetic details and artistic excellence with providing them the greatest tools for developing and strengthening dramatic writing. Migdalia Cruz credits Fornes with teaching her how to listen to difficult voices and reveal painful truths. Moraga commends Fornes as a teacher who asks students to "go to the hardest/ ugliest truths (the writer's truths) of what it is to be Latina, hungry of body and sex and spirit in this pitiful country. She encouraged those journeys into the forbidden" (qtd. in Delgado and Svich 1999: 184). Notably, Fornes's Playwrights Lab brought together, for the first time, significant numbers of Latina/o playwrights who otherwise would likely have remained isolated. The lab also helped to unify and empower many Latina dramatists who, before coming to the workshop, experienced alienation within both mainstream and Latino arts spaces.

Leading Contemporaries

Jose Rivera, like so many in Fornes's workshops, began writing drama with fixed beliefs: "I thought playwriting meant social and political awareness and activism" (qtd. in Savran 1999: 170). Rivera's plays include *Marisol* (1992), *A Tiger in Central Park* (1992), *Cloud Tectonics* (1995), *Each Day Dies with Sleep* (1990), *The Promise*, *The House of Ramon Iglesia* (1983), *Giants Have Us in Their Books*, *The Street of the Sun*, *Sonnets for an Old Century*, *References to Salvador Dali Make Me Hot*, *Sueno*, and *Lovers of*

Long Red Hair. His works have been produced nationally by the Public Theatre, Playwrights Horizons, Berkeley Repertory, the Magic Theatre, Mark Taper Forum, and South Coast Repertory. Rivera's Obie Award-winning *Marisol*, originally commissioned and developed by INTAR, received its world premiere at the Humana Festival of New American Plays at the Actors Theatre of Louisville. It was subsequently produced by the New York Shakespeare Festival in association with the Hartford Stage.

Alberto Sandoval-Sanchez locates Rivera within the new generation of Nuyorican playwrights who "revisit, re-vision, and reimagine the history of Latino diaspora, exile, and nostalgia, as new hybrid identities are articulated and constructed on the stage. They are professionals who have received a formal education, who are an integral part of the middle class, and whose home is here in the U.S." (1999: 116). Rivera credits his studies with Gabriel Garcia Marquez at the Sundance Institute (1989) as influencing his use of magical realism as an artistic means to address culture, history, and, perhaps more subtly, politics. Rivera explains, "Things in theatre don't have to be what they are in life" (Savran 1999: 171); "What makes magic realism are the unpredictable effects produced by myriad and common causes" (173). Rivera also credits reading Sam Shepard with helping him form his sensibilities as a dramatist (see chapter 18). Other influences include Thomas Pynchon for what David Savran describes as Rivera's "ability to elongate character and mess with time and space" (171), exemplified in *Each Day Dies with Sleep*, a work Rivera describes as "toying with our notions of cause and effect in a completely non-naturalistic way" (qtd. in Savran 1999: 172). Rivera has also written for both television and film.

Nilo Cruz, another Fornes protégée, holds the distinction of the first Latino playwright to have his work recognized by a Pulitzer Prize for Drama (2003) for *Anna in the Tropics*. The play focuses on the cigar-making industry in 1929 Tampa, Florida. The lives of the cigar workers include a parallel with the plot of Leo Tolstoy's *Anna Karenina*. Cruz's other works are *A Bicycle Country, Night Train to Bolina, Graffiti, Hortensia and the Museum of Dreams, Of Storks and Angels, A Park in Our House, Dancing on Her Knees, Betty and Gauguin, Drinking the Sea, Not Yet Remembered,* and *Two Sisters and a Piano*, which has also been performed as a radio play. He has written adaptations of Marquez's *A Very Old Man with Enormous Wings* and Federico Garcia Lorca's *The House of Bernarda Alba*. Cruz's work has been developed and performed throughout the United States, including at the Joseph Papp Public Theatre, the Magic Theatre, South Coast Repertory, The Group at Strasberg in Los Angeles, INTAR, and the New York Theatre Workshop. It has also been featured as part of several major festivals, including the Bay Area Playwrights Festival and the New York Shakespeare Festival. Among Cruz's many awards is an Alton Jones Award for *Night Train to Bolina* as well as the Joseph Kesselring Award for *A Park in Our House*.

While some critics read Cruz as writing within a Latin American tradition of magical realism, Cruz himself actually rejects the label: "I prefer to exclude my work from the school of Magic Realism, because I always like to start from a raw, tangible reality and then have the characters of my plays transform their reality into something magical. I believe in the power of creativity and imagination, not in an existing magical reality" (qtd. in Svich and Marrero 2000: 117). In his discussion of Cruz's writing about Cubania ("Cubanness as a way of being in the world"), Jose Munoz highlights Cruz's use of emotion as "an instrument to see Cuba beyond a certain ideological fog" (2000: 457). Cruz is candid about the role politics occupies in his writing: "The characters in my plays usually, if not always, interrogate displacement, religion, postcolonial promises, sexuality, existential void, and corruption of power" (qtd. in Svich and Marrero 2000: 116). Following his mentor Fornes, Cruz writes plays with a distinct sense of the visual as its own dramatic language: "In my plays language functions in the same way that color operates in painting – creating contrast, hues and dimensions, but overall as a sense of composition and harmony. I firmly believe that in theatre language must be poetic, rhythmic and sensorial. I use lyrical language to dictate action. My plays are also very visual" (Svich and Marrero 2000: 117).

Another artist highly invested in visual language is Luis Alfaro, playwright, performer, producer, and director. He is co-founder with Diane Rodriguez of the Latino Theatre Initiative at the Mark Taper Forum and Director of New Play Development at the Mark Taper Forum. Alfaro is also the recipient of a prestigious John D. and Catherine T. MacArthur Foundation Fellowship (1997–2000) for his wide-reaching contributions to American theatre. His plays include first short works (1987), *True Stories from Pico Union, Downtown* (1993), *BitterHomes and Gardens* (1994), *Cuerpo Politizado* (1995), *Speaking in Tongues* (1995), *Straight as a Line* (1997), *Breakfast, Lunch and Dinner* (2001), *Electricidad* (2003), *Body of Faith* (2003); the spoken word CD *down town* (New Alliance/SST Records, 1994); and a short film of his solo performance work, *Chicanismo* (PBS/KCET, The Works IV, 1996), which was nominated for an Emmy and won Best Experimental Film at the 1998 CineFestival. His collaborative works include *Black Butterfly, Jaguar Girl*, and *Pinata Women and Other Super Hero Girls Like Me* (based on the poetry of Alma Cervantes, Sandra Munoz, and Marisela Norte). His distinctions and awards include an NEW/TCG Playwrights Fellowship (2000–1), 2002–3 Kennedy Center Fund for New American Plays Awards (for *Breakfast, Lunch and Dinner* and *Electricidad*), and visiting artist at the Kennedy Center in Washington, DC (for *Black Butterfly*). He has toured his solo performance work throughout the United States, England, and Mexico with performances at Highways Performance Space, Cornerstone Theatre Company, the Getty Center, the Goodman Theatre, New York's Soho Rep, Hennepin Center for the Arts (Minneapolis), Playwrights' Arena, and The Actor's Gang (Los Angeles).

Alfaro's work largely focuses on the people and landscape of Los Angeles. *Downtown* spotlights a wide array of social issues, including domestic and political violence, in the context of Alfaro's childhood Pico-Union neighborhood; *Black Butterfly* presents the stories of five girls and their quest to realize their dreams while growing up in East Los Angeles. Critics have noted the exemplary ways Alfaro writes about Chicana/o political issues while also focusing on related concerns of gender and sexuality.

Maria Teresa Marrero remarks, "Alfaro opens up a traditional Chicano political space to include Chicano gay rights" (2000: 144), while David Román observes, "From his marginality he offers a cultural politics that foregrounds ethnicity or sexuality depending on his point of emphasis at any given moment in time" (2004: 188). Alfaro based his first "docudrama," *Body of Faith*, on interviews with gay, lesbian, bisexual, and transgender people of faith. Set in a three-generation gang-member family, *Electricidad* offers a Chicano version of the Sophocles classic *Electra*. In *Breakfast, Lunch and Dinner*, Alfaro writes about the emotional life of women struggling with issues of food and family.

Migdalia Cruz's work has long held the attention of her contemporaries Luis Alfaro and Cherrie Moraga, both of whom praise Cruz for occupying the cutting edge of American theatre in her insistent breaking of taboos and bold explorations of the multiple forms of violence that shape Latina/o identity. A Nuyorican playwright from the South Bronx, Cruz studied under Fornes at the INTAR Hispanic Playwrights Lab during the early to mid-1980s. Her plays have been commissioned by numerous theatres, including Crossroads Theatre, Latino Experimental Fantastic Theatre (LEFT), Latino Chicago, Brooklyn Academy of Music, Playwrights Horizons, Cornerstone Theatre Company, INTAR, the WOW Café, Theatre for a New Audience, Arena Stage, and the Working Theatre. Cruz has written over 30 dramatic works for the stage, including: *The Have-Little* (a.k.a. *Lillian*) (1987), *Lucy Loves Me* (1988), *Miriam's Flowers* (1988), *Telling Tales* (1990), *Fur* (1991), *Running for Blood No. 3* (a radio play, 1992), *Rushing Waters* (1993), *Cigarettes and Moby Dick* (1993), *Dreams of Home* (1993), *Latins in La-La Land* (1994), *Lolita de Lares* (1995), *-Che-Che-Che!* (1997), *Salt* (1998), *Mariluz's Thanksgiving* (1998), *Welcome Back to Salamanca* (1998), *Yellow Eyes* (1999), *Primer Contacto* (2001), *El Grito del Bronx* (2002), and *X & Y Stories* (2003). Her play *Another Part of the House* (1995), inspired by Lorca's *The House of Bernarda Alba*, elaborates on the sexual life of Maria Josefa and daringly brings Pepe el Romano onstage. Cruz's work has been widely produced across the United States and abroad at notable venues including: Classic Stage Company, Playwrights Horizons, INTAR, Brooklyn Academy of Music, HOME, Theatre For the New City, The Group at Strasberg, the WOW Café, American Repertory Theatre, Cornerstone Theatre Company, Foro Sor Juana Ines de la Cruz (Mexico City), Old Red Lion (London, England), Vancouver Players, and Théâtre d'aujourd hui (Montreal). In 1995, Latino Chicago Theatre Company produced a season of her work that included *Fur*, *Cigarettes and Moby Dick*, and *Lolita de Lares*. Among Cruz's many distinctions are: an NEA/TCG Workshop residency with INTAR, Sundance Institute Screenwriting Workshop (for *Salt*), Kennedy Center's Fund for New American Plays (for *Another Part of the House*), 1991 finalist for the Susan Smith Blackburn Prize (*Salt* and *The Have-Little*), an NEA and McKnight Playwriting Fellow, and a TCG/PEW National Artist in Residence at Classic Stage Company.

Cruz's plays encompass a variety of genres with such wide-ranging works as *Frida: The Story of Frida Kahlo* (a musical), *Telling Tales* (a collection of monologues), *The Have-Little* (a family drama), and several screenplays. Cruz's willingness to experiment with different types of aesthetic forms and thematic content stems from her five-year experience under Fornes's tutelage. In interviews, she credits the lab, most especially witnessing Moraga's political boldness and Fornes's inimitable commentary, with most challenging her vision as a playwright. Of her time with Fornes, Cruz says, "I was thinking this is what I should be writing, or this is how writing sounds, or this is how you sound intelligent. Instead, she made me look inward and think about how people talk, what people say, who are the people I know best to write about" (qtd. in Arrizon and Manzor 2000: 207). Cruz focuses on the members of her community she knows intimately: poor people and those whose life stories are most often reduced to convenient stereotypes. Her series of monologues, *Telling Tales*, depicts a young girl responding to her neighborhood's horrifying displays of vigilantism; *Fur*, her darkly comic take on *Beauty and the Beast*, centers around a hirsute girl named Citrona, sold by her mother to a deranged pet shop owner who keeps her locked in a cage in the basement of his store; *Miriam's Flowers* examines an impoverished young girl who releases her inexpressible feelings of grief over the tragic death of her baby brother through ritual acts of scarification; *Lolita de Lares* portrays the life of outlaw Puerto Rican freedom fighter Lolita Lebron; *Lucy Loves Me* presents a reinterpretation of the Cinderella fairy tale; and *El Grito del Bronx* explores the story of a Puerto Rican prisoner on death row.

Violence plays a central role in Cruz's work as part of her focus on the emotional and physical poverty of women, for the body is all some women may ever fully control. To the charge that her characters and themes are of unredeeming darkness, Cruz responds, "I write about the people searching for liberation of their souls despite the shackles of their social, economic or physical conditions. My characters see only what is under the skin. Each must face the reality of their flesh before freeing their souls. To me, there is no trip more beautiful than the one from dark to light" (author's personal correspondence with the playwright).

Dramatic Comedy

John Leguizamo is perhaps the most broadly known Latino solo performer. Raised in New York, Leguizamo studied acting with Lee Strasberg and Wynn Handman at New York University. Among his other influences, he lists Lily Tomlin, Richard Pryor, and Whoopi Goldberg. Leguizamo's work in theatre, television, film, and literature covers a range of genres. His written and performed works for the stage include *Mambo Mouth* (1990), *Spic-O-Rama* (1991), *Freak, John Leguizamo Live!*, and *Sexaholix*. Leguizamo's first two plays were performed off-Broadway; both *Freak* and *Sexaholix* were subsequently produced on Broadway, and both received special presentations on HBO. Among the many venues where Leguizamo has performed are: Nuyorican Poets Café, Knitting Factory, Home for Contemporary Theatre and Art, PS 122, Dixon Place, Goodman Theatre, and the Ahmanson Theatre. In 1995, Leguizamo created and starred in the first Latino comedy/variety show, the Emmy Award-winning *House of Buggin'* (Fox). His other honors and awards include: an Obie; 1992 Dramatists' Guild Hull–Warner Award for Best Play (*Spic-O-Rama*); four CableACE Awards for Best Comedy Special Writing/Acting (*Spic-O-Rama*); Tony Award nominations (*Freak*); and Drama Desk and Outer Critics' Circle Awards (*Freak*). Driven by irreverent portraits of Latino identity, *Mambo Mouth* and *Spic-O-Rama* focus on issues of family and masculinity. *Freak*, subtitled "a Semi-Demi-Quasi-Pseudo Autobiography," presents a rich exploration of Latino family life with an emphasis on father–son relationships and their impact on individual subject formation. *Sexaholix* continues these explorations through a wildly comic and dramatically poignant engagement with questions of birth, death, fatherhood, maturity, and sex.

Like Leguizamo, Culture Clash designed their work for television (Fox), with the first Latino-themed sketch comedy television show to be exclusively produced and written by its stars. Culture Clash is Richard Montoya, Rick Salinas, and Herbert Siguenza, a three-person troupe of writers and performers who have been working together since 1984. The creators of over 12 plays for the national stage, they are critically acclaimed for their eclectic use of theatre, most especially comedy and social satire, to explore issues of race, culture, and community in America. Their plays often incorporate original research and community interviews. For *Chavez Ravine*, for example, Culture Clash engaged in conversations with Chicano historian Rudy Acuna and photographer Don Normark and with many of Chavez Ravine's original residents. Their other plays include *Bowl of Beings*, *Radio Mambo: Culture Clash Invades Miami*, *Culture Clash in Bordertown*, *Nuyorican Stories*, *Mission Magic Mystery Tour*, *Anthology*, *Carpa Clash*, and *Anthems: Culture Clash in AmeriCCa*. They have performed at major theatres in the United States, including Lincoln and Kennedy Centers, the Public Theatre, La Pena Cultural Arts Center, South Coast Repertory, San Jose Repertory Theatre, Berkeley Repertory Theatre, and the Arena Stage.

Chicano Secret Service, a multimedia, avant-garde performance troupe, also utilizes comedy to explore issues of politics, community, and identity. Their work has been described as "a cross between the radical theories of Franz Fanon and Paolo Friere and the hijinx of Monty Python" (Jan Breslauer, *Los Angeles Time*, February 28, 1993). The group was first conceptualized and founded by Elias Serna and Eduardo Lopez (a.k.a. Lalo Alcaraz) during the mid-1980s when the two were student activists at the University of California at Berkeley. The group was soon joined by Tomas Carrasco, a fellow student activist at San Diego State College, thus formally defining the core group as Chicano Secret Service. Their work incorporates film, live video, photography, and improvisational performance. From 1988 to 1990 the group studied with Luis Valdez and the San Francisco Mime Troupe while crafting their sense of style and assembling material at various student rallies, protests, and street gatherings. In the early 1990s, Lopez left Chicano Secret Service in order to pursue a solo career as a comic writer and visual artist (with "La Cucaracha," he has become the first syndicated Chicano cartoonist). In 1993, Susan Carrasco joined, adding such acclaimed characters as "MC Chata" and "Tia Lucita." The troupe approaches laughter as revolutionary.

Their work is edgy, topical, irreverent, and oftentimes unabashedly silly. Their performances fluidly incorporate improvisation in order to immediately address pressing political issues for each specific audience.

Their performance history includes *Don't Panic Get Hispanic* (1988–90), *Do the Riot Thing* (1992), *Locura Lo Cura: A Little Menace Will Cure It* (1992), *Madness is the Cure* (1993), *Fear of a Brown Planet* (1998), *Latinoliscious L.A.* (1999), *Latinoliscious* (2003), *S.P.I.C. – Space Prison Industrial Complex* (2003), and *Mex-presso (Hold the Consciousness)* (2003). Their work has been performed nationwide at numerous arts spaces, theatres, universities, and colleges, including the New World Theatre, El Teatro Campesino, Asian American Theatre, Los Angeles Contemporary Exhibits (LACE), and Highways (Santa Monica, California), where they debuted *Latinoliscious*, a compilation of sketches featuring such characters as Chata Stewart and Sadam Jose. Among the group's signature performance pieces, "Frida Kahlua" and "The Wizard of Aztlan" exemplify their mastery in making humorous painful matters, such as deep-seated cultural exclusions.

Latinas have also used comedy to confront various forms of oppression, often with special attention to issues of gender and sexuality. Diane Rodriguez, one of the core members of El Teatro Campesino, occupies a central role as an actress, playwright, and director. She is founding member of the comedy group Latins Anonymous, and co-founder and director of the Latino Theatre Initiative at the Mark Taper Forum. Her plays include *The Lalo Project* (2003), the monologue *Water*; and several co-written works with Luis Alfaro: *The Ballad of Ginger Esparza* (1995); *Diva L.A.* (1995); *Spirits Rising* (1996); and *Los Vecinos/The Neighbors* (1997). Rodriguez has also directed several significant productions including the 2002 West Coast premiere of Migdalia Cruz's *The Have-Little*. Monica Palacios, a founding member of Culture Clash, is recognized as working at the forefront of feminist, Latina/o, and queer performance. Among her most critically acclaimed works are: *Queer Soul: A Twenty-Year Retrospective* (2002), *Besame Mucho* (2000), *My Body and Other Parts* (1998), *Greetings from a Queer Senorita* (1994), and *Latin Lezbo Comic* (1991). She is the recipient of a Rockefeller Fellowship (2002–3) for *Sweet Peace*. Other significant voices in Latina comic drama and performance include Carmelita Tropicana (*Milk of Amnesia, Chicas 2000*; collaborative works with Uzi Parnes, *Memorias de la Revolucion/Memories of the Revolution* and *The Conquest of Mexico as Seen through the Eyes of Hernan Cortes's Horse*; and collaborative works with Ela Troyano, *Sor Juana: The Nightmare* and *Carmelita Tropicana: Your Kunst is Your Waffen*, a screenplay); Marga Gomez (*Memory Tricks, Marga Gomez is Pretty, Witty and Gay*, and *Hung Like a Fly*, a CD); and Maria Elena Gaitan, a veteran activist performer, among whose many works include *Chola Con Cello* and *The Teta Show*, a work created for Latina survivors of breast cancer. Foundational contemporary Latina dramatists also include Estella Portillo Trambley, whose *Day of the Swallows* (1970) is a precursor for Chicana lesbian playwrighting, and Dolores Prida, whose *Beautiful Senoritas* (1977) explores bilingualism, biculturalism, and body issues in the shaping of contemporary Latina identity.

Frustrated with the lack of complex roles for Latinas in both mainstream and Latino playwriting, many Latina actresses began writing plays to create plays by, for, and about women. Evelina Fernandez's *How Else Am I Supposed to Know I'm Still Alive* (1989) is a landmark play for its depiction of two older Latinas and the intensity of their friendship. Fernandez's other works include the screenplay *Luminarias* and the play *Dementia*, a gripping drama that addresses AIDS and mental health. Josefina Lopez's signature works include *Confessions of Women from East L.A.* (1996), *Real Women Have Curves* (1990), and *Simply Maria or the American Dream* (1988). Lopez is the founder of CASA0101, located in the heart of Boyle Heights, one of Los Angeles's poorest and most historically populated Mexican American neighborhoods, an arts space that offers playwriting and screenwriting courses, filmmaking workshops, and youth theatre labs. Like Fornes, Lopez is sowing the seeds for a new generation that will continue to expand our thinking about American theatre.

Other historically pivotal works include Denise Chavez's *Novenas Narrativas*, featuring the TeatroPoesia/Tongues of Fire festival in the early 1980s. The play inspired Latina playwrights by demonstrating the urgency of creating works that boldly address matters of gender and sexuality. Chavez is primarily considered a novelist and short story writer; however, her play must be read as part of a tradition of Latina/o work adapted for the stage. Other Latina/o work adapted for the stage includes: Rodrigo Garcia's *Ten Tiny Love Stories*, a series of monologues by ten women recalling particular relationships with men, based on his film; Joe Loya's prison play based on his memoir *The Man Who Outgrew His Prison Cell*; Sandra Cisneros's *The House on Mango Street*; Luis Rodriguez's translations of work into spoken word performance; Rueben Martinez's *Border Ballads*; and the Taco Shop Poets' *Chorizo Tonguefire*.

Notably, there are numerous other established as well as emerging playwrights whose work significantly expands fixed notions of Latina/o drama: Jorge Cortino Ignacias, Carlos Murillo, Joe Hurtua, Carmen Rivera, Candido Tirado, Naomi Iizuka, John Michael Garces, Janis Astor del Valle, and Lisa Loomer. Performance art occupies a particularly significant role in the dismantling of strictly delineated categories for identity and performance. Noted performers include Harry Gamboa, Jr., ASCO, Guillermo Gomez-Pena, Elia Arce, Nao Bustamante, Coco Fusco, Aya de Leon, and Caridad "La Bruja" de la Luz. It is precisely these artists who inspire new research and challenge existing readings of Latina/o voices on the American stage.

BIBLIOGRAPHY

Algarin, M. and Griffith, L. (1997). *Action: The Nuyorican Poets Café Theater Festival*. New York: Simon and Schuster.

Alvarez, L. (1998). *Collected Plays*. Lyme, NH: Smith and Kraus.

Antush, J. (ed.) (1991). *Recent Puerto Rican Theater: Five Plays from New York*. Houston: Arte Público.

——(ed.) (1994). *Nuestro New York: An Anthology of Puerto Rican Plays*. New York: Penguin.

Arrizon, A. (1999). *Latina Performance: Traversing the Stage*. Bloomington: Indiana University Press.

——and Manzor, L. (eds.) (2000). *Latinas on Stage*. Berkeley, CA: Third Woman Press.

Bonney, J. (ed.) (2000). *Extreme Exposure: An Anthology of Solo Performance Texts from the 20th Century*. New York: Theatre Communications Group.

Bowles, N. and Rosenthal, M. E. (eds.) (2001). *Cootie Shots: Theatrical Inoculations Against Bigotry for Kids, Parents, and Teachers*. New York: Theatre Communications Group.

Broyles-Gonzalez, Y. (1994). *El Teatro Campesino: Theater in the Chicano Movement*. Austin: University of Texas Press.

Carillo, J. and Gonzalez, J. C. (eds.) (2001). *Latino Plays from South Coast Repertory*. New York: Broadway Play Publishing.

Cortina, R. (ed.) (1991). *Cuban American Theater*. Houston: Arte Público.

Culture Clash (Richard Montoya, Rick Salinas, and Herbert Siguenza) (1999). *Culture Clash: Life, Death and Revolutionary Comedy*. New York: Theatre Communications Group.

——(2003). *Culture Clash in AmeriCCa*. New York: Theatre Communications Group.

Delgado, M. M. and Svich, C. (1999). *Conducting a Life: Reflections of the Theatre of Maria Irene Fornes*. Lyme, NH: Smith and Kraus.

Feyder, L. (ed.) (1992). *Shattering the Myth: Plays by Hispanic Women*. Houston: Arte Público.

Fusco, C. (1995). *English is Broken Here*. New York: New Press.

——(ed.) (2000). *Corpus Delecti: Performance Art of the Americas*. New York: Routledge.

——(2001). *The Bodies That Were Not Ours and Other Writings*. New York: Routledge.

Gamboa, Jr., H. (1998). *Urban Exile: Collected Writings of Harry Gamboa, Jr.*, ed. Chon Noriega. Minneapolis: University of Minnesota Press.

Gonzalez, L. S. (2001). *Boricua Literature: A Literary History of the Puerto Rican Diaspora*. New York: New York University Press.

Herrera Sobek, M. and Viramontes, H. M. (eds.) (1988). *Chicana Creativity and Criticism: Charting New Frontiers*. Houston: Arte Público.

Houghton, J. (ed.) (2001). *Signature Theater 1999 Presents Maria Irene Fornes*. Lyme, NH: Smith and Kraus.

Huerta, J. (1979). *Nuevos Pasos: Chicano and Puerto Rican Drama*. Houston: Arte Público.

——(1982). *Chicano Theater: Themes and Forms*. Tempe: Bilingual Press.

——(1989). *Necessary Theater: Six Plays About the Chicano Experience*. Houston: Arte Público.

——(2000). *Chicano Drama: Performance, Society, and Myth*. Oxford: Oxford University Press.

Leclerc, G., Villa, R., and Dear, M. J. (eds.) (1999). *La Vido en L.A.: Urban Latino Cultures*. Thousand Oaks, CA: Sage.

Lopez, J. (1996a). *Food for the Dead and La Pinta*. Woodstock, IL: Dramatic Publishing.

——(1996b). *Real Women Have Curves*. Woodstock, IL: Dramatic Publishing.

——(1997a). *Confessions of Women from East L.A.* Woodstock, IL: Dramatic Publishing.

——(1997b). *Unconquered Spirits*. Woodstock, IL: Dramatic Publishing.

Marrero, M. T. (2000). "Out of the Fringe? Out of the Closet: Latina/Latino Theatre and Performance in the 1990s." *Drama Review* 44, 3: 131–53.

Meyer, O. (1996). *Blade to the Heat*. New York: Dramatists Play Service.

Moraga, C. (1983). *Loving in the War Years: lo que nunca paso por sus labios*. Boston: South End.

——(1993). *The Last Generation: Prose and Poetry*. Boston: South End.

——(1994). *Heroes and Saints and Other Plays*. Albuquerque: West End.

——(1997). *Waiting in the Wings: Portrait of a Queer Motherhood*. Ithaca, NY: Firebrand.

——(2001). *The Hungry Woman: A Mexican Medea and Heart of the Earth: A Popul Vuh Story*. Albuquerque: West End.

——(2002). *Watsonville/Circle in the Dirt*. Albuquerque: West End.

Morton, C. (1983). *The Many Deaths of Danny Rosales and Other Plays*. Houston: Arte Público.

Munoz, J. E. (1999). *Disidentifications: Queers of Color and the Performance of Politics*. Minneapolis: University of Minnesota Press.

——(2000). "The Onus of Seeing Cuba: Nilo Cruz's Cubania." *South Atlantic Quarterly* 99, 2/3: 455–9.

Osborn, E. (ed.) (1987). *On New Ground: Contemporary Hispanic Plays*. New York: Theatre Communications Group.

Perkins, K. and Uno, R. (eds.) (1996). *Contemporary Plays by Women of Color*. New York: Routledge.

Piñero, M. (1974). *Short Eyes*. New York: Hill and Wang.

——(1980). *La Bodega Sold Dreams*. Arte Público.

——(1984). *The Sun Always Shines for the Cool; A Midnight Moon at the Greasy Spoon; Eulogy for a Small-Time Thief*. Houston: Arte Público.

Portillo Trambley, E. (1983). *Sor Juana and Other Plays*. Ypsilanti: Bilingual Press.

Prida, D. (1991). *Beautiful Senoritas and Other Plays*. Houston: Arte Público.

Ramirez, E. (2000). *Chicanas/Latinas in American Theatre: A History of Performance*. Bloomington: Indiana University Press.

Rivera, J. (1997). *Marisol and Other Plays*. New York: Theatre Communications Group.

——(2003). *References to Salvador Dali Make Me Hot and Other Plays*. New York: Theatre Communications Group.

Rivera, R. Z. (2003). *New York Ricans from the Hip Hope Zone*. New York: Palgrave.

Rodriguez, L. (2001). *Hearts and Hands: Creating Community in Violent Times*. New York: Seven Stories Press.

Román, D. (1998). *Acts of Intervention: Performance, Gay Culture, and AIDS*. Bloomington: Indiana University Press.

——(ed.) (2000). *Theater Journal* 52, 1, Special issue on Latino Performance.

——(ed.) (2004). *Downtown and Elsewhere: A Luis Alfaro Reader*. Ann Arbor: University of Michigan Press.

——and Hughes, H. (1998). *O Solo Homo: The New Queer Performance*. New York: Grove.

Russell, M. (ed.) (1997). *Out of Character: Rants, Raves, and Monologues from Today's Top Performance Artists*. New York: Bantam.

Rosenberg, J. (1995). *Aplauso: Hispanic Children's Theater*. Houston: Arte Público.

Sanchez, E. (1997). *Plays by Edwin Sanchez*. New York: Broadway Play Publishing.

——(1999). *Icarus*. New York: Broadway Play Publishing.

——(2000). *Barefoot Boy with Shoes On*. New York: Broadway Play Publishing.

Sandoval-Sanchez, A. (1999). *Jose, Can You See? Latinos On and Off Broadway*. Madison: University of Wisconsin Press.

——and Sternbach, N. S. (eds.) (2000). *Puro Teatro: A Latina Anthology*. Tucson: University of Arizona Press.

——and Sternbach, N. S. (2001). *Stages of Life: Transcultural Performance and Identity in U.S. Latina Theater*. Tucson: University of Arizona Press.

Savran, D. (ed.) (1999). *The Playwright's Voice: American Dramatists on Memory, Writing and the Politics of Culture*. New York: Theatre Communications Group.

Svich, C. and Marrero, M. T. (eds.) (2000). *Out of the Fringe: Contemporary Latina/Latino Theatre and Performance*. New York: Theatre Communications Group.

Taylor, D. (2003). *The Archive and the Repertoire: Performing Cultural Memory in the Americas*. Durham, NC: Duke University Press.

——and Costantino, R. (2004). *Holy Terrors: Latin American Women Perform*. Durham, NC: Duke University Press.

——and Venegas, J. (eds.) (1994). *Negotiating Performance: Gender, Sexuality, and Theatricality in Latin/o America*. Durham, NC: Duke University Press.

Troyano, A. (2000). *I, Carmelita Tropicana: Performing Between Two Cultures*. Boston: Beacon Press.

Valdez, L. (1990). *Luis Valdez – Early Works: Actos, Bernabe, and Pensamiento Serpentino*. Houston: Arte Público.

——(1992). *Zoot Suit and Other Plays*. Houston: Arte Público.

Yarbro-Bejarano, Y. (2001). *The Wounded Heart: Writing on Cherrie Moraga*. Austin: University of Texas Press.

24

"Off the Porch and into the Scene": Southern Women Playwrights Beth Henley, Marsha Norman, Rebecca Gilman, and Jane Martin

Linda Rohrer Paige

Was it enough for the Southern woman playwright, rocking on her porch swing and sipping a mint julep, to etch out a character for her next play? No. Neither the scent of magnolias nor the dazzling azaleas poking their heads through the porch railings could keep Southern women playwrights at home. We have come a long way from Zora Neale Hurston's backroads journeys, Ada Jack Carter's forging streams, and Bernice Kelly Harris's mountainous retreats – all fine efforts to engage in theatre, mostly folk dramas. Not only has Hurston's dream of "A Negro Theatre" been realized, but also the 2002 Pulitzer Prize has been awarded to a Southern-born African American female, Suzan-Lori Parks, for *Top Dog/Underdog*. Though today's playwriting women of the South engage in regional theatre far beyond that of which their female predecessors dreamed – and certainly, beyond the confines of their homes and local communities – their works often retain the flavors of the South: from Southern landscapes, traditions, and sometimes quirky characters to themes of loss, disintegration, inheritance, and issues of identity. Now Southern women playwrights are open to a range of new and exciting possibilities, including innovations in stage techniques and design, as well as an array of complex gender issues. Just as regional theatre has grown and diversified, so too has the Southern woman playwright, expanding her range of interests and themes to include pornography, prostitution, domestic violence, stalking, child abuse, autonomy, racism, and "white guilt," among others. As diverse as their themes, women playwrights of the New South (some homebred, others a result of migrations to this region where they can work best) benefit from a melting of cultures in big cities like Atlanta, community theatre groups and writing workshops, and opportunities to see their plays staged. Some of these playwrights have been catapulted beyond regional theatre to Broadway, with playwrights such as Beth Henley (*Crimes of the Heart* and *Miss Firecracker*) and Marsha Norman (*'night, Mother*) gaining further success by adapting their plays for the screen.

Beth Henley, the first woman to win the Pulitzer Prize in 24 years with her play *Crimes of the Heart* (1981), unlike the other playwrights to be considered here, locates most of her plays in the South. Her early plays, primarily set in Mississippi and Louisiana, and even her later play, *Impossible Marriage* (1999), which takes place in coastal Georgia, make use of common Southern themes: close family ties, disintegration and dissolution of relationships, the intractable will to persevere despite loss, and connection to the land and its creatures. Because so much about Henley already has been written, this chapter sheds light on some of the playwright's less noticeable themes, including her characters' attachment to animals.

When queried about animal imagery in her plays, Beth Henley remarked, "I hadn't ever realized there was animal imagery until my friend, playwright Frederick Bailey, pointed it out to me. I don't know what it means" (qtd. in Betsko and Koenig 1987: 216). Pressed further about the "symbolic value" of these animals, Henley quixotically retorted, "Well, humans are animals. We're mammals; I think we should stop pretending that we're not" (ibid.). The playwright's words may at first appear puzzling owing to their simplicity, yet Henley speaks truth: we are closer to our "brothers and sisters" in nature than we care to admit.

Henley creates strong characterizations and unravels knots of human motivations by carefully interlocking animal attributes to specific characters. This intermingling of human and non-human achieves its greatest clarity in *Crimes of the Heart* and in *The Miss Firecracker Contest* (1985). Introducing audiences to a virtual zoo of the animal kingdom – dogs, cats, chickens, horses, frogs, apes, monkeys, whales, shrimp, snakes, and even worms – Henley captures and reveals through this motif the strange dichotomies within us all. This "guilt by association" is emblematic of humanity and the animal world: the grotesquely beautiful, the kindly corrupt, the defeated hopeful, hilarity amidst suffering – opposites that uncomfortably jockey together for space. Moreover, by interjecting laughter into her characterizations, the playwright demonstrates how the human spirit copes and survives despite despair. Her plays depict human resiliency, with characters rising above earthly dilemmas to become ennobled through their capacity to love.

Crimes of the Heart tells the story of the Magrath sisters, reunited due to the arrest of the youngest sister, Babe, for attempted murder of her husband, State Senator Zackery Botrelle. Each fearful of recurring pain, the Magrath sisters carry with them the burden of their mother's suicide years earlier (their mother hanged herself, alongside her old yellow cat, after her husband had abandoned her). Meg Magrath, the oldest sister, exhibits a kind of world-weariness (*Weltschmertz*); yet, similar to her mother and sisters, she defensively eschews pain. Meg's sensitivity to suffering manifests itself in a shell of protectiveness. In her youth, she had waltzed into the local Hazelhurst, Mississippi, drugstore, past the poster of crippled children, without donating a penny to the suffering youth. Instead, she ordered a double-decker scoop of ice cream, impervious to others' suffering: "I can stand it. I can," she triumphantly convinced herself (40–1). Further, Meg's reading "favorites" included books such as

Diseases of the Skin, which illustrates sickening pictures of drooping eyeballs and rotting-away noses. Her self-inflicting obsession with pain reminds audiences of her vulnerability in a precarious world.

Just as her mother connected with animals (the cat), Meg, too, finds a kinship with animals. Having deserted Hazelhurst, she procures a job in Los Angeles working as a clerk in a dog food company. There she provides customers with "cold storage" bills, an appropriate metaphor for her attempt to become desensitized to life's anxieties. Meg's heart, metaphorically, is also in "cold storage," numbed by her attempts to avoid emotions. Ironically, Meg's association with animals through her job links her subtly (and indirectly) to *food* for animals – in this case, for dogs. This association serves as a sign of the eldest Magrath's humanity and establishes her kinship with nature. Ultimately, audiences realize that Meg's problem lies not in a lack of caring, but in caring too much: so intense is her fear of destruction and obliteration of self that Meg's connection with animals is her way of avoiding an overly sensitive bond with humans. Speaking to her sister Lennie about avoiding reading letters from home, Meg confesses negligence but pleads, "Oh, Lennie! Do you think I'd be getting slicing pains in my chest, if I didn't care about you! If I hated you? Honestly, now, do you think I would?" (15).

Meg's association with animals further ties her to her old flame, Doc Porter, who once aspired to be a veterinarian and who was jilted by Meg during a hurricane. Back home now and years later, she reveals that she left Doc out of fear: "I don't know why... 'Cause I didn't want to care. I don't know. I did care though. I did" (50). Porter's nickname of "Doc" is a sign of the character's interest in healing wounded animals and people. Like Meg, Doc has a generous heart; he offers Lennie the use of his land so that her horse, Billy Boy, might graze on it, thus indicating his inclination to nourish animals.

The common bond between Henley's characters and animals becomes likewise noticeable in Babe, the youngest of the Magrath women. What precipitates Babe's adulterous affair with Willie Jay, a 15-year-old African American, is the bond they share in nurturing "an old stray dog" found by Willie Jay. Willie Jay's mother realized that they could not afford to feed it, "so she was gonna have to tell [her son] to set him loose in the woods" (30). In need of assistance, Willie Jay's mother enlists Babe, asking her to provide a home for the dog – generically named "Dog" – and the youngest Magrath happily honors the request. Just as the horse, Billy Boy, offers Lennie a surrogate relationship with a "male," so too does Babe (whose husband, significantly, remains absent throughout the play) crave male companionship:

Babe: Well, I said I like dogs and if he wanted to bring the dog over here, I'd take care of him. You see, I was alone by myself most of the time 'cause the senate was in session, and Zackery was up in Jackson.

Meg: Uh Huh. (*Meg reaches for Lennie's box of birthday candy. She takes little nibbles out of each piece, throughout the rest of the scene.*)

Babe: So the next day, Willie Jay brings over this skinny, old dog with these little crossed-eyes. Well, I asked Willie Jay what his name was, and he said they called him Dog. Well, I liked the name; so I thought I'd keep it. (30)

Willie Jay and Babe establish a friendship based on mutual understanding, compassion, and affection, most evident in their joint endeavor to help a "stray." Upon Willie Jay's departure, leaving Dog behind, Babe confesses to "feeling something for him" – the pronoun "him" pertaining, of course, to Willie Jay, but extending, tangentially, to the dog:

Babe: . . . so I told him he could come back and visit with Dog any time he wanted, and his face just kinda lit right up. (30)

Frequently visiting the Botrelle estate, Willie Jay proudly boasts of how "fat Dog is getting" (30). Over time his visits extend to Babe, another creature in need of emotional "nourishment."

With Willie Jay, Babe shares what she cannot with her husband, Zackery. We discover through the course of the play that he has beaten his wife on more than one occasion (27–8). Upon finding Babe one day with Willie Jay and Dog, Zackery snarls at them both: "Don't you ever come around here again, or I'll have them cut out your gizzard!" (31). Frightened and crying, Willie Jay runs home, followed by a terrified Dog. Babe then draws the gun Zackery had bought for burglars from a drawer just in time to greet her oppressor as he enters the house (31). At first, she considers suicide, as her despairing mother had years before. But Babe reconsiders her initial intentions, shooting her husband instead:

Why I was gonna shoot off my own head! That's what I was gonna do. Then I heard the back door slamming and suddenly, for some reason, I thought about mama . . . how she'd hung herself. And there I was about ready to shoot myself. Then I realized – that's right I realized how I didn't want to kill myself! And she – she probably didn't want to kill herself. She wanted to kill him, and I wanted to kill him, too. I wanted to kill Zackery, not myself. 'Cause I – I wanted to live! (31–2)

Babe's ambiguous reference to "him" – when she says that her mother "wanted to kill him, and I wanted to kill him, too" – connects her abusive husband, Zackery, with her father, whose abandonment of his wife constitutes another kind of abuse. Both men lack heart, symbolically, and feelings for others, especially love – that which the Magrath sisters and those closest to them need. In her essay "A Population and Theater at Risk: Battered Women in Henley's *Crimes of the Heart* and Shepard's *A Lie of the Mind*," Janet V. Haedicke is partially correct when she ascribes to Babe's actions the "defense of her fifteen-year-old black lover," for she assumes that Babe's motives have nothing to do with self-defense (1993: 85). In defending the underdog, the youngest Magrath simultaneously defends herself. Babe's anger ultimately discovers its rightful target. Though her initial intention may have been to "kill"

Zackery, to aim for his heart, her bullet misses its mark, lodging instead in her persecutor's gut. Of course, figuratively, Zackery has no "heart," so it comes as no surprise to Henley's audience that the bullet should adeptly find its target at the "seat" of Botrelle's bile, his liver. When Zackery's sister, Lucille, later phones with news that her brother's liver will be spared, Babe responds merely by asking if Dog has returned home yet (37). This apparent lack of interest in her "crime" and in the welfare of her estranged husband indicates Babe's true interests lay elsewhere – in *underdogs*.

The respect for animals by the Magrath women reaches its pinnacle in the Magrath mother's suicide, which Henley further links to the animal motif. By drawing analogies between the now missing father and the old yellow cat, a stray for which the mother cared, the playwright implicates the father who abandoned the family.

> *Babe*: And that old yellow cat. It was sad about that old cat.
> *Meg*: Yeah.
> *Babe*: I bet if Daddy hadn't of left us, they'd still be alive. [. . .] 'Cause it was after he left that she started spending whole days just sitting there and smoking on the back porch steps. She'd sling her ashes down on the different bugs and ants that'd be passing by.
> *Meg*: Yeah. Well, I'm glad he left.
> *Babe*: That old yellow cat'd stay back there with her.
> *Meg*: God, he was a bastard. (21)

The playwright's nuanced intermingling of dialogue about animals establishes a kinship between the father and the cat, as the one constitutes a comment upon the other. Thus, Henley's animals teach us about complicated characterizations and relationships.

The Miss Firecracker Contest finds despair, not suicide, pivotal to the audiences' understanding of characterization. Essentially, animal images in *Firecracker* break into three major groups: those associated with inhuman characters, those linked to the despairing and pitiable "uglies" of the world, and those connected to the imaginative and loving healers of humanity. For instance, in *Firecracker*, Delmount and Elain's mother, Mrs. Rutledge, who inspired fear in her children, is referred to by her own son as an "ape" (11), one step removed from humanity. Penetrating the source of Mrs. Rutledge's strained relationship with her children proves no small task. Nonetheless, by examining this absent character in light of her animal associations, one uncovers clues to her all-consuming drive for her daughter's success, using beauty, not values, as a mark of achievement. Unfortunately a product of her mother's teachings, Elain marries a rich "toad," not a prince at all, and only through Popeye, the seamstress, who makes "queens" out of frogs, sewing them elaborate costumes and dressing them up, will the characters of *Firecracker* learn to love themselves. Both Carnelle Scott, the Rutledges' once-homeless cousin with a marred reputation, and Delmount, the aimless drifter and one-time city worker, assigned the task of picking up dead dogs from the highway, become transformed by their association with Popeye, this lover of all animals. As a result, animals in Henley's dramas serve as indicators of human capacities to connect or disconnect. If audiences wish to unravel the enigma that is Henley's characters, one way they might begin understanding is by examining the playwright's use of animal metaphors.

Though less likely to incorporate animal symbols in her plays, Marsha Norman experiments with other motifs, such as "housing" and "building." Born in Louisville, Kentucky, September 21, 1947, and raised by religious fundamentalist parents, Norman spent a solitary childhood, without television or movies, and was even forbidden by her parents to play with other children. During her teenage years, she worked on her high school's yearbook and newspaper. At Agnes Scott College in Decatur, Georgia, the future playwright majored in philosophy and took creative writing classes. Graduating Agnes Scott in 1969, Norman returned to Louisville. After her two-year marriage to a high school English teacher dissolved, she entered the University of Louisville, earning her MFA in playwriting.

The socially conscious Norman tackled various jobs, including work at a hospital burns unit and another job with disturbed youth at the Kentucky Central State Hospital, which later became the catalyst for *Getting Out*. But not until becoming a budding newspaper columnist did she meet Jon Jory, artistic director of the thriving Actors Theatre of Louisville. Recognizing her talent, Jory encouraged Norman to write a play for Actors Theatre. Norman met the challenge with *Getting Out*, which premiered in 1977, winning acclaim not just from Louisville theatregoers, but also from regional theatres across the country. As her popularity intensified, Norman's plays appeared on Broadway, where she won the Pulitzer Prize for *'night, Mother* (1983). With amusement, the playwright counts translations of *'night, Mother* like a peacock spreads its glittering colors to the sun: "already, Jessie and Mama...speak Spanish, French, German, Swedish, Danish, Finnish, Dutch, Portuguese, Greek, Italian, Polish, Yiddish, Chinese, Japanese, and Afrikaans" (qtd. in Norman 1988: 404).

'night, Mother, which premiered in 1982, reminds us that gender lines exist and sometimes cut like razors. Ideas of what constitute "good drama" differ, and in the case of *'night, Mother*, the ideas move along gender lines. For example, the exasperated critic Robert Asahina reports being bored with Jessie's character to the degree that he was not even "interested enough...to stay for the second act" of the play (although there is no second act):

> Nor would I have lasted past the intermission of Marsha Norman's *'night, Mother* – except there wasn't one; it had only one act, stretched to the almost unbearable length of exactly ninety minutes. That's right: exactly ninety minutes. I know; I timed it. So did everyone else at the John Golden [Theatre] – audience, cast, and crew. (100)

Exhibiting a male bias and misunderstanding Norman's message about a woman's need for autonomy, Asahina lacks appreciation of – indeed, fails to grasp – the playwright's point. The difference lies in the perspectives of the viewers: women look at the play from a female perspective, recognizing that the drama deals with women's experience, one diametrically opposed to that of males. Bored, uncomfortable in their seats, many males quickly exit the theatre at the end of *'night, Mother*, whereas women remain, pensive and absorbed in Jessie's suicide and Norman's message of female autonomy.

Norman's drama consists of one evening in the lives of two women. Significant male figures, while mentioned, never appear. Within the first 200 lines of *'night, Mother*, Jessie announces her intent to commit suicide using her father's gun, which her mother, unwittingly, has helped her locate. Also unwittingly, Jessie's brother, Dawson, has supplied the bullets with which his sister will end her life. In the intervening time (marked by clocks onstage, in the kitchen and living room), the two characters talk, and the audience learns about their lives and about absent characters who affect them: Cecil, Jessie's husband, and Ricky, her delinquent son; Jessie's unnamed father; and Mama's friend, the apparent pyromaniac, Agnes. We also observe what has led Jessie to death's precipice as well as her mother's demise to the point that – despite her attempted protests – she partially accepts Jessie's suicide. Abandoned by her husband and son, Jessie has moved back into her mother's house (the locale, a generically suburban mid-America, is purposefully not designated by the playwright). She attends to her now widowed mother's needs by performing household chores and upkeep, which includes replenishing the supply of assorted candies for Mama's sweet tooth.

'night, Mother moved quickly, even spectacularly, from regional theatre to Broadway. It enjoyed considerable critical acclaim with Kathy Bates performing the role of Jessie and Ann Pitoniak playing her mother, Thelma. In New York, the play proved remarkably successful with enthusiastic female theatregoers, and less so with male audiences, many of whom were incited to downright distaste for or disinterest in the drama. Women, by and large, felt that *'night, Mother* spoke to them in a personal way, providing pause for contemplation.

Autonomy is the central issue of *'night, Mother*, as Jessie Cates points out. Frantically, she explains to her mother that living on is impossible, for everything lacks meaning, even her relationship with her mother. She requires control – autonomy – over her destiny. Prior to the evening of the play, Jessie felt invaded by outsiders and family members, including the incident of the mail-ordered bra her brother opened, her ring that her son, Ricky, stole, and her husband's abandonment of her to the emergency attendant during her particularly bad fit of epilepsy. Ironically, on the night during which the play takes place, Jessie proclaims her good fortune; she feels well enough to do something about her body from which she feels alienated. Observing her baby picture, Jessie confesses to Mama that she "lost" that child, a carefree baby, long ago.

Structuring an intermission-less, 90-minute play, Norman builds the drama on the tension of Jessie's impending suicide. Her declarations as mother and child, including her admitted shortcomings, run the gamut of past causes or perceived wrongs motivating Jessie's suicidal decision. Denying that the act is instigated by anger or revenge, Jessie claims to be someone unable to solve the puzzle of a Rubik's cube; the pieces of her life, like the cube, symbolically fail to fit and are misunderstood by others. Jessie closes her bedroom door and carries out her one act of self-determination and autonomy. The play warrants comparison with the last act of Lillian Hellman's *The Children's Hour*, in which Martha's suicide provides the climax around which the drama pivots (see chapter 8).

Critical responses differ significantly in regard to the motivation of Jessie's suicide. In "Speaking Silences: Women's Suicide," Margaret Higonnet posits that female suicide is inextricably linked to the issue of autonomy (1986: 74). Along these lines, Harriet Goldhor Lerner, in her book *The Dance of Anger*, suggests that females are less likely than males to admit to anger, though they may try to "blot out awareness of [their] own anger" (1989: 6). Psychologists generally concur that anger is at the root of most suicides. Jessie denies anger as a motivation for the suicide in *'night, Mother* (so, too, do the critics); however, a close reading of the text reveals that anger does indeed motivate Jessie's suicide. For example, consider the anger Jessie feels toward Dawson's violation of her privacy, or her anger when Mama threatens to call Jessie's brother. Jessie replies that Dawson is not invited to this farewell moment. Jessie's anger occurs when she describes her husband's prowess as a craftsman: a builder of things, such as houses, porches, bridges, and baby cribs. Compared to him, Jessie thinks herself incapable. She even notes that had Mama not first enticed Cecil to their rural home to build a porch onto the house, she never would have met, much less married, him. Norman's protagonist associates her inadequacies as a builder with her body (her failure to control it). Though not inclined to think herself a rebel, Jessie demonstrates both rebellious-ness and anger when she becomes enlivened by Mama's story of Agnes Fletcher. Agnes serves as a sort of alter ego for Jessie: as the play progresses and Thelma unsuccessfully tries to convince her daughter to live, the dialogue moves to the subject of Agnes:

> *Mama*: I'm serious! Agnes Fletcher's burned down every house she ever lived in. Eight fires, and she's due for a new one any day now.
> *Jessie*: (*Laughing*) No!
> *Mama*: Wouldn't surprise me a bit.
> *Jessie*: (*Laughing*) Why didn't you tell me this before? Why isn't she locked up somewhere?
> *Mama*: 'Cause nobody ever got hurt, I guess Agnes woke everybody up to watch the fires as soon as she set 'em. One time she set out porch chairs and served lemonade.
> *Jessie*: (*Shaking her head*) Real lemonade?
> *Mama*: The houses they lived in, you knew they were going to fall down anyway, so why wait for it, is all I could ever make out about it. Agnes likes a feeling of accomplishment.
> *Jessie*: Good for her. (38–9)

If men are considered "builders" and owners of houses, then women's treatment of these edifices seems highly ironic. Just as Mama resents the fact that her husband stuck her in this house (where she now lives) out in the country (46), Thelma's friend, Agnes the pyromaniac, acts on her resentments, burning all the houses in which she ever lived (38). Importantly, by committing suicide, Jessie will destroy, metaphorically, her own temple or "house," her body, just as Agnes Fletcher burns down her houses. Likewise Jessie, who destroys her own body in an effort to gain autonomy, Agnes's burning down of her houses provides her with a "feeling of accomplishment" (39). In destroying houses, literally and symbolically, women paradoxically experience growth and cause for celebration. On one level, the destruction of real houses symbolically represents women's fiery response to patriarchy (which "imprisons" them within the confines of the "house"). On another level, the destruction of the "house," at least in Jessie's case, signals women's rebellion against patriarchy's claim to her body.

Audiences associate males as the builders of houses, especially in the scene in which Jessie questions Mama's story about Agnes's pyromania. Ironically, Jessie is incredulous at the idea that her mother's friend would burn down her own house, reasoning that Agnes would then have no place to live (39). After all, Jessie surmises, now that Buster, Agnes's husband, has died, no man is around "to build her a new one" (40). With a man – namely, a husband – Agnes, like Jessie, would be metaphorically "homeless." Jessie misses the point that in many respects she and Agnes are in a similar bind. Both of their acts, Agnes's burning and Jessie's suicide, defy logic. Yet Agnes and Jessie invite audiences to share in their "celebrations." For instance, Agnes awakens the neighbors to view her houses burning just as Jessie "wakes" Mama and sets out a symbolic "porch chair" for her to witness the night's events. It is characteristically poignant of Norman's play that Mama, who has adhered to patriarchal demands of passivity and waiting ("waiting" is another motif in *'night, Mother*) asks, "so why wait" for houses to fall (39). Being the principal rebel, Jessie is similar to Agnes in that both – through their actions – rebel against patriarchal authority. This, insinuates Norman, is the way that her heroine asserts a modicum of autonomous free will. Mama, unknowingly, agrees with Jessie that "houses," which would have collapsed anyway, should be destroyed.

Norman's other plays include *Getting Out, Third and Oak: The Laundromat*, and *The Pool Hall*. Set in the South, *Getting Out* introduces audiences to the "divided" Arlene/Arlie, a parolee and ex-prostitute determined to succeed in life despite patriarchal constraints – past, present, and future. Formerly in prison for second-degree murder and armed robbery, Arlene discovers that bars exist not merely in prison; Norman's protagonist quite literally notices iron bars spanning the length of her new apartment's windows. Even more poignantly, she begins to recognize that "bars" may not always be visible.

The play unfolds on two levels: Arlie lives in the past, while Arlene represents the present. The play's first moment with Arlie, the juvenile delinquent, divulges a dark side to her character. It begins with a repulsive monologue about throwing another child's frogs into the street just to watch them splatter under the wheels of passing cars. As the play progresses, however, the audience learns the circumstances that have informed her character, in particular an abusive father who raped her during her childhood. Audiences observe her struggle to redefine herself as Arlene, a new personality (and portrayed by another actress). In *Getting Out*, Norman introduces additional threatening father figures: Carl, the cynical pimp, who tries to bully the protagonist back into his employment, and the more insidious Bennie, a former guard at the Alabama prison, who wants control of Arlene's life, and almost rapes her (33–4). When her estranged mother visits, Arlene explains how she acquired her new name: "There was this chaplain, he called me Arlene from the first day he come to talk to me" (20). Perhaps the only character demonstrating genuine good will in the play is Arlene's neighbor Ruby, who offers the newcomer a job washing dishes. Though less profitable than prostitution, dishwashing is at least legal. Arlene explains to Ruby that the chaplain urged her to shed "Arlie," her wicked self, and how, having taken this advice to extremes, she had attacked herself with a kitchen fork from the prison commissary:

> There's all these holes all over me where I've been stabbing myself an I'm sayin' Arlie's dead for what she done to me, Arlie's dead an it's God's will . . . I didn't scream it, I was jus' sayin' it over and over . . . Arlie's dead, Arlie is dead . . . (54)

The play also demonstrates that the chaplain's analysis of the situation, which fails to take into account Arlene's background, is simplistic. Arlene has to make peace with her younger and angrier self, Arlie. The play ends with these two characters alone onstage together, speaking, for the first time, in unison, laughing.

Norman's drama *Third and Oak* (1980) combines two plays, the first and second parts originating separately as *The Laundromat* and *The Pool Hall*. Norman specifies a preference that the plays be performed together. Part I takes place in a laundromat at night, where two white women are washing their husbands' clothes. They are the right sort of ages respectively to be mother and daughter, late fifties and twenties, and although they meet as strangers, Norman underscores the pseudo-configuration of mother–daughter by providing them with similar surnames, Johnson. Talking about their lives, they discover and reveal comparable pain and loss: Alberta, Mrs. Johnson senior, has recently lost her husband (deceased), while Dee Dee, Mrs. Johnson, Jr., fears she is losing hers to other women. Washing the clothes becomes a metaphor for working through their separate pains. Part II, set in a pool hall, introduces the audience to two black men. This play mirrors the first in that these two characters link emotionally, but not biologically, as surrogate father and son. Both struggle to come to terms with a common loss (the biological father of the younger man was also the older man's close friend). Further, Norman formally connects the plays as a character from each briefly steps into the other's play: Shooter drops off his clothes in *The Laundromat*, throwing them in the washer, and Dee Dee enters *The Pool Hall* looking for Shooter, hoping that he will go with her for pancakes.

Like her predecessors, Rebecca Gilman represents a new generation of Southern women playwrights who possess the skills and talent for spinning tales. Combining Marsha Norman's rebelliousness and Beth Henley's comic grotesque, Gilman's *Spinning into Butter* (1999) draws its title from the children's controversial story of *Little Black Sambo*, who escapes being eaten by the tigers by watching them spin so fast around the tree that they churn into butter. The play takes place in an imaginary liberal arts college in Belmont, Vermont, where it explores issues of sexism and racism through the experiences of Dean Sarah Daniels, a middle-aged white woman, described by Gilman's stage direction as "earnest in her desire to do right by her students" (7). The play presents three intertwining actions: Sarah's painful rejection at the hands of a younger male colleague; her well-intentioned, but clumsy, attempt to secure a special minority scholarship for a Nuyorican student; and a frightening eruption of anonymous racist rhetoric aimed at a black student on campus. This abuse produces a flurry of defensive activity on the part of the college administrators, who attempt to spin their political correctness by engaging in open forums with the students. Not only does the play offer an insightful critique of political correctness regarding racial discrimination, but it also attempts to deal with the phenomenon of "white guilt." Sarah, the most sympathetic character in the play, confesses her own suppressed racist feelings at the play's climatic moment:

> I thought I was fine, I thought I was making progress, until I got that job at Lancaster [College]. I thought I was fine. But then I had to move to Chicago, and I don't know. Everything seemed different. All my newfound self awareness and societal insight and . . . and all that crap, all that crap just flew out the window. So quickly. Because in the abstract, black people were fine. But in reality, they were so rude. (75)

Sarah grows aware of the reason for her being hired at Belmont: not because of her qualifications, but because of her liberal resume, which indicates experience teaching at a black college. Indeed, the resume led the hiring committee to assume that she was likely African American. Confiding these feelings in a notebook, which is found by her senior colleague and used against her, Sarah resigns before being fired. Sarah's "crime" is that she fails to observe individuals, only seeing African Americans as a homogeneous group. When the college discovers that Simon Brick, the supposed victim of the racist abuse, is responsible for the threatening letters and creating a hoax, the administration expels him. In the play's poignant conclusion, the two outcasts join in an act of reconciliation as Sarah phones Simon:

> So how are you feeling today? (*Long pause. She listens.*) Oh, Simon. (*Pause.*) Listen, don't be so hard on yourself. Okay? (*Beat.*) Simon? (*Beat.*) Simon. It's okay. You hear me? Simon? (*Beat. Softly*). It's okay. (106)

Critics frequently compare this play to those by Beth Henley. A more apt comparison, however, may be found in Gilman's play *The Land of Little Horses* (premiering in

1989, published 1997), a compelling drama that reflects many of Marsha Norman's major themes and action in *'night, Mother*. Pivotal to both plays is the father, a patriarchal figure characterized as "silent," a man who fails to relate to his wife, but relates, to some extent, to his daughter or daughters. Marrying women unable to please them, these absent males ignore their spouses. The relationships with their wives have profound and lasting impact upon the play's action as the mothers and daughters feel not only estranged from themselves, but also tangled in strained and tortuous encounters with others.

Rebecca Gilman is part of a continuing generation of Southern playwrights, especially with *The Land of Little Horses*. Though not exactly set in a Southern locale, audiences hear the characters debate their origins and the Southern location where they currently reside. Gilman's play appears to be influenced by Henley's *Crimes of the Heart*, for the action centers on three sisters, one of whom – the glamorous one – abruptly returns to her Southern family roots. The character, Jessica, exudes brittle defiance toward social convention just as Meg does in *Crimes of the Heart*, and she is insensitive to the emotional needs of her sisters. She leaves stockings, for instance, strewn about the house for her sister Evelyn to pick up. Though inspired by Henley's drama, *Little Horses* is more than a replica of *Crimes*. While Jessica has much in common with sexually successful Meg of *Crimes*, Evelyn and Jean Louise, Jessica's sisters, combine characteristics of Babe and Lennie (*Crimes*). Audiences meet Evelyn, the sister with the most common sense, who from the beginning of the story becomes engaged to the dullard Charles. Living at home, the youngest sister, Jean Louise, feels static and manages to escape, not with a man, but with her eccentric Aunt Dot. Their escape leads them to a horse ranch, where they free the corralled miniature horses. Janet Gupton argues in her essay "Comedy and the Plays of Beth Henley" that this "transgressive behavior" typifies Henley's female characters and "destabilizes the identity of the Southern lady." This characteristic brands Henley's "group[s] of women" as "unruly," rebels against patriarchy (2002: 132). Whereas in *Crimes* the older generation remains absent – granddaddy dies off-stage and the mother has committed suicide before the play begins – in *Little Horses* representatives of the past generation (Aunt Dot and Laura, the mother) remain integral to the play's action.

Laura has worked laboriously in the past to gain attention from her husband, using her daughters as bait to incite reaction from him. She, like Thelma Cates of *'night, Mother*, develops jealous feelings over her daughters' special relationship with their father. Ultimately, the result of Laura's unseemly "scenes" in the marriage work to end her relationships with her children as they are filled with a sense of disgust and guilt. In *'night, Mother* and *Little Horses*, daughters complain of their inability to "fix" relationships for their parents and for themselves. Thelma in *'night, Mother*, for instance, become so estranged from her daughter Jessie that the child, though grown, refuses to believe herself capable of "fixing" anything, least of all herself. Though Laura of *Little Horses* and Jessie of *'night, Mother* make pleas for absolution, their words go almost unnoticed; however, both Gilman and Norman insist on accountability for their "mother" characters. In each play the playwrights challenge audiences to consider whether the triumph of communication brings fresh air to a diseased house, or if the family secrets, finally exposed, arrive too late.

Born in Trussville, Alabama, Rebecca Gilman belongs to a generation of Southern women playwrights raised in the creative world of regional theatre. Comfortable with the process of college and regional workshops, where their plays often undergo many drafts before publication, these new Southern playwrights work well within a community of other playwrights as well as actors. Additionally, they are acutely aware of timely social issues. By the time of her graduations from the prestigious Middlebury College in Vermont and the creative writing program at the University of Iowa, Gilman already had received many rejections of her plays from various regional theatres. Not until submitting to the Circle Theatre in the Midwest did she finally discover a professional theatre willing to present her work.

In an effort to repay the debt, Gilman premiered her new play, *Boy Gets Girl*, at the Circle Theatre in 2000. Comparing *Boy Gets Girl*'s plot to that of the early 1980s film *Looking for Mr. Goodbar*, some critics find the play more gripping than the movie, given the fact that Gilman's protagonist, Theresa Befell, is a responsible, hardworking journalist, lacking the recklessness of *Goodbar*'s Diane Keaton character, who jeopardizes her safety by bar-hopping and picking up strangers. Gilman's play asserts that no one deserves to become the object of a stalker, no matter what mistakes are made. In *Boy Gets Girl*, Theresa innocently accepts a blind date, set up by a friend, with a computer technician, Tony. She agrees to have a beer with him and nothing more. Initially, Theresa notices nothing strange about Tony; neither buzzers signal nor lights flicker huge letters saying "STALKER, STALKER." Thus, Gilman's heroine agrees to a second meeting; however, this time Theresa sees that the two have nothing in common and politely tells Tony that she is uninterested in continuing. What should end with Theresa's excusing herself and leaving becomes an exasperated struggle to make an exit:

Tony: Look, I'm just trying to walk away with a little of my pride here. At least let me pay for the meal. (*Pause*).

Theresa: All right, then. Thank you.

Tony: You know, last night I turned on the TV and I saw there wasn't a game on. I thought, if there was a game, I'd learn some of the names of the players and then I could impress you tonight. Because, you know, when we first met, I just thought that you must think I'm an idiot.

Theresa: I didn't think that.

Tony: Because I don't read books like you do. I mean, I took a lit class in college and all that, but I didn't know who you were talking about the other night. That woman.

Theresa: Edith Wharton?

Tony: Yeah, her. Is it because I didn't know who Edith Wharton was?

Theresa: No. I would never in my whole life not like somebody for not knowing who Edith Wharton was. It's just me. It's entirely me. (30)

Incited by this dismissal, Tony soon meets his rebuttal with determined flame: beginning with flowers and phone calls, he insistently invades the journalist's life, inveigling her silly young assistant into supplying him with private information about her boss. Embarrassed, Theresa informs her co-workers and calls the police. Everyone seems sympathetic, tries to help, but Tony progresses from verbal (obscene mail and phone calls) to physical violence, trashing Theresa's apartment. *Boy Gets Girl* ends with Theresa's leaving her current job (though she likes it) for Denver, where she will take on a new name and identity. In a frightening exchange, New York policewoman Madeleine Beck makes clear that Theresa has no choice:

Theresa:	Well, what's the worst thing you've ever seen?
Beck:	You don't want to know.
Theresa:	Have you seen people killed?
Beck:	I've seen that.
Theresa:	That wasn't the worst thing? (*Beat.*) Detective? (*Pause.*)
Beck:	You don't want to know. (60)

Other plays by Gilman deal with equally complex social concerns, ideas which seem often inspired by real-life incidents. In *The Glory of Living* (1999), set in the rural deep South, we observe the dismal career of Lisa, daughter of a prostitute, picked up by a psychopath and ultimately faced with execution for killing on his orders. *The Crime of the Century* (2001) presents the forgotten portraits of Richard Speck's murder rampage, Chicago nurses whose lives are snuffed out by the killer. Premiering in 2001, *Blue Surge* explores tough gender issues, especially prostitution, as it matches two policemen with two prostitutes, what might seem at first an impossible pairing. Garnering critical praise, the play received England's Prince Prize for commissioning original work.

For playwrights Henley, Norman, and Gilman, a would-be biographer might easily refer to their personal histories; however, with Jane Martin, biographers must be content to record merely that the playwright hails from Kentucky. Though one may refer to a long list of awards and successful plays by Martin, including the American Theatre Critics' Award in 1993 for the year's best play, not to mention the nomination of *Keely and Du* for the Pulitzer, the issue of anonymity raises as much critical response as do the plays themselves. Most people in theatre circles nowadays accept the notion that Jane Martin is Jon Jory (who currently directs at the Guthrie Theatre, and quite noticeably takes the premieres of Jane Martin's new plays along with him). Nevertheless, years of speculation as to Jane Martin's identity have tantalized theatre critics. In my co-edited volume with Robert L. McDonald, *Southern Women Playwrights: New Essays in Literary History and Criticism*, J. Ellen Gainor finds fault with the issue of pseudonym and Jane Martin: "When I sent a letter of inquiry to the theater [Actors Theatre of Louisville] ... I was shocked to receive an early morning telephone call from Mr. Jory himself, who cordially, but firmly, informed me that Jane Martin actively discourages scholarly explorations of her work" (2002: 141).

Though Jane Martin continues to mask "her" identity, the playwright unmasks society's ills, unveiling its myths and secrets. An early play by Martin, *Coup/Clucks* (1984), provides a sort of Southern extravaganza of farce, satirically pushing the Southern envelope of tradition, ideals, and prejudices: the idea of the Southern Lady and landed gentry, the lost paradise of *Gone With the Wind*, and the camaraderie of the Ku Klux Klan. In *Coup*, the first part of the play, the white inhabitants of Brine, Alabama, prepare for the annual *Gone With the Wind* parade, under the direction of 60-year-old Miss Zifty, who plays Scarlett O'Hara. Everything goes wrong as the redneck taking the part of Rhett refuses and Dr. Kennedy, the local black dentist, "inherits" the role. Aghast, the offended Miss Zifty resigns in disgust and Don Savannah, the old lady's flamboyant, gay hairdresser, dons the dress of Scarlett, though ultimately relinquishing it to the black maid, Beulah. *Clucks*, the second part of Martin's farce, presents the aftermath of the parade. A dispirited rally of indignant Klansmen, filled with bravado (yet clearly under the thumbs of their women) and incensed at the "desecration" of their parade, retaliate with a "ride" on the dentist's home, where the cast of Mitchell's classic has gathered. Carting a "dynamite sandwich" and an 11-foot cross, the half-hooded remnants of the Invisible Empire huddle curiously, arguing, outside in the dentist's front yard:

> *Travis*:   Ryman, gimme that hand-gun. . . . Pritch, I'm forty years old, been laid off six
> months, my wife's turned colored on me, m' oldest boy ran over m' neighbor's
> blue-ribbon Pekinese on his motorbike, I can only git it up oncet a week an'
> I'm goin' t' light that cross lyin' down. . . . (*Gives pistol to Pritchard and goes to the
> cross. Searches in pocket for matches, finds nothing.*) Somebody give me a light. (*A
> pause. They look at each other.*) Gimme a match. (*They look in their pockets.*)
> Gimme a lighter! (*They look at him.*) Gimme two goddamn sticks! (*Bobby Joe
> does. Travis breaks them and throws them at him.*) Colored, hell. We oughta run
> *ourselves* outta' Alabama. (59)

Taking a serious subject, racial hatred, Martin transforms it into a comedic uproar, turning tragedy into farce. By the end of the play, the redneck Travis reluctantly learns a new song from his wife: the "Ode to Joy" theme of Beethoven's *Ninth*, which he proclaims to be "nigger music" (72).

Martin's better-known play, *Keely and Du* (first performed in 1993), examines another serious subject: abortion rights. Kidnapped by religious extremists, Keely, a young woman pregnant as a result of a rape, gradually develops an unexpected alliance with one of her abductors, an older woman named Du. Set not in the South but somewhere near Cincinnati, the play introduces another variation of a "mother–daughter" relationship. Unlike Walter, the pastor who masterminded the kidnapping, Du talks to Keely in personal terms, telling her about her own religious awakening, artfully embellished by its sexual overtones:

> *Du*:   The fact is he [her husband] was an uninteresting man, but he got into the
> storage business and turned out a good provider. Now, listen close here, we went

along 'til he bored me perfectly silent, if you can imagine, and God found us pretty late when the kids were gone or near gone, and when God found that man he turned him into a firebrand and an orator and a beacon to others, and I fell in love with him and that bed turned into a lake of flame and I was, so help me, bored no more, and that's a testament. (276)

Keely's marital experience has differed considerably: she has been raped by her ex-husband. Despite herself, Du begins to side with Keely against Walter, the ex-spouse, and in one scene of kindness, tries to cheer up her captive, bringing her a change of dress from the nightgown she previously wore. Left alone for a moment, Keely, in a frenzy of disgust after a visit from her now "reformed" ex-husband, uses the dress-hanger to abort herself (297). In the last scene of the play, Martin reverses the situations of the characters: Keely is now free from both the baby and her imprisonment, and Du serves time in prison for kidnapping. Having suffered a stroke in the interim, Du can hardly speak. Keely calms her, exposing a depth of friendship and also indicating a hint of regret for her lost baby (300). In *Keely and Du*, the "mother–daughter" relationship congeals with Keely's abortion as Keely describes to Du a concert that she has recently attended with personal affection and inferences:

Keely: I went to a Judd concert. You know the one that sings without her mother now…(*She stops*.)…without her mother now…There was this guy next to me…had a little girl on his lap, maybe two. (300)

Another subject as topical as abortion rights emerges with *Mr. Bundy*, premiering five years after *Keely and Du*. Here, Martin explores another current subject: how to treat a convicted pedophile after his release from prison. Mr. Bundy, a retired school teacher in his sixties, has recently moved next door to Cathryn and Robert Ferreby and their 8-year-old daughter, Cassidy, with whom he makes friends. Another couple, a trucker named Jimmy Ray and his unappealing wife Tianna (a pure Southern stereotype, part "spa-day girl," part hell-fire preacher), warn the Ferrebys that Mr. Bundy has recently been in prison for molesting teenage boys. Robert and Cathryn are repelled by this couple, who are vulgar and ignorant (Jimmy Ray insists that Mr. Bundy "turn[ed]" his victims homosexual) (117), but the news, nonetheless, alarms them. A child psychologist, Cathryn wants Mr. Bundy to have a second chance, but Robert, outraged, ultimately attacks his neighbor physically, pummeling him to the floor with groin and face kicks. Shocked by her husband's brutality, Cathryn then leaves, taking Cassidy with her. Mr. Bundy leaves as well. The play begins and ends with Cassidy's rhyme about the "oogey-boogey" (93, 137), but Martin leaves the audience in doubt quite who the "oogey-boogey" really is. As with *Keely and Du*, the playwright challenges audience assumptions. Never appearing as anything but a harmless, gentle old man, Mr. Bundy, nonetheless, inspires fear in Robert because of the potential danger he represents. But the play queries, when is one's debt to society paid? Though at times actions of the characters seem contrived, they demonstrate that the playwright tackles difficult societal problems and refuses to settle for easy solutions. Even the unappealing Jimmy and Tianna deserve a degree of sympathy, Martin insinuates, having lost their own child to a murderous pedophile. Martin, like Henley, Norman, and Gilman, is unafraid to examine topical issues. These four playwrights understand the Southern world, making them outspoken representatives of their region as well as spokeswomen for larger thematic concerns.

BIBLIOGRAPHY

Asahina, R. (1984). "The Real Stuff." *Hudson Review* 37, 1 (Spring): 99–104.

Betsko, K. and Koenig, R. (1987). "Beth Henley." In *Interviews with Contemporary Women Playwrights*. New York: Beech Tree, 211–22.

Gainor, J. E. (2002). "Pseudonym and Identity Politics: Exploring Jane Martin." In Robert L. McDonald and Linda Rohrer Paige (eds.), *Southern Women Playwrights: New Essays in Literary History and Criticism*. Tuscaloosa: University of Alabama Press, 139–53.

Gilman, R. (1997). *The Land of Little Horses*. New York: Dramatists Play Service.

—— (1999). *The Glory of Living*. New York: Faber and Faber.

—— (2000a). *Boy Gets Girl*. New York: Faber and Faber.

—— (2000b). *Spinning into Butter*. New York: Faber and Faber.

—— (2002a). *Blue Surge*. New York: Faber and Faber.

—— (2002b). *The Crime of the Century*. New York: Faber and Faber.

Gupton, J. (2002). "Comedy and the Plays of Beth Henley." In Robert L. McDonald and Linda Rohrer Paige (eds.), *Southern Women Playwrights: New Essays in Literary History and Criticism*. Tuscaloosa: University of Alabama Press, 124–38.

Haedicke, J. V. (1993). "A Population and Theater at Risk: Battered Women in Henley's *Crimes of the Heart* and Shepard's *A Lie of the Mind*." *Modern Drama* 36: 83–95.

Henley, B. (1982). *Crimes of the Heart*. New York: Dramatists Play Service.

—— (1985). *The Miss Firecracker Contest*. New York: Dramatists Play Service.

—— (1999). *Impossible Marriage*. New York: Dramatists Play Service.

Higonnet, M. (1986). "Speaking Silences: Women's Suicide." In Susan Rubin Suleiman (ed.), *The Female Body in Western Culture: Contemporary Perspectives*. Cambridge, MA: Harvard University Press, 68–84.

Lerner, H. G. (1989). *The Dance of Anger: A Woman's Guide to Changing the Patterns of Intimate Relationships*. New York: Harper Perennial.

McDonald, R. L. and Paige, L. R. (eds.) (2002). *Southern Women Playwrights: New Essays in Literary History and Criticism*. Tuscaloosa: University of Alabama Press.

Martin, J. (1984). *Coup/Clucks*. New York: Dramatists Play Service.

—— (1992). *Criminal Hearts* [*A Comedy in Two Acts*]. In *Jane Martin: Collected Plays, Volume 1: 1980–1995*. Lyme, NH: Smith and Kraus (1995), 201–51.

—— (1993). *Keely and Du*. In *Jane Martin: Collected Plays, Volume 1: 1980–1995*. Lyme, NH: Smith and Kraus (1995), 253–300.

—— (1995). *Jane Martin: Collected Plays, Volume 1: 1980–1995*. Introduction by Marcia Dixcy. Lyme, NH: Smith and Kraus.

—— (2000). *Mr. Bundy*. In *Jane Martin: Collected Plays, Volume 2: 1996–2001*. Lyme, NH: Smith and Kraus (2001), 91–138.

—— (2001). *Jane Martin: Collected Plays, Volume 2: 1996–2001*. Foreword by Michael Bigelow Dixon. Lyme, NH: Smith and Kraus.

Norman, M. (1979). *Getting Out*. New York: Dramatists Play Service.

—— (1980). *Third and Oak: The Laundromat*. New York: Dramatists Play Service.

——(1983). *'night, Mother*. New York: Noonday.

——(1988). "Time and Learning How to Fall." In *Marsha Norman: Collected Works, Volume 1*. Lyme, NH: Smith and Kraus (1997), 398–408.

——(1995). *The Pool Hall*. In *Marsha Norman: Collected Works, Volume 1*. Lyme, NH: Smith and Kraus (1997), 59–108.

25

David Mamet: America on the American Stage

Janet V. Haedicke

Born in Chicago on November 30, 1947, David Mamet is perhaps the most quintessentially American of contemporary playwrights. Not only has he taken as his explicit subject America and its mythic Dream, but he has also taken as his form the multiple media of American culture to explore the potency of America's national and international myth. In original plays, adaptations, film, television, essays, novels, poetry, and interviews, Mamet examines the potentially destructive, if not violent, effect of the American Dream. The American Dream, he observes, "was basically about raping and pillage. . . . We are finally reaching a point where there is nothing left to exploit. . . . The dream has nowhere to go so it has to turn on itself" (qtd. in Savran 1988: 133). This dynamic of individualism and the "Dream" gone awry permeates the bulk of Mamet's work, but for Mamet it is in drama that the critique of the "Dream" has its roots and it is in drama that the possibility of redemption emerges most provocatively.

Even within this single form – drama – Mamet exhibits an exploratory impulse, moving from experimental one-acts to realistic full-length plays. Having grown up on Chicago's Jewish South Side and working menial jobs at Hull House Theatre and at Second City, Mamet drafted his first plays while attending Goddard College in Vermont. During his junior year, he studied acting under Sanford Meisner at New York's Neighborhood Playhouse, forming a lifelong interest in the craft but eventually concluding that his abilities lay elsewhere. In 1968, his senior thesis, a satirical review entitled *Camel*, was presented at Goddard, and *Lakeboat* was produced in 1971 at another Vermont school, Marlboro College, where Mamet taught acting. Returning as artist-in-residence to Goddard later that year, Mamet formed the St. Nicholas Theatre Company with students William H. Macy and Steven Schachter and, with no money for royalties, staged two of his earlier plays (in draft form): *Sexual Perversity in Chicago* and *The Duck Variations*. Returning to Chicago in 1972, Mamet became artistic director of the St. Nicholas Theatre Company in 1974 with Patricia Cox joining Macy and Schachter in performing *Squirrels*. That same year *Sexual Perversity in Chicago* opened at the Chicago's Organic Theatre under the direction of Stuart Gordon, winning a Joseph Jefferson Award. Its production in New York on a double-bill with *Duck Variations* at the off-off-Broadway St. Clement's Theatre earned Mamet the 1975 Obie Award for Best New Play. Another Joseph Jefferson winner in Chicago, *American Buffalo* premiered in October 1975 at the Goodman Theatre's Stage 2, directed by Gregory Mosher and featuring Macy. Both director Mosher and actor Macy were to become long-term Mamet collaborators. The play moved in December to open the new St. Nicholas Theatre space on Halstead Street in Chicago, where *Reunion* was also staged before Mamet resigned in 1976. Mamet's play *Water Engine* soon followed this production in 1977. Opening in New York in 1976, also at St. Clement's Theatre, and winning an Obie for Distinguished Playwriting, *American Buffalo* marked Mamet's emergence into national prominence. The *American Buffalo* production moved to Broadway in 1977 featuring Robert Duvall in the lead role of Teach, and subsequently won the New York Drama Critics' Circle Award. Success in New York eventually gave birth to the Atlantic Theatre Company, which grew out of workshops conducted by Mamet and Macy in the mid-1980s. The Company continues to stage Mamet's dramas.

Although Mamet continues to write less traditionally realistic plays, such as *Edmond*, which won an Obie in 1982, and even children's drama, it is in what Ruby Cohn terms his "Business Trilogy" (1982: 109) – the three plays *American Buffalo*, *Glengarry Glen Ross*, and *Speed-the-Plow* – that Mamet's reputation as a leading American playwright is solidified. In 1978, *American Buffalo* became the first American play staged in England's new National Theatre space. In 1984, *Glengarry*, having opened first in London and then at the Goodman, won the Pulitzer Prize as well as the Drama Critics' Award and garnered four Tony nominations for a Broadway run of 378 performances. In 1988, *Speed-the-Plow* attracted popular attention for the casting of the singer Madonna, but even more controversy was generated in 1992 by the female character in *Oleanna* (more on this controversy shortly). The production of *The Cryptogram* in 1994 in London and in 1995 in Boston and New York placed Mamet in the American theatrical tradition of domestic realism. Recalling similar shifts in focus and form by Eugene O'Neill and Sam Shepard, Mamet was confirmed as the principal American dramatist by the overtly autobiographical *The Old Neighborhood*, a play that had runs in Boston and New York in 1997. As the title indicates, *Boston Marriage*, produced in Boston in 1999, is also considered domestic realism, though the family here is lesbian.

Although Mamet's indictment of American cultural myths appears in popular culture (film, stories) as well as in theatre, he hastens to distinguish between writing for mass entertainment, whose task "is to cajole, seduce, and flatter consumers," and the artist's purpose, whose job is to report "everything that we have thought is wrong" (Mamet 1997b). His first film project was *The Postman Always Rings Twice* in 1981; Mamet's other screenplays include *The Verdict*, *The Untouchables*, *We're No Angels*, *Hoffa*, *Deerslayer*, and *Glengarry Glen Ross*. He both wrote and directed *House of Games*, *Things Change*, *Homicide*, *Oleanna*, *The Spanish Prisoner*, and *State and Main*.

The first major American playwright in a line of many Hollywood hopefuls to achieve success in screenwriting, Mamet has met with less success in writing for television, with the exception of two episodes for *Hill Street Blues* in the 1980s and an HBO production of *Lansky* in 1998. Many of his scripts involve a con game, reflecting one of Mamet's most profound influences: "As Thorstein Veblen in *Theory of the Leisure Class* says, sharp practice inevitably shades over into fraud" (qtd. in Kane 2001). Deliverance from the criminal elements of the American Dream emerges most vitally for Mamet in drama: "the theatre affords an opportunity uniquely suited for communicating and inspiring ethical behavior." He adds that, "in a morally bankrupt time we can help to change the habit of coercive and frightened action and substitute for it the habit of trust, self-reliance, and co-operation" (Mamet 1986: 26–7).

In his 1998 book *Three Uses of the Knife*, Mamet uncannily prophesied a post-9/11 America poised at the brink of moral bankruptcy, remarking that "Our World Position is not tenuous, but our mental balance is. . . . We are determined to squander all . . . to defend ourselves against feelings of our own worthlessness, our own powerlessness" (44–5). The division in the world, which according to Thomas Friedman was the "overarching feature" (2002: 4) of the Cold War system, has yielded to the integration of globalization. As a result, when Americans "hear all the hate and anger boiling out there against them, . . . the natural instinct is to want to build walls against it" (375). With globalization emerging as Americanization, the myth of this country and its Dream has ascended to new heights. Americans yearn for the Cold War divisions in an era in which the enemy was clearly defined. As Mamet observes:

> Our endorsement of violence in art, like our endorsement of violence in our nation's behavior, is a compulsive expression of the need to repress – to identify a villain and destroy it. The compulsion must be repeated because it fails. It fails because the villain does not exist in the external material world. The villain, the enemy, is our own thoughts. . . . The "information age" is the creation by the body politic, through the collective unconscious, of a mechanism of repression, a mechanism that offers us a diversion from our knowledge of our own worthlessness. (1998b: 52–3)

Mamet's perspective, one that permeates his major plays, finds validation in the work of diverse cultural critics. Canadian social scientist Sacvan Bercovitch, in his dissection of American myths, observes: "What I discovered in America was the simultaneity of violence and culture formation." America, Bercovitch observes, transformed into "a barbaric dream documented by a procession of 'great minds and talents,' and an interpretive process through which the worlds out there had been triumphantly repressed" (1993: 9). If, as political scientist Benedict Anderson claims, nations are "imagined political communities, products of an invented past" (qtd. in Kammen 1991: 394), then dwelling within this collective fantasy and cultural symbol creates a past and imagines a present not only for our own progeny but also for those of other nations. As "Selves" who are America "internalized, universalized" as well as "naturalized" (Bercovitch 1993: 1), we dominate to express our potency.

According to Catherine Lutz, after the Cold War a "bunkered" self-image emerged of a national security state, wherein a "militarized civilian subjectivity" operated within "an ideology of total defense" (1997: 263). This defensiveness could root out "undesirable categories of people – the Communist, the misfit, the homosexual, the egghead, the dupe" (254). Mamet eerily predicted the resurrection of this impulse in the war on terrorism. We may extol our shout praise in flag-waving, he says, "but after the shouting we are empty and alone." The feelings "inform us that everything – understanding, world domination, happiness – is within us and within our grasp ('We're Number One!'), and that life, for those as powerful, perceptive, and blessed as we, should be and will be simple" (1998b: 52–3). However, "as soon as 'our' victory is proclaimed, the anxiety reasserts itself. We knew it [the victory] was a false struggle, and we now must cast about for another opponent/another villain/another action film/ another oppressed people to 'free,' so we can reassure ourselves again, of what we know to be untrue: that we are superior to circumstance (that we are, in effect, God)" (19–20).

Mamet's characters are thus American selves, embracing a "common language of self-hood," which is rooted in "'truths'" (Schnog 1997: 4) such as Freudian repression and the Oedipal complex. Regarding the psychological as invented, theorists attempt to examine the power of America's psychological society "to naturalize hierarchies of social identity through its labels and formulas of emotional life" (Schnog 1997: 8). This power of labels, formulas, and discourse underlies all of Mamet's dramas. Citing Veblen once again, Mamet notes that "the more that jargon and technical language is involved in an endeavor, the more we may assume that the endeavor is essentially make-believe. . . . As in Law, Commerce, Warfare" (1986: 5). Mamet's dramas speak ever more profoundly to a terrorist-hunting and haunted America as the characters fight for a piece of a disintegrated Dream, struggling hopelessly to conquer by performing popularized American roles. Mamet's characters are "entropic figures" (Bigsby 1985: 253), confined by spaces emptied of meaning, an emptiness they attempt to fill with a diarrheic language that only perpetuates the hollowness of life. Having internalized a competitive obsession, Mamet's characters unleash disjointed fragments, sound bites that aim not to communicate but, in Mamet's words, to dominate: "not to speak the desire but to speak that which is most likely to bring about the desire" (qtd. in Savran 1988: 137). The desire is for power and for an identity defined against a vanquished Other; ironically, the words of these competitors only circumscribe them, reflecting Mamet's perception of subjectivity as mediated by language: "Our rhythms describe our actions – no, our rhythms *prescribe* our actions. I'm fascinated by the way, the way the language we use, its rhythms, actually determines the way we behave, rather than the other way around'" (qtd. in Wetzsteon 1976: 39, emphasis in original).

In Mamet's drama, then, language – banal, fragmented, contradictory – represents people who are disjointed and emptied of communicative value in a world where perceived value lies only in perceived power. The often-leveled charge that Mamet's plays lack plot misses the point that the plot itself is the very plotlessness of too many

American lives emulating the vacuity of a sit-com. The "action" of a Mamet play reverberates in the tension beneath the words, which fail to connect the characters to each other and to their world: "What I write about is what I think is missing from our society. And that's communication on a basic level" (qtd. in Dean 1990: 33). Pushed to the fringes of society, Mamet's characters often channel their desperation into what becomes a litany of obscenities, the incantatory rhythms of which exceed an accurate rendering of urban speech patterns. Critics have focused attention on the language of "our foremost warrior-philologist" (Savran 1988: 132), but too few have perceived that "Mamet-speak" (Kroll 1995: 72) is a language attenuated to the point of implosion; like its speakers, language represents the character's theatricalized worlds, one ready to implode at any minute. Mamet insists that his dialogue is "not an attempt to capture language as much as it is an attempt to create language.... The language in my plays is not realistic but poetic" (qtd. in Kane 2001: 48–9), albeit poetry on the edge.

As with the language and dramatic form, Mamet's putative realism cracks under its own excess. Admittedly, Mamet advocates theatre as "story-telling" (qtd. in Kane 2001: 50), dismissing his earlier "episodic glimpses" (1988b: 78) as immature, and endorses the well-made play structure as best imitating our perceptual ordering of experience into a beginning, middle, and end. Awareness, however, of the illusory nature of perception itself, which contrasts realism and its ensuing causality, permeates his drama. His concerns are epistemological as well as sociological; Mamet examines America and its promise of the Dream as purely perceptual. At root, power struggles persist as performances to install one version of reality against another. Theatre scholar C. W. E. Bigsby remarks that Mamet's characters "may seek to impose a simple realism on events"; however, this realism is not a condition that Mamet "is willing to endorse" (1985: 288). Mamet's subversive realism captures the labyrinth involved in the mediation of subjectivity (identity) by language, the complication of causality by the intrusion of chaos, and the undermining of surfaces caused by subterranean emptiness. The playwright himself states that his "true métier lies somewhere in between" (qtd. in Savran 1988: 133) the esoteric and the realistic and that neither form alone can release or enlighten (Mamet 1986: 111). The more his characters desire to elevate their places in an ordered, hierarchical universe (in other words, climb the greasy pole), the more their illusions of identity are exposed as fictional and entropic.

Mamet's business trilogy captures the entropy of the economic system, an "out-growth of the intrinsic soul of a culture" (qtd. in Savran 1988: 141) and hence not readily transformed. Since business is "what America is about" (qtd. in ibid.: 137) and the subtext of business is always power, Mamet predicts an ever-worsening polarization in the country that ultimately constitutes his subject. In his attempt to expose the "national unconscious" (qtd. in Bigsby 1985: 274), Mamet dramatizes our sanctified separation of the personal and the professional, which permits the exoneration of criminality or even violence in the name of business. In this corrosive, "hierarchical business system," it is legitimate for "those in power... to act unethically" (qtd. in Kane 2001: 47). Cherished all-American values are summoned to the service of the American Dream, which "interests me because the national culture is founded very much on the idea of strive and succeed." The American myth, he contends, is "the idea of something out of nothing" where "only one guy is going to get to the top" (qtd. in Kane 2001: 46–7). Mamet, having declared his main project to be the demystification of the American Dream (Savran 1988: 133), maintains that the Dream's divisiveness permeates his drama: "American capitalism comes down to one thing. . . . The operative axiom is 'Hurrah for me and fuck you.' Anything else is a lie" (qtd. in Dean 1990: 190).

In his focus on this "fucking," whose literal as well as figurative manifestation is encapsulated in the family, Mamet has thus tacitly conflated the business and familial systems, the public and private realms, exposing a landscape of spiritual bankruptcy as the illusionary border between the two dissolves. America as theatre, as linguistic construction, is reflected in Freud's proclaiming, according to Ernest Jones, that "America is a mistake" (qtd. in Demos 1978: 63). This is an ironic recognition of the unique elevation of psychoanalysis in this country, a phenomenon traced by historian John Demos to the late nineteenth-century shift in the American family system to a gender and generationally divided unit, reduced in its "cast of characters" (73) and relegated to the newly separated private sphere. Centered on a "structural triangle," this "hothouse" or "Oedipal family" (73) promoted individuation, guilt, and linearity (the process by which an individual progresses and gains wealth), the very dynamic for which America's theatrical tradition of realism, especially of the domestic variety, has been disparaged for upholding. Mamet's characters inhabit a stage, whether capitalistic or domestic, where their attempt to perform themselves into being against an antagonistic "Other" perverts the communal theatrical impulse: "In the family, as in the theater, the urge to control only benefits the controller. Blind obedience saves him the onerous duty of examining his preconceptions, his *own* wisdom, and, finally, *his own worth*" (Mamet 1986: 32).

Although this linkage of economic, theatrical, and familial systems illuminates the possibilities to examine and critique gendered hierarchies in domestic drama, its influence on Mamet only confirms the charges of misogyny leveled against him. The early plays gave rise to a conflation of playwright with his characters, notably *Lakeboat*'s Stan, who defines women as "Soft things with a hole in the middle" (59). In Mamet's dramaturgy, aggressive males predominated and, until recently, women were not merely marginalized but excluded. As Hersh Zeifman points out, in *American Buffalo*, the oft-mentioned Ruth and Grace remain "ghosts" (1992: 126), who, like those in *Glengarry*, "haunt the margins of the text but never break through to the stage. Their presence is evoked only metonymically, as terms of abuse, or else in the form of 'spirits' whose essence threatens male values" (132). What is onstage is the "Phallus in Wonderland" (125), a homosocial realm of American business, where homophobia and misogyny collude. Guido Almansi more harshly condemns Mamet's dramaturgy, noting that in his plays,

[t]he subject of [males'] complaints is often a woman, or that more forward, buxom, and aggressive woman, America, who has bestowed upon them a dream, the Great American Dream, only to prove a prick-teaser, or that other woman, more mammary, plump, and vigorous yet, Mother Nature, a female God, rancorous and vindictive, who fucks up every single thing and every single man. (1986: 193)

Mamet, however, persistently rails against hierarchy, noting that a byproduct of the failed American Dream is that "the people it has sustained – the white males – are going nuts" (qtd. in Savran 1988: 134), and acknowledges rampant misogyny in America, noting, "if you look around the United States of America you will see that we do have a certain amount of misogynistic men. For example, all of them" (Mamet 1988b: 84). Admittedly, the emptiness, impotence, and violence of the male environment fail to counter its hegemony, but Mamet signals transformative possibilities in bringing the feminized Others from the margins of the world into view. If indeed America's actions embody the limits of possibility, and if it is our actions, not our values, which incur international division (Rinder 2003: 17), then Mamet's call for change without a betrayal of moral principles is within our grasp. The Oedipal polarization of Self/Other wielded as weapon on Mamet's stage, according to Rinder, was fired on the world stage in President Bush's 2001 proclamation that "Either you are with us or you are with the terrorists," an apparent trigger in "the decline of the United States in global public esteem" (21). Observing that "As somebody said, all great crimes are committed in the name of public tranquility. . . . It's a confidence trick for taking power" (1997b), Mamet underscores the treacherous challenge, exacerbated at the inauguration of the twenty-first century, of securing the homeland without replicating the crimes against it.

American Buffalo signals in title, setting, and subject matter Mamet's unwavering focus on a homeland both threatened and threatening, buffaloed and buffaloing. This home, where the buffalo no longer roam, is grounded in mythic feats of oppression and repression, the frontiersmen's conquest over nature immortalized on a nickel. This is the coin of the realm in a republic where, according to the play's epigraph, the Lord who marched in glory in "The Battle Hymn" is now "peeling down the alley in a black and yellow ford" (Mamet 1976). This is an America whose values are pawned and sold (the play takes place in a pawnshop, or "junkshop") as junk in a cluttered landscape like "Don's resale shop"; as the play opens, the proprietor of the pawnshop is preaching to his young "gopher," Bob, the gospel of capitalism: "there's business and there's friendship" (7) while he swears revenge on the buyer of a buffalo-head nickel who he is convinced has conned him. That this impulse to polarize finds its paradigm in the family system is evidenced in Mamet's comment that "*American Buffalo*, sneakily enough, is really a tragedy about life in the family" (1988b: 93). Thus, Bob becomes the child-object of an Oedipal triangle with the appearance of Walter, tellingly nicknamed Teach, who, ranting against Ruthie and Grace for beating Teach at poker, concludes that in the world at large, "The only way to teach these people is to kill them" (11). A gambler himself who was nicknamed "Teach" by the petty thieves in his daily poker game at a Chicago junk shop, Mamet in his book *Three Uses* posits gambling as an analogue to America's global policy: "In our devotion to the ideas of our own superiority, we are like compulsive gamblers who destroy themselves by enacting a drama of their own worthlessness.... But we cannot gamble enough to find peace,... [we] arm ourselves and strut enough to feel secure" (1998b: 45, 52). In his history of the American Dream, Jim Cullen echoes Mamet's sentiments when he observes that America itself "is a world built on gambling" (2003: 161). The logic of capitalism, he adds, "tries to square the circle wherever possible in the name of maximizing profit as efficiently as possible." The American Dream, therefore, "focuses on getting something for nothing. Yet an air of exertion, even anxiety, suffuses this dream," because it is "the gambling, not the winning or losing, that finally matters" (166, 167).

Having been humiliated by his poker loss to a woman, Teach proceeds to appropriate Don's position as the turf boss, extolling the godhead of capitalism as America's founding force:

> *Teach*: You know what is free enterprise?...
> The freedom...
> Of the *Individual*...
> To Embark on Any Fucking Course that he sees fit...
> In order to secure his honest chance to make a profit. Am I so out of line on this?...
> Does this make me a Commie?...
> The country's *founded* on this, Don. You know this....
> Without this we're just savage shitheads in the wilderness...
> Sitting around some vicious campfire. That's why *Ruthie* burns me up. (72–3)

These illogical linguistic turns and gender assaults typify the Mametian litany and exemplify an Oedipal domination for self-aggrandizement. Sacvan Bercovitch puts it this way: "To define injustice through particular violations of free enterprise (or its constituent elements, such as equal opportunity and representative individualism) is to consecrate free enterprise as *the* just society" (1993: 366). This is precisely what Teach does, defining injustice as a violation of free enterprise, thereby consecrating individualism (vis-à-vis free enterprise) through power, authority, and violent domination.

The corrosive effect of such a stance is revealed in the corruption of Don, whom Teach coerces, "simply as a business proposition" (31), into excising Bob from their "thing," the ludicrously planned heist of the buffalo nickel from the "fucking fruit" (54) who bought it. Teach's "either him or us" (84) stance inevitably breeds violence as prefigured by his toting of a gun, "a silly personal thing" (85) that "helps [him] to relax" (84) during the robbery. Striking Bob after their plan is foiled (Teach actually oversleeps), Teach, in his refusal to transport Bob to the hospital despite Don's orders, reveals his dominance and individuality: "I am not your nigger. I am not your wife" (100), Teach says. Although Don is initially complicit in Teach's violence, the revelation of Bob's loyalty provokes his turning the violence on Teach, striking him as he condemns his "poison." "You make life of garbage" (101), Dan says to (and of) Teach. Trashing the junkshop, Teach exits, calling himself a "sissy" in defeat; however, Don, who, according to Mamet, has been "tempted by the devil into betraying all his principles" (1988b: 94), rejects an identity defined in terms which polarize society. Comforting Bob, he conjures the presence of Grace in a Ruth-less, white-male, junked world and evokes the possibility of community with his final "That's alright" (Mamet 1976: 106).

The rapacity and claustrophobia of capitalism materialize again in Mamet's *Glengarry Glen Ross*. Despite its awards, Mamet maintains that this multi-protagonist "gang comedy" "[is] not as good a play as *American Buffalo*" (1988b: 92), which he explicitly compared to *Death of a Salesman*; however, the character of Shelly "The Machine" Levene, an aging, self-inflating, desperate salesman, who is both exemplar and victim of free enterprise, is often compared to Willy Loman (Kane 1999: 64). Unlike the unspecified product that Willy peddles, however, Shelly's "business" is pointedly real estate as America's once fruited plain. However, real estate is not only bereft of buffalo but also subdivided into profit centers, such as Glengarry Highland and Glen Ross Farms. Mamet, himself having worked in a Chicago real estate agency from 1969 to 1970, depicts the competition and con games frenetically deployed to make a sale and gain ascendance on the real estate "board." Selling the land manifests the inevitable end of an American Dream enmeshed in an exalted system of free enterprise; thus, Mamet's epigraph for the play is a "*Practical Sales Maxim*: ALWAYS BE CLOSING" (1982: 13).

Hemmed in and frantic for a close, Levene opens the play by badgering the younger business manager, Williamson, to provide him with more and better leads so that he can regain his place on the board and not be forced to hustle "Polacks." Seated in a booth at a Chinese restaurant, the two men verbally vie before agreeing on a kickback scheme, which falls through when Levene cannot pay the initial bribe. In the next scene, the racist scapegoating continues in another booth where Moss consoles Aaronow for missing a sale: "How you goan'a get on the board sell'n a Polack? And ... don't ever try to sell an Indian" (29). Consolation, however, gives way to coercion as one aging salesman cons the other into complicity in a scheme to stage an office robbery as cover for removing the leads from the file and selling them to a competitor:

> *Moss*:   I lied. (*Pause.*) Alright? My end is my business. Your end's twenty-five. In or
>   out. You tell me, you're out you take the consequences.
> *Aaronow*: I do?
> *Moss*:   Yes. (*Pause.*)
> *Aaronow*: And why is that?
> *Moss*:   Because you listened. (46)

Again words are weaponry, not tools of communication, prescribing rather than describing action. The office is indeed trashed and the leads stolen, yet it is Levene, not Aaronow, whom Moss has convinced to act for him. Having been near suicide, Levene instead "got *out* there" (101), not only in the office robbery but also in the sales arena, to "convert the motherfucker," closing a big deal by selling the unsuspecting couple Bruce (or Ozzie?) and Harriet on that *"thing"* (72), which implies their unaffordable dreams. Boasting his victory (he thinks he has closed the deal), Levene cashes in his colleagues. Even the slick-wisecracking Roma's charade to dupe a reneging client is motivated by his belief that Levene is back on his way to being "Number One," driving Roma to keep pace with his competition (Levene). Once his uncontrolled verbiage trips him up and reveals his guilt in the break-in to steal the leads, Levene undertakes a bravado effort to bribe his supervisor, Williamson, into silence with the investigating detective; instead, he is silenced himself by the revelation that his American Dreamer clients had no intention of buying, but are instead "insane. They just like talking to salesmen" (104). Pleading futilely to Williamson in the name of his daughter, Levene seems to be offered salvation by Roma, who has also lost his contract with the client for whom they performed their spiel; as he exits his interview with the detective, Roma proposes to "Machine" Levene a partnership since the world they inhabit is "not a world of men . . . there's no adventure *to* it" and "We are the members of a dying breed" (105). This frontier connection between the younger and older salesmen yields to the dollar; Roma sells out Levene, who is still under interrogation. Proclaiming that "I GET HIS ACTION" (107), the hotshot salesman Roma exits for the restaurant to foist more land on American Dream aspirants so that he can ride his bonus Cadillac over the range while Levene, now implicated in his crime, faces a closed frontier. In the business landscape, according to Mamet, "one can only succeed at the cost of the failure of another. . . . The effect on the little guy is that he turns to crime. And petty crime goes punished; major crimes go unpunished" (qtd. in Kane 2001: 47). In this trashed office reminiscent of the junked shop in *American Buffalo*, only Aaronow provides an ethical presence – and that an impotent one: "Oh, god, I hate this job" (108).

The detritus of the American Dream is both subject and setting of the third of the trilogy, *Speed-the-Plow*, which dramatizes the Machiavellian machinations of Hollywood – dream factory not only for the nation but also for the world. According to Jim Cullen, a new version of the American Dream emanates from this new perspective, one that exalts "effortless attainment" (2003: 160) rather than hard work, and personality rather than character (176). Despite his success at screenwriting, Mamet condemns Hollywood for "flooding the market with trash" (1988b: 78), a verdict echoed by the play's protagonist, recently promoted production head Bobby Gould: "It's not all garbage but most of it is" (1985a: 29). Now an adult pawning values in a Los Angeles studio rather than a Chicago junk shop, Bobby is again the center of a conflict for his soul. The Teach figure is Charlie Fox, who seeks gold through Gould, pressuring him to produce a *"Buddy* picture" (11). To this Hollywood staple – the Buddy film – exalting the American (white) male, Fox has added a prison setting in the backdrop, in which the white star wins over "the black guys going to rape his ass" (11). Despite Gould's insistence that "Money is not Gold" (21) in their "People

Business" (22), Fox predicts that "We're going to kick the ass of a lot of them fucken' people" (28) since "it's Boy's Choice: Skate in One direction Only" (23). The competition that must be skated over is a female, the first to materialize onstage in a full-length Mamet play and the harbinger of those to follow in each subsequent play. Karen, Gould's temporary secretary, challenges Hollywood's values when she says, "But why should it all be garbage?" (29), and eventually counters Fox's film proposal with one of her own, an adaptation of a book entitled *The Bridge*. Although Gould has given Karen the "artsy" and apocalyptic book by some "Eastern Sissy Writer" (58) as a ruse to get her to his apartment, he does approve of the project after having sex with her. Apparently as comically obtuse and circular as Fox's script is obvious and linear, *The Bridge* nonetheless makes Karen feel empowered and signals her call for connection across gender borders.

It is indeed her transgression of borders which threatens Fox, who has inadvertently propelled her cause with his $500 wager with Gould that she will not "schtup" (have sex with) him. Fox's initial assessment that Karen "falls between two stools" (35) – neither "floozy" nor career woman – is confirmed by her acknowledgment to Gould of a shared desire for connection that superseded her awareness of his sexual ploy. Defying the polarized scripting of women as Madonna or whore, Karen's sexuality is transgressive, as emphasized by the casting of the pop singer Madonna in the original role. It is this gender transgression and its transformative potential that must be quashed to secure the hold of a mythic (and macho) capitalism and individualism. Enraged at the revitalized Gould, Fox resorts to violence to reestablish hierarchical divisions between male and female, West and East, professional and personal. Scorning Karen's project as a "sissy film" and Gould as "an old *woman*" (70) and "some Eastern Fruit" (66), Fox strikes him. His violent lashing out is similar to Teach in *American Buffalo*; when frustration overwhelms, violence overtakes. But it is Karen's coerced confession that sex was contingent upon Gould's endorsement of her proposal that secures Fox's victory and exile of the woman to the proverbial "A & P" (80), i.e., to bag groceries. Unable to embrace an identity beyond gendered scripts, Gould rejects *The Bridge*, which to Karen "brought grace" (4), in favor of Fox's male ethos: "And what *if* this fucken' 'grace' exists? It's not for you. . . . You have a different thing" (81). This "thing" is a perversion of the nineteenth-century novelist William Makepeace Thackeray's call for "duty," an idea chosen by Mamet as epigraph: "to each some work upon the ground he stands on, until he is laid beneath it." Gould's response to Fox's question, "What are we put on earth to do?" signals his damnation: "We're here to make a movie" (82), a fate confirmed by Mamet's 1989 play *Bobby Gould in Hell*. Redemption is denied any who both reproduce and produce in things the repressive "thing" of the American Dream.

In *Oleanna*, produced in 1992, Mamet shifts settings from business to academia, yet the focus remains the "corrosive hierarchies" implicit in the American Dream and the complicity of language to foster power. Perhaps the most controversial of his plays, *Oleanna* dramatizes the issue of sexual harassment, perhaps reflective of a previously "staged" version in the televised confirmation hearings of Clarence Thomas for

Supreme Court Justice. Mamet's public persona, macho characters, and lack of clearly defined female characters in his plays now found a different situation in *Oleanna*'s putative attack on political correctness and contemporary feminism. Yet, as Leslie Kane points out, "It is simply too easy to dismiss the play as antifeminist, even misogynist" (1999: 184). Male and female share the stage here, admittedly the male's office in the public sphere, but both are ultimately entrapped in its claustrophobic space. Not feminism but hierarchical doctrine is the target of the play as John, an actual professor on the verge of receiving tenure, assumes the role of "Teach." Language again emerges as performative and formative when Carol, befuddled by the verbiage in John's book, finds no reprieve in personal contact during her office visit. Intercutting John's monologues to his student about her grade with telephone monologues to his wife, Grace, about their impending purchase of a house, John is patronizing and patriarchal in both his professional and personal lives. His diatribe against the "Artificial Structure" (21) of the educational system notwithstanding, John intimidates Carol, validating Mamet's assertion that "we say we want to 'help, teach and correct.' But the end of each is oppression" (1998b: 25). His proposal of an "A" based on personal meetings and his arm around her shoulder only exacerbate Carol's frustration.

In the next act power positions invert, when Carol files charges of sexual harassment with the tenure committee, which will determine the stability of John's identity and future. Having joined a vague and unnamed "Group," Carol hurls a counterblow at John, charging him with rape. The suggestion of sexual abuse in childhood arises as Carol's initial panic at John's insistence that "I'm not your *father*" (9) explodes into her equating "paternal prerogative" (67) with rape. Though perhaps not as dramatically, John shares with Carol a sense of early disempowerment: "my earliest and most persistent memories are of being told that I was stupid" (16). It is a sense that Mamet shares as well: "I was like the professor in *Oleanna* . . . who all his life had been told he was an idiot so he behaved like one" (qtd. in Lahr 1997: 73). Mamet's indictment of the Oedipal dynamic in childhood exposes the damaging effects to both sexes.

Although the criminal charge of rape may be unfounded, John's oppression of Carol is sexualized, if not sexual. He believes in "an elitist, in, in a protected hierarchy" (67) and he mocks students, like Carol, who "slave to come here" (52). The "teacher–student paradigm" in Mamet's plays, identified by Pascale Hubert-Leibler (1992: 73), characterizes parent–child, male–female, and lord–serf relationships, all of which emulate the master–slave structure evoked by the folk-song epigraph:

> Oh, to be in *Oleanna*
> That's where I would rather be.
> Than be bound in Norway
> And drag the chains of slavery.

Each chained and therefore dangerous in their bunker mentality, John and Carol trade positions only to leave the hierarchies of the system unchanged. Its inevitable violence erupts as John beats Carol after his rejection by the Committee; cowering on the floor as he shuffles papers on his desk, Carol ends the play ambiguously, with neither side claiming victory.

In *The Cryptogram*, produced in 1994, it is the husband and father (another character named Bobby) who remains off-stage, although the father's absence represents not a marginalized position but a dominating one. In this play, Mamet turns his focus from the public world of business to the private world of home. In his venture into domestic realism (a realism illustrating home life), Mamet parodies the Oedipal triangle overtly rather than covertly as in *American Buffalo*. The setting is a living room in 1959, when the American Dream of "Ozzie and Harriet" reached its apex. It is also the setting of David Mamet's boyhood (John is a surrogate for the author in the play). With a family "cobbled together" after his parents' divorce, Mamet lived in a model house, where the glass kitchen tabletop came to be associated "with the notion of blood" so frequently was it shattered by his enraged stepfather. Suffering what Mamet's sister terms "emotional terrorism" (qtd. in Weber 1997), Mamet was left with a "great longing to belong" (Mamet 1986: 73), much like the 10-year-old John in *Cryptogram*, who, anxious about a camping trip with his father the next day, cannot sleep. His anxiety seems confirmed by the "Camping song" of the play's epigraph: "Last night when you were all in bed / Mrs. O'Leary left a lantern in her shed" (1997a). Although the ostensible object of his opening line, "I couldn't find 'em" (1), is his slippers, the true object of John's search is his father. Constantly descending the stairs (descending into hell), he seeks assurance from the adults. They, however, no more "belong" than the child since both the housewife mother, Donny, and the homosexual pseudo-patriarch, Del, are relegated to the margins and longing for validation from the male – a white heterosexual hunter – who dominates the world of the play. While the mother stammers, "He's at the Office" (11) or "He'll be here when he gets here, I think" (38), Del futilely attempts to distract the hypersensitive child with an observation game. Mamet's identification with John (and his Judaism) emerges clearly in his assertion that the world of the outsider "is based on observation." Observing is the "habit of the young child," but also, in Mamet's words, "historically it is the habit of the Jew" (1986: 73).

These outsiders find the family home, that *sanctum sanctorum* of the American Dream, a cryptogram, "something written in code or cipher," the latter term referencing a "person or thing without influence or value; a nonentity" (*American Heritage Dictionary*, 1976). Child, mother, and homosexual are all reduced to ciphers by Robert (who is never seen in the play) and forced to turn on each other in their fear of their own worthlessness. When Donny learns that her husband is leaving her, she attacks Del, who has lent the adulterous Robert his room despite knowing that he would never accord attention to "Some Poor Geek" (74). Donny and Del are demeaned by sex or sexuality; as a result, they betray the powerless child: Del by dismissively giving John his father's knife ("Take the knife and go," 100), and Donny by leaving unanswered her son's cries that he hears voices. Though it can be inferred that the play's outcome will be John's suicide, the play's ending is in fact ambiguous, with the boy poised on the stair landing, symbolic of his oscillation between childhood and adulthood.

Even more overtly autobiographical, Mamet's play *The Old Neighborhood*, produced in 1997, portrays Bobby Gould (Mamet's sometime alter ego) attempting to reconstruct his identity through three one-acts. In Act 1, titled *The Disappearance of the Jews*, originally written in 1983, Bobby reminisces with his high school friend Joey in a prototypical male diatribe against homosexuals; yet the tone is longing as Bobby confesses to his wife's blaming the Jew for their victimization. In Act 2, titled *Jolly*, Bobby recalls with his sister the abuse in their stepfamily. Though their memories diverge, the effects are the same, Jolly now dreaming of opening a door to a murderous mother, Bobby feeling "pathetic" (1998a: 79). Having left his own family, he resists Jolly's assurances that he was the one loved and that his kids will not suffer: "*We're* not okay" (77). In Act 3, titled *Deeny*, Bobby reunites with an old lover in a bar; his final "Good-bye, love" (100) seems to bid farewell not only to the person but also to the possibility of reawakening passions that are as doomed as his desire to reinvent the past.

Mamet's dissection of the American home takes another twist in *Boston Marriage*, produced in 2002. The title referring to a Victorian euphemism for a long-term lesbian relationship, the play portrays a nineteenth-century Boston household maintained by the aging and elitist Anna. This satire, in tone similar to Oscar Wilde, replaces the male triangle of *American Buffalo* with the female triangle of Anna, her partner, Claire, and her maid, Catherine. Still the play, like most of Mamet's dramas, continues the assault on American power structures and the barrage of language that creates reality. Wearing an emerald necklace that Claire finds "excessive for the morning" (2002: 2), Anna explains with pride that she has secured a male benefactor to support the household:

Anna: Well, we do love shiny things.
Claire: In unity with our sisters the Fish.
Anna: Men . . .
Claire: What can one do with them.
Anna: Just the One Thing.
Claire: Though, in your case, it seems to've been effective. (3)

This cynical repartee between the women characterizes their relationship as they alternate between crude and intellectual banter. Anna's reaction to Claire's proclamation that she has fallen in love with a young girl ranges from melodramatic despair ("I receive nothing but the tale of your new rutting. (*Pause.*) Oh, how lonely you make me feel," 15) to detached analysis ("You know so many of our ills proceed from a corporeal imbalance," 17). Eventually, she consents to aid Claire in her seduction scene by entertaining the mother on the condition that she function as "a *stage manager*" (33) and be allowed to watch. When their planned performance is foiled, by the young girl's off-stage recognition of her mother's necklace, both Anna and

Claire are deprived of sexual targets. Initially blaming each other, they unite in a plan to stage another performance – a séance – using the jewel as a prop to recuperate both father and daughter. This act fails as well when a letter terminating Anna's funds and demanding return of the necklace answers their invitations.

Mixed with Anna and Claire's thrust-and-parry are their outrageous assaults on the Scottish maid whose name and nationality elude Anna: "Cringing Irish Terror, is it? What do you want? Home Rule...?... An apology for your potato famine? IT CAME FROM THE LACK OF ROTATION OF CROPS!!!" (9, 16). Fired for fornicating, the maid returns to reveal to Claire the falsity of Anna's claims of a missing necklace and impending imprisonment; nevertheless, Claire leaves her love waiting to accompany Anna into "Exile," pledging loyalty, if not love: "The world you see is not cruel. It possesses neither falsity nor guile. And it shall be my mission to protect you from it" (112). They exit only to have the wily Anna return to instruct the maid to obtain a receipt for the necklace. If not ethical, these women are competent and resilient performers of their identities and creators of their destinies; worthy opponents, they flaunt gender and class conventions. While they mercilessly regale the aggressively heterosexual and lower-class maid, the maid, too, participates in their staged lives and she, too, survives. Unlike in some of his other plays, none here evinces a bunker defense against her own worthlessness. *Boston Marriage* evokes speculation as to the direction of Mamet's future drama. Unlike his defeated, if not doomed, male characters, these women seek another stage on which to perform their identities, readily abandoning all notions of a fixed sense of self.

Although his characters wage combat with words, Mamet's audience may perceive in the poetic rhythms of his language the possibility of poetry in our lives and of passage beyond the dead end of a predatory American Dream. "All plays are about decay," Mamet asserts. "They are about the ends of a situation which has achieved itself fully, and the inevitable disorder which ensues until equilibrium is again established.... That is why theatre has always been essential to human psychic equilibrium" (1986: 111). Forays into other genres notwithstanding, Mamet finds solution, if not resolution, in the theatre:

> The solution... which will enable us to function happily in the midst of rational uncertainty to a personal and seemingly unresolvable psychological problem – is the dream; the solution to a seemingly unresolvable social (ethic) problem is the drama (poem). For the sine qua non of both the dream and the drama is the suspension of rational restrictions in aid of happiness. (1986: 9)

As uncertainty becomes rational and the unresolvable solvable, borders dissolve, polarization implodes, and dreams (through drama) revision the American Dream into something less solipsistic. Believing that playwrights must address, as did Tennessee Williams, "that which we desire most, which is love and a sense of belonging" (1986: 36), Mamet strives "to bring to the stage the life of the human soul so that the community can participate therein" (1988b: 91). The soul's salvation is described in embracing terms: "When you come into the theater, you have to be willing to say, 'We're all here to undergo a communion, to find out what the hell is going on in this world'" (1998b: 19). In this communal ritual lies the magic of Mamet, the redemption of America and its Dream, and the presence of grace on the world stage.

BIBLIOGRAPHY

Almansi, G. (1986). "David Mamet, a Virtuoso of Invective." In Marc Chenetier (ed.), *Critical Angles: European Views of Contemporary American Literature*. Carbondale: Southern Illinois University Press, 191–207.

Bercovitch, S. (1993). *The Rites of Assent: Transformations in the Symbolic Construction of America*. New York: Routledge.

Bigsby, C. W. E. (1985). *Beyond Broadway:A Critical Introduction to Twentieth-Century American Drama*, vol. 3. Cambridge: Cambridge University Press.

Cohn, R. (ed.) (1982). *New American Dramatists, 1960–1980*. New York: Grove.

Cullen, J. (2003). *The American Dream: A Short History of an Idea that Shaped a Nation*. New York: Oxford University Press.

Dean, A. (1990). *David Mamet: Language as Dramatic Action*. Rutherford: Associated University Presses.

Demos, J. (1997a). "Oedipus and America: Historical Perspectives on the Reception of Psychoanalysis in the United States." In Joel Pfister and Nancy Schnog (eds.), *Inventing the Psychological: Toward a Cultural History of Emotional Life in America*. New Haven, CT: Yale University Press, 63–78.

Demos, J. (1997b). "History and the Psychological: Reflections on 'Oedipus and America.'" In Joel Pfister and Nancy Schnog (eds.), *Inventing the Psychological: Toward a Cultural History of Emotional Life in America*. New Haven, CT: Yale University Press, 79–83.

Friedman, T. (2002). *Longitudes and Attitudes: Exploring the World After September 11*. New York: Farrar.

Hubert-Leibler, P. (1992). "Dominance and Anguish: The Teacher–Student Relationship in the Plays of David Mamet." In Leslie Kane (ed.), *David Mamet: A Casebook*. New York: Garland, 69–85.

Kammen, M. (1991). *Mystic Chords of Memory: The Transformation of Tradition in American Culture*. New York: Knopf.

Kane, L. (ed.) (1992). *David Mamet: A Casebook*. New York: Garland.

——(1999). *Weasels and Wisemen: Ethics and Ethnicity in the Work of David Mamet*. New York: St. Martin's.

——(ed.) (2001). *David Mamet in Conversation*. Ann Arbor: University of Michigan Press.

Kroll, J. (1995). "Phantoms in the Dark." Review of Mamet's *The Cryptogram*. *Newsweek* 20 (February): 72.

Lahr, J. (1997). "Fortress Mamet." *New Yorker*, November 17: 70–82.

Lutz, C. (1997). "Epistemology of the Bunker: The Brainwashed and Other New Subjects of Permanent War." In Joel Pfister and Nancy Schnog (eds.), *Inventing the Psychological: Toward a Cultural History of Emotional Life in America*. New Haven, CT: Yale University Press, 245–67.

Mamet, D. (1976). *American Buffalo*. New York: Grove.

——(1981). *Lakeboat*. New York: Grove.

——(1982). *Glengarry Glen Ross*. New York: Grove.

——(1985a). *Speed-the-Plow*. New York: Grove.

——(1985b). "Two Gentlemen of Chicago: David Mamet and Stuart Gordon" (with Hank Nuwer). *South Carolina Review* 17 (Spring): 9–20.

——(1986). *Writing in Restaurants*. New York: Viking.

Mamet, D. (1988a). "Celebrating the Capacity for Self-Knowledge" (with Henry I. Schvey). *New Theatre Quarterly* 4 (February): 89–96.

—— (1988b). "Interview with David Mamet." In Esther Harriott (ed.), *American Voices: Five Contemporary Playwrights in Essays and Interviews*. Jefferson, NC: McFarland, 77–97.

——(1992). *The Cabin*. New York: Turtle Bay.

—— (1995). *Oleanna*. New York: Grove.

—— (1997a). *The Cryptogram*. New York: Vintage.

—— (1997b). "The *Salon* Interview" (with Richard Covington). *Salon*, October 24; http://www.salon.com/feature/1997/10/cov_si_24mamet3.html.

—— (1998a). *The Old Neighborhood*. New York: Vintage.

—— (1998b). *Three Uses of the Knife: On the Nature and Purpose of Drama*. New York: Columbia University Press.

—— (2002). *Boston Marriage*. New York: Vintage.

Pfister, J. and Schnog, N. (eds.) (1997). *Inventing the Psychological: Toward a Cultural History of Emotional Life in America*. New Haven, CT: Yale University Press.

Rinder, L. (2003). "The American Effect." In Lawrence Rinder et al. (eds.), *The American Effect: Global Perspectives on the United States, 1990–2003*. New York: Whitney Museum, 15–44.

Savran, D. (1988). *In Their Own Words: Contemporary American Playwrights*. New York: Theatre Communications Group.

Schnog, N. (1997). "On Inventing the Psychological." In Joel Pfister and Nancy Schnog (eds.), *Inventing the Psychological: Toward a Cultural History of Emotional Life in America*. New Haven, CT: Yale University Press, 3–16.

Weber, B. (1997). "At 50, A Mellower David Mamet May Be Ready to Tell His Story." *New York Times* online edition, November 16; http://www.nytimes.com/archives.

Wetzsteon, R. (1976). "New York Letter." *Plays and Players* (September): 37.

Zeifman, H. (1992). "Phallus in Wonderland: Machismo and Business in David Mamet's *AmericanBuffalo* and *Glengarry Glen Ross*." In In Leslie Kane (ed.), *David Mamet: A Casebook*. New York: Garland, 123–35.

26
1970–1990: Disillusionment, Identity, and Discovery

Mark Fearnow

The 1960s saw the dismantling of the heterosexual family drama as the home of American theatre and its replacement with a drama of radical questioning and idealism. The 1970s flooded those dream estates with pessimism, ushering in what could be called a "drama of malaise." In the 1980s, the energy that built up a new and positive theatre came largely from formerly silenced groups – feminist, gay and lesbian, African American, Latina/o, and Asian American playwrights – and a renewed political drama arose in response to the conservative environment of 1980–92. Many of these playwrights, in addition to Albee, Guare, Shepard, Mamet, and August Wilson, are considered in separate chapters. The goal here is to identify some key voices of the period and to define the era's possible links among drama, theatre, and the rest of culture.

The notion of a negative drama may sound absurd, but such periods have a purpose: rest, reflection, and recovery. Plays such as Michael Weller's *Moonchildren* (1972), Mark Medoff's *When You Comin' Back, Red Ryder?* (1973), Robert Patrick's *Kennedy's Children* (1975), David Rabe's *Streamers* (1976), and Lanford Wilson's *Fifth of July* (1978) reflected a level of exhaustion and anger with the failures of the 1960s.[1] The 1970s offered cause for disillusionment and despair. The disarray of the Democratic Party following the assassinations of Martin Luther King and Robert F. Kennedy in 1968, and the tumultuous Democratic Convention, led to the election of the Republican candidate, Richard Nixon. The new president claimed to have a "secret plan" to end the war in Vietnam. He markedly reduced American ground forces in Southeast Asia, but at the same time conducted an unauthorized campaign of carpet bombing against military and civilian targets in Vietnam, Laos, and Cambodia. Reports of the escalation fired the already volatile atmosphere on university campuses, and in May 1970, National Guardsmen firing into a crowd of demonstrators killed four students at Kent State University in Ohio; 11 days later, two African American students were killed when local and state police fired at protesters at Mississippi's Jackson State University (Carruth 1989: 393). Neither the 1971 leaking of the "Pentagon Papers" (revealing Defense Department deceptions) nor the arrest of White House operatives who broke into the Democratic Party headquarters in the Watergate complex in June 1972 was enough to damage Nixon's popularity. He won easy reelection in 1972 over the liberal anti-war candidate, George McGovern. As the Watergate scandal unfolded, the White House reacted as to a siege; Vice President Spiro Agnew pleaded no contest to criminal charges and resigned. The president was soon proven to have conspired to cover up his administration's involvement with the Watergate break-in. Faced with impeachment, Nixon resigned the presidency in August 1974. The United States handed off military operations to the South Vietnamese, and the forces of the Communist North quickly overran the peninsula. Americans watched on television in April 1975 as Vietnamese civilians clung to helicopters evacuating American personnel in the southern capital of Saigon, soon renamed Ho Chi Minh City. The sacrifice of countless lives on multiple sides had been, it seemed from an American perspective, for nothing. While the election of Georgia governor Jimmy Carter as president in 1976 promised a recovery from the miasmas of Watergate and Vietnam, the economy grew worse. At one point in 1980, inflation reached 12.4 percent despite interest rates at a record 20 percent (Henretta et al. 1987: 969). This "misery index," along with Carter's failure to free 53 American hostages taken by Iranian militants in November 1979, precipitated the landslide election of conservative icon Ronald Reagan in 1980.

Writers from previous generations resurfaced in the 1970s, but most failed to match the *zeitgeist* of this post-lost-war, post-revolutionary era. Familiar authors such as Robert Anderson, William Gibson, Frank D. Gilroy, Arthur Laurents, Jean Kerr, and N. Richard Nash offered plays, but none rivaled their earlier successes in public acceptance or critical admiration. A revered cultural figure, Archibald MacLeish (1892–1982) saw his play *Scratch* (1971) close after two performances. Figures of the 1960s avant-garde such as Jean-Claude van Itallie and Jack Gelber continued to experiment, but the time of their flourishing seemed past. Van Itallie's *The Serpent* (1970), a startling theatrical event based on the Open Theatre's improvisations on the Book of Genesis, was among the last of the improv-based rituals to reach a wide audience. The Open Theatre disbanded in 1973. (For discussion of the Open Theatre and 1960s drama more generally, see chapter 15.)

One example of successful adaptation to the times was a project of Jerome Lawrence (1915–2004) and Robert E. Lee (1918–94). The pair had enjoyed a series of Broadway successes, beginning in 1955 with *Inherit the Wind*, a reworking of the 1925 Scopes trial (see chapter 11). Their plays tended toward large casts, historical sources, and optimistic conclusions propelled by the triumph of progressive forces. The plays could not be seen as stretching public morals. Rather, they identified and articulated intellectual and moral positions already held by the middle-class audience, set those positions against representatives of a vanquished opposition, and offered a means through which to celebrate one's own enlightenment. *The Night Thoreau Spent in Jail* (1970) was a timely adaptation of this technique. The hundreds of productions of the play around the United States were testament to the continued viability of realism as vehicle for the "play of ideas."

Like Lawrence and Lee's other work, *Thoreau* simplifies complex persons and ideas into readily understandable terms, relying upon empathy with a likable protagonist as a carrier for sentiments. The young Thoreau is imprisoned for refusal to pay taxes to support President Polk's undeclared war on Mexico. The playwrights emphasized Thoreau's "relevance" (a ubiquitous noun in 1970): he rebels against the power of the state and its militarist adventures, against materialism, against the degradation of nature, and – in rejecting the limitations of his mentor Ralph Waldo Emerson – against even the progressive elements of the previous generation. Thoreau became the perfect 1970 hero – anti-war, anti-establishment, ecologically aware, a free thinker. The actor playing Thoreau was directed by the playwrights to leap from the stage at play's end and stride "up the aisle of the theatre to the sound of his own different drummer" (Lawrence and Lee 1970: 90). Lawrence and Lee's approach in offering their play to the public was innovative, reflecting the anti-materialist sentiments of their text, but also the decline of Broadway, with its systems of out-of-town try-outs, high-stakes opening nights, and fateful reviews. *Thoreau* opened at Ohio State University and then the authors toured the country 1970–2, witnessing and in some cases directing productions at more than 100 college and university, community, and regional theatres, all the while continuing to revise the play and engage in dialogue with directors, actors, designers, reviewers, academics, and audiences. This process, which came to be known as "workshopping" a play, grew in prominence during the 1970s and 1980s and by the turn of the century was the normal route for "play development." Interviews with playwrights conducted in the 1980s and 1990s found most describing Broadway as "dead," "irrelevant," or "ridiculous" (see Bryer 1995; Greene 2000; Savran 1988). The resident (or "regional") theatre movement, which took root in the 1960s, blossomed in the 1970s, with resident professional companies producing new work throughout the country. The decentralized system produced significant returns. Jerome Lawrence told an interviewer in 1991 that despite its never having been produced on Broadway, the acting version of *The Night Thoreau Spent in Jail* had sold 480,000 copies (Bryer 1995:174).

Tennessee Williams and Arthur Miller, however unwillingly, took on in the 1970s the mantles of living legends. Like all legends, they were rife for worship and imitation as well as parody and derision. Lanford Wilson was the outstanding inheritor of what might be called the Williams tradition, but a longer list of writers can be seen as moving in orbits affected primarily by the undeniable gravity of the planet Williams. The style and form of these plays can be defined as intensely character-driven drama in which the plot is submerged beneath the cumulative events in the lives of characters. Plot points emerge suddenly, often surprisingly, and reveal hitherto unseen workings of the characters' psyches. This branch of realism is often identified with Chekhov, Williams himself – as well as Wilson and others – having devoted considerable time to the study of that writer's work. Added to the Chekhovian structure is the mark of Williams – a Romantic attraction to the grotesque, the beautiful spirit in an ugly body, compassion for the broken, the miserable, and the deformed. The plays are neither unrelievedly grim nor the damaged characters doomed, as one would expect in a work by Sartre or Genet. The plays suggest a vague hope, if not redemption, resulting from the characters' suffering.

Mart Crowley (b. 1935) was one of the most promising of the "School of Williams." Crowley followed his sensational *The Boys in the Band* (1968) with a delicate memory play about childhood and coming of age, *A Breeze from the Gulf* (1973). The boy who is the play's central character is pulled between his devoutly Catholic father and his mentally ill mother, who ends in an asylum. Its autobiographical tone, setting on the Mississippi Gulf coast, and gay subtext strengthen the comparison with Williams. Though a soundly structured and poetically crafted play, it received only 48 performances in New York, and has rarely been revived (Hischak 2001: 63). In a move that, in its typicality, has come to be seen as a major threat to the future of American playwriting, Crowley turned to television writing and producing, writing only two additional plays in 30 years.

Paul Zindel (1936–2003) was an established author of "young adult fiction" when *The Effect of Gamma Rays on Man-in-the-Moon-Marigolds* was awarded the Pulitzer Prize in 1970. The play, like much of Zindel's fiction, takes place among a poor family headed by a mentally disturbed mother. One daughter finds potential escape through her talent for science, but the mother wrecks plans for a triumph over the community at the school science fair, remaining at home and killing the children's pet rabbit. The play is not without hope. The scientist-daughter wins the science fair, and her narration regarding her project, its demonstration of how a subtle, invisible but powerful force from outside may affect living things, is a memorable statement of the scientifically unexplainable assertion of disciplined intelligence and good will in young people deprived of these things in their environment.

While *Marigolds* was still running, Zindel's second play opened in on Broadway. *And Miss Reardon Drinks a Little* (1971) was another drama of family horror and retribution. Now the domineering mother has died, and the eldest of three Reardon sisters (a Superintendent of Schools) agrees to have her sister – a teacher who has been accused of sexual assault on a student – committed to an institution. This nearly plotless sort of realism has occasionally succeeded (Carson McCullers's *The Member of the Wedding* is an example), but Zindel's work lacked the poetic magic that could sustain his characters' permutations over the course of two hours. *The Secret Affairs of Mildred Wild* (1972) and *Ladies at the Alamo* (1977) disappeared from view after quick Broadway closings, and Zindel withdrew from playwriting.

Michael Weller's *Moonchildren* (1972) came to Broadway from Washington's Arena Stage in a production directed by Alan Schneider. The play ran only briefly in New York, but became an iconic play about the 1960s, observed from the next decade. *Moonchildren* is set in a student apartment in a college town during the 1965–6 academic year. The characters' drug use, sexual experiments, tricks and spoofs, political activities, philosophical obsessions, and practical concerns about food and money are intertwined in a subtle arc of action defined by the academic calendar (beginning in early fall and ending the day after graduation). The delicate plotting and group protagonist are reminiscent of Chekhov. At the end of the play, with the finality of graduation, we have a sense of the future direction for each of the core characters, similar to Chekhov's *The Cherry Orchard*. As in that play, the end shows everyone having left except for one (Bob). The characters leave without saying goodbye, or say goodbye with utter coolness, unwilling to admit dependency. In the play's final interaction, Bob confesses to Kathy that he has been hiding the fact that his mother died during Christmas break. In a more conventional drama, this opening-up would lead to an embrace, a breakthrough. But Weller avoids this resolution. As Bob continues to describe his feelings of loss and unhappiness, Kathy exits, leaving him alone except for the group's cat, who has been forgotten and left behind. Bob puts the cat out and is suddenly overcome with emotion. The play ends with Bob giving in to spasms of weeping. Weller adds the stage direction, "his mother's death has nothing to do with it" (179).

Lanford Wilson's *The Fifth of July* (1978) is in some ways about the same *Moonchildren*, observed now from the high disillusionment of 1978. Like the Weller play, the plotting is diffuse and subtle, though compressed in time. The action takes place during two continuous scenes: early evening of Independence Day 1977, and the following morning, and centers around choices to be made by Ken Talley, Jr., who lost both legs in Vietnam. Ken has inherited what remains of the family farm and its comfortable house. The play represents a new maturity in American drama; Ken is gay, but the play is not about his gayness. He has come back to his hometown of Lebanon, Missouri, with his lover, Jed, a quiet horticulturalist. Gathered for the holiday are Ken's sister (June) and her teenaged daughter (Shirley), as well as their friend John, now married to another college friend, Gwen, an aspiring singer who inherited wealth. Ken and June's Aunt Sally is present, as well as the ashes of her husband, Matt. John and Gwen have a musician in tow (Wes), who functions as observer of the eccentric group and as victim of John's sadistic personality. The journey of the eight characters over 18 hours, the interweaving of motivations and reflection of one story upon another, the pulling together of a string of time to collapse the hopes and disappointments of three generations into one coherent dramatic action, is a superb accomplishment. If American drama of the 1970s can be said to have a masterpiece, it is surely *The Fifth of July*.

The spirit of Chekhov is very present. Like Madame Ranevskaya, Ken must decide whether or not to sell the family place – in his case to John and Gwen, who want to create a recording studio. Linked to this question is whether or not Ken will return to his career of teaching, offered to him by the high school principal. Over the course of the play, we learn of Ken's terror at appearing before teenagers with his crutches and artificial legs; June's disappointment at the failure of her utopian dreams; Shirley's ambition for fame and glamour; Sally's desire to preserve the family's rootedness; John's resentments against the Talleys; Gwen's actual talent. The outcome of the play differs from *The Cherry Orchard* – Ken turns down John and Gwen's offer, choosing a web of tradition and responsibility over his impulse to escape and retire from the world. Sally and Jed deposit Matt's ashes; Jed's plantings will grow to maturity; Ken will face a classroom; Shirley assumes a mantle of responsibility for the future of the Talleys; Wes forms a musical alliance with Gwen, suggesting the future removal of John. The play has the compression and focus of art, but the truth and texture of real life. Within a structure of co-reflective decisions by psychologically complex and plausible characters, the interlopers are subtly vanquished, while the small braveries of hanging on and going on are placed before us. Throughout the play, Ken has been attempting to transcribe a recording of a story made by a boy with a severe speech defect. He had nearly given up, but by the end of the play, he has succeeded and reads aloud the boy's concluding paragraph:

> After they had explored all the suns in the universe, and all the planets of all the suns, they realized that there was no other life in the universe, and that they were alone. And they were very happy, because then they knew it was up to them to become all the things they had imagined they would find. (127)

Touches such as this nearly forgotten story element, which reappears with sudden-ness and grace, distinguish the play from those of Tennessee Williams and his other "children." Wilson eschews Williams's tragic sense of life, the cosmic fatalism suggesting that the sensitive and good are bound to be trodden under by the bullies of the universe; that their destruction is sad, but inevitable. Nor does Wilson embrace the treasured irony of Chekhov, with heroes struggling on at play's conclusion toward some illusory goal, the struggle itself providing sole meaning. Wilson accomplishes a surprising feat in modern drama: he manages to be hopeful without being sentimental or dishonest. There is no guarantee of a happy future for the Talley family at the end of *The Fifth of July*, but they have, on their separate though interlinking paths, chosen to remain, and to remain together. Unlike the choices made by Chekhov's three sisters, the Talleys' choice is not resignation, but defiance. The way of the late twentieth century was to pull apart, cut bonds, get ahead, keep looking for something better. The Talleys resist that call, and choose instead two words more of the nineteenth than the twentieth or twenty-first centuries: *family* and *home*. These are perhaps surprising hallmarks for Wilson – a gay writer who left the Midwest to make a life in New York. Wilson challenges his audience to redefine these words with courage and without sentimentalizing.

Talley's Folly (1979) and *Talley & Son* (1985, originally *A Tale Told*, 1981) join with *The Fifth of July* to form a trilogy. All concern the Talley family and take place on the same piece of land on and around Independence Day. *Talley's Folly* and *Talley & Son* take place on July 4, 1944, as the family struggles over control of the property and family business, while outside, on the river, Sally meets with Matt Friedman, a German Jewish accountant from the city, who has been courting her but was chased off by her family. *Talley's Folly* has been the most performed Wilson play, making its

Plate 17. *Talley's Folly,* by Lanford Wilson. Jeannine Hutchings (Sally Talley) and David Schuster (Matt Friedman). Courtesy of the Missouri Repertory Theatre.

way after a successful Broadway run into regional, university, community, and even high school theatres. It features charming characters, a short running time, and one set, when the economics of American theatre made such plays necessities. *The Fifth of July* is by almost any literary measure a better play, but *Talley's Folly* presents none of the difficulties of *The Fifth of July* – complex themes, subtle motivations, and, an obstacle for some audiences, a romantic kiss between two men.

Wilson's plays of 1969–96 were written in the context of a playwright-centered company, the Circle Repertory Theatre, which Wilson co-founded with a director and two actors in 1969. Like Chekhov at the Moscow Art Theatre or Odets with the Group, Wilson had the advantage of writing for particular actors, and having actors and directors constantly available for readings and suggestions. This context explains the high degree of naturalism in the writing. The playwright could hear in his head the voices of the company and write with the confidence that they shared an approach and acting style and so could realize a complex text. The plays *Lemon Sky* (1970), *The Hot l Baltimore* (1973), *The Mound Builders* (1975), *Serenading Louie* (1976), *Angels Fall* (1982), and *Burn This* (1987) emerged from the creative matrix of this home company. This body of work, in addition to his writing of the 1990s and after, comprises a substantial creative contribution, impressive in both its quality and range, a collection of writing perhaps equaled in this period only by Edward Albee and David Mamet.

Other fine plays emerged from Circle's workshops and productions. Mark Medoff's *When You Comin' Back, Red Ryder?* (1973) resembled Robert E. Sherwood's *The*

Petrified Forest (1935) in its depiction of a criminal's domination of travelers at a remote diner (see chapter 8), but the differences highlight the cultural change of 40 years. Sherwood's Duke Mantee takes over the diner as a hideout and leaves the inhabitants alone, killing the poet only when forced. Medoff's Teddy taunts and humiliates his victims because it amuses him. His behavior seems motiveless unless one counts the pleasure of sadism. Albert Innaurato's *Gemini* (1977) was daring in its subject matter – a crisis of sexual orientation in the life of a Philadelphia man who is traumatized when two college friends descend upon his family's row house. Innaurato's outrageous depiction of the mores of working-class South Philly may have overwhelmed the story material, but the comedy succeeded in attracting audiences for a long Broadway run that might not have been expected for a "coming-out" play. Jim Leonard's *The Diviners* (1980) came to Circle from the American College Theatre Festival, where it had won the top prize. The play echoes Faulkner in its characters and Shakespeare in its dramatic structure, moving freely through a poeticized rural Indiana of the 1930s and culminating in a tragedy that is no one's fault. Leonard continued to write for Circle until – like so many others – he moved into television writing and production.

If Lanford Wilson stretched his audience to embrace a wider moral perspective, David Rabe (b. 1940) may sometimes be said to have stretched his audience to the breaking point. Rabe forged a drama of shock, respecting few limits on language, stage action, and aesthetic perspective, making him perhaps the most walked-out-on playwright of the 1970s. Rabe was drafted in 1966 and sent to Vietnam. After his return, he was adopted as one of Joseph Papp's discoveries at the Public Theatre, and the enduring success of Rabe's work has to some degree overshadowed other Papp protégés such as Miguel Piñero, Thomas Babe, John Ford Noonan, and Dennis Reardon, all of whom created substantial bodies of work. In her biography of Papp, Helen Epstein describes a macho environment at the Public in the 1970s, a "hotbed of creativity" with Papp as father figure to a hard-drinking, cigar-smoking circle of aggressive young male playwrights (Epstein 1994: 311–18). Rabe emerged as a standout with *The Basic Training of Pavlo Hummel* (1971). He followed this sensational work with three more plays about the Vietnam experience: *Sticks and Bones* (1971), *The Orphan* (1973), and *Streamers* (1976). His non-war plays focus on brutality in daily life. Of the 1970s plays, *In the Boom Boom Room* (1973) is the story of a go-go dancer who moves through a shadowy demi-monde and is eventually beaten to death.

The Basic Training of Pavlo Hummel exploits the power of the grotesque. Rabe creates an aesthetic relation between stage and audience that is fraught with anxiety and ambiguity. As an audience member, one is not sure how to react – is it safe to laugh? Is violence about to break out? Rabe avoids familiar forms of plot except to twist them inside out. There is in *Hummel* something of the dreaminess of Megan Terry's *Viet Rock* (1966) as well as the violence and threat of Kenneth H. Brown's *The Brig*, produced by the Living Theatre in 1963 (see chapter 15). But *Hummel* is denser and more complicated than these works. It begins with Hummel's absurd death – a grenade is thrown into a brothel and he clutches it to his stomach. Hummel is then led Scrooge-like through realities back home and in the military. The action seems to occur in Pavlo's mind during the four days it took him to die, or perhaps these visions are instantaneous with his death, or perhaps they are presented to the dying man from some outside source. Rabe leaves this question unanswered. In its depiction of the military as an absurd machine into which an innocent is fed, the play is reminiscent of the Piscator/Brecht *Good Soldier Schweik* plays. As in Brecht, a strange humor animates the most violent stage action and, conversely, what seem safely comic scenes shift suddenly into violence. The play ends with Pavlo being placed into an aluminum coffin, his protests cut off when the lid is slammed and locked.

Whereas *Hummel* might be described as an odd, mocking, violent vaudeville, *Sticks and Bones* uses the television situation comedy as its ironic foil. David comes home from Vietnam, blind, haunted by flashbacks. His family is bizarre: they are named for the characters in the television sitcom *The Adventures of Ozzie and Harriet* (ABC, 1952–66), and their home suggests a television reality. The family responds to David with the chirpy good humor that prevails in that world. When he is unwilling to join their sitcom reality, the family suggests suicide and, in an unforgettable scene – almost unbearable in its grotesquerie – they assist him in slashing his wrists. Rabe, more markedly than any other American writer, combined the double consciousness of Brecht with the psychic cruelty demanded by Antonin Artaud. That such a play ran for more than a year in a Broadway theatre (having transferred from the Public) is a testament to its intellectual originality, relevance to its cultural moment, and undeniable theatrical effectiveness.

Rabe took a different course with *Streamers*, seen by many as his finest work. Here the contract with the audience is recognizable as realism, but this is no guarantee of predictability. Set in an army barracks in the United States in 1965, the play begins with a fragile soldier, Martin, displaying his wrist, which he has just slashed in a suicide attempt and then wrapped in a towel. Rabe deftly suggests the psychology of the seven principal characters so that our insight into their potential is limited, as in real life. He plants suggestions of underlying primal urges grounded in sexuality and race. We come to care about the characters, but are constantly aware that violence may erupt at any moment, especially with the arrival of Carlyle, a hostile, apparently mentally unstable African American soldier who resents another soldier's friendship with whites and, we learn eventually, is equally driven by a sexual agenda. In the end, two are dead. As in *Sticks and Bones*, the tension, violence, and cosmic injustice in the play are hard to endure. The first production of *Streamers* (directed by Mike Nichols) at the Long Wharf Theatre in New Haven, Connecticut, became famous for the number of audience members who walked out. The play eventually opened on Broadway, where it was praised by critics and ran for more than a year.

Another writer skilled in the grotesque was cartoonist-playwright Jules Feiffer (b. 1929). *The White House Murder Case* (1970), set in a future "several Presidential elections hence," was staged at Circle in the Square on a two-level set, with the White House above and the war scenes below. An administration bent on war as a means to popularity has ordered an invasion of Brazil. The president authorizes use of poison gas, but the gas blows the wrong way, killing hundreds of Americans. About to go public with the truth, the First Lady is stabbed to death with a wooden stick holding an anti-war sign. A cabinet member confesses to the crime in exchange for a pardon and a post in the next administration. Among other satires was Gore Vidal's *An Evening with Richard Nixon* (1972), using Nixon's own words as weapons. The play's power to wound was blunted by Vidal's inclusion of satirical portraits of other presidents, ranging from Washington to John F. Kennedy, suggesting that Nixon was not peculiar in his dishonesty and desire for empire.

A "School of Miller" would be difficult to discern in the 1970s. Arthur Miller himself continued to offer new works (see chapter 14), but the tightly structured serious play with a strong social message was not in abundance. A shining exception was by Jason Miller (1939–2001). *That Championship Season* (1972) may have been the last great three-act work of American realism. The play takes place in a small town in Pennsylvania, where each year the former basketball coach hosts a reunion of his championship team from 20 years earlier. In the mode of Arthur Miller, the characters suffer through personal crises – accusations of betrayal and deception – that lead to articulation of a larger social truth. The play won rave reviews and multiple awards, including the Pulitzer Prize, but Jason Miller turned away from writing to pursue film acting.

A vogue for topical realistic plays developed in the 1970s. This trend was likely influenced by television, where made-for-TV movies specialized in realistic dramas on current issues. Michael Christopher's *The Shadow Box* (1977), about the struggles of three hospice patients and their loved ones, was the most admired of these plays, winning the Pulitzer Prize. Opening in New York the same week was Ronald Ribman's *Cold Storage* (1977), about two dying men who share their grief and anger. Like *The Shadow Box*, Ribman's play relied upon the device of a secret revealed in the final scene, which breaks an emotional earthwork and allows emotion and forgiveness to flow. Brian Clark's *Whose Life Is It Anyway?* was truest to the thesis-play tradition, presenting through the form of drama the arguments pro and con regarding the right to die. The debate takes place in the hospital room of a man paralyzed from the neck down and who wishes to be taken off of life support. Two doctors represent differing moral and scientific positions. This play and *The Shadow Box* were widely produced around the United States and made into films.

Related to these topical works was an insurgent thread of documentary drama, reviving interest in a form that faltered after the suppression of the Federal Theatre Project and its Living Newspapers in the 1930s. *The Trial of the Catonsville Nine* (1971) was adapted by Saul Levitt from transcripts of proceedings against Catholic priests Daniel and Philip Berrigan and seven others who destroyed draft records at a Selective Service office in 1968. The event ran for three months off-Broadway and then briefly on Broadway. Eric Bentley's *Are You Now or Have You Ever Been?* (1978) was adapted by the Brecht scholar and translator from transcripts of the House Un-American Activities Committee (HUAC) hearings of the 1950s. Bentley emphasized interrogations of theatre people – Abe Burrows, Ring Lardner, Jr., Paul Robeson, and

Lillian Hellman, among others. The piece was elegantly designed and cast with well-known actors, such as Colleen Dewhurst as Hellman.

The playwright-director Emily Mann invented a new iteration of the documentary with *Anulla: An Autobiography* (1977), based on transcripts of interviews with a Holocaust survivor and produced at the Guthrie Theatre in Minneapolis. In *Still Life* (1980), Mann assembled a piece from interviews she conducted with a Vietnam veteran, his abused wife, and a female artist with whom he was having an affair. Though the work is entirely monologic, Mann's intercutting of the statements and the interpretation of the persons/characters by actors created a disturbing event. Mann later extended her technique with *Execution of Justice* (1984), employing interviews, court transcripts, and other documents to dramatize the trial of Dan White, who murdered gay City Supervisor Harvey Milk and Mayor George Moscone in San Francisco in 1978 and was convicted only of manslaughter. The piece premiered at Actors Theatre of Louisville and played on other regional stages before a brief Broadway run in 1985.

The burgeoning regional theatre movement of the 1970s contributed many outstanding works to the national repertoire. Plays by Marsha Norman and Beth Henley (see chapter 24) emerged from Actors Theatre of Louisville, as did D. L. Coburn's two-character comedy, *The Gin Game* (1977), which transferred to a Broadway house and won the Pulitzer Prize. A major dramatic event of the decade was Preston Jones's *A Texas Trilogy* (1976), three full-length plays performed in repertory. They were produced at the Dallas Theatre Center and seen there by agent Audrey Wood and director Alan Schneider, who arranged for a Washington performance at the Kennedy Center. The three plays – *Lu Ann Hampton Laverty Oberlander* (spanning 20 years and two marriages in the life of a cheerleader), *The Last Meeting of the Knights of the White Magnolia* (the last gasp of a Klan-like organization), and *The Oldest Living Graduate* (about a World War I veteran still suffering from shellshock) – present an elaborate tapestry of interconnected lives in a forsaken Texas town. The *Trilogy* was an expensive undertaking in its transfer to New York, and despite positive reviews ran for less than a month. The plays were produced at regional theatres and universities around the country. Jones (1936–79) remained in Texas, where he wrote two more plays before dying unexpectedly after ulcer surgery.

The work of Terrence McNally (b. 1939), Tina Howe (b. 1952), and Israel Horowitz (b. 1939) in the 1970s was similar in their tendency toward serious comedies, their skill at satire, and their refined abilities with linguistic humor. McNally's *Where Has Tommy Flowers Gone?* (1970) was a loosely structured collection of short scenes and monologues linked by the rebellious Tommy and his quest for meaning. The character drifts through New York City in a magical foray with a red shopping bag, into which he occasionally places objects he has stolen or otherwise acquired, finally vowing to use its contents to construct a bomb to blow himself up. *Bad Habits* (1974) allowed McNally to satirize American obsessions with perfection and therapy. The play consists of two contrasting one-acts set in contrasting hospitals. An amiable doctor who indulges his patients in excesses of drinking, smoking, and sex runs Dunelawn, the first hospital. A doctor who punishes his straitjacketed charges runs Ravenswood, the other hospital. *The Ritz* (1975) was a major break-through for McNally. The farce takes place inside a gay bathhouse with 35 doors leading to steamrooms and cubicles. An Ohio garbage contractor flees to this place, fearing his Mafioso brother-in-law, who intends to kill him. Hi-jinks ensue when he is pursued by various males and by a female singer, who auditions constantly, having mistaken him for Joseph Papp. The play was McNally's proof that he could sustain a full-length evening of comedy in a Broadway theatre. If the play was not exactly a gay pride vehicle, it did introduce mainstream audiences to a world they had not seen before and in a comic setting they could accept. *The Ritz* ran for more than a year and was made into a film.

Tina Howe's *Museum* (1978) and *The Art of Dining* (1979) experimented with linking theatre to other venues and art forms. Highly unusual in their conceptions, her plays merged theatre and performance art. *Museum* satirizes the pretentious who drift through an exhibit of contemporary art, one group destroying a set of sculptures when the guard steps out. *The Art of Dining* was performed with a fully functioning restaurant kitchen on stage, preparing high-quality food for the characters, whose menu choices and responses to the food offer information about their personal dreams and limitations.

In addition to his breakthrough, violent play, *The Indians Want the Bronx* (1968, starring Al Pacino), Israel Horowitz's outstanding work of the 1970s was the one-act *Line* (1971), showing the machinations of people struggling for position in a queue. *The Primary English Class* (1976) ran for four months at Circle in the Square. The play uses a translator to tell the audience what the non-English speakers in the class are saying, but the teacher is flustered and unable to maintain order. The extreme character types engage in various seductions, misunderstandings, and conflicts, until the teacher chases them from the room. Like many of Horowitz's plays, this one may be said to exploit a gimmick, but Horowitz's intellect is typically a step ahead of the audience, and the gimmick (or device, to be less judgmental) carries the work beyond the level of sketch comedy and into the realm of revelation.

The election of Ronald Reagan in 1980 brought a wave of pro-business policies and the pursuit of proxy wars in El Salvador and Nicaragua. The Reagan presidencies (1980–8) coincided with the ascendancy of the "religious right" to new levels of political power. After 1982, the economy improved, and a spirit of entrepreneurial capitalism swept popular culture, epitomized by a much-quoted line from Oliver Stone's film *Wall Street*, "Greed is good." The arts came under continuous attack by religious and ideological conservatives, who fought for the defunding of public support for the arts – especially the National Endowment and Corporation for Public Broadcasting. Conservative and religious activists organized protests outside theatres and pressured government and private funding agencies to cut off support to theatres accused of "anti-family" productions. These developments created a widening gulf between government and the intellectual and artistic communities.

Many American playwrights reacted to these cultural shifts with satires of American mores and with effective political drama. Plays dealt with the new national ethic of "get your own" by exposing savagery in American life. Among the most enduring of these plays is David Rabe's *Hurlyburly* (1984). More conventional and realistic in form than *Pavlo Hummel* or *Sticks and Bones*, the play has the characteristic knife-edge tension of Rabe's work. So numbed are its characters to whatever conscience they possess, one senses they are capable of great and sudden violence. The play is set in a sun-drenched house in the Hollywood Hills, where two casting agents (Mickey and Eddie) operate a constant open house for their film business friends. The men snort cocaine routinely and exchange women as property. A failing character actor (Phil) has a history of criminal violence. The other men enjoy Phil's presence, as a dangerous pet or walking projection of their inner desires. Late in the play, Phil commits suicide, leaving a puzzling note. Alone, Eddie contemplates suicide, but is interrupted by the return of a homeless young woman who had fled the house. Her innocence, as well as the timing of her arrival, is meaningful to Eddie, and the play ends ambiguously but with hope for Eddie's recovery of himself.

Lanford Wilson's outstanding play of the 1980s – *Burn This* (1987) – has much in common with *Hurlyburly*. With the exception of the double-murder ending of *Serenading Louie* (1976), Wilson had not emphasized violence and threat as primary dramatic techniques. Now he introduced an enraged character with a strange name – Pale. The play is set in a SoHo loft which Anna, a dancer, has shared with two gay men. Anna and Larry return from the funeral of Robbie, the other roommate, who died in an accident. During the night, Robbie's brother Pale bursts into the apartment under the pretense of getting his brother's things. He wants answers about why things happen, about his brother's sexuality, about what his own life is worth. Pale's language, the savagery of his constructions, his scatological inventiveness, is reminiscent of George and Martha's dueling in Albee's *Who's Afraid of Virginia Woolf?* (see chapter 16). He accuses the surviving pair of various crimes, humiliates Anna's boyfriend, and breaks down. The performance of John Malkovich as Pale dominated the production, but the play, not dependent on that performance, was produced around the country and successfully revived off-Broadway in 2002.

Comedy and satire were resurgent in the 1980s, as if the conservative social climate provoked comedic attack. Christopher Durang (b. 1949) rose to prominence with a relentless satire of the teachings and structures of the Catholic Church called *Sister Mary Ignatius Explains It All for You* (1981). The play, workshopped in 1979 at the Ensemble Studio Theatre, was paired with Durang's farce, *The Actor's Nightmare*, and directed by Jerry Zaks at Playwrights Horizons. *Sister Mary* does indeed explain it all, beginning her adult education class with a chart of our solar system, then the universe, then outside the universe where exist heaven, hell, and purgatory. Sister introduces a boy (Thomas) to assist her in presenting the lesson, asking him to read such things as a list of people who will burn in hell. The list includes Zsa Zsa Gabor and Betty Comden, but "is added to constantly." Sister proceeds to answer questions, but is interrupted by four former pupils who put on a religious pageant. Sister exposes the four as sinners – one had two abortions, another had a child out of wedlock, one man is gay (which Sister says "makes Jesus puke"), and the other is an alcoholic and spouse abuser. As this last man still maintains the sacraments, Sister rejoices that at least one has turned out a good Catholic. When one of the former pupils threatens Sister with a gun, the nun distracts her, produces her own gun and shoots her dead. Learning that the gay man has just that morning confessed his sin of homosexual acts, she kills him as well, proclaiming, "I've sent him to Heaven!" Sister falls asleep, but little Thomas sits on her lap, aiming the gun at the remaining pupil. The furor provoked by this play when it was performed around the country was the first of many waves of anti-theatrical protest in the 1980s and 1990s. As often happens, picketing and threats created interest and filled theatres to capacity. Durang's other plays of the 1980s included satires of marriage and parenthood – *Baby with the Bathwater* (1983) and *The Marriage of Bette and Boo* (1985) – and of therapy culture (*Beyond Therapy*, 1981, and *Laughing Wild*, 1987).

Like Durang, A. R. Gurney (b. 1930) studied drama at Yale and gained attention as a comic playwright in the 1970s. Gurney's work is puzzlingly self-contained – appealing to audiences, but oddly timeless, cut off from social and political concerns of the moment. Gurney's plays typically are peopled with well-to-do Easterners, highly articulate, well educated, superficially civilized, struggling to keep instincts and emotions in check. The plays are unified by a consistent technique and tone, reminiscent of the 1930s comedies of S. N. Behrman and Philip Barry. *The Dining Room* (1981) employs a theatrical device similar to ones used by Alan Ayckbourn and Thornton Wilder. Into a beautiful dining room, set in a void "as if on display in some museum, many years from now," pass a panoply of white, upper-middle-class characters, pursuing their own lives and then moving on, oblivious to the other realities inhabiting the room. Over the course of the parade of persons and scenes, one senses the value of gathering together over food and drink around polished wood, and of the sadness of its loss in a technological world.

Gurney was productive in the 1980s. *The Middle Ages* (1982) followed four characters over 40 years in their relation to a private men's club; *The Perfect Party* (1986) chronicled the extreme measures taken by a literature professor to become a party consultant; *Sweet Sue* (1987) divides a woman and the young man she desires into inner and outer selves; *Another Antigone* (1988) was a serious work about a student's charges against a professor; and *The Cocktail Hour* (1989) is a realistic comedy about a playwright who presents his well-to-do family with a play he has written about them and plans to produce. *The Cocktail Hour* displays Gurney's talent in top form. Soundly structured over two acts, with characters who are believable, whose changes are surprising yet make psychological sense, the play unfolds with grace and ease.

Tina Howe's work continued to grow in complexity in the 1980s and – like Gurney – she found a distinct path that seemed somehow unaffected by cultural change. *Painting Churches* (1983) was a departure – a sustained two-act realistic play. Howe's fascination with art continued. The adult daughter of a patrician Boston couple (named Church) comes home to paint their portrait before they relinquish their longtime home. The play's tone is comic, but relies upon exposure of painful childhood experiences, including the daughter's eating disorder, which abated when she discovered the power of making art. In *Coastal Disturbances* (1987), Howe returned to her collage technique, making a dramatic picture of visitors to a New England beach. The play is delicate, humorous, leaving the audience to interpret its events, as in a Chekhov short story.

Many accomplished works of realism appeared in the 1980s. Horton Foote contributed to his nine-play *Orphans' Home Cycle* tracing generations in rural Texas. Terrence McNally wrote the romance *Frankie and Johnny in the Claire de Lune* (1987) and a comedy about competition among "opera queens" called *The Lisbon Traviata* (1980). Mark Medoff wrote an outstanding play about the politics of deafness in *Children of a Lesser God* (1980). William Mastrosimone emerged with a forceful melodrama about rape and vengeance (*Extremities*, 1982). John Patrick Shanley became a regular presence in theatres around the country with character-driven plays very popular with actors, such as *Danny and the Deep Blue Sea* (1984), *Women of Manhattan* (1986), and *Italian American Reconciliation* (1988). But perhaps the most original, disturbing, and quintessentially 1980s work was Wallace Shawn's *Aunt Dan and Lemon* (1985).

Audiences best know Shawn as a short, doughy character actor who has appeared most memorably as the protagonist of the film *My Dinner with André* (Louis Malle, 1981); but Shawn had been an active playwright since the 1970s, closely associated with the Public Theatre. His plays *Our Late Night* (1974) and *Marie and Bruce* (1980) fascinated and puzzled audiences. Shawn's work is strange, nonconforming to dramatic genres or familiar aesthetic contracts between audience and stage. *Aunt Dan and Lemon* takes this strangeness to new levels, leaving many people frustrated and angry when the play ends, and provoking some to interrupt the performance by shouting at the characters. Lemon is a fragile-looking young woman who begins by welcoming the audience to her simple London flat. Because of her delicate health, she is unable to eat food, and drinks only the purified juices that she displays on a table. Lemon wishes to tell her story, about her Aunt Dan, and how Aunt Dan came to be her hero. So far, so good. The past begins to unfold as characters enter to enact Lemon's memories. The more we see of Aunt Dan, the more disturbing does the evening become. Dan (short for Danielle) is an Oxford professor who espouses an elaborate philosophy of might makes right, the necessity and even desirability of violence against the weak, the elimination of "vermin" such as the Viet Cong. Her idol is Henry Kissinger, whom she worships and desires for his willingness to take on the great responsibility of killing. Aunt Dan regales Lemon with stories of her friend Mindy, a prostitute who glories in her ability to blackmail men for huge sums and who murders a police informant by strangling him during sex. What makes the play especially strange is that – unlike most plays of ideas – there is no one in the play to argue with Dan's elaborately reasoned Naziesque philosophy. Lemon's mother objects, but is no match for Dan, who defeats her handily again and again. The play ends with Lemon's own articulation of the philosophy she has learned. She aspires, when she is well enough, to teach others to give thanks to those "who are willing to take the job of killing on their own backs." She sips her juice and the play ends.

Shawn has taken the notion of dialectic a step beyond Brecht. He puts the entirety of the thesis in the mouth of an intelligent and persuasive character. There is no antithesis in the play. Rather, Shawn puts the responsibility to react onto the individual audience member. In watching this play, one's mind is racing, constructing arguments to counter Aunt Dan (thus it is not surprising that at some performances people shout them out). The playwright forces us to think and decide what we believe or – if we are unwilling to do so – to accept Aunt Dan's views. Quite arguably, Shawn achieves Brecht's goal of the transformation of consciousness better than Brecht's own plays have done. One leaves this theatre transformed, charged up, angry, and ready to articulate a counter-philosophy – a philosophy that values human life for its own sake and not for what it can get for us.

NOTE

1   Production dates, casting information, and length of run data are taken from Hischak (2001).

BIBLIOGRAPHY

Bigsby, C. W. E. (1992). *Modern American Drama, 1945–1990*. New York: Cambridge University Press.

Brustein, R. (1980). *Critical Moments: Reflections on Theatre and Society, 1973–1979*. New York: Random House.

Bryer, J. R. (1994). *Lanford Wilson: A Casebook*. New York: Garland.

——(1995). *The Playwright's Art: Conversations with Contemporary American Dramatists*. New Brunswick, NJ: Rutgers University Press.

Carruth, G. (1989). *What Happened When: A Chronology of Life and Events in America*. New York: Harper and Row.

Epstein, H. E. (1994). *Joe Papp: An American Life*. Boston: Little, Brown.

Greene, A. (ed.) (2000). *Women Who Write Plays: Interviews with Contemporary American Dramatists*. Lyme, NH: Smith and Kraus.

Henretta, J. A. et al. (1987). *America's History since 1865*. Chicago: Dorsey.

Hischak, T. S. (2001). *American Theatre: A Chronicle of Comedy and Drama, 1969–2000*. New York: Oxford University Press.

Hoffman, T. (ed.) (1988). *Famous American Plays of the 1970s*. New York: Dell.

Hughes, J. R. and Cain, L. P. (2002). *American Economic History*, 6th ed. Boston: Addison-Wesley.

King, W. D. (1997). *Writing Wrongs: The Work of Wallace Shawn*. Philadelphia: Temple University Press.

Kolin, P. (1988). *David Rabe: A Stage History and Bibliography*. New York: Garland.

Lawrence, J. and Lee, R. E. (1970). *The Night Thoreau Spent in Jail*. New York: Samuel French.

Marx, R. (ed.) (1988). *Famous American Plays of the 1980s*. New York: Dell.

Savran, D. (1988). *In Their Own Words: Contemporary American Playwrights*. New York: Theatre Communications Group.

Weller, M. (1971). *Moonchildren*. New York: Delacorte.

Williams, P. M. (1993). *A Comfortable House: Lanford Wilson, Marshall W. Mason, and the Circle Repertory Theatre.* Jefferson, NC: McFarland.

Wilmeth, D. and Bigsby, C. (eds.) (2000). *The Cambridge History of American Theatre: Post-World War II to the 1990s.* Cambridge: Cambridge University Press.

Wilson, L. (1978). *The Fifth of July.* New York: Hill and Wang.

27

Maria Irene Fornes: Acts of Translation

Andrew Sofer

One of the most significant figures to emerge from the avant-garde off-off-Broadway movement of the 1960s, Cuban American playwright, director, and designer Maria Irene Fornes defies categorization. As much inspired by film and painting as by dramatic literature, Fornes's poetic theatre highlights disturbing, often violent images composed with exquisite attention to visual composition. A woman shoots a rabbit; defying logic, the bullet wounds her friend as well (*Fefu and Her Friends*). A painfully intimate scene of marital disharmony is replayed, verbatim, with hand puppets manipulated by the actors (*The Danube*). Furiously mute, a Latin American soldier in military breeches and riding boots performs jumping-jacks as long as can be endured by actor and audience (*The Conduct of Life*). By turns antic and somber, manic and freeze-framed, a Fornes play obeys its own, sometimes surreal, logic. Avant-garde by taste – she has never been interested in straightforward realism – Fornes is neither abstract nor abstruse onstage. Always one step ahead of her critics, this mercurial playwright continually breaks new theatrical ground, challenging us to register the emotional specificity of the moment without jumping to interpretive conclusions.

Although less well known than her contemporaries Sam Shepard, Lanford Wilson, and Terrence McNally, Fornes's more than 40 plays have received nine Obies – more than any other dramatist except Shepard – including a 1982 Sustained Achievement Obie "for the wit, imagination, and social outrage she has brought to off-Broadway for twenty years" (Kent 1996: 212). Among Fornes's many other awards are a two-year Playwriting Fellowship from the National Endowment for the Arts (1984), a Home Box Office Award (1985), and an Award in Literature from the American Academy and Institute of Arts and Letters (1985). She was a Pulitzer Prize finalist for *What of the Night?* (1988), and New York's Signature Theatre Company inaugurated a season-long retrospective of her work in 1999, the same year that a collection of tributes from colleagues and critics appeared in print (Delgado and Svich). According to Tony Kushner, "America has produced no dramatist of greater importance than Maria Irene Fornes" (1999: xxxiii).

An early champion of the right of playwrights to direct their own plays, Fornes has directed most of her own as well as plays by Ibsen, Chekhov, Calderon, and several contemporaries. As mentor, Fornes's impact on American theatre has been still greater. She has taught worldwide and nurtured a generation of Latino/a playwrights at INTAR (International Arts Relations) in New York, where she directed the Hispanic Writers-in-Residence Workshop until 1995, using visualization exercises to free students from predictability (see chapter 23). Shepard, Migdalia Cruz, David Henry Hwang, Cherrie Moraga, Suzan-Lori Parks, Paula Vogel, and many others attest to Fornes's influence.

Yet despite her eminence in theatrical circles, Fornes remains a coterie dramatist, "the reigning playwright of the ninety-nine-seat house" (Robinson 1999a: ix). This is in part because her spare scripts – many of which are unpublished and exist in multiple versions – are mere blueprints for the theatrical events she mounts with a painter's exactitude. Fornes is an inveterate reviser and often changes a text in rehearsal or when restaging. An auteur in the mode of Richard Foreman and Robert Wilson, Fornes possesses an imagination as much visual as verbal. Her crisp stage images recall those of Edward Hopper; their impact derives from a carefully choreographed interplay between language and silence, gesture and stillness, shadow and light. Formal, hesitant dialogue floats on the surface of these turbulent plays.

Fornes is an autodidact writing in her second language, and her plays explore acts of translation as emblems for self-transformation. Her characters continually struggle to translate thought into language, writing into speech, speech into action, action into coherent being. Quiet scenes of onstage reading recur, as characters carve out precious breathing spaces amidst painful circumstances. Diaries, letters, and journals come to life on the stage. Found texts and foreign languages invade Fornes's dialogue, as if challenging the playwright's claim to speak from a place of authority. The right to speak, indeed language itself, is never taken for granted. Expression is a hard-won achievement for both characters and playwright: "It is as if words are dampness in a porous substance – a dampness which becomes liquid and condenses. . . . I want to catch the process of the forming of thought into words" (Cummings 1985: 55).

In Fornes's denuded, often claustrophobic environments, literacy represents escape from a soul-destroying sense of exclusion and incompleteness. Reading and writing are steps toward personhood. Fornes's women, especially, struggle to translate disjointed, often traumatic experiences into a coherent narrative of self. "I feel sometimes that I am drowning in vagueness – that I have no character. I feel I don't know who I am," confesses the child-bride Marion in *Abingdon Square* (Fornes 1998: 4). For Fornes, a sense of self-worth is a prerequisite for the joys of love, companionship, and community. Yet even as her characters aspire to transcendence and communion, sexuality remains the bedrock of their experience. The tension between the demands of physical passion and the urge to purify the self impels Fornes's carnal theatre.

Fornes was born in Havana in 1930 and immigrated to the United States with her widowed mother and sister in 1945. Having grown up in a Bohemian household, she originally intended to become a painter, living in Europe from 1954 to 1957 with that goal in mind. Fornes by chance attended Roger Blin's 1954 Paris production of Samuel Beckett's *Waiting for Godot* and, despite knowing no French, was galvanized by Beckett's visual poetry: "When I left that theater I felt that my life was changed, that I was seeing everything with a different clarity" (Cummings 1985: 52). Fornes inherited not only Beckett's vaudeville sensibility (especially in her early, absurdist plays), but also Beckett's insistence on meticulous visual composition.

After returning to the United States to work as a textile designer in 1957, Fornes wrote her first play, *The Widow* (1961, unproduced until 1978), based on her translation of family letters. *Tango Palace* (originally *There! You Died*, 1963), her second play, was produced in San Francisco, Minneapolis, and New York and anthologized in a college textbook. Encouraged by its success, Fornes abandoned painting and joined the thriving avant-garde off-off-Broadway scene in the mid-1960s. She worked with such groups as the Actors Studio, where she observed Strasberg's Method; the Open Theatre, whose "transformational" style of acting she absorbed (see chapter 15); New Dramatists Workshop; and the Judson Poets Theatre. Her growing list of honors included several Obies, as well as awards from the Whitney Foundation (1961), the University of Minnesota (1965), Cintas Foundation (1967), Yale University (1967–8), Boston University (1968), the Rockefeller Foundation (1971), the Guggenheim Foundation (1972), the National Endowment for the Arts (1973), and the New York State Council on the Arts (1976). By the mid-1960s, Fornes was teaching playwriting at the Teachers and Writers Collaborative in New York and at drama festivals and workshops. Fornes also branched out into directing, designing, and producing. In 1973 she became president of the New York Theatre Strategy, an organization that produced the work of experimental American playwrights, a post she held until 1979. Taking control of the mise en scène proved a necessary step in her artistic development, and Fornes asserted directorial control over her plays beginning with the wistful fantasy-Western *Molly's Dream* (New Dramatists Workshop, 1968).

Fornes's early plays are existential vaudevilles, often in exuberant musical form inspired by 1930s film. Exposure to the Actors Studio led Fornes to experiment with aleatory compositional techniques in order to produce free-flowing action and characterization. Besides *Tango Palace* (San Francisco Actors Workshop, 1963), plays from this fertile period include *The Successful Life of 3* (Firehouse, Minneapolis, 1965); *Promenade* (Judson Poets Theatre, 1965, revised 1969), with music by Reverend Al Carmines; *Molly's Dream*; and *Dr. Kheal* (Village Gate and New Dramatists Workshop, 1968).[1] The latter, a monologue spoofing academic claims to knowledge, has become her most-produced play after *Fefu and Her Friends*. Fornes also wrote a failed Broadway sex farce, *The Office* (Henry Miller, 1966), and two anti-war plays, the burlesque satire *The Red Burning Light; or, Mission XQ3* (Open Theatre, 1968), and an audience-participation piece, *A Vietnamese Wedding* (Washington Square Methodist Church,

1967). In the latter, members of the audience were invited to enact a traditional Vietnamese wedding as a gentle exercise in empathy. With typically understated irony, Fornes offered *A Vietnamese Wedding* as her contribution to "Angry Arts Week," a week-long anti-war protest.

The struggle to quell internalized voices that claim authority over subjective experience animates the absurdist *Tango Palace*. In a padlocked room that features a shrine and a Beckettian assortment of found props (masks, swords, a whip, beetle masks, banderillas), a straightlaced young businessman, Leopold, emerges from a canvas sack to find himself tortured by Isidore, an androgynous clown and would-be tutor: "This is my whip. (*Lashing Leopold.*) And that is pain" (Fornes 1987: 72). Isidore and Leopold play out sadomasochistic scenarios – a tango, a bullfight, a duel – while their dialogue is pre-scripted on cards that Isidore flips at Leopold as he recites his canned speeches. Leopold tries to break free but finds his every move predetermined by the cards; when he defies Isidore's warning and tries to burn the cards, Isidore trips him up and announces, "There! You died" (76). Leopold remains trapped (as in Hegel's parable of master and slave) by his demand for recognition. The Pozzo and Lucky-like pair are caught in a symbiotic relationship with no exit. Despite the antic zest of Isidore's routines, *Tango Palace* is a claustrophobic nightmare from which the callow Leopold, doomed to seek Isidore's love for eternity, can never escape.

Less didactic than *Tango Palace*, *The Successful Life of 3* is a charming sketch-comedy that burlesques the delusions of romantic love. Eschewing psychological realism, the play braids comic vignettes and wry non-sequiturs. He, "a handsome young man," and She, "a sexy young lady," find their conventionally dull marriage continually infiltrated by 3, "a plump, middle-aged man," who enjoys a parasitic life of erotic and professional fulfillment at He's expense. Fornes insists on the surrealism of everyday behavior, the comic extent to which we reinvent reality to suit ourselves. Nowhere is this more evident than in the absurdities of marriage. 3 and She enjoy various absurd adventures but always return to the triangular arrangement that ultimately suits their complacency. Older but no wiser, the trio conclude their drama with a cheerful, Brechtian Song to Ignorance: "Let me be wrong / But also not know it" (Fornes 1987: 64).

Fornes's greatest commercial success, the musical *Promenade*, broadens the scope of her social satire to include the hypocrisy of the justice system, the exploitation of the poor, and the complacency of the rich. Two prisoners, 105 and 106, dig a hole under the nose of a jailer more concerned with extorting sex from the jail's female visitors than preventing escape. These innocents then take a tour of human folly and misery, averting their gaze from the horror as they fill their pockets with booty: "When I was born I opened my eyes, / And when I looked around I closed them; / And when I saw how people get kicked in the head, / And kicked in the belly, and kicked in the groin, / I closed them" (Fornes 1987: 37). Class satire dominates: the poor find themselves conscripted on the battlefield, while flirtatious and bubble-headed aristocrats celebrate a banquet featuring a naked lady, Miss Cake, bounding from the pastry. Joined by a saucy servant, 105 and 106 embark on a carefree life of crime, noting that costume alone separates criminal and capitalist (they pin their convict jackets on a hit-and-run victim who is hauled off to jail in their stead). Comically reunited with their long-lost mother, 105 and 106 return to their cell content at the world's inequities: "And for those who have no cake, / There's plenty of bread" (45). A vaudeville with a sting in its tail, the play was a critical hit and moved uptown, where its theatre was renamed The Promenade in honor of the play's extraordinary nine-month run.

The early 1970s was a fallow period for Fornes, as she concentrated on her administrative work for New York's Theatre Strategy and produced few plays: *The Curse of the Langston House* (Cincinnati Playhouse in the Park, 1972), *Aurora* (Theatre Strategy, 1973), and *Cap-a-Pie* (INTAR, 1975). But *Fefu and Her Friends* (Theatre Strategy, 1977; American Place Theatre, 1978) proved her greatest critical success. This landmark feminist play marks a shift in Fornes's work from vaudevillian playfulness toward a darker, more socially aware and psychologically probing dramaturgy.

Fefu also features Fornes's boldest staging innovation to date. Part 1 takes place in a living room, behind a proscenium frame in the mode of "fourth wall" realism. For the middle section of the play, the audience is divided into four groups, each of which moves to a different space in the theatre to witness four intimate chamber scenes set in lawn, study, bedroom, and kitchen, respectively. The scenes take place simultaneously for the characters (several characters move from scene to scene), and the audience can watch them in any order. After each scene has been played identically four times, the spectators regroup in the main auditorium to watch the final act, their frontal perspective on the action deepened and disturbed by Fornes's site-specific staging.[2]

On the surface, the play celebrates theatre's ability to create a female community. In 1935, eight women gather at a country house owned by Stephany (Fefu) to rehearse a fund-raising presentation on women's education. In the course of the day, the women drift apart and come together, often in a tone of blithe improvisation, as when the rehearsal devolves into a water fight, or when Fefu introduces her off-stage husband, Phillip, to conventional Christina by shooting blanks at him:

Fefu: You haven't met Phillip. Have you?
Christina: No.
Fefu: That's him.
Christina: Which one?
Fefu: (*Aims and shoots.*) That one!
(*Christina and Cindy scream. Fefu smiles proudly. She blows on the mouth of the barrel.*) (Fornes 1992: 10–11)

But the play's freewheeling surface is deceptive. No man ever appears onstage, yet Phillip, together with Fefu's younger brother and a gardener, constantly threatens to impinge on this tenuous community of women, which remains confined in the house. "They are well together," Fefu observes of the men. "Women are not. Look at them. They are checking the new grass mower.... Out in the fresh air and the sun, while we sit here in the dark" (15).

Fefu exposes the dark side of women's experience. Each woman has in some way been damaged or limited in life choices (with the possible exception of the ebullient Emma, who joins the men outside). Trapped in an unhappy marriage, Fefu is in the early stages of clinical depression. Working-class Paula has been abandoned by Cecilia, her lover; Cindy has just broken up with a man. Julia, Fefu's friend, has been injured in a bizarre hunting accident: we are told that when a nearby hunter shot a deer, Julia suffered convulsions. She is now confined to a wheelchair. Julia's disability literalizes the other women's emotional paralysis and acquires an added, symbolic dimension in the course of the play. Julia suffers from visions in which she is tormented by invisible judges, who have punished her refusal to accept a patriarchal prayer (which begins, "The human being is of the masculine gender") by paralyzing her. Julia's hallucinatory monologue in Part 2 makes Fornes's most explicit feminist statement: "They say when I believe the prayer I will forget the judges. And when I forget the judges I will believe the prayer. They say both happen at once. And all women have done it. Why can't I?" (35).

The judges threaten Fefu, who chafes at the restrictions placed upon her by her gender yet shares her husband's distaste for female sexuality. Fefu's anger at her husband is displaced into shooting Phillip with a gun loaded (by him) with blanks: "It suits our relationship... the game, I mean. If I didn't shoot him with blanks, I might shoot him for real" (13). Fefu is capable of love and tenderness toward the other women, but at root she is isolated and fearful: "I am in constant pain.... It is as if normally there is a lubricant ... not in the body... a spiritual lubricant ... it's hard to describe ... and without it, life is a nightmare, and everything is distorted" (29).

In Part 3, rehearsal brings the fractured community of women together. Emma performs an extract from pioneer children's educator Emma Sheridan Fry's *The Science of Educational Dramatics*, a 1917 textbook whose call to embrace the spirit through artistic expression counterpoints the judges' repressive prayer. Yet the tone shifts abruptly when Fefu has a vision of Julia walking. Determined to prove that her friend's illness is psychosomatic, Fefu pulls Julia from the wheelchair. When Julia refuses to fight her condition, Fefu reaches for her gun and exits. *"There is the sound of a shot.... Julia puts her hand to her forehead. Her hand goes down slowly. There is blood on her forehead. Her head falls back"* (61). A bewildered Fefu reenters holding a dead rabbit, and the lights fade as the other women surround Julia's body.

No other moment in Fornes's writing has provoked as much debate. Some critics view Fefu's killing of Julia as a necessary, liberatory act: "Fefu is acting out the role of subject. To act has been Fefu's triumph" (Moroff 1996: 55). But while the play's final image is ambiguous, Fornes's parable is clear. Just as the hunter's shooting of a helpless deer enables the numinous judges to punish Julia, so Fefu's shooting of a helpless rabbit allows them to dispose of her. Although Fefu claims, "I'm never angry," and has supposedly given up hunting, her frustration eventually explodes – only to find the wrong target (14). Unless channeled productively, warns Fornes, repressed female rage will harm other women. Yet the play is not fatalistic, for the friends' antic solicitude holds out the possibility that if women can free themselves from the judges' prayer, they can become each other's spiritual guardians (as Emma guards Fefu). Despite its shocking denouement, *Fefu* is ultimately hopeful.

Fefu's deepening commitment to psychological exploration concludes the first phase in Fornes's career (1961–77).[3] In 1978, Fornes began a nearly decade-long relationship with the Padua Hills Festival in Los Angeles. Staging works-in-progress outdoors liberated her use of space still further, as did her longstanding collaborations with lighting designer Anne Militello, set designer Donald Eastman, and costume designer Gabriel Berry. Fragmentary scenes, disruption of perspective, chiaroscuro lighting, and distortions of scale characterize Fornes's work of the 1980s and 1990s, as does her incorporation of found props and objects, such as the Hungarian language tapes that inspired *The Danube* (Padua Hills, 1982), her most apocalyptic play.

For Fornes, the tapes' mundane transactions and polite exchanges evoked a lost world of working-class civility, a Europe destroyed by war. *The Danube* takes place on a bare platform, features simple props and postcard-style backdrops, and proceeds in short episodes that follow language instruction convention. At the start of most scenes, a tape plays a sentence in English and then in Hungarian, followed by enough blank tape for the actor to speak the same line naturalistically. Between scenes ominous smoke rises from several places on the stage floor.

The play traces a gentle courtship between two young people from different cultures. Paul, a young American working in Budapest on the eve of World War II, falls in love with shy Eve, who studies both German and English – a sign of Hungary's uncertainty about the future. Fornes limns a culture in jeopardy. A waiter warns, "You should eat when you can. The crops have not been good" (Fornes 1986: 51). Eve faints at the restaurant; Paul comes down with what seems like anemia. A starving barber politely begs Paul for milk and meat. Soon the characters are wearing goggles, suffering skin ailments, and experiencing mysterious spasms. Paul marries Eve and joins the Hungarian army, but the stresses of war and sickness pull the couple apart. Stiff, formal speeches become almost unbearably poignant. Confined to a sanatorium, Paul laments: "We are all useless to Hungary. We cannot save her. Oh, Hungary, we cannot save you" (57). "My dearest," Eve writes to Paul at the front, "Life escapes from us like blood out of a wound" (58).

The play departs from chronological narrative and spins into nightmare. A scene in which Paul accuses Eve is repeated by puppets whose appearance is identical to the characters; the puppets then perform a scene of packing suitcases that is repeated, with slight variation, by the actors playing Eve and Paul. The family unit fractures as the couple take leave of Eve's ailing father. Eve delivers a valediction – "We die at last, my

Danube" – and the play closes with "*a brilliant white flash of light*" that engulfs the characters (64). *The Danube* contrasts Paul's love affair with Old Europe with the threats of cultural imperialism, economic exploitation, and nuclear Armageddon. Fornes comments in an interview, "To me the loss of that innocence and over sophistication is a crime against humanity. It's like a violation of the personality or the environment with pollution" (Fornes 1999a: 229).

The Danube features a rarity for Fornes: a loving father–daughter relationship. Absent parents are recurrent Fornes motifs, as in her play *Mud* (Padua Hills, 1983). *Mud* focuses on a young woman's relationship with two sexual rivals who are, respectively, brother- and father-figure. Mae, Lloyd, and Henry are impoverished rural characters perched almost literally on the edge of an abyss. *Mud* takes place in a wooden room that sits on a 5-ft-high promontory of earth. The wood "*has the color and texture of bone that has dried in the sun*," in contrast with the soft, red earth of the promontory. There is a blue sky but "*no greenery*" (Fornes 1986: 15). Against this bleak background a tragedy takes place, as Mae, "a spirited young woman," struggles to escape the men's dependence on her for affection, food, and shelter (14).

Co-dependent Mae and Lloyd have grown up together since Mae's father adopted Lloyd as a child. Now in their twenties, they live together as man and wife on Mae's subsistence ironing wages. Lloyd tends their meager farm but is impotent, unemployable, and ill. Threatened by Mae's attempts to gain literacy at school, the unlettered Lloyd keeps Mae through a combination of threats and guilt. Mae holds Lloyd in contempt, but her low self-esteem prevents her from emancipating herself: "I feel I am hollow…and offensive" (24). The dynamic changes when Mae brings Henry, an intelligent but barely literate man in his fifties, into the household. Alive to the beauty of Henry's mind, Mae takes Henry as her lover, displacing the jealous Lloyd, who takes money from Henry's purse to pay for medicine. In a twist of irony, Henry is paralyzed by a stroke and must be fed slop, like Lloyd's pigs. Henry steals the money Lloyd owes him from Mae, enraging her. Exhausted by the responsibility of supporting both men, Mae places Henry in Lloyd's care and walks out. The desperate Lloyd shoots Mae to prevent her abandoning him. As she dies, Mae identifies with the starfish she has read about in her grammar school textbook: "Like the Starfish, I live in the dark and my eyes see only a faint light. It is faint and yet it consumes me. I long for it. I thirst for it. I would die for it. Lloyd, I am dying" (40).

While it is tempting to read the play as a parable of gender oppression, Fornes views the trio's tragedy as a product of socioeconomic circumstance and depicts the characters as essentially decent but abandoned children. Fornes bristles at the suggestion that Mae is the men's victim or somehow more selfless than they are, and she does not condemn Lloyd for shooting Mae, who has used him emotionally and sexually (Fornes 1999b: 231). *Mud* is feminist not because the men are oppressors, but "because the central character is a woman, and the theme" – the hunger of the mind to educate itself – "is one that writers usually deal with through a male character" (Fornes 1999a: 227). Fornes insists that these characters are too caught up in the struggle to survive to act out concepts of traditional sex roles; yet, as so often in her work, a spirited young woman is destroyed as a result of the conflict between dependence and self-realization.

This conflict replays itself in *Sarita* (INTAR, 1984), a study in sexual dependency set in the South Bronx between 1939 and 1947. Cuban American teenager Sarita Fernandez lives with her mother, Fela. Sarita's father, a merchant seaman, abandoned Fela when he discovered she was pregnant, and the pattern of parental abandonment recurs in the next generation. At 13, Sarita falls in love with the charismatic but feckless Julio. Pregnant at 14, Sarita abandons her son two years later to be with Julio, from whom she repeatedly fails to break free. Sarita is saved from suicide by Mark, a soldier whom she tries to love in return for his kindness. Nevertheless, she finds herself drawn back to Julio, who eventually attempts to blackmail her. Sarita stabs Julio and ends the play incarcerated in a mental hospital.

Whereas *Mud* suggests that Mae's fate might have been different in other circumstances, *Sarita* implies that biology is destiny. Sarita is doomed by her passionate attraction to Julio, whereas "[men] don't want a family. They don't feel like women that they want to have a baby.... For them it's a weight on their backs. It's being chained" (Fornes 1986: 119). Consumed by sexual jealousy, Sarita cannot conceive of a life of her own beyond childhood fantasies of law and medical school: "Other people don't have to learn how to be. But I'm a savage. I have to learn how to live my life" (100). Although the play implicates both Fela's neglect and the Church's repressive attitude toward female sexuality, the stages of Sarita's descent into madness resemble Stations of the Cross in a passion play. Suffering is leavened by occasional musical numbers and by brief celebrations of female companionship, as when Sarita and Fela dance a gleeful jitterbug before an altar to the Virgin of La Caridad del Cobre. But the play's expressionistic set dwarfs the women's aspirations for a better life.

The Conduct of Life (Theatre for the New City, 1985) is a violent melodrama shorn of Fornes's characteristic playfulness and wit. Orlando, a lieutenant in an unnamed Latin American country, rises to lieutenant commander by conducting torture on behalf of the state. The play links state and domestic violence through the three people Orlando controls: Leticia, his trophy wife; Olimpia, a middle-aged servant; and Nena, a 12-year-old girl whom Orlando abducts and sexually tortures, first in a warehouse and then in the basement of his own home. The set externalizes Orlando's compartmentalized psyche. Four receding horizontal planes represent living room, dining room, hallway, cellar, and (10 feet above the cellar) warehouse. As the play unfolds, Orlando's secret life invades the upper-middle-class home's "civilized" spaces of social interaction. Nena moves from warehouse to cellar to dining room (where Nena and Olimpia sort beans, the play's only glimpse of female solidarity) to living room.

The Conduct of Life examines the interlocking systems of sexual, economic, and gender exploitation. Orlando's career path demands a sadism he strives to sublimate: "Man must have an ideal, mine is to achieve maximum power.... I must no longer be overwhelmed by sexual passion or I will be degraded beyond hope of recovery" (Fornes 1986: 68). Orlando proves unable to separate the genteel and horrific conduct of his domestic and professional lives, installing Nena as a domestic servant/slave and convincing himself that his exploitation is a form of love.

The adult women respond according to their social positions. Leticia realizes that Orlando married her for social advancement but protects him nonetheless. She at first lives in denial of Nena's presence in the house, but then connives in Orlando's actions. Leticia takes out her frustration on her maid, Olimpia, whose life of menial chores secures Orlando's and Leticia's middle-class status. Class prevents Leticia and Olimpia from forming an alliance based on gender; to Olimpia, Leticia is simply the "boss." Olimpia comforts Nena and eventually lashes out at Orlando, risking her job. By contrast, when Orlando threatens Leticia physically, she shoots him out of an urge for self-preservation and, panicked, places the revolver in Nena's hands. Nena takes the gun *"in a state of terror and numb acceptance"* (88).

As in *Fefu*'s shooting of the rabbit/Julia, Leticia's rage backfires on a more vulnerable woman. Like Fornes's earlier study in patriarchal oppression, *The Conduct of Life* is a *Lehrstück* (learning-play, a dramaturgical device devised by Bertolt Brecht to encourage didactic drama), but the question of whether torturers are made rather than born – whether Orlando is symptom or root of state violence – is left undecided. Orlando's sadism pushes the play in the direction of melodrama despite its determination to avoid voyeurism. Fornes has argued that the invisible generals (a parallel to *Fefu*'s judges) are the true oppressors in the play; that Orlando is "just a peon in the political system"; and that "those women are strong" (Savran 1988: 68, 67). But it is hard not to see Orlando as monstrous or the three women as his victims, despite Fornes's claim that the women resist rather than maintain the situation. If Orlando is demonized, Nena is sanctified as a martyr: "I want to conduct each day of my life the best possible way. I should value the things that I have.... And if someone should treat me unkindly, I should not blind myself with rage, but I should see them and receive them since maybe they are in worse pain than me" (Fornes 1986: 84–5).

Besides *The Conduct of Life*, the mid-1980s observed Fornes adapting Virgilio Piñero (*Cold Air*, INTAR, 1985), Ibsen (*Hedda Gabler*, Milwaukee Repertory Theatre, 1987), and Chekhov (*Drowning*, Acting Company National Tour, 1985; *Uncle Vanya*, CSC Repertory Theatre, 1987); staging history (*The Trial of Joan of Arc at Rouen in a Matter of Faith*, Theatre for the New City, 1986); and collaborating with Tito Puente and Fernando Rivas on a musical play (*Lovers and Keepers*, INTAR, 1986). Her most substantial work of this period, *Abingdon Square* (Seattle Repertory Theatre, 1984; American Place Theatre, 1987), crystallizes many key Fornes concerns in a muted style.

Like *Sarita*, *Abingdon Square* anatomizes female sexual guilt. In 1908, Marion, a 15-year-old orphan, marries the lonely widower Juster out of gratitude and a sense of obligation. In abrupt, often impressionistic scenes, the play follows Marion between the ages of 15 and 24 as she fights the benign claustrophobia of Juster's house on

Tenth Street in New York City. Finding herself attracted to Juster's son Michael, who is her age, Marion seeks atonement through a private rite in Juster's attic, where she stands on her toes and recites from Dante's *Purgatorio* until she collapses. After inventing a love affair in her diary, Marion becomes pregnant through a chance encounter with a workman and eventually takes a lover, Frank, renting an apartment in Abingdon Square for their liaisons. When Juster discovers a rent receipt, he ejects Marion and takes custody of her son, Thomas. Failed by Frank and enraged by Juster's refusal to let her see Thomas, Marion degenerates into promiscuity and paranoia. *Abingdon Square* concludes with another act of violence whose impact backfires, recalling *Fefu*. Juster shoots at Marion in a rage and falls into a coma, having suffered a stroke. Abandoned by Frank, Marion returns to the house on Tenth Street to nurse her dying husband. In the play's final scene, Marion and Juster embrace as Michael returns from the army (where he enlisted to escape rival tugs of loyalty to father and stepmother). The riven family unit reconstitutes itself; but although *"a bright light"* shines in the final tableau, Fornes once more confines Marion in the household that has stifled her (Fornes 1988: 10). Unusually for Fornes, all the major characters, with the exception of the spineless young lover, are sympathetic. *Abingdon Square* is Fornes's most delicate treatment of the conflict between duty and passion.

Having achieved an intimate domestic drama with *Abingdon Square*, Fornes combined four one-act plays (*Nadine*, *Springtime*, *Lust*, *Hunger*) into an epic sequence, *What of the Night?* (originally *And What of the Night?*, Milwaukee Repertory Theatre, 1988; Trinity Repertory Company, 1989). Recalling O'Neill's generational sagas, the sequence indicts the hardening of the American soul and the leaching of our compassion for the poor. *What of the Night?* begins in the economically depressed Southwest of 1938 and traces 60 years in the life of three siblings, Ray, Charlie, and Rainbow. Each hungers for love but falls prey to the implacable forces of brutalization.

Nadine recalls Erskine Caldwell in its unsparing portrayal of poverty. Homeless Nadine prostitutes herself to support her children, Charlie and Rainbow, and her sick baby, Lucille. While Nadine trades sex for money from the brutish Pete, Pete extorts clothes to sell from Charlie, an innocent teenager. When Charlie refuses to strip the clothing from an unconscious bum, Pete beats him. Economic desperation frays bonds of familial affection: "I have nothing good to give [my children], nothing to teach them," remarks Nadine (Fornes 1993: 171). But Birdie, a tough, streetwise orphan of 14 befriended by Nadine's family, represents hope for escape. Pursued by Pete and drawn in to a dead-end marriage with Charlie, Birdie walks out at the end of *Nadine*, suggesting that escape from heredity and environment may be possible.

Springtime portrays a delicate love affair that flares up only to disappear in darkness. Rainbow, now 29, tries to save her sick German lover, Greta, first by stealing and then by engaging in pornography at the behest of the mysterious Ray, who (unbeknownst to them) is Rainbow's brother, given away for adoption by Nadine when Rainbow was a baby. Love between two women is taken for granted as an alternative to male coercion: "If I don't like men why should I pretend that I do?" asks Rainbow. "Why should I try to love someone I don't love when I already love someone I love? And besides, do you think it makes a difference to anyone?" (Fornes 1993: 184). Rainbow's lines are the closest Fornes has come to declaring a lesbian poetics. But Ray literally invades the women's domestic scene of caregiving to prey on Greta, and at the play's end Rainbow, feeling exhausted and unloved, abandons her lover. The pattern of abandonment in the face of male brutality repeats itself.

If *Springtime* is a delicate love story, *Lust* is an operatic marriage play that moves the work further into O'Neill territory. Ray, now 37, is *"passionate and driven"* (Fornes 1993: 192). *Lust* traces Ray's ferocious rise to power as he cynically marries the privileged Helena, takes over her father Joseph's business, and seduces the now middle-aged Birdie. In one of Fornes's most shocking scenes, Joseph matter-of-factly violates Ray sexually as the men discuss setting up a scholarship fund for an underprivileged boy. Fornes grotesquely parodies a parental relationship, suggesting that capitalist relations preempt any need for female presence. Although Ray holds Helena in contempt, repeated references to milk suggest that both hunger for maternal love (a trait shared by all the characters). Ray, whose sexual conflicts are externalized in an expressionistic dream sequence, sublimates his emotional needs into will-to-power, at the price of Helena's and Birdie's happiness. Helena is another Fornes study in female dependence; although refined, as the others are not, she is merely a collection of neurotic symptoms.

Hunger concludes the tetralogy *"after an economic disaster"* (Fornes 1993: 219). The now elderly characters are reduced to foragers seeking shelter in a warehouse. In this bleak, Beckettian wasteland, Ray is destitute and in rags, Charlie is senile, and Birdie collapses. The Great Depression of 1998 takes place in a crueler America than that of 1938: homelessness is bureaucratized and the poor are literally ware-housed. Charlie acts as caretaker of the shelter; Ray, evicted from the compound that houses the privileged class, must forage for scraps to sell (as Charlie once did in *Nadine*). Simple acts of kindness and generosity, as when Birdie shares her loaf of bread with Ray, punctuate a general air of decay. *Hunger* ends with the characters kneeling before a broken-winged angel who offers animal entrails – omens of a hopeless future – rather than sustenance. *What of the Night?* is a dance of death to the music of time.

Having plumbed the lower depths in *What of the Night?*, Fornes turns from the tragedy of familial relations to the possibility of artful connections. She revisits the erotic absurdism of *The Successful Life of 3* in *Oscar and Bertha* (Padua Hills, 1991), a tale of two lascivious siblings whose exuberant sexuality is unconstrained by convention. Fornes's plays of the 1990s ultimately celebrate the value of art, creativity, and play as responses to America's current spiritual and economic crisis. Although less well received than her passion plays of the previous decade, they constitute an important chapter in Fornes's unpredictable career.

Enter the Night (1993, New City Theatre, Seattle), Fornes's response to AIDS, asks whether grace can be wrested from illness and suffering without falling into "victim art" or the easy solutions proffered by domestic realism (the same question that motivates Kushner's *Angels in America*). The three friends Jack, Tressa, and Paula each have serious problems but refuse hysteria, embracing politically incorrect role play – Tressa dresses as the Oriental character from D. W. Griffith's film *Broken Blossoms* – as a force for spiritual healing. *Enter the Night* celebrates rituals of performance, from Jack's own play to enacted scenes from movies. However, Jack's grief for a dead lover, together with survival guilt, leads him to a bloody, sadomaso-chistic off-stage encounter with a gang of thugs. The women comfort him by reciting passages from Capra's *Lost Horizon*, a therapeutic ritual in which the power of art triumphs over Jack's death-drive. *Enter the Night* insists that sustaining connections can be forged beyond the nuclear family; Paula has a husband and children, but her closest tie is to Tressa. Unlike Rainbow and Greta, this couple has transcended possessiveness in favor of tenderness unsustainable in *What of the Night?* For once, domestic space becomes a space of comfort and replenishment, and Fornes's wit returns as Jack sardonically envisions a future theatre in which "The leading charac-ters will have the illness most common among theatergoers. . . . Plays will be funded by pharmaceutical laboratories" (Fornes 1996: 159).

The Summer in Gossensass (1997, The Women's Project at the Harold Clurman Theatre, New York) pays tribute to *Hedda Gabler*, the only play Fornes claims to have read before embarking on her writing career. Set in London in 1891, the play reconstructs the attempts of two actresses – American Elizabeth Robins (suffragette author of *Votes for Women!*) and her friend Marion Lea – both to stage the first English production of Ibsen's notorious play and, since they lack a complete English transla-tion of the script, to piece together clues to Hedda's character and motivation from textual fragments. A literary detective story with Hedda's elusive motivation as the quarry, *Gossensass* affectionately portrays the actresses' oscillation between elation and despondency. In this sunny work, female artistic collaboration triumphs over feminine rivalry; the dour Norwegian, about whose love life the women giddily speculate, brings Elizabeth and Marion together in an act of translation that for once does not result in violence. Their inspired guesses about Hedda produce a comedy of misreading.

Fornes's most recent play, *Letters from Cuba* (2000), is the first since *Sarita* directly to address female Cuban American identity. Juxtaposing the pathos of exile with the longing to make art, the play takes place in a New York apartment shared by three aspiring artists in their twenties. Marc and Joseph both love Fran, a Cuban dancer who receives a series of letters from her brother Luis in Cuba (culled from Fornes's letters from her own brother), poetically tossed from a stage rooftop. *Letters from Cuba* harks back to Fornes's first play, *The Widow*, in which family letters convey the Cuban émigré experience, even as the theme of exile – resulting in family reunion thanks to the power of art – invokes Shakespearean romance. By magically translating Luis and his son, Enrique, from Cuba to the New York apartment, the play brings Fornes's art full circle. Fornes received her ninth Obie for her writing and direction, evidence that the two aspects of her artistry are inseparable.

Given her four-decade career in the theatre, Fornes has received less critical attention than she deserves. Nevertheless, the number of Fornes monographs, essays, and dissertations increases yearly. Broadly speaking, Fornes critics tend to fall into two camps (with some crossover; see Garner 1994): "phenomenologists" and "materialists." Beginning with Michael Smith's and Robert Pasolli's appreciative *Village Voice* reviews in the 1960s, the former camp focuses on communicating the exhilarating, sometimes disorienting experience of attending a Fornes play, and the ways in which it resists conventional literary analysis. These critics often characterize Fornes's drama by analogy to artistic movements such as absurdism (Zinman), metatheatre (Moroff), hyperrealism (Wetzsteon), and Latin American surrealism (Robinson 1999b; Fuchs). Fornes advocates such as Cummings (1999), Drukman, Marranca, and Sontag emphasize the way Fornes strips away the trappings of realism – including coherent narrative, plot development, and psychological motive – to convey her characters' essential subjectivity. The phenomenologists do not shy away from dramaturgical analysis or textual explication, but in general stress Fornes's *theatrical* innovation and its immediacy in performance. By contrast, materialist critics foreground Fornes's treatment of ethnicity, sex, class, and gender from the perspective of social critique. Almost all emphasize the feminist dimension to Fornes's work (a dimension she has warily acknowledged), together with her empathy for the underprivileged and marginalized.[4] Thus Fornes's deeply humanist aesthetic has been analyzed through the lenses of materialist feminism (Kent), poststructuralism (Wolf, Geis), and Bakhtinian heteroglossia (Keyssar), amongst others. Plainly a multiplicity of critical categories exists through which to explore this protean playwright.

Fornes herself remains suspicious of critics and categories. While the Latina and lesbian aspects of her work have attracted attention, Fornes names Chekhov, Beckett, Brecht, and Ionesco as her forebears and has, not uncontroversially, praised the humanist "standard of excellence" by which she wishes to be judged. Yet despite her disavowal of identity politics, Fornes acknowledges that her founding of the INTAR Hispanic Playwrights Lab in 1981 was inspired by "trying to discover a Hispanic sensibility," and her nurturing of a generation of Hispanic playwrights remains her most visible legacy to the American theatre (Svich 1999: xvi). While her own work has never found a permanent home in the regional theatres, Maria Irene Fornes deserves a wider audience as well as a broader readership. Hers is the dynamic, "plastic" theatre her fellow stage poet Tennessee Williams once called for.

NOTES

1. Parenthetical venues and dates refer to a play's first production. For production histories of Fornes's plays through 1998, see Delgado and Svich (1999: 280–91). As of 1998, *Fefu and Her Friends* received 45 professional, amateur, and college productions; *Dr. Kheal*, 39; *The Successful Life of 3*, 33; *Mud*, 27; *Promenade*, 20; *The Conduct of Life*, 16; and *The Danube*, 12,

making these Fornes's most staged works. Many Fornes plays have never received a second professional production.

2. While Worthen and others interpret Fornes's prismatic staging as an ideological critique of realism, Fornes claims that she was serendipitously inspired by a visit to the Relativity Media Lab, whose spaces suggested various

rooms in Fefu's house (Marranca 1978: 108). Many critics have joined the debate over whether *Fefu*'s stage experimentation establishes a feminist, anti-realist poetics; for a representative sample, see Fuchs (1999), Keyssar (1991), Wolf (1992), and Zinman (1990). In 1996 Fornes wrote a one-set version of the play to maximize the number of theatres that may perform the work.

3. Most critics note *Fefu* as a clear turning point, but the fact that so many Fornes plays remain unpublished renders it difficult to divide her prolific career into neat phases. For instance, the period between *Fefu* and *The Danube* includes *Lolita in the Garden* (1977); *In Service* (1978); *Eyes on the Harem* (1979); *Evelyn Brown* (1980); the adaptations *Blood Wedding* (1980)

and *Life is a Dream* (1981); and *A Visit* (1981). My overview silently omits from discussion these and other unpublished plays, translations, libretti, and adaptations.

4. In a 1985 interview, Fornes states: "I am a feminist in that I am very concerned and I suffer when women are treated in a discriminatory manner and when I am treated in a discriminatory manner because I am a woman. But I never thought that I should not do certain work because I'm a woman nor did I think I should do certain work because I'm a woman" (Cummings 1985: 55). Fornes resists ideological labels, insisting that it is art's function to teach an audience without sloganeering.

BIBLIOGRAPHY

Cummings, S. (1985). "Seeing with Clarity: The Visions of Maria Irene Fornes." *Theater* 17: 51–6.

——(1999). "'The Poetry of Space in a Box': Scenography in the Work of Maria Irene Fornes." In Marc Robinson (ed.), *The Theater of Maria Irene Fornes*. Baltimore: Johns Hopkins University Press, 174–85.

Delgado, M. M. and Svich, C. (1999). *Conducting a Life: Reflections on the Theatre of Maria Irene Fornes*. Lyme, NH: Smith and Kraus.

Drukman, S. (2000). "Notes on Fornes (With Apologies to Sontag)." *American Theatre* 17: 36–9, 85.

Fornes, M. I. (1986). *Plays*. New York: Performing Arts Journal Publications.

——(1987). *Promenade and Other Plays*. New York: Performing Arts Journal Publications.

——(1988). *Abingdon Square. American Theatre* 4: 1–10.

——(1992). *Fefu and Her Friends*. New York: Performing Arts Journal Publications.

——(1993). *What of the Night?* In Rosette Lamont (ed.), *Women on the Verge: Seven Avant-Garde American Plays*. New York: Applause, 157–235.

——(1996). *Enter the Night*. In Bonnie Marranca (ed.), *Plays for the End of the Century*. Baltimore: Johns Hopkins University Press, 121–79.

——(1999a). "From an Interview with Allen Frame." In Marc Robinson (ed.), *The Theater of Maria Irene Fornes*. Baltimore: Johns Hopkins University Press, 207–8.

——(1999b). "Creative Danger." In Marc Robinson (ed.), *The Theater of Maria Irene Fornes*. Baltimore: Johns Hopkins University Press, 230–3.

Fuchs, E. (1999). "Fefu and Her Friends: The View from the Stone." In Marc Robinson (ed.), *The Theater of Maria Irene Fornes*. Baltimore: Johns Hopkins University Press, 85–108.

Garner, Jr., S. B. (1994). *Bodied Spaces: Phenomenology and Performance in Contemporary Drama*. Ithaca, NY: Cornell University Press.

Geis, D. R. (1999). "Wordscapes of the Body: Performative Language as *Gestus* in Maria Irene Fornes's Plays." *Theatre Journal* 42: 291–307.

Kent, A. B. (1996). *Maria Irene Fornes and Her Critics*. Westport, CT: Greenwood.

Keyssar, H. (1991). "Drama and the Dialogic Imagination: *The Heidi Chronicles* and *Fefu and Her Friends*." *Modern Drama* 34: 90–106.

Kushner, T. (1999). "One of the Greats." In Maria M. Delgado and Caridad Svich (eds.), *Conducting a Life: Reflections on the Theatre of Maria Irene Fornes*. Lyme, NH: Smith and Kraus, xxxiii.

Marranca, B. (1978). "Interview: Maria Irene Fornes." *Performing Arts Journal* 2: 106–11.

—— (1984). "The Real Life of Maria Irene Fornes." *Performing Arts Journal* 8: 29–34.

Moroff, D. L. (1996). *Fornes: Theater in the Present Tense*. Ann Arbor: University of Michigan Press.

Robinson, M. (1999a). "Preface." In Marc Robinson (ed.), *The Theater of Maria Irene Fornes*. Baltimore: Johns Hopkins University Press, ix–xi.

—— (1999b). "Introduction," In Marc Robinson (ed.), *The Theater of Maria Irene Fornes*. Baltimore: Johns Hopkins University Press, 1–21.

Savran, D. (1988). "Maria Irene Fornes." In *In their Own Words: Contemporary American Playwrights*. New York: Theatre Communications Group, 51–69.

Sontag, S. (1986). "Preface." In Maria Irene Fornes, *Plays*. New York: Performing Arts Journal Publications, 7–10.

Svich, C. (1999). "Conducting a Life: A Tribute to Maria Irene Fornes." In Maria M. Delgado and Caridad Svich (eds.), *Conducting a Life: Reflections on the Theatre of Maria Irene Fornes*. Lyme, NH: Smith and Kraus, xv–xxix.

Wetzsteon, R. (1986). "Irene Fornes: The Elements of Style." *Village Voice* 31: 42–5.

Wolf, S. (1992). "Re/presenting Gender, Re/presenting Violence: Feminism, Form, and the Plays of Maria Irene Fornes." *Theatre Studies* 37: 17–31.

Worthen, W. B. (1989). "*Still Playing Games*: Ideology and Performance in the Theater of Maria Irene Fornes." In Enoch Brater (ed.), *Feminine Focus: The New Women Playwrights*. New York: Oxford University Press, 167–85.

Zinman, T. S. (1990). "Hen in a Foxhouse: The Absurdist Plays of Maria Irene Fornes." In Ruby Cohn (ed.), *Around the Absurd: Essays on Modern and Postmodern Drama*. Ann Arbor: University of Michigan Press, 203–20.

28

From Eccentricity to Endurance: Jewish Comedy and the Art of Affirmation

Julia Listengarten

The roots of contemporary Jewish American playwrights such as Neil Simon, Wendy Wasserstein, Herb Gardner, and Barbara Lebow are embedded in the Jewish comic tradition whose origin in American theatre traces back to the late nineteenth century and whose development spans the entire twentieth century. In fact, it was in the late nineteenth and early twentieth centuries when an impressively large number of Jewish comedians, including the famous George Burns, Milton Berle, Jack Benny, Sophie Tucker, and Fanny Brice, entered the world of American vaudeville and burlesque, introducing a series of Jewish character types into American theatre. Their performances became a bridge between the Yiddish theatre[1] intended solely for Yiddish-speaking Jews — recent immigrants from Eastern Europe — and mainstream American theatre (see chapter 3). By incorporating the aspects of the Yiddish performance tradition such as *klezmer* folk songs, topical *shtetl* ("ghetto") jokes, and Jewish comic stereotypes into their vaudeville and burlesque routines, Jewish American entertainers made the specifics of ethnic humor accessible to the more diversified, if still mostly Jewish, audience. As Sarah Cohen writes, "In crowded vaudeville and burlesque halls, primarily owned and operated by Jews, [Jewish American comedians such as Eddie Cantor, Sophie Tucker, and Fanny Brice] catered to former Yiddish theater fans who now wanted entertainment that was more American than Yiddish but still had a Jewish flavor" (1983: 3). This was the beginning of Jewish American comedy, a tradition, characterized by its richness in content and versatility in style, which would continue to evolve under the influence of various cultural and historical developments during the twentieth century.

The first Jewish American entertainers thrived on discovering humor in ethnic idiosyncrasies of their characters. Indeed, in portraying eccentric people caught in a web of hilarious circumstances, these performers unabashedly exploited their cultural background. Some of the most popular character stereotypes portrayed in vaudeville and burlesque routines by Jewish comedians were the "*Yiddische* mama";[2] the *schlemiel*, "a clumsy, maladjusted hard-luck loser" (Epstein 2001: xv); and the social critic with often radical political views. Rather than merely mocking their characters' eccentric qualities, these performers explored the particularity of ethnic humor with great affection, showing an intimate knowledge of their own Jewish sensibility. Sarah Cohen observes that, "Unashamed of being Jewish, they seasoned their acts with spicy Yiddish to amuse, not malign, their people" (1983: 3–4).

While their audience grew more ethnically diversified, Jewish American comedians began to draw their jokes from a larger immigrant context, focusing on the issues of cultural misunderstanding that resulted from the immigrants' efforts, not always successful however, to assimilate into the American mainstream. As the popularity of Fanny Brice and Sophie Tucker rose, "[t]heir Jewishness, their particular subcultural world," writes June Sochen, "gave them a perspective on life, an angle of vision, that enabled them to transcend their particularity and become one with large, diverse audiences" (qtd. in Cohen 1983: 44). For them as well as many performers of that era, Sochen writes, it was never a question of abandoning their ethnicity but transcending the ethnic particularity and finding the universality in humor in order to "connect with Gentile as well as Jewish audiences" (ibid.). Still, the sharpness of language, the quirkiness of characters, and the eccentricity of situations in vaudeville and burlesque routines of early Jewish American entertainers were unavoidably rooted in the Jewish comic sensibility and laid the foundation for the further development of the Jewish comic tradition. This tradition in the twentieth century has encompassed such outstanding comedians as the Marx brothers, Mel Brooks, Woody Allen, and Jerry Seinfeld. It has also found its way into dramatic literature, especially over the past two decades, in Neil Simon's farces as well as his semi-autobiographical *Brighton Beach* trilogy, in Wendy Wasserstein's comedies *Isn't It Romantic* and *The Sisters Rosensweig*, in Herb Gardner's dramatic works populated by eccentric but incredibly self-conscious characters, and in Barbara Lebow's poignant Holocaust drama, *A Shayna Maidel*.

The nature of Jewish humor is intertwined with the Jewish sensibility, a relationship that has been tackled by both critics and artists. Commenting on the Jews' propensity to "denigrate their own character flaw," Sigmund Freud writes that Jewish jokes "are stories created by Jews and directed against Jewish characteristics.... I do not know whether there are many other instances of a people making fun to such a degree of its own character" (qtd. in Curry 1996: 199). Jewish humor is indeed imbued with self-deprecation. This self-deprecating quality of Jewish humor, as Epstein posits in his study of Jewish American comedy titled *The Haunted Smile: The Story of Jewish Comedians in America*, originates from "the Yiddish cultural tradition [that] nurtured both self-mockery and the mockery of the powerful" (2001: xiii). Satire therefore – whether it manifests itself in self-parody or derision of others, most likely anti-Semites – becomes tightly woven into the subversive fabric of Jewish humor. Through the criticism of the oppressors as well as the deprecation of themselves, Jews have been able to transcend fear and humiliation and overcome anxiety and alienation, resulting from their feeling of being the "other," the outsiders in mainstream culture.

As a matter of fact, humor has always prevailed in Jewish culture to celebrate life as well as existing as a means of survival. Cohen avers that over the centuries, humor "has helped the Jewish people to . . . confront the indifferent, often hostile universe, to endure the painful ambiguities of life and to retain a sense of internal power despite external impotence" (qtd. in Konas 1997: 60). Jewish writers often comment on the necessity for humor and comic relief in Jewish culture stemming from the tragic history of Jews. Arthur Miller, for instance, contemplates on the sense of tragedy in the world, in this particular case in relation to Jewish history: "there is tragedy in the world but . . . the world must continue: one is condition for the other. Jews can't afford to revel too much in the tragic because it might overwhelm them" (qtd. in Cohen 1983: 124). Indeed, the feeling that life must continue even though it seems to have achieved its tragic impasse characterizes the Jewish sensibility and pervades Jewish comedy. This feeling, enriched by the necessity for endurance and the yearning to celebrate life even under dire circumstances, emerges from the Jewish history of continuous persecutions and pogroms culminating in the Holocaust tragedy.

It can be argued that the best examples of Jewish comedy, while rooted in its ethnic humor tradition, convey a particular philosophy, one that recognizes the profusion of tragedy in life but refuses to dwell on it. Instead, it emphasizes the importance of spiritual faith, strong familial bond, and communal support. It is noteworthy that the recognition of life's ambivalence, permeated with the comic-*cum*-tragic spirit, also existed in Eastern European Yiddish comedy, a forerunner of Jewish American comedy, particularly in the works of Sholom Aleichem.[3] It was an essential part of the worldview and sensibility of Russian drama which could be seen as one of the vital influences on Yiddish theatre in Russia.[4]

Both Wendy Wasserstein and Neil Simon speak of this tragicomic ambivalence in life as it relates to their dramatic works. Wasserstein, somewhat alluding to the Chekhovian perception of the comic, refers to her plays as wistful comedies. In regards to *The Sisters Rosensweig*, she explains: "This is neither a serious nor a comedic play. It's hopefully both. The trick in writing it, playing it, or even reading it, is to find the balance between the bright colors of humor and the serious issues of identity, self-loathing, and the possibility for intimacy and love, when it seems no longer possible" (Wasserstein 1993: x). Simon, too, dramatizes the worldview in which the fusion of laughter and tears, joy and sorrow, optimism and self-doubt manifests itself. "I can't think of a humorous situation that does not involve some pain," Simon maintains in relation to his comedies (qtd. in Cohen 1983: 153). This perception of life is more universal than purely ethnic or parochial, which explains the widespread popularity and appeal of contemporary Jewish comedy to mainstream American audiences. In fact, Jewish comic playwrights over the past several decades, while emerging as the voice of contemporary American Jewry and expressing concerns stemming from their ethnic background, have effectively related their anxiety-ridden comic-*cum*-tragic perception of life to the general American spectator, achieving recognition and often commercial success.

Among contemporary Jewish comic playwrights, Neil Simon is perhaps the most commercially successful. Bigsby writes that in 1991 Arthur Miller expressed his "dismay at the decline of a Broadway, which at that time . . . was staging only one play with any serious pretensions, and that was a Neil Simon comedy" (2000: 114). Bigsby further contends that by the 1990s Simon became "the quintessential Broadway writer, highly skillful and creating plays which probe anxieties in such a way as to cauterize the wounds which he momentarily opens" (2000: 160). There is obvious recognition of the tragic in Simon's comedies but the pain never lasts long and the tragedy is always averted, a philosophy that to an extent lies in the nature of Jewish comedy, whose function has been not to explore tragedy and injustice but rather to celebrate life in the face of its most tragic circumstances. Simon's comedies do not search for answers or attempt to challenge the status quo. In most of his dramatic works, Simon does not dramatize the pervasiveness of life's tragic uncertainty; his wit provides an immediate relief, thereby significantly downplaying the seriousness of his characters' plight. This "technique of deflecting pain through humor," as Bigsby notices, "accounts for [Simon's] popular appeal and the critical suspicion that he inspires" (2000: 159).

Simon's success as a comic playwright began with *Barefoot in the Park* (1963) and *The Odd Couple* (1965) both becoming Broadway long-running hits in the 1960s. His talent as a writer of comedy blossomed, however, a decade earlier in the 1950s when he was writing comic sketches for television comedians, including Sid Caesar, who would become a prototype for his character Max Prince in one of his later plays, *Laughter on the 23rd Floor* (1993). This early experience as gag-writer informed Simon's playwriting method: his dramatic dialogue in all of his subsequent plays is known for its effective one-liners that his characters brilliantly fire at one another. It is also noteworthy that during this period, Simon, through his collaborations with television comedians and comedy writers such as Sid Caesar, Phil Silvers, Mel Brooks, and Woody Allen, immersed himself into the world of popular Jewish American entertainment rooted in ethnic humor and, perhaps more significantly, in the recognition of the healing power of comedy.

Simon himself acknowledges the influence of the Jewish cultural heritage on his writing. The Jewish background is "so deeply embedded in me and so inherent in me," Simon says, "that I am unaware of its quality" (qtd. in Koprince 2002: 8). The spirit of Jewish comedy is in fact present in all of Simon's plays even when the Jewishness of his characters is not emphasized. In some, mostly early comedies, Simon focuses on urban rather than Jewish comic types, but in doing so he explores the eccentricities of his characters trapped in a series of absurd circumstances, in the style of Jewish American vaudeville and burlesque. The two main characters in Simon's early comedy-farce *The Odd Couple* (1965), Oscar Madison and Felix Ungar, are indeed reminiscent of a comically contrasting vaudevillian pair whose mutual incompatibility becomes a source for a variety of humorous incongruities in the play. Thus, in the best tradition of Jewish American vaudeville or burlesque, their habits are rendered extreme and their eccentric qualities become exaggerated. The sense of comedy is no longer a result of misunderstanding or mistaken identity, as in a majority of comic plays and farces; rather, it emerges out of the characters' mismatched personalities stemming from differing life attitudes, which become explicitly manifest when Oscar and Felix enter into their pseudo-marriage, a domestic partnership of two heterosexual men.

Oscar is a laid-back, recent divorcé and passionate poker player whose spacious Manhattan apartment, once a lovely place, is at the start of the play "a study in slovenliness," packed with "dirty dishes, discarded clothes, old newspapers, empty bottles, . . . opened and unopened laundry packages, mail and disarrayed furniture" (5). Oscar's counterpart, Felix, is, on the contrary, fixated on cleanliness and immaculate order. He is a humorous but also very neurotic and extremely self-conscious personage, evocative of the *schlemiel*, Yiddish comic stereotype of an unfortunate loser.[5] It is through the character of Felix that Simon introduces a note of distress, even if only for a fleeting moment, into the otherwise comic world of amusing absurdities and eccentric manners of *The Odd Couple*. In fact, the domestic partnership between Oscar and Felix, which is clearly doomed from the beginning, is formed as a result of Oscar's attempt to avert his friend's possible suicide attempt; Felix's threats have indeed dramatically intensified after the breakup of his marriage. Oscar's offer to share his apartment leads, however, to a series of hilarious mishaps, and it takes only a brief moment for the audience to realize that Felix's threats are never real and can actually be attributed to his constant hypochondria. As Oscar comments on his friend's neurosis, "You know what he's like. He sleeps on the window sill. 'Love me or I'll jump' . . . 'Cause he's a nut, that's why" (19).

Simon is not interested in exploring the causes – whether social or personal – of Felix's neurotic behavior and the sense of inadequacy that plagues him; instead, he offers a string of hilarious encounters between the self-assured and easy-going Oscar and the extremely insecure and frustrated Felix. Comic situations are fused with brilliant dialogue, which is superbly peppered with one-liners. Simon is aware of his comic language, which he hones and shapes continuously. His one-liners seem particularly in place when they are spoken by characters who are either comic writers themselves or stand-up comedians. In *The Sunshine Boys* (1972), Simon's other early comedy, as well as in his later play *Laughter on the 23rd Floor*, he fuses comic gags and sharp one-liners with the characters' verbal idiosyncrasies stemming from their lifelong careers in show business.

Commenting on the abundance of one-liners in *The Sunshine Boys*, Simon appropriately attributes it to the characters' vaudeville roots: "I spent my life growing up with these men. If they spoke in one-liners and punch lines instead of conversation, it's because it was the only language they knew" (qtd. in McGovern 1979: 5). The inspiration for Simon's *The Sunshine Boys* came from the world of early Jewish American comedians. "Spend a few afternoons around the Friars Club, a hangout for aging comedians," writes Simon, "and a pencil, a pad, and a discriminating ear will record for you some of the funniest and saddest dialogue you ever heard" (ibid.). The characters of Willie Clark and Al Lewis in the play are the prototypes of famed Joe Sultzer and Charlie Marks, who in the early twentieth century successfully incorporated Yiddish dialects and Jewish stereotypes in their well-received comic skits, most famous of which involved "Dr. Kronkhite" (Yiddish for "Dr. Sickness"). In Simon's play, the aged comedians – the Sunshine Boys – who broke their partnership years ago, are reconnected again to perform "the doctor sketch" for a CBS television show. "The doctor sketch" itself, as well as a handful of incongruities resulting from this reunion of the old team partners, forms the basis of comedy in Simon's *The Sunshine Boys*. The language in "the doctor sketch" is filled with hilarious exchanges like:

Al:	Are you married?
Willie:	I am looking.
Al:	Looking to get married?
Willie:	No. Looking to get out. (52)

The humor in *The Sunshine Boys* also arises out of the characters' incompatible personalities, similar to the mismatched character qualities of Oscar and Felix in *The Odd Couple*. Willie's unwillingness to perform the sketch with his former partner, as well as his unfortunate attempts to change its verbal and physical routine, results in heated arguments between the feeble comedians. The exchange ultimately leads to Willie's collapse during the recording of their performance. The nature of their arguments seems preposterous but their consequences are rather grave: owing to his conflict with Al, Willie suffers a heart attack, becomes bedridden, and consequently requires constant medical assistance.

Notwithstanding his play about alcoholism, *The Gingerbread Lady* (1970), *The Sunshine Boys* is arguably Simon's most serious comedy among his early dramatic works; it is a comedy whose world is shaped by the playwright's recognition of life's ambivalence, in which humor coincides with sorrow and laughter is tinged by sadness. The decline of vaudeville – once a popular genre – is directly connected to the characters' old age, associated with solitude, sickness, and death. Once wealthy and successful, Willie now lives alone in an old, dilapidated hotel, struggling to accept but in the end still denying his loneliness, loss of memory, and debilitating illness. Willie's partner from their "sunshine" days, Al Lewis, likewise has lost his zest for life after his wife passed away and, unable to take care of himself, is temporarily residing with his daughter in suburban New Jersey. At the end of the play, both Willie and Al, who seem to have settled their old grudges, find out, rather ironically, that their circumstances force both of them to move to the Actors Home in New Brunswick. The reconciliation of the old vaudeville partners provides them with one more opportunity to sharpen their wits. It also coincides with the feeling of virtual abandonment they experience – abandoned by their respective families, friends, fans, and ultimately society as a whole. This fusion of comedy with sadness allows Simon to avoid sentimentalizing over the loss of fame and their old age. As Ruby Cohen argues, "Out of the public eye, old age is dramatized as dirty, demeaning, confusing, and utterly lonely. Yet Simon also makes it funny, so that we laugh with a sympathy that the selfish old souls scarcely deserve" (qtd. in Konas 1997: 30). Wit, human resilience, and the ability to enjoy life always prevail in Simon's comedies, even when laughter is momentarily interrupted by sentimentality.

Throughout his playwriting career Simon has been attracted to depicting the life of comedians onstage and behind the scenes, capturing precious moments of their comic talent at work. Simon's recent semi-autobiographical play *Laughter on the 23rd Floor* is a glorification of a community of television comedy writers, "an affectionate salute to [the] gifted writers and comedians, much as *The Sunshine Boys* is a tribute to the lost art of vaudeville" (Koprince 2002: 141). Based on Simon's own early experience as a writer of television sketches, particularly for Sid Caesar's famous TV series *Your Show of Shows*, the play displays a dazzling array of characters, prototypes of Simon's celebrated colleagues. *Laughter on the 23rd Floor* also becomes a demonstration of Simon at his best as a Jewish comic playwright, synthesizing the self-deprecating humor with the satire of the powerful, delineating as well as inverting Jewish stereotypes, and celebrating the communal spirit.

The play focuses on a few days in the "Writers' Room" of the Max Prince Studio, seen through the eyes of the recently hired young writer Lucas Brickman (Simon himself). The gallery of Simon's eccentric character types includes the hypochondriac Ira Stone, a variation of the Yiddish *schlemiel*, whose brilliant sense of humor coincides with extreme self-consciousness; the overbearing Carol Wyman, a "Yiddische mama," in the otherwise masculine community of the writers; and the politically aware Russian émigré Val Skolsky, a social observer and critic. Their sense of humor is based on ethnic characteristics and the quirkiness of their personalities.

The idiosyncrasies of the characters in Simon's *Laughter on the 23rd Floor* and the brilliance of their incessant gags are toppled by the enormity of Max Prince's eccentric personality and comic genius. His outstanding talent as a television comedian is combined with his exceptional physical power and emotional overabundance; he is clearly a patriarch in a writers' family, protecting their welfare and exuding admiration for their talent. Being painfully aware of the impending dispersion of his team due to NBC's latest strategy to reduce the airtime, Prince is nevertheless unable to avert the disintegration of the writers' community, which makes him extremely vulnerable. His fierce, satirical attacks on authority – the NBC's executives linked in Prince's paranoid mind with McCarthy's censorship – result from his feeling of helplessness and his perception of injustice, both in his personal life and in society at large. Max Prince's variety show indeed closes but the communal spirit prevails. "No goodbyes, alright? . . . Come on. Let's celebrate" (95) becomes Prince's motto on the verge of his show's demise. In his early dramatic works, Simon emphasized the urban rather than Jewish personality traits of his characters. In his later plays he is interested in infusing his recognition of life's ambiguity with the particularly Jewish sensibility. In fact, most of the characters in *Laughter on the 23rd Floor* are Jewish comedy writers.

In his trilogy consisting of *Brighton Beach Memoirs*, *Biloxi Blues*, and *Broadway Bound*, the focus of Simon's attention shifts to the trials and tribulations of Eugene Jerome (Simon himself), a Brooklyn-born Jewish boy whose journey is one of growing up in the Depression era, surviving the psychological as well as physical brutalities of military training during World War II, and maturing into a successful comic writer in the postwar period. Since Eugene Jerome is a narrator in all of the three plays, it is his voice, blending humor with sadness, that brings a comic-*cum*-tragic perspective to this story of one person's survival on his road to fame. In the course of relaying his personal ordeals, Eugene reaches the realization that "Contrary to popular belief, everything in life doesn't come to a clear-cut conclusion" (1987: 102). It is the ability to rejoice together as a family or community that provides him and his relatives with the spiritual and psychological power to continue.[6] There is a precious moment in *Broadway Bound*, taking place between Jerome and his mother Kate. Facing the disintegration of her marriage, Kate is reminiscing about her childhood's most memorable experience: the night when she danced with the famous dancer George Raft:

> Eugene: (*holding out his arms to her*) Come on. I'll dance with you … I'm George Raft. … Everybody is watching us. … Don't let 'em down, Mom. (*Kate looks at Eugene for a moment, listening to the music. Then she slowly stands and they begin to dance – awkwardly at first, then more gracefully.*) (87–8)

As the mother and son dance together, their bond grows stronger, bringing Kate a temporary relief from the disruptions of her family life.

The feeling of nostalgia for the loss of this familial comfort permeates Simon's later plays. At the end of the trilogy, the family is no longer together to celebrate life and endure pain; Kate, the family stronghold, is the only person left in the house to "wax her grandmother's table and bask in the joy of her son's success" (102). Simon has often been criticized for offering "a softened [somewhat sentimentalized] view of history, especially in *Brighton Beach Memoirs*, in which he nostalgically recalls his childhood during the Depression" (Koprince 2002: 10). Indeed, Simon avoids the social causes that eventually led to the erosion of the family structure during the postwar period; instead, he affectionately renders a family portrait while both admiring and slightly ridiculing the subjects of his drawing. Kate is a traditional Jewish mother sacrificing her life for the wellbeing of her family; Jack is a weak father-figure alienated from society and ultimately his own children ("Either you've grown too fast … or I've outlived my place in this house," 73); Ben is a socialist grandfather who rejects life's unnecessary luxuries and refuses to join his wife in wealthy Miami Beach. The self-deprecatory nature of Simon's humor especially manifests itself in a short radio sketch written by the two aspiring comedy writers Eugene and his older brother Stanley, in which they poke fun at their family's eccentric personalities, very much in the tradition of early Jewish American entertainers.

Plate 18. Brighton Beach Memoirs, by Neil Simon, Missouri Repertory Theatre. Richard Halverson (Jack) and Sonja Lanzener (Blanche). Courtesy of the Missouri Repertory Theatre.

Simon, similarly to his characters Eugene and Stanley from the *Brighton Beach* trilogy, is not particularly interested in writing political satires. "To me, comedy has to have a point," contends Ben in *Broadway Bound*. "What was the point of all this?" he asks, referring to the radio sketch. "To make people laugh," responds his grandson Eugene (68). The serious issues such as ethnic prejudice, social injustice, anti-Semitism, the Holocaust, psychological and physical abuse (particularly in *Biloxi*

Blues), and the disintegration of community and familial relations are certainly mentioned, but only in passing. Simon's comedies by and large ignore the dichotomy between the desire for assimilation and the loss of ethnic identity, a concern that both Wasserstein and Gardner investigate in their plays.

The Jewish ambivalence about assimilation stems from the urge Jews have expressed for centuries to integrate into a cultural majority by becoming social "insiders" and identifying with the mainstream, which always risks forfeiting one's ethnic roots. The self-deprecatory nature of Jewish humor is directly linked to this paradox for, in addition to functioning both as an escape and defense mechanism against the powerful majority, the self-mockery, as argued by Heda Jason, "reveals the Jew's feeling of cultural ambiguity" (qtd. in Curry 1996: 202).[7] Cultural ambiguity can partially be identified with the sense of guilt for having rejected their roots. Infused with the feeling of alienation from both Jewish and non-Jewish cultures, this sense of guilt may ultimately transform itself into a sense of resentment of one's own Jewish identity.[8] Self-deprecation allows Jews to avoid self-loathing and provides them with a necessary distance to gain a new insight into their cultural assimilation. In fact, Jewish comedy, as "an intellectual outlet of self-deprecating-humor," has a possibility for Jews to reconcile "their guilt feelings and [reveal] their 'need to search for self-identity'" (Bleiweiss, qtd. in Curry 1996: 203).

In both *Isn't It Romantic* (1981) and *The Sisters Rosensweig* (1992), Wasserstein's female characters are compelled to reevaluate their identity and Jewish roots, ultimately redefining the role of the Jewish female within familial and social structures. Their feeling of "otherness," which could easily lead to the sense of alienation, stems from being both Jewish and female. Wasserstein's characters are thus contemporary Jewish women dealing with their identity crisis as they struggle to establish themselves in today's society. Janie Blumberg in *Isn't It Romantic* is a 28-year-old aspiring writer who, as Bigsby asserts, tries to "escape the stereotype awaiting her, to become herself rather than conform to the expectations of others" (1999: 340). The expectations imposed upon Janie by her extravagant mother are centuries old: to marry a nice Jewish boy, "preferably a doctor with a six-figure salary" (Bigsby 1999: 340) and become a traditional Jewish wife who would wear a mink coat "to walk the carriage" (*Isn't It Romantic*, qtd. in Cohen 1997: 67). Janie, on the contrary, is dreaming about true love and a meaningful relationship, as her voice on the answering machine turns into a leitmotif of the play: "Isn't it romantic, merely to be young on such a night as this?" (Cohen 1997: 23).

Even though the overweight, idealistic, and somewhat confused Janie is self-conscious and extremely insecure – "a female *schlemiel* figure, mocking herself for the habitual mistakes she makes" (Cohen 1997: 20) – she finds an inner strength to defy conventional norms. As she gradually matures in the course of the play, she comes to the realization that her relationship with the young Jewish doctor Marty (a.k.a. Murray) Schlimovitz, whose family Americanized their last name to Sterling and who himself is now in search of his own Jewish roots, is far from being meaningful and satisfying. Janie refuses to marry the quintessential "nice Jewish doctor." As she explains: "Marty, you're not right for me. I can't move in with you now. If I did that, I'd always be a monkey, a sweet little girl" (61); and she is no longer afraid to disappoint her invasive, overbearing mother: "Look, I'm sorry. Things didn't work out as you planned. There's nothing wrong with that life, but it just isn't mine right now" (Cohen 1997: 67).[9]

The pain of self-realization does not last long, however; the sense of comedy in this play diffuses the remaining traces of sadness and frustration, not unlike the comic quality permeating Neil Simon's plays. Bigsby argues that the play "in some ways elaborates a familiar vaudeville and Jewish routine, and much of its humour derives precisely from the familiarity of the central character [who] is vulnerable, unclear what she wants, but aware that she is, indeed, a comic figure" (1999: 340). What also makes her a comic figure is the incongruity between the image she projects as an insecure "sweetheart" and her courageous strife, even if unconscious, for independence and self-assertion. Janie is also a writer – one of the play's autobiographical characteristics – and therefore she exudes sharp verbal responses. Her clever remarks are both self-deprecating and satirical of others, and her wit sometimes counteracts against the seriousness of her circumstances. Wasserstein herself aims at juxtaposing pain and laughter, disillusionment and optimism, constantly disrupting the audience's emotional involvement through the play's episodic structure and refusing to provide them with any all-encompassing solutions. As the play reaches its ending, Janie's journey of self-discovery has barely begun. In a tradition of a wistful Jewish comedy, Janie is spotlighted as she is "dancing beautifully, alone" (Cohen 1997: 70), with the music from "Isn't It Romantic" underscoring the closing moment of the play.

Similarly to Neil Simon, Wendy Wasserstein recognizes the effect of her Jewish roots on her sensibility as a writer. In her plays as well as short stories such as the recently published collection *Shiksa Goddess*, she capitalizes on her knowledge of Jewish culture and ethnic idiosyncrasy. Wasserstein often speaks of "being raised on Jewish comics and of suspecting that her sense of community, melancholy and spirituality can be traced back to her experience of temple" (qtd. in Bigsby 1999: 332). In *The Sisters Rosensweig*, Merv Kant (a.k.a. Mervyn Kantlovitz), a Jewish American furrier who unexpectedly shows up at Sara's fifty-fourth birthday party in London, is fervently compelled to remind Sara Goode (née Rosensweig) of her Jewish roots that she, a successful international banker, has rejected. She mocks Mervyn's attempts to "revive" her Jewishness by telling him not to "proselytize" her. She ridicules her sister's religious observance; as Gorgeous prays over the candles performing the Sabbath ceremony, Sara rudely interrupts her sister, calling her prayers "an ancient tribal ritual" (38).

Wasserstein universalizes the search for self-identity in *The Sisters Rosensweig*, making it pertinent to both Jews and non-Jews. According to the playwright, the words of Geoffrey, a bisexual boyfriend of one of the sisters, surmise the characters' quandary in this play: "You don't know what it is to have absolutely no idea who you are!" (88). Wasserstein continues, "Despite their maturity, most of the characters in the play are struggling with who they are. There's a reason why these three sisters are from Brooklyn and the play takes place in Queen Anne's Gate, London" (ix). Whereas Sara has come to terms partially with her lack of identity, trying hard to negate her feelings of loneliness and alienation, her daughter Tess is yearning, instead, for the sense of belonging to one's community. Consequently, she attempts to join her British-born Lithuanian boyfriend on his way to Vilnius, only realizing later that there is, in fact, no place for her in the Lithuanian resistance. In the play she passionately questions Sara: "Mother, if I've never really been Jewish, and I'm not actually American anymore, and I'm not really British or European, then who am I?" (106).

Wasserstein's *The Sisters Rosensweig* is a journey of self-discoveries and mutual revelations, filled with joy and sorrow, and influenced by Chekhov's *Three Sisters* in more ways than merely the title. Sara eventually finds emotional comfort in her reunion with Pfeni and Gorgeous, her two sisters, as well as in the recognition, even if temporary, of her Jewish roots.[10] Geoffrey leaves Pfeni for his homosexual friend, finally realizing that "he misses men" (89). Pfeni, an international journalist, returns to her role of a "wandering Jew," departing for Tajikistan, yet another conflict-ridden country, to collect materials for her new book project. Tom, Tess's boyfriend, takes a flight to Lithuania to reconnect with his ethnic background. Tess remains with her mother in London continuing to wonder, "Are we people who will always be watching and never belong?" (100).

In the midst of crucial character self-explorations, Wasserstein reveals her own self-deprecating comic personality. Sara, herself being a representation of "the [Jewish] moneylender stereotype with a feminist twist" (Frank 1995: 251), expresses the voice of the playwright as she pokes fun at Merv's ethnic parochialism, insisting on his "persistently narrow perspective" (Wasserstein 1993: 53). Merv himself ridicules the most popular stereotype about Jewish men propagated by Jews themselves: "I don't think it's particularly true that Jews don't drink. I think it's a myth made up by our mothers to persuade innocent women that Jewish men make superior husbands" (27). Gorgeous, whose personality combines eccentricity with suburban conservatism and whose radio program – Dr. Gorgeous Show – inspires its listeners to "maintain a warm traditional home" (30), is involved in the act of self-mocking, referring to herself as a "housewife, mother, and a radio personality" (99).

Wasserstein shares the ability to derive humor from the character's incongruous personality and behavior with both Neil Simon and Herb Gardner. The character-driven humorous situations and hilarious gags are, however, not the only characteristics that unite the writing styles of Simon and Gardner – the older-generation Jewish American playwrights – with the younger generation, Wasserstein. Gardner's personages in *A Thousand Clowns* (1962) and *I'm Not Rappaport* (1985) are as eccentric and unconventional as Simon's quirky Jewish vaudevillians and zany comedy writers from *The Sunshine Boys* and *Laughter on the 23rd Floor*. The identity quest, crucial for Wasserstein's characters and often imbued in her comedies with poignancy, frustration, and hope, is the journey that Gardner creates with his character Charlie in *Conversations with My Father* (1991). What distinguishes Gardner's comedies from those of Simon and Wasserstein is the insidious satire on social and political institutions that pervades the fabric of his writing. Gardner, in this regard, could be seen as a successor of the Marx Brothers, who in the early days of Jewish American comedy "mercilessly lampooned [social] institutions that had so deeply disappointed Americans, thus allowing audiences to vent their anger on the institutions that had failed them (the government) or that ignored or condescended to them (the wealthy and powerful)" (Epstein 2001: 89).

Gardner astutely weaves satire into the context of his plays. For instance, in *A Thousand Clowns*, the New York Bureau of Child Welfare has determined that Murray Burns, an unemployed comedy writer, is unfit to be the guardian of his nephew, Nick, and subsequently threatened to remove the child from his albeit unofficial custody. Whereas the private life of entertainers (presented in this comedy by eccentric Murray, his brash brother and agent Arnold, and the neurotic Leo Herman, a host of the children's television show "Chuckles the Chipmunk" and Murray's former employer) is unconventional and erratic, the world of the welfare institution is bureaucratic and hostile. In Gardner's later comedy *I'm Not Rappaport*, both characters, two feisty octogenarians, have been marginalized by society. In *Conversations with My Father*, Gardner expresses his concern over the systematic betrayal of Jews by society at large: by the government institutions of tsarist Russia, allowing pogroms, as well as the World War II American government, keeping silent about the Holocaust.

Gardner, however, is not a political writer; he is a socially aware comedian who entered the world of Jewish comedy in the 1950s with the cartoon strip "Nebbishes" and whose sense of humor allows a fusion of politically biting satire with purely entertaining vaudeville routines and absurd situations that he creates for his eccentric characters. In *I'm Not Rappaport*, the two elderly New Yorkers, the Jewish socialist and union activist Nat and the African American superintendent Midge, regularly meeting on the same bench in Central Park, are akin to vaudevillian partners who crave companionship but find themselves in constant dispute. Moreover, the play title is derived from an old vaudeville number in which one of the characters refuses to admit that a person he is speaking to is not a friend but a complete stranger. The inability to acknowledge the truth has constructed Nat's own fluid personality: the multiple identities that this character consecutively assumes compel him to weave a series of lies about his life. Is he indeed a retired waiter as he proclaims himself to be to the bewildered and frustrated Midge at the end of the play, or is it yet another identity assumed by the character? More importantly, is this merely an absurd game for Nat who makes up various adventures he never experienced in life, or is it a manifestation, both painful and funny, of the elusiveness of his memory?

In *Conversations with My Father*, Gardner's most ambitious play, the structure of this work is that of a memory play in which the main character, Charlie, is on an identity quest, compelled to revisit his immigrant childhood and adolescent years during the Depression and World War II periods. The majority of Jewish American playwrights have recognized the necessity for Jews to reexamine their roots in order to reconstruct or reclaim their Jewish identity. This need to "revisit past experience, to return repeatedly to one form or another of history (e.g., persecution in Europe, the immigration experience, the Depression, and the Holocaust)," which, according to Michael Woolf, has always been "a characteristic of Jewish-American culture" (qtd. in Koprince 2002: 10), receives a new urgency in the context of intensified ethnic and religious hatred.

Charlie's memory in Gardner's play transports him back to his childhood in New York where his father, Eddie Ross, owned a saloon on Canal Street, "the epicenter of several ethnic enclaves"(1995: 246), in Glenda Frank's description. She lists three ethnic groups presented in the play, Jewish, Irish, and Italian, arguing that "the critical cultural dynamic" in this dramatic work lies "not between minorities but [in] the influence of the mainstream on ethnic identity" (246). Gardner's more scrupulous attention, however, is on the life of Jewish American immigrants whose ethnic pride conflicts, at times tragically, with their relentless desire for assimilation. The reality that Gardner predominantly focuses on in this play is a world of two cultures: the Yiddish culture inherited by the characters from their homeland, the Eastern European *shtetl*, and the mainstream culture of assimilated ethnic identities; it is also a world of several languages – mainly Yiddish and English with an occasional Hebrew prayer and an Italian expression – existing simultaneously and complementing each other, while Yiddish songs such as "Rumania, Rumania" intermingle with American popular tunes.

The collision of these two worlds results in a series of disappointments and frustrations often combined with comic absurdities. Eddie, for instance, equates American success with one's ability to be accepted by the mainstream. In his eagerness to assimilate, he changes his family name from Goldberg to Ross; his wife's accented English embarrasses him and he is utterly baffled by her lack of desire to switch from Yiddish to English ("Twelve years – twelve years of English with Mr. Katz you're still sayin' 'turn me off the Lokshen'!," 321). Moreover, under tragic circumstances, Eddie is quick to forfeit his ethnic background altogether. Having just heard that his older son was killed in action, he shouts in rage, disrupting the old Yiddish lullaby chanted by his grieving wife: "get *this*, God, I ain't a Jew no more! Over, pal! Fifty years of bein' a Jew Loser; over, baby!" (377). It is ironic that Eddie's conflicted personality flourishes when he feels comfortable with his ethnic background and is able to discover spiritual power and find joy in the communal celebrations characteristic of Jewish culture. As he chases two mobsters away from his saloon, he dances with Zaretsky, his boarder and famous Yiddish actor, "to an irresistible Freylekeh rhythm – irresistible . . . to any triumphant Jew in the room" (345).

Unlike the somewhat oversimplified world of Neil Simon's plays, the picture rendered by Gardner in *Conversations with My Father* is complex, multicolored, and infused with tragedies and celebrations; it tells the story of one family's disasters and survivals through the mixture of vibrant voices, languages, attitudes, and cultures.[11] This world is often disrupted by the threats of anti-Semitism and the tragedies of World War II. Furthermore, the characters in Gardner's play are painfully aware of, and emotionally affected by, the horrors of the Holocaust, but its devastating reality is never as tangible and terrifyingly close as it becomes in Barbara Lebow's *A Shayna Maidel* (1985).

Lebow remembers that right after the war her family was visited by her third cousins, Holocaust survivors, an encounter that made a tremendous psychological impact on the playwright, then a 10-year-old girl. Commenting on her interest in the Holocaust history, Lebow writes that the focus of her exploration is not on the concentration camp experiences. "There is no mention of atrocities in my play. I was more interested in what happened to these people after they were liberated from the camps" (qtd. in Cohen 1997: 74). In *A Shayna Maidel* she creates Lusia, a concentration camp survivor who gradually faces reality while struggling to cope with her sense of guilt for living. She also learns to appreciate life again, as she becomes reunited with her father and younger sister, both of whom were fortunate to emigrate from Poland long before the Nazi occupation of Europe. In the course of discovering the will and spiritual power to carry on, Lusia dreams about her past and future. Lebow insists that the events in the present (post-World War II New York) are mixed together with memory and fantasy scenes rather than flashbacks: "A flashback is objective. A memory scene has some reality, but the facts are somewhat distorted or colored by the person's mind who is remembering. Fantasy scenes . . . are events that never happen at all" (qtd. in Cohen 1997: 74).

Lusia's reality and fantasy blur as she looks for solace, reminiscing about her prewar life in a small Polish town. She finds comfort in reliving the moments she enjoyed so much in the past when she was part of a larger Jewish community in a small *shtetl*, surrounded by her loved ones, most of whom, including her 3-year-old daughter, were exterminated. Trying to overcome the cultural barriers but, instead, feeling confused and alienated in a foreign country, she turns to her perished relatives for help and encouragement. The healing power of the communal spirit prevails as Lusia's poignant memories of her family and friends allow her to endure the pain and also discover hope and affirmation in the present. The spiritual connections that Lusia establishes with her Americanized sister Rose (a.k.a. Rayzel) provide her temporary emotional relief, if not cure. Still, the connection with her sister colors her life with new meaning. Rose, in turn, is compelled to reevaluate the significance of her Jewish roots, eventually identifying herself with the millions of Eastern European Jews murdered in the Holocaust.

As the inner beauty of this newly found but still fragile familial closeness manifests itself, comic situations abound. The nature of Lebow's comedy, however, is far from being either farcical or satirical; the sense of comedy in this play emerges from the persistent human need to celebrate compassion, spiritual beauty, and communal faith. While the play's title *A Shayna Maidel* translates into "a pretty girl," the phrase also connotes "inner beauty" and is often used as "an expression of love and of yearning of hope" (qtd. in Cohen 1997: 73). It is the search for love, hope, and the potentially therapeutic function that constitute the essence of Jewish humor. One could also argue that in this fusion of poignancy and optimism, resilience and affirmation, lies the universal appeal of Jewish American comedy.

NOTES

1. Yiddish theatres enjoyed their popularity in America until the early 1930s, catering exclusively to Yiddish-speaking Jews emigrated from Eastern Europe between the 1880s and early 1900s. In recreating the life and character types of the Eastern European *shtetl*, Yiddish theatres in America aimed at preserving "the familiar within the unknown and [making] the new aliens less homesick" (Cohen 1983: 1).

2. The overbearing Jewish mother is present in numerous comic sketches of American vaudeville as well as more serious dramatic works.

3. Sarah Cohen implies that the works of Sholom Aleichem contain much more tragic awareness of life's injustice and complexity than Broadway adaptations of his stories ever revealed (1983: 11).

4. The Yiddish theatrical tradition flourished in Russia especially in the 1920s and 1930s.

5. Felix can be seen as a forerunner of Woody Allen's character types who are rooted in the same Yiddish stereotype of a maladjusted hypochondriac.

6. Avner Ziv emphasizes the emotional significance of Jewish laughter in reaction to a tragic circumstance. He writes that "[u]nlike the individual experience of crying, Jews share their laughter with one another and, through common emotional release, they can look to one another for comfort" (qtd. in Curry 1996: 200).

7. One could argue that the self-deprecatory characteristic of Jewish humor has become increasingly stronger and more pervasive in postwar Jewish comedies as Jews have continued to assimilate at a faster rate into a mainstream non-Jewish culture.

8. This gamut of contradictory feelings is arguably at work in Woody Allen's films such as *Hannah and Her Sisters*, *Annie Hall*, *Sleeper*, and *Zelig* among others.

9. Janie is not the only character in *Isn't It Romantic* to defy social conventions and traditional norms. Paradoxically, Tasha, Janie's intrusive, overwhelming mother, who attempts, somewhat unsuccessfully, to instill the traditional Jewish values into her disobedient daughter, hardly fits the description of a traditional Jewish wife herself. Dressed in a cape and exercise leotards, Tasha is rather an extravagant dance teacher who "order[s] up breakfast from a Greek coffee shop every morning" (67–8).

10. As Tess records her mother's biography for a college project, Sara begins her story: "My name is Sara Rosensweig. I am the daughter of Rita and Maury Rosensweig. I was born in Brooklyn"(107).

11. The play's complexity – in both structure and content – could perhaps explain the rather short commercial success of this work in production, especially compared to the continued commercial popularity of Simon's comedies. *Conversations with My Father* was originally produced by the Seattle Repertory Theatre in 1991 and then subsequently performed at the Royal Theatre in New York in 1992 in which the role of Eddie was played by Judd Hirsch, who previously portrayed Nat in the 1985 Broadway production of *I'm Not Rappaport*.

BIBLIOGRAPHY

Bigsby, C. W. E. (1999). *Contemporary American Playwrights*. Cambridge: Cambridge University Press.
—— (2000). *Modern American Drama, 1945–2000*. Cambridge: Cambridge University Press.
Cohen, S. B. (ed.) (1983). *From Hester Street to Hollywood: The Jewish-American Stage and Screen*. Bloomington: Indiana University Press.
—— (ed.) (1997). *Making a Scene: The Contemporary Drama of Jewish-American Women*. Syracuse, NY: Syracuse University Press.
Curry, R. R. (ed.) (1996). *Perspectives on Woody Allen*. New York: G. K. Hall.
Epstein, L. J. (2001). *The Haunted Smile: The Story of Jewish Comedians in America*. New York: Public Affairs.
Frank, G. (1995). "The Struggle to Affirm: The Image of Jewish-Americans on Stage." In Marc Maufort (ed.), *Staging Difference: Cultural Pluralism in American Theatre and Drama*. New York: Peter Lang.
Gardner, H. (2000). *The Collected Plays*. New York: Applause.
Konas, G. (ed.) (1997). *Neil Simon: A Casebook*. New York: Garland.
Koprince, S. (2002). *Understanding Neil Simon*. Columbia, SC: South Carolina University Press.
McGovern, E. M. (1979). *Neil Simon: A Critical Study*. New York: Frederick Ungar.
Simon, N. (1973). *The Sunshine Boys*. New York: Samuel French.
—— (1984). *Brighton Beach Memoirs*. New York: Samuel French.
—— (1986). *Biloxi Blues*. New York: Samuel French.
—— (1987). *Broadway Bound*. New York: Samuel French.
—— (1994). *The Odd Couple*. New York: Samuel French.
—— (1995). *Laughter on the 23rd Floor*. New York: Samuel French.
Wasserstein, W. (1993). *The Sisters Rosensweig*. New York: Harcourt Brace.

29

Repercussions and Remainders in the Plays of Paula Vogel: An Essay in Five Moments

Ann Pellegrini

she was given to increasing the bounds of the moment by flights into past or future; or sidelong down corridors and alleys . . .

Virginia Woolf, Between the Acts

"Let Me Go Way Back"

Paula Vogel believes in ghosts. In an interview with theatre studies scholar David Savran, she provides a memory of her childhood as a way of explaining the "enormous emotional repercussions" of her connection with the past. "Let me go way back," she begins:

> I remember a teacher in the fourth grade . . . bringing an early Edison gramophone into the classroom. And she said, "Paula, why don't you turn the crank of the phonograph," so that we could see how it worked. I think I burst out crying, and she said, "What's wrong," and I said, "I can't." And she said, "Why?" And I said, "Because there's a dead man's hand on that crank." I didn't want to put my hand out and occupy the space that belonged to somebody else. It was actually quite tangible to me. I don't think there's a neat demarcation, politically, ethically, between history and the present moment. (Vogel 1999a: 283)

Vogel's childhood memory (a ghost story by any other name) constitutes a theory of history as an ongoing and deeply felt relationship.[1] For Vogel, history's meaning

I want to express my thanks to David Krasner for his editorial kindnesses, very plural! Sarita Rainey offered invaluable research assistance. Along the way, conversations with Jennifer Louise Dunning, Heather Lukes, Molly McGarry, and Rebecca Schneider provided much-needed buoyancy and contact. I am grateful.

resides less in facts and who did what when than in affect and the pulse of feeling. Remember: "The connection I have with time is something that causes enormous emotional repercussions for me" (1999a: 283). Crucially, the percussive effects of the past in the present are not the same thing as "fate" or "causality." Rather, and more optimistically, this living edge of the past (another term for this is "psychic life") holds out the possibility of connecting otherwise, connecting with a difference.

This awareness of the disturbing capacity of the past to reach into and disrupt the present, for better and for worse, is a through-line in her plays. (Just think of that dirty sock in *The Mineola Twins* [1995].) Granted, "through-line" may not be the right word for a playwright who consistently refuses the niceties of linear narration in favor of circular structures that up-end, or at least muddle, neat distinctions among past, present, and future. In *The Baltimore Waltz* (1992), for example, which was Vogel's first major critical success, we meet a main character, and a playwright, painfully attuned to history's haunting touch and to time's limitations when we tell it "straight."

The play tells the story of two siblings, Anna (a surrogate for Vogel herself) and Carl, and their imaginary journey to Europe in search of a cure for Anna's ATD (Acquired Toilet Disease). ATD is, obviously, a stand-in for AIDS. It turns out that the traveling only happens in Anna's head as she sits vigil at her brother's bedside. He is the one who is ill, with AIDS. The various scenes of their travel – vignettes, really, postcard-like in their self-containment – represent her daydreams. Her flights of imagination are her way of taking leave from the awful unfolding present, that moment when she learns her brother is dead. He has died.

The play is haunted by Vogel's own loss, the AIDS-related death of her beloved brother Carl, in 1988. *The Baltimore Waltz* is dedicated to her brother's memory, "because [Vogel] cannot sew" (1996: 3). The prefatory materials to the published version of the play even include a letter Carl wrote to her, in March 1987, in which he provides (often hilarious) instructions for his funeral. In an author's note, Vogel offers her explicit permission to all future productions of *The Baltimore Waltz* to include his letter in the accompanying program. She wants, she says, to let Carl "speak to us in his own words" (4). This is one of the many ways in which the play defiantly and wishfully bends time: a brother speaks from beyond the grave in a letter written before it.

In that same author's note, Vogel informs us that Carl had invited her to travel to Europe with him in 1986. "Due to pressures of time and money," though, "[she] declined, never dreaming that he was HIV positive" (4). *The Baltimore Waltz* is not merely Anna's imaginary journey; it is also Vogel's *and* the audiences, too, as she sends out postcards of a trip that never occurred. Layering his letter on hers, absence with presence, this patchwork quilt of a play breaks open cramped notions of time and space and loosens proprietary understandings of kinship and affiliation. It is true that neither Anna's daydreams, nor the play built around them, can finally halt time's passage, but so much else depends on how one tells it.

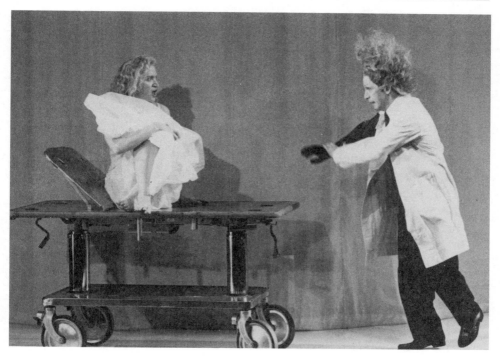

Plate 19. The Baltimore Waltz, by Paula Vogel, Yale Repertory Theatre. Mary Schultz (Anna) and Tim Blake Nelson (Carl), photo by T. Charles Erickson.

Scrapbook Dramaturgy

In *The Baltimore Waltz*, as elsewhere in Vogel's dramas, circularity does not mean a return to or of "the same." Rather, as Savran observes in an essay introducing *The Baltimore Waltz and Other Plays*, even when we are returned to "the scene of the crime," this return also involves us in a contradiction: "everything has remained the same and, simultaneously, changed radically" (1996: xiii). Consider in this vein *The Oldest Profession* (1980), Vogel's reworking – repetition with a difference – of David Mamet's play *The Duck Variations*. Like Mamet, Vogel uses the formal device of setting the entire action of the play in one place (a park bench). However, she replaces *The Duck Variations'* two elderly male protagonists with five old women, all lifelong prostitutes who are barely scratching out a living in the "oldest profession" of the play's title.

Perched on a "long bench at 72nd Street and Broadway, New York City" (in the heart of their professional territory) "shortly after the election of Ronald Reagan" (Vogel 1996: 131), the five aging prostitutes alternately argue about contemporary politics and reminisce about the good old days. After a brief blackout, the second scene begins as the first one did, except now the women number only four. With the exception of blackout four, a subtraction by one happens after each subsequent blackout, until, by the last scene, only Vera is left onstage. She does not speak. "She just sits, plaintively quiet," to await, as does the audience, the sixth and final blackout of the play.[2] In several ways, the main event of *The Oldest Profession* – death – occurs between the scenes, during the blackouts. The play's subtitle seems even to emphasize this reading: *A Full-Length Play in Six Blackouts*. The audience does not so much see the main event or events as witness the aftermath: absence. Structurally, these absences and the device that marks them, the repeated blackouts, appear the same, and yet each loss is also unique and individual.

The Oldest Profession is not the only one of Vogel's plays in which she explicitly sets out to reimagine someone else's work. In *How I Learned to Drive* (1997), she retells Vladimir Nabokov's *Lolita*, a story of pedophilia, from the perspective of the abused girl. *And Baby Makes Seven* (1984) lifts – and hilariously repurposes – the imaginary children of Edward Albee's *Who's Afraid of Virginia Woolf?* The structure of *The Baltimore Waltz* is borrowed from an 1891 short story by Ambrose Bierce, "An Occurrence at Owl Creek Bridge." Vogel has said that Thornton Wilder's *Our Town*, in particular its "homage to the ghost plays of Noh," is one of the inspirations behind her 2003 play, *The Long Christmas Ride Home*.

David Savran has described these borrowings as "acts of retaliation" (qtd. in Vogel 1996: x). This is a helpful and witty formulation, which aptly underscores Vogel's interest in exposing and unsettling the guiding assumptions of her (usually) male predecessors. But Vogel's willingness, not to mention her *nerve*, to rewrite the dramatic texts of others also signals something else, namely, generous modes of historical contact and (dis)identification.

Strange Ordinary

Vogel uses somewhat more colorful language to describe the origins of her 1986 play *Desdemona: A Play About a Handkerchief*: "rip-off." In a prefatory note to the play, she writes that it was "written as a tribute ('rip-off') to the infamous play, *Shakespeare the Sadist* by Wolfgang Bauer" (1996: 176). As Ann Linden observes, *Desdemona's* influences, what I would call its "historical relations," are visible on two levels: form and content (Linden 2002: 238). At the level of content, the play rewrites Shakespeare's *Othello* from the perspective of the female characters: Desdemona, of course, but also Emilia and the courtesan Bianca. This reflects Vogel's feminist wish to develop "fully dimensional" female characters, something, she has argued, male dramatists of the past have rarely accomplished or even attempted. As a result, "there's a very small legacy for women dramatists to use" (1999a: 273). She wants to portray women as more than functions of privatized family relationships as daughters, mothers, and wives. Vogel's imaginative rewriting of Shakespeare's *Othello*, for example, can be viewed as a reaching back into theatre history in order to broaden the identificatory field for future dramatists as well as future audiences.

The formal innovations of *Desdemona* are borrowed from Bauer, yet tweaked. *Desdemona* was written in "thirty cinematic takes," and in her note to directors, Vogel encourages them to stage the play in such a way as to simulate the process of filming, with jump cuts and repetitions (1996: 176). Bauer's *Shakespeare the Sadist* was also divided into "takes," its cinematic associations underscored through the use of music from films and slides of film studio logos.[3] While Vogel does not explicitly invite the "intercutting" of materials from other artistic media in *Desdemona*, the creative mixture of various media elements, especially the use of music to conjure a particular historical scene or mood, has become a hallmark of Vogel's later work.

Vogel wrote *Desdemona* while enrolled in the PhD program at Cornell University. The play, in fact, had its first staged reading at Cornell in 1977, and Vogel herself directed. She credits this educational period for introducing her to the ideas of the Russian formalist Viktor Shklovsky (1893–1984). Shklovsky was significant to Vogel because he was interested, as was Vogel, in how art produces its effects on an audience. Although his particular focus was literature, his investigation into the techniques by which literary language can make ordinary events appear "strange" had implications for other forms of art such as theatre, as well as politics. His best-known concepts are "defamiliarization" (*ostranenie*, or "making strange") and "laying bare" (in which art calls attention to its devices). These ideas were eventually taken up and explicitly politicized in Bertolt Brecht's (1898–1956) well-known "alienation effect" (*Verfremdungseffekt*),[4] which advocates finding new ways to turn obvious and normative events into something unusual, extraordinary, and startling.

Both Shklovsky and Brecht have made their mark on Vogel's plays, although she identifies far more closely with Shklovsky. Her self-described "Russian Formalist mind" can be observed in her already noted preference for circularity and repetition over linearity, as well as in the way she has come to mix – or "*juxtapose*," as Linden aptly notes (2002: 234) – dialogue with musical and visual elements.[5] Nor are her formal experimentations bound by conventions of western drama. Most recently, in *The Long Christmas Ride Home*, Vogel turns with great effect to elements of traditional Japanese theatre (more on this play shortly).

Vogel is not experimenting with form for form's sake. Rather, she is interested in disrupting routinized habits of response, and this, too, derives from her engagement with Shklovsky's Russian formalism. She shares Shklovsky's concern with the way habits of perception have been dulled to the point of becoming automated. In his important essay "Art as Technique" (1917),[6] he criticized the "habitualization" of everyday life, warning that it "devours work, clothes, furniture, one's wife, and the fear of war" (qtd. in Vogel 1998c). By defamiliarizing "the normal," art can help to recover or refresh our faculties of perception so that we might feel – and, perhaps, make – the world anew.

The stakes here are high. As the range of Shklovsky's list indicates ("work, clothes, furniture, one's wife, and the fear of war"), habitualization does not merely dull the complexities of ordinary life. A related concern is that we might grow so accustomed to extreme or *non-ordinary* experiences that we not only accept them as normal, but we also become immobilized in our ability to challenge them; sexual violence, for example, or the organized violence of war might come to feel ordinary, automatic, and, in a word, "natural," thereby stifling any resistance to the status quo. This is not to suggest that "the" problem with violence is that contemporary American society has come to think of it as "normal," when in actuality we need to view it as exceptional. This change of focus would actually *not* help us recognize the ubiquity of some forms of violence. Regrettably, the everyday encounters of homophobia, racism, and sexism suggest that violence does not belong only or even principally to the realm of non-ordinary experience.[7] For those who are the objects of such repeated violence, there is no respite from the everyday.

This disturbing possibility is provocatively explored in Vogel's 1993 play *Hot 'N' Throbbing*, which documents the brutality of domestic violence. In the split-screen world of the play, we follow two stories – two worlds, really – at once. There is the domestic reality of the Woman/Charlene (who writes screenplays for erotic films), her children (Girl/Leslie Ann and Boy/Calvin), and her estranged husband (the Man/Clyde), against whom she has a restraining order. Next to or, more provocatively, *encircling* this reality is a world of fantasy: an erotic dance hall with peep shows and porno booths. Two glass booths, at stage left and stage right, actually bracket the living room at the center of the stage. The effect here is to suggest the volatile porousness of the boundaries between fantasy and reality and between archetype (Woman, Man, Girl, Boy) and lived particular (Charlene, Clyde, Leslie Ann, and Calvin).

Over the course of this innovative play, scenes out of a peep show are juxtaposed with scenes of a life-and-death struggle for power between the Man and the Woman, in which she loses. Adding to the tragedy is the fact that the Boy and the Girl have witnessed their father murdering their mother. The play ends by suggesting that this history of violent loss will be borne and repeated in the next generation. In the disturbing last scene of *Hot 'N' Throbbing* the Girl ages before our eyes: she pulls back her hair; exchanges her tight pants and halter top for knee socks, a long-sleeve shirt, thick jeans, and running shoes; and, finally, dons her mother's glasses. The looking-glass image complete, the cycle begins again. The play's final words return us to the beginning: the Girl sits at her mother's computer and types the words her mother was typing at the play's start (see Linden 2002: 244).

But, must history repeat itself? *Hot 'N' Throbbing* cannot or will not answer this question. Its task is rather to press *us* to ask it. Here I am parting company somewhat from Linden, who sees the play ending with a "continuation of patterns" of violence (2002: 244). In my view, the play's conclusion is more open-ended than terms like "continuation" or "patterns" suggest. The Girl's future does not have to be foreclosed, or bound, by the mother's past. The altered context in which the Girl repeats her mother's dialogue is significant in this regard. Where her mother's words were part of a screenplay, the daughter's are part of a play, of a production of *Hot 'N' Throbbing*, perhaps. The Girl begins to type: "'Setting: At the beginning of the play we see a living room in a suburban townhouse.... At the top of Act One, the mother is typing a screenplay'" (Vogel 1996: 294). Alongside the possibility of history repeating itself, the play thus counterposes theatre as a locale where different histories – different "befores" and "afters" – might unfold. A potential for change and for alternative endings is signaled in this change of genre, in the shift from the formulaic screenplays of the mother to the incomplete play of the daughter. It is for the audience to complete the work of writing the daughter's story.

On the Value of being a "Bad" Feminist

It has been noted earlier that the women of Vogel's plays are never reduced to their functions as wives, mothers, and daughters. At the same time, though, Vogel is keenly interested in exposing the debilitating effects of being reduced to such functional roles. One of the feminist achievements of *Hot 'N' Throbbing* is that it is unafraid to show the Woman's participation in the gendered dynamics that ultimately result in her murder. This is not the same thing as blaming the victim; it is, however, a refusal to see violence against women as all-or-nothing scenarios in which a woman is either all good, and thus an "innocent victim," or else she must have had it coming. As Vogel argues in a 1998 interview with Arthur Holmberg, "Wherever there is confusion or double, triple, and quadruple standards, that is the realm of theatre. Drama lives in paradoxes and contradictions" (1998b). Her object in *Hot 'N' Throbbing* and elsewhere is to shine a light on the lived consequences of living with "paradoxes and contradictions." In a play like *Hot 'N' Throbbing* this willingness to speak honestly about the intricate lines that connect one person to another means portraying the Woman's ongoing feelings for her abusive husband: feelings of pity, anger, and desire, too. This ambivalence is the stuff of drama because it is the stuff of life. *Hot 'N' Throbbing* is not a pretty feminist fable; then again, Vogel's feminism is not about "showing a positive image of women" (Vogel 1998b). Her feminist vision is far more complicated – and messy – than that.

This messiness may even be among the reasons *Hot 'N' Throbbing* has had so few professional productions (two). Indeed, the play's topic is "controversial"; the scenes that simulate peep shows and porno booths are deliberately pushing the envelope, as Vogel avows in the author's note to the play (1996: 230). But, arguably, responses to *Hot 'N' Throbbing* would have been less ambivalent and less nervous if Vogel had told the audience what it already thought it knew about domestic violence – if, in other words, she had given the audience back an obvious story of absolutely powerless victims and absolutely empowered abusers. This, however, is not the story Vogel creates. Nor does she cleanly delineate lines between representation and reality.

Even her humor stings. We are encouraged to laugh out of place, that is, at politically serious topics like domestic violence (*Hot 'N' Throbbing*), child abuse (*How I Learned to Drive*), and AIDS (*The Baltimore Waltz*). She uses humor to disarm and defamiliarize, crediting her "Jewish genes" (1998b) for the way she combines terror and comedy. This may not add up to an easy or seamlessly pleasant theatrical experience. But, Vogel does not see theatre's task as reassurance: "To me a play doesn't need to make me feel good. It can be a view of the world that is so upsetting that when I leave the theatre, I want to say no to that play, I will not allow that to happen in my life" (1998b). She courts this kind of upset in her own audiences; in the service of renewing the ordinary, she is willing to disrupt or qualify their pleasure as spectators. These theatrical disturbances are more than dalliances with formalism. At times, theatre needs to shock audiences out of their complacencies in order to challenge our accustomed ways of seeing the world, even, sometimes, our accustomed *feminist* ways.

In other plays, too, Vogel refuses to offer sanitized or politically "correct" views of complex social realities. Eschewing a theatre of positive images, she instead invites resistance and risks pushing her audience back in their seats with "negative empathy." For example, consider how hard it would be to fashion a "polling-group safe case" for lesbian and gay families out of *And Baby Makes Seven*'s strange tribe. The play depicts a lesbian couple, their gay male friend (who is also the biological father of their child), and their three imaginary children. Vogel does not offer us a cozy homosexual version of the idealized heterosexual family unit (mother, father, and baby makes three); instead, she blows the lid off the fantasy that *any* family structure is normal. This refusal to present lesbian and gay families as carbon copies of the "traditional" family (add same-sex couple and stir) requires the audience to work harder to find its way "in." Empathic identification across difference has to be forged, not given in advance as some sort of liberal gesture of inclusion. In its willingness to transgress political comfort zones, right, left, and sideways, Vogel's *And Baby Makes Seven* ultimately offers something far richer and more complex than mirror images: a deliriously queer vision of kinship outside the bounds of the expected. "Non-traditional" families are not the only beneficiaries of such expansion.

Twisted kinship of a different sort is on view in Vogel's *The Mineola Twins*. Its identical twins, Myra and Myrna, are divided by politics, but similar in their inability to see shades of gray. This gravity-defying farce is a time capsule – and maybe a time bomb – of social and political upheaval in the United States in the second half of the twentieth century. The play's hilarious conceit – one actress plays both sisters (with the audience very much in on the joke) – works as a dizzying commentary on the straightjacket of gender roles and the limitations of binary thinking. This is not to say that *The Mineola Twins* wears its, or Vogel's, politics on its sleeve. Vogel is not interested in promoting a single political message –

agree with me or else! – but in providing a dramatic text that exposes the explosive political and social consequences of not listening to perspectives other than one's own. In a 1997 interview, Vogel said that she wrote the play as her response to the "political schizophrenia that's dividing us, dividing us into communities, into warring factions, into enraged siblings" (qtd. in Linden 2002: 247–8). Vogel's hope for *The Mineola Twins* is that it might work "toward that moment – even if it's only in our dreams – that we'll talk to each other, that we won't be divided anymore" (qtd. in ibid.: 248).

Vitally, this is not a dream of coercive sameness. Ending violent social divisions of the sort portrayed in *The Mineola Twins* does not mean making everyone the same or quarantining supposedly dangerous difference to the private sphere. For democracy to flourish, there must be more space made available to be different and *act* differently in private and in public.[8] This may be the democratic promise of Vogel's theatrical vision: the possibility that for an evening or an afternoon a group of strangers gathers in a common space, and out of this shared time they produce not a singular version of what occurred, but multiple and sometimes even competing memories of one and the "same" thing. This eruption of difference at the site of the same is not unlike the ways in which identical twins are not. As *The Mineola Twins* shows us, the twins may be much more alike than they'll ever admit, but this does not make them the same, nor even *self*-identical. In other words, we can change our minds about what we saw and experienced at the theatre; re-vision is part of the pleasure, and risk, of remembering events and relationships.

Time's Pulse (This is Not an Ending)

Given the political hopes that Vogel brings to her own plays and to theatre in general, it seems surprising that she does not identify more closely with Brecht or his theories. Her resistance makes sense, though, in the context of her profoundly empathic response to history. History just does not work as a distancing mechanism for Vogel in the same way it does for Brecht (Vogel 1999a: 275). For Brecht, a cool rationality and a "pulling back" must prevail in order to examine history. Vogel feels time's pulse too keenly to hold it at arm's length (think again of the dead man's hand on the gramophone's crank). Obviously, Vogel is well aware of, and herself exploits, various distancing techniques in her plays. She recognizes that distance is necessary to the work of theatre. In the program notes to *The Long Christmas Ride Home*, she argues: "To feel emotion, one must have distance, distance in years, distance in seats (framed by a proscenium) to experience the emotion of the play – emoted by living, breathing and very empathic actors" (2003: Playbill). Thus, her self-described "love/hate relationship" with Brecht's theories (1999a: 275) is not a reaction against distancing techniques *per se* or even to the use of historical distance as a defamiliarizing device. It is, rather, a reaction against a view of history as safe (distanced) or somehow containable in its effects.

In *How I Learned to Drive*, for which Vogel won the 1998 Pulitzer Prize for Drama, the play unfolds as a series of memories, recounted by the narrator Li'l Bit. The play is launched in an indeterminate present, and then we travel with Li'l Bit both backward and forward in time, viewing snapshots – out of sequence, out of time – as her story comes together and falls to pieces. By play's end, we are returned to the present, but it is a present elsewhere than Li'l Bit, or her audience, began. We have learned at what cost Li'l Bit learned to drive – and to love.[9]

The play's central drama is the incestuous relationship between Li'l Bit and her Uncle Peck. None of the terms usually used to characterize their relationship – "incest," "child abuse," "pedophilia," "trauma" – is adequate to either the complexity or weight of Li'l Bit's connection to her uncle. His legacy to her – love and loss, recognition and refusal – fails to resolve into pious and self-contained certainties. Uncle Peck is the only one of Li'l Bit's relatives who really sees her. But this recognition is also a form of seduction, and worse, in the play. He validates what he calls the "fire" in her head (1998a: 70) and teaches her to drive a car with confidence, like a man, even as he strips her of confidence in her body. The first driving lesson, when she was 11 years old, was also the first time he molests her. From that first lesson onwards, Li'l Bit has ceased to live in her body: "I retreated above the neck, and I've lived inside the 'fire' in my head ever since" (90).

Both the fire in Li'l Bit's head and the bodily sensation that she says she can feel only while driving connect her to her uncle across time and across the boundaries of life and death. In the haunting final image of the play, Li'l Bit steps into the car of memory and welcomes Uncle Peck's ghost.

> Ahh . . . (*Beat.*) I adjust my seat. Fasten my seat belt. Then I check the right side mirror – check the left side. (*She does.*) Finally, I adjust the rearview mirror. (*As Li'l Bit adjusts the rearview mirror, a faint light strikes the spirit of Uncle Peck, who is sitting in the back seat of the car. She sees him in the mirror. She smiles at him, and he nods at her. They are happy to be going for a long drive together. Li'l Bit slips the car into first gear; to the audience.*) And then – I floor it. (92)

She cannot escape her past; that is her burden and her gift. It is an ambivalent embrace.[10]

The burdens of our history with others weigh also heavily on the family of *The Long Christmas Ride Home*. The play opens and closes with memories of a long ago Christmas and a near-fatal car crash. In the wake of this almost-was, the car's five passengers – three children and their parents – will suffer from their desire to halt time, that is, to go back in time and fix what was damaged. This wish effectively blocks them from making a different kind of contact with time's accidents. As it circles round, *The Long Christmas Ride Home* reveals the fragility and the hope of human (re)connection.

The play makes detailed use of elements from traditional Japanese theatre. Large lifelike puppets represent the younger versions of the play's three siblings, Claire,

Stephen, and Rebecca. This is a borrowing from the premodern Japanese puppet theatre of *joruri* or *bunraku* (Viswanathan 2003: Playbill). The puppets float above the stage, but not too high; they are held by the actors who portray the children as adults, compellingly symbolizing the psychic grip of the past on the present. The characters are literally carrying around earlier "freeze-framed" versions of themselves. In a sense, the children have become their own ghosts; the puppets are a haunting theatrical conceit, spectral traces of a past the children cannot let go. As Meera S. Viswanathan observes in a program note to *The Long Christmas Ride Home*, these ghostly allusions connect the play to medieval Noh theatre. In Noh, which was "grounded in Zen Buddhist sensibilities . . . the central character of the first half of the play is revealed in the second to be in fact a ghost, haunted by his lingering attachments to the illusory world of phenomena" (Playbill). In *The Long Christmas Ride Home* the problem is not that characters are haunted by lingering attachments to the sensual world; it is that they do not know *how* to attach or connect in the present one. The adult children are haunted by a past they can feel, but whose meaning they have not yet apprehended. They yearn for contact with each other, with the past, with lost parts of themselves. Each of the three children attempts to connect with a lover who has literally shut them out by locking the door. As the three characters enjoin their lovers (we never see the objects of their love embodied) to unlock the door, we are also connecting to a past event of communicative breakdown (their father violently struck their mother while riding in a car during the ride home from Christmas visits). The children's struggles to remember are struggles to re-member, for flesh to touch flesh. In the final moments of the play, *The Long Christmas Ride Home* proposes theatre, and its shared time and space, as a place for flesh and blood contact. The adult Stephen, who is dying from AIDS, invites the audience to imagine with him a broken group breathing as one. The collision of these "multiple breaths" creates "entire symphonies of air and color and light" (qtd in Coale 2003: Playbill). It looks so beautiful from a distance, he tells us. *Come closer*, Vogel dares.

Collision and contact. Color and light. Living with an openness to history and its reverberations does not promise wholeness or the safety of the known. Vogel's plays certainly do not offer anything as simple as "closure." The plays are scrapbook-like in their presentation of time's remainders: fragments of memory, quick political references to ground a moment, and bits of song to mark an historical time or place. The dramatic action often circles around the characters' struggles to hold it together and bring order to these shards of memory without being cut to pieces. Characters do not always succeed. Or, if they do succeed, the achievement alters the terms of measurement. Time's pulse is not slight. And yet, out of the past and out of renewed relationships to it might flash up alternative ways of inhabiting the present and imagining the future. That is Paula Vogel's ghostly gift to us.

NOTES

1. This may be a distinctively "queer" way to understand – and relate to – time. Certainly, there are striking overlaps between Vogel's conception of historical contact and that of a number of queer theorists. I am thinking in particular of the "queer historical touch" developed by Carolyn Dinshaw (1999). Judith Halberstam pursues questions of queer time in her forthcoming book (2004). See also Elizabeth Freeman (2002) and Molly McGarry (2003).

2. See Ann Linden's elegant and brief discussion of *The Oldest Profession*; my summary largely follows hers (2002: 234–5).

3. For more on this, see Linden (2002: 238), where she credits Christopher Bigsby (1999: 298–9).

4. For a brief discussion of the political limits of formalism, see Terry Eagleton (1983: 136).

5. For Vogel's "Russian Formalist mind," see Vogel (1999a: 288).

6. For a helpful and brief discussion of this essay, see Raman Selden (1986: 8–9).

7. For more on this issue, see Ann Cvetkovich (2003), Ann Cvetkovich and Ann Pellegrini (2003), and David L. Eng and David Kazanjian (2003). I have also benefited from Laura Levitt's discussion of what it means to claim the ordinary (2003).

8. My own thinking about these issues has been nourished by conversations and collaborations with Janet R. Jakobsen.

9. The arguments in this section condense my more extensive discussion about mourning and traumatic memory in *How I Learned to Drive* in Pellegrini (2004).

10. I am borrowing this term from Laura Levitt (2003).

BIBLIOGRAPHY

Bigsby, C. W. E. (1999). *Contemporary American Playwrights*. Cambridge: Cambridge University Press, 289–329.

Coale, S. (2003). "The American Family: Fantasy, Failure, Fulfillment?" Playbill. In Paula Vogel, *The Long Christmas Ride Home*. Providence, RI: Trinity Repertory Company.

Cvetkovich, A. (2003). *An Archive of Feelings: Trauma, Sexuality, and Lesbian Public Cultures*. Durham, NC: Duke University Press.

——and Pellegrini, A. (eds.) (2003). *Public Sentiments*. Special issue of *The Scholar and Feminist Online* 2, 1 (Summer); www.barnard.edu/sfonline/ps.

Dinshaw, C. (1999). *Getting Medieval: Sexualities and Communities, Pre- and Postmodern*. Durham, NC: Duke University Press.

Eagleton, T. (1983). *Literary Theory: An Introduction*. Minneapolis: University of Minnesota Press.

Eng, D. L. and Kazanjian, D. (eds.) (2003). *Loss: The Politics of Mourning*. Berkeley: University of California Press.

Freeman, E. (2002). "Time Binds, or, Erotohistoriography." Unpublished paper.

Halberstam, J. (2004). *In a Queer Time and Place: Essays on Postmodernity and Gendered Embodiment*. New York: New York University Press.

Levitt, L. (2003). "Gendered Pictures, Generational Visions." In Laura Levitt (ed.), *Changing Focus: Family Photography and American Jewish Identity*. Special issue of *The Scholar and Feminist Online* 1, 3 (Winter); www.barnard.edu/sfonline/cf.

Linden, A. (2002). "Seducing the Audience: Politics in the Plays of Paula Vogel" and "Interview with Paula Vogel." In Joan Herrington (ed.), *The Playwright's Muse*. New York: Routledge, 231–52; 253–60.

McGarry, M. (2003). "Ghosts of Futures Past." Unpublished paper.

Pellegrini, A. (2004). "Staging Sexual Injury: *How I Learned to Drive.*" In Janelle G. Reinelt and Joseph R. Roach (eds.), *Critical Theory and Performance*, 2nd ed. Ann Arbor: University of Michigan Press.

Savran, D. (1996). "Loose Ends: An Introduction." In Paula Vogel, *Baltimore Waltz and Other Plays*. New York: Theatre Communications Group, ix–xv.

Selden, R. (1986). *A Reader's Guide to Contemporary Literary Theory.* Lexington: University of Kentucky Press.

Shklovsky, V. (1965 [1917]). "Art as Technique." In Lee T. Lemon and Marion J. Reis (eds.), *Russian Formalist Criticism: Four Essays*. Lincoln: University of Nebraska Press.

Viswanathan, M. S. (2003). "A Slender Margin." Playbill. In Paula Vogel, *The Long Christmas Ride Home*. Providence, RI: Trinity Repertory Company.

Vogel, P. (1996). *The Baltimore Waltz and Other Plays.* New York: Theatre Communications Group.

—— (1998a). *The Mammary Plays: How I Learned to Drive and The Mineola Twins.* New York: Theatre Communications Group.

—— (1998b). Interview by Arthur Holmberg. *ARTicles Online*; www.amrep.org.

—— (1998c). "A Dis-Orientation for the Class of 2002." *Brown Alumni Magazine Online* (November/December); www.brownalumnimagazine.com.

—— (1999a). Interview with David Savran. In David Savran (ed.), *The Playwright's Voice: American Dramatists on Memory, Writing and the Politics of Culture*. New York: Theatre Communications Group, 263–88.

—— (1999b). Interview with Mary-Louise Parker. In Betsy Sussler (ed.) (with Suzan Sherman and Ronalde Shavers), *Speak Theater and Film: The Best of Bomb Magazine's Interviews with Playwrights, Actors, and Directors*. New York: New Art, 1–11. (Originally published in *Bomb* 61 [Fall 1997].)

—— (2003). Playbill. *The Long Christmas Ride Home.* Providence, RI: Trinity Repertory Company.

30

Lesbian and Gay Drama

Jill Dolan

Historians and critics, theorists and practitioners define and chronicle lesbian and gay theatre from a variety of perspectives. Some believe this genre derives its power and definition from identity, infusing its content with preoccupations, styles, and concerns "true" and "authentic" to lesbian, gay, bisexual, transgendered, and/or queer communities. Other theorists and artists believe "lesbian and gay drama" is already an archaic category, no longer necessary because such work has gradually assimilated into mainstream theatre and performance. Queer theorists see lesbian and gay performance as a transgressive social practice that demonstrates, through notions of "performativity," the profitable instability and fluidity of sexuality, as well as of gender, race, and ethnicity. They suggest that queer performativity demonstrates, through socially constructed everyday life performance – as well as in solo perform-ance art and other forms that reject the normalizing tendencies of domestic dramatic realism – that sexuality is not essential to identity (that is, not biological) but ideologically delimited in various ways in different historical moments across cultures.

Early histories of the genre look back to the first half of the twentieth century to chart how sexuality became a determining factor in creating, attending, and cri-tiquing drama and performance. Kiaer Curtain's *We Can Always Call them Bulgarians* (1987) begins in the early twentieth century. He explores lesbian and gay theatre against a backdrop of social mores enforced by legislation such as New York's Com-stock Law (the "Act for the Suppression of Trade in, and Circulation of, Obscene Literature and Articles of Immoral Use," passed through Congress by Anthony Comstock in 1873) and the Wales Padlock Act of 1927, which allowed the New York police department to penalize theatre owners who allowed homosexuality (or so-called sexual degeneracy or perversion) to be portrayed onstage. Curtain discusses *The*

I would like to thank Jaclyn Pryor for her superb research assistance on this chapter, and Stacy Wolf for her very helpful remarks on earlier drafts.

Captive (1926), a play adapted from a story by Edouard Bourdet, in which lesbian desire drives the plot. Police, three months into the show's run, rushed into the theatre and arrested the director and the entire cast during a performance. Mae West's play *The Drag* (1927), one of the earliest expressions of openly homosexual content on a public stage, described two gay men, one married, involved in a love triangle that ends in murder and stages, in the process, a drag ball. Although the play was successful out of town, New York police threatened to shut it down if West tried to open it on Broadway (see chapter 6).

Lillian Hellman's *The Children's Hour* (1934) uses "deviant" sexuality to build the plot's tension and begin its characters' unraveling. A student's fabricated story about a lesbian relationship between two teachers who run a girl's school propels the play to its tragic conclusion, in which one of the teachers, decried for her desire, finds that what began as a vicious rumor does indeed describe her feelings for her colleague. She confesses her tortured love and promptly kills herself. The tragic ends of lesbian or homosexual male characters in conventional drama of the 1930s through the 1950s affirmed the staunchly heterosexual proscriptions of the time; they remained unhappy, isolated, singular examples of their kind (see chapter 8).

American drama of the 1940s and 1950s, as David Savran points out in his book *Communists, Cowboys, and Queers* (1992), often used latent homosexuality as a plot device, writing titillating, compelling, coded undercurrents of longing and yearning for the banished, sinful pleasures of same-sex affection and passion. Savran cites Arthur Miller's *A View From the Bridge* (1955), as well as Tennessee William's *Cat on a Hot Tin Roof* (1954), to demonstrate that often, in canonical American drama, thematizing same-sex longings and desire helps to shape characters' personalities and destinies, while alternative sexual practices remained taboo in American culture. Senator Joseph McCarthy's House Un-American Activities Committee (HUAC) in the 1950s blacklisted homosexuals along with Communists, since gay identity, which HUAC purposefully linked to anti-democratic politics, threatened national values. Such inculcation of homosexuality as a political as well as a moral menace meant that playwrights, actors, directors, and producers who might have called themselves lesbian or gay had to cloak their identities in innuendo. Such artists signaled their desire indirectly, through vocal, gestural, and other semiotic codes lesbian or gay spectators might read but that would slip by government censors. Gay playwrights like Edward Albee, who began his career in the early 1960s (see chapter 16), shrouded gay themes in his plays' subtext and symbolism and left homosexuality incidental to their larger meanings. For example, in Albee's *The Zoo Story* (produced in 1960 in Greenwich Village's Provincetown Playhouse), which takes place at a bench in Central Park, Jerry, a young man who has been to the zoo (and who identifies as "queer," having had sex with a "Greek boy"), provokes Peter, a reticent married man with two children whose sexuality is left ambiguous, to kill him. When Peter stabs him to death, Jerry thanks him, saying, "See, you're an animal, too."

As a result of social repression, many gay and lesbian playwrights gravitated to less commercial, less visible theatres to develop and present their plays among a more liberal, supportive community of artists and audiences. Joe Cino's Caffé Cino, a storefront coffeehouse and impromptu performance space that opened in Greenwich Village on Cornelia Street in 1958, also offered a fertile workshop for playwrights eager to experiment outside of realist formal conventions that typically ostracized or punished lesbians and gay men. Cino offered his 8 ft by 8 ft stage to any artist who had something to say until the Caffé closed in 1968. Doric Wilson, one of the first gay playwrights to flourish at Caffé Cino, staged *And He Made a Her* for Cino, a play that became ubiquitous in the Caffé's repertoire. Wilson went on to form TOSOS (The Other Side of Silence) Theatre, which produced much of his later work. As a Caffé Cino denizen, Wilson wrote the popular *Street Theatre*, first produced in 1982 at the Theatre Rhinoceros in San Francisco, a regional gay theatre whose formation was inspired by Cino's Caffé.

Cino also produced Robert Patrick's early play *The Haunted Host* (1964), in which the ghost of his ex-lover visits a playwright. The ghost helps him realize that he has closed himself off from love. London's prominent queer theatre, Gay Sweatshop, included the play in its first season in 1975. Lanford Wilson's *The Madness of Lady Bright* (1964), about the mental deterioration of a drag queen, proved significant to many of the artists for whom Caffé Cino provided formative, generative artistic and social possibilities. William Hoffman, one of the first gay playwrights to write about the AIDS crisis, also began his career at Cino's, with *Thank You, Miss Victoria* (1965). Playwrights often used Cino's whole storefront theatre and café as their environmental set, even involving the bathroom in a sound cue for a toilet flush in Wilson's *Babel, Babel, Little Tower*. Caffé Cino was constrained by the tiny stage and the nearness of the audience to the performers, but the electricity (what Cino called "magic time" [see Crespy 1996]) that often comes from such intimate performance conditions helped the work ride a current of relevance and need in the gay and lesbian subculture.

The Stonewall riots of 1969 proved a major turning point for lesbian and gay liberation in America that deeply affected the future of gay and lesbian drama and performance. Although police raided gay and lesbian bars in Greenwich Village throughout the 1950s and 1960s, patrons faced the New York Police Department's invasion of the Stonewall Inn on Christopher Street the night of Judy Garland's funeral in 1969 with righteous resistance (see Duberman 1993). Gay people who had permitted themselves to be led off to jail in prior raids now refused to bow to authority, and fought against the police instead of acquiescing. Stonewall began the public American movement for homosexual liberation, and gay and lesbian theatre groups sprang up around the country to develop new plays and new ways of working in drama and performance.

Early overtly lesbian drama adopted experimental forms, sometimes didactic in their style and tone. For example, Martha Boesing's feminist theatre, At the Foot of the Mountain in Minneapolis, produced performances for mostly women-only audiences, stressing the importance of a separate space to explore a forum that for too long had excluded women's voices and experiences. Boesing's play *Love Song for an Amazon* (1976), a ritual ceremony performed by two women, uses transformational theatre techniques to create a positively charged onstage community. Lesbian and feminist theatre companies in New York which, because of the city's visibility and the density of lesbian and gay drama flourishing simultaneously there, came to represent the national references for the history of the form, tended to be aesthetically and politically aggressive. It's Alright to be a Woman Theatre (established in 1970), one of the first women's agit-prop theatre groups, used the street performance styles of the era to promulgate new political stands on women's and lesbians' experiences. Margo Lewitin established Women's Interart, a producing house in Hell's Kitchen that helped lesbian and feminist theatre thrive despite the competitive, pricey real estate of Manhattan. A group of downtown experimental playwrights including Rosalyn Drexler, Rochelle Owens, Sam Shepard, Ed Bullins, and lesbian writers Megan Terry (*Viet Rock*, 1966) and Cuban American Maria Irene Fornes (see chapter 27), formed the New York Theatre Strategy in 1973, a workshop that allowed playwrights to test their ideas without worrying about pleasing audiences. Fornes led Theatre Strategy for five years; her early plays, like *Tango Palace* (1963), were heavily influenced by Beckett and the Theatre of the Absurd; her later work includes the significant feminist play *Fefu and Her Friends* (1977).

The Women's Experimental Theatre (WET, established in 1977) branched off from Joseph Chaikin's Open Theatre, when Roberta Sklar – who had served as the Open Theatre's co-director, but never captured the attention and acclaim of her collaborator – left the theatre. Inspired by the new lesbian and feminist political analysis, she began her own company with Sondra Segal and Clare Coss. WET produced performances that quoted canonical texts like Aeschylus's *The Oresteia* to invest them with new meanings about gender and sexuality. *The Daughter's Cycle Trilogy*, which included the play *Electra Speaks* (1980), rewrote and repopulated the House of Atreus from a feminist perspective. WET's work refused the typical separation of audience and performer, choosing instead to use elements of audience participation in devising their productions, and inviting their performance collective to generate material from their own lives that might offer new viewpoints on old, patriarchal stories. WET's work serves as a useful example of the close affiliation between lesbian and feminist cultural politics. Their productions addressed mother/daughter relationships – one of the most ubiquitous tropes of the second-wave women's movement in the United States – along with food, body image, and labor, all women's issues instilled with a lesbian perspective.

Rather than forming theatre collectives, as did many lesbian artists influenced by feminist politics, or following the newly envisioned tenets of the experimental theatre movement, white gay male playwrights adopted more conventional forms to describe their experiences and their liberatory practices after Stonewall. Mart Crowley's pre-Stonewall *Boys in the Band* (1968), which was produced off-Broadway, served as the generic model for many plays that followed. *Boys* – which has become a classic of gay drama, despite its less than sympathetic representations of gay men – uses realism to tell the story of a group of close friends gathering to celebrate a birthday, whose drunken revelries and game of truth inspire vicious accusations and painful confessions and revelations. The play's portrayal of gay men as self-loathing spoke of homophobia that the play thoroughly internalized. Despite its retrograde political meanings, *Boys in the Band* was the first visible, widely produced, and eventually filmed gay American drama (see chapter 15).

By the early 1980s, playwright/actor Harvey Fierstein took *Torch Song Trilogy* (1982) to Broadway. Fierstein's play formed three smaller sketches that told, from an affirming, sometimes campy perspective, stories about the peccadilloes of white gay male life in New York. In the solo play, *International Stud*, playing Arnold Beckoff, a gay, Jewish New Yorker who is also a professional female impersonator (not unlike Fierstein himself), he enacted gay sex acts, describing his experience with an anonymous partner in a club. While the moment probably marked the first simulation of anonymous anal sex in Broadway history, Fierstein's Jewish, campy shtick made him familiar to New York audiences. His slightly self-deprecating comic style invited the audience to laugh with him, rather than at him, and, in the process, to accept his differences. Fierstein went on to write the book for the musical *La Cage Aux Folles* (1983), a comedy based on a French film about a female impersonator, his gay partner, his son, and the heterosexual family into which his son intends to marry. Although full of slapstick humor, *La Cage* preaches tolerance and pride, ideas sanctified by the musical's long Broadway run, 1,761 performances.

Martin Sherman's play *Bent* (1979) used similar familiarizing devices to deliver gay content to New York audiences, after it moved to Broadway from its run at London's Royal Court. The production starred Richard Gere, and while it detailed in horror and sorrow gay men's treatment during the Holocaust, the themes of genocide in which it embedded its gay love story were well known to New York spectators. *Bent's* imprisoned lovers move heavy stones from one pile to another, caught in an endless, dehumanizing concentration camp trial through which only their passion for each other keeps them alive under the eyes of Nazi guards. In *Bent*, gay male love represents human struggle against a culture of death; the play's realism and its historical themes made its depiction of a gay relationship redemptive and tolerable. As these examples show, gradually, white gay men writing gay plays saw their work successfully produced in mainstream forums, rather than by the collective, alternative theatres that welcomed lesbians and people of color.

Jane Chambers, the first openly lesbian American playwright, produced her work with the Glines, an organization that championed gay theatre. Chambers's breakout success, *Last Summer at Bluefish Cove* (1980), played an extended run at Westbeth Theatre, which is housed in a city-subsidized artists' building near the west side pier in Greenwich Village. The realist play describes a group of lesbian friends taking their annual beach vacation on Long Island. Most of the couples share a dense history of sexual relationships with each other; the lightly bickering pairs establish themselves as "typical," assimilating lesbians' lives to the familiar hetero-sexual model. While Chambers types the characters predictably – from the gruff butch to the mothering femme – their affection for each other, and their commitment to their friendships as sustaining, provided one of the first positive, complex illustra-tions of lesbian community onstage. Lil, the womanizing single and senior member of the community, falls in love with Eva, a straight woman whose subsequent coming out story steers the plot. In a twist that became typical for lesbian plays, Lil dies, in this case of cancer, but symbolically because of her non-monogamous, butch, tomcat behavior, which threatened the normative, conventionalized, insistently coupled world of the play.

Death or exile as plot devices appear often in lesbian plays of the 1980s, as if the playwrights, while describing lesbian life, could only write their characters' strengths and budding sense of community by later punishing them with tragedies that continued to emblematize their singularity and oppression in American culture. Another trope that appears in many of these plays – such as Sarah Dreher's *8 × 10 Glossy* (1988) and Chambers's *Quintessential Image* (1983) – is the lesbian as an outsider, often a photographer, who can see clearly other people's relationships, but feels only distanced from her own. Lesbian characters, even as written by lesbian playwrights in this period, seemed odd and alone, or if part of a community as in *Bluefish Cove*, one or two were regularly singled out and symbolically punished for being too "butch," or too "male-identified," testifying to this genre's attachment to gender liberation and conventional monogamous relations over more radical sexual identity politics.

Many critics argued that much self-described gay and lesbian realist drama pro-moted damaging representations of lesbian and gay characters and their place in American culture. They saw danger in realism's ideological entrenchment in insist-ently normal (or "normative") values that promote heterosexuality as the appropriate standard in the middle-class lives of American families, and whiteness as the default perspective from which drama speaks (see Dolan 1993, 2001). As playwrights and directors tried to add lesbian and gay drama to the conventional American canon, escalating costs also obstructed their attempt at visibility and parity in mainstream venues.

Some lesbian and gay theatre artists found other forums for their artistic visions, starting venues modeled by Cino's Caffé. The WOW Café in New York's East Village (established in 1980), for instance, became a vital proving ground for a generation of lesbian performers who rejected the tenets of realism, the proscenium stage, and commercial theatre. WOW's core organizing committee decided early on not to apply for grants, so that they would not be beholden to anyone but their audiences and their own artistic collective for financial and creative support. Artists worked at WOW with few resources, in a "poor theatre" style that lent their performances an edgy immediacy. First housed in a long, narrow storefront on East 11th Street, the Café soon moved to a walk-up, old factory space on East 4th

Street at the Bowery, where the theatre still makes its dusty home. No signage adorns the door to the theatre; spectators climb past boarded-up businesses on other floors and wait in line in the stairwell to pay for their inexpensive ticket. They enter a small, funky, jerry-rigged theatre where, rather than box sets housing normative domestic arrangements, WOW's artists created unusual settings (sometimes, for instance, stories took place in outer space) in imaginative ways. They concentrated on their performances and their reception by spectators to offer a vision of new social relationships. Productions at WOW were usually off-the-cuff, affecting, and pleasurable, especially for lesbians who had grown tired of realism's failures and more conventional theatre's refusal to risk investigating the complexity of their social and sexual lives.

Performance artist and playwright Holly Hughes, who came to New York from Michigan in the early 1980s to be a visual artist, found herself at WOW instead. Disillusioned by the political correctness she found constraining in the feminist art world, Hughes reveled in WOW's anarchy, its unwillingness to be held accountable to anyone's party line. Hughes's underground classic *The Well of Horniness* (1983), whose name parodied Radclyffe Hall's archetypal lesbian novel *The Well of Loneliness* (1928), caused a sensation at WOW. Written as a radio play but originally performed live by artists who had already become infamous as part of WOW's core collective (Alina Troyano, Peggy Shaw, Sharon Jane Smith, and Hughes, among others), the play stages a hilarious, parodic romp through lesbian subculture that quotes the conventions of radio drama, detective fiction, soap operas, melodrama, early television shows, and vaudeville. Hughes also wrote the eloquent, absurdist lesbian duet *Dress Suits for Hire* (1987), which was performed by Peggy Shaw and Lois Weaver. She continued writing autobiographical solo performances, including the poetic *World Without End* (1989), Hughes's reverie for her mother; *Clit Notes* (1990), a ribald comedy whose title couldn't be printed in most newspapers; and *Preaching to the Perverted* (2000), among other widely toured performances.

The Split Britches Company – Peggy Shaw, Lois Weaver, and Deb Margolin – whose work began at WOW with their signature play *Split Britches* (1982), an autobiographical, impressionistic homage to Weaver's reclusive female relatives in the Blue Ridge Mountains of Virginia – became WOW's founding and sustaining force. Shaw and Weaver, partners in everyday life as well as in the theatre, took on leadership roles, Weaver by teaching acting, directing, and performance composition to WOW members, Shaw by providing unmitigated artistic and physical support for experimentation on WOW's boards. Deb Margolin, the trio's straight and Jewish member, wrote many of Split Britches' performances, although they devised them, based on their own dreams and longings, collectively. Margolin brought her idiosyncratic presence into their performances in ways that, if they could not be called lesbian, could certainly be called "queer."

Plate 20. Split Britches (Lois Weaver, Peggy Shaw, and Deb Margolin) in *Upwardly Mobile Home.* Courtesy of Deb Margolin.

Shaw, Weaver, and Margolin all moved on to solo careers, Shaw in *You're Just Like My Father* (1995), *Menopausal Gentleman* (1999), and *To My Chagrin* (2001), autobiographical renderings of her life as a butch lesbian grandmother. Weaver's solo shows, likewise, detail her experiences as a theatrical femme. Shaw and Weaver maintain a separate collaboration that began with *Anniversary Waltz* (1989), which celebrated their tenth anniversary as partners; *Lust and Comfort* (1995), a bittersweet, absurdist inquiry into the costs and benefits of long-term, public relationships; and *It's a Small House and We Live in it Always* (2003), a nearly silent performance piece in which Shaw and Weaver slightly fictionalize and theatrically crystallize the complications of their relationship.

Margolin's solo career has also flourished, with *Joy Rides, Car Thieves* (1995) and *O Wholly Night and Other Jewish Solecisms* (1996), among other performances.

With Split Britches as its reigning example, WOW fostered many notable collectives and solo performers, who developed work at the Café then often moved out into other downtown Manhattan (and sometimes mainstream) venues. The Five Lesbian Brothers (Lisa Kron, Peg Healey, Moe Angelos, Babs Davy, and Dominique Dibbell), for example, began their group performance career with *Voyage to Lesbos* (1989), a fantastical, parodic, episodic rendering of rampant, wild, completely unconventional sexual exploration. The contradictions of the group's name signal their challenges to the proprieties of gender and sexuality. Their subsequent productions, some at New York Theatre Workshop, an off-off-Broadway theatre a short way down East 4th Street from WOW, included *Brave Smiles* (1992), a parody of genre films that stereotype lesbians; *The Secretaries* (1994), an outrageous take-off on killer lesbian horror films, in which a cabal of secretaries at a logging plant sacrifices local men in monthly rituals; and *Brides of the Moon* (1997), a queer space odyssey that satirized family conventions and middlebrow American aspirations.

The Brothers maintain a loose affiliation, although most of them now concentrate on solo performance. Lisa Kron, one of the early denizens of WOW, tours American regional theatres with her autobiographical monologue, *2.5 Minute Ride* (1996). First produced by George C. Wolfe at the Joseph Papp Public Theatre, *Ride* tells an elegiac story about traveling to Auschwitz with her father, a survivor of the Holocaust, intercut with a story about Kron bringing her lesbian partner to a family reunion at a large amusement park in Ohio. The visually simple, emotionally tender piece uses irony to soften the pain of revisiting the past, and just as delicately (and with less camp than Harvey Fierstein used 15 years earlier) mingles Kron's Jewish ethnicity with her lesbian identity.

Although gay men in the 1980s and 1990s never fostered their own version of the WOW Café or Caffé Cino, queer performance artist Tim Miller co-founded P.S. 122 (established in 1980) in the East Village. (The P.S. originally stood for Public School, in New York City's educational lexicon; when the building became available for reuse, the initials came to stand for Performance Space.) The venue remains essential to the development of solo performance and other iconoclastic dance, drama, and theatre, much of which is lesbian, gay, transgendered, by people of color, or queer. In addition to co-founding P.S. 122, Miller co-founded Highways Performance Space and Gallery (established in 1989) with critic Linda Frye Burnham in Los Angeles, another venue that supports work by both white and of color gay men and lesbians. One of the first openly gay male solo performance artists, Miller's monologue- and movement-based, activist, autobiographical work addresses issues of civil liberty and sexual liberation. Miller and fellow queer theatre artists Holly Hughes and John Fleck, and feminist firebrand Karen Finley, became known collectively in the 1990s as the "NEA Four," when the National Endowment for the Arts withheld grants that its own peer review panel approved for the four performers. His subsequent entanglement with the United States justice system became fodder for Miller's self-reflective, politically dissident work.

Miller is also renowned for the signature nudity in his performances. In *Naked Breath* (1994), during the height of the HIV/AIDS pandemic, Miller disrobed and moved into the audience to interact with spectators. He sat on people's laps, talking openly and affectionately with strangers about what it meant to be a naked gay man inviting himself into close proximity with other people's bodies. Audiences, at first embarrassed, soon tolerated and applauded Miller's naked interactions, which purposefully counteracted the physical degradation with which the dominant culture stereotypes people with AIDS and openly celebrated gay male sexuality at a time when the queer community was ravaged by the loss of those dying from the disease. In another groundbreaking moment in that performance, Miller directly addressed his naked penis, entreating it to "get hard" as a way of celebrating sexuality's necessity to life, rather than its association with death.

Much of Miller's now over 20-year opus refers to the AIDS pandemic, a social crisis that gay, lesbian, and queer theatre continues to address. William Hoffman wrote one of the first so-called AIDS plays (see Román 1998), *As Is* (1985), a dark comedy about HIV's impact on several gay men, their families, and the medical community. The play focuses on one gay man who learns to accept his HIV-positive lover "as is." Larry Kramer's realist play *The Normal Heart* (1985) solicits identifications with an ill gay man and his partner, and exhorts gay and heterosexual spectators to express their outrage at the lack of public funding for AIDS research and virus intervention. David Román's book *Acts of Intervention: Performance, Gay Culture, and AIDS* (1998) chronicles the canon of HIV/AIDS plays and performances, and engages critically with the complex ethical issues they raise about theatre and performance, activism and advocacy, and the efficacy of performance toward positive social change.

Solo performance continues to appeal to gay men and lesbians, since even toward the end of the twentieth century, the queer experiences accommodated by mainstream theatre tended toward two-dimensional assimilation rather than full-fledged radicalism. Autobiographical solo performance allows more room to explore difficult social truths, and requires less expensive sets, lighting, costumes, and props, and obviously, no other actors. Gay and lesbian solo performers often find special poignancy in performing, through their own perspectives, the familial and cultural characters who have acted as delivery systems for their oppression and their redemption throughout their lives. When gay men and lesbians play multiple characters, they explore a range of assimilations and rejections of white, middle-class, heterosexual American values and measure, against the length of their own bodies and experiences, the distance between the margins they inhabit and the mainstream to which they're inevitably, ambivalently connected (see chapter 32).

Queer people of color also succeed with this form. For example, Alina Troyano, an early member of WOW, creates solo performances that usually begin at theatres in Lower Manhattan, then go on to tour the country. Troyano's alter ego/persona Carmelita Tropicana buoys many gay, lesbian, or queer events, often serving as a quick, witty, and kind emcee for performance festivals or community political events.

Troyano's solo show *Milk of Amnesia* (1994), performed at P.S. 122, details her necessary forgetting and remembering (or literally reassembling) of her very early childhood in Cuba, and uses cross-gender impersonations to represent not only the differently gendered sides of herself and her culture, but the binational ethnic loyalties inspired by immigrant life. Puerto Rican lesbian solo performer Marga Gomez, too, in her show *A Line Around the Block* (1996), which she performed at the Public Theatre in New York and toured across the country, impersonates various members of her family and her multiple identifications with various subcultures.

Chicano queer playwright/performance artist Luis Alfaro, although he usually doesn't play other characters in his poetically rhythmic performances, describes the visceral experience of growing up gay in Mexican American culture, falling between the cracks of the tightly knit bonds of both communities. Alfaro uses his body literally and metaphorically in his piece *Cuerpo Politizado* (*Politicized Body*) (1996), at one point in his piece "A Mu-Mu Approaches" stuffing himself with boxes and boxes of Hostess Twinkies while a taped monologue describes the compromises necessary to assimilate into American life. In "Bachelor Party," Alfaro drinks shots of tequila in very quick succession, using the crisp, loud bang of the shot glass on a small table beside his microphone to insistently punctuate the ironies of the stories he tells while he drains the bottle of liquor. Alfaro, who received a John D. and Catherine T. MacArthur Foundation "genius" award, is affiliated with the Latino Initiative Project of the Los Angeles Theatre Center; he also tours solo work.

Pomo Afro Homos (established in 1991), a collective of three African American gay men originally based in San Francisco, toured performances in the early 1990s that investigated gay male and African American identity. One of their most well-known plays, *Dark Fruit* (1994), illustrates the social stigmas caused by both homophobia and racism in a series of vignettes that continually shift cultural perspectives. The piece works with irony, parody, and poignant optimism to describe the difficult pleasures of being gay men of color. Brian Freeman, one of the original Pomos, also tours solo performances, including *Civil Sex* (1997), a piece in which he plays Bayard Rustin, the first African American to participate in the civil rights struggle as an out gay man, and as an African American in the nascent gay rights movement.

Autobiographical solo performance appeals to queer artists financially as well as aesthetically and politically, as it is relatively inexpensive to present and easy to tour. The trade-off, however, is that a generation of lesbian, gay, and queer artists has generated drama that really only they can perform. Their contribution to the archive of queer performance is fundamental and impressive, but too little of it can circulate through other modes of production to be mounted by other performers at other theatres. Hughes's *The Well* and some of the Five Lesbian Brothers' plays have been reproduced with other casts in other locations, but much of this drama is tied to the artists by whom it was generated and depends on their physical presence to be meaningful. While solo performance offers a rich vein of lesbian and gay drama, other gay, lesbian, and queer theatre artists soldier on in more conventional forums, determined to see their work produced and recognized and recirculated through the medium of the play's text.

Although some of these lesbian and gay writers, directors, and actors remain committed to the somewhat essentializing category of "gay or lesbian play," for many successful, visible mainstream artists, their gay identity hasn't constrained or necessarily shaped their artistic careers. Playwright Terrence McNally, for example, one of the first out gay men to be accepted into mainstream American theatre, writes plays about gay men – such as *Lisbon Traviata* (1985), *Lips Together, Teeth Apart* (1991), the musical theatre adaptation of *Kiss of the Spiderwoman* (1992), and *Love! Valor! Compassion!* (1995) – while also working on Broadway, writing, for example, the book for the musical theatre version of *The Full Monty* (2000), the popular movie about a group of unemployed British working-class men who decide to make money by staging their own strip routine, and *Master Class*, a play about opera diva Maria Callas (1995). While Lanford Wilson and John Guare, along with others of their 1960s gay male compatriots, experimented with absurdism and hybrid theatrical forms, McNally and other gay male playwrights (such as Richard Greenberg) have succeeded with more conventional drama, placing their gay male characters in familiar domestic situations and allowing them to suffer some of the traumas (including coming out, death, and illness) into which such realist forms often devolve.

McNally's *Love! Valor! Compassion!*, for example, tells the story of several gay male couples' annual vacations at the country home of Gregory, their talented dancer friend. Much like Chambers's *Last Summer at Bluefish Cove*, the play constructs their community through their relationships. After narrating a series of personal, artistic, and health crises, the play's bittersweet epilogue describes how the couples bravely live out their lives together (for whatever lengths of time) in comfortable, domestic ways. This play uses nudity as decoration more than activism – the men gleefully disrobe to swim together in the pond on Gregory's property, a moment the play blesses with charming naturalness. This more distanced, aesthetic nudity counters the activist way in which Tim Miller wields his nakedness as a political tool. After opening at the Manhattan Theatre Club, *L!V!C!* transferred successfully to Broadway, was made into a film, and now enjoys a healthy shelf life in regional theatres.

Lesbian drama, like drama by women in general, has been less successful finding its way into visible commercial venues. The only lesbian productions that played to Broadway acclaim have been Lily Tomlin's solo shows *Appearing Nightly* (1977) and *Search for Signs of Intelligent Life in the Universe* (1985; revived 2000), although to call either of them "lesbian" would be hyperbolic. Although Tomlin and her artistic and life partner Jane Wagner are openly lesbian, and although both performances refer directly to lesbian and gay culture, their one-woman plays encompass a wide range of issues and identities. Likewise, Sandra Bernhard makes oblique or casual references to her own ambiguous sexual identity or to lesbians and gay men in general in her popular concert-like performances *Without You I'm Nothing* (1990) and *I'm Still Here...Damn It!* (1998), both of which began downtown at the Westbeth Theatre, then transferred to Broadway for limited runs before being made into art films. Bernhard works with an edgy social palette that draws on Jewish and African American culture more than the elusive lesbian desires in which she sometimes trades.

On the other hand, while she has never seen her work produced on Broadway, lesbian playwright Paula Vogel has achieved success off-Broadway and in regional theatre. Her play *The Baltimore Waltz* (1992), originally presented at the Circle Repertory Theatre – starring the openly lesbian actor Cherry Jones and directed by openly lesbian Anne Bogart – addresses allegorically Vogel's brother's death from AIDS. In theatrical flights of comic fantasy, Vogel's three-character play follows a brother and sister on their whirlwind search through Europe for a cure for "Acquired Toilet Disease," the sister's sexually contracted disease, which turns out to be a displacement of the brother's HIV/AIDS. Regional theatres and universities all over America have produced the play. Vogel's *And Baby Makes Seven* (1987), in which a lesbian and a gay male couple fantasize – in another curious, absurdist environment – about having a child, while not commercially successful, exemplifies the range of Vogel's theatricality and her social imagination. *Hot 'N' Throbbing* (1990) and *The Mineola Twins* (1995) also dig under the surface of normative heterosexual life to root out with generous humor insidious ideological presumptions and complacencies about gender, sexuality, and class. Her play *How I Learned to Drive* (1997) won the Pulitzer Prize in 1998, making Vogel the first out lesbian to win the award (out gay playwright Tony Kushner won the 1993 Pulitzer Prize for *Angels in America* [1992]). *Drive* narrates L'il Bit's sexual awakening (or child abuse, depending on one's perspective) by her Uncle Peck, in a rather sadly nostalgic, presentational yet nuanced style that is both moving and liberating. The play's content, while only obliquely lesbian (in certain pronominal usages in off-hand remarks), addresses sexual identity in powerful, ambivalent, poignant ways. Vogel extends *Drive* away from domestic realism – and even comments on it sardonically, making the family dinner table a scene of anarchy, misogyny, and lewdness rather than a hallowed setting for normative family values – to illustrate the unwieldy enormity of desire and longing. (See chapter 29 for further discussion of Vogel's work.)

While Vogel has now become a noted playwright off-Broadway and in regional theatres, as a woman, she remains outside a certain circle of influence. On the other hand, the Broadway production of Kushner's *Angels in America* was heralded as prophetic. Critics agreed that it spoke with breathtaking scope and intellectual, political, and theatrical daring to the concerns of a country living through the AIDS pandemic and the reign of Ronald Reagan in the 1980s. The two-part saga has been performed around the world; often, its productions are boycotted or censored. Kushner lends his energy and insights to protest these and other repressions of free speech and artistic expression. Perhaps because of his success with *Angels*,

Kushner affords the luxury of thematic diversity, writing other plays about the Russian Revolution (*Slavs*, 1995), and about the personal and political strife of an international cast of characters in *Homebody/Kabul* (2001), both of which have little to do with queer sexual identity.

But gender politics still operate in the different receptions of gay men's and lesbians' plays. As a white male, although gay, Kushner's opportunities seem unlimited, while Vogel, as a white lesbian, still plies her trade at least one status level below. Gay and lesbian playwrights of color often find themselves even more compromised by a lack of social approbation. Asian American playwright Chay Yew produces his plays at the Los Angeles Theatre Center, the Cornerstone Theatre Company, and the Mark Taper Forum, in Los Angeles; at La Jolla Playhouse in San Diego; and at the New York Theatre Workshop, the Public Theatre, and the Manhattan Theatre Club in New York. But like Vogel, Yew has never received a Broadway production, although his work stages political and sexual, racial and ethnic inquiries similar to those through which Kushner garners wide appeal. Yew's plays, such as *Language of Our Own* (1997), lyrically evoke the ways gay and racial identity bump up against each other in subtly shaded scenes whose images evoke the hybrid nature of both Asian and American cultures.

Chicana playwright Cherrie Moraga, a prolific political essayist, poet, and activist, began her career with *Giving Up the Ghost* (1984), an evocative tone poem about a young butch Chicana lesbian in love with an older femme who comes to represent everything the younger woman idealizes about her Mexican ethnicity. In a fragmented, postmodern form that eschews structural coherence for rich, singular visual and narrative images, the play evokes the social schizophrenia of binary distinctions between lesbian and straight, Chicana and white. Moraga rewrote the play in a more realist form later in her career, and committed herself stylistically to more conventional structures to accommodate Chicano domestic dramas such as *Shadow of a Man* (1985) and the more expressionist *Heroes and Saints* (1989).

Racial and ethnic distinctions contribute to differing degrees of visibility for much gay and lesbian drama, theatre, and performance, although to make a strict corollary between race and access to resourceful, influential venues would be misleading. For example, although an African American gay man, George C. Wolfe's artistic direction of the Public Theatre regularly puts his work among the most critically noticed theatre in New York. Wolfe demonstrates his commitment to racial, ethnic, and sexual diversity in the consistently varied seasons he directs or produces at the Public, from plays by Chay Yew to solo performances by Marga Gomez and Lisa Kron. Under Wolfe's leadership, the Public Theatre regularly transfers promising work to Broadway; these plays typically include progressive themes, often addressing the lives and concerns of people of color and gay men, whether or not they are marketed as gay or minoritarian. For example, a production of gay playwright Richard Greenberg's Tony Award-winning *Take Me Out* (2003), about a successful African American baseball player who comes out to his team, his profession, and his fans, transferred from the Public to Broadway, where its valentine to the sport as the apex of American democracy is as moving as the beautiful hero's adamant refusal of the closet.

The 2003 Tony Awards demonstrated openly gay men's incursion into the most powerful, well-rewarded ranks of Broadway production when Marc Shaiman and Scott Wittman, the lyricists/composers of the musical adaptation of John Waters's film *Hairspray*, won a Tony for Best Original Score. Delighted with their win, the two men joked about the preponderance of gay and Jewish men in Broadway musical theatre as they accepted their award. They ended with an affectionate public kiss, enthusiastically applauded by the audience. Of course, these two weren't the first gay men to be rewarded with accolades in the high-profile business of American musical theatre (see Wolf 2002). Composer/lyricist Stephen Sondheim, whom some consider the national treasure of the form, has gradually allowed his gay identity to be part of his public persona. While his intelligent, musically and thematically sophisticated musicals rarely take on gay themes (except, some might argue, for *Company* [1970]), his example as a successful openly gay man in an important, financially lucrative form illustrates that gay men and lesbians leave their imprint on all kinds of theatre production.

Queer camp traditions and gay male drag have long been a staple of American performance, theatre, and drama, from performance artist Ethyl Eichelberger's solo performances in New York in the 1970s and 1980s, to the Cockettes, a group of drag queens performing fantastical glamour art in San Francisco in the 1970s, to Hot Peaches, another drag troupe that traveled Europe (after "discovering" Peggy Shaw in New York's Sheridan Square). *Hedwig and the Angry Inch* (2000), John Cameron Mitchell's rock musical about a transsexual's botched gender-change operation, ran for an extended time off-Broadway in New York. Even ex-Brat Packer Ally Sheedy took a turn as the male-to-female transgendered lead. *Hedwig*, which was made into a well-received independent film, has become a popular choice for regional theatres. *Zanna Don't* (2002), a new off-off-Broadway musical parody, playfully disdains and degrades heterosexuals as social pariahs instead of lesbians and gay men. Even *Avenue Q* (2003), another off-Broadway musical, with puppets playing most of the characters, includes campy queer content.

Playwright/performer Charles Busch was one of the avatars of off-off-Broadway drag performance, writing parodic confections as vehicles for his own glamour drag. One of his earliest plays, *Vampire Lesbians of Sodom* (1985), ran for five years at the Provincetown Playhouse off Washington Square in Greenwich Village. Busch, whose acerbic humor and cutting wit flattened generations of queer audiences, successfully expanded his career by writing comedy for heterosexual performers and mainstream audiences, such as *The Tale of the Allergist's Wife* (2000), which transferred to Broadway. Other drag artists chose to remain downtown (literally and figuratively), as did Charles Ludlam and his Ridiculous Theatre Company, which parodied high art and other cultural forms for 20 years at its Sheridan Square location. Ludlam and his business partner and life companion Everett Quinton regularly served up biting satires of sexual and social mores, queering melodramas like *Camille* (1973) and a host of other generic conventions, such as the penny-dreadful Gothic parody *The Mystery of Irma Vep* (1984), now another favorite on the regional theatre circuit. Ludlam performed in drag, but his costumes never completely hid his gender; he played Camille with his curly chest hair bristling purposefully out of his bodice. After Ludlam died of AIDS in the 1980s, Quinton kept alive the Ridiculous tradition and began his own solo career, presenting in 2003 a one-man show called *Twisted Olivia*, in which he uses the Ridiculous conventions of drag, multiple characters, multiple costume changes, and excessive symbolic and hilarious props to skewer (and sweetly honor) the Dickens classic, *Oliver Twist.*

Female-to-male drag performance appeared on the cultural radar in the late 1990s, in a succession of "drag king" shows playing at bars around the country that made drag an even more ubiquitous and fluid performative sign. Bisexual and transgender activism – for visibility and respect in queer communities and for civil rights in American society – flourishes in performance, gracefully and articulately represented by transsexual performer Kate Bornstein in her solo show, *Virtually Yours: A Game for Solo Performer with Audience* (1998), and in her book, *Gender Outlaw: On Men, Women, and the Rest of Us* (1994); by *Hedwig*; and by, among many others, the duo Kiki and Herb, two gay men who began their gender-bending performances at small clubs like the Fez, on Manhattan's Lower East Side, in the late 1990s. They moved off-Broadway to the Cherry Lane Theatre to ply their idiosyncratic theatrical pairing in a rather louche lounge act called *Kiki and Herb: Coup de Théâtre* (2003) that attracts large, varied audiences.

Contemporary lesbian, gay, and queer theatre continues to stretch the boundaries of sexual identity and to expand the cultural archive of American stories and experiences, perceptions and critiques, as it has done for the last 40-odd years of the twentieth century. While some lesbian and gay drama continues to attract coterie audiences – especially at gay-, lesbian-, or queer-identified venues like the now defunct Alice B. in Seattle, the long-lived Theatre Rhinoceros in San Francisco, and Theatre Offensive in Boston (see McCully 1997) – those crowds are no longer as homogeneous as they were in the 1970s, 1980s, and 1990s. That is, while much gay, lesbian, or queer theatre production began in communities for which it mirrored the complications of living as gay and lesbian Americans, this "preaching to the converted" (see Miller and Román 1995) no longer exclusively defines the creation or reception of lesbian and gay drama. Community-or social movement-oriented theatre continues to sustain a diverse gay and lesbian population, but lesbian and gay drama, whether assimilationist or more radical, whether queer in content, intent, or form, disperses into the mainstream of American culture more and more frequently.

In fact, over the course of the end of the twentieth century and at the beginning of the twenty-first, the criteria of "authenticity," which once demanded that gay, lesbian, and queer experience be represented only by those who had lived it, gradually relaxed into a more open standard in which issues of alternative sexual identity could be addressed, performed, and received by anyone. Remarkably, the twenty-first century has already provided impressive social gains for gay men, lesbians, bisexuals, and trans-people. The Supreme Court decision to throw out the Texas sodomy laws; the Canadian government's legalization of gay marriages; even the decision of Wal-Mart, one of the nation's largest and most politically conservative employers, to add sexual orientation to its anti-discrimination clause, all mark progressive change. Gains in the law, the legislature, and the public sphere will no doubt influence the kind of drama, theatre, and performance produced by (and for) gay men, lesbians, bisexuals, trans-gendered, and queer people for generations.

None of the fierce Christopher Street drag queens and butches who began the first wave of queer liberation with the Stonewall rebellion could have anticipated how far gay men and lesbians would come under the legal doctrines of equal protection, or under the loosening (at least in larger urban areas) of American cultural morality. And yet there remains a long way to go. With the Defense of Marriage Act signed into federal law by President Bill Clinton in 1996; with the religious right in the United States fulminating against all gay and lesbian requests for authorization and legaliza-tion of our relationships; with ever-higher incidents of queer-bashing and other forms of backlash at our social achievements; and with the reluctance of even liberal legislators, judges, and city administrators to embrace the full sexual, racial, ethnic, and gendered diversity of the queer community in the largest possible sense, lesbian, gay, and queer drama, theatre, and performance remains a vanguard creative move-ment whose most incisive, persuasive work is perhaps only just beginning.

Bibliography

Case, S.-E. (ed.) (1996). *Split Britches: Lesbian Practice, Feminist Performance.* New York: Routledge.

Clum, J. M. (1996). *Staging Gay Lives: An Anthology of Contemporary Gay Theater.* Boulder, CO: Westview.

Crespy, D. A. (1996). *Off-Off Broadway Explosion: How Provocative Playwrights of the 1960s Ignited a New American Theater.* New York: Back Stage Books.

Curb, R. K. (ed.) (1996). *Amazon All Stars: Thirteen Lesbian Plays.* New York: Applause.

Curtain, K. (1987). *We Can Always Call them Bulgarians: The Emergence of Lesbians and Gay Men on the American Stage.* Boston: Alyson.

Dolan, J. (1993). *Presence and Desire: Essays on Gender, Sexuality, Performance.* Ann Arbor: University of Michigan Press.

——(2001). *Geographies of Learning: Theory and Practice, Activism and Performance.* Middleton, CT: Wesleyan University Press.

Duberman, M. (1993). *Stonewall.* New York: Penguin.

Hoffman, W. (ed.) (1979). *Gay Plays: The First Collection.* New York: Avon.

McCully, S. (1997). "How Queer: Race, Gender and the Politics of Production in Contemporary Gay Lesbian and Queer Theatre." Dissertation, University of Wisconsin-Madison.

Marra, K. and Schanke, R. A. (eds.) (2002). *Staging Desire: Queer Readings of American Theater History.* Ann Arbor: University of Michigan Press.

Miller, T. and Román, D. (1995). "Preaching to the Converted." *Theatre Journal* 47, 2 (May): 169–88.

Munoz, J. E. (1999). *Disidentifications: Queers of Color and the Performance of Politics.* Minneapolis: University of Minnesota Press.

Román, D. (1998). *Acts of Intervention: Performance, Gay Culture, and AIDS.* Bloomington: Indiana University Press.

——and Hughes, H. (eds.) (1998). *O Solo Homo: The New Queer Performance*. New York: Grove.

Savran, D. (1992). *Communists, Cowboys, and Queers*. Minneapolis: University of Minnesota Press.

——(2003). *A Queer Sort of Materialism: Recontextualizing American Theater*. Ann Arbor: University of Michigan Press.

Shewey, D. (ed.) (1988). *Out Front: Contemporary Gay and Lesbian Plays*. New York: Grove.

Solomon, A. and Minwalla, F. (eds.) (2002). *The Queerest Art: Essays on Lesbian and Gay Theatre*. New York: New York University Press.

Wolf, S. (2002). *A Problem Like Maria: Gender and Sexuality in the American Musical*. Ann Arbor: University of Michigan Press.

31

American Drama of the 1990s
On and Off-Broadway

June Schlueter

There were moments of excitement in the 1990s theatre, to be sure, but if New York's Broadway offerings were the measure of achievement for American drama, the closing decade of the century left much to be desired. Venues that had opened their velvet curtains to the work of America's most promising playwrights earlier in the century were increasingly focused on entertainments; with notable exceptions, Broadway in the 1990s was not the place for serious drama but for the musical with popular appeal. Yet the musicals of the 1990s were generally not blockbusters. As the decade began, *Chorus Line*, the longest-running musical in Broadway history, was winding down, making way for *Miss Saigon* (1991), the most expensive production in Broadway history. But in the 1990s, the American entries on Broadway were mostly revivals: *Fiddler on the Roof* and *Peter Pan* (1990); *The Most Happy Fella, Guys and Dolls*, and *Man of La Mancha* (1992); *My Fair Lady* (1993); *Damn Yankees* and *Show Boat* (1994); *The King and I, A Funny Thing Happened on the Way to the Forum, Chicago*, and *Grease!* (1996); *Annie* (1997); *The Sound of Music* (1998); *Annie Get Your Gun* and *Kiss Me Kate* (1999); and *Jesus Christ Superstar* (2000). And the new musicals that won *Theater Yearbook*'s "Best" awards, with the exceptions of *Titanic* (1997), for its scope, and *The Lion King* (1998), for its design, were hardly landmarks in the development of musical theatre: *Grand Hotel* and *City of Angels* (1990), *Crazy for You* (1992), *The Who's Tommy* and *Kiss of the Spiderwoman* (1993), *Passion* (1994), *Sunset Boulevard* (1995), *Rent* (1996), *Parade* (1999), and *James Joyce's The Dead* (2000).

One might conclude that the talent pool in the 1990s was, for whatever reasons, deficient. But the fact is that it was the climate for the legitimate theatre that was the problem. By the 1990s, *being* on Broadway was not sufficient; even with ticket prices at record highs – $50 typically, $100 for *Miss Saigon* – plays needed to *stay* on Broadway for long runs to full houses even to recoup their investment, much less realize a profit. Hence artistic choices yielded to financial imperatives, with investors placing their money on the big-cast, full-orchestra, star-powered spectacular that would fill a five-hundred-plus-seat house nightly with audiences not only from New

York but also from the city's thriving tourist trade. Throughout the decade, and particularly in its later years when the stock market was bullish and the economy thriving, Broadway was making money. But the Great White Way's one hundredth birthday season in 1994–5 proved emblematic of what Broadway had become: that year, there were no new musicals or new plays of consequence by Americans on the Broadway stage. This was a lean year even for musicals, and the "Best" award went to Andrew Lloyd Webber's *Sunset Boulevard*, a British import.

A number of circumstances made the challenges to the Broadway theatre more pronounced. Although the legitimate theatre was largely unaffected by the National Endowment for the Arts' (NEA's) sobering discouragement of "obscene" art or by cuts in funding to the NEA and the New York State Council for the Arts, high-priced plays were competing not only with films but also with high drama on "reality" TV: close-ups of the wars in the Persian Gulf, Yugoslavia, and Rwanda; the Branch Davidian confrontation with federal agents; the nerve gas attack on Tokyo; the bombing of the federal building in Oklahoma; the Clarence Thomas/Anita Hill hearings; the Rodney King riots in Los Angeles; O. J. Simpson on the freeway. Joseph Papp died in 1991, ending a life that many felt was a beacon for the American stage, and putting the Lower East Side Public Theatre, an alternative and a stimulus to Broadway, at risk. A few years later, the *New York Times*, recognizing the inordinate influence that theatre critic Frank Rich had on the viability of a play, assigned others to do the reviews, which may or may not have helped the vulnerable Broadway stage.

If the challenges to Broadway had any positive effect, it was to secure the transition, already in place for decades, to off-Broadway, that group of theatres outside New York's entertainment district – the Manhattan Theatre Club, Playwrights Horizon, the Circle Repertory Theatre, the Joseph Papp Public Theatre, the Vineyard Theatre, the Roundabout Theatre Company, Circle in the Square, and Lincoln Center, for example (though the last three are technically classified as "Broadway") – where high profit margins and conservative audiences were simply not a concern. Off-Broadway – unlike its non-profit cousin off-off-Broadway, which had its origin in the 1960s at Caffé Cino and La Mama and which typically mounted performances in lower Manhattan's basements and lofts – was still "commercial" theatre, with Equity actors, but the venues were smaller and the financial pressures were greatly reduced. New Yorkers familiar with "beyond" Broadway had had a long relationship with such alternative venues, which were host to numerous new plays; for them, it was unnecessary to look north to the lights of Times Square.

American playwrights also respected off-Broadway. Following the landmark production of Samuel Beckett's *Waiting for Godot* in 1956, those who were writing for Broadway recognized the discrepancy between European drama and their own and realized they needed to test the possibilities of the form. Among the off-Broadway pioneers was Edward Albee, who, in 1960, restyled Beckett's absurdist vision into two plays about the American experience: *The Zoo Story* and *The American Dream*. As off-Broadway came of age, David Mamet and Sam Shepard became regular presences, providing forceful voices on New York's smaller stages. By the 1990s, the full range of living American playwrights associated with serious drama – Albee, Mamet, Shepard, Christopher Durang, John Guare, A. J. Gurney, Beth Henley, Tony Kushner, Donald Margulies, Terrence McNally, Arthur Miller, Anna Deavere Smith, Wendy Wasserstein, August Wilson, for example – were being produced off-Broadway. Even Neil Simon, the Norman Rockwell of Broadway and a staple of non-musical Broadway fare, who had won both a Tony Award and a Pulitzer Prize in 1991 for *Lost in Yonkers* and, two years later, had done *Laughter on the 23rd Floor* on Broadway, decided, during Broadway's centennial year, to stage his *London Suite* (1995) at the Union Square Theatre. With the disgruntled Arthur Miller, it looked like Simon agreed that the Broadway theatre was not a place for serious drama.

This is not to say that Broadway did not host American playwrights. But the inventory of new plays that originated on Broadway in the 1990s is short. *Theater Yearbook* lists 430 productions of plays, musicals, revues, and revivals in the 11 seasons from 1989–90 through 1999–2000, for an average of 40 productions per year. Of these, about five each year were new American plays and five were revivals of American plays. Most of the new plays proved inconsequential, though some – August Wilson's *The Piano Lesson* (1990) and *Two Trains Running* (1992), Margulies's *What's Wrong with This Picture?* (1994), and Miller's *Broken Glass* (1994) – added to those playwrights' already distinguished canons, as did Tennessee Williams's posthumously produced *Not About Nightingales* (1999), McNally's *Master Class* (1995), and three transfers from off-Broadway – Guare's *Six Degrees of Separation* (1990), Craig Lucas's *Prelude to a Kiss* (1990), and Wasserstein's *The Sisters Rosensweig* (1993). Two choices stand out, though, as particularly notable: the 1993 staging of Robert Schenkkan's *The Kentucky Cycle* and the spring 1993 and fall 1993 mountings of Kushner's two-part *Angels in America*.

Schenkkan's play, a nine-part cycle that took six hours and two evenings to perform, cost its producer $2.5 million: it was the most expensive straight play in Broadway history to that time. William A. Henry III, writing for *Time* magazine about this epic treatment of 200 years in the lives of seven generations of three interrelated Kentucky families, called *Kentucky Cycle* a play of "undeniable power," then observed: "Industry leaders say its fate will measure the maturity of the Broadway audience – and hardly anyone gives it much chance" (1993: 72). *Kentucky Cycle* opened on November 14 and closed on December 12, 1993.

Despite Schenkkan's force as a storyteller, his was an unknown name in the New York theatre scene and few were willing to invest two nights in so unrelenting a portrait of moral corruption, even with Stacy Keach performing the role of the patriarch. Though Broadway had enthusiastically embraced the lengthy British import *Nicholas Nickleby* some years before, theatregoers seemed less enamored of an eastern Kentucky tale, even though Kentucky was an emblem – some would say a caricature – of America. Reviewers admired the courage that went into the marathon and the agility of the 21 actors who played 70 roles. But Schenkkan's characters were judged by many to be stereotypical, with predictable, if grotesque, reactions to the dilemmas that 200 years of history imposed upon them. Hence Keach as Michael

Rowan gives blankets infested with smallpox to the local Indians, killing them all; slits his Cherokee wife's heel tendons so she cannot run away; and kills his infant daughter. The saga goes on, documenting acts of violence, murder, betrayal, and revenge. Some called it great storytelling; others lamented Schenkkan's "clunky" writing; and others, despite the fact that the play won a Pulitzer Prize, thought it more of a TV miniseries than a serious Broadway play. One or two of the reviewers noted the competition with *Angels in America*, a play that had received rave reviews for *Part One: Millennium Approaches* the previous season and that was now staging *Millennium* and *Part Two: Perestroika* in repertory. Did Appalachia stand a chance against gays in the Reagan years?

Subtitled *A Gay Fantasia on National Themes*, *Angels in America* was also an ambitious project. Though it focused on the mid-1980s, the heart of the Reagan era, rather than surveying 200 years of history, it, too, was a story about America, told through the prism of homosexuality and AIDS. Three men with ties to the courthouse command Kushner's stage. One is a sexually ambivalent Mormon, who is increasingly unhappy with his Valium-sedated wife; one is a gay who tests positive for AIDS and whose partner of four years is afraid to remain. The third is Roy Cohn, the outspoken right-wing attorney of the McCarthy years who is still attacking gays and denying his own homosexuality. Like *Kentucky Cycle*, the play asked audiences to spend two evenings in the theatre, with each part lasting three and a half hours. And Kushner, despite his *A Bright Room Called Day* (1991) and his having won a Pulitzer Prize for *Angels* before it reached New York, was relatively unknown. Still, his nuanced writing, George C. Wolfe's deft direction, accomplished performances by eight actors playing some 20 roles, and enthusiastic reviews insured the vitality of *this* account of the moral degeneration of America. Responding to Part 1, Jack Kroll called *Angels in America* "the biggest, most intelligent, most passionate American play in recent memory" (1993: 70), and Frank Rich added that it was "the most thrilling American play in years" (1993: 15). After Part 2 – which followed the lives of the two couples, spotlighted Cohn and his circle as he was dying of AIDS, and asked grand and intimate questions – the critics made their approval even more emphatic. Some were chary, to be sure, pointing to the rough edges of this bulky epic, which was still under revision in previews; but most were hyperbolic. David Patrick Stearns offered the judgment that "*Perestroika* is more bizarre, visionary, poetic and profound than its predecessor" (1993: 1D); Jeremy Gerard called Part 2 "a sprawling complex work with incomparable elegance and clarity" (1993: 34); and Clive Barnes offered this opinion of the two-part cycle: "it is one of those plays defining an era, a work of today's imagination and sensibility, and today at least, can on no account be missed." The play, in short, let audiences know what Broadway theatre could be.

The 1990–1 Broadway season had a promising start. There were nine new plays that year – more than in any other season of the decade. Theatregoers flocked to *Miss Saigon*, of course, when it opened in April 1991. But those who preferred the straight play had splendid choices: Wasserstein's *The Heidi Chronicles*, following a run off-Broadway, had transferred to Broadway in 1989; as the 1990–1 season opened, that production was just winding down. It was replaced by other important American plays: Lucas's *Prelude to a Kiss*, August Wilson's *The Piano Lesson*, Guare's *Six Degrees of Separation*, and, later in the season, Simon's *Lost in Yonkers* and Paul Rudnick's *I Hate Hamlet*. By contrast, at the end of the decade, the Broadway menu of straight plays was lean. Major long-running musicals – including *Cats*, *Les Miserables*, *The Phantom of the Opera*, *Chicago*, and *The Lion King* – were filling Broadway houses, but if box office receipts are a measure of achievement, the five new American plays that season – by John Pielmeier, Larry Coen and David Crane, David Hirson, Elaine May, and Claudia Shear – were minor events. For serious plays that season, audiences were endorsing the revivals.

Indeed, Broadway deserves ongoing credit for renewing familiar plays by the veterans of American theatre. Eugene O'Neill, for example, held a prominent place in the revival repertory. In 1993, the Roundabout staged *Anna Christie*; in 1996, Circle in the Square did *Hughie*; in 1998, Lincoln Center Theatre offered *Ah, Wilderness!*; and late in the 1999–2000 season, the Walter Kerr Theatre was home to *A Moon for the Misbegotten*. Most notably, in 1999, the Brooks Atkinson Theatre hosted a three-month run of *The Iceman Cometh*, the playwright's four-and-a-half-hour study of the dissolute habitués of Harry Hope's saloon. Fourteen years earlier, there had been a revival of *Iceman* with Jason Robards as a cheerful, well-intending Hickey, who had discarded his "pipe dreams" and encouraged his drinking partners to reform. Now, in a production based on London's Almeida Theatre Company, Kevin Spacey played Hickey in another mode, foregrounding the icy intensity of the man who had killed his wife but whose self-righteous platitudes pervaded his advice to his friends. The performance won him an Outer Critics' Circle Award.

Williams was also a presence, repeatedly, on the Broadway stage. The 1990s saw revivals of *Cat on a Hot Tin Roof* (1990), *A Streetcar Named Desire* (1992), *The Glass Menagerie* (1994), *The Rose Tattoo* (1995), *The Garden District* [*Something Unspoken* and *Suddenly Last Summer*] (1995), *The Night of the Iguana* (1996), and *Summer and Smoke* (1996), which preceded the posthumous premiere of *Not About Nightingales*, an early "lost" play produced first at London's Royal National Theatre, then at Houston's Alley Theatre, and, in 1999, at New York's Circle in the Square. Set in 1938, *Not About Nightingales* is a prison play, dramatizing the inhuman treatment of inmates by a vindictive warden. Although written before *The Glass Menagerie* and the canon of plays that established Williams's reputation in the 1940s, *Nightingales* had all of the power of the better-known works; audiences responded in disgust to the ruthless relegation of inmates to the scalding temperatures of the isolation cell, ironically called the "Klondike." That year, the Outer Critics' Circle gave *Nightingales* its Best Broadway Play award, reminding playgoers of how substantial Williams's contributions to the theatre were.

O'Neill and Williams were attracting audiences years after their deaths. But it was the still active Miller who commanded the attention of Broadway that final season of the century. It was the fiftieth anniversary of *Death of a Salesman*, the most familiar of all American plays, and audiences paid top prices for this celebrated event. In 1949,

Lee J. Cobb established the role of Willy Loman, that tired hulk of a man so powerfully visualized on the cover of the Viking edition of the play. George C. Scott took on the role in 1975 at Circle in the Square, but there was no other Broadway production until 1984, when Dustin Hoffman, a "shrimp" of a man (unlike Cobb, the "walrus"), played Willy to audiences fascinated by his individualized reading of the role. That year, Miller oversaw a production of *Salesman* at the Beijing People's Art Theatre in China, and the following year the Hoffman production was televised, reaching some 25 million viewers. Now, with Brian Dennehy starring in the Broadway revival, which opened on February 10, 1999, 50 years to the day after its premiere, there were few in the audience who had not been exposed to the play. Yet for nine months (274 performances), the house was full and the production received four Tony Awards plus a lifetime achievement award for Miller.

There was a special significance – and poignancy – to the century's culminating in this 50-year-old play, particularly when Kushner's *Angels in America* seemed to have laid the groundwork for the new millennium. Yet reviewers uniformly recognized not only the strength of Miller's writing but also the archetypal power of Willy Loman. Here was a character who, in post-World War II America, encapsulated the spirit of the ordinary man, whose work ethic, pride, and self-deceptions did not admit defeat; here was a man who was tired to the bone yet still involved in the American Dream, a man who thought himself the head of the household, the provider husband, the caring father, but who simply failed to see how he – and life – had changed. Willy was the man everyone in the audience feared he would become, the man who unwittingly schooled us as a society on the need to accommodate our failures. On the eve of the new millennium, as in 1949, the force of Miller's *Death of a Salesman*, the great American tragedy of the common man, was secure.

There were other revivals of Miller's plays in the 1990s as well. Although Miller had turned his affections to the British stage in the 1980s and celebrated his eightieth birthday in London with a festival of his work, by the beginning of the 1990s New York was once more courting America's elder playwright. When Tony Randall established the National Actors Theatre in 1991, the first production was Miller's *The Crucible*, which played to sold-out houses. The Roundabout Theatre Company did revivals of *The Price* in 1992 (with Eli Wallach as Gregory Solomon), *All My Sons* in 1997, and *A View from the Bridge* in 1997 (the last reopened at the Neil Simon Theatre). The Royale Theatre hosted another revival of *The Price* in 1999. Off-off-Broadway, the Signature Theatre, which featured a playwright a year, devoted its 1997–8 season to Miller, with productions of *The American Clock*, a double-bill of *The Last Yankee* and *I Can't Remember Anything*, and the world premiere of *Mr. Peters' Connections*, an interior meditation, or "procession . . . of moods" (Miller 1999: viii), involving living and dead characters as well as characters constructed from Mr. Peters's imagination.

Mr. Peters' Connections, in fact, was one of four new plays by Miller in the 1990s. The others, which all appeared on Broadway, though only after United Kingdom premieres, were *The Ride Down Mount Morgan* (1991, revived in 1999), *The Last Yankee*

(1993, revived by the Signature in 1997–8), and *Broken Glass* (1994). *The Last Yankee*, a one-act character study done at the Manhattan Theatre Club, brought the audience into a mental facility, first to the waiting room, where two men meet and converse, and then behind the wall, where their wives struggle against clinical depression, analyzing their lives and their husbands as a third woman lies motionless, an arm covering her eyes. Also a one-act play, *Broken Glass* treats similarly pained people living in Brooklyn in 1938, immediately following *Kristallnacht* and during the Depression years. The focus is on Sylvia Gellburg, a Jewish woman who suffers an unexplained paralysis that renders her unable to use her legs (see chapter 14). Both plays deal with self-deprecation, self-deception, and the cruel corners of experience.

It was *The Ride Down Mount Morgan*, though, that proved a major event for Miller. Following its world premiere in 1991 in London's Wyndham's Theatre, its American premiere in 1996 at the Williamstown Theatre Festival in Massachusetts and an off-Broadway production by the Public Theatre in 1998, the play opened late in the 1999–2000 season at Broadway's Ambassador Theatre, with Patrick Stewart as the lionized – and lying – figure at the center of Miller's drama and his own. Lyman Feld has an appetite for life that leads him to claim a double share. But when a car crash puts him in hospital and two wives arrive, his deception is exposed: Theo, his Upper East Side wife of 30 years and mother to their grown daughter, meets Leah, a youthful Elmira businesswoman, his wife of nine years and mother to their son. Miller is at his best in this sophisticated play, which moves teasingly between truth and fiction as it explores the psyche of the self-centered, insatiable man who may himself have scripted this devastating moment as his own final scene. As Gerald Nachman, writing for the *San Francisco Chronicle*, observed, "It is hard to tell if [Lyman Feld] is living in a fantasy, having a delusion, is in a coma or has died and is reassessing his life as he watches it play out" (1991: E2). Although the play provides neither the assurances nor the closure playgoers crave, it summons us into the dangerous and powerful space where the psychic and the artistic converge.

Albee's work received attention in the 1990s as well, with a 1993–4 off-off-Broadway Signature Theatre featured-artist season of several plays, including *Counting the Ways* and *Listening*, *Sand* (*Box*, *The Sandbox*, and *Finding the Sun*), *Fragments* (*A Concerto Grosso*), and *Marriage Play*; the Vineyard Theatre's mounting, at the Promenade Theatre, of *Three Tall Women* in 1994; and a Broadway revival of *A Delicate Balance* that won a "Best Revival" award in 1996, 30 years after its premiere. *Marriage Play* and *Three Tall Women* (as well as *Finding the Sun* and *Fragments*) were new to New York – and were vintage Albee. Commissioned and performed by Vienna's English Theatre in 1987 and 1991, respectively, each had a United States premiere before New York, and each was met with excitement by a New York audience that had not seen a new Albee play in a decade.

For *Marriage Play*, however, the critics' reactions were reserved. Responding to the Princeton production, Alvin Klein lamented the play's "80 numbing minutes" (1993: 16); Jonathan Kalb wrote of a "leitmotiv in the key of ZZZ" (1992: 90); and Mel Gussow saw it as "a kind of coda" (1994: 487) to the unmistakably resonant *Who's*

Afraid of Virginia Woolf? Even when one grants the play's repetitions and the clear genetic link between Gillian and Jack and Martha and George, though, *Marriage Play* establishes an identity of its own. More than a tactic of the absurdist 1960s, Jack's four replay announcements that their marriage is ending gain force as a contemporary demonstration of the inauthenticity of language and experience. Each time Jack tells Gillian "I'm leaving you," the couple test ways to penetrate the moment, emotionally and linguistically, so they might validate it as theirs. At the same time, in a theatrical culture dominated by the conventions of domestic drama, Albee searches for a way to write a play about marriage without repeating, recycling, and falsifying the relationship he wishes to dramatize.

Less angst-ridden than *Marriage Play*, *Three Tall Women* won the approval of critics and earned its 66-year-old playwright a third Pulitzer Prize. Occasioned by the memory of his mother, the play presents the life of a 92-year-old woman who is about to die. In the present tense of Act 1, the elderly woman, still feisty but showing signs of dementia, converses with her middle-aged nurse-companion and a youthful female lawyer, both tending to, and interfering with, the woman's wishes. In the past tense of Act 2, the woman has had a stroke and, possibly, died: a lifeless dummy stretched out on the bed becomes the backdrop for the reenactment of the woman's life. Now the two attendees become the woman at earlier stages of her life, as the trinity presents an emotionally compelling and dramatically complex portrait of a life burdened with problems, including a bisexual son. Ben Brantley of the *New York Times* called the play a "startlingly personal work" (1994: 13); others, noting that Albee exorcised demons in the play, commented not only on the fictional treatment of Albee's adoptive mother but also on the Boy in the play, who remains mute throughout. Kroll's assessment in *Newsweek* summarized the sentiment of the critics: the deeply personal *Three Tall Women* was "Edward Albee's strongest play in two decades" (1994: 62) (see chapter 16).

The next generation of American playwrights was also prominent in the last decade of the twentieth century. Mamet contributed three plays, the first of which, *Oleanna*, was an off-Broadway sensation in 1992. With ongoing attention being paid to feminist causes and a new focus on sexual harassment, particularly in the academy, Mamet styled what may well have been the most provocative play of the decade. In it, a college professor, about to be awarded tenure, is in conversation with a female undergraduate inquiring about a grade. As the play moves through its three acts, Carol is transformed from a naive student, aware of her professor's authority over her, into an aggressive feminist wielding extraordinary power. When Carol files a sexual harassment charge with John's tenure committee, the conversation that John as professor and master of academic discourse controls yields to his expression of disappointment. Though wounded, he tries to maintain the upper hand and does not give Carol a chance to explain why she is offended – or himself a chance to understand her concern. In Act 3, John's frustration escalates, culminating in physical violence that surprises even him; audience members variously conclude "This is a man out of control" or "She deserved it." Programs for the event at New York's Orpheum

Theatre encouraged the divide: some featured a target with Carol as the bull's eye, others the same target but with John in the middle. This was indeed a contemporary version of the war between the sexes and the failure of language to intervene.

Mamet's other two plays, though intriguing, had less of an impact. *The Cryptogram*, like *Oleanna*, premiered in London, then followed with a production at the American Repertory Theatre in Cambridge, Massachusetts, before opening in 1995 at New York's Westside Arts Theatre. Focused on the power of language, as was *Oleanna*, the play draws attention to the coded controls and cryptic exclusions of the language parents use in the presence of their children. *The Old Neighborhood*, staged at the Hasty Pudding Theatre in Cambridge in 1997 and, several months later, at the Booth Theatre, New York, connects three one-acts – *The Disappearance of the Jews, Jolly*, and *Deeny* – through a common character, Bobby Gould. Though not a major work, the play records Mamet's interest in exploring his own Jewish background and the relationship between one's ethnic and personal identity and one's collective and individual past (see chapter 25).

Off-Broadway's Atlantic Theatre Company staged revivals of Mamet's *Edmond* in 1996 and his *American Buffalo* in 2000. A one-actor, *An Interview*, was included in *Death Defying Acts* in 1995, with works by May and Woody Allen. Off-off-Broadway, the Ensemble Studio Theatre, for its 1995–6 season, offered five of Mamet's one-acts under the title *No One Will Be Immune*; three of these – *A Sermon, Sunday Afternoon*, and *No One Will Be Immune* – were new.

Although less visible in the 1990s than in earlier years, Shepard also enjoyed the support of a number of New York venues. *Buried Child* was revived in 1996 at the Brooks Atkinson Theatre, *True West* in 2000 (its 20-year anniversary) at Circle in the Square. In its 1996–7 season, the Signature mounted several Shepard plays: *When the World Was Green (A Chef's Fable)* (conceived with Joseph Chaikin); *The Tooth of Crime*; *The Sad Lament of Pecos Bill on the Eve of Killing His Wife, Killer's Head*, and *Action*; and *The Curse of the Starving Class*. The playwright contributed new works as well to the 1990s repertoire: *States of Shock* in 1991 at the American Place Theatre and *Simpatico* in 1994 at the Public (plus *Eyes for Consuela*, based on an Octavio Paz story, in 1998 at the Manhattan Theatre Club).

In *States of Shock*, Shepard's first new entry in New York since *Lie of the Mind* in 1985, the principals are two veterans: the elder, Colonel (played by John Malkovich), is Shepard's generic soldier, decorated in paraphernalia from several wars; the younger, Stubbs, in a wheelchair, wears his missile wound as a badge of honor, acquired, presumably, when he unsuccessfully tried to save the life of Colonel's son – unless, the play implies, Stubbs himself is Colonel's son. Staged in the aftermath of the Persian Gulf War, the play reflects the sardonic tone of Shepard's earlier work and the playwright's characteristic assault on mythic America (see chapter 18). In a family restaurant, where a couple in white tarry before their shopping trip, awaiting their order of clam chowder, a soundtrack plays war sounds to the accompaniment of percussive drums and flashing lights, the menacing Colonel erupts into violence, and both Stubbs and White Man follow their sexual urges. Though critics welcomed this latest chapter in Shepard's saga of America, most found the play obscure, and none thought it more than a minor contribution.

Three years later, *Simpatico* fared only modestly better in its three-hour Public Theatre presentation. The kind of detective story that sends critics into plot summaries, *Simpatico* opens with Carter, a prosperous breeder of race horses, meeting with Vinnie, his less-than-prosperous friend, in a seedy motel room. The two had been partners 15 years earlier, embroiled in a scam that left Carter with all the advantages: cash, a car, and Vinnie's wife. But Vinnie has been blackmailing Carter with a shoebox of sexually explicit photographs that, if released, would compromise his "respectable" friend. Complications develop as others are introduced into the intricate plot, which culminates with Carter trembling on the floor, having unwittingly yielded power to Vinnie. This was a theatrical strategy Shepard had explored before, most notably in *True West*, where two brothers vie for position and exchange roles at the end of the play. Noting the structural and strategic links to the earlier work, *New York Times* critic Stephen Holden dismissed *Simpatico* as "a long, reflective epilogue" (1994: 15). Indeed, most critics saw this excursion into staged film noir as merely a footnote in the career of the 50-year-old playwright, who had previously won 12 Obie Awards and a Pulitzer Prize.

It is ironic that critics saw Shepard's 1990s work as 1960s nostalgia, for Shepard had been immensely influential in the challenge to domestic realism, the (still prevailing) staple of the American stage. Shepard's plays moved audiences into a surreal world in which the icons of American culture, including the nuclear family, became caricatures in an emerging, revisionary culture and a resistant dramatic form. With other playwrights in the final decade of the twentieth century, Shepard was asking, implicitly, where the theatre could go from here. A cohort of fine American playwrights – Horton Foote, A. R. Gurney, Romulus Linney, Terrence McNally, Neil Simon, and August Wilson, for example – continued to write in a predominantly realistic mode, creating plays that were often compelling contributions to the American stage. August Wilson's *The Piano Lesson*, for example, which had runs in New Haven, Boston, Chicago, San Diego, Washington, DC, Los Angeles, and off-Broadway, before it reached the Broadway stage, is a model of domestic realism. New York – indeed, America – needed to see black families on the commercial stage, and Wilson obliged, creating the story of a Pittsburgh family, with roots in Mississippi, whose Boy Willie tries to persuade his sister to sell the heirloom piano so he might buy farmland back home. The piano, though, has a history that records the journey of blacks from slaves to homeowners, and Boy Willie's sister is not about to part with it. Wilson's work, like his plays of the 1980s – *Ma Rainey's Black Bottom*, *Fences*, and *Joe Turner's Come and Gone* (and *Two Trains Running* [1992]) – were important to the Broadway stage, which had seen few American plays by and about blacks since Lorraine Hansberry's *Raisin in the Sun* in 1959. But like that powerful exploration of society's exclusions and African American dignity, August Wilson's work, directed by Lloyd Richards, had a secure moral and artistic home within the mainstream of American drama (see chapter 20).

Female playwrights, who were not abundant at any point in the history of American drama, were nonetheless doing important work. By the 1990s, several were established playwrights, and each made further contributions that decade: Beth Henley with *Abundance* (1990); Wendy Wasserstein with *The Sisters Rosensweig* (1992, 1993), a revival of *Uncommon Women* (1994), and *An American Daughter* (1997); Maria Irene Fornes with *Terra Incognito* (1997); Tina Howe with *One Shoe Off* (1993) and *Pride's Crossing* (1997); Marsha Norman with *Trudy Blue* (1999); and Adrienne Kennedy with a 1995–6 Signature season at the Public that included revivals of *Funnyhouse of a Negro* and *A Movie Star Has to Star in Black and White*; the premiere of *June and Jean in Concert*; one-acts (*Dramatic Circle*, *Ohio State Murders*, and *Motherhood*) collected under the title *The Alexander Plays . . . Suzanne in Stages*; and, with her son Adam Kennedy, *Sleep Deprivation Chamber*, based on Adam's experience as a black man for whom an alleged traffic violation led to an arrest and beating.

Less familiar playwrights whose work insured that female characters and perspectives were center stage included Catherine Butterfield (*Joined at the Head*, 1992); Paula Vogel (*The Baltimore Waltz*, 1992; *And Baby Makes Seven*, 1993; *Desdemona: A Play About a Handkerchief*, 1993; and *How I Learned to Drive*, 1997); Emily Mann (*Having Our Say*, 1995); Elaine May (*The Way of All Fish*, 1998); Margaret Edson (*Wit*, 1998); Anna Deavere Smith (*Fires in the Mirror*, 1991; and *Twilight: Los Angeles, 1992*, 1994); and Eve Ensler (*The Vagina Monologues*, 1999). There was considerable structural variety in women's work. *Wit*, for example, realistically depicts the final moments in the life of a woman dying of ovarian cancer, adding a possibly imagined visit from an admired professor. *How I Learned to Drive*, a frank look at women's sexuality, proceeds through a series of vignettes. *Abundance*, which includes the story of a woman who was captured by Indians, then writes a commercially successful book about her ordeal, is epic in its coverage of the history of the Old West. And *The Vagina Monologues*, a digest of female sexuality, is a one-hander, an increasingly popular (and practical) genre staged both on and off-Broadway (by such writer/ actors as Deavere Smith, Spalding Gray, Wallace Shawn, and Eric Bogosian) (see chapter 32).

Plays about homosexuality and AIDS also held a secure place in the repertory of the 1990s, as did plays with gay characters. *Angels in America* was the most prominent example, but there were other notable entries as well: Craig Lucas's *Prelude to a Kiss* (1990) and *The Dying Gaul* (1998), William Finn and James Lapine's musical *Falsettoland* (1990), Jon Robin Baitz's *The Substance of Fire* (1991), David Drake's *The Night Larry Kramer Kissed Me* (1992), Paula Vogel's *And Baby Makes Seven* (1993), Paul Rudnick's *Jeffrey* (1993) and *The Most Fabulous Story Ever Told* (1998), and numerous others. By the end of the decade, gay plays were routine off-Broadway, and even on Broadway they were not mere occasions for snickering at a less familiar lifestyle. Still, in 1998, Terrence McNally's *Corpus Christi* rankled a few reactionaries, whose violent objections to anticipated irreverence caused the Manhattan Theatre Club (temporarily) to cancel the production. The play proved merely suggestive in its pursuit of its thesis, "What if Jesus were gay?"

Donald Margulies was among the more frequently produced playwrights in the 1990s. The decade saw revivals of *The Loman Family Picnic* (1993), *What's Wrong with This Picture?* (1994), *The Model Apartment* (1995), and *Collected Stories* (1998), as well as two plays new to New York: *Sight Unseen* (1992) and *Dinner with Friends* (1999), in off-Broadway venues. With his sure grasp of dialogue, wry sense of humor, deft craftsmanship, and sheer intelligence, Margulies always managed to engage his audiences. In *Sight Unseen*, the subject is an artist of reputation who, in a visit to the farmhouse home of a woman he once loved, discovers angles of vision and optics on art and life that earlier were unseen. As Jonathan Waxman submits to the piercing questions of a German interviewer in gallery scenes juxtaposed with those in the farmhouse and with flashbacks to his earlier life, the portrait of the artist fills in, reflecting at each stage a bit more of Margulies's Picasso-like conception of the complexities of self. His writing was also strong in *Dinner with Friends*, which captures the nuances of conversation in a play that may well be the definitive statement on the anxieties of a married couple facing the failure of their friends' marriage. As in *Sight Unseen*, Margulies jumps around in time, inviting the audience to texture the picture he incrementally reveals. The production, which came to New York from the Humana Festival in Louisville, won the playwright a Pulitzer Prize.

John Guare had one Broadway entry in the 1990s – *Four Baboons Adoring the Sun* (1992) – and was the Signature's featured artist in 1998–9, with revivals of *Marco Polo Sings a Solo* and *Bosoms and Neglect* as well as the premiere of *Lake Hollywood*. *Six Degrees of Separation*, though, which transferred from off-Broadway to Lincoln Center in 1990 and won a "Best Play" award, remained his signature contribution. In it, an Upper East Side couple open their apartment door, and their lives, to a wounded (gay) black man, who shows up bleeding and pleading for help. The obliging couple gradually learn that they have been conned: this is neither Sidney Poitier's son nor their own son's friend from Harvard. Yet the "tenancy" of this dissembler leads them to question their own relationships and assumptions. The power of Guare's play is in its focus on connections – broken and whole – that make up the human community (see chapter 22).

Durang's name might also have been on the "remarkable" list, but the playwright who had shocked and delighted 1980s audiences with his spoofing spirit in such plays as *Sister Mary Ignatius Explains It All To You* (1981) and *The Marriage of Bette and Boo* (1985) had a harder time in the 1990s. In the 1994–5 season, the Manhattan Theatre Club presented several of his one-acts under the title *Durang Durang: Mrs. Sorken, For Whom the Southern Belle Tolls, A Stye of the Eye, Nina in the Morning, Wanda's Visit*, and *Business Lunch at the Russian Tea Room*. But the full-length *Sex and Longing* (1996), with its sweep of sexual and political satire, had an undistinguished run at Lincoln Center. And *Betty's Summer Vacation* (1999), with its rude assaults on sexual and political mores, fell short of success. Noting how the political – and theatrical – climate had changed by the 1990s, David Lefkowitz shrewdly observed: "When the sensational becomes commonplace, a satirist's options are more limited" (1999: 38).

Still, there were successful political plays that used humor to engage audiences intellectually. Among the better examples were Suzan-Lori Parks's *The America Play* (1993), Jose Rivera's *Marisol* (1993), and Russell Lee's *Nixon's Nixon* (1996). In *The America Play*, Parks gives us a tall, lean black man who resembles Abe Lincoln and plays the president at a theme park, where customers pay to be John Wilkes Booth for just long enough to shoot the president and utter one comment – usually "Thus to the tyrants!" In *Marisol*, Rivera gives us a nightmare vision of New York, in which a young Latina needing help in navigating its violent corners engages an unlikely guardian angel. In Lee's *Nixon's Nixon*, the president who claimed not to be a crook is the subject of an ironic, funny, empathetic portrait designed to fascinate the American public. In all three plays, the dramatists are searching for a form and a tone to accommodate the climate of a country that had lost its innocence. Knowing that audiences brought more and more baggage with them to the theatre as the country approached the millennium, writers invested their confidence in the power of art to negotiate the line between the comic and the tragic in order to make patent our country's arrogance and fears. For many, political theatre that "enables us to see our moral choices, our mixed aspirations, and our difficult upsets" (Havis 2001: xiii) was a timely response.

Throughout this chapter, my focus has been on the Broadway and off-Broadway New York theatre. I have said little about off-off-Broadway, which is a genre unto itself; nothing about foreign plays hosted by New York's stages; and nothing of the many homegrown and imported productions of Shakespeare and other classic play-wrights that appear every season. Although several major United States cities host thriving theatres and offer opportunities for emerging playwrights to showcase their work, New York remains the gold standard for the American theatre. With some 35 Broadway theatres and a host of off-and off-off-Broadway venues, on any weekend night one can choose from a menu of 70 to 100 plays. As Arthur Miller put it back in 1955 (before the off-and off-off-Broadway theatre movements), "The American theater is five blocks long, by about one and a half blocks wide" (Miller 1978: 31).

Once the primacy of New York theatre is acknowledged, however, it is important to emphasize that many of the plays produced in Manhattan venues neither originate nor end there, for New York theatre is in every respect reciprocal. Broadway shows often have touring productions in cities across the nation. Even plays considered "new" by the editors of *Theater Yearbook*'s annual *Best Plays* volumes often have had premieres elsewhere, in any number of regional theatres throughout the country or, for that matter, in London. *Kentucky Cycle*, for example, originated in Seattle's Intiman Theatre and had runs in Los Angeles' Mark Taper Forum and Washington, DC's John F. Kennedy Center for the Performing Arts; indeed, the play was recognized in 1992 with a Pulitzer Prize even before it reached Broadway. Similarly, before coming to New York, *Angels in America* won a Pulitzer Prize for the production at the Mark Taper Forum in Los Angeles and an *Evening Standard* Award for the production at the Royal National Theatre in London. And when *The Piano Lesson* went up on Broadway, several theatres were billed as associates: the Eugene O'Neill Theatre Center, the

Huntington Theatre Company, the Goodman Theatre, the Old Globe Theatre, and off-Broadway's Manhattan Theatre Club. Indeed, many of the plays with Broadway runs in the 1990s – *Six Degrees of Separation*, *Prelude to a Kiss*, and *The Ride Down Mount Morgan*, for example – transferred from off-Broadway to their midtown neighbor. Much of the credit for that well-greased pipeline belongs to Joseph Papp, whose Public Theatre served both as a venue in its own right and as an incubator for subsequent productions. As Jeffrey Sweet noted in the 1991–2 *Theater Yearbook* volume: "So thoroughly did Papp and his colleagues in other non-profit companies transform the theater that all but one of the works selected as this year's 'Best Plays' reached New York via institutional venues either in this country or abroad" (5).

The story of American drama in New York in the 1990s, then, is the story of theatre in America. For Cambridge's American Repertory Theatre, Boston's Huntington Theatre Company, the Williamstown Theatre Festival, New Haven's Yale Repertory and Long Wharf Theatre, Providence's Trinity Repertory Company, Princeton's McCarter Theatre, Chicago's Goodman Theatre, Minneapolis's Guthrie Theatre, the Actors Theatre of Louisville, Houston's Alley Theatre, Seattle's Intiman Theatre, the Seattle Repertory Theatre, San Francisco's Eureka Theatre Company and ACT, Los Angeles's Mark Taper Forum, Costa Mesa's South Coast Repertory, San Diego's Old Globe Theatre, and an array of fine regional theatres across the country, though only occasionally referenced in this chapter, are all players in a thriving national theatre, a theatre well positioned to meet the challenges of the new millennium.

BIBLIOGRAPHY

Barnes, C. (1993). "*Angels* Soars (Sorta)." *New York Post*, November 24.
Bigsby, C. W. E. (1999). *Contemporary American Playwrights*. Cambridge: Cambridge University Press.
Brantley, B. (1994). "Edward Albee Conjures Up Three Ages of Women." *New York Times*, February 14: 13.
Gerard, J. (1993). "*Angels in America: Perestroika*." *Variety*, December 6: 33–4.
Guernsey, O. L., Jr. (ed.) (2000). *The Best Plays of 1999–2000*. New York: Limelight.
Gussow, M. (1994). "Off-Off-Broadway." In Otis L. Guernsey, Jr. and Jeffrey Sweet (eds.), *The Best Plays of 1993–1994*. New York: Limelight, 487–91.
Havis, A. (ed.) (2001). *American Political Plays: An Anthology*. Urbana: University of Illinois Press.
Henry, W. A., III (1993). "America's Dark History." *Time*, November 22: 72.
Hischak, T. S. (2001). *American Theater: A Chronicle of Comedy and Drama, 1969–2000*. Oxford: Oxford University Press.
Holden, S. (1994). "Laying Odds on America's Soul." *New York Times*, November 15: 15.
Kalb, J. (1992). "A Decrepit Balance." *Village Voice*, March 3: 90.
Klein, A. (1993). "Albee's *Marriage Play*." *New York Times*, New Jersey Section, February 23: 16.
Kroll, J. (1993). "Mourning Becomes Electrifying." *Newsweek*, May 17: 70.
——(1994). "Trinity of Women." *Newsweek*, February 21: 62.
Lefkowitz, D. (1999). "Broadway and Off-Broadway." In Otis L. Guernsey, Jr. (ed.), *The Best Plays of 1998–1999*. New York: Limelight, 3–47.

Miller, A. (1978 [1955]). "The American Theater." In Robert A. Martin (ed.), *The Theater Essays of Arthur Miller*. New York: Viking, 31–50.

—— (1999). "Preface." In *Mr. Peters' Connections*. New York: Penguin, vii–viii.

Nachman, G. (1991). "An American View of the London Stage." *San Francisco Chronicle*, December 30: E2.

National Theatre Critics' Reviews (1995–2000). Woodside, NY: Theatre Critics' Reviews.

New York Theatre Critics' Reviews (1990–4). New York: Critics' Theatre Reviews.

Rich, F. (1993). "Embracing All Possibilities in Art and Life." *New York Times*, May 5: 15.

Stearns, D. P. (1993). "Spirit of *Angels* Lifts *Perestroika*." *USA Today*, November 24: 1D.

Sweet, J. (1992). "Broadway and Off-Broadway." In Otis L. Guernsey, Jr. and Jeffrey Sweet (eds.), *The Applause/Best Plays Theater Yearbook of 1991–1992 Featuring the Ten Best Plays of the Season*. New York: Applause, 3–51.

Willis, J. and Lynch, T. (ed.) (2000). *Theatre World*. New York: Applause.

32

Solo Performance Drama:
The Self as Other?

Stephen J. Bottoms

Jimmy paints.... There's one piece / one / a black boy / a black boy in a chair with colors / colors of Orange / Red / Black 'n' Blue / This boy sits in a chair by a kitchen window in Harlem / looking through locked bars onto an empty street / The boy's eyes are wide / sad / Know what I call that piece / I call it *Solo* / that's the name of it, man / *Solo.*

Dael Orlandersmith, The Gimmick (2000: 89–90)

Monologue-based performance has a long and rich history in the United States, encompassing everything from sermons and political oratory to sales pitches and medicine show hucksterism. Within entertainment contexts, the solo voice has also been prominently apparent, in vaudeville, stand-up, and other comedic forms. In the realm of character-based drama, however, self-standing monologues have historically been a rather marginal form, usually confined to the realm of short sketches and one-act plays, or to one-man shows such as those in which actors impersonate "great men" like Mark Twain and Abraham Lincoln. Prior to the 1980s, it was generally considered obvious that having two or more characters interact onstage was better than having single characters talking to themselves (or to invisible addressees, or to the audience). The last two decades of the twentieth century, however, saw a sudden expansion both in the number of artists making monologue-based theatre, and in audience demand for such work.

It must be acknowledged, from the outset, that the reasons for this shift have been economic as much as aesthetic. "Why are so many theatre artists choosing to [make] solo performance pieces rather than creating ensemble works or even plays?" writer-performer Holly Hughes asks rhetorically: "I'd guess that 75 percent of that question can be answered by looking at the economic situation of most theatres in this country. Solos are all that they can (barely) afford to produce" (Hughes and Román 1998: 2). Significantly, it was amidst the relative penury of New York's "underground" arts scene, at the turn of the 1980s, that solo performance first became a popular and widely practiced form of theatrical expression. In the non-commercial, unfunded contexts of loft studios and underground clubs and cabarets, particularly in the East Village, one-person shows proved cheap, portable, and easy to program as part of longer bills.

A similar underground theatre movement had emerged "off-off-Broadway" during the 1960s, yet with a few notable exceptions, such as Jeff Weiss's oft-revived *And That's How the Rent Gets Paid* (1966), this scene had featured little in the way of solo work (cf. Bottoms 2004). What had changed during the interim was the 1970s evolution of "performance art." Initially an extension of the individual studio practices of visual artists, performance art began largely as a gallery-based form, with practitioners treating their own bodies (rather than clay or canvas) as their primary medium and material. The ephemerality of such work was, in part, a reaction against the commodification of art objects as things to be bought, sold, and speculated on. Yet performance art quickly evolved into a form of theatricality that could also be sold to paying customers. By 1983, Laurie Anderson's eight-hour epic, *United States* – a mixed-media fusion of projected visuals, synthesized music, songs, and spoken narratives – had propelled her onto the huge stage of the Brooklyn Academy of Music.

During the 1980s, the term "performance art" came to be used as a catch-all descriptor for events that did not easily fit established aesthetic categories. In particular, it was widely used as a label for solo theatrical work in which the performer was also "the artist" – that is, the originator or author of the material, rather than "merely" its interpreter. However, several of the monologuists who emerged from the downtown scene of this period have been at pains to reject such categorization: in a piece posted on his website, for example, Eric Bogosian (who presented much of his early work in art-world venues like The Kitchen) specifies that he is an actor and writer, *not* a performance artist. The latter term he regards as better applied to visual artists whose work has extended into the fourth dimension (time). By contrast, Bogosian locates himself in relation to theatre traditions, on the grounds that his primary concern is with the creation of character and situation through performed language. Based on this distinction, perhaps, most contemporary solo performers belong more to the theatre than to the art world. Yet the performance art tradition has been vital in establishing the now commonplace idea of performing one's own work, without intermediaries. It is this development that has made monologue performances a significant arena for theatrical experimentation since the 1980s.

The central question for anyone planning to perform their own material alone onstage is how best to *dramatize oneself*. Given that one must inevitably adopt a performing persona or role of some sort, in presenting oneself to an audience (simply "being oneself," whatever that is, is a practical impossibility), the artist has to decide which "face" or "faces" will best serve his or her creative objectives. Even if one wants to present material drawn directly from personal experience, the task is still to find an appropriate representational strategy by which to do this – just as "Jimmy," in this chapter's epigraph, paints an image of a figure, quite separate from himself, in order to express his own innermost feelings. Conversely, though, even if one presents a wholly fictitious character onstage, just as one might in any dialogue-based play, the decision to perform it oneself, solo, will nonetheless mean that an audience will tend to see the character presented as an expression of something very personal to the writer-performer. After all, this is not simply an actor playing a part, but an artist presenting him-or herself as the art. Solo performance thus constitutes a kind of *Extreme Exposure* (to borrow the title of Jo Bonney's excellent anthology of work by American monologuists): when an individual confronts the audience alone, the exterior mask that s/he presents is widely assumed to offer a refracted expression of some aspect of her or his interior subjectivity.

Being fully aware of the intense scrutiny they place themselves under, most contemporary soloists use direct audience address as a means of taking on the audience's gaze and acknowledging its presence. Rather than being permitted to pretend that they are mere "flies on the wall," audiences find themselves interpolated directly into the theatrical exchange, as figures to be conversed with, questioned, and even harangued. Such tactics result in the distinction between monologuists and stand-up comedians often being somewhat blurred, but whereas the conventions of comedy permit vocal responses and even heckling from spectators, audiences at anything framed as "theatre" or "art" will tend to assume that their only options for audible response are laughter and applause. Rather than expecting comebacks, monologuists will instead engage spectators by inviting them to take on dramatic "roles" of one sort or another. This is quite literally the case in much of Eric Bogosian's work: for example, in *Funhouse* (1983), he offers the audience a series of perverse sales pitches and mock lectures, by becoming a sidewalk barker inviting "gentlemen" into his X-rated peepshow, a torture specialist lecturing a training group on the use of electrodes on the body, a televangelist addressing his couch-bound congregation, and so on. In each case, the audience is invited to "play along" with their implied characterization, while also appreciating the comic ironies arising from their being so "miscast." In other sequences again, Bogosian addresses imagined figures invisible to the audience, and thus implicitly excludes his actual listeners from the exchange, as if pushing them away rather than drawing them in. This kind of interplay between intimate involvement and ironic or critical distancing is a common feature of solo performances, even when the audience is "cast" simply as "themselves."

The Mask of Autobiography

The most common form of contemporary solo performance is the autobiographical monologue, and in most cases, such work seems predicated on the attempt to present the performer's "self" to the audience, as directly as possible, by minimizing any sense that this s/he is playing a role, or presenting "an act." That strategy also frequently implies an attempt to minimize the distance between actor and audience: the performer recounts ostensibly true, personal narratives as if s/he were addressing concerned friends, rather than a group of strangers sitting in the dark. For spectators, of course, this is a very agreeable role to be cast in, and this factor – along with the voyeuristic intrigue inherent in confessional storytelling – has helped make autobiography a popular theatrical form.

The most celebrated practitioner of this approach is Spalding Gray, whose solo performances propelled him, during the 1980s, from the relative obscurity of New York's downtown scene to international acclaim.[1] As a founder member of the experimental theatre company the Wooster Group, Gray's initial forays into autobiography provided the basis for that company's *Rhode Island Trilogy* (1975–8). These complex, multi-layered theatre pieces used fragments of personal narrative and "found objects" from Gray's past (such as pictures and sound recordings) as raw materials, which director Elizabeth LeCompte juxtaposed and intercut with other source materials. This collage approach seemed to invite audiences to view "selfhood" as a kind of patchwork of scraps and memories: the character named "Spalding Gray" appeared to be composed of "a multiplicity of masks" (Savran 1988a: 64). When he moved on to develop solos, however, Gray rejected such layering, and instead pursued a seeming artlessness in presentation. Sitting behind a desk with a notebook and pen, he would simply recount personal anecdotes to his audience, by improvising around his notes. Indeed, when he later began publishing texts to his monologues, they were based on edited transcripts of these improvisations, rather than on anything consciously written as a "play."

Gray's performances have always maintained a strong sense of being created "in the moment" onstage, even when presented many times over: "even though Gray may be repeating an anecdote as he remembers it from a previous performance," Michael Peterson notes, "the quality of active remembering separates this experience from that of a scripted reenactment" (1997: 55). This is, of course, a triumph of performance technique, and Gray always describes himself as an actor playing a character called Spalding Gray. Yet the impression created for spectators is of a man appearing onstage "in person," rather than "in character." The titles of his earliest monologues – *Sex and Death to Age 14* and *Booze, Cars and College Girls* (both 1979) – aptly articulate the idea that Gray is simply cataloguing his memories in as straightforward and unmediated a manner as possible, for the entertainment of his audience. Indeed, his disarmingly conversational tone and close attention to seemingly trivial detail make his work reminiscent of observational comedy: critics have often described him as a "sit-down comic," as if his performances offered a more genteel, sophisticated form of the "lowbrow" stand-up form.

Gray is, then, more raconteur than dramatist. Indeed, if "drama" can be loosely defined as a narrative form in which embodied conflict of some kind is explored, and

to some extent resolved, through dialogue and action, then Gray's amiably uncon-
flicted monologues are perhaps not very "dramatic" at all. Yet as Peterson argues
persuasively in his book *Straight White Male*, Gray's work does generate tensions of its
own. By casting the audience as intimates, he invites them to share a certain
complicity with him, just as if he were gossiping with like-minded friends. As a
result, though, a frisson of unease is often generated: do we as spectators want to be
"in" with this character? Gray speaks, often quite self-consciously, as a member of
America's dominant demographic of straight, white, middle-class WASPs, a privileged position which he insistently ironizes, but never questions to the point of
explicit critique. "Gray wants us to be fascinated and repelled at the same time,"
argues Henry Sayre: we must deal for ourselves with the question of whether or not to
accept his welcoming smile (Sayre 1989: 27–8).

Gray's generation of a schism between his interpolated "us" and an implicitly
excluded "them" is particularly apparent in his most famous piece, *Swimming to
Cambodia* (1985), which recounts his experiences in Thailand during the making of
the feature film *The Killing Fields*, in which he acted. While sharing numerous gossipy
intimacies about fellow western artists like John Malkovich and Roland Joffe, Gray
only ever refers to his Thai hosts collectively, as groups of nameless film extras,
prostitutes, and servants. In doing so, he tends to reinforce the stereotypical American
view of Asians as inscrutably smiling Orientals. "The waiters were running
and jumping over hedges because they couldn't get to us fast enough," he notes in
his opening anecdote, about a rest day from filming: "They were running and
jumping and smiling – not a silly smile but a profound smile, a deep smile. . . . Some
people say that the Thais are the nicest people that money can buy" (Gray 1987: 19).
Gray invites his audience to share in this quizzical amusement toward Asians as the
exotic "other," but the "money can buy" line is the kicker, raising an ironic question
mark over western assumptions about their "availability" as commodities. Nonetheless, as Gray's critics have forcefully pointed out, such light irony is probably insuffi-
cient to subvert such culturally entrenched views – and may merely end up
reinforcing them.

This same phenomenon of the complicitous spectator is used to more progressive
effect in the work of various autobiographical performers from minority communities.
Gay and lesbian artists, in particular, have used personal narratives as a way of
confirming and validating the life experiences of identity groups usually rendered
"other" by the dominant culture (when visible at all). Queer spectators are interpolated into the "us" of artists like Tim Miller and Holly Hughes, as they share stories
of sexual awakening, of "coming out," of abuse and marginalization at the hands of
the straight majority, and so forth. Conversely, heterosexual audience members often
find themselves conscious of being "othered" in these contexts: to see a Tim Miller
piece as a straight person is to be made to feel welcome, but also to be made aware that
one is not the primary addressee. The resulting sense of semi-exclusion provides an

instructive inversion of the usual cultural hierarchy of straight as privileged, gay as other (see chapter 30).

Miller, like Gray, adopts a friendly, conversational tone in his performances, but unlike Gray, he also involves spectators through very physical engagement. At the start of *Naked Breath* (1994), for example, he enters from the back of the auditorium, and talks directly to individual spectators, before sitting himself in the lap of one unsuspecting individual. His approach is always playful and unthreatening, but Miller makes a point of emphasizing his physical presence: indeed, he usually removes his clothes at some point during each performance, to stand naked before his audience. Confronted by a heterosexist culture that still compels "closetedness," Miller's insistence on the explicit visibility of *My Queer Body* – as the title of a 1992 piece puts it – is for him a political imperative. His personal narratives, likewise, tend to adopt an overtly activist slant. *Glory Box* (1998), for example, recounts the development of Miller's relationship with his Australian partner as a means of protesting the injustice of United States immigration laws, which permit residency status for foreign spouses of heterosexual Americans, but fail to recognize homosexual partnerships.

Miller's performances are always impassioned and persuasive, but like Gray, he tends to prioritize the creation of a seemingly unmediated flow of autobiographical anecdotes, and thus the illusion of personal immediacy onstage. His monologues shift back and forth in time between the present of performance and the past events he describes, but do little to disrupt or query the governing impression of Miller's own centeredness and self-confidence, both as a performer and as a "character." For a gay artist, this has the advantage of projecting a strong sense of personal *pride*. Yet I would argue that the more intriguing – and more strictly "dramatic" – forms of autobiographical monologue are those which, rather than seeking to minimize the differences between actor and character, and the gap between performer and audience, instead play actively *with* those distinctions. For example, the performances of Holly Hughes and other veterans of the WOW Café (an East Village storefront venue, run self-sufficiently by a collective of lesbian artists since the early 1980s; see chapter 30) often use very self-conscious structural devices to emphasize the depiction of "self" as a character, or series of characters, constructed by and through dramatic circumstances (rather than as a stable entity whose experiences simply happen to it). The spectator is also, therefore, allowed greater freedom to respond to the work on her own terms, rather than being drawn into a complicitous "we" with the performer.

Hughes's *Clit Notes* (1994) is a good example of this approach. It opens with her delivering a breezily witty account of her first adolescent inklings of desire for other women – a coming-to-awareness which she purports to have embraced enthusiastically from the outset. Yet it becomes clear that, far from offering any pretense at unadorned autobiography, Hughes is here playing up to the "brazen lesbian" image constructed for her by the media during the "NEA Four" controversy of 1990, when she, Miller, John Fleck, and Karen Finley were stripped of their grants from the

National Endowment for the Arts, on the grounds that their work was "indecent." The title *Clit Notes*, and Hughes's bright red (scarlet-harlot) dress are also indicative of this ironically defiant attitude to such censure. Yet as the piece progresses, Hughes also adopts a number of other, less brash personae to recount other recollections – including those of her "softer, older self" and "the sullen, overprivileged brat she once was" (Hughes and Román 1998: 427, 429). She frames these shifts through the use of yet another figure, a professorial type giving a mock-alarmist lecture (with subheadings) on "Performance Art: What Causes It? Where It Comes From and What Can Be Done About It" (427). These "titles" parody the metonymic link between homosexuality and performance art so often implied by press and politicians (three of the "NEA Four" were gay), while also creating for the audience a kind of critical distance on the various selves that Hughes presents: is any one of these the "real" her, or are they all just performative masks? Toward the end of the performance, Hughes then hits her audience with a seemingly very personal confession that openly undermines the "brazen" persona. "What my girlfriend and I are good at is *acting* shameless," she stresses: "I wish I had no shame. Maybe there are shameless queers. But I know that I'm not one of them" (436, my emphasis). Switching to a third-person narrative about her girlfriend's coming out, she then offers an alternative account of lesbian awakening, marked this time not by gung-ho enthusiasm but by the sense that "a hole has opened up inside her. All of a sudden, a deep hole filling up with the cold water of shame" (437).

Clit Notes, despite its throwaway pun of a title, turns out to be a passionate outcry against a deeply judgmental, homophobic American culture, which has forced upon Hughes (and so many others) a kind of split selfhood. While playing up to her outer image of proud defiance, Hughes's character(s) can never entirely shake this deeply inculcated sense of shame. This sense of unease is underlined further by the way that Hughes intercuts her coming-out narratives with the more recent story of her father being diagnosed with cancer. The sense of jarring disjuncture set up by the insertion of this very different subject matter forces the audience to ask further questions: why this, now? It eventually becomes clear that Hughes sees her father's disappointment in her as the root source of her unshakeable guilt. Indeed, her very public involvement in the NEA controversy is described as the "thing that my father says is what's really killing him" (425). Still, almost despite herself, she continues to care deeply for this dying man who, in her childhood, "had done everything he could to make the world safe for me" (423). On one level, then, *Clit Notes* is a "family drama" in the great American tradition, as Hughes conjures up a profound sense of her central character's ambivalence toward her chief antagonist: "Fuck! I didn't just say I loved my father, did I? I meant to imply that I loved his *body*. Which is not *him*. My *father*, his *body*... two completely separate entities" (420).

Hughes creates a complex layering of comedy and pathos by presenting herself not simply as a raconteur but as a multi-faceted and fundamentally unresolved character. Some of her colleagues from the WOW Café have pursued similar dramatic strategies still further. Carmelita Tropicana, for example, in *Milk of Amnesia* (also 1994), pushes the fragmentation of "self" to disorienting extremes, in addressing her desire to revisit Cuba, from which she was exiled as a child. Her stage name is itself a blatantly artificial persona – a mock-stereotypical pseudonym adopted by the artist Alina Troyano to ironize her own "otherness" before American audiences. Yet the autobiographical "Carmelita" character discovers that she is not only a Cuban "other" in America, but also an American "other" in Cuba. Her sense of displacement becomes vividly apparent during the performance, as "Carmelita" repeatedly disappears behind a string of other stage personae, like a bus driver, a doctor, and even a pig. In these moments, the *absence* of the authorial central character (further complicated by the disembodied presence of "the Writer" in taped voiceovers) evokes a powerful sense of self-loss – of Tropicana having drunk the "milk of amnesia" and forgotten fundamental things about her identity as a Cuban. The piece's final stage directions describe her "stepping out of the Carmelita character and addressing the audience," but without that persona, it is not at all clear who or what she becomes (Hughes and Román 1998: 47).

Given such complex dramatizations of self not as a stable essence but as a series of masks, the next logical step, perhaps, is to abandon any overt claim to "autobiography" and to fictionalize one's experiences entirely (just as some of Tennessee Williams's and Eugene O'Neill's plays fictionalize aspects of their own family histories). This is the strategy adopted by African American poet-playwright Dael Orlandersmith, who in the 1990s created a trilogy of one-woman shows telling the stories of young women growing up in Harlem – just as she did. Pressured from all sides, these characters all seek to reshape and redeem their experiences through poetry, but they are never called "Dael," and Orlandersmith is adamant that she is not simply playing herself. "It's not the fact that it's based on somebody's life that interests me," she stresses: "My work is basically fictional" (qtd. in Coleman 1999: 32). Nevertheless, her performances are as grounded in the fact of her own bodily presence as are Miller's. In her 1998 piece *The Gimmick*, for instance, the adolescent central character, Alexis, repeatedly stresses her painful awareness of being "big and fatter than other kids" (Orlandersmith 2000: 80). Onstage, Orlandersmith cuts a large, striking figure, and though she is certainly not "fat" (whatever that is), one can well imagine that Alexis's acute body-consciousness is based on personal experience. A strange tension is thus established, as the spectator is drawn in to sympathize with Alexis, while at the same time wondering, from a certain distance, about the degree to which her story is also Orlandersmith's own. *The Gimmick*'s use of language generates a similar push–pull effect. There is an immediacy about the storytelling because, in contrast to most autobiographical monologues, Alexis tells her story in the present tense, as if experiencing it, or "reliving" it, in the onstage moment. Yet while directing her story toward the audience, she never explicitly acknowledges them *as* an audience, or engages in chatty repartee with them. The language is, instead, insistently poetic – with phrases building, circling, and repeating as if this were an extended solo by a jazz or blues musician. Orlandersmith thus conjures up vividly immediate imagery in the mind's eye, while also retaining a certain formal distance from her listeners.

Perhaps the most striking aspect of Orlandersmith's work, though, is the way she succeeds in cutting across lines of cultural difference. Since she performs primarily in subscription-subsidized, not-for-profit theatres, Orlandersmith's audiences are often made up largely of middle-class whites, for whom Harlem might as well be another planet. Yet Alexis's story is immediately accessible and comprehensible even to these "others," because the play's emphasis, at least initially, is on the universal struggles of childhood and adolescence – on the need to find friendship and accept-ance, the urge to define oneself as an individual, the fear of rejection and ridicule. At the play's outset, these are far more pressing issues for Alexis than her blackness, since everyone around her is black, too. It is only as she and her painter friend Jimmy seek to spread their wings beyond Harlem, and explore New York's downtown art world, that they begin to understand the implications of racial difference. Jimmy's paintings are quickly latched onto as a new, authentic expression of black youth, and then just as quickly dropped. The results are devastating for him, but Alexis comes to see the destructive shallowness of the art market as simply another life-sapping "gimmick," like the other gimmicks she sees around her in the relative poverty of Harlem – the numbing allure of drugs, sex, and violence. Her struggle is to find her own voice as an individual, rather than anesthetizing herself by giving in to these familiar temptations. Yet her pain and anger at her situation become vividly manifested through a sense of split identity, as she hides the vulnerability she feels on the inside behind a hardened, stereotyped mask of self-defense:

> I see a girl / see / a rich, white girl / what I perceive to be a rich, white girl / I'm walking downtown / She's walking uptown. . . . She looks at me / smiles / smiles at me / I stop / knowing she's smiling at me / I stop / block her / not touching her / don't have to / I'm bigger / taller / I block her and say, "What you laughing at / what're you lookin' at? I'll fuck you up, bitch." / . . . She says, "Why? What did I do to you? I wasn't laughing at you." . . . / Outside I say, "Fuck you, bitch / You think I'm funny" / Inside I say, What am I doing? . . . My God, what am I doing? (97–8)

Alexis's explosion in this moment comes as release of built-up pressure, and is just one small incident in the narrative. Yet it epitomizes Orlandersmith's achievement in *The Gimmick*: in dramatizing Alexis's sudden, traumatized response to "what I perceive to be a rich, white girl," she simultaneously makes behavior that whites might "perceive to be" threateningly alien seem comprehensible and even sympa-thetic. Where Spalding Gray's monologic address tends, perhaps, to reinforce cultural divisions between "us" and "them," Orlandersmith's seeks actively to high-light them and, as far as possible, to overcome them through the cultivation of understanding.

Multiple-Character Selves

The search for understanding also lies at the heart of the work of another leading African American soloist, Anna Deavere Smith. Rather than basing her work on personal experience, however, Smith's practice is about listening to others. Her performances, which she groups together under the collective title of *On the Road: A Search for American Character*, consist of minutely observed recreations of the words, speech patterns, and gestures of people whom she has interviewed. Smith's conviction is that, by listening not just to what people say but to the ways in which they say it, one can learn important things about their underlying "characters" as shaped by their surroundings and experiences. Smith launched *On the Road* in the early 1980s, initially as an extension of her practice as an acting teacher, but the project really came into its own in the early 1990s, when she interviewed some of the people caught up in the race riots in Crown Heights, Brooklyn, in 1991, and in Los Angeles the following year. The resulting performances, *Fires in the Mirror* (1992) and *Twilight: Los Angeles, 1992* (1993), succeeded in shedding much-needed light on complex events that had been shamefully trivialized and sensationalized by the mass media. Rather than reducing the riots' victims and participants to the level of sound bite and stereotype, Smith sought to inhabit their words and give sustained voice to a multiplicity of conflicting perspectives on what had happened, and on what needed to change. Thus, *Twilight* is carefully structured so as to map out, first, "the territory" of racial division in Los Angeles, before going on to focus on specific reactions to the brutal beating of Rodney King by white police officers in South Central Los Angeles, and to the acquittal of those officers by an all-white, suburban jury – the event that sparked the rioting. Smith provides plausible humanity to representatives of the jury and police force, as well as to victims of police violence; to those who rose up in arms, as well as to those harmed in the rioting; to Hispanics and Koreans as well as to blacks and whites. The result is a kaleidoscopic depiction of vastly complex, genuinely tragic circumstances.

Smith's work stands in an alternative lineage of monologue performance to that of the autobiographically based work discussed thus far. Multiple-character solos were pioneered in the 1980s, most notably by Eric Bogosian. The actor performs a series of monologues, sequentially, each one depicting a different character. These gradually accumulate to create a collage-like array of takes on a particular theme or subject. Where autobiographical work tends, as we have seen, to create a fairly intimate relationship with audiences, multiple-character work tends to require spectators to adopt a more critical or ironic attitude toward the material presented. No one character sticks around long enough to become the audience's "friend," and instead the careful juxtaposition of different characters implies that their different attitudes and viewpoints are being presented for our scrutiny. This proves an ideal format for Smith's investigation of social tensions, because it means that no one voice is prioritized or privileged as the singular arbiter of "truth." "Few people speak a language about race that is not their own," Smith notes: "In order to have real unity, all voices would have to first be heard or at least represented" (Smith 1994: xxv).

Multiple-character solos might appear, at first glance, to evade completely the self-presentation approach of autobiography, but this is not really the case. Bogosian, for example, claims that all his characters are based on his own internal voices – his *Men Inside*, as the title of his first, 1981 piece puts it. His monologues develop as he "listens" to the voices of characters that emerge from his subconscious, through improvisation. Bogosian has come to the conclusion that all of these characters can be categorized according to "12 distinct male archetypes, ranging from a threatening street punk to a redneck deer hunter to a little boy playing" (Bogosian 2002: 17). On one level, it seems, his audiences are being invited to participate in the self-mocking, ironic display of his personal neuroses, much as are Spalding Gray's. Yet where Gray is lightly self-deprecating, Bogosian's is a high-octane performance style, strongly influenced by the punk-rock aesthetic he grew up with in the late 1970s – "aggressive and loud . . . awkward was good; grotesque was fascinating" (17). Indeed, the chief attraction of his performances is the sense of raw energy and charisma that he brings to his chameleon-like role switches. Yet his punky aggression also tends to imply a kind of blanket negativity toward the world at large, rather than seeking to enlighten his audiences in any way. His "archetypes" are never far from being "stereotypes," and are usually foolish or arrogant or obsessive or obnoxious to a degree that makes them either repellent or laughable (or both). Bogosian's work thus points, unintentionally, toward an underlying problem with the multiple-character approach to monologue work: the act of channeling a series of voices through a single performing body can too easily create the impression that the actor himself is in possession of knowledge and vision superior to that of any of the individual characters depicted.

Anna Deavere Smith has also sometimes been accused of appearing to privilege herself over her subjects, by caricaturing their speech patterns and gestures. Yet the edge of exaggeration that some see in her performances is an inevitable result of her studied reproduction of behavior that was once spontaneous, in the moment of the interview. In this respect, her performances are as far from Gray's illusion of self-presence as could be: she seeks, instead, to highlight and underline the specific, *gestic* qualities of her subjects' behavior, almost as if pursuing Brechtian "estrangement techniques." In doing so, Smith implicitly dramatizes *herself* as a careful listener and observer (her memoir of 2000 is entitled *Talk to Me*), and invites spectators to take on a similar role. Her own gender and color simultaneously foreground the fact that she, as an individual, is inherently different from many of the characters presented, and can never fully "inhabit" their subjecthood. Still, Smith's light complexion also helps audiences to see her in a kind of "in-between" position, physically bridging the racial gulf that her most famous pieces dramatize. (As a young actress, she recalls, casting agents had trouble placing her in roles because she wasn't considered to look either "black" or "white.") Smith thus literally embodies the underlying message of *Twilight: Los Angeles, 1992*, which implies the need to progress beyond the simplistically bifurcated, "black and white" language of most discussions over race (as in "right and wrong," "us and them"), and instead to inhabit the uncertain, liminal zones in which hope must be found. This perspective is summarized in the play's closing monologue by Twilight Bey, one of the organizers of the Los Angeles gang truce:

> So twilight / is / that time / between day and night. / Limbo, I call it limbo....Like the sun is stuck between night and day / in the twilight hours...a lot of times when I've brought up ideas to my homeboys, / they say, / "Twilight, / that's before your time, / that's something you can't do now." / [But] I cannot forever dwell [only in] identifying with those like me / and understanding only me and mine. (Smith 1994: 254–5)

Among other notable multiple-character monologuists are New Yorkers John Leguizamo and Danny Hoch, both of whom have fused Bogosian's high-energy approach to the presentation of character with a keenly observed focus on actual social circumstances, which at times makes their work reminiscent of Smith's more "documentarian" approach. Smith's dramatization of interview material has also proved influential on soloists such as Eve Ensler, who spoke with women of varying ages and backgrounds in creating *The Vagina Monologues* (1996). This seemingly risqué, but ultimately rather sentimental, celebration of female sexuality has enjoyed worldwide commercial success, thanks largely to the seemingly endless stream of celebrities who have proved willing to step in for star turns in individual monologues.

Offending the Audience

Leaving these figures aside, I want to conclude by discussing some more disconcertingly abrasive approaches to solo performance. As we have seen, most contemporary monologue-based theatre tends either to seek a friendly intimacy with its spectators, or to provide them with a certain critical distance on the characters depicted – or indeed to achieve both, through a kind of push–pull dynamic of simultaneous attraction and questioning. A few artists, however, have sought to confront and discomfort their audiences more overtly. The most notorious exemplar of this approach is Karen Finley, another of the leading East Village artists of the 1980s, whose work represents a radical feminist critique of patriarchal power structures. In *The Constant State of Desire* (1986), for example, this entails a twin assault on both America's capitalist economic system and the dominance of the father in the domestic sphere – both of which she portrays as creating a culture of appalling violence and abuse, and of equally appalling neglect toward those truly in need of help, such as AIDS sufferers. Reacting to social realities she perceives as obscene, Finley presents obscenity itself as the only viable response: her monologues are "never just a litany of four-letter expletives," notes critic Cynthia Carr, "but an attempt to express emotions for which there are perhaps no words. An attempt to approach the unspeakable" (1993: 121). Take, for example, the layered imagery of forced sexual penetration in this extract from *Constant State of Desire*:

> Joanne sleeps with a gun under her pillow because every time she has intercourse with her husband he defecates uncontrollably as he has an orgasm . . . it's that loose, runny diarrhea shit that splatters all over the room . . . even though he pays all the bills and spends time with the kids – SHE'LL TAKE HIS CASH BUT SHE WON'T TAKE HIS SHIT! So she takes her husband's gun and sticks it up his ass as he's about to cum. (Finley 1990: 11)

As this extract indicates, Finley's work is also disturbing for its use of grotesque, jet-black humor, which prompts laughter so involuntary that it is liable to induce self-disgust in the spectator. She never allows audiences the comfort of coolly objective scrutiny. What is perhaps most unnerving about Finley's work, however, is the way she slides seamlessly between different performative masks, so that the question of exactly who is speaking from moment to moment becomes tortuously unclear. "There's no nonsense here about taking the audience out of itself and into the performer's world," Carr notes, drawing an explicit contrast with Spalding Gray: "Finley doesn't offer such wholeness; she presents a persona that has shattered, a self unable to put a face on things" (1993: 123). Fusing autobiographical and multiple-character approaches, she moves from first-person confessions to third-person narrative and from grotesque revenge fantasies to delirious, gender-switching embodiments of incest and rape: "Then I mount my own mama in the ass. That's right. I fuck my own mama in the ass because I'd never fuck my mama in her snatch. She's my mama!" (Finley 1990: 19). In Finley's work, moreover, the lines of demarcation between abusers and victims are never clear-cut: *The Constant State of Desire* foregrounds the metaphor of "the father in us all" – of the inbred urge to violate and dominate that Finley sees in herself and all around her – and concludes with a monologue titled "White Man's Guilt," which implicates herself, as a Caucasian, in the continued exploitation and oppression of Native Americans.

The problem with Finley's work, though, lies precisely in the extremity of emotional display that is also its primary strength. Matching her shocking language with performance tactics often involving confrontational nudity, and the smearing of her body with substances resembling blood and feces, Finley sets herself up as such a force of horror that she necessarily "others herself" from her observers. It is thus all too easy for her to be dismissed as freakish and gratuitously revolting by those not already sympathetic with her objectives. Not surprisingly, Finley became the primary hate figure in the "NEA Four" controversy of the early 1990s – and indeed is cited as such by the voice of Holly Hughes's father in *Clit Notes*.

A much subtler approach to upsetting the audience is adopted by Wallace Shawn in *The Fever* (1991), whose basic mode of address is as innocuous and conversational as that of Spalding Gray. Indeed, this piece was originally written for performance in the living rooms of well-to-do friends, and even when transferred to conventional theatre spaces, Shawn continued to perform the entirety of the monologue while sitting in an armchair, as if delivering a Roosevelt-style "fireside chat." What is disturbing about *The Fever* is the way that Shawn succeeds in drawing audiences into his circle of address, and then confronting "us" with ideas that one would never raise in polite society.

Shawn normally writes plays for more than one actor, but many of his pieces nonetheless hinge around unsettlingly direct address to spectators. In *The Fever*, Shawn appears simply to be Shawn (no other character name is given), and he uses his personal presence as a means to present his most direct, personal expression of what he has described as the "embarrassing" urge to "get [audiences] to worry about the things that are bothering me" (Savran 1988b: 220). As with Orlandersmith's *The Gimmick*, however, this is a semi-fictional mono-drama delivered largely in the present tense. This character is, it seems, speaking to us while on a trip to an unnamed foreign country where the torture of prisoners is regarded as a legitimate tool of government policy. Here, he has been struck down by a fever and by compulsive attacks of vomiting – a violently physical reaction both to the barbarities he has witnessed, and to his growing awareness that he himself is implicated. The economic domination of the West, which allows him to live in comfort and attend charming artistic events such as this one, is the root cause behind the continuing deprivation and depravity of this "under-developed" country. In a particularly telling metaphor, Shawn proposes that it is only physical distance that prevents westerners from seeing this every day:

> Shouldn't we decorate our lives and our world as if we were having a permanent party? . . . Yes, but we can't have celebrations in the very same room where groups of people are being tortured and killed . . . isn't there any other room we can use? Yes, but we still could hear the people screaming. Well then – can't we use the building across the street? (Shawn 1991: 20)

Moreover, such discomforting realizations are not limited to relations between "first" and "third" worlds. Shawn's character, in his delirium, homes in unerringly on the ways in which the relatively privileged in any context justify their own lifestyles to themselves:

> there's a reason why *I'm* the one who *has* the money in the *first* place, and *that's* why I'm not going to give it all away . . . for God's sake, I *worked* for that money. . . . Why is the old woman sick and dying? Why doesn't she have money? Didn't she ever work? You idiot, you pathetic idiot, of course she worked. She worked sixteen hours a day in a field, in a factory. She worked, the chambermaid worked – you say *you*

work. But why does your work bring you so much money, while their work brings practically nothing? (57)

The to-and-fro flow of questions and answers apparent in the sequences quoted is indicative of Shawn's strategy of involving his audience by almost *obliging* them to ask these questions of themselves, too — to implicate themselves in these same appalling rationalizations. (Theatregoers, after all, tend to be among the more privileged members of any society.) *The Fever*, moreover, addresses its spectators with increasing directness as it progresses. At first, it appears we are simply being made privy to an unorthodox travelogue, but Shawn's "I" tends to be displaced increasingly by a "we" that encompasses his spectators, and eventually even by a "you" of direct address: "Look, here's a question I would like to ask you — have you ever had any friends who were poor?" (49). The implied answer is that nobody can cope for long with the guilt and discomfort of spending time with those substantially less fortunate than themselves.

Shawn's logic is difficult to contest in good conscience — so much so that, by the end of *The Fever*, his startlingly simple conclusions seem almost unavoidable: "All right, go ahead. Go ahead. Say it. / The life I live is irredeemably corrupt. It has no justification" (95). The audience is invited to confront this as a truth more real than their own day-to-day rationalizations: "just let it happen just for this moment, just for tonight, and then tomorrow we'll go back to lying again" (95). In performance, this moment can exert an unnerving power over spectators, as they contemplate the accuracy of this judgment in their own lives. *Will* we just go back to justifying ourselves as "good people," in the manner that has been exposed as sick farce this evening? What can we do to make this not true? Shawn has been accused by some critics of simply leaving his character — and perhaps his listeners — in the position of irredeemability; of failing to articulate any potential for change. Surely though, such potential must be sought out by the listener, for him-or herself, in the solo isolation of individual conscience. Having forcefully interpolated his spectators into the play's conflicts, Shawn refuses to let them off the hook on which he has so deftly hung them.

The directness of monologue-based performance can take many forms, but the most compelling works in this genre are those that actively highlight and interrogate the interdependent relationships between actor and spectator, and between actor and character, on which the theatrical event always pivots. It is worth acknowledging, finally, that many of the pieces discussed here *can* be performed as plays by actors other than their authors. This would be rather pointless with strictly autobiographical narratives like Gray's and Miller's (why not simply present one's own?), but once a degree of self-consciously "playwriterly" character construction comes into play, there is no reason to suppose that works as diverse as *Clit Notes* and *Twilight* could not be meaningfully performed by others. I have seen both *The Fever* and Bogosian's *Funhouse* in accomplished British productions. Still, in both those cases, I was insistently aware of their authors' absence from the stage. Solo work, it seems, tends to point back toward the singularity of its originating voice far more directly than dialogue-based drama. Indeed, this is the case even with some of the monologue plays by non-actor playwrights that have emerged since the 1980s boom in solo performance. For example, Neil LaBute's celebrated trilogy of one-acts, *Bash: Latterday Plays* (1999), which reworks Greek-tragic narratives in contemporary American contexts, almost compels the spectator to reflect on LaBute's own clearly conflicted relationship with his Mormon background. Ultimately, it seems, solo performance is one of the most tellingly personal dramatic forms available, and it has been American artists who, over the last two decades or so, have been at the forefront of exploring its many possibilities.

NOTE

1. Please note that this chapter was written prior to Spalding Gray's tragic death early in 2004. Rather than amend everything here to "past tense," however, it seemed appropriate to leave the discussion as is, in recognition of the "present-time" spirit of Gray's performances.

BIBLIOGRAPHY

Bogosian, E. (1994). *The Essential Bogosian*. New York: Theatre Communications Group.

——(2002). "Cutting Loose." *American Theatre* (April): 16–19, 57–60.

——(n.d.). "Who the Fuck is Eric Bogosian?" http://www.ericbogosian.com.

Bonney, J. (2000). *Extreme Exposure: An Anthology of Solo Performance Texts from the Twentieth Century*. New York: Theatre Communications Group.

Bottoms, S. J. (2004). *Playing Underground: A Critical History of the 1960s Off-Off-Broadway Movement*. Ann Arbor: University of Michigan Press.

Carr, C. (1993). *On Edge: Performance at the End of the Twentieth Century*. Hanover, NH: Wesleyan University Press.

Coleman, C. (1999). "On Beating the Odds: An Interview with Dael Orlandersmith." *American Theatre* (September): 32.

Ensler, E. (2001). *The Vagina Monologues*. London: Virago.

Finley, K. (1990). *Shock Treatment*. San Francisco: City Lights.

Gray, S. (1987). *Swimming to Cambodia: The Collected Works of Spalding Gray*. London: Picador.

Hughes, H. and Román, D. (1998). *O Solo Homo: The New Queer Performance*. New York: Grove.

LaBute, N. (2000). *Bash: Latterday Plays*. New York: Overlook.

Miller, T. (1997). *Shirts and Skin*. Los Angeles: Alyson.

Orlandersmith, D. (2000). *Beauty's Daughter, Monster, The Gimmick: Three Plays*. New York: Vintage.

Peterson, M. (1997). *Straight White Male: Performance Art Monologues*. Jackson: University Press of Mississippi.

Savran, D. (1988a). *Breaking the Rules: The Wooster Group*. New York: Theatre Communications Group.

——(1988b). *In Their Own Words: Contemporary American Playwrights*. New York: Theatre Communications Group.

Sayre, H. (1989). *The Object of Performance*. Chicago: University of Chicago Press.

Shawn, W. (1991). *The Fever*. London: Faber and Faber.

Smith, A. D. (1993). *Fires in the Mirror: Crown Heights, Brooklyn and Other Identities*. New York: Anchor.

——(1994). *Twilight: Los Angeles, 1992*. New York: Anchor.

——(2000). *Talk To Me: Travels in Media and Politics*. New York: Anchor.

33

Experimental Drama at the End of the Century

Ehren Fordyce

The following chapter focuses on experimental drama in the United States during the 1980s and 1990s, with occasional references to previous decades when it is important to show the legacy influencing an artist or work. By "experimental," I am trying to cover a wide variety of dramatists working outside the aesthetic of psychological realism, its familiar settings of home and work, and its predominantly linear forms of narrative and dialogue. Additionally, I have sought to include dramatists who clearly write for theatre in a manner that could not be confused for television or film writing.

I also refer to "avant-garde" works, although for several reasons I have chosen not to use that as a blanket term for the works discussed here. One reason for this is my desire to avoid the important and complicated debates about whether the American avant-garde is dead (see Schechner, Aronson, Mufson, and others), as well as the related, albeit separate, debates about the theoretical "death" of the author (see Barthes and Foucault) and, more significantly for drama, the "death" of character (see Fuchs). Another reason why I use the term "avant-garde" selectively stems from the fact that not all playwrights discussed in this chapter are informed by the European historical avant-garde (symbolism, futurism, dadaism, expressionism, constructivism, surrealism, and others) or the American performance avant-garde of the 1950s and 1960s (Black Mountain College, happenings, early performance art, Judson Dance, and others). The 1980s and 1990s observed the rise of many playwrights emerging from previously marginalized identities: playwrights of color, female playwrights, and gay and lesbian playwrights, to name only some of the most commonly used categories of identity. Some playwrights and performing artists write in relation to the avant-garde and its tradition of predominantly white, male

Thanks to Adelina Anthony, Tommy DeFrantz, Harry Elam, James Frieze, David Krasner, Daphne Lei, Daniel Mufson, Brad Rothbart, Arden Thomas, and Gary Winter for their suggestions and assistance with scripts.

artists. For instance, African American dramatist Suzan-Lori Parks writes partly in dialogue with Samuel Beckett. Still, many American playwrights seeking to write from the perspective of identity-based issues have had to consider legacies other than the avant-garde for models. Additionally, the avant-garde has occasionally been associated, albeit reductively, with a stridently oppositional tone, a desire to *épater la bourgeoisie* (shock the middle class). Many of the writers included here resist parts of American society and culture, but many also seek artistic affirmations that would fail to surface simply through easy plot resolutions, pat sentiments, and moral lessons. Since the term "experimental" seems more encompassing than "avant-garde," I use it as the guiding term, reserving "avant-garde" for reference to historical connections. In what follows I move chronologically whenever possible. However, when it is more effective to demonstrate a pattern through a confluence of trends rather than sequential causality, I depart from chronology. In general, I have tried to be more inclusive than exclusive, emphasizing small-scale experiments as much as thorough-going attempts at avant-gardism. I have sought at all times to remember the words of a youthful and slightly overenthusiastic Samuel Beckett, who wrote the following in defense of Joyce's *Finnegans Wake*:

> Here form *is* content, content *is* form. You complain that this stuff is not written in English. It is not written at all. It is not to be read – or rather it is not only to be read. It is to be looked at and listened to. His [Joyce's] writing is not *about* something; *it is that something itself.* (1984: 27)

I say "overenthusiastic" because the equation of form and content is by no means simple. There is no essential fit between the structure and style of a piece and its subject matter, but there are ways in which the two levels may be more consciously congruent or more consciously in friction than psychological realism conveys, with its illusion that form is primarily an empty vessel that holds content. Suzan-Lori Parks puts it this way: "Form should not be looked at askance and held suspect – form is not something that 'gets in the way of the story' but is an integral part of the story" (Parks 1995: 7).

The 1980s: Expanded Realism and Language Plays

The focus begins with a discussion of early 1980s experimental drama by three dramatists well known from previous decades: Tennessee Williams, Maria Irene Fornes, and Adrienne Kennedy. All use the convention of dramatic character, each to different effect, while expanding the boundaries of realism, influenced in part by sociopolitical reasons. They recognize that in submitting slavishly to the requisite of the "reality principle" by imitating a sociological slice of life, the theatrical experience may in fact be closing off imaginary and material alternatives, possibilities for transformation, and potentials for aesthetic and political change. Although famous primarily for his pre-1960s plays, Williams continued to write until his death in 1983. Recently critics have begun to reappraise Williams's late work, recognizing its debt to European avant-garde sources and coming to terms with the more overtly homosexual and less (or "too") obviously lyrical character of the late writing (see chapter 12). From *The Gnädiges Fräulein* (1966, included in experimental playwrights Messerli and Wellman's 1998 anthology *From the Other Side of the Century II*) to *The Remarkable Rooming-House of Mme. Le Monde* (1984), Williams's oeuvre is capacious, and much of it, like the latter play, still unstaged. Although Williams continued to use character and, to a lesser extent, plot, his late plays are apt to take advantage of these concepts in expressionistic or grotesque ways that threaten and mock theatrical conventions.

Fornes's work of the 1980s and 1990s is classical in form, given its use of nominally psychological versions of character and linear narrative. However, Fornes's apparent realism frequently carries self-conscious qualities and unease with speech, a feature that is especially clear in Fornes's direction of silences in her own work. Susan Sontag puts it nicely in her preface to Fornes's *Plays*: "Her work is both a theatre about utterance (i.e. a meta-theatre) and a theatre about the disfavored – both Handke *and* Kroetz, as it were" (Fornes 1986: 9). *Mud* (1983) is a well-known example (see chapter 27).

Like Williams and Fornes, Adrienne Kennedy uses story and the convention of character, but she, too, redirects these basic dramatic forms in unusual ways. On the surface, a play like *Motherhood 2000* (1994, included in Marranca 1996) appears to be a documentarian monologue, a kind of victim testimony that lightly fictional-izes Kennedy's own autobiography and the police beating of her son Adam. But the play's laconic, testimonial style is ironic, in a serious way. Kennedy juxtaposes the seeming lack of affect in the Writer/Mother's speech with a hyperbolically apocalyp-tic, almost sci-fi description of New York City's Upper West Side; she then further distances the narrator's monologue by introducing a medieval passion play-within-the-play in which the narrator confronts the abusive cop while he plays Christ on the cross. It is worth dwelling on Kennedy's play because it uses a number of techniques that appear in other experimental dramas, such as the self-referentiality of the structure and the *bricolage* or pastiche of different verbal idioms and textual sources (monologue and passion play, for instance). As the play ends, Kennedy achieves an elegant formal resolution in which the meta-frame of the monologue and the inner frame of the passion play snap shut. While emotionally distanced, this formal synching of different narrative levels reasserts the importance of the narrator's final gesture: hitting the Christ cop in the head with a hammer. Kennedy's point is that drama is a social action, not just an aestheticized, distant "elsewhere" separate from reality. Through a play, the narrator can perform "rhetorical violence" on the policeman; this violence is a "real" but less destructive act than the physical violence her son experienced. The formal experimentation is necessary to make this point, while maintaining the most clear-sighted and least sentimentally emotive expression.

In the generation of New York off-off-Broadway writers who span the 1970s and 1980s, three playwrights deserve mention as a group: Mac Wellman, Len Jenkin, and Jeffrey Jones. Acquainted and often published together, they also share similarities in the forms of their experimentalism. Along with playwright Eric Overmyer, each of these dramatists, in different measures, has an interest in exploring the depth and range of the American vernacular. At times they appear to suffer from logorrhea. At their best, however, their language is ecstatic and even visionary, effusively overloading itself in a restless search for feelings not yet tamed, thoughts not yet defined. Furthermore, they often demonstrate how and why so much of American speech has become impoverished, owing to reductive political partisanship, crudely manufactured political consensuses, incessant commercialization, regional and ethnic flattening, mediatized homogenization, and facile identifications fostered through stereotyping. Plays like Wellman's *Harm's Way* (1978, in Wellman 1994); Jenkin's *Gogol* (1977, in Wellman 1985), *Dark Ride* (1981), and *American Notes* (1988, both in Jenkin 1993b); and Overmyer's *Native Speech* (1984) and *In a Pig's Valise* (1989) all transmit an undercurrent of American hucksterism and Carney-talk. Language is both the tool of the Great Communicator and the principal con game in these works. *Native Speech*, for example, concerns unlicensed radio DJ Hungry Mother and his punning deconstructions of American talk. As he puts it, "What's happening to the language? It's scary, Jim. The Great Nuance Crisis is upon us" (10). Mother's verbal twists turn on him, however, when his listeners begin to take his invented Junk reports on the local heroin trade as real. In a move reminiscent of French theorist Jean Baudrillard's arguments that the simulacrum takes the place of the real, the play pinpoints how in our world there is no longer truth versus falsity, or reality versus illusion; there is only simulation. Clearly Mother's "Junk report" does not represent heroin alone. "Junk" is also an allegory about the American addiction to cultural kitsch and socioeconomic waste. Other works worth mentioning by Overmyer include the frequently produced *On the Verge* (1985), about three female adventurers in Terra Incognita, and the noir mystery *Dark Rapture* (1992).

Of the four playwrights, Wellman is the most prolific. His *7 Blowjobs* (1991, in Wellman 1994) will be remembered as an overt attempt to counter the bluster of Senator Jesse Helms and others who sought to block public funding of photographer Robert Mapplethorpe's homoerotic works. *A Murder of Crows* (1992) and *The Hyacinth Macaw* (1994), the first two parts of a four-part series, strike a fine balance between verbal virtuosity and a parodic deconstruction of the American family drama. These plays are social psychologies, each using individual characters as figures in a national psychodrama. Indeed, the notion of character often breaks down in these works because a character can turn into its psychic double; or a character can simply eschew the ideal of consistency, that "bubble of sham" (13), while noting that "Identity is a hellish burden.... The trap of being something definite" (144–5). One outcome in Wellman's plays, as well as in many other experimental works, is the discarding of psychological subtext. Characters will simply declare or mis-declare their thoughts and feelings. Indeed, contrary to that old truism of playwriting – "show, rather than tell" – Wellman and others occasionally find successful ways to turn theatre back into narrated storytelling, as Kennedy does in *Motherhood 2000*.

Jeffrey Jones is least like the other three playwrights, although each is quite individual in his own way. Jones's most produced play is *Seventy Scenes of Halloween* (1980, in Wellman 1985). In terms of genre, the play is lodged in an uncanny place somewhere between hyperreal domestic drama and cartoonish expressionist horror flick. The play also uses a relatively uncommon technique of the avant-garde: permutation. As the opening stage direction suggests, the scenes in Jones's play are interchangeable: "different arrangements create different 'stories' with different 'meanings'" (63). Since the scenes' published arrangement actually sets up and then deconstructs genre expectations rather neatly, it is debatable whether or not one would actually want to permutate the play's structure.

However, Jones's direction is indicative of a new attitude in experimental play-writing after the 1960s and 1970s, which saw the rise of the director and collectives. Like Jones, a director/playwright such as Richard Foreman suggests that other directors might rearrange the order of his dialogues. Jones and Foreman are willing to disavow not only linear development, but also the author's mastery over his own text, provided that displacement of authority leads to productive engagement with and interpretation of the text. Other works by Jones, such as *Der Inka von Peru* (1984, in Wellman 1988) or *Tomorrowland* (1985, in Jones 2001), further disassociate the author from ownership of his text when he constructs entire plays out of "plagiarized" historical source materials.

Let me conclude the discussion of 1980s playwrights by mentioning a final New York writer, also deeply interested in issues of history and myth. Charles L. Mee, often referred to as Chuck Mee, was trained as a historian. His major collection of plays is, in fact, entitled *History Plays*. Linguistically, Mee is a bit more restrained than the previously discussed playwrights, and his plays loosely use the conventions of character and plot. However, there is frequently a self-referential awareness of theatre in his pieces and, more importantly, he explores character primarily as a function of history and social systems rather than psychology. His work *Vienna: Lusthaus* (1986), written for the choreographer Martha Clarke, won an Obie for Best Play that year. Without a linear plot and collaged from various historical sources, the text also demonstrates a basic experimental willingness to break down disciplinary boundaries, in this case between dance and theatre. Other works by Mee, such as *Orestes* (1992) and *The Trojan Women A Love Story* (1996), rework Greek myths, but they do so without trying to turn the Greeks into classical icons of "noble simplicity and calm grandeur," to borrow the eighteenth-century art historian Johann Winckelmann's well-known phrase. These plays are anachronistic; baroque in the range of their literary and historical allusions; and full of changes in idiom, from the pop-cultural to the lyrical to the occasional use of specialized scientific discourses. Most recently, Mee's writing has taken a comic turn as he increasingly explores the theme of love in *Summertime* (2000), *Big Love* (2000), and *Wintertime* (2003).

In an experimental move relative to the distribution of scripts, Mee has also made almost all of his scripts available online at www.charlesmee.org. Mee is not alone in this regard. Richard Foreman has also shared his works freely on the Internet. In part, the move is an invitation to others to produce their work. However, an implicit capital-critique may also exist in these "copyleft" strategies, an attempt to treat literature as part of a cultural commons, rather than to isolate it in the commodity structure of the publishing industry. As the appropriative techniques of some experimental writers would indicate, culture is arguably in common in any case.

A final point about Mee: his writing for a director/choreographer like Martha Clarke and the stage history of his unpublished play *Another Person is a Foreign Country* (directed by Anne Bogart and written for a site-specific production in an abandoned New York City insane asylum) suggest how Mee comes from a generation of writers working after the rise of the director in America. One effect of this trend is the writing of plays developed less with an eye to traditional considerations of dramatic structure (inciting action, narrative rise, tragic fall) and more attuned to the possibilities of other structures: for instance, plays shaped by the architecture and history of a building (see also Mac Wellman's site-specific play *Crowbar* [1989], in Wellman 1994); or by the phenomenology of consciousness (Gertrude Stein to Richard Foreman); or by the exigencies of production itself (the Wooster Group, Reza Abdoh).

Performance Texts

In his essay "Metaphysics and the *Mise en Scène*," Antonin Artaud famously argued to make theatrical staging predominant over dramatic writing when he wrote that "What is essential... is to determine what this physical language consists of, this solidified, materialized language by means of which theatre is able to differentiate itself from speech" (1958: 38). And he goes on to assert that "it is the *mise en scène* that is the theater much more than the written and spoken play" (41). Although the director Edward Gordon Craig had proposed something similar at the turn into the twentieth century, Artaud's argument for mise en scène – that the overall conception and staging of a piece of theatre is an art with its own autonomy – has had the most lasting impact on experimental work in the theatre. In the United States, since the translation of Artaud's text in 1958, one can follow both his direct and oblique influence on artists like Judith Malina and Julian Beck of the Living Theatre (see chapter 15), Rachel Rosenthal, and other early proponents of performance art; on through the New York "Theatre of Images" of the 1970s and 1980s; to the work of director-writers like Reza Abdoh in the 1990s, as well as collective creation groups like Elevator Repair Service, GAle GAtes, and others.

Artaud's critique of the overweening use of language in theatre at the expense of other forms of expression poses more than a technical challenge to artists. Such critiques of "logocentrism" – to borrow a term made popular in the United States in the 1970s and 1980s with the rise of philosophical deconstruction and the writings of Jacques Derrida, himself influenced by Artaud – also constitute an assault on history in the sense that the practice of documenting history almost always entails writing. So when creators of theatre begin to forego the use of dramatic scripts in an attempt to create beyond language, what remains to document the performance? As Richard Schechner lamented in a 1981 essay announcing the decline of the American theatrical avant-garde, "But as performance itself – ways of staging, performers creating their own 'performance texts' – becomes the main focus there needs to be a way of directly transmitting these scores from one generation to another. . . . It's hard to see how this work will be transmitted if not either by developing an actual repertory or by passing on the techniques of workshop" (56).

Fortunately, a number of theatre artists – many combining the position of director/choreographer with that of writer/performer/designer – began in the late 1960s and afterwards to create documents, or "performance texts," to record a kind of theatrical work that resisted traditional dramatic conventions while it still used language. In some cases, it can be argued that these performance texts are so period and person specific that they cannot be recreated by other performers. Although this claim has validity, a number of the texts about to be discussed can be restaged. Often by the nature of these works, they beg to be recreated with more respect to the textual "spirit" than "letter." Moreover, late twentieth-century experimental theatre practices still linger in the sense that they have inspired dramatists who think of themselves primarily as dramatists. As Mac Wellman notes in his introduction to the 1985 anthology of experimental plays *Theatre of Wonders*, "The idea [of wonder] was suggested by critic Bonnie Marranca's excellent notion of a theatre of images, which she developed to discuss the seminal works of Richard Foreman, Robert Wilson, and Lee Breuer. Indeed, much of the work contained here reveals a debt to these three notable members of the New York avant-garde" (ix).

These three artists provide a good place to begin a discussion of how notions about *mise en scène* have contributed to new forms of dramatic and performance-based writing. Foreman began his career in the theatre as a set designer, studied playwriting at Yale, and then became widely known as a writer-director-designer of his own works in the New York City off-off scene of the early 1970s. Influenced by Brecht's alienation techniques, by Jack Smith's proto-camp, quasi-durational performances, with their unusual mix of the intensely mundane and the highly theatrical, and by Gertrude Stein's writing of a continuous present (see chapter 9), Foreman's scripts evoke figures that pass for characters while their dialogue is actually a staging of the phenomenology of consciousness. Foreman, in fact, often writes textual fragments and only assigns those fragments an order and an actor once he is in rehearsal. In terms of staging practice, Foreman keeps turning and altering an audience's perception of the possible context for any given stage utterance, teasing out continuity here, upsetting expectation there. In an echo of Beckett's comments on Joyce, Foreman writes succinctly, "The plays are about what they do" (1985: 209). Foreman's output is copious, and it is difficult to single out a text from his oeuvre. *Film is Evil Radio is Good* (1987, in Foreman 1992) and *The Mind King* (1992, in Foreman 1995), with their relatively clear themes, might be two places to approach his work for the first time. Foreman's essays on performance are also as significant as the writings of Strindberg, Shaw, Stein, and other major playwright-theoreticians.

Robert Wilson's work, like Foreman's, is frequently a self-reflexive examination of the act of observation. However, while Foreman's design aesthetic is self-consciously ugly and anti-art-ish, Wilson's is clean, beautiful, and often eerily sublime. Moreover, Wilson's staging of performers' bodies differs fundamentally from Foreman's. Wilson's performers strike more hieratic poses, and their gestures are frequently, but not always, slowed. His movement vocabulary bears traces of the geometric extensions of form found in Martha Graham's dance, while Foreman's figures are often contorted, turned back in on themselves, and stooped. Regarding texts, in the 1970s, Wilson sometimes used non-linear, declarative works written by the autistic child actor Christopher Knowles as a way to explore what alternative forms of perception might be like. Wilson has said of Knowles's writing that "he would write something both for the sound and for the way it looked on the page. The words looked the way they sounded" (Marranca 1977: 48). In the 1980s and 1990s, Wilson increasingly staged classical texts, but he also engaged a number of dramatic and non-dramatic writers to create performance texts. Examples include Darryl Pinckney's text for *Orlando* (1989), a monologue adaptation of Virginia Woolf's novel; William Burroughs's libretto for the musical *The Black Rider*, music by Tom Waits (1990); and Paul Schmidt's libretto for *Alice*, music also by Waits (1992). Each is worthy of being staged by others. Regardless of the type of text he uses, however, Wilson does not recreate a text's semantics as much as he creates a frame to offset the text, counterpointing the text and its materiality rather than highlighting any transparency in signification. In a favorite metaphor, Wilson describes his staging as a kind of silent film layered over and against the radio play of a text. In that sense, Wilson continues the avant-garde practice of artists like Cage, Cunningham, and Rauschenberg who created music, movement, and sets together without any preliminary agreement about how to unify their competing sign-systems.

Third in this trio is Lee Breuer, one of the founders of the New York City experimental company Mabou Mines, along with a number of other writer-director-performers including director JoAnne Akalitis (see her *Dressed Like an Egg* in Marranca and Dasgupta 1984). Breuer's writing methods can vary from work to work, although they often share a slight tone of punk intellectualism. His 1970s works like the *Animations* trilogy are alternately lyrical and parodic in their self-reflexive look at the act of storytelling. A series of 1980s texts, based around the figure of a warrior ant, intercut and mix an exoticized pseudo-lyricism of the "Orient" with an ironic allegory about the proletariat. These texts are also significant because Breuer attempts to synthesize Asian puppetry forms, like Japanese *bunraku* and Balinese *wayang kulit*, with western avant-garde alienation techniques. Breuer will probably be most remembered for his adaptation of Sophocles's *Oedipus at Colonus* into the musical *The Gospel at Colonus* (1983). With music by Bob Telson and a choir that included several of America's finest gospel groups, the work makes a stunning analogy between the choral odes of Greek tragedy and styles of worship in the black church. Like much experimental art of the period, *Gospel* depends upon a basic intercultural pastiche of normally different idioms and also plays with the idea of art as a form of ritual. Unlike some avant-garde work, however, *The Gospel at Colonus* does not veer away from powerful emotionality. It is rapturous, affirmative, proud, and dignified.

Other artists whose work extends from the 1970s to the 1990s include Meredith Monk and Ping Chong, who have worked together on several occasions. Monk's work is difficult to classify in numerous ways. She is both a creator and a performer, and has been trained as a singer, composer, dancer, and visual artist. Her tone is precise, dispassionate, and lightly comic. Like much experimental theatre, Monk's work is set intentionally at the boundary between disciplines. As she puts it in a "Mission Statement," she wants an art that is "inclusive, rather than exclusive"; "that cleanses the senses"; "that seeks to reestablish the unity existing in music, theater, and dance"; and "that reaches toward emotion we have no words for" (Jowitt 1997: 17). Like Wilson, whose work she predates, Monk sometimes uses text as much for sonorous as semantic purposes, and she frequently dispenses with character and narrative. Also like Wilson, although with a more affirmative affect, Monk does not try to inundate the stage as a signifying field; she leaves gaps for the spectator to fill. The positive, community-oriented tone of Monk's work lends itself to a mildly essentialist form of feminism, although such a description may understate the sense of irony and play and the lack of didacticism in her art. Some of her more well-known theatrical "operas" include *Education of the Girlchild* (1973), *Quarry* (1976), and *Atlas* (1991).

Monk also created a number of dance/music/theatre pieces with Ping Chong, such as *Paris* (1982) and *The Games* (1983). In *Paris*, the two evoke the quirky experimentalism of French Left Bank modernism, but the piece is more of a danced and sung tone poem about the spirit of the Parisian avant-garde than an "actorly" imitation of figures and events. Other works by Chong, such as *Nuit Blanche: A Select View of Earthlings* (1981), *Kind Ness* (1986), and *Snow* (1989), are more traditionally dramatic in form, using characters and nominally realistic dialogue. However, Chong's narrative structures often intercut radically discontinuous periods and places or embed allegorical resonances into quotidian events. Narrative context becomes intercultural and global rather than a local, naturalistic slice of life. Regarding *Kind Ness*, James Frieze writes that it is less the "frail map of a performance than a blueprint for other, future productions" and that "Chong has said that [this work] is the item in his oeuvre that can most squarely be described as 'a play,'" albeit a play "very much in quotation marks" (2002: 169).

Emerging in the late 1970s and early 1980s (after the so-called Theatre of Images and artists like Monk and Chong) are director-writer John Jesurun, director Peter Sellars, and, most significantly, the ensemble the Wooster Group, with director

Elizabeth LeCompte. Some dramatic texts have come directly out of the Wooster Group's work, such as Jim Strahs's play about NATO, *North Atlantic* (1984, in Marranca 1986). Wooster Group performer Ron Vawter, along with writer Gary Indiana, created the superb one-man show *Roy Cohn/Jack Smith*, a script that merits performance by others. However, the Wooster Group has especially influenced other artists by showing how rich the possibilities of collage texts and performance styles are (see *Frank Dell's The Temptation of St. Anthony* [1987] in Marranca 1996) and through its creation of a whole new theatrical vocabulary and set of conventions for integrating multimedia with live performance. Most recently, it has returned to classical dramatic texts such as Chekhov's *Three Sisters* (*Brace Up!*, 1991), O'Neill's *The Hairy Ape* (1995), and Racine's *Phèdre* (*To You, the Birdie!*, 2002). The Chekhov and Racine plays were translated for the Group by Paul Schmidt, and they deserve mention as examples of what might constitute contemporary experimental translation. Schmidt not only translates for the semantic value of a word; he also tries to recast syntactical and rhythmic values that are too often lost in word-for-word translations (for more on Schmidt, see the interview with director Liz Diamond in Diamond and Sellar 2000).

Another artist who incorporates multimedia into dramatic writing is John Jesurun. He emerged in New York's off-off scene with his "living film serial" *Chang in a Void Moon* (1982–6), staged in nightclubs and theatres. Later scripts, such as *Deep Sleep* (1986, in Marranca 1986), which won an Obie, *White Water* (1986, in Osborn 1987), and *Everything That Rises Must Converge* (1990), all incorporate multimedia directly into their stage directions and dialogue. Frequently Jesurun plays games of address and reception in which a live actor speaks in dialogue with a televised actor, but whether the characters are actually communicating with each other or carrying on a *dialogue de sourds*, a dialogue of the deaf, remains open to question. The child of Puerto Rican parents, Jesurun also plays with issues of identity, albeit in ontological as much as ethnic ways. Many of his scripts are multilingual. Jesurun received a MacArthur Award in 1996, and his work deserves critical and artistic attention.

While Peter Sellars is also known for incorporating multimedia into his stage work, his primary contribution to experimental dramatic writing has been the promotion, in conjunction with composer John Adams, of new American operas and musicals, namely Alice Goodman's librettos for *Nixon in China* (1987) and *The Death of Klinghoffer* (1991) and poet June Jordan's libretto for *I Was Looking at the Ceiling and Then I Saw the Sky* (1995).

Also in the 1990s, San Francisco-based director George Coates, who began working in the 1970s, continues to create multimedia "operas," often based on emerging technologies from Silicon Valley. In New York and elsewhere, the director Anne Bogart also creates dramatic texts from pastiches, such as *The Medium* (1993), based on various writings by media theorist Marshall McLuhan; *Going Going Gone* (1996), based on quantum physics; and *American Silents* (1997), which explores American silent film. Finally, the Los Angeles-and New York-based director Reza Abdoh produced a variety of savage collages before his death from AIDS in 1995. *The Hip-Hop Waltz of Eurydice* (1990, in Mufson 1999) is the text perhaps most amenable to recreation by others, although it is stylistically difficult in its non-linear, associative leaps. "A parable of the repression of homosexuality" (Mufson 1999: 3), *Eurydice* juxtaposes classical myth and contemporary sitcom; image theatre and word play; and quotidian banalities with Artaudian flights of fatalistic imagery. Abdoh's *The Law of Remains* (1991, in Marranca 1996) is an apocalyptic fantasia which intercuts the life of serial killer Jeffrey Dahmer with the world of Andy Warhol's Factory. *Tight Right White* (1993) brutally riffs off the kitschy Hollywood film *Mandingo* (1975) to create a scathing image of America's continuing reliance on ethnic and sexual exploitations. While all the artists in this section take up Artaud's suggestion to redefine drama by exploring the theatre's non-textual dimension, Abdoh probably provides the fullest embodiment of other Artaudian ideas. In effect, Abdoh's work is an Artaudian "theatre of cruelty" that clarifies the world by corrosively stripping away kitsch, masks, sentimentality, and sham panaceas.

New Dramatic Voices of the 1990s

Since the legacy of the 1990s is still unsettled, it remains to be seen which dramatists will be remembered in future decades, or indeed which will continue to write for the theatre. Older experimental playwrights like Eric Overmyer have increasingly been drawn to film and television; many younger writers have followed suit. Geographically, New York City remains the hub for new, experimental play production at theatres such as the Public Theatre, Playwrights Horizons, New Dramatists, Soho Repertory Theatre, P.S. 122, The Kitchen, The Flea, Clubbed Thumb, New Georges, and others. Nevertheless, many of these theatres are producing less work than in the past, and often less of it is experimental. Increasingly cities outside of New York – Seattle, Minneapolis, Austin, San Francisco, for example – are havens for new production. Initiatives like the RAT Conference, proposed by playwright Erik Ehn in 1993 and still ongoing, have also moderately helped regional alternative theatres to support each other.

The remaining chapter provides a three-part hierarchy that examines well-known and widely performed experimental drama, the moderately known with solid production histories, and "The Lesser Known," to borrow Suzan-Lori Parks's eponym for the main character in her *The America Play*. It needs to be acknowledged that these classifications are, by necessity, arbitrary. Moreover, public familiarity should not be taken as a sign of intrinsic value.

Parks herself is the only person included in the first category. Along with Tony Kushner, Parks is arguably the most important American playwright of the 1990s, experimental or otherwise. She received recognition early for her play *Imperceptible Mutabilities in the Third Kingdom* (Obie Award for Best New Play, 1989–90). Early works like *Mutabilities* and *The Death of the Last Black Man in the Whole Entire World*

(1992) are, in some respects, Parks's most idiosyncratically experimental works. Marked by seriocomic linguistic play, discontinuous settings, characters that are choruses, and characters that are historical syntheses as much as psychologies, her plays are meditations on history and the American black experience (among other experiences). But as the play's fractured and multiplied worlds suggest, there is also "no single 'Black Experience'" (Parks 1995: 21). In this sense, her plays *do* what they mean, rather than deliver a thesis to an audience. *The America Play* (1993) marked Parks's first production at the Public Theatre, home of many of her subsequent openings. Set in the "Great Hole of History," the first act of *The America Play* depicts the Foundling Father, an African American who makes his living by acting the role of Abraham Lincoln while patrons come up and pretend to assassinate him. In the second act, the Father's wife Lucy and child Brazil appear; they dig into the Hole of History, remember the Father, and finally dig his grave. *Venus* (1996) concerns Saartjie Baartman, the so-called "Venus Hottentot," a South African woman whose large posterior was publicly exhibited in Europe during the nineteenth century. Mingling conceptual and verbal play about black women and butts, "booty" (in several senses), the butt of history, and so on, Parks creates a historical phantasmagoria about racial exploitation; but the play is also about love and desire. Her dramas *In the Blood* (1999) and *Fucking A* (2000) repeat and revise Hawthorne's *The Scarlet Letter*; each concerns, in different ways, motherhood. Finally, *Topdog/Underdog* (2001), winner of the 2002 Pulitzer for Drama, depicts two brothers, Lincoln and Booth, vying with each other to see who can lay claim to their parents' inheritance money. While the settings and structures of Parks's plays have appeared increasingly realistic, they remain marked by modes of allegory and verbal gaming that undermine their seeming verisimilitude.

Playwrights Cherrie Moraga and Naomi Wallace, like Parks, share an interest in drama as a place where the ghosts of history can be reborn. Moraga's *Heart of the Earth: A Popul Vuh Story* (1994) and *The Hungry Woman: A Mexican Medea* (1995), in their use of mythic materials, are among her least realistic work. Set in the "second decade of the twenty-first century," in a "metaphysical border region," *The Hungry Woman* reenvisions the Medea myth through multiple lenses: the Chicana-American urban experience; Aztec divinities; and queer feminism. Moraga's work, like much drama in the 1990s, takes up issues of identity politics, but recasts identity into multiple dimensions. She writes about "hyphenated Americans," to paraphrase the title to a set of plays by Chay Yew; but she writes about a doubly, triply, multiply hyphenated America.

Wallace's work also reveals a feminist perspective, although this definition hardly defines her dramas. *One Flea Spare* (1995), set in the plague-ridden London of 1665, makes a cloistered household in the city an allegory for the class and sexual debates of the body politic. Relatively restrained and nominally realistic in its language, the play occasionally gives vent to fierce lyricism. *Slaughter City* (1996) is set in a modern industrial meat-packing factory. While primarily linear in narrative, the play also uses epiphanic moments that break up that linearity and reveal a kind of synoptic vision of a workers' history. Gender and sexuality also figure in the plot of the play, although the emphasis remains on questions of labor. Wallace's language is nominally realistic, but suffused with a sardonic poetry.

While spiritual and allegorical modes interrupt or run as undercurrents through the historical perspectives of Moraga and Wallace, they tend to predominate in the writing of Erik Ehn. *Wolf at the Door* (1991) takes domestic family drama and turns it into a kind of tone poem. The plays collected in *Beginner* (1995) and *The Saint Plays* (2000) are ethereal, surrealistic, imagistic, and religious, but also leavened by a kind of homey wit. They are "Big Cheap Theater," according to Ehn, because they are "past reach of discourse [i.e. Big] . . . common, public [i.e. Cheap]" and because " 'Theater' is hospitality – a living act of corporal mercy" (Ehn 2000: x).

Finally, among this group of moderately known writers, David Greenspan is a writer-performer-director more closely associated with the New York off-off scene than the previous three authors. Besides appearing in the works of fellow artists, such as Richard Foreman, Greenspan often also acts in his own work. His plays, like *2 Samuel 11, Etc.* (1990) and *The HOME Show Pieces* (1991), appear almost hypernaturalistic in their dialogue, but he undermines their realism through structural twists in which characters turn into each other or different worlds are set in analogy to each other. The first act of *Son of an Engineer* (1994) appears like a slightly absurdist domestic drama until the end of the act when "the Earth is destroyed by missiles" (78); Act 2 takes place on Mars, where the family struggles to make a new order. A number of Greenspan's texts touch on homosexuality, but the expression of gay identity is usually taken for granted in the works, rather than their raison d'être.

Among the relatively unfamiliar dramatists listed next are a number of superb playwrights, many of whom also direct and/or perform. Some have been working since the 1970s, while others have begun to write in the 1990s. Laurie Carlos (*Feathers at the Flame*, 1998) is a director-choreographer-writer-maker of devised theatre. Relatively well known for her work with Urban Bush Women, she has also helped to produce the works of a number of younger African American artists. Some of these artists include Sharon Bridgforth, whose works like *dyke/warrior-prayers* (1996) explore the formal possibilities of Ntozake Shange's choreopoems to express black lesbian identities; Daniel Alexander Jones (*Ambient Love Rites*, 1998); and Carl Hancock Rux. Rux works in many different fields, from spoken word to directing to writing. His *Talk* (2004) is a dramatic play of ideas; *Pagan Operetta* (1998) is a book of poems, but they could be staged as theatre or spoken word in their own right.

New music texts have often become vehicles for high-quality writing. Some of the artists working in this genre include Robert Ashley (*Perfect Lives*, 1991; *Now Eleanor's Idea*, 1992), who began composing in the music and performance avant-garde of the 1970s; Matthew Maguire (*The Tower*, 1993); Rinde Eckert, whose *And God Created Whales* won an Obie for Music in 2000; Janet Allard (*The Unknown Attraction*, 2000); and, perhaps the most notable emerging artist in this list, Ruth Margraff (*Wallpaper*

Psalm, 1995; *The Elektra Fugues*, 1996; *Night Vision: A First to Third World Vampyre Opera*, 2000). Also worth mentioning as a piece of writing between disciplines – in this case between theatre and dance, rather than theatre and music – is former Judson Dance member David Gordon's *The Mysteries and What's so Funny?* (1991, in Feingold 1993). At the boundary between drama and performance art there are also a variety of significant writers, such as Kathy Acker, Karen Finley, Coco Fusco, Guillermo Gómez-Peña, and Rachel Rosenthal.

Finally, several other dramatists of interest follow and, when published, some plays: Robert Alexander, *I Ain't Yo' Uncle* (1992, in Elam and Alexander 1996); Shelley Berc, *A Girl's Guide to the Divine Comedy* (1994, in Marranca 1996); Barbara Cassidy; Breena Clarke and Glenda Dickerson, *Remembering Aunt Jemima: A Menstrual Show* (1992, in Elam and Alexander 1996); Constance Congdon, *Tales of the Lost Formicans* (1989); Migdalia Cruz, particularly her more non-realistic plays such as *Fur* (1995, in Svich and Marrero 2000); Gordon Dahlquist; Lisa D'Amour; Karl Gajdusek; Rinne Groff; David Hancock, winner of two Obies, but not published; Karen Hartman, *Gum* (2003); Naomi Iizuka, *Skin* (1995, in Svich and Marrero 2000) and *Polaroid Stories* (1999); Carson Kreitzer; Victor Lodato; Karen Malpede, *Us* (1992, in Lamont 1993); Keith Antar Mason, *for black boys who have considered homicide when the streets were too much* (1993, in Elam and Alexander 1996); Richard Maxwell, *House* (1998, winner of a 1999 Obie); Carlos Murillo; Lynn Nottage, *Las Meninas* (1995); Aishah Rahman, *Only in America* (1997); Kate Robin; Joan Schenkar, *The Universal Wolf* (1990, in Lamont 1993); Caridad Svich, *Alchemy of Desire/Dead Man's Blues* (1994, in Svich and Marrero 2000); Split Britches' *Belle Reprieve* (1991, in Case 1996); Denise Uyehara; and Elizabeth Wong, *Letters to a Student Revolutionary* (1989, in Lamont 1993).

In summary, the legacy of the 1980s and 1990s in America suggests a number of avenues for future exploration. The need to write about the experiences of a multi-ethnic, polysexual, multi-class, intergenerational society – and to find a form to do so – will surely remain. Unquestionably the redefinition of performance will continue to redefine what dramatic writing might mean. Technological innovation will, no doubt, continue to exert new pressures on how humans perceive and communicate, and hence on how they represent themselves. There may be nothing *absolutely* new under the sun, but the promise of the *relatively* new remains open. Dramatists still desire to stir up the truth by wedding new perceptions to new forms; as long as that happens, experiment lives.

BIBLIOGRAPHY

Abdoh, R. (1994). *Tight Right White. TheatreForum* (Fall/Winter): 63–81.

Aronson, A. (2000). *American Avant-Garde Theatre: A History.* New York: Routledge.

Artaud, A. (1958). *The Theater and its Double*, trans. Mary Caroline Richards. New York: Grove.

Barthes, R. (1977). "The Death of the Author." In *Image, Music, Text*, trans. Stephen Heath. New York: Hill and Wang.

Baudrillard, J. (1994). "The Precession of Simulacra." In *Simulacra and Simulation*, trans. Sheila Glaser. Ann Arbor: University of Michigan Press.

Beckett, S. (1984). *Disjecta: Miscellaneous Writings and a Dramatic Fragment*, ed. Ruby Cohn. New York: Grove.

Breuer, L. (1979). *Animations*. New York: Performing Arts Journal Publications.

——(1987). *Sister Suzie Cinema: The Collected Poems and Performances, 1976–1986*. New York: Theatre Communications Group.

——(1989). *The Gospel at Colonus*. New York: Theatre Communications Group.

Bridgforth, S. (1996). *dyke/warrior-prayers*. Unpublished typescript.

Carlos, L. (1998). *Feathers at the Flame*. Unpublished typescript.

Case, S.-E. (ed.) (1996). *Split Britches: Lesbian Practice, Feminist Performance*. New York: Routledge.

Chong, P. (1986). *Kind Ness*. Plays in Process, vol. 8, no. 9. New York: Theatre Communications Group.

——(1989). *Snow*. Plays in Process, vol. 10, no. 9. New York: Theatre Communications Group.

Congdon, C. (1994). *Tales of the Lost Formicans and Other Plays*. New York: Theatre Communications Group.

Diamond, L. and Sellar, T. (2000). "The Labyrinth of Words." *Theater* 30, 1: 91–101.

Ehn, E. (1992). *Wolf at the Door*. Plays in Process, vol. 12, no. 10. New York: Theatre Communications Group.

——(1996). *Beginner*. Los Angeles: Sun and Moon Press.

——(2000). *The Saint Plays*. Baltimore: Johns Hopkins University Press.

Elam, H. and Alexander, R. (eds.) (1996). *Colored Contradictions: An Anthology of Contemporary African-American Plays*. New York: Plume.

Feingold, M. (ed.) (1993). *Grove New American Theater*. New York: Grove.

Foreman, R. (1985). *Reverberation Machines*. Barrytown, NY: Station Hill.

——(1992). *Unbalancing Acts: Foundations for a Theater*. New York: Random House.

——(1995). *My Head Was a Sledgehammer: Six Plays*. Woodstock, NY: Overlook Press.

——(2001). *Paradise Hotel and Other Plays*. Woodstock, NY: Overlook Press.

Fornes, M. I. (1986). *Plays*. New York: Performing Arts Journal Publications.

Foucault, M. (1977). "What is an Author?" In *Language, Counter-Memory, Practice*, ed. Donald F. Bouchard, trans. Donald F. Bouchard and Sherry Simon. Ithaca, NY: Cornell University Press.

Frieze, J. (2002). "The Interpretation of Difference: Staging Identity in the United States (1986–92)." Dissertation, University of Wisconsin-Madison. Ann Arbor: University of Michigan.

Fuchs, E. (1996). *The Death of Character: Perspectives on Theater after Modernism*. Bloomington: Indiana University Press.

Greenspan, D. (1990). *2 Samuel 11, Etc.* Plays in Process, vol. 11, no. 5. New York: Theatre Communications Group.

——(1992). *The HOME Show Pieces*. Plays in Process, vol. 13, no. 6. New York: Theatre Communications Group.

——(1995). *Son of an Engineer*. Los Angeles: Sun and Moon Press.

Hartman, K. (2003). *Gum; and The Mother of Modern Censorship*. New York: Dramatists Play Service.

Jenkin, L. (1993a). *Careless Love*. Los Angeles: Sun and Moon Press.

——(1993b). *Dark Ride and Other Plays*. Los Angeles: Sun and Moon Press.

Jesurun, J. (1997). *Everything That Rises Must Converge*. Los Angeles: Sun and Moon Press.

Jones, J. (2001). *Plays by Jeffrey Jones*. New York: Broadway Play Publishing.

Jowitt, D. (ed.) (1997). *Meredith Monk*. Baltimore: Johns Hopkins University Press.

Lamont, R. C. (1993). *Women on the Verge: Seven Avant-Garde American Plays*. New York: Applause.

Maguire, M. (1993). *The Tower*. Los Angeles: Sun and Moon Press.

Margraff, R. and Ho, F. (2000). *Night Vision: A First to Third World Vampyre Opera*. New York: Autonomedia/Big Red Media.

Marranca, B. (ed.) (1977). *The Theatre of Images*. New York: Drama Book Specialists.

——(1986). *Wordplays 5, New American Drama*. New York: Performing Arts Journal Publications.

——(ed.) (1996). *Plays for the End of the Century*. Baltimore: Johns Hopkins University Press.

——and Dasgupta, G. (eds.) (1984). *Wordplays 4, New American Drama*. New York: Performing Arts Journal Publications.

Maxwell, R. (1999). *House. Performing Arts Journal* 21, 3: 79–92.

Mee, C. L. (1998). *History Plays*. Baltimore: Johns Hopkins University Press.

Messerli, D. and Wellman, M. (eds.) (1998). *From the Other Side of the Century II, A New American Drama, 1960–1995*. Los Angeles: Sun and Moon Press.

Moraga, C. (2001). *The Hungry Woman*. Albuquerque: West End Press.

Mufson, D. (1999). *Reza Abdoh*. Baltimore: Johns Hopkins University Press.

——(2001). "Just How Dead is the Avant-Garde?" *American Theatre* (April): 47–9.

Nottage, L. (2003). *Crumbs from the Table of Joy, and Other Plays*. New York: Theatre Communications Group.

Osborn, M. E. (1987). *On New Ground: Contemporary Hispanic-American Plays*. New York: Theatre Communications Group.

Overmyer, E. (1993). *Collected Plays*. Newbury, VT: Smith and Kraus.

Parks, S.-L. (1995). *The America Play, and Other Works*. New York: Theatre Communications Group.

——(1997) *Venus*. New York: Theatre Communications Group.

——(2001a). *The Red Letter Plays*. New York: Theatre Communications Group.

——(2001b). *Topdog/Underdog*. New York: Theatre Communications Group.

Rahman, A. (1997). *Plays by Aishah Rahman*. New York: Broadway Play Publishing.

Rux, C. H. (1998). *Pagan Operetta*. New York: Fly by Night Press.

——(2004). *Talk*. New York: Theatre Communications Group.

Schechner, R. (1981). "The Decline and Fall of the (American) Avant-Garde: Why It Happened and What We Can Do About It." *Performing Arts Journal* 14: 48–63; 15: 9–19.

Svich, C. and Marrero, M. T. (eds.) (2000). *Out of the Fringe: Contemporary Latina/Latino Theatre and Performance*. New York: Theatre Communications Group.

Wallace, N. (2001). *In the Heart of America, and Other Plays*. New York: Theatre Communications Group.

Wellman, M. (ed.) (1985). *Theatre of Wonders: Six Contemporary American Plays*. Los Angeles: Sun and Moon Press.

——(ed.) (1988). *Seven Different Plays*. New York: Broadway Play Publishing.

——(1994). *The Bad Infinity*. Baltimore: Johns Hopkins University Press.

——(2000). *Crowtet I: A Murder of Crows and The Hyacinth Macaw*. Los Angeles: Green Integer.

——(2001). *Cellophane*. Baltimore: Johns Hopkins University Press.

Williams, T. (1984). *The Remarkable Rooming-House of Mme. Le Monde*. New York: Albondocani.

Index